MANAGEMENT INFORMATION SYSTEMS

CONCEPTUAL FOUNDATIONS, STRUCTURE, AND DEVELOPMENT

McGraw-Hill Series in Management Information Systems

Gordon B. Davis, *Consulting Editor*

Davis and Olson: *Management Information Systems: Conceptual Foundations, Structure, and Development*
Davis and Everest: *Readings in Management Information Systems*
Dickson and Wetherbe: *The Management of Information Systems*
Dickson and Wetherbe: *The Management of Information Systems Casebook*
Everest: *Database Management: Objectives, Organization, and System Function*
Lucas: *The Analysis, Design, and Implementation of Information Systems*
Lucas: *Information Systems Concepts for Management*
Lucas and Gibson: *A Casebook for Management Information Systems*
Meadow and Tedesco: *Telecommunications for Management*
Weber: *EDP Auditing: Conceptual Foundations and Practice*

MANAGEMENT INFORMATION SYSTEMS

CONCEPTUAL FOUNDATIONS, STRUCTURE, AND DEVELOPMENT

SECOND EDITION

Gordon B. Davis
Honeywell Professor of Management Information Systems
University of Minnesota

Margrethe H. Olson
Associate Professor
New York University

McGRAW-HILL BOOK COMPANY

New York   St. Louis   San Francisco   Auckland   Bogotá
Hamburg   Johannesburg   London   Madrid   Mexico   Montreal   New Delhi
Panama   Paris   São Paulo   Singapore   Sydney   Tokyo   Toronto

This book was set in Times Roman by University of Minnesota.
The editors were Christina Mediate and Joseph F. Murphy;
the production supervisor was Marietta Breitwieser.
The drawings were done by Fine Line Illustrations, Inc.
R. R. Donnelley & Sons Company was printer and binder.

MANAGEMENT INFORMATION SYSTEMS
Conceptual Foundations, Structure, and Development

4567890DOCDOC89876

ISBN 0-07-015828-2

Library of Congress Cataloging in Publication Data

Davis, Gordon Bitter.
    Management information systems.

    (McGraw-Hill series in management information systems)
    Includes bibliographies and index
    1. Management information systems.   I. Olson,
Margrethe H.   II. Title.   III. Series.
T58.6.D38   1985   658.4'038   84-12606
ISBN 0-07-015828-2

CONTENTS

v

PREFACE

A major contribution of the first edition of this text was to define the scope or domain of management information systems. The text was very well received by the information systems academic community. It was used across a wide variety of courses ranging from introductory undergraduate courses to graduate seminars. The reason for the diversity of use is the unique contribution of the book. It is a conceptual study of information systems in organizations, and therefore the material can be surveyed at an introductory level or explored in more depth in a graduate seminar. The first edition was identified as a "classic" in the field in a study of information systems books and journals (Scott Hamilton and Blake Ives, "Knowledge Utilization among MIS Researchers," *MIS Quarterly*, 6:4, December 1982, pp. 61-77).

Although there are several terms to describe the content of the book, the term "management information systems" is used because it is well accepted. Alternative terminology such as information systems or organizational information systems would have been acceptable. The conceptual structure implied by the terms is the same—a computer-based information system to support organizational processes. In other words, the information system is a support system for an organization. That part of the information system designed to support organizational operations is an operational support system, the part designed to support decision making is a decision support system (DSS), and the part that supports knowledge work is a knowledge work support system. The information system concept is also broad enough to include information processing support for office work (office automation).

The scope of the text is an organizational information system as broadly defined. It includes standard operational information systems, information systems for management control, information systems for strategic management, decision support systems, office information systems, and knowledge work support systems.

The second edition is a major revision. The features of the revision are the following:

- Reorganization of the chapters. The description of the structure of a management information system is the second chapter.

- Rewriting of the technology chapters and moving them forward as the second section of the book. These are written as an optional section for students without prior exposure or as a review.

- Expansion of the Conceptual Foundations section. A chapter has been added on Concepts of Planning and Control (Chapter 10). The chapter on value of information has been dropped, with some of the material incorporated in the chapter on Concepts of Information.

- Expansion of the material on support systems. Two chapters are devoted to the subject: Chapter 12 on Support Systems for Planning, Control, and Decision Making and Chapter 13 on Support Systems for Management of Knowledge Work.

- Inclusion of a section of four chapters on Information System Requirements. The determination of information requirements and formulation of an information system plan are key problems in information systems. The section has chapters on the information system plan, strategies for information requirements determination, database requirements, and user interface requirements.

- Reorganization and rewriting of the section on Development, Implementation, and Management of Information System Resources.

- Inclusion of short vignettes or incidents in each chapter to illustrate the concepts. These are based on news articles, personal experiences of the authors, or reports from colleagues.

- Addition of short discussion cases at the end of each chapter.

There are selected references at the end of each chapter for further reading. The rapid expansion of literature in the field and the breadth of the topics in the book preclude a complete bibliography of interesting articles or books, and many worthwhile references have not been included. However, the selected references provide a useful starting point for further investigation.

The text does not assume any special background. It can be used by computer science students to introduce them to the concepts of organizational information systems, by business students interested in entering the field of information systems, and by students in a variety of disciplines who are users or potential users of information systems and wish to understand them. The book is suitable as the text in the MBA survey course in information systems. The material is written for the serious student—it is not a "gee whiz" survey. At the same time, the material is written in an understandable style, and students with a wide variety of backgrounds and skills have found the book readable.

There are a number of vignettes and minicases that are excerpted from general newspaper articles, computer newspaper articles, and business journals.

Excerpts from *Business Week* are used by special permission from Business Week, McGraw-Hill, Inc.

Excerpts from *Computerworld* are used by permission from CW Communications, Framingham, MA.

Excerpts are reprinted by permission from *The Christian Science Monitor* © 1981. The Christian Science Publishing Society; all rights reserved.

Other excerpts, figures, and quotations are used by permission of the respective publishers. All rights are reserved by them.

The book has benefited from the outstanding services of Janice DeGross in typing the manuscript, making corrections, adding codes for the automated printing of the book, and managing the production processes assigned to the authors. A large number of professors have made suggestions on the revision: Aran Srinivasan, Hubert Dunsmore, Paul Cheney, and William King made suggestions prior to the revision; detailed review comments on the manuscript were provided by Gerardine DeSanctis, James Senn, Gad Ariav, Mary Culnan, Jack Baroudi, Blake Ives, and Jane Fedorowicz. Gordon Everest, Sal March, Yannis Vassiliou, and other colleagues at the University of Minnesota and New York University were very helpful when we needed assistance with individual chapters or with specific issues.

Gordon B. Davis
Margrethe H. Olson

The authors are very interested in feedback. Comments and suggestions can be sent to:

Gordon B. Davis
Honeywell Professor of
  Management Information Systems
School of Management
University of Minnesota
271 19th Avenue South
Minneapolis, Minnesota 55455

Margrethe H. Olson
Associate Professor
Graduate School of Business
  Administration
New York University
90 Trinity Place
New York, New York 10006

INTRODUCTION TO MANAGEMENT INFORMATION SYSTEMS

The first section of the text is definitional. The two chapters introduce the subject matter of the book and define the boundaries of the topics included in the study of information systems in organizations.

Chapter 1 presents the definition of a management information system. Its relationship to other concepts and the scope of MIS as an academic discipline are explained. The management information system is also described from the perspective of a user. The definition of a management information system introduced in the chapter is a broad one and encompasses various information support systems including decision support systems and office information support systems.

Chapter 2 presents the structure of a management information system and uses three different perspectives to build a synthesis of the conceptual structure.

Frameworks such as those presented in this section aid users and designers to understand their current information system relative to the concept of a comprehensive management information system. The frameworks also highlight issues in the design of a more complete information system.

The section is an introduction to the text; it can also be a summary. After studying the remainder of the book, these two chapters (especially Chapter 2) can provide an integrating summary.

CHAPTER 1

AN OVERVIEW OF MANAGEMENT INFORMATION SYSTEMS

THE MIS PROFESSIONAL
PURPOSE AND ORGANIZATION OF THIS TEXT
  Purpose of the Text
  Organization of the Text
SUMMARY
MINICASES
EXERCISES

Information processing is a major societal activity. A significant part of an individual's working and personal time is spent recording, searching for, and absorbing information. As much as 80 percent of a typical executive's time is spent in the processing and communication of information. More than 50 percent of the United States work force is employed in jobs that primarily involve some form of information processing. A large proportion of these employees are "knowledge workers"; their duties involve the production and use of information outputs—documents, reports, analyses, plans, etc.

Computers have become an essential part of organizational information processing because of the power of the technology and the volume of data to be processed. The application of computers to information processing began in 1954 when one of the first computers was programmed to process payroll. Today, computerized processing of transaction data is a routine activity of large organizations. Moreover, the capability to automate information processing has permitted an expansion in the scope of formalized organizational information use. The current challenge in information processing is to use the capabilities of computers to support knowledge work, including managerial activities and decision making. The wide variety of computer resources to perform transaction processing, to provide processing for a formal information and reporting system, and to accomplish managerial-decision support are broadly classified as the organization's *management information system* or MIS.

The focus of this text is management information systems rather than routine data processing. MIS is a broad concept rather than a single system. Some MIS activities are highly integrated with routine data processing, while other MIS applications are designed for a particular knowledge work activity or decision-making function. The office use of computer and communication technology to support person-to-person communications and clerical support functions is also included in this text as part of management information systems.

The design and implementation of management information systems in an organization necessitates the identification of information requirements. The requirements for routine transaction processing tend to be stable and relatively easy to identify; information requirements for management and decision making activities are more changeable and more difficult to define. The content of this text is useful both for those who design, implement, and manage information systems and for those who specify information requirements and use the systems. The text can help systems analysts to understand the structure of a management information system and the type of requirements to be included; it can aid information systems executives in planning and management; it can help users to understand how their information requirements fit into the system and how to analyze and formulate those requirements. It can also aid users who develop their own systems.

HOW LONG CAN AN ORGANIZATION OPERATE WITHOUT COMPUTER INFORMATION PROCESSING?

When asked how long different business functions would be able to operate without the information processing capabilities of computers, 36 companies responded with the following results for all operational applications: On average, the companies estimated that only 28 percent of the operational activities would be functioning within 5.5 days without computer data processing. Finance companies in the sample estimated that only 13 percent of operations would be functioning after 5.5 days without computing. (Figure 1-1).

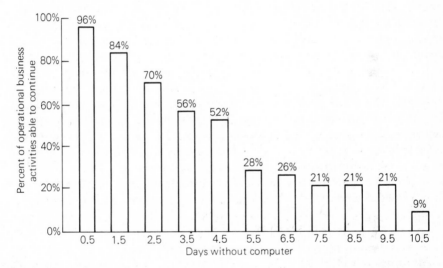

Figure 1-1
Decline in operational business activities following a complete computer data processing failure. (Source: D. O. Aasgaard, P. P. R. Cheung, B. J. Hulbert, and M. C. Simpson, "An Evaluation of Data Processing 'Machine Room' Loss and Selected Recovery Strategies," University of Minnesota, Management Information Systems Research Center WP-79-04, p. 70.)

DEFINITION OF A MANAGEMENT INFORMATION SYSTEM

There is no consensus on the definition of the term "management information system." Some writers prefer alternative terminology such as "information processing system," "information and decision system," "organizational information system," or simply "information system" to refer to the computer-based information processing system which supports the operations, management, and decision-making functions of an organization. This text uses "MIS" because it is descriptive and generally understood; it also frequently uses "information system" instead of "MIS" to refer to an organizational information system.

WHAT'S IN A NAME?

A 1983 survey of 334 large organizations identified the following names used for the information systems function:

Name	Percent
Management information systems	33
Information services	17
Information systems	14
Data processing	12
Information resource management	3
Other	21
	100

Information Systems Planning to Meet Business Objectives: A Survey of Practice, Cresap, McCormick and Paget, New York, 1983, p. B-7.

A definition of a management information system, as generally understood, is *an integrated, user-machine system for providing information to support operations, management, analysis and decision-making functions in an organization. The system utilizes computer hardware and software; manual procedures; models for analysis, planning, control and decision making; and a database.* The fact that it is an integrated system does not mean that it is a single, monolithic structure; rather, it means that the parts fit into an overall design. The elements of the definition are highlighted below.

DEFINITION OF A MANAGEMENT INFORMATION SYSTEM

A management information system is
- An integrated user-machine system
- For providing information (not just data)
- To support the operations, management, analysis, and decision-making functions
- In an organization

The system utilizes
- Computer hardware and software
- Manual procedures
- Models for analysis, planning, control, and decision making, and
- A database

The management information system has been described as a pyramid structure (Figure 1-2) in which the bottom layer consists of information for transaction processing, status inquiries, etc.; the next level consists of information resources in support of day-to-day operations and control; the third level consists of information system resources to aid in tactical planning and decision making for management control; and the top level consists of information resources to support strategic planning and policy making by higher levels of management. Each level of information processing may make use of data provided for lower levels; but new data may also be introduced. For example, some of the information to support management and decision making is provided by the data obtained for transaction processing, while some may be new data about activities external to the organization.

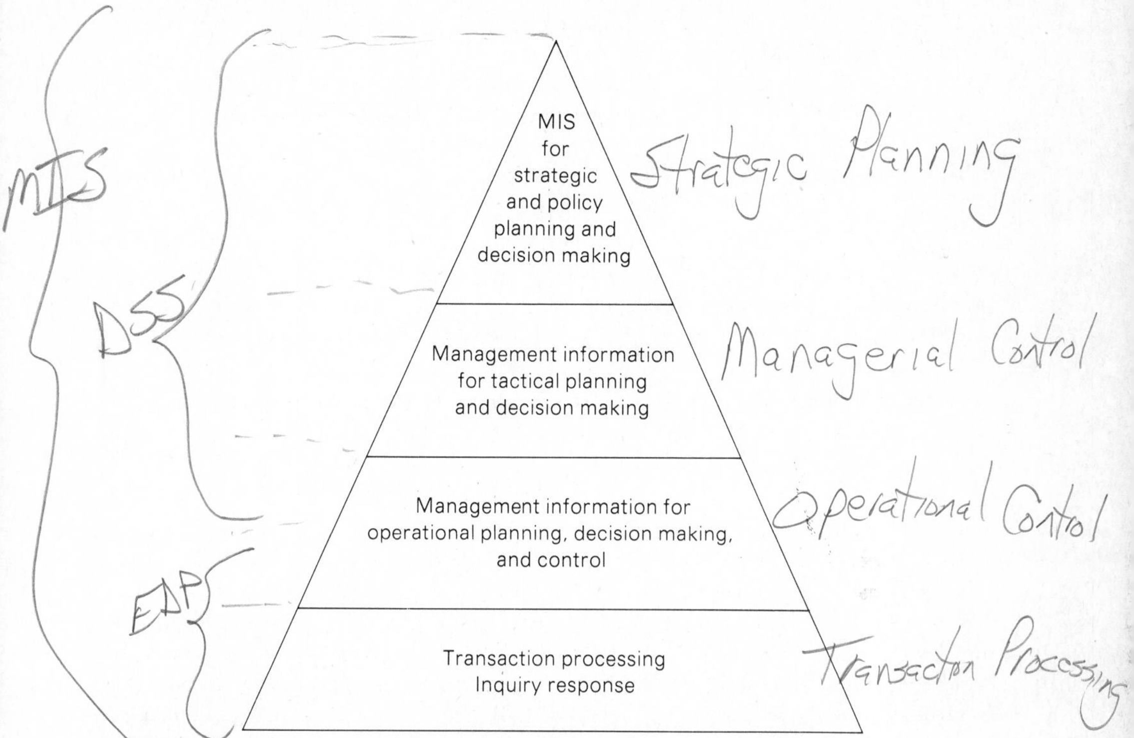

Relation: among EDP, MIS, + DSS

MIS

DSS

EDP

MIS
for
strategic
and policy
planning and
decision making

Strategic Planning

Management information
for tactical planning
and decision making

Managerial Control

Management information for
operational planning, decision making,
and control

Operational Control

Transaction processing
Inquiry response

Transaction Processing

Figure 1-2
Management information system. (Adapted from Robert V. Head, "Management Information Systems: A Critical Appraisal," *Datamation,* May 1967, p. 23.)

In order to further clarify the definition, the following sections elaborate on certain key concepts: the user-machine system, the concept of an integrated system, the need for a database, and the role of planning and decision models. In addition, there is a discussion of the relationship of MIS to other information system structural concepts: information resource management (IRM), decision support systems (DSS), and data processing (DP).

Computer-Based User-Machine System

Conceptually, a management information system can exist without computers, but it is the power of the computer which makes MIS feasible. The question is not whether computers should be used in management information systems, but the extent to which information use should be computerized. The concept of a user-machine system implies that some tasks are best performed by humans, while others are best done by machine. The user of an MIS is any person responsible for entering input data, instructing the system, or utilizing the information output of the system. For many problems, the user and the computer form a combined system with results obtained through a set of interactions between the computer and the user.

User-machine interaction is facilitated by operations in which the user's input-output device (usually a visual display terminal) is connected to the computer. The computer can be a personal computer serving only one user or a large computer that serves a number of users through terminals connected by communication lines. The user input-output device permits direct input of data and immediate output of results. For instance, a person using the computer interactively in financial planning poses "what if" questions by entering input at the terminal keyboard; the results are displayed on the screen in a few seconds.

The computer-based user-machine characteristics of an MIS affect the knowledge requirements of both system developer and system user. "Computer-based" means that the designer of a management information system must have a knowledge of computers and of their use in information processing. The "user-machine" concept means the system designer should also understand the capabilities of humans as system components (as information processors) and the behavior of humans as users of information.

 Information system applications should not require users to be computer experts. However, users need to be able to specify their information requirements; some understanding of computers, the nature of information, and its use in various management functions aids users in this task.

Integrated System

Management information systems typically provide the basis for integration of organizational information processing. Individual applications within information systems are developed for and by diverse sets of users. If there are no integrating processes and mechanisms, the individual applications may be inconsistent and incompatible. Data items may be specified differently and may not be compatible across applications that use the same data. There may be redundant development of separate applications when actually a single application could serve more than one need. A user wanting to perform analysis using data from two different applications may find the task very difficult and sometimes impossible.

The first step in integration of diverse information system applications is an overall information system plan. Even though application systems are implemented one at a time, their design can be guided by the overall plan, which determines how they fit in with other functions. In essence, the information system is designed as a planned federation of small systems.

Information system integration is also achieved through standards, guidelines, and procedures set by the MIS function. The enforcement of such standards and procedures permits diverse applications to share data, meet audit and control requirements, and be shared by multiple users. For instance, an application may be developed to run on a particular small computer. Standards for integration may dictate that the equipment selected be compatible with existing computers and that the application be designed for communication with the centralized database.

The trend in information system design is toward separate application processing from the data used to support it. The separate database is the mechanism by which data items are integrated across many applications and made consistently available to a variety of users. The need for a database in MIS is discussed below.

Need for a Database

The terms "information" and "data" are frequently used interchangeably; however, information is generally defined as data that is meaningful or useful to the recipient. Data items are therefore the raw material for producing information.

The underlying concept of a database is that data needs to be managed in order to be available for processing and have appropriate quality. This data management includes both software and organization. The software to create and manage a database is a *database management system*.

When all access to and use of the database is controlled through a database management system, all applications utilizing a particular data item access the same data item which is stored in only one place. A single updating of the data item updates it for all uses. Integration through a database management system requires a central authority for the database. The data can be stored in one central computer or dispersed among several computers; the overriding requirement is that there be an organizational function to exercise control.

Utilization of Models

It is usually insufficient for human recipients to receive only raw data or even summarized data. Data usually needs to be processed and presented in such a way that the result is directed toward the decision to be made. To do this, processing of data items is based on a decision model. For example, an investment decision relative to new capital expenditures might be processed in terms of a capital expenditure decision model.

Decision models can be used to support different stages in the decision-making process. "Intelligence" models can be used to search for problems and/or opportunities. Models can be used to identify and analyze possible solutions. Choice models such as optimization models may be used to find the most desirable solution.

USING INFORMATION IN FINDING PROBLEMS

"Communities across the U.S. are starting to use information as well as fire hoses to combat arson. Boston, New Haven, Knoxville, Phoenix, San Francisco, and Seattle all run programs that collate fire department records with tax, building ownership, and other data....And growing numbers of insurance companies...are using similar surveys to reduce arson fraud by policy-holders.'

"The new arson information tracking programs are already paying off.... Last year the Federal Bureau of Investigation reported a 12% drop in arson in the U.S. Although experts say it is too early to link the national drop in arson directly to information management systems, the results from cities that have installed such systems are encouraging. For example, in Phoenix, which installed an arson information program in 1978, arson cases dropped last year to 497, or 35% of all fires, from 739, 49% of the total, in 1978.'

For an arson information system to be effective, cities have found they must strike up a cooperative relationship with insurance companies, which already collect many of the same data. The new arson prevention system encourages the exchange of information instead of duplicating efforts.

Excerpts from "Data Programs Help Stamp Out Arson," *Business Week*, June 13, 1984, pp. 110D–110H.

In other words, multiple approaches are needed to meet a variety of decision situations. The following are some examples of problems and the type of model that might be included in an MIS to aid in analysis in support of decision making:

Problem	Example of model
Amount of inventory safety stock	Inventory model which computes safety stock under a variety of assumptions
Personnel selection	Personnel search and ranking-of-alternatives model
New product pricing	New product introduction model
Expenditure control	Budgetary control model

In a comprehensive information system, the decision maker has available a set of general models that can be applied to many analysis and decision situations plus a set of very specific models for unique decisions. Similar models are available for planning and control. The set of models is the model base for the MIS.

Models are generally most effective when the manager can use interactive dialog to build a plan or to iterate through several decision choices under different conditions.

MIS AS AN EVOLVING CONCEPT

When the concept of MIS was first introduced, many proponents envisioned a single, highly integrated system that would bring together processing for all organizational functions. Others questioned whether it was possible to design adequate computer-based information systems to support management planning and decision making functions, especially strategic planning.[1] They questioned the value of applying advanced information technology to an ill-defined judgmental process.

Over time, the concept of a single, highly integrated system was demonstrated to be too complex to implement. The MIS concept is now that of a federation of subsystems, developed and implemented as needed but conforming to the overall plan, standards, and procedures for the MIS. Thus, rather than a single, global MIS, an organization may have many related information systems which serve managerial needs in various ways.

 MIS as a concept continues to evolve. It is related to, but not equivalent with, data processing and other information systems-related concepts. Two such concepts that can be considered extensions of the MIS concept are decision support systems (DSS) and information resources management (IRM). An emerging trend consistent with the evolution of the MIS concept is end-user computing.

MIS versus Data Processing

A data processing system processes transactions and produces reports. It represents the automation of fundamental, routine processing to support operations. Prior to

<hr />

[1] John Dearden, "MIS is a Mirage," *Harvard Business Review*, January–February 1972, pp. 90–99, and "Myth of Real-Time Management Information," *Harvard Business Review*, May–June 1966, pp. 123–132.

computers, data processing was performed manually or with simple machines. A management information system is more comprehensive; it encompasses processing in support of a wider range of organizational functions and management processes. However, every MIS will also include transaction processing as one of its functions.

What does it take to make a data processing system into a management information system? Can a rather mundane data processing system be an MIS if a simple database, retrieval capabilities, and one or two decision models are added? This is not a useful question. MIS is a concept and an orientation toward which an information system design moves rather than an absolute state. Therefore, the significant issue is the extent to which an information system adopts the MIS orientation and supports the management functions of an organization. The answer is usually a matter of degree rather than a simple yes or no.

One important aspect of the difference between MIS and routine data processing is the capability to provide analysis, planning, and decision making support. An MIS orientation means users have access to decision models and methods for querying the database on an ad hoc basis; the database is also, of course, an essential part of routine transaction processing and reporting. Furthermore, an MIS orientation means information resources are utilized so as to improve decision making and achieve improved organizational effectiveness. Information resources are also used as a means of achieving a competitive advantage.

AIRLINES THINK INFORMATION SYSTEMS MAKE A COMPETITIVE DIFFERENCE

In 1983 the Justice Department initiated an investigation to decide whether computer reservation systems were being used unfairly to reduce competition.

The major airlines provide travel agents with access to computer reservations systems that include data on the schedules of all airlines. Eighty percent of all travel agents use them. The listed airlines pay to be listed, but the airline providing the service displays its flights to an advantage (such as listing them first). There are three large systems, but the American Airlines system dominates.

	Percent of use
American Airlines Sabre	39
TWA PARS	16
United Apollo	29
Others	13
	100

MIS and Decision Support Systems

A decision support system (DSS) is an information system application that assists decision making. DSS tend to be used in planning, analyzing alternatives, and trial and error search for solutions. They are generally operated through terminal-based interactive dialogs with users. They incorporate a variety of decision models. DSS represent a significant class of MIS applications which will be discussed in detail in Chapter 12.

USING INFORMATION ANALYSIS TO WIN AT FOOTBALL

"We can describe everything to the computer, says Chuck Clausen, defensive line coach for the Philadelphia Eagles. We can identify formations, draw pictures, define pass patterns, who caught the ball, yardage, what every receiver was doing, and how the blocking was.'

"Because of the number of players on the field and the diversity of possible plays, football is particularly suitable to computer analysis. Neal Dahlen, a scout for the San Francisco 49ers, says he can analyze and evaluate nearly 40 variables in any individual play on the team's computer. Based on information gleaned from computer printouts, 49er coach Bill Walsh often scripts the first 20 plays of a game before he even arrives at the stadium.'

As an example of the value of this analysis, a weakness was uncovered by a computer analysis of the lineup patterns of the Kansas City Chiefs. When the ball was between the 20-yard line and the goal line, the Chiefs lined up in the same formation 70 percent of the time. The San Diego Chargers' 372F Shoot Pump play was developed to exploit the weakness.

"Currently an NFL rule bars computer terminals from the sidelines or the press boxes. The hometown advantage would be too great for teams that have complex computer systems on their own turf, says Pete Adimante, an NFL spokesman. Nevertheless, football insiders expect that the rule will be made more liberal within the next few years.'

Excerpts from "The Computer Scores Big on the Gridiron," *Business Week,* October 24, 1983, pp. 185-188.

MIS and Information Resource Management

Information resource management (IRM) is an approach to management based on the concept that information is an organizational resource. Given that view, the task of the information system executive is to manage the resource. The resource is defined very broadly. The scope of IRM includes data communications, word processing, and personal computers as well as traditional data processing. The IRM concept tends to emphasize the organizational effectiveness of the information system resource rather than the technical sophistication or efficiency of the hardware and software. The MIS concept, as defined in this text, includes the resource view of information. The IRM concept is applicable to management of the MIS function, as discussed in Chapter 20.

End-User Computing

A recent major development affecting the structure and design of MIS is end-user computing. Users are provided with terminals or personal computers and powerful software for accessing data, developing models, and performing information processing directly. This development, made possible by the increasing power and decreasing cost of the technology, is a significant force for change in the way information resources are organized, provided, and used. In many organizations, the MIS function is undergoing a transition from centralized control of information systems resources toward provision of support to users who control their own development and operation of information systems. System support for end user computing and issues of MIS management in the end user environment are discussed in detail in the text.

HANDLING INCREASED DEMAND FOR INFORMATION

"The Essex Group, a unit of United Technologies Corp., is taking a pragmatic approach to office automation....Much of the company's $900 million in annual sales depends on two highly cyclical industries: housing and automobiles. Timely information on housing starts, auto order backlogs, and production schedules was increasingly crucial in fine-tuning Essex's costly inventories.'

"Employee requests for data soared 45% in 1982, to 429 inquiries. But the backlog of the central data processing department was so large that it was taking a year or more to fill many of these requests for information." Had Essex not acted to provide better response to information needs, disgruntled managers might have started installing their own personal computers. The result would have been loss of access and control over organizational information maintained on the micros.

"Managers who have completed training through Essex's newly-formed information center no longer have to wait for the data processing department. They can use one of 550 terminals linked to Essex's mainframe computer or one of the company's 40 personal computers to gain access to and analyze copies of data files themselves. Since the center opened, in early 1982, about 400 Essex employees—from senior executives to engineers and secretaries—have completed one or more computer courses.'

Excerpted and adpated from "Taking the Anxiety out of Office Automation," *Business Week,* September 19, 1983, pp. 96D-96F.

MIS AND OTHER ACADEMIC DISCIPLINES

Many of the ideas which are part of management information systems are found in other academic disciplines. Four major academic areas are especially significant to the MIS concept: managerial accounting, operations research, management and organization theory, and computer science.

Managerial Accounting

It is useful to think of the field of accounting as having two major areas: financial and managerial accounting. Financial accounting is concerned with the measurement of income for specific periods of time such as a month or a year (the income statement) and the reporting of financial status at the end of the period (the balance sheet). Financial accounting reports are oriented toward investors. As a result, financial accounting has limited usefulness for managerial decision making. Managerial accounting, on the other hand, is concerned with determining relevant costs and performing other analysis useful for managerial control and managerial decisions. It tends to be the focus for the preparation of budgets and performance analysis based on budgets. Historically the accounting department was always responsible for data processing because the first applications were related to accounting functions.

The MIS concept includes much of the content of managerial accounting; however, the support systems which provide users with access to data and models are beyond the scope of traditional managerial accounting. Current organizational practice is usually to retain cost and budget analysis within the managerial accounting function and to have the MIS function provide data and model support.

Operations Research

Operations research is the application of the scientific method and quantitative analysis techniques to management problems. Some of its key concepts are:

1 Emphasis on systematic approaches to problem solving
2 Use of mathematical models and mathematical and statistical procedures in analysis
3 Goal of seeking optimal decisions or optimal policy

Operations research is important relative to management information systems because it has developed procedures for the analysis and computer-based solutions of many types of decision problems. The systematic approach to problem solving, use of models, and computer-based solution algorithms are generally incorporated in the decision support system component of MIS.

Management and Organization Theory

Since the MIS is a support system for organizational functions, it draws upon concepts of organization, organization behavior, management, and decision making. The fields of management (or organization behavior) and organization theory provide several important concepts which are key to understanding the function of an MIS in an organization. Some of these concepts are:

1 Behavioral theory of organizational and individual decision making
2 Individual motivation
3 Group processes and group decision making
4 Leadership techniques
5 Organizational change processes
6 Organizational structure and design

These concepts are discussed in Chapter 11.

Computer Science

Computer science is important to management information systems because it covers topics such as algorithms, computation, software, and data structures. However, the academic field of management information systems is not an extension of computer science; rather it is an extension of management and organizational theory. The fundamental processes of management information systems are more related to organizational processes and organizational effectiveness than computational algorithms. The emphasis in MIS is on the application of the technical capabilities computer science has made possible.

SUBSYSTEMS OF AN MIS

MIS has been introduced as a broad concept referring to a federation of subsystems. Two approaches to defining the subsystems of an MIS are according to the organizational functions which they support and according to managerial activities for which they are used.

Organizational Function Subsystems

Because organizational functions are somewhat separable in terms of activities and are defined managerially as separate responsibilities, MIS may be viewed as a federation of information systems—one for each major organizational function. There may be common support systems used by more than one subsystem, but each functional system is unique in its procedures, programs, models, etc. Typical major subsystems for a business organization engaged in manufacturing are:

Major functional subsystem	Some typical uses
Marketing	Sales forecasting, sales planning, customer and sales analysis
Manufacturing	Production planning and scheduling, cost control analysis
Logistics	Planning and control of purchasing, inventories, distribution
Personnel	Planning personnel requirements, analyzing performance, salary administration
Finance and accounting	Financial analysis, cost analysis, capital requirements planning, income measurement
Information processing	Information system planning, cost-effectiveness analysis
Top management	Strategic planning, resource allocation

The database is the primary means of integration of the various subsystems. A data item that is stored or updated by one subsystem is then available to the other subsystems. For instance, the sales and inventory information used by the marketing subsystem is supplied through the logistics subsystem; the same data is used by the manufacturing subsystem for production planning and scheduling (Figure 1-3).

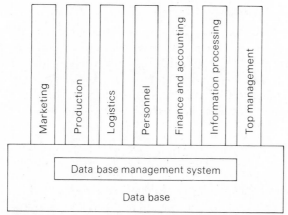

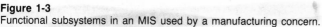

Figure 1-3
Functional subsystems in an MIS used by a manufacturing concern.

Activities Subsystems

Another approach to understanding the structure of an information system is in terms of the subsystems which perform various activities. Some of the activities subsystems will be useful for more than one organizational function subsystem; others will be useful for only one function. Examples of major activities subsystems (to be explained further in Chapter 2) are:

Activity subsystem	Some typical uses
Transaction processing	Processing of orders, shipments, and receipts
Operational control	Scheduling of activities and performance reports
Management control	Formulation of budgets and resource allocation
Strategic planning	Formulation of objectives and strategic plans

Note that these activities subsystems correspond to the levels of the pyramid structure that defines MIS (see Figure 1-2). The relationship of activities subsystems to functional subsystems is illustrated in Figure 1-4.

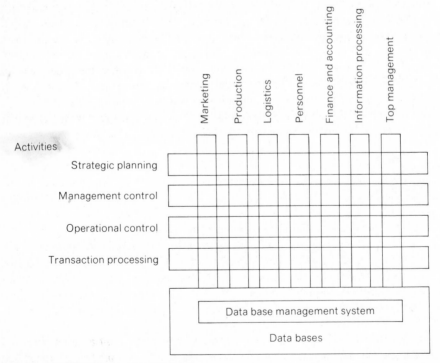

Figure 1-4
Relation of activities to functional subsystems.

MIS AS SEEN BY THE USER

The major users of a computer-based information system are the following:

User	Uses
Clerical personnel	Handle transactions, process input data and answer inquiries.
First-level managers	Obtain operations data. Assistance with planning, scheduling, identifying out-of-control situations, and making decisions.
Staff specialists	Information for analysis. Assistance with analysis, planning, and reporting.
Management	Regular reports. Ad hoc retrieval requests. Ad hoc analyses. Ad hoc reports. Assistance in identifying problems and opportunities. Assistance in decision-making analysis.

Clerical personnel are responsible for input and data control rather than being primary users of the output of the system. The job of the clerical person may be altered significantly when transaction processing is changed from manual to computer-based, especially if the system is online. For instance, an order clerk who takes orders over the phone previously worked with paper order forms and used an inventory book to check whether requested items were in stock. Now the clerk sits at a terminal; when an order is received, the clerk can instantly check inventory and complete the order, making substitutions if necessary while the customer is still on the telephone. In addition, the address and credit status of the customer can be verified immediately.

Since most of the information required by first-level managers is operational in nature, it can be supplied through the database and transaction processing systems. These also provide access to status information. For instance, an inventory status report can show the on-hand quantity for every item in inventory, flagging those items whose levels are too low or too high based on the inventory model used. Thus the supervisor can easily take action on items needing attention; without the report they would be difficult to identify.

The staff specialist assisting management in particular functional areas makes substantial use of the capabilities of MIS. The database is searched for problems. The data is analyzed to find possible solutions. Planning models are utilized to arrive at a first approximation of plans for management to examine. The model base provides the means for intelligence and design as staff specialists formulate data for managerial use. They may also examine and analyze data from external sources and incorporate them into models.

Since, currently, many decision models are somewhat difficult to use and require some knowledge of data processing, higher-level managers may not take the time to do analyses themselves. There is a trend toward the creation of specialist staff positions to handle such processing for managers.

Higher levels of management are affected by MIS through improved response to inquiries, continuous monitoring of important variables (rather than periodic reporting), and improved capability to identify problems or opportunities. Management control is enhanced by planning models and analytical models. For the highest level of management, strategic planning is aided by strategic planning models and analysis methods which support their use.

INFORMATION AS A STRATEGIC WEAPON

Sears sends reminders to customers that it is time to renew their service contracts. "It also sends letters offering special package deals to customers who have bought several appliances but have not purchased maintenance contracts for any of them. By keeping track of the appliance purchases made by each customer, as well as the service plans and maintenance calls for those appliances, Sears has been able to create a powerful marketing tool that is helping to boost service revenue and win customer goodwill."

"Owens-Corning Fiberglass Corp. ... is turning information developed by in-house research and development into what could prove a lucrative new marketing tool. The Toledo company generated substantial data on the energy efficiency of a wide variety of house designs when it was conducting research to develop new insulation materials several years ago. Now, to boost sales of its home insulation products, Owens-Corning has developed a computer program that uses these data to come up with energy-efficiency ratings for new designs. Owens has begun to offer builders free evaluations of their designs if they agree to buy all of their insulation from the manufacturer and meet a minimum standard of energy efficiency."

"Fidelity Brokerage Services Inc. spent $8 million for a proprietary system that has vaulted it into the No. 2 slot in the discount brokerage business—a move that was made against much larger rivals. Its system allows a broker using a terminal on his desk to execute stock trades more quickly and less expensively than most competitors who buy their services from outside computing companies."

"Xerox Corp. decided to put a good deal of value on faster information, and it is reaping significant rewards. By year end, Xerox expects it will have cut manufacturing costs in its copier division by 18% from those of three years ago. To accomplish that, it had to revamp 10 key manufacturing operations and change a number of business practices, including those in materials handling and inventory control. Xerox now exchanges quality-control information with its suppliers via computer terminals to eliminate the expensive inspection of incoming parts. In turn, the copier maker gives suppliers its master manufacturing schedule so they can ship parts at precisely the time that Xerox needs them on its production line, thus keeping inventories lean."

Excerpted from "Business is Turning Data into a Potent Strategic Weapon," *Business Week,* August 22, 1983, pp. 92-98.

THE MIS PROFESSIONAL

An organization typically has a separate MIS function which is responsible for acquiring and operating system hardware, acquiring or developing software, and managing the overall MIS resource. MIS professionals with a diverse array of skills are required to staff the MIS function. There is also a need for MIS professionals whose primary role is to adequately service the needs of a diverse user community.

The field of computing did not, in the beginning, emphasize formal education as a preparation. The field is now so broad and complex that some amount of formal education is generally necessary for a career in information systems. Two obvious alternatives are computer science and management information systems.

Although very useful, computer science alone is generally not sufficient for the management information systems specialist. Understanding basic organizational functions (marketing, finance, manufacturing, accounting, management, etc.) is as important as knowledge of computers. Understanding decision making and human behavior in interaction with computer systems is as important as knowledge of programming. Understanding the dynamics of organizational change is as important as technical skills.

An example of academic preparation suitable for MIS is the curriculum recommendation of the Association for Computing Machinery (ACM) for those who wish to specialize in computer-based organizational information systems.[2] The curriculum is a post-bachelor's degree program to provide educational preparation for a career in information systems. Figure 1-5 shows the basic structure of the proposed curriculum. A similar, but scaled-down, curriculum has been proposed for undergraduates.[3] A somewhat comparable curriculum has been proposed by a committee of IFIP (the International Federation for Information Processing). A curriculum with a slightly different orientation has been developed by DPMA (the Data Processing Management Association).[4]

The ACM curriculum is especially interesting in the context of MIS because it specifies academic preparation for two types of information systems professionals: the information analyst who works with users to define information requirements and the system designer who specifies hardware and software requirements. The information analyst is concerned with organizational information needs, whereas the system designer has more technical computer training. The role of the information analyst includes facilitation of organizational change; an information analyst should be conversant with the basic organizational functions and may even report to the functional area for which information services are being provided.

PURPOSE AND ORGANIZATION OF THIS TEXT

The text is designed to serve the purposes of two sets of readers. The first group includes people who are or will be managers of an organizational function that is supported by MIS or their staff support specialists. Such persons need to know how MIS can provide them with information that will help them function more effectively. They also need to understand principles of information systems in order to effectively develop and use end user systems. The second group are computer professionals who need to broaden their

---

[2]Jay F. Nunamaker, J. Daniel Couger, and Gordon B. Davis, "Information Systems Curriculum Recommendations for the 80s: Undergraduate and Graduate Programs—A Report of the ACM Curriculum Committee on Information Systems," *Communications of the ACM*, 25:11, November 1982, pp. 781–805.

[3]Nunamaker, Couger, and Davis, "Information Systems Curriculum Recommendations for the 80s."

[4]The IFIP Curriculum had not yet been published; it is expected to be published by North Holland. "DPMA Model Curriculum for Undergraduate Computer Information Systems Education," prepared by the Data Processing Management Association Education Foundation Committee on Curriculum Development, 1981.

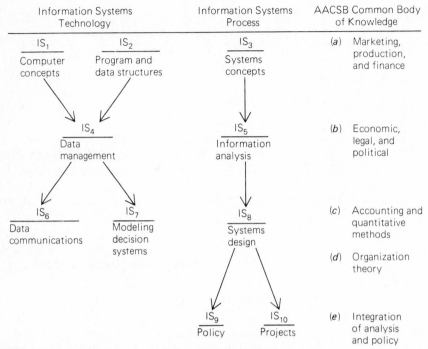

| Information Systems Technology | Information Systems Process | AACSB Common Body of Knowledge |

Figure 1-5
Curriculum for professional program in information systems. (Figure 1 from J. F. Nunamaker, J. D. Couger, and G. B. Davis, "Information Systems Curriculum Recommendations for the 80s: Undergraduate and Graduate Programs—A Report of the ACM Curriculum Committee on Information Systems," *Communications of the ACM*, 25:11, November 1982, p. 787.) ©1982, Association for Computing Machinery, Inc. By permission.

knowledge of information systems and learn to comprehend user needs for information. This group needs an orientation to MIS as a concept and philosophy.

The book emphasizes the role of the user in the design, development, and operation of information systems. The design methods and design principles presented in the text are applicable both to the MIS professional as a designer and to the end user who specifies requirements and/or develops applications.

Purpose of the Text

This text is different from most other books on computers and information systems. Its purpose is to be more than descriptive; its purpose is to explain "why" and "under what conditions." A person who studies or works in information systems in organizations may be able to describe the different components of a system but still not understand how and why the parts fit together. The text emphasizes not only alternatives in information system development, design, and use; it also specifies conditions and decision criteria for selecting among alternatives. The book thus contains descriptive material for conceptual understanding, but emphasizes developing an ability to discriminate and select among alternatives.

The last point is often related to contingency theory. The idea is that the selection of a method, format, design, procedure, etc., is *contingent* on the characteristics of the problem or situation. A contingency theory specifies the characteristics, the alternatives, and the rules or criteria for selection. The text presents contingency theories for a number of important decisions in MIS design, implementation, and operation.

Organization of the Text

The text is divided into seven sections. In the remainder of this section, the structure of an MIS will be explained (Chapter 2). In Section Two, the technical environment surrounding MIS will be described. This includes an overview of hardware, software, and communication facilities (Chapter 3); storage and retrieval of data (Chapter 4); and transaction processing, office automation, and information processing control functions (Chapter 5).

A complete understanding of computer-based organizational information systems requires an understanding of information use and information value, and how they relate to the organization and humans as information processors. Section Three of the text (Chapters 6 through 11) covers these conceptual foundations. It is a key section of the text. To illustrate the coverage, the concepts covered are listed below with comments on their relevance to an MIS.

Concept	Comments
The decision making process	MIS design should reflect not only rational approaches for optimization in making decisions but also the behavioral theory of organizational decision making.
Concepts of information	Information is that which adds to a representation. It has attributes of age and quality. It also has value in that it changes decisions.
Humans as information processors	The capabilities of humans as information processors impose limitations on information systems and suggest principles for their design.
System concepts	Because a management information system is a system, and also part of an organizational system, the concepts of systems are useful in designing approaches to information system development.
Concepts of planning and control	Information processing is a significant part of the important organizational activities of planning and control.
Organizational structure and management concepts	An information system exists within an organization and is designed to support management functions; information is an important determinant of organizational form.

An underlying assumption is that information systems add value to an organization. Information is viewed as a resource much like land, labor, and capital. It is not a free good. It must be obtained, processed, stored, retrieved, manipulated and analyzed, distributed, etc. An organization with a well-designed information system will generally have a competitive advantage over organizations with poorer systems.

The MIS as a support system for all forms of organizational knowledge work is the focus of Section Four. This is divided into information support for decision making (Chapter 12) and general support for knowledge work (Chapter 13).

Section Five is concerned with determining information requirements for MIS. There are four areas of concern: developing a long-range plan (Chapter 14), strategies for determining information requirements (Chapter 15), data modeling for database requirements (Chapter 16), and user interface requirements (Chapter 17).

The translation of information requirements into an installed system that is utilized effectively and accepted by its users is a difficult process. Section Six covers development, implementation and ongoing management of information systems. Chapter 18 covers techniques for design and development of information systems, including implementation as an organizational change process. Chapter 19 reviews techniques for maintaining information system efficiency and effectiveness, while Chapter 20 provides an overview of management of the MIS function. The final chapter of the text summarizes important current issues, future developments, and societal implications of MIS.

SUMMARY

Information is a vital ingredient for the operations and management of any organization. The scope of a formal information system in an organization is limited by the data that can be obtained, the cost of obtaining, processing, and storing the data; the cost of retrieval and distribution; the value of the information to the user; and the capability of humans to accept and act on the information. A computer-based management information system is designed to both reduce the costs and increase the capabilities of organizational information processing.

A definition of a management information system is an integrated, user-machine system for providing information to support the operations, management, and decision-making functions in an organization. The system utilizes computer hardware and software; manual procedures; models for analysis, planning, control, and decision making; and a database. Online operations facilitate user-machine dialog and interactive analysis, planning and decision making. MIS is an evolving concept. Rather than a single large system, an MIS is a federation of loosely integrated subsystems. Functional subsystems of an MIS may be developed separately, guided by a master development plan, and integrated through the database. Rather than being distinct from data processing, MIS is an orientation which guides the development and operation of data processing systems. Three concepts which are incorporated into the MIS orientation are decision support systems, information resource management, and end user computing.

The concept of MIS may be viewed as a substantial extension of the concepts of managerial accounting, operations research, and organizational theories related to management and decision making. The content of computer science is relevant, but management information systems as an academic discipline is more of an extension of organizational behavior and management than computer science.

Subsystems of MIS can be described in terms of organizational functions (such as marketing and production) or activities (such as planning and transaction processing). Each functional subsystem can be viewed as containing activity subsystems related to that function.

Different classes of users of MIS will use it differently. Clerical users primarily provide input and data control. First-line supervisors use it for operational control and detailed exception reporting. Management uses it for special reports and analyses, often employing a staff specialist to manipulate decision models and perform analyses. Because of the complexity of the process of MIS development and need for judgment, there is a need for comprehensive academic training for MIS professionals.

The text is directed at both users and developers of an MIS. It has a unique emphasis on conceptual foundations and contingency theory. The study of the text should aid in developing an understanding of what MIS is, why it is that way, and how it is developed and managed.

MINICASES

1 AMERICAN EXPRESS WITHDRAWS $1 BILLION IDS OFFER

The following excerpts are from a news article in the Minneapolis *Star and Tribune*, August 17, 1983, p. 58.

"American Express Co. called off its acquisition of Investors Diversified Services, Inc. (IDS), Tuesday, saying that $1 billion was too high a price." (IDS has investment funds such as mutual funds and money market funds. It would therefore allow American Express to expand its range of services to customers.)

"Although American Express officials would not comment further, several observers said that problems discovered at IDS probably lay behind the decision....[The] article [in the *Wall Street Journal*] said that American Express feared that IDS's data-processing system was inadequate to handle the new products planned for the IDS sales staff. American Express officials also were concerned about the 30 percent annual turnover among sales person-nel....Walter Scott, IDS president, responded that IDS's data-processing was quite competent and has absorbed at least one new product a month for two years." (Note: The acquisition was completed after a revised offer.)

Questions

a Why should American Express be so concerned about the capabilities of IDS's data processing?

b What competitive advantages to a financial services company may be provided by an information system?

2 HOW LONG CAN OPERATIONS AND MANAGEMENT ACTIVITIES CONTINUE WITHOUT INFORMATION?

In the chapter, estimates were given for how long an organization could operate without computer data processing. The concept of survival without information can be refined by dividing the organization's activities into operations, operational planning and control, management control, and strategic planning. The length of time for information deprivation to affect the organization differs in much the same way that deprivation of the elements required for human survival take different times to adversely affect human existence:

TIME FOR DEPRIVATION TO HAVE SERIOUS EXTREME EFFECT

Deprivation of human needs		Information deprivation		
Element	Time for serious adverse effect	Element	Activities affected	Time for serious adverse effect
Oxygen	Few minutes	Transaction documents	Operations	Hours to days
Water	Few days	Daily or weekly operations reports	Operational control	Days to weeks

**TIME FOR DEPRIVATION TO HAVE
SERIOUS EXTREME EFFECT**

Deprivation of human needs		Information deprivation		
Element	Time for serious adverse effect	Element	Activities affected	Time for serious adverse effect
Food	Few weeks	Planning and control reports	Management control	Weeks to months
Emotional support	Few months or years	Long term trend reports	Strategic planning	Months to years

Even though emotional support is as necessary for complete and normal human development as oxygen, death will occur in minutes without oxygen, whereas months or years may pass before serious effects surface with emotional deprivation. By analogy, if transaction documents (bills, invoices, checks, etc.) are not produced, organizations will quickly cease to function, but if strategic planning information is not made available and used, the organization will eventually fail because it does not adapt to change.

Questions
a If you were a chief executive, how would the above analysis affect your policies and plans for information systems?
b Explain the decision you would make with respect to the following alternative projects.
   (1) Transaction system backup project versus a decision support system for strategic planning.
   (2) A weekly inventory control report versus a yearly inventory analysis.

3 REQUIREMENTS TO PROGRAM NUMERICALLY CONTROLLED MACHINE
Company A does machining, welding, finishing, and assembling. The company uses two large numerically controlled work centers containing tools controlled by a computer. There were several problems, one of the major ones being programming of the machines. Errors in the programming created conflict between the programmers and operators.

In studying this situation, it was noted that machine programmers were segregated from machine operators not only by physical location, but also educational and vocational backgrounds. As a result, communication between them was very low. Machine programmers had difficulty in programming the machines efficiently. For example, a drill bit was programmed to withdraw over two feet in order to rotate a piece of work; a movement of a few inches would have been sufficient.

  Source: W. C. Giauque and W. J. Sawaya, "Automated Manufacturing: Two Cases Where It Failed to Match Its Promise," *Exchange*, Winter 1984, p. 9.

Questions
a What are the important components of academic knowledge required for an in-depth analysis of the problem and design and implementation of solutions?
b Suggest a solution based on the limited facts given.

EXERCISES

1 Read several articles on MIS and develop your own definition of MIS.
2 Describe the effect of applying computer technology to information systems in terms of:
  a Speed of processing
  b Scope of information system
  c Complexity of system design and operation
3 How does MIS differ from:
  a Managerial accounting?
  b Operations research?
4 Why is a database generally a feature of an MIS?
5 Read the following two articles by John Dearden and write an analysis covering the following points:
  a Valid objections
  b Irrelevant points
  c Invalid objections
    Dearden, John: "MIS is a Mirage," *Harvard Business Review*, January–February 1972, pp. 90–99.
    Dearden, John: "Myth of Real-Time Management Information," *Harvard Business Review*, May–June 1966, pp. 123–132.
    (Hint: You may wish to read the Letters to the Editor in May–June 1972 following the article "MIS is a Mirage.")
6 Some critics of the MIS concept (see John Dearden, "Myth of Real-Time Management Information") say that management does not generally need completely up-to-date information and therefore online systems for management cannot be justified. Comment.
7 Explain the concept of an integrated system.
8 Why is the MIS developed as a federation of systems rather than as a single, total system?
9 MIS has been "pushed" by computer technology. Explain.
10 How might the following employees be affected by a comprehensive MIS:
  a Accounts receivable clerk?
  b Sales representative?
  c Sales manager?
  d Plant manager?
  e Staff analyst for financial vice president?
  f President?
11 What are the functions commonly found in an information system for:
  a A manufacturing company?
  b A department store?
12 What management activity modules might one find in a rather complete MIS?
13 Explain the difference between information analyst and computer systems designer. (Hint: Read Jay F. Nunamaker, J. Daniel Couger, and Gordon B. Davis, "Information Systems Curriculum Recommendations for the 80s: Undergraduate and Graduate Programs—A Report of the ACM Curriculum Committee on Information Systems," *Communications of the ACM*, 25:11, November 1982, pp. 781–805.)
14 A person who understands all about computer hardware, software, and programming may not be suited to design a computer-based management information system. Why not?
15 Explain in your own words the following relationships:
  a MIS to DSS
  b MIS to IRM
  c MIS to data processing
  d MIS to computer science

STRUCTURE OF A MANAGEMENT INFORMATION SYSTEM

What does a management information system look like? What is its conceptual structure? What is its physical structure? This chapter addresses these questions. There is no standard, agreed-upon framework for describing management information systems. However, the central tendency is reflected in the chapter.

This chapter emphasizes the scope of MIS as a broad concept and thus reflects an "ideal" toward which an organization may move as it designs or redesigns its information systems. The organization's management information system is not a distinct entity, separate from its other information systems. Rather it represents a broad framework within which individual information systems (or subsystems) fit. In the text, "management information system" and "information system" are used interchangeably to refer to this broad framework.

Like most complex systems, a management information system can be described in a number of different ways. For example, imagine describing an automobile to someone without prior experience with a car. It might be explained in terms of its physical characteristics of shape, color, seating capacity, number of doors, etc. It could also be described in terms of the component systems such as chassis, engine, or transmission, and how these components are related to achieve a working automobile. One might also classify cars in terms of major use, such as a station wagon, sedan, and sports car. Each of these classifications would provide insight to the person seeking to understand automobiles.

Multiple approaches are used in this chapter to explain the structure of an organizational information system or management information system. The information system is described in terms of four separate but related classifications:

1 Operating elements
2 Decision support
3 Management activity
4 Organizational function

After describing management information systems from these four perspectives, the chapter presents a synthesis of the last three categories into a single model of a management information system.

OPERATING ELEMENTS OF AN INFORMATION SYSTEM

If one requested to be shown the information system of an organization, he or she would probably be shown its physical components. An inquiry as to what these physical components do might be answered in terms of processing functions or perhaps in terms of system outputs for users.

Physical Components

The physical components required for an organizational information system are hardware, software, database, procedures, and operations personnel. These elements, shown below, are described in further detail in Chapters 3, 4, and 5.

Physical component	Description
Hardware	Hardware refers to phyical computer equipment and associated devices. Hardware must provide for five major functions: 1 Input or entry 2 Output 3 Secondary storage for data and programs 4 Central processor (computation, control, and primary storage) 5 Communications
Software	Software is a broad term given to the instructions that direct the operation of the hardware. The software can be classified into two major types: system software and application software.
Database	The database contains all data utilized by application software. An individual set of stored data is often referred to as a file. The physical existence of stored data is evidenced by the physical storage media (computer tapes, disk packs, diskettes, etc.) used for secondary storage.
Procedures	Formal operating procedures are physical components because they exist in a physical form such as a manual or instruction booklet. Three major types of procedures are required: 1 User instructions (for users of the application to record data, employ a terminal to enter or retrieve data, or use the result) 2 Instructions for preparation of input by data preparation personnel 3 Operating instructions for computer operations personnel
Operations personnel	Computer operators, systems analysts, programmers, data preparation personnel, information systems management, data administrators, etc.

Processing Functions

A description of an information system in terms of physical components does not explain what the system does, just as a description of a hardware configuration does not explain

Process transactions

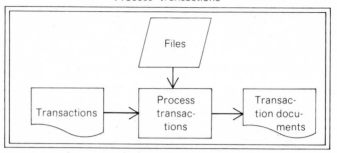

Maintain history (master) files

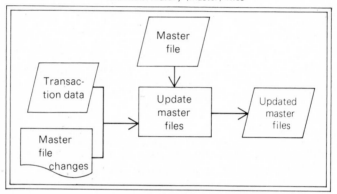

Produce reports

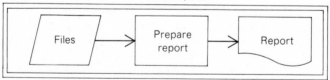

Process inquiries

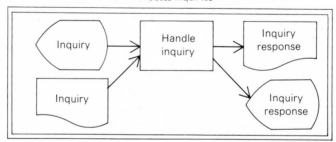

Process interactive support applications

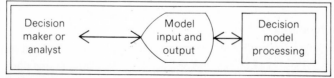

Figure 2-1
Processing functions.

why it is configured in that way. Another way to describe an information system is in terms of processing functions (Figure 2-1). The major processing functions are the following:

Processing function	Comments
Process transactions	A transaction is an activity such as making a purchase or a sale or manufacturing a product. It may be internal to the organization or may involve the organization and an external entity. Performance of a transaction requires records to (1) direct a transaction to take place, (2) report, confirm, or explain its performance, or (3) communicate the transaction to those needing a record for background information or reference.
Maintain master files	Many processing activities require creation and files maintenance of master files, which store relatively permanent or historical data about organizational entities. For example, processing to prepare an employee's paycheck requires data items for the employee's rate of pay, deductions, etc. When transactions are processed, master file data items are updated to reflect the most current information.
Produce reports	Reports are significant products of an information system. Scheduled reports are produced on a regular basis. An information system should also be able to produce special reports quickly based on ad hoc (unscheduled) requests.
Process inquiries	Other outputs of the information system are responses to inquiries using the database. These may be regular inquiries with a preset format or ad hoc inquiries. The essential function of inquiry processing is to make any record or any item in the database easily accessible to authorized personnel.
Process interactive support applications	The information system contains applications designed to support systems for planning, analysis, and decision making. The computer performs processing based on a planning model, decision model, etc.; the mode of operation is interactive with the user responding to questions and requests for data and receiving immediate results in order to alter inputs until a solution or satisfactory result is achieved.

Outputs for Users

The user of a management information system provides inputs and receives outputs. The user's assessment of the information system is therefore dependent somewhat on the ease of input but is primarily based on the usefulness of the output the user sees. The outputs thus form one description of an information system and can be classified as being of five major types:

1 Transaction documents or screens
2 Preplanned reports
3 Preplanned inquiry responses
4 Ad hoc reports and inquiry responses
5 User-machine dialog results

Examples of transaction documents are items such as sales invoices, payroll checks, customer billings, and purchase orders. Transaction documents refer directly to the operations of the organization, while the other types of outputs support management and control of those operations.

Transaction document type	Explanation and examples
Informational	Reports or confirms that action will be or has been taken. Examples are a sales order confirmation verifying receipt of an order from a customer and a report describing receipt of goods previously ordered. Their purpose is to provide feedback to persons connected in some way with the action or later reference.
Action	Requests or instructions for action. A purchase order initiates a purchase, a check instructs the bank to pay, a production order instructs production actions.
Investigational	Reports exceptions, errors, or other conditions that may require investigation. Used for control and future reference.

Reports, inquiry responses, and dialog results provide four types of information:

1 Monitoring information. The information confirms that actions have been taken and reports status in financial or other terms. The information also provides the recipient with background for understanding other reports and analyses. Monitoring information may provide a basis for problem finding and diagnosis and may lead to action, but no action is specified by the information itself.

2 Problem finding information.[1] The information is presented in a format that promotes identification of problems. Examples are comparisons between enterprise data and standards (internal standards, industry averages, or competitor data) and projections of current performance to the end of a reporting period.

3 Action information. The information is presented with action specified or implied.

4 Decision support. The report, inquiry, result, or dialog is oriented to performing analysis and making a decision.

Preplanned reports have a regular content and format and are usually run on a regularly scheduled basis. Examples are sales analysis, inventory status, and budget variance reports. Prepared at a given time, they reflect one of three conditions with respect to the time period they cover:

1 They describe status or condition at a point in time (such as inventory status as of January 31, 1985);

2 They summarize what has occurred during a period such as a week, month, or year (e.g., sales during month of March 1985);

3 They present results to date and project to the end of the period (such as a year).

Preplanned inquiries are generally associated with limited output, usually with respect to a small number of items, and result in such output as inventory on hand of part 37518, pay rate of employee 518238142, or balance due from customer XYZ Industries.

---

[1] Based on C. H. P. Brookes, "A Framework for DSS Development," Information Systems Forum Research Report, Department of Information Systems, University of New South Wales, 1984.

Inquiries are typically handled online, which means the inquiry is entered and response received immediately via terminal. Since the inquiry has been preplanned, the input format of the inquiry is generally quite simple, and therefore the terminal may be operated directly by the user requesting the information.

Ad hoc reports and inquiry responses occur at irregular intervals and require data or analysis whose format has not been preplanned. If the data items needed are not available, a data collection procedure must be planned and implemented. If the data is already stored in the information system, the ad hoc request may be handled in two ways:

1 The user may be provided with a means for preparing and processing the request. The inquiry may, for example, be formulated by use of an inquiry language using either an online terminal or special coding forms for subsequent transcription to machine-readable form.

2 An information service (often called an information center) may be available to process ad hoc requests. Specialists staffing the information service aid users to analyze requests and specify the retrieval and processing necessary to provide the requested data or analysis.

Regardless of how the request is handled, the capability for the system to respond to the inquiry within a reasonable period of time (from a minute to a day) to support the current needs and activities of the organization is crucial.

User-machine dialog differs from reports or inquiries. It is essentially a way in which a user can interact with a model to arrive at an analysis or a solution. User-machine interaction employs a terminal such as a visual display terminal or a stand-alone personal computer plus computer processing of a model such as an analysis, planning, or decision model. Examples are site planning models, capital investment analysis models, and portfolio management models.

MANAGEMENT INFORMATION SYSTEM SUPPORT FOR DECISION MAKING

Decisions vary with respect to the structure that can be provided for making them. A highly structured decision can be preplanned or prespecified, whereas a highly unstructured decision cannot. A structured decision can be said to be programmable, in the sense that unambiguous decision rules can be specified in advance. The term does not necessarily mean that the decision is automated, although many programmable decisions are automated. An unstructured decision is said to be nonprogrammable. The structured, programmable decision tends to be routine and frequently repeated; the unstructured decision tends to occur with less frequency and tends to be nonroutine. Decision making will be explained in more detail in Chapter 6.

Information system support will differ for the two types of decisions. Some decisions will fit easily into this classification, but many decisions are more or less structured and have some elements that are programmable and some that are not.

Structured, Programmable Decisions

When a decision can be programmed, an organization can prepare a decision rule or decision procedure. This can be expressed as a set of steps to follow, a flowchart, a decision table, or a formula. The decision procedure will also specify the information to be acquired before the decision rules are applied. Since structured, programmable decisions can be prespecified, many of these decisions can be handled by lower-level personnel with little specialized knowledge. In fact, many highly structured decisions may be completely automated, although human review is generally considered desirable. Examples of highly structured decisions are inventory reorder formulas and rules for granting credit.

The information system requirements for structured decisions are clear and unambiguous procedures for entering the required input data, validation procedures to ensure correct and complete input, processing of the input using the decision logic, and output of the programmed decision in a form that is useful for action. A useful output should be clear as to how it is to be used and should contain enough data to assist the recipient to assess the reasonableness of the decision.

In many cases, it is not possible to define a decision procedure or decision rule to handle all possible situations. In these cases, the decision rules are written to apply to the most common situations, and the uncommon or unusual situations that do not apply are referred to a human decision maker, usually one with some specialized knowledge.

Unstructured, Nonprogrammable Decisions

The unstructured decision has no preestablished decision procedure, either because the decision is too infrequent to justify the organizational cost of preparing a decision procedure (even though it may be partly programmable) or because the decision process is not understood well enough or is too changeable to allow a stable preestablished decision procedure. The support requirements for unstructured decision making are access to data and a variety of analysis and decision procedures that can be applied to the solution of the problem. The data requirements are not completely known in advance, so data retrieval must allow for ad hoc retrieval requests. Interactive decision support systems with generalized inquiry and analysis capabilities are appropriate information system support for unstructured decision making. Decision support systems will be discussed in more detail in Chapter 12.

MANAGEMENT INFORMATION SYSTEM STRUCTURE BASED ON MANAGEMENT ACTIVITY

Management information systems support management activity. This means that the structure of an information system can be classified in terms of a hierarchy of management planning and control activities.

Hierarchy of Management Activity

The following categories of management planning and control were defined by Anthony:[2]

---

[2]R. N. Anthony, *Planning and Control Systems: A Framework For Analysis*, Harvard University Press, Cambridge, 1965.

Level	Comments
Strategic planning	Definition of goals, policies, and general guidelines charting course for organization. Determination of organizational objectives.
Management control and tactical planning	Acquisition of resources. Acquisition tactics, plant location, new products. Establishment and monitoring of budgets.
Operational planning and control	Effective and efficient use of existing facilities and resources to carry out activities within budget constraints.

The three levels of management activity can be differentiated on the basis of the planning horizon for each level. Strategic planning deals with long-range considerations. The decisions to be made are concerned with the choice of business direction, market strategy, product mix, etc. Management control and tactical planning has a medium-term planning horizon. It includes acquisition and organization of resources, structuring of work, and acquisition and training of personnel. It is reflected in the capital expenditure budget, the three-year staffing plan, etc. Operational planning and control is related to short-term decisions for current operations. Pricing, production levels, inventory levels, etc., are a result of operational planning and control activities.

A particular manager may have responsibility for a mix of management activities, but proportions shift with management level. For instance, a shop floor supervisor will spend most of his or her time on operational planning and control. An executive vice president will devote, by comparison, more time to strategic planning.

The activities and information processing for the three levels are interrelated. For example, inventory control at the operational level depends on accurate processing of transactions; at the level of management control, decisions made about safety stock and reorder frequency are dependent on correct summarization of results of operations; at the strategic level, results in operations and management control are related to strategic objectives, competitor behavior, and so forth to arrive at inventory strategy. There is a marked contrast between characteristics required of information for strategic planning and for operational control, with management control and tactical planning being somewhat in the middle. Table 2-1 shows the differences for seven information characteristics. Given these differences, information system support for strategic planning should be quite different from information system support for operational control. These differences are explored in further detail later in this chapter and in subsequent chapters.

TABLE 2-1 INFORMATION REQUIREMENTS BY LEVEL OF MANAGEMENT ACTIVITY

Characteristics of information	Operational control	Management control	Strategic planning
Source	Largely internal	←————————————————→	External
Scope	Well-defined, narrow	←————————————→	Very wide
Level of aggregation	Detailed	←————————————————→	Aggregate

TABLE 2-1 INFORMATION REQUIREMENTS BY LEVEL OF MANAGEMENT ACTIVITY

Characteristics of Information	Operational control	Management control	Strategic planning
Time horizon	Historical ←――――――――――――――――――――→		Future
Currency	Highly current ←―――――――――――――――――→		Quite old
Required accuracy	High ←―――――――――――――――――――→		Low
Frequency of use	Very frequent ←――――――――――――――――――→		Infrequent

Reprinted from "Framework for Management Information Systems" by G. A. Gorry and M. S. Scott Morton, *Sloan Management Review*, Fall 1971, p. 59, by permission of the publisher. ©1971 by the Sloan Management Review Association. All rights reserved.

Decisions vary as to the degree of structure within each level of management activity, although the majority of decisions at the operational control level are relatively structured and the majority of decisions at the strategic planning level are relatively unstructured. Table 2-2 shows examples of structured and unstructured decisions at each management level. The table also shows that information systems to support structured versus unstructured decisions are characteristically different. Structured decision systems provide decision rules and exception reports but are relatively inflexible as to content and format. Decision support systems (DSS), on the other hand, are characterized by flexible access to the database, a variety of flexible output formats, and a collection of decision models to "support" the manager in the decision-making *process*.

TABLE 2-2 TYPES OF DECISION BY MANAGEMENT ACTIVITY

		Operational control	Management control	Strategic planning
	Structured ↑			
Structured decision systems		Inventory reorder decisions	Pricing of bids	Acquisition of a company
		Production scheduling	Selection of credit line institutions	Addition of new product line
		Selection of vendor	Allocation of advertising	Entry into new market
Decision support systems		Hiring of new supervisor	Internal organization of a department	New organization of company
	Unstructured ↓			

The following three sections summarize the characteristics of information system support for the three levels of the hierarchy of management planning and control.

Information Systems for Operational Control

Operational control is the process of ensuring that operational activities are carried out effectively and efficiently. Operational control makes use of preestablished procedures and decision rules. A large percentage of the decisions are programmable. The procedures to follow are generally quite stable. The operating decisions and resulting actions usually cover short time periods (a day to a week). Individual transactions are often important, so that the operational system must be able to respond to both individual transactions and summaries of transactions.

Processing support for operational control consists of (Figure 2-2):

1 Transaction processing
2 Report processing
3 Inquiry processing

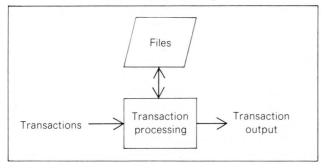

Transaction processing

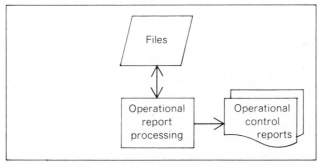

Control reports

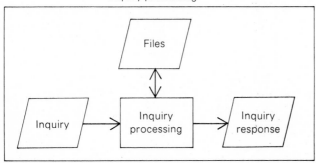

Inquiry processing

Figure 2-2
Processing to support operational control.

These three types of processing contain various decision-making routines which implement prespecified decision rules or provide output describing the decision that will be taken unless the user responsible overrides it. Some examples will illustrate the type of decision procedures that can be designed into operational control systems.

- An inventory withdrawal transaction produces a transaction document. The transaction processing program can also examine the balance on hand, etc., and decide (using preestablished criteria) if a replenishment order should be placed. If so, the order quantity is calculated by use of an order quantity algorithm, and an action document is produced which specifies the need for an order plus the order quantity. The human recipient (e.g., inventory analyst) may accept the order as it is or may choose to override the programmed decision by canceling it or adjusting the order quantity.
- An inquiry to a personnel file describes the requirements for a position. The computer search of the employee file uses preprogrammed rules to select and rank candidates.
- A telephone order clerk taking an order enters the data online using a visual display terminal. In the case of a stockout, programmed decision rules are applied to identify substitute items which the order taker can suggest to the customer.
- A programmed decision rule in a report processing procedure may cause issuance of special reports to provide information in a problem area. An example might be a report showing orders still outstanding after 30 days, produced as a result of an unusually high (the limit prespecified) 30-day balance.

The database for operational control and operational decision making contains primarily internal data generated from transactions. The data items are generally quite current. Care must be taken to interpret data being recorded from operations, since the sequence of processing is often significant; for example, additions to inventory are processed before withdrawals in order to avoid the appearance of being out of stock when new stock has been received.

Information Systems for Management Control

Management control information is required by managers of departments, profit centers, etc., to measure performance, decide on control actions, formulate new decision rules to be applied by operational personnel, and allocate resources. Summary information is needed; it must be processed so that trends may be observed, reasons for performance variances may be understood, and solutions may be suggested. The control process requires the following types of information:

1 Planned performance (standard, expected, budgeted, etc.)
2 Variances from planned performance
3 Reasons for variances
4 Analysis of possible decisions or courses of action

The database for management control consists of two major elements: (1) the database provided by operations, and (2) the plans, standards, budgets, etc., which define management expectations about performance. There may also be some external data such as industry comparisons and cost indices (Figure 2-3).

The processing requirements to support management control activities are the following:

1 Planning and budget models to assist managers in finding problems in direction and preparing and revising plans 'and budgets. This includes projections of effects of current actions.

2 Variance reporting programs to process scheduled reports showing performance and variances from planned performance or other standards such as competitor performance.

3 Problem analysis models to analyze data to provide input for decision making.

4 Decision models to analyze a problem situation and provide possible solutions for management evaluation.

5 Inquiry models to assist in responding to inquiries.

The outputs from the management control information system are plans and budgets, scheduled reports, special reports, analyses of problem situations, decisions for review, and inquiry responses.

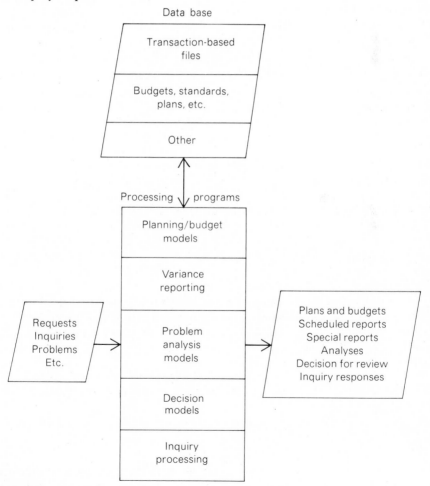

Figure 2-3
Management control database and processing support.

Information Systems for Strategic Planning

The purpose of strategic planning is to develop strategies by which an organization will be able to achieve its objectives. The time horizon for strategic planning tends to be fairly long, so that fundamental shifts in the organization may be made. For example:

- A department store chain may decide to diversify into the mail order business.
- A department store chain with stores in the central city may decide to change to a discount type of operation in the suburbs.
- A company manufacturing industrial products may decide to diversify into consumer lines.

Strategic planning activities do not have to occur on a periodic, regular cycle as do management control activities. They can be somewhat irregular, although some strategic planning may be scheduled into the yearly planning and budgeting cycle. Data requirements for strategic planning are generally for processed, summarized data from a variety of sources. There is need for considerable external data. Some examples of types of data that are useful in strategic planning illustrate the nature of the data requirements:

1 Outlook for the economy in the company's current and prospective areas of activity
2 Current and prospective political environment
3 Current capabilities and performance of the organization by market, country, etc. (based on current policies)
4 Prospects for the industry in each country
5 Capabilities of competitors and their market shares
6 Opportunities for new ventures based on current or expected developments
7 Alternative strategies
8 Projections of resource requirements for the alternative strategies

This database contains some "hard" facts, but much is based on judgment. Much of the data cannot be collected on a regular basis, and much of it cannot be specified completely in advance. For this reason, some have argued that it is impossible (or certainly impractical) to have a management information system for strategic planning activities. They point out the difficulty of efficiently coding, storing, and retrieving the multitude of rumors, facts, hunches, etc., that enter into an assessment of prospects for an industry, a market, or an economy.

An alternative to this view is that information system support cannot be as complete for strategic planning as it is for management control and operational control, but the system is one source of information that can provide substantial aid to the process of strategic planning. For example:

- The evaluation of current capabilities is based on internal data generated by operational processing requirements, but it may need to be summarized in a special way for planning use.
- The initial projections of future capability can be developed by analysis of past data. This first approximation is adjusted by management on the basis of judgment and experience.
- Fundamental market data on the industry and competitors can probably be kept in the organization's database.

- Databanks of public information regarding the industry and competitors may be purchased in machine-readable form for use with planning and decision models.

MANAGEMENT INFORMATION SYSTEM STRUCTURE BASED ON ORGANIZATIONAL FUNCTION

The structure of an information system can also be described in terms of the organizational functions which use information. There is no standard classification of functions, but a typical set of functions in a manufacturing organization includes production, sales and marketing, finance and accounting, logistics, personnel, and information systems. Top management can also be considered as a separate function. Each of these functions has unique information needs and each requires information system support designed for it. An organization may not actually be organized along functional lines (to be discussed in detail in Chapter 11), but in general the logical information subsystem will follow functional lines.

As explained in Chapter 1, a management information system is essentially a federation of information systems that are designed to support the functional subsystems of the organization. Each functional subsystem requires applications to perform all information processing related to the function, although this may involve calling upon a database, a model base, and some computer programs which are common to all functional subsystems. Within each functional subsystem, there will be applications for transaction processing, operational control, managerial control, and strategic planning (Figure 2-4).

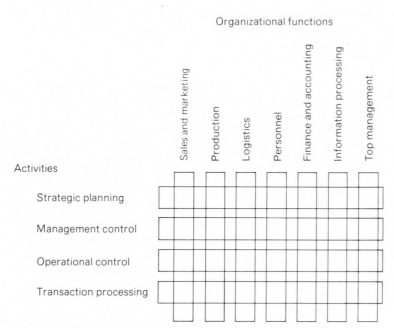

Figure 2-4
The matrix of functional subsystems and management activities.

Sales and Marketing Subsystems

The sales and marketing function generally includes all activities related to the promotion and sales of products or services. The transactions are sales orders, promotion orders, etc. The operational control activities include the hiring and training of the sales force, the day-to-day scheduling of sales and promotion efforts, and periodic analyses of sales volumes by region, product, customer, etc. Managerial control concerns comparisons of overall performance against a marketing plan. Information for managerial control may include data on customers, competitors, competitor products, and sales force requirements. Strategic planning for the marketing function involves consideration of new markets and new marketing strategies. The information requirements for strategic planning include customer analyses, competitor analyses, consumer survey information, income projection, demographic projections, and technology projections.

Production Subsystem

The responsibilities of the production or manufacturing function include product engineering, planning of production facilities, scheduling and operation of production facilities, employment and training of production personnel, and quality control and inspection. Typical transactions to be processed are production orders (based on an explosion of the sales orders and inventory requirements into component parts), assembly orders, finished parts tickets, scrap tickets, and time-keeping tickets. Operational control requires detailed reports comparing actual performance to the production schedule and highlighting areas where bottlenecks occur. Management control requires summary reports which compare overall planned or standard performance to actual performance for such classifications as cost per unit and labor used. Strategic planning for manufacturing includes alternative manufacturing approaches and alternative approaches to automation.

Logistics Subsystem

The logistics function encompasses such activities as purchasing, receiving, inventory control, and distribution. The transactions to be processed include purchase requisitions, purchase orders, manufacturing orders, receiving reports, tickets for inventory, shipping orders, and bills of lading. The operational control function uses information contained in reports such as past-due purchases, past-due shipments to customers, out-of-stock items, overstocked items, inventory turnover reports, vendor performance summaries, and shipper performance analyses. Managerial control information for logistics consists of overall comparisons between planned and actual inventory levels, costs for purchased items, stockouts, inventory turnover, etc. Strategic planning involves the analysis of new distribution strategies, new policies with regard to vendors, and ''make versus buy'' strategies. Information on new technology, distribution alternatives, etc., is required.

Personnel Subsystem

The personnel subsystem includes hiring, training, record keeping, payment, and termination of personnel. The transactions result in documents describing employment requisitions, job descriptions, training specifications, personnel data (background, skills, experience), pay rate changes, hours worked, paychecks, benefits, and termination notices. Operational control for personnel requires decision procedures for action such as hiring, training, termination, changing pay rates, and issuing benefits. Management control of the personnel function is supported by reports and analyses showing the variances resulting from differences between planned and actual performance for such classifications as number of employees hired, cost of recruiting, composition of skills inventory, cost of training (by employee, by program), salary paid, distribution of wage rates, and conformance with government equal opportunity requirements. Strategic planning for personnel is involved with evaluating alternative strategies for recruiting, salary, training, benefits, and building location to ensure that the organization obtains and retains personnel necessary to achieve its objectives. The strategic information required includes analyses of shifting patterns of employment, education, and wage rates by area of the country (or world).

Finance and Accounting Subsystem

Finance and accounting are somewhat separate functions but are sufficiently related to be described together. Finance is responsible for ensuring adequate organizational financing at as low a cost as possible (in a manner consistent with other objectives). This function covers granting of credit to customers, collection processes, cash management, and financing arrangements (loans, sales of stock, leasing). Accounting covers the classification of financial transactions and summarization into the standard financial reports (income statement and balance sheet), the preparation of budgets, and classification and analysis of cost data. Budget and cost data are input for managerial control reports, which means that accounting provides input for managerial control applications in all functions. Among the transactions associated with finance and accounting are credit applications, sales, billings, collection documents (statements), payment vouchers, checks, journal vouchers, ledgers, and stock transfers. Operational control over the function itself requires daily error and exception reports, records of processing delays, reports of unprocessed transactions, etc. The managerial control level for accounting and finance utilizes information on budgeted versus actual cost of financial resources, cost of processing accounting data, and error rates. The strategic planning level for accounting and finance involves a long-run strategy to ensure adequate financing, a long-range tax accounting policy to minimize the impact of taxes, and planning of systems for cost accounting and budgeting.

Information Processing Subsystem

The information processing function is responsible for ensuring that the other functions are provided the necessary information processing services and resources. Typical transactions for information processing are requests for processing, requests for corrections or changes in data and programs, reports of hardware and program performance, and project proposals. Operational control of information processing operations requires information on the daily schedule of jobs, error rates, and equipment failures; for new project development it requires daily or weekly schedules of programmer progress and test time. Managerial control over information processing requires data on planned versus actual utilization, equipment costs, overall programmer performance, and progress compared to schedule for projects to develop and implement new applications. Strategic planning for information systems involves the organization of the function (such as centralized or decentralized), the overall information system plan, selection of strategic uses of information, and the general structure of the hardware and software environment. For example, a major strategic decision might be to implement microcomputer workstations for all analysts, planners, and managers.

Office automation may be defined as a separate subsystem or included within information processing. Office automation includes a wide range of support facilities for knowledge work and clerical activities. Examples are word processing, electronic mail, electronic filing, and data and voice communications.

Top Management Subsystem

The top management function (chief executive officer plus staff) operates separately from the functional areas, but also includes the functional vice presidents acting in a top management capacity such as in management committees. The transactions processed by top management are primarily inquiries for information and support of decisions. The transaction documents, therefore, tend to be letters and memoranda. Responding to the inquiries and making decisions requires either access to the database and decision models of the organization or transmittal of the requests to other parts of the organization. The information for operational control in the top management function includes meeting schedules, correspondence control files, and contact files. Managerial control by top management uses information which summarizes the management control being exercised by other functions to evaluate whether the functions are performing as planned. This requires access to the plans and actual performance of all the functions. Strategic planning activities relate to matters such as direction of the company (which business it should be in) and plans for ensuring necessary resources. The strategy determined by top management sets the framework for strategic planning within function and also coordinates planning to remove major inconsistencies. Strategic planning at the top management level requires a wide variety of summarized external and internal data. Information system support for strategic planning may include ad hoc retrieval of data, ad hoc analyses, and decision support systems.

EXTERNAL INFORMATION DOMINATES EIS

In the design of an executive information system (EIS) for the chief officers of a large regional banking system, the requirements were dominated by external information not produced by the transaction system of data processing. Examples of external information requirements were:

- Competitor information
- Regultory information
- Regional economic indicators
- Customer preferences for services
- Quality of services being provided

SYNTHESIS OF A MANAGEMENT INFORMATION SYSTEM STRUCTURE

The MIS structure has been described in terms of support for decision making, management activity, and organizational functions. These three approaches will now be synthesized into a management information system structure. This is essentially a conceptual framework which allows one to describe an existing or planned information system. There is also a physical structure which defines the way an MIS is implemented.

Conceptual Structure

The conceptual structure of a management information system is defined as a federation of functional subsystems, each of which is divided into four major information processing components: transaction processing, operational control information system support, managerial control information system support, and strategic planning information system support. Each of the functional subsystems of the information system has some unique data files which are used only by that subsystem. There are also files which need to be accessed by more than one application and need to be available for general retrieval. These files are organized into a general database managed by a database management system.

A further amplification of the structure is the introduction of common software. In addition to application programs written especially for each subsystem, there are common applications which serve multiple functions. Each subsystem has linkages to these common applications. There are also many analytical and decision models that can

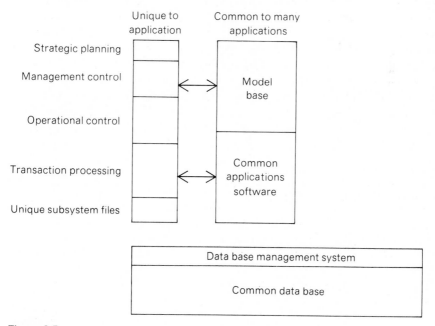

Figure 2-5
The information subsystem for a function (such as marketing or production).

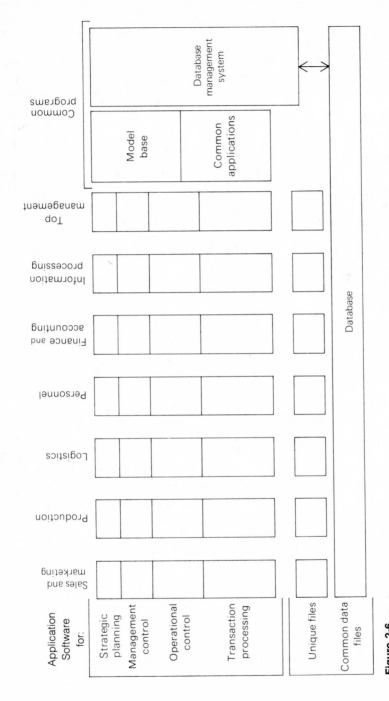

Figure 2-6
The organizational MIS.

be used by many applications. These form the model base for the information system. (The concept of a model base will be discussed in Chapter 12.)

This structure is diagrammed for a functional subsystem in Figure 2-5. The subsystem has unique programs and unique files for its basic activities. It shares the use of common applications software, a model base, a database, and the database management system. The database management system controls all files in the common database, and may also be used for storage and retrieval of the files unique to a function. The combination of all subsystems forms the management information system for the organization. This is diagrammed in Figure 2-6.

Within the three management activity classifications of a functional subsystem of the information system, applications can be classified as to the type of management information support provided. These can be monitoring information, action information, and decision support. This is illustrated in Figure 2-7.

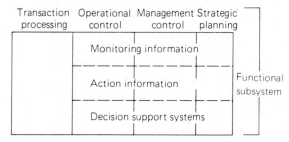

Figure 2-7
Type of management information support within a functional subsystem.

The amount of information processing resources required varies by level of management activity. Transaction processing is substantially more significant in terms of processing time, data volume, etc., than strategic planning. Transaction processing systems provide the base for all other internal information support. This concept of the large transaction processing base and a fairly small strategic planning component can be visualized as a pyramid (Figure 2-8). The lower part of the pyramid describes structured, well-defined procedures and decisions, while the top part of the pyramid represents more ad hoc, unstructured processes and decisions. The bottom levels of the pyramid are of more use to clerical personnel and lower-level managers, while the higher levels apply primarily to top management.

Physical Structure

The physical structure of an MIS would be identical to the conceptual structure if all applications consisted of completely separate programs used by only one function, but this is frequently not the case. Substantial economies can be achieved from:

1 Integrated processing
2 Use of common modules

Integrated processing is achieved by designing several related applications as a single system in order to simplify the interconnections and reduce the duplication of input. A

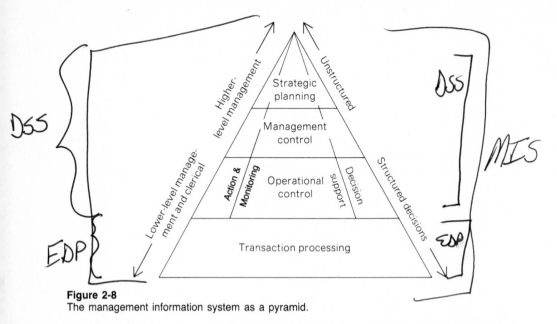

Figure 2-8
The management information system as a pyramid.

good example is an order entry system. The recording of an order initiates a sequence of processing, each step using new data but also much of the data from prior processing. The major steps in a typical sequence are:

Step	New data entered	Documents produced
Order entry	Sales representative identification	Order acknowledgment
	Customer identification	Credit exception notice
	Items ordered	Order register
	Quantity of each item	Picking document
		Items out of stock
		Items to be ordered
Shipping	Actual quantity shipped	Shipping document
Invoicing	Freight cost	Invoice register
		Sales journal
		Back-order register
Collection	Amounts received	Customer statements
	Returns and allowances	Returns and allowances register
		Cash receipts journal
		Accounts receivable aging
Analysis		Inventory status
		Sales by representative, district, customer, or other category

Note that a large number of documents and reports are prepared from the initial entry of the order plus later entry of actual quantity shipped, freight, amounts received on account, and returns and allowances. The assumption is made that the customer name,

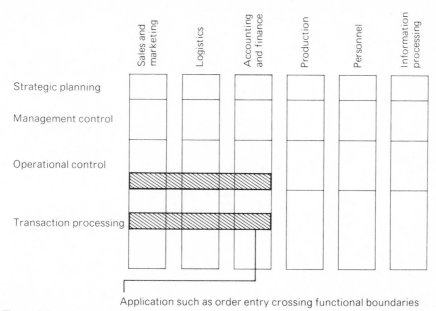

Figure 2-9
Applications crossing functional boundaries.

address, and credit status, plus price of each item, are contained in customer files and billing files. The documents and reports from order entry are not associated with a single function but with the sales and marketing, logistics, and accounting and finance functions. In other words, an integrated order entry system crosses functional boundaries (Figure 2-9).

Modularity is the design of an information system as a number of small sets of processing instructions called modules. Some modules are used only once in a single application; others are used in a large number of applications. The use of modules even in cases where each has a single purpose is desirable because it improves control over system development and modification. The modules can be written and tested separately, allowing more efficient maintenance by identification of the boundaries of the module being changed. The use of modules is thus an application of system principles (see Chapter 9).

The physical structure of an information system is affected by the use of common modules for many processing operations. For example, a common input data validation routine may be used for all applications. If an application consists of major modules for input, input validation and error control, processing, and output, the use of a common module for input validation and error control means that no application is complete without using this module (Figure 2-10).

SOME ISSUES OF MANAGEMENT INFORMATION SYSTEM STRUCTURE

There are several issues regarding the structure of management information systems about which there is ongoing debate. Among these are the extent of formal versus

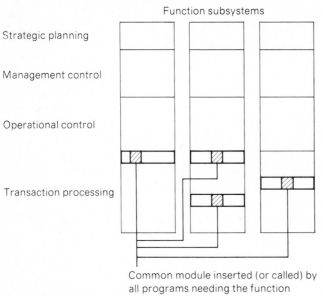

Function subsystems

Strategic planning

Management control

Operational control

Transaction processing

Common module inserted (or called) by
all programs needing the function

Figure 2-10
Use of common modules in physical structure of MIS.

informal information systems, manager resistance to formal information systems, the extent of integration of files and processing, the extent of user-machine interaction, and generalized versus individualized systems.

Formal versus Informal Information Systems

The management information system as described in this chapter encompasses only part of the total information processing that takes place in an organization. The complete information processing system of an organization consists of both public systems and private systems. "Public" is used in the sense of being known to relevant persons in the organization and available to all who have authority to access the information. Private systems are kept by individuals. These may supplement or duplicate the public systems, and they may be unsanctioned and discouraged or sanctioned and encouraged. There are within the public and private systems both formal and informal information systems. The formal information system is manifested by documents and other records, usually indicating compliance with prespecified rules and procedures. The informal information system may process information that is vital to organizational functioning but without formal records of that process.

The management information system defined in this chapter, with its prespecified procedures and programs for applications, is part of the formal public system. It is organizationally public and access is dependent only upon having appropriate organizational authority to enter or retrieve data or to receive reports or inquiry responses. There is also an informal public system that serves all persons in the organization who connect with it. The informal system has few predetermined rules. Examples of the public informal information system are electronic mail, telephone calls, conversations at gathering points such as the water cooler, notes on the bulletin board, articles and other publications distributed in the office (perhaps annotated), and presentations by external information sources such as sales representatives.

In addition to these formal and informal public systems, many private information systems tend to exist in organizations. Some of these are quite formal, at least for the individual owner and any support staff who help maintain it. For example, an industrial sales manager might maintain a separate file of performance data on sales representatives which she uses to augment the information received from the formal sales information system. The manager's secretary might collect and maintain the data (for instance, from the sales representatives' daily customer call reports), but the information is available only for the sales manager's use, possibly without the sales representatives' knowledge. This is a formal private system. It is based not upon the function or the job title but upon the person who occupies the position. Many individuals also have their own private informal information systems. Primarily through personal contact they maintain a flow of information which may be critical to decision making but is available to them as individuals rather than as occupiers of a formal position.

The organizational information system

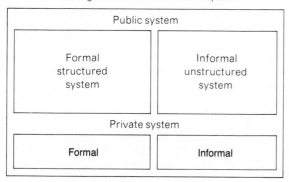

Effect of MIS on relative sizes of information system components

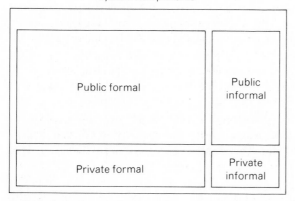

Figure 2-11
Public or private and formal versus informal information systems.

PRIVATE, FORMAL SYSTEM TO TRACK ADMISSIONS

The Graduate Program Office keeps the formal public files on all students who apply for admission to the doctoral program of the School of Management. If someone who is authorized wants to look at an applicant's file, they have it. However, they keep no records on applicants by program. The MIS area secretary has a private formal system. Anyone who wants "tracking data" asks her. It is her private system; if she leaves, it is unlikely the system would persist. There is no formal documentation.

As shown in Figure 2-11, the public information system of an organization tends to be larger than the private system, but the latter includes a significant portion of organizational information flows. The effect of a comprehensive information system of the type described in this chapter is to increase the scope of the formal, public system. This increase reduces the need for private, formal systems and probably reduces the need for both public and private informal systems. One advantage of the formal public system over private information systems is that it belongs to the position rather than the person, so that when a new person comes into a position he or she will have in place the necessary information support to function in that position.

Increasing the scope of the public formal system also has associated costs. There are the costs of eliciting requirements, designing the system, programming, testing, and writing procedures for operating and using the system. Because of the high cost of developing systems, the tendency has been to only automate systems that can be justified as public systems so that the costs are shared over many users. However, the trend to end user computing, as described in Chapter 1, means users have access to terminals or personal computers and powerful application development languages which facilitate having them develop their own systems. Many applications developed by users on personal computers are highly individualized, and are thus formal, private systems.

There is ongoing debate as to how much organizational information processing can effectively be made part of the formal system and how much should remain in the informal systems. It can be argued that many important decisions are based on information received through informal channels that cannot be formalized, especially at top management levels. A well-known study by Mintzberg[3] shows that as much as 80 percent of a chief executive's time is spent in verbal communication. A study of information systems managers by Ives and Olson[4] showed a similar pattern. This is especially noteworthy because these managers cannot be said to be unfamiliar with the capabilities of the formal, public information system.

Advocates of increasing the scope of the formal public system claim that if it can reduce the time spent by managers in informal communication, their productivity will increase and thus benefit the organization. Skeptics of this view claim that the only information systems that will affect managerial productivity are enhancements to informal systems such as electronic mail and to formal private systems such as user-developed decision support systems. This debate will be considered again in later chapters.

---

[3]Henry Mintzberg, *The Nature of Managerial Work*, Harper & Row, New York, 1973.

[4]B. Ives and M. H. Olson, "Manager or Technician? The Nature of the Information System Manager's Job," *MIS Quarterly*, 5:4, December 1981. pp. 49-63.

Extent of Integration

Some advocates of "total systems" have argued for complete integration of all formal information processing. The experience to date suggests that such a tightly integrated system is impractical. There are too many factors to consider all at once, and maintenance is difficult. For this reason, information systems tend to have a modular design with integration only where required (as in the order entry system example). Inconsistencies among subsystems are reduced by the use of standards and the common database.

Data integration is accomplished by the use of a common database. A common database does not necessarily eliminate the need for separate files. Some files are significant only to one application and therefore may be designed for and maintained by that application.

Data requirements for different levels of management activity also suggest the need for more than one database rather than complete integration. For example, the data collected from external sources and stored for strategic planning is so different from internal data for operational control that some different databases may be desirable.

Extent of User-Machine Interaction

The information system structure does not specify online user-machine interaction; it indicates only support for various operational and management activities. Online processing of transactions is often desirable because the transaction is completed immediately. Inquiries are generally more effective if immediate response is available. The use of analysis, planning, and decision models is frequently enhanced if the analyst, planner, or decision maker can interact directly with the computer program, asking "what if" questions during problem analysis. With the decreasing costs of both computer and communications technology, the trend is to online interactive processing for both transaction processing and decision support systems.

The computer system that supports online transaction processing may not be able to support interactive models. However, having an information system does not imply that a single computer system must be used. An organization may use its in-house computer for transaction processing but provide alternatives for interactive models such as providing a small in-house interactive system, renting time on an outside computer through timesharing, or providing personal computers. These approaches encourage managers and staff specialists to develop their own support models, rather than depending on the staff of the information processing function to provide them.

SUMMARY

This chapter has defined a conceptual structure for a management information system. An actual organizational information system will differ from this model because certain elements are not cost-justified or because the implementation is performed in an evolutionary manner rather than all at once.

The information system may be described in terms of its operating elements. Its physical components are hardware, software, database, procedures, and personnel. Its processing requirements are to process transactions, maintain master files, produce reports, process inquiries, and process interactive support applications. The outputs for users are transaction documents, preplanned reports, preplanned inquiry responses, ad hoc reports and inquiry responses, and user-machine dialog responses. These provide management and other decision makers with monitoring information, action information, and decision support. Information can be provided for both structured, programmable decisions and unstructured, nonprogrammable decisions.

Management information system structure is affected by management activity and organizational function. Information requirements vary with the level of management activity supported: strategic planning, managerial control, or operational control. They also vary depending on the degree of structure of the decision supported. Each organizational function supported by the information system has its own unique information processing requirements as well as some which are common to several functions.

The conceptual structure of an information system consists of a federation of information subsystems for different functions. Each subsystem provides support for transaction processing, operational control, management control, and strategic planning. Some typical subsystems might be marketing, production, logistics, personnel, finance and accounting, information systems, and top management. The conceptual structure includes some unique files for each subsystem plus a common database. There is unique software for each subsystem, and there is common software used by or available to all subsystems—a database management system, common software routines, and a model base of analysis, planning, and decision models.

Some issues of MIS structure around which there is an ongoing debate are the extent of the formal information system versus informal systems, the extent of integration of processing and data, and the extent of user-machine interaction.

MINICASES

1 TIME TO REVIEW

The GBD Company has had a computer for several years and has added applications based on the power or persuasion of executives of different functions. They now wish to examine their status relative to the concept of a management information system. The following is the list (portfolio) of applications currently on the system for sales and marketing, accounting and finance, production, and information systems.

— Payroll
— Accounts receivable
— Competitive intelligence notes
— Accounts payable
— Data processing error log
— Daily cash report
— Weekly production schedule
— Competitive position analysis (yearly)
— Weekly payroll report
— Monthly cash flow projection
— Sales variance report
— Five-year rate of return projection
— Sales order accounting
— Weekly data processing error report

Questions

a Classify these applications according to the management information system conceptual model.

b If the applications reflect the areas where information is most needed, what can you say about the nature of the business and the factors critical to its success? *Cash flow & sales oriented*

c Assuming that the most critical success factor for the company is on-time delivery of high quality products, where in the conceptual model should future applications be developed? *They must start from scratch, with the possible exception of weekly reporting*

2 THE COMPUTER IN THE RESTAURANT

The installation of a minicomputer-based information system has enabled Dailey's Restaurant in Atlanta to streamline their operations and promote tighter internal controls over their business.

A waiter takes an order at a table, and then enters it online via one of the six terminals located in the restaurant dining room. The order is routed to a printer in the appropriate preparation area: the cold-item printer if it is a salad, the hot-item printer if it is a hot sandwich, or the bar printer if it is a drink. A customer's meal check listing the items ordered and the respective prices is automatically generated. This ordering system eliminates the old three-carbon-copy guest check system as well as any problems caused by a waiter's handwriting. When the kitchen runs out of a food item, the cooks send an ''out of stock'' message, which will be displayed on the dining room terminals when waiters try to order that item. This gives the waiters faster feedback, enabling them to give better service to the customers.

Other system features aid management in the planning and control of their restaurant business. The system provides up-to-the-minute information on the food items ordered and breaks out percentages showing sales of each item versus total sales. This helps management plan menus according to customers' tastes. The system also compares the weekly sales totals versus food costs, allowing planning for tighter cost controls. In addition, whenever an order is voided, the reason for the void is keyed in. This may help later in management decisions, especially if the voids are consistently related to food or service.

Acceptance of the system by the users is exceptionally high since the waiters and waitresses were involved in the selection and design process. All potential users were asked to give their impressions and ideas about the various systems available before one was chosen.

Based on Ann Dukes, ''Side Order of (Computer) Chips Speeds Meals,'' *MIS Week*, June 17, 1981, p. 14.

Questions

a In managing the business of a restaurant, what are some decision that must be made in the areas of:
—strategic planning
—managerial control
—operational control

b What information would you require from this system in order to aid in making such decisions? (In other words, what would make this system a more complete management information system rather than just doing transaction processing?)

c Compared to this system, most restaurant information systems are relatively informal. Explain the probable effects that making the system more formal would have on:
—customers
—waiters
—management

EXERCISES

1 The implementation of computer-based information systems to replace manual systems generally requires:

a Greater formalization

b More predetermination of rules for recording and providing information

c Higher requirements for accuracy

List the good and bad results of the above factors as they affect individuals who work in the organization.

2 Information processing for decision support will differ depending on whether the decision is structured or unstructured. Explain why this is true. Choose one structured decision and one unstructured decision to illustrate your explanation.

3 Basic transaction processing will always be performed; providing information for strategic planning may never occur, and no one will notice. Explain why this statement is true in many organizations.

4 The conceptual structure of an information system encompasses a complete portfolio of applications that populate all of the cells in Figure 2-4. In actual implementation, some cells may not have any applications. Explain why.

5 The transaction processing application must usually be done before operational control applications can be implemented. What organizational processes must take place in order to have the necessary input for management control applications?

6 Discuss the advantages and disadvantages of extending the formal, public system at the expense of the formal private system and the informal public system.

7 Personal computers allow individuals in an organization to have private files and private systems. Discuss advantages and disadvantages of this trend.

8 As sales manager, you have been provided with a personal computer that can act as a terminal to the main computer as part of an electronic mail network or as a stand-alone computer for doing modeling, maintaining files, and word processing. How might this system be used in connection with your private versus public information systems, both formal and informal?

9 A company decided to implement a highly integrated management information system. Any transaction entered into the system would immediately affect all related functional subsystems at all levels of activity. The system was never implemented successfully. Why do you think it was a failure?

10 Why is user-machine interaction not required for an information system? Why is it considered very desirable?

SELECTED REFERENCES

There are a few now classic references that were significant in the development of the concept of a management information system; other references describe doubts about the concept or define problems in its implementation. There are also some current readings to give some breadth of background for later chapters.

Significant Historical MIS Concept References

Aron, J. D.: "Information Systems in Perspective," *Computing Surveys*, December 1969, pp. 216–236.

Blumenthal, Sherman: *Management Information Systems: A Framework for Planning and Development*, Prentice-Hall, Englewood Cliffs, NJ, 1969.

Drucker, Peter F.: "What the Computers Will Be Telling You," *Nation's Business*, August 1966, pp. 84–90.

Gorry, G. A., and M. S. Scott Morton: "A Framework for Management Information Systems," *Sloan Management Review*, Fall 1971.

Zani, William M.: "Blueprint for MIS," *Harvard Business Review*, November–December 1970, pp. 95–100.

Pro and Con Discussion of MIS Concept (Historical)

Ackoff, R. L.: "Management Misinformation Systems," *Management Science*, December 1967, pp. B147–B156.

Dearden, John: "Can Management Information Be Automated?" *Harvard Business Review*, March–April 1964, pp. 128–135.

Dearden, John: "Computers: No Impact on Divisional Control," *Harvard Business Review*, January–February 1967, pp. 99–104.

Dearden, John: "MIS Is a Mirage," *Harvard Business Review*, January–February 1972, pp. 90–99. See Letters to Editor in May–June 1972 issue.

Dearden, John: "Myth of Real-Time Management Information," *Harvard Business Review*, May–June 1966, pp. 123–132.

Will, Hart J.: "MIS—Mirage or Mirror Image?" *Journal of Systems Management*, September 1973, pp. 24–31.

Current Readings

Dickson, G. W.: "Management Information Systems: Evolution and Status," in *Advances in Computers*, M. Youts (ed.), Academic Press, New York, 1981.

Keen, Peter G. W.: "'Interactive' Computer Systems for Managers: A Modest Proposal," *Sloan Management Review*, Fall 1976, pp. 1–17.

McFarlan, F. Warren and James E. McKenney: A series of three articles in the *Harvard Business Review*: "The Information Archipelago—Maps and Bridges," September–October 1982; "The Information Archipelago—Plotting a Course," January–February 1983 (with Philip Pyburn); "The Information Archipelago—Governing the New World," July–August 1983.

Mintzberg, Henry: "Managerial Work: Analysis from Observation," *Management Science*, 18:2, October 1971, pp. B97–B110.

TWO

SURVEY OF INFORMATION SYSTEMS TECHNOLOGY

Many readers of this book will already be familiar with the basic technology for information systems; others will not. This section is therefore optional depending on prior background. Parts of the section can be skimmed; others can be studies in detail. The technology for information systems changes rapidly, but the emphasis of the section is on fundamental technology rather than on specific details that become quickly outdated.

Other chapters in the text will assume that the reader has basic familiarity with technology and will use the definitions and concepts presented in this section. Some topics introduced in these chapters will be explained in greater detail in subsequent chapters. The topics covered in the three chapters include:

Chapter 3 Hardware, Software, and Communications Technology for Information Systems

- A computer system
- Data representation
- Microelectronics
- Instructing (programming) a computer
- A user view of a computer system
- Communications facilities
- Communications networks
- Distributed systems

Chapter 4 Storage and Retrieval of Data

- Models of data
- Logical data concepts
- Physical storage devices
- File organizations
- Database organizations

Chapter 5 Transaction Processing, Office Automation, and Information Processing Control Functions

- Transaction processing
- Document preparation
- Message and document communication
- Public data services
- Information processing controls
- Information systems availability controls

CHAPTER 3

HARDWARE, SOFTWARE, AND COMMUNICATIONS TECHNOLOGY FOR INFORMATION SYSTEMS

This chapter is a short survey of three major elements of information systems technology—hardware, software, and communications. A knowledge of basic information systems technology will be assumed in subsequent chapters; this chapter provides a review.

A COMPUTER SYSTEM

There are a wide variety of computer systems available in terms of size, complexity, and power. Regardless of size, every computer system includes hardware and software to perform processing functions.

Computer Hardware

Basic hardware equipment in a computer system supports the following functions:

1 Entry or input to the computer
2 Output from the computer
3 Secondary storage
4 Computation, control, and primary storage (central processing unit or CPU)

Two additional functions may be present:

5 Data communications
6 Data preparation

Equipment connected directly to the computer (through cables or communications lines) is termed "online"; equipment used separately and not connected is "offline." The

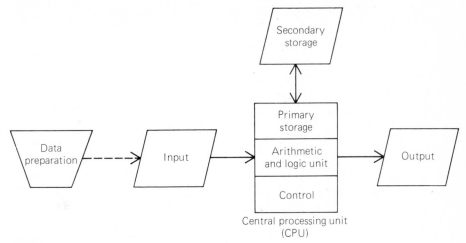

Figure 3-1
Basic functions in a computer system.

relationship between these equipment functions in a basic computer system is shown in Figure 3-1.

Data for computer processing comes from four sources:

1 Direct online entry at a terminal
2 Data preparation in which transactions are converted to machine-readable form for later input and processing
3 Data in machine-readable document form
4 Previously processed data in secondary storage

Direct entry of data for immediate processing generally requires a keyboard for entry and a visual display terminal (VDT) for display of data, instructions, messages, etc. A visual display terminal is often called a CRT (cathode ray tube) because most use a cathode ray tube of the type used in television sets. The terminal can be an intelligent terminal or a dumb terminal:

1 *Intelligent terminal.* This type of terminal contains the logic to perform some data processing such as input validation and may also have storage for transactions, formats, error messages, etc. It can also operate offline, preparing and storing records for subsequent transmission to the computer.
2 *Dumb terminal.* They usually have neither processing capability nor storage capacity. They merely send and receive; all processing is performed by the computer to which they are connected.

Direct entry may also use other devices which augment the keyboard: a touch sensitive screen, a mouse (a small box that is moved on a flat surface to direct the visual display cursor around the screen), or very limited voice entry.

Data preparation may be online or offline; the type of input device used will vary accordingly. Offline data preparation prior to input may use a key-to-disk system in which keyed data is stored on a disk and then transferred to magnetic tape for input to processing. Some older systems use punched cards for data preparation.

There are also a variety of specialized input devices that read data documents coded with machine-readable data. Such devices are optical character readers (OCR), magnetic ink character readers (MICR), and point-of-sale scanners. An example is the scanning device in a supermarket checkout counter which reads the "universal product code" on the package.

The "computer" is the central processing unit (CPU) of a computer system. It typically consists of the control unit, the arithmetic and logic unit, and primary storage or "memory."

The arithmetic and logic unit contains electronic circuitry components called registers, where logic for processing of data and instructions is performed. Data and instructions to be processed are stored in primary storage for fast access. For instance, if two numbers are to be added together, the following processing sequence takes place:

1 The first number is accessed in primary storage and transferred to a register in the arithmetic and logic unit.

2 The second number is accessed in primary storage and added electronically to the first number in the register.

3 The result is copied from the register to a third location in primary storage.

The control unit of the CPU contains the circuitry for synchronization and control of the activity between the arithmetic logic unit and primary storage.

Secondary storage is supplementary to the primary storage contained in the CPU. It has larger capacity, and is less expensive but slower relative to primary storage; it is therefore used to hold data files plus programs not currently in use. The most common secondary storage media are magnetic disk, magnetic diskettes, and magnetic tape (reel and cassette). Storage technology is changing rapidly with the storage capacity of each storage medium increasing and the cost per character stored decreasing. In general, a diskette of the type used with small computers or word processors will store several hundred thousand characters or, at most, a few million characters. Larger, rigid nonremovable disks (often called hard disks, rigid disks, or Winchester disks) on small computers can store in the tens of millions of characters. Disk packs on larger systems hold hundreds of millions of characters. Magnetic tape storage capacities vary depending on a number of factors, but a typical tape can store from a few million up to tens of millions of characters of data. For comparison, a textbook contains two to three million characters.

Most secondary storage utilizes magnetic media. A medium such as metal disk, plastic diskette, or plastic tape is coated with a metallic oxide. The coating can be magnetized. Tiny areas on the coating are treated as small magnets whose polarity is set in one of two ways in order to store one of two values. Data can be read without altering the polarity. Secondary storage is read or written by passing the magnetic media under a read-write head that either reads the polarity that is present in each tiny segment or changes the polarity to record new data.

The tradeoff between cost of storage and speed of access suggests a hierarchy of storage in a computer system. For example, a small computer system may use a rigid disk for storage of programs and data records that need to be readily available with very little delay (programs frequently used and data files being processed), and floppy disks (diskettes) or magnetic tape for low cost, slower access speed applications and backup storage. Other storage media are available, but they are not as widely used.

The most common output device is the printer, but output can be on a visual display terminal, a typewriter terminal, graph plotter, computer output microfilm, or other devices. There is a wide range of printer technology with high-speed printers using electrostatic printing (method used by most office copiers) and impact printing. Slow-speed printers use typewriter-like thimbles, daisy wheels, or dot matrix printing mechanisms. A high-speed printer may print thousands of lines per minute; a slow-speed printer at a personal workstation will usually print at less than 100 lines per minute.

Classes of Computer Systems

There are a wide variety of computer systems in terms of size and power. Five classes illustrate the differences:

1 Supercomputers
2 Large-scale computers
3 Medium-scale computers
4 Minicomputers
5 Microcomputers

Supercomputers are designed for applications requiring very high speed computation and large primary storage. Large-scale computers have very large secondary storage capacities, very powerful CPUs, and highly sophisticated operating systems. They can support multiple jobs executing concurrently and online processing from many remote locations at once. Medium-scale computer systems have reduced capacity and speed compared to large-scale computers.

Minicomputers are usually small (less than the size of an office desk) and relatively inexpensive. Each minicomputer may support online processing from multiple remote locations. In many organizations, multiple minicomputers with communications capabilities replace a single large-scale computer.

Microcomputers are very small (will easily fit on a desktop) and typically have a simple operating system and small primary storage, one input unit (visual display

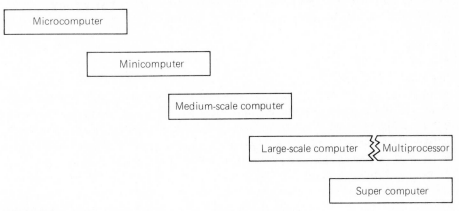

Figure 3-2
Relative positions for processing power of computer systems.

terminal), one output unit (a slow printer), and limited secondary storage through diskettes or cassettes. They are frequently termed personal computers.

The classes of computers are approximate, and they overlap in various dimensions of speed, cost, etc., as shown in Figure 3-2. Multicomputer configurations (several CPUs linked together) of large computers can be as powerful as supercomputers. Supermini computers, especially multicomputer minisystems, are comparable in power to low-end large-scale computers. The low end of the minicomputer range and the high end of the microcomputer range are used for small business computers. The lower range of microcomputers are personal computers and small, portable briefcase computers.

MICROCOMPUTERS PLUS BIG COMPUTER FOR PEPSI

Fear was one reaction of the Pepsi delivery crew in Tupelo, Mississippi when their company replaced the drivers' manual system with suitcase computers. Each driver now has a microcomputer which is used as a remote processor. The microcomputers are linked up to Pepsi's central computer system daily to update inventory information. Billing and accounting information is collected at each delivery location and each truck's daily inventory flow is monitored. Customers appreciate the computerized receipt, and there are financial benefits to the firm.

At the end of each day, all unsold merchandise is unloaded from the trucks and inventory is checked against the driver's records. The following day, the trucks are reloaded. The cost of taking inventory has been reduced and drivers are returning with less unsold merchandise. Because there is less loading and unloading of merchandise from trucks, fewer bottles are broken. Management estimates that over $25,000 per year may be saved because of the system.

"Remote Micros in Briefcases Make Rounds with Pepsi Crew," *Computerworld*, February 23, 1981, p. 65.

Computer Software

The sets of computer program instructions that direct the operation of the hardware are called *software*. A set of instructions for a specific task is termed a *routine*; a complete set of instructions to execute a related set of tasks is a *program*. Software instructions are also termed *code*. As mentioned in Chapter 2, software can be divided into two major categories:

1 System software
2 Application software

Examples of system software are the operating system which directs and assists the execution of application programs, utility programs which do common tasks such as sorting, compilers which translate programs coded by the programmer into machine-level instructions, and database management systems which manage storage and access to databases. System software is also required for data communications.

System software is usually purchased rather than developed by internal personnel. The operating system is sometimes included in the price of the hardware and provided by the hardware vendor. Database management system software is usually purchased separately, either from the hardware vendor or from independent software vendors.

Application software includes computer programs written for an individual application such as payroll processing or personnel skill analysis. They generally require system software in their execution. For example, the application program may specify reading data from a record stored on a disk; the operating system provides the instructions to manage the physical reading of the record from disk storage.

Software programs vary widely in size. For example, a very simple application program may consist of a few hundred lines of instructions in a programming language, while a large application program or system software program may consist of tens of thousands of lines of instructions.

An application system consists of a set of programs and related manual procedures to accomplish information processing. The cost of developing a large application system can be very high. The main advantage of developing a system "in house" is to obtain a unique system designed to fit specific needs of an organization. In many cases, it is more appropriate to lease or buy application software. There is a growing trend toward purchasing generalized application *packages* (such as payroll, accounts receivable, production scheduling) and using internal development personnel to tailor the packages to unique organizational needs. Application packages are sold or leased from companies which specialize in software development; application packages for small (personal) computers are sold in computer stores, by mail, and other similar channels.

DATA REPRESENTATION FOR COMPUTERS

Computers perform all calculation and storage with elements which have only two possible states. These elements include electronic switches which are open or closed, electrical pulses that are high or not high, or magnetized elements that have two directions of polarity. The two states are represented symbolically by 0 and 1; they are called binary digits or bits. In essence, the computer moves strings of 0s and 1s through the circuitry to perform operations and stores strings of 0s and 1s in storage devices.

Since the computer needs to move and store a large number of characters but only represents the two values of 0 and 1, there must be a method to represent and manipulate decimal numbers and alphanumeric characters (alphabetic, numeric, and special characters such as period and asterisk). Also, numeric data is coded in a form which is suitable for computation.

The Binary Code for Alphanumeric Data

The way to represent many different characters using only binary digits is to take sets of 1s and 0s and establish a code such that a certain pattern of 0s and 1s represents A, another pattern B, etc. The set of 0s and 1s to represent the alphanumeric characters has to have enough different 1 and 0 combinations for each of the alphanumeric characters and any other characters needed. For example, a 3-bit set will have eight different combinations, as shown below.

Combinations of 0 and 1 with 3 bits	
000	100
001	101
010	110
011	111

The number of bits required to encode the most common alphanumerics is at least 6, which permits 64 different combinations. Because of the need for more codes to distinguish between upper- and lowercase alphabetics and utilize many special characters, most computers use a set of 8 bits to encode a character. Each set of 8 bits is called a byte. For example, the three characters 1 – A may be coded with three bytes as follows (an actual code being given only for illustrative purposes):

1	–	A
11110001	01100000	11000001

In other words, the computer moves and stores 1s and 0s (as represented by the two possible states), but 8-bit sets of the 1s and 0s represent (code) alphanumeric characters. The computer stores strings of these binary representations, moves them about, rearranges them, compares them, and so on.

In theory, each computer system could utilize a different set of 8-bit combinations to encode alphanumeric characters. In practice, two standard coding schemes are used. One is called ASCII (American Standard Code for Information Interchange); the code in use on most IBM machines is called EBCDIC (Extended Binary Coded Decimal Interchange Code).

When data items first enter the computer (say from keyboard input), the characters are coded into ASCII or EBCDIC, character by character. The codes also define the sequence by which data are sorted and ordered. This is termed the *collating sequence*. The numeric value of the 8-bit code representing A is less than for B, and so on.

Binary Coding of Numeric Data for Calculations

The coding of each character by an 8-bit byte works for numeric digits as well as for alphabetics and special characters. However, this is not an efficient scheme for arithmetic processing. For numbers on which calculations will be performed, some computers will split the 8 bits into two 4-bit numeric coding sets. The coding concept is the same as with alphanumerics, with each 4-bit set representing a separate decimal digit. For example, the code for 103 is:

1	0	3
0001	0000	0011

The computer can perform arithmetic on these sets much like arithmetic on decimal numbers. Arithmetic operation on these sets is termed ''binary-coded decimal'' or ''packed-decimal arithmetic.'' Besides improving calculation efficiency, less storage space is required for numeric characters.

Another method of representing a decimal number for arithmetic processing is to encode numbers by using a string of binary digits, which holds the actual binary equivalent of the number. Depending on the computer, the string of bits can be 24, 32, 36, etc., bits in length. For example, the quantity 103 would be coded by a 32-bit binary string as:

00000000000000000000000001100111

Arithmetic performed on such strings is termed ''binary arithmetic.'' In general, it is faster and less complicated for computer hardware than binary-coded decimal arithmetic.

WHO OR WHAT IS ASCII?

A new student learned to access the university timesharing system. A text editor appealed to her. She could write a paper, store it, and make corrections after the professor reviewed her draft. She entered the text using the text editor and stored it. The next day, she printed it out. To her dismay, everything was in capital letters. She had keyed:

   Now is the time for all good men....

The printout read:

   NOW IS THE TIME FOR ALL GOOD MEN....

She called the HELP line at the computer center and was told she had not specified ASCII. "Who or what is ASCII?" she moaned.

   A friend with more computer experience explained it. On that computer system, the computer codes all letters as uppercase, using a six-bit code. For most jobs, use of the short code reduces the storage space required by about 25 percent. If upper- and lowercase are necessary, the user must specify a larger code (in terms of number of bits). The ASCII code (American Standard Code for Information Interchange) is a 7-bit code (usually extended to 8 bits) for encoding upper- and lowercase, a large set of special characters, etc. Note the relative number of characters that can be coded by a 7- or 8-bit code versus a 6-bit code (the one with only uppercase).

	6 bits	7 bits	8 bits
Maximum number of characters	64	128	256
Can be used for:			
Alphabetics, uppercase	26	26	26
Numbers	10	10	10
Alphabetics, lowercase	0	26	26
Special characters	28	66	194

   Many (if not most) computers do not require the user to make this choice; this one does.

MICROELECTRONICS

The basic building block for all computer hardware is the chip. This section will explain the concept of the chip and how chips are assembled onto boards that connect into a bus that carries signals. It will also explain how general-purpose chips are made specific through microcode. The purpose of the section is to provide a broad survey rather than an explanation of all the technical options.

Logic and Memory Chips

A chip is a rectangular piece of silicon on which an integrated circuit has been etched. A crystal of silicon is sliced into thin circular slices called wafers. Circuits are etched on the wafer by a process of masking and diffusion that forms and connects transistors, resisters, diodes, etc., and the wafer is sliced into chips. Several chips are produced from each wafer. The chips can be microprocessor chips, memory chips, or chips for other functions. After completion, the chips are separated from the wafer and each chip is mounted in a package with pins for plugging the chip into a board.

   Memory chips are of two major types: read-only memory (ROM) and random access memory (RAM). The ROM chips are used for permanent programs (such as the microprograms or firmware described later). The programs are written as part of the manufacturing process, and a user cannot alter them. The program instructions are read from ROM as part of processing, but there is no writing to it.

RAM chips are used for primary storage containing user data and application programs being processed. Data may be read from this storage and data stored in it. It is volatile in the sense that data stored in it is lost if power is interrupted, as opposed to magnetic secondary storage.

Boards and Buses

A microprocessor is a chip which contains the traditional functions of the central processing unit. It contains an arithmetic and logic unit and a control unit (to synchronize operations). The microprocessor also uses a bus architecture. In early computers, wires were used to interconnect the various functional units in the central processing unit. As circuitry became smaller and large-scale integration was implemented, wiring everything together became infeasible. The alternative was to establish a common electrical "roadway" along which all signals are sent. All functional units connect to the roadway, called a *bus*. An electrical signal is sent down the bus and selects the connecting path that will take it to its destination. Different signals are kept from interfering by synchronizating signals and controls.

Internal architecture of the microprocessor varies depending on the number of buses. For example, a single bus architecture uses a single internal bus to move signals among registers in the arithmetic logic unit. A single bus architecture is simple but slow. Two or three buses may be used to increase speed.

The complete central processing unit requires not only microprocessor chips but also memory chips and input-output interface chips. They are all interconnected by external buses. The different chips are packaged and connected to the external buses by the use of boards. A number of chips will be placed on a board and interconnections made by wiring circuits printed on the boards. The board has connections to the buses as well as a power supply.

The explanation to this point is most appropriate to small computers. Very large computers also use integrated circuits. However, the circuits are very dense and require special cooling and other design features. There are several technologies for microprocessor and memory chips, and some tend to be used mainly for microcomputers; others are used primarily with very large computers.

Microcode and Machine-Language Instructions

Computer instructions are usually written in a programming language, to be explained later in the chapter. The computer does not execute the programming language instructions directly; they must be translated into sets of machine-language instructions which are very specific and elementary. Examples of machine-language instructions are an instruction to read data from a memory location into a register, an instruction to add the contents of a second memory location to the data in the register, and an instruction to store the sum from the register in a memory location. The machine-language instructions are in turn each composed of a set of very elementary instructions called microinstructions. The machine-language instructions are interpreted and executed by a special computer program (a microprogram or microcode) permanently recorded in read-only memory. The microprogram is also called firmware to distinguish it from hardware and software. With microcode, general-purpose chips can be tailored to specific single applications for permanent use. This allows chips to be manufactured for use as control devices in equipment using only standard components. For instance, a simple calculator may contain a chip with a set of microcoded instructions for executing the necessary calculator functions.

In the design of computers, both microcode and software can be used to present the user with a machine that has different characteristics from the physical hardware. The machine the programmer or user deals with is a conceptual or logical machine; the details of how the conceptual machine is implemented in the circuitry or software is not provided to the user. The term *virtual* is frequently used in information systems to refer to the conceptual system. For example, virtual storage refers to primary storage that is unlimited as far as the programmer is concerned, even though there are well-defined physical limits to the size of primary storage.

INSTRUCTING A COMPUTER

As noted above, the computer hardware is instructed by a program of machine-language instructions in primary storage. For all practical purposes, programmers never write computer instructions in machine language. The programmer writes instructions in a language more suited to human use, which is then translated to machine language.

When programs are needed which are very specific to machine efficiency, they are generally written in an assembler language. However, except for operating system programs and some applications that require close coordination with hardware characteristics, most programming is done in high-level languages. Some important types of high-level languages for instructing a computer are procedure-oriented languages, query languages, report generators, program generators, analysis and modeling facilities, and very high level languages. Each of these types of languages will be explained briefly.

Assembler Language

Coding a program in machine language is very complex, tedious, and prone to error. Assembler languages are close to machine language but allow the programmer to use symbolic operation codes and symbolic addresses. For example, a symbolic instruction to add two quantities stored in memory might be:

AP WKGRDTOT,MPLYANS

where AP is the symbolic code for adding the contents of a storage location given the symbolic name MPLYANS to the contents of a storage location given the symbolic name WKGRDTOT. In this case, the names are programmer shorthand: WKGRDTOT for a storage location for a grand total and MPLYANS a storage location containing the result of a multiplication.

The symbolic operation codes and symbolic addresses must be translated to actual machine operation codes and machine storage addresses. This translation is performed by an assembly program or assembler. Each class (or brand) of computers has a somewhat unique assembler language appropriate to the machine architecture.

The Human-Machine Productivity Tradeoff

With a machine-oriented assembler language, the programmer must learn to "think like the computer." High-level languages emphasize instructions that are understandable to the human programmer. The core statements in a high-level language are also the same regardless of the type of computer. High-level language programs are converted by compiler or generator programs associated with each language.

There is a tradeoff implicit between the use of high-level languages and machine-oriented assembler languages. The high-level languages obtain human productivity at the expense of extra storage and inefficiencies in execution. The human productivity gains come through reduced time to code instructions and less time to debug and document the programs; the languages are less error-prone and at least partly self-documenting. High-level languages are also easier to learn and are not dependent on a particular type of computer, so that the programmer's skills are more transferable. Machine costs have decreased to the extent that high-level languages are almost always preferred.

High-level languages differ with respect to ease of use. There is a clear trend toward languages that reduce the need for programmers to understand technical details of the computer and data storage. These languages (often termed "very high level languages") make it more feasible for users to develop their own applications rather than relying on professional programmers; this is one aspect of the trend to end-user computing described in Chapter 1. The programming staff can then be concerned with complex large multiuser applications that require a formal development and programming process.

Procedure-oriented Languages

The languages most commonly used for development of information processing applications are procedure-oriented languages. There are two general types: data processing languages for programming the processing of large volumes of data records and algorithmic languages for programming of algorithms and mathematical computations. High-level languages can also be used for coding a wide variety of other applications.

The common element of procedure-oriented languages is that the programmer specifies the step-by-step procedures to be followed. There are many commonalities of form and logic among procedure-oriented programming languages. Once a person has learned programming in one procedure-oriented language, it is generally simpler to learn another. Some commonly used procedure-oriented languages are the following:

Language	Description and example
COBOL (*Common Business Oriented Language*)	Utilized primarily for applications requiring repetitive processing of large amounts of data records. It is the most commonly used data processing language. A simple but complete COBOL program is shown in Figure 3-3.
FORTRAN (*FOR*mula *TRAN*slator)	Utilized for algorithms and mathematical computation and scientific applications where many computations are to be performed on a relatively small amount of numeric data. A simple FORTRAN program is shown in Figure 3-4 (and explained in the example below).
PL/1 (*Programming Language 1*)	Oriented to applications which require both computation and processing of large amounts of data records.
PASCAL (named after the mathematician)	Algorithmic language; excellent for instructional purposes because it enforces elements of good programming style.
BASIC (*Beginners All-Purpose System for Interactive Computing*)	Very simple to learn and use. Only eleven fundamental statements. It is the most widely used procedure-oriented language for personal computers.
APL (*A Programming Language*)	An interactive language for algorithmic processing. It is especially powerful in programming computational procedures involving vectors and matrices.
ADA (named after Augusta Ada, the Countess of Lovelace, daughter of the poet Lord Byron; she is called the "world's first programmer")	A comprehensive procedure-oriented language combining features for programming, data processing, algorithmic, realtime (time-sensitive), and system software applications.

DECIDING WHICH PRIZE TO TAKE

Many sweepstakes contests give the winner an alternative of an immediate amount or a yearly payment for a stated number of years. A financial advisor offers not only investment advice but advice on the option to choose. Since the yearly payments occur later, the comparison should be between the present value of the future stream of payments and the immediate payment. A simple FORTRAN program to do this comparison is shown in Figure 3-4. It accepts input of immediate payment, yearly future payments, number of years for future payout, and the current interest rate for investment. The output consists of the labels on the results, input values, the comparison, and a decision message.

```
        IDENTIFICATION DIVISION.
        PROGRAM-ID. PAYROLL-REPORT.
        AUTHOR. GORDON B DAVIS.
            REMARKS.  SIMPLE COBOL PROGRAM TO READ HOURS-WORKED AND
            RATE-OF-PAY AND TO COMPUTE REGULAR-PAY, OVERTIME-PAY,
            AND GROSS-PAY.  OVERTIME-PAY IS ONE-AND-ONE-HALF THE
            REGULAR RATE FOR HOURS OVER 40.
*
        ENVIRONMENT DIVISION.
        CONFIGURATION SECTION.
        SOURCE-COMPUTER. CYBER.
        OBJECT-COMPUTER. CYBER.
        INPUT-OUTPUT SECTION.
        FILE-CONTROL.
            SELECT PAYROLL-FILE ASSIGN TO FILE1.
            SELECT PAYROLL-REPORT-FILE ASSIGN TO OUTFILE.
*
        DATA DIVISION.
        FILE SECTION.
        FD  PAYROLL-FILE LABEL RECORD IS OMITTED
            DATA RECORD IS PAYROLL-RECORD.
        01  PAYROLL-RECORD.
            05 PAYROLL-ID                PICTURE X(5).
            05 HOURS-WORKED              PICTURE 99.
            05 RATE-OF-PAY               PICTURE 9V999.
            05 FILLER                    PICTURE X(69).
        FD  PAYROLL-REPORT-FILE LABEL RECORD IS OMITTED
            DATA RECORD IS PRINT-PAY-LINE.
        01  PRINT-PAY-LINE.
            05 FILLER                    PICTURE X(10).
            05 PAYROLL-ID                PICTURE X(5).
            05 HOURS-WORKED              PICTURE ZZ99.
            05 RATE-OF-PAY               PICTURE ZZ9.999.
            05 REGULAR-PAY-PRINT         PICTURE $$$$$$9.99.
            05 OVERTIME-PAY-PRINT        PICTURE $$$$$$9.99.
            05 GROSS-PAY-PRINT           PICTURE $$$$$$9.99.
            05 FILLER                    PICTURE X(89).
        WORKING-STORAGE SECTION.
            77 REGULAR-PAY               PICTURE S999V99.
            77 OVERTIME-PAY              PICTURE S999V99.
            77 GROSS-PAY                 PICTURE S999V99.
            77 MORE-RECORDS              PICTURE X(3) VALUE "YES".
*
        PROCEDURE DIVISION.
        MAINLINE-ROUTINE.
            PERFORM INITIALIZATION.
            PERFORM PAY-PROCESSING UNTIL MORE-RECORDS EQUAL "NO".
            PERFORM CLOSING.
            STOP RUN.
        INITIALIZATION.
            OPEN INPUT PAYROLL-FILE OUTPUT PAYROLL-REPORT-FILE.
            READ PAYROLL-FILE AT END MOVE "NO" TO MORE-RECORDS.
        PAY-PROCESSING.
            IF HOURS-WORKED OF PAYROLL-RECORD IS GREATER THAN 40
                PERFORM PAY-CALCULATION-WITH-OVERTIME
            ELSE
                PERFORM PAY-CALCULATION-NO-OVERTIME.
            COMPUTE GROSS-PAY = REGULAR-PAY + OVERTIME-PAY.
            PERFORM WRITE-REPORT-LINE.
            READ PAYROLL-FILE AT END MOVE "NO" TO MORE-RECORDS.
        PAY-CALCULATION-NO-OVERTIME.
            MULTIPLY HOURS-WORKED OF PAYROLL-RECORD BY RATE-OF-PAY OF
                PAYROLL-RECORD GIVING REGULAR-PAY ROUNDED.
            COMPUTE OVERTIME-PAY = 0.
        PAY-CALCULATION-WITH-OVERTIME.
            MULTIPLY RATE-OF-PAY OF PAYROLL-RECORD BY 40 GIVING
                REGULAR-PAY ROUNDED.
            COMPUTE OVERTIME-PAY ROUNDED = ((HOURS-WORKED OF
                PAYROLL-RECORD - 40) * 1.5 * RATE-OF-PAY OF
                PAYROLL-RECORD).
        WRITE-REPORT-LINE.
            MOVE SPACES TO PRINT-PAY-LINE.
            MOVE CORRESPONDING PAYROLL-RECORD TO PRINT-PAY-LINE.
            MOVE REGULAR-PAY TO REGULAR-PAY-PRINT.
            MOVE OVERTIME-PAY TO OVERTIME-PAY-PRINT.
            MOVE GROSS-PAY TO GROSS-PAY-PRINT.
            WRITE PRINT-PAY-LINE.
        CLOSING.
            CLOSE PAYROLL-FILE, PAYROLL-REPORT-FILE.
```

Figure 3-3
Simple but complete COBOL program to compute gross pay and produce list.

Program
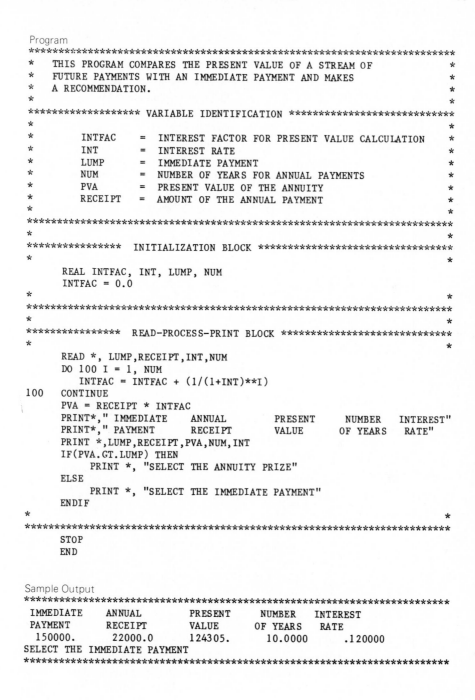

```
********************************************************************
*    THIS PROGRAM COMPARES THE PRESENT VALUE OF A STREAM OF        *
*    FUTURE PAYMENTS WITH AN IMMEDIATE PAYMENT AND MAKES           *
*    A RECOMMENDATION.                                             *
*                                                                  *
****************** VARIABLE IDENTIFICATION ***********************
*                                                                  *
*        INTFAC    =    INTEREST FACTOR FOR PRESENT VALUE CALCULATION *
*        INT       =    INTEREST RATE                              *
*        LUMP      =    IMMEDIATE PAYMENT                          *
*        NUM       =    NUMBER OF YEARS FOR ANNUAL PAYMENTS        *
*        PVA       =    PRESENT VALUE OF THE ANNUITY               *
*        RECEIPT   =    AMOUNT OF THE ANNUAL PAYMENT               *
*                                                                  *
********************************************************************
*                                                                  *
*************** INITIALIZATION BLOCK ****************************
*                                                                  *
      REAL INTFAC, INT, LUMP, NUM
      INTFAC = 0.0
*                                                                  *
********************************************************************
*                                                                  *
*************** READ-PROCESS-PRINT BLOCK ***********************
*                                                                  *
      READ *, LUMP,RECEIPT,INT,NUM
      DO 100 I = 1, NUM
         INTFAC = INTFAC + (1/(1+INT)**I)
100   CONTINUE
      PVA = RECEIPT * INTFAC
      PRINT*," IMMEDIATE     ANNUAL        PRESENT      NUMBER     INTEREST"
      PRINT*," PAYMENT       RECEIPT       VALUE        OF YEARS   RATE"
      PRINT *,LUMP,RECEIPT,PVA,NUM,INT
      IF(PVA.GT.LUMP) THEN
           PRINT *, "SELECT THE ANNUITY PRIZE"
      ELSE
           PRINT *, "SELECT THE IMMEDIATE PAYMENT"
      ENDIF
*                                                                  *
********************************************************************
      STOP
      END
```

Sample Output
```
********************************************************************
 IMMEDIATE     ANNUAL        PRESENT      NUMBER     INTEREST
 PAYMENT       RECEIPT       VALUE        OF YEARS   RATE
  150000.       22000.0       124305.      10.0000     .120000
SELECT THE IMMEDIATE PAYMENT
********************************************************************
```

Figure 3-4
Simple FORTRAN program to compare future monthly payments with immediate payment.

Database Query Languages

The database query languages are not universal languages such as the procedure-oriented languages described above. They are specific to the database management system with which they are used. In other words, each database management system has its own query language with unique rules and instruction formats.

There are two reasons for accessing data from files and databases: The first is to use the data in data processing and reporting applications, the second is for ad hoc queries of the database. Many database query languages are oriented to programmers and are designed to be used in data processing applications; often they are special commands used in combination with a procedure-oriented language such as COBOL. Others are sufficiently simple that they can be used by a nonprogrammer (i.e., a manager) for ad hoc queries.

Report Generators

The procedures for formatting a report and performing subtotals and breaks for each group of items, page breaks, page headings on first and subsequent pages, page numbering, grand totals, etc., can be quite complex. Yet they follow fairly regular rules. The regularity of the procedures and rules for report layout are the basis for report generators.

Using a report generator, the programmer describes the format of the report and characteristics of the data. The detailed procedures are generated by the software. An older but rather widely used report generator on small business computers is RPG (Report Program Generator). Report generators are now generally incorporated in very high level languages and database query languages.

Program Generators

Following the concept of a report generator, program generators prepare an application program from specifications of display terminal screen layouts, interactive dialogs, and processing to be performed. Using a program generator, a programmer need not write the detailed procedures for programming a dialog for a visual display terminal. Instead, the programmer uses a screen-dialog layout to provide simple specifications to the program generator, which generates the program instructions.

Statistical Packages

Both programmers and nonprogrammers may need to perform statistical and other data analysis. It is not generally either necessary or efficient to write a statistical program in a procedure-oriented language. Statistical packages perform the analysis based on simple input parameters describing the data and the analysis to be performed. The formulas and data manipulation routines performed by the packages are based on standard, well-defined algorithms. There are a large number of these statistical packages. The most widely used are SPSS (Statistical Package for the Social Sciences), BMDP (BioMedical Data Analysis Package), and SAS (Statistical Analysis System).

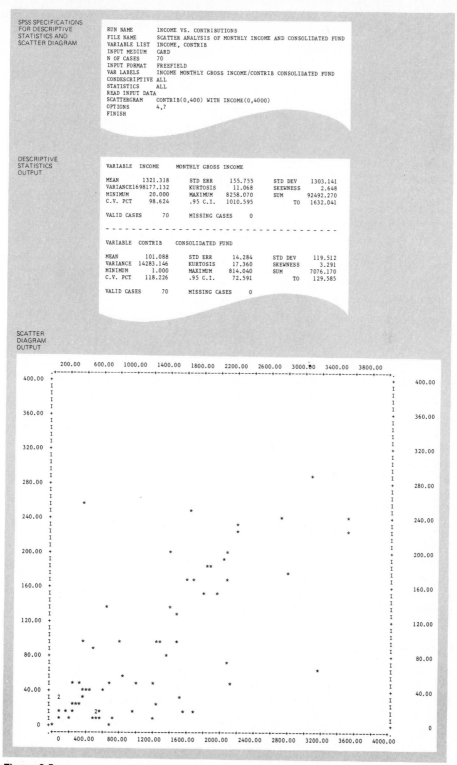

Figure 3-5
Example of specification input to SPSS statistical package and resulting outputs (for comparing contributions to Consolidated Fund with income).

ANALYZING DATA USING A STATISTICAL PACKAGE

The personnel manager was in charge of the Consolidated Fund Drive. One of the most frequent questions asked by contributors was how their contributions compared to the average for their income level. To respond to this question, an analysis was performed on contributions for the prior year. The amount contributed to the Consolidated Fund was compared to the monthly income of the contributor. There were 70 contributors. The results were plotted as a scatter diagram, excluding two high income contributors in order not to identify them to people seeing the chart. The analysis was performed using SPSS (Statistical Package for the Social Sciences). It allowed the contributors to decide how they wanted to position their contributions relative to the norm for their income. Figure 3-5 shows the specifications for the analysis, the descriptive statistics output, and the scatter diagram output.

Modeling Languages

Modeling languages are designed to build and test models of "real-world" problems. There are various modeling languages for different types of problems. For example, there are languages for "queuing" problems having waiting lines (such as grocery store checkout lanes), languages for modeling the behavior of various economic systems, and languages for financial modeling. The financial modeling facilities are the most significant for management activities and related analysis. Modeling languages are available on both large computer systems and microcomputers.

The modeling systems for large-scale computers are comprehensive and include a number of options for analysis. Examples of major packages are IFPS (Interactive Financial Planning System) and EXPRESS. Simple statements are used to describe variables, to define the elements of the model, and to input data. There are facilities such as the following to enhance the model:

- Change values for "what if" analysis
- Goal seeking to find values necessary to achieve a goal (for example, sales to achieve a profit goal)
- Simulation using probabilities

An example of a simple quarterly sales and profit model programmed using IFPS is shown in Figure 3-6.

The most widely used software packages for modeling on personal computers are the "electronic spreadsheet" packages (also termed "calcs" after the first major program called VisiCalc). The user has available a large work space divided into rows and columns and uses it like a spreadsheet. Values and relationships are assigned to rows and columns. When a value is changed, all other data values that are affected by that value are automatically changed as well. The application of modeling facilities and spreadsheet programs to decision making will be described in more detail in Chapter 12.

Very High Level Languages

Very high level languages or fourth generation languages (4GL) are a general class of languages designed to improve the efficiency of the applications development process.

NORTHWEST INDUSTRIES: AN EXECUTIVE INFORMATION SYSTEM

Executives at Northwest Industries (1980 sales: $2.9 billion) use very high level languages to access data and perform analysis and modeling. The development of this system began in 1976 when Ben Heineman, president and chief executive of Northwest, decided that he needed a specially tailored database to aid him in monitoring, projecting, and planning the progress of his nine operating companies. A great believer in the advantages of "not being the captive of any particular source of information," Heineman wanted to be able to analyze various aspects of the business himself but saw little opportunity to do so without a computer-based system to reduce data-handling chores.

In January 1977, the six top executives at Northwest were given access to an experimental system through which they could retrieve more than 70 reports and perform such limited analyses as compound growth calculations, variance analysis, and trend projections. By February, Heineman had reached the limits of the system's capabilities and was demanding more.

Additional capabilities were provided by an access and analysis language, EXPRESS, which facilitated not only simple file handling and data aggregation but also extensive modeling and statistical analyses of data series. To complement these improved capabilities, Northwest has since added to its executive database:

350 financial and operational items of data on planned, budgeted, forecasted, and actual monthly results for each operating company for the past eight and the next four years.

Forty-five economic and key ratio time series.

Several externally subscribed databases.

Northwest's Executive Information System (EIS) with its extensive and continually growing database is now used by almost all managers and executives to perform their monitoring and analytic functions. But the driving force behind the system and its most significant user remains Heineman. Working with the system is an everyday thing for him, a natural part of his job. With his special knowledge of the business and with his newly acquired ability to write his own programs, Heineman sees great value in working at a terminal himself rather than handing all assignments to staff personnel.

"There is a huge advantage to the CEO to get his hands dirty in the data," he says, because "the answers to many significant questions are found in the detail. The system provides me with an improved ability to ask the right questions and to know the wrong answers." What is more, he finds a comparable advantage in having instant access to the database to try out an idea he might have. In fact, he has a computer terminal at home and takes another with him on vacation.

Supporting Heineman and other Northwest executives are a few information systems people who function as system coaches. They train and assist users in determining whether needed data are already available and whether any additional data can be obtained. They also help to get new information into the database, train users in access methods, and teach them to recognize the analytic routines best fitted to different types of analyses. Only for major modeling applications do these coaches actually take part in the system design and programming process.

John F. Rockart and Michael E. Treacy, "The CEO Goes On-Line," *Harvard Business Review,* January-February 1982, pp. 85-86.

```
100 COLUMNS JANUARY,FEBRUARY,MARCH,TOTAL
110 *          SHANE COOK CO.
120 SALES = 20000, PREVIOUS * 1.10
130 COST OF SALES = 0.60 * SALES
140 GROSS MARGIN = SALES - COST OF SALES
150 EXPENSES = 2000 + 0.20*SALES
160 PROFIT = GROSS MARGIN - EXPENSES
170 COLUMN TOTAL FOR SALES THRU PROFIT = SUM(C1 THRU C3)
END OF MODEL
INPUT: SOLVE
ENTER SOLVE OPTIONS
INPUT: ALL
```

	JANUARY	FEBRUARY	MARCH	TOTAL
SHANE COOK CO.				
SALES	20000	22000	24200	66200
COST OF SALES	12000	13200	14520	39720
GROSS MARGIN	8000	8800	9680	26480
EXPENSES	6000	6400	6840	19240
PROFIT	2000	2400	2840	7240

Figure 3-6
Simple IFPS program to prepare quarterly sales and profit forecast.

Some of these languages are designed to improve the productivity of programming professionals, while others are designed to be used directly by the end user. The user-oriented report generators and modeling languages already described in this chapter are examples. In very general terms, these languages are designed for specification of what needs to be accomplished, as opposed to the procedure-oriented languages which specify *how*. An example of a simple program in a very high level language called FOCUS and the resulting output are shown in Figure 3-7.

A USER VIEW OF COMPUTER SYSTEMS

Most computer users do not have to deal with the technical details of the computer or programming language, but they do have to follow rather specific procedures. The procedures for use depend on the design of the information system. Major differences in procedures can be observed for users of batch systems, users of terminals with online processing, and users of personal microcomputers.

Batch System Use

With a batch system, the user prepares data to be processed at a later time by the computer. The input data consists of a batch of transactions prepared over a period of time such as a day or week. A user responsible for processing data in a batch system must prepare input data in the exact format and with the exact codes required by the processing program, prepare control information used to ensure that no records are lost or remain unprocessed, and check output received for errors (including checking against the control information prepared with input data). The user is also responsible for reviewing error reports, preparing corrections, and submitting corrections for processing. A user

PROGRAM IN FOCUS

```
        PROJECT: TS3017           MEMBER: GORDON3          DATE: 84/02/24
        LIBRARY: SPFSRC           LEVEL:  01.01            TIME: 18:27
        TYPE:    CONTROL          USERID: TS3017           PAGE: 01 OF 01
START
COL  ----+----1----+----2----+----3----+----4----+----5----+----6----+----7----+----8

   1  REPORT EMPLOYEE
   1  SUM CSAL MAX.CSAL MIN.CSAL AVE.CSAL
   1  BY CJC
   1  END
```

OUTPUT

CURR_JOBCODE	CURR_SAL	MAX CURR_SAL	MIN CURR_SAL	AVE CURR_SAL
A01	$9,500.00	$9,500.00	$9,500.00	$9,500.00
A07	$20,000.00	$11,000.00	$9,000.00	$10,000.00
A15	$26,862.00	$26,862.00	$26,862.00	$26,862.00
A17	$56,762.00	$29,700.00	$27,062.00	$28,381.00
B02	$34,580.00	$18,480.00	$16,100.00	$17,290.00
B03	$18,480.00	$18,480.00	$18,480.00	$18,480.00
B04	$42,900.00	$21,780.00	$21,120.00	$21,450.00
B14	$13,200.00	$13,200.00	$13,200.00	$13,200.00

PROGRAM IN FOCUS

```
        PROJECT: TS3017           MEMBER: GORDON4          DATE: 84/02/24
        LIBRARY: SPFSRC           LEVEL:  01.02            TIME: 18:27
        TYPE:    CONTROL          USERID: TS3017           PAGE: 01 OF 01
START
COL  ----+----1----+----2----+----3----+----4----+----5----+----6----+----7----+----8

   1  REPORT EMPLOYEE
   1  HEADING CENTER
   1  "SALARY ANALYSIS BY JOB CODE"
   1  " "
   1  SUM CSAL AS 'CURRENT,SALARY'
   5      MAX.CSAL AS 'MAXIMUM,SALARY'
   5      MIN.CSAL AS 'MINIMUM,SALARY'
   5      AVE.CSAL AS 'AVERAGE,SALARY'
   1  BY CJC AS 'JOB,CODE'
   1  END
```

OUTPUT

SALARY ANALYSIS BY JOB CODE

JOB CODE	CURRENT SALARY	MAXIMUM SALARY	MINIMUM SALARY	AVERAGE SALARY
A01	$9,500.00	$9,500.00	$9,500.00	$9,500.00
A07	$20,000.00	$11,000.00	$9,000.00	$10,000.00
A15	$26,862.00	$26,862.00	$26,862.00	$26,862.00
A17	$56,762.00	$29,700.00	$27,062.00	$28,381.00
B02	$34,580.00	$18,480.00	$16,100.00	$17,290.00
B03	$18,480.00	$18,480.00	$18,480.00	$18,480.00
B04	$42,900.00	$21,780.00	$21,120.00	$21,450.00
B14	$13,200.00	$13,200.00	$13,200.00	$13,200.00

Figure 3-7
Simple programs in FOCUS and output from execution. Top program uses FOCUS data names in output; bottom program prints specified headings.

manual describes how to prepare input data in the correct format, interpret error reports, prepare corrections, and interpret the output. Generally, the user submits prepared input data to, and receives output from, computer operations personnel rather than operating the computer directly. Batch processing of transactions is explained in more detail in Chapter 5.

Online System Use

In online processing, the user has a terminal for input of transactions and output of results. The terminal is connected by communication lines to a remote computer where processing actually takes place. Transactions are entered and processed one at a time as they occur (in "realtime"). The user generally has to be identified to the system as an authorized user before transactions are accepted. System sign on and authorization usually uses a password protection scheme. Users may have different authorization levels which determine what types of transactions they may perform. For instance, a user may be authorized (via his or her password) to process certain update transactions (e.g., a sale) but not others (e.g., alteration of payroll data). The mode of operation is for the terminal to provide a dialog with the user. The dialog may be extensive and provide tutorial and help information for entry of data, or it may be very limited and require the user to understand what data to enter and how it should be entered.

A user responsible for processing data in an online system must sign on properly; enter transactions in the proper format based on a dialog, a visual form, or instructions in a manual; respond to error messages (since the system should reject any invalid data) with corrected input; and review control information. At the end of a period of processing transactions, the user signs off, so that an unauthorized user may not subsequently enter data. The computer application will normally provide some control information or control list of transactions entered during the period, so that the user may check the processing or be able to reference the work done during the session. During entry of transactions, the system provides both instructions and warning and error messages. Ideally, the messages should be so complete and clear that a user can respond with corrections or adjustments. This ideal is not always achieved, and so a separate user manual may explain error codes and error messages and explain how to make corrections and adjustments.

Microcomputer Use

A microcomputer (or personal computer) is operated through an interactive dialog; unlike online processing with a remote computer, all processing takes place locally. As an alternative, a microcomputer may be used as a terminal device for online processing. Frequently microcomputers are utilized in both fashions; transaction data from a centralized computer may be copied online to the microcomputer's memory and then processed locally. Newer microcomputers are designed to communicate directly with each other (and with other devices such as printers, large disk storage, etc.) rather than with a large mainframe computer. The significant factor is that the user of the microcomputer has direct control over processing.

Microcomputer use places additional responsibilities on the user. The user must prepare for processing by "booting" the system (to load the operating system into primary storage) and loading the application program to be used. He or she must directly deal with setting up output and storage devices, inserting diskettes in the proper disk drive, and placing paper in the printer. The instructions for loading and preparing are not difficult in themselves; however, they require a period of learning (and relearning if use is intermittent). The user may develop applications or use prewritten applications.

In addition, the user of a personal computer has more technical responsibility. Error messages may come from both the application itself and the operating system. For instance, a message such as BDOS ERROR can result from a variety of technical conditions sensed by the operating system. The user is also responsible for backup of files and programs. Currently, security features for microcomputers are very limited, and so the user must establish security controls if needed.

COMMUNICATIONS FACILITIES

The capability for a computer to communicate with remote devices and for physically separate (distributed) computers to communicate with each other is important in the design of many information systems. In this section, the basic facilities for communication will be described. The additional requirements for data communications networks to support distributed systems will be discussed in the next section.

Model of a Communications System

A simple conceptual model of a communications system is shown in Figure 3-8. A transmitter provides coded symbols to be sent through a channel to a receiver. The message which comes from a source to the transmitter is encoded before being sent through the communications channel and decoded by a receiver. The channel is not usually a perfect conduit for the coded message because of noise and distortion.

The bits that encode data are carried through the channel by an electrical signal or waveform. The waveform has three characteristics that can be used in encoding data: strength of the signal (amplitude), direction of the "flow" of the signal in a cycle time (phase), and number of times the waveform is repeated during a specified interval (frequency). These three characteristics are diagrammed in Figure 3-9. The standard unit of signalling speed is a *baud*, which is one pulse or code element.

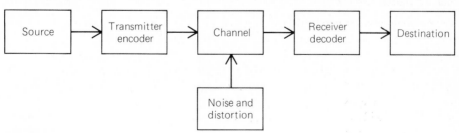

Figure 3-8
Simple conceptual model of communications system.

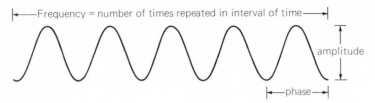

Figure 3-9
Diagram of wave form.

The purpose of a communications system is to reproduce at the destination a message selected at the source. The conceptual significance of this model as it applies generally to information and communication will be discussed in Chapter 7. In this section, the hardware and software components of data communications will be related to this general model.

Communications between a "host" computer and a remote device such as a terminal contain all the components of the conceptual model in Figure 3-8. When a message is sent from a terminal (source), the input codes are converted to signals (encoded) to be transmitted over a line (channel) such as a telephone line. When the message reaches the computer (destination) it is first converted back to the internal computer codes (decoded) for computer use. When the computer sends a message back to the remote device, the sequence is reversed, with the computer as the source and the remote device as the destination.

Most older communications systems have used analog encoding in which the frequency of the signal changes continually to approximate the frequency changes of the voice signal. When an analog transmission is used for the two values in binary coding, a modulator is used to encode the data before transmission and a demodulator reverses the process (Figure 3-10). The device, called a *modem* (abbreviation of *Mod*ulator/*demodu*lator), is not required if the communication carrier is designed for digital transmission. Digitally encoded transmission is more efficient and has fewer errors. It can also be used for voice transmission by encoding voice frequencies using digital codes and then reversing the process to reproduce the voice from the codes.

There are generally two types of data transmission: synchronous and asynchronous. With asynchronous transmission, each character is transmitted separately and therefore has a "start" signal transmitted in front of it and a "stop" signal at the end of it. In synchronous transmission, a number of characters are sent as a unit, and "start" and "stop" signals are required only for the whole unit. It is used where faster transmission rates are required. The receiving device (e.g., terminal) is "synchronized" bit for bit

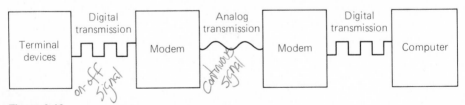

Figure 3-10
Use of modems with analog transmission.

with the sending device; clocking mechanisms are required at both ends to achieve synchronization.

Communications Channels

Communications channels, commonly known as "lines," may use one or more of the following technologies:

- Physical connection lines
  - —twisted pair of copper wires
  - —coaxial cables
  - —fiber optics lines
- Microwave "lines"
  - —line of sight earth microwave
  - —satellite
  - —radio

The full transmission capacity of a physical line is rarely required for transmitting data or voice. The physical line is divided into narrower virtual lines based on the capacity required by users and technical considerations on keeping them separate. The bandwidth of a channel or line is the range of frequencies assigned to it. A wideband or large range of frequencies allows more data to be transmitted per unit of time than a narrowband, where the speed of the channel is in bits per second (bps). The speed is proportional to the bandwidth of the channel:

Speed and bandwidth	Explanation
Low speed (narrowband)	Data is transmitted in a range of up to 300 bits per second. This speed is usually used for slow speed terminals.
Medium speed (voice band)	These channels are provided by the Bell operating companies and other telephone and data communications companies. The typical transmission rates are from 300 to 2400 baud, with 9600 baud or more possible on a special dedicated line (see below). Based on typical coding, these speeds are 30, 240, and 960 characters a second.
High speed (broadband)	Where it is necessary to transmit very high volumes of data at high speeds, a broadband service is appropriate.

For medium-speed channels, the user has the option of leased (dedicated) or dial-up lines. With a leased or dedicated line, the channel is always connected and is only used for communication between the two points. In addition, a leased line can be "conditioned" since it is only used for digital transmission and not for voice; the line is treated to improve the transmission rate and decrease the number of errors in transmission. The cost of an unlimited-use leased line is usually a flat monthly charge based on the distance between the two points.

In dial-up lines, the channel is connected only during the duration of the particular communication. The source is linked into a common carrier's public switching network which assigns a channel. The charge for use of the public switched network is roughly comparable to that of a long-distance telephone call. Because of the complex process of establishing a connection, delays in initial response times for dialing and connections may be 15 to 20 seconds which would be unacceptable for some realtime response systems. Also, connecting through a telephone dial-up may be delayed when channels are busy. On the other hand, usage of dial-up lines has the advantage of portability (a terminal device at any location may be connected to the computer).

Data communication in general is performed in either half-duplex or full-duplex modes. Half-duplex is transmission in only one direction at a time; to provide a response back to the entry terminal, the line must switch directions. Full-duplex provides communication in both directions at once. Data entered at the terminal is sent to the computer and simultaneously echoed back to the terminal.

A single slow-speed device, such as a terminal, will not use the capacity of a medium- or high-speed line. Therefore, a number of devices can share the same line by the use of a *multiplexor*. There are several approaches to multiplexing, but essentially the multiplexor divides the line into small segments and interleaves the slow transmissions of many devices to use the line capacity. A multiplexor at the receiving end reverses the process. A *concentrator* is a small computer that performs the same function as a multiplexor but also performs other functions related to validation of data, formatting of data, backup, etc.

Front-End Processors

The management of data communications requires a complex set of computer programs. Terminals may need to be checked for transmission and messages assembled and

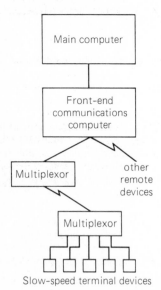

Figure 3-11
Use of front-end communications computer and multiplexor.

checked prior to any processing. Error checking and error recovery procedures are required. Many computer systems use a special front-end processor to handle all data communications. Usually a small computer, it performs all functions required to assemble and check a message that is then sent to the main computer for processing (Figure 3-11).

COMMUNICATIONS NETWORKS

In many instances a computer within an information system is "stand-alone" and self-contained with no data communications; however, the more typical situation is that the information system is a network of devices interconnected by a communications network. The communications network is needed to connect:

- Remote devices to a central computer
- A computer in one location to a computer in another
  —within an organization
  —among organizations (such as airlines)
- An "intelligent" device (having microprocessor logic and processing capability) to other intelligent devices

These communications capabilities are significant because they allow the following functions to be accomplished:

- Communication among users of computer systems
- Communication among applications being executed on different systems
- Sharing of computer resources
- Distribution of computer applications among computers in different locations

There are two broad classes of communications networks—local area and wide area networks. A local area network (LAN) can be used to support interconnections within a building or set of buildings close together; a wide area network (also termed long haul network) can be used for communications among remote devices, including those close by if there is no local area network.

Concept of a Communications Network

Communications networks are formed from the interconnection of a number of different locations through communications facilities. There are multiple devices on the network with multiple users able to choose among them.

One way of describing the concept of a network is in terms of "layers" of function or interconnection.[1] The *end user* is the source or destination of a message. In network terminology, an end user is not necessarily a person; it may be an application program inquiring into a file, an application program interacting with another application, a terminal user talking to another terminal user, etc. The *access path* is the connection between the two end users that allows them to communicate.

---

[1]P. E. Greene, "An Introduction to Network Architecture and Protocols," *IBM Systems Journal*, 18:2, 1979; and Ralph G. Berglund, "Comparing Network Architectures," *Datamation*, February 1978.

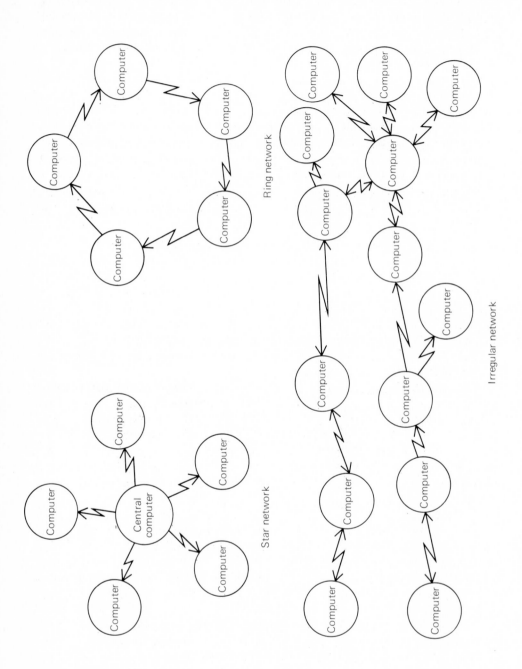

Figure 3-12
Star, ring, and irregular networks for data communications.

A path is established by pairwise linking of *nodes* in the network. A node is a physical box that can accept and redirect a message along an access path: it may be a computer, a multiplexor, or a terminal controller. It also buffers messages (holding characters and waiting until it receives the entire message before transmitting it to the next node) and performs error control.

A network can be configured in many different ways, depending primarily on the applications and geographic locations to be supported. The placement of the nodes and the number of alternate communications paths between them determine the configuration. The common network configurations (star, ring and irregular) are shown in Figure 3-12. In a star network, all messages are received by the central computer and switched to the proper location; this process is called *message switching*. In the ring network, messages are passed from one node to another in a given direction. A multiple-connected irregular network may be structured to have multiple access paths between any two nodes. The control and management of an irregular network is usually more complicated than a star or ring.

Local Area Network (LAN)

If the professionals in an organization each have a workstation (a personal microcomputer system) and every clerical person doing typing, filing, retrieval, etc., has a word processing computer, it is probably useful to communicate among the devices. Stringing wires between devices is feasible if there are only a few devices to interconnect, but it rapidly becomes infeasible with larger numbers. The alternative is to connect the devices to a local area network (LAN).

A local area network is constructed of high-capacity lines, such as a coaxial cable. If the cable is long, electronic devices are attached to keep signals strong and clear as they move along the line. A device to be attached to the network cable has an interface (connection) containing a microprocessor that manages the logic of the attachment and transmission. If the local area network is small, the attachment logic may be handled by a computer that controls the entire network. There are a number of proprietary designs for building a local area network. Examples are Ethernet (Xerox), Wangnet (Wang), and Decnet (Digital Equipment).

Messages to be sent over the local area network are assembled by the sending device into short packets of data with a code that indicates the destination. The communications interface decides if the line is available; if it is, the message is sent. The communication protocol of a local area network determines how a receiving device is addressed and how contention for the line is handled. The most important local area network contention-handling designs are *token ring* and *carrier-sense multiple-access collision detection* (CSMA/CD)

In token ring design, the line has a token consisting of a code (set of bits) that is continuously circulated around the ring on the line connecting the devices. A device ready to send "takes the token" by changing the set of bits in the token code. Transmission from that device then has full use of the line. When transmission is complete, the token code indicating network availability is put back on the line. In carrier-sense multiple-access collision detection design, the transmitting device checks to see if there is a signal on the line; if not, it puts the message to be sent on the network. Only if it detects a collision (another device started at the same time) does it retransmit, waiting a random interval before attempting to do so.

Another alternative to local communications is to have all devices connected to a PABX (Private Automatic Branch Exchange) which acts as a central switchboard to connect devices needing to communicate. This is a natural method of integrating voice and data communications.

Local area networks designed only for data communications (and perhaps telephones) are termed *baseband* networks. A *broadband* network is a larger capacity cable that can be divided into separate channels, each channel acting as a separate line. The extra capacity means the broadband network can carry data communications, television, telephone, etc., on the same cable. It is more expensive than a baseband network and is therefore cost-justified only where there is a consistently high volume of communications.

Wide Area Network

In contrast to local area networks in the same building or small area, the wide area network provides communication over long distances. For almost all organizations, long-distance communications make use of facilities and services of public communications companies. In most countries, this is a government monopoly; in the United States, it can be one of the Bell System companies, AT&T, or other private communications companies (GTE Telenet, Satellite Business Systems, etc.).

Wide area network communications can use the regular telephone network, but this is expensive and relatively poor for large volumes of data transmission. The alternative is a *packet switching network*. The packet switching network is accessed via a local connection, typically through the telephone. The data to be transmitted is received by a node in the network (a special purpose computer operated by the packet switching vendor) and divided into packets (strings of data characters) with each packet having a sequence number and address of destination. The packets are sent over high speed communications facilities with error detection on each packet. At the destination, the packets are assembled in the proper order to form the original message.

Protocols

When two devices are communicating, there must be agreement as to the meaning of control information being sent with the data and agreement as to how the control information and data shall be packaged. This agreement is the *protocol*. There are a number of standard communication protocols. A common standard protocol is the international RS-232 physical connection standard for connecting two devices with a cable. It specifies, for example, what each pin on the cable is used for. Most microcomputers use RS-232 cables.

A broader standard approach to communications protocols is the international standard X.25 *open systems interconnect* model. The X.25 model consists of seven layers in a hierarchy of communication protocols. The first three layers are physical, link, and network:

Physical layer   Physical interface between data terminal equipment

Data link layer   Flow of data control between adjacent nodes

Network layer   Public packet-switching interface for public data networks

There are standard protocols for these three levels, and standards are being developed for the remaining layers of transport, session, presentation, and application. Thus, using X.25, networks can have a common protocol for communicating with packets. IBM has SNA (System Network Architecture) for interconnecting devices in data communications. SNA uses SDLC (Synchronous Data Link Control) which is a subset of the X.25 data link layer standard.

DISTRIBUTED SYSTEMS

Each CPU represents processing power, each terminal device represents power to enter and retrieve data, each input device represents power to input data, and each output device represents the capability to receive output. All these devices can be grouped in

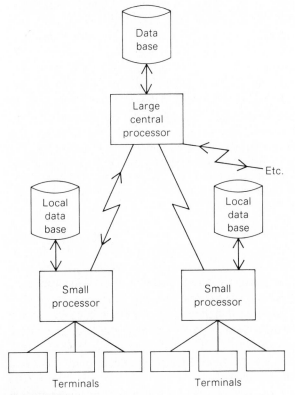

Figure 3-13
Distributed processing using hierarchy of processors.

one location (centralized); they can also be dispersed, so that the power is distributed to different locations. There are a number of variations of distributed systems depending on the distribution of hardware and data:

- Separate computer system in each location
  —each system has own data
  —systems share data
  —systems share data managed by a designated computer
- Central computer with
  —input/output devices in other locations connected to central computer
  —data preparation and data entry equipment at other locations

When physically separated computers are interconnected through communications facilities, the configuration is called *distributed computing*. Distributed computers may be organized as a *hierarchy* or a *ring*. A hierarchy of processors is shown in Figure 3-13. The lowest level of processors consists of microcomputers or minicomputers which have some local data storage and perform local processing. Tasks too large to be processed at this level or requiring data not available in the local database are transmitted to a higher-level regional or centralized computer. The highest level in the hierarchy of processors has the capacity to handle large-scale problems.

Alternatively, there may be a ring structure of minicomputers of equal power and no large central processor. Each minicomputer does local processing and accesses data from the other locations as required. The way a distributed processing system is configured usually depends on the needs of the application.

There are several advantages of distributed computing over a centralized computer. Since the bulk of computing is performed at the local site, communications costs can be significantly reduced. Furthermore, if one processor is "down" (cannot function), its processing can be shifted to other processors, and there is minimal disturbance to the entire system; if, on the other hand, a central computer "goes down," all processing stops. In the case of the hierarchical configuration in particular, users may benefit from local control over a relatively inexpensive system and still have access to more powerful computers as needed.

SUMMARY

Hardware, software, and communication facilities are required for information system development and operation. The basic elements were surveyed in the chapter. Computers operate with two-state logic or 0 and 1 bits. A basic computer system consists of a central processing unit containing primary storage, an arithmetic and logic unit, and a control unit. There are also secondary memory, input and output devices, and software for both system operations and specific applications. Building blocks for hardware are logic and memory chips that make up a microprocessor and magnetic media for storage of data.

A computer is directed by software instructions. Most programming of instructions is done in high-level languages which trade off programmer productivity against extra machine resources. A number of types of high-level languages used in information processing applications are described.

Communications is an important element in many existing systems and in most new systems. The chapter surveys basic communications facilities. Both local area and wide area networks are briefly described. Distributed systems are elements in a trend to more closely tie processing facilities and data to the location of use.

MINICASES

1 DISTRIBUTED PROCESSING: EASY AS A, B, C

While school districts around the country strain against tightening budgets to sustain services and contain costs, Michigan's Wayne County Intermediate School District is delivering more services at less cost. According to district officials, a switch to distributed data processing made a big difference.

Wayne County Intermediate School District, the nation's third largest, serves 36 constituent districts, with a combined student population of over 450,000 in the Detroit metropolitan area. Its new distributed system now links 28 small computers to a powerful central computer at Intermediate's headquarters.

"Converting from a centralized to a distributed system enables us to put computer power out where the action is—in the local school and school board offices," notes Jerry L. Henderson, Wayne County Intermediate's director of data processing. "At the same time, it sharply reduces the workload on the central computer, extending its life and freeing its time for other administrative and instructional tasks." The result, according to Mr. Henderson, is improved and expanded data processing service to local district administrators, staff, and students at a substantially lower cost. "Dollar savings are impressive," he declares. "It would have cost $5.4 million to maintain established services with the former centralized system. With the new distributed system, our budgeted costs are less than $4.6 million, a savings of more than $800,000, while providing more services than before."

Currently, 28 of Wayne County Intermediate's constituent school districts are on the computer system network. The small processors now installed at local district facilities maintain their own record files and are also online to the host computer, which maintains the master database. Some 235 visual display terminals in local school and board offices are linked to the computers and are used to access the local computer databases to enter or retrieve information.

Adapted from "Easy as A, B, C," *IBM Information Processing*, 1:5, December 1982.

Questions

a What major administrative applications would such a system serve? Could this system serve educational functions as well?
b To what can be attributed the reported cost savings? *People, transporting of info*
c What disadvantages might this system have compared to a centralized system? *less control, harder to maintain security, harder to upgrade*

2 HARDWARE REORGANIZATION PRESSURES

The director of information systems of a major engineering firm is pondering whether to break apart and totally reconfigure his computer operations center. At present, a single large computer supports the company's batch and online systems. Work loads are quite erratic and in the past year long response time delays on the online systems, combined with batch schedules, have put him under considerable pressure to provide more responsive service.

Questions

a Suggest several alternative hardware configurations and evaluate them in terms of both overall efficiency and responsiveness to user needs.
b What other actions might be taken to improve responsiveness to user needs without reconfiguring the hardware?

EXERCISES

1 Define the following terms:
   a Bus
   b System software
   c VDT
   d LAN
   e Modem
   f Concentrator
   g Application
   h Distributed computing
2 Define and contrast the following pairs of terms.
   a Microcode and machine language
   b Multiplexor and concentrator
   c Front-end and main computer
   d Intelligent terminal and dumb terminal
   e Local area and wide area networks
   f Token ring and CSMA/CD
3 Why is a high-level language less error-prone?
4 Many people in the industry say COBOL is dead, yet over 60 percent of all application programs are coded in COBOL. What programs might not be suitable for coding in a very high level language instead of COBOL?
5 Explain the need for a variety of programming languages.
6 Describe how a local area network could be used to connect microcomputers in an office building.
7 Describe how a PABX could be used to do the same interconnection as a local area network.
8 Describe the advantages and disadvantages of distributed computing.
9 Why do protocols make a difference in data communications?
10 What is the X.25 standard communications protocol?
11 If packets of data from a file are being sent, they may be routed on different transmission paths. How do they get to the right location and get reassembled in the right order?
12 What is the difference between digital and analog communications? Why is digital favored for most new networks?
13 Explain the hardware configuration alternatives in distributed processing.

SELECTED REFERENCES

Most elementary texts on computers cover the material in the chapter.

STORAGE AND RETRIEVAL OF DATA

Organizational activities require data. Making sales, producing products, billing, collecting amounts due, and assigning personnel are examples of activities that use data. Data items have value to the extent that they are useful in the performance of useful organizational activities. However, the data items are of value only if they can be retrieved, processed, and presented to those who need them within the time allowed for the decision or action to which they apply. Data that cannot be located or processed in time has no value. Storage and retrieval of data are therefore important issues in information system design and operation.

There are both economic and physical limitations on the storage and retrieval of data. An organization must therefore determine which data should be in its files and databases. Data items are not stored in a random or arbitrary fashion; they are organized and stored for efficient retrieval. The storage organization must also take into account the characteristics of the storage media and storage devices being used. This chapter surveys data concepts, physical storage devices, and file and database organizations. The models and procedures for establishing database requirements are described in Chapter 16.

PHYSICAL VERSUS LOGICAL MODELS OF DATA

Data consists of symbols which represent, describe, or record reality, but the data symbols are not the same as reality. In other words, a name identifies a person, but the name is not the same as the person. Data symbols can never be a complete representation of reality; they describe objects and events and their characteristics incompletely. Decisions about what to extract from reality and how to represent it using symbols should therefore reflect the needs and views of the users of the data. For example, an organization may ask employees about prior work experience, code their responses, and store the data items because personnel administration views prior work experience as important in understanding employee ability. Another user of employee data (such as the employee's medical plan insurer) may be interested in the characteristics of childhood illnesses because of their importance in employee immunity to certain diseases.

Humans input huge amounts of data into their brains, but data items are not stored as individual items. They are categorized and related to other data items already stored. The same concept applies to computer data storage; data to be stored must be categorized and related to other stored data. It is therefore necessary to understand the structure of data items as they relate to the organization and data users in the organization. This understanding is expressed as a data model.

A *data model* is an abstract representation of data. It defines the way data items are organized and related. The model can use a variety of representations. Examples are graphs, mathematical formulas, and tables. The objective is to represent the essential elements of the data without the detail.

There are two major classes of data models—logical data models and physical data models. These two classes reflect the fact that efficient physical storage and retrieval of data must be designed around the physical characteristics of storage media and devices, but users of data should be able to describe, think about, and use data without being concerned about its physical storage. The user-oriented ways of describing and understanding data are termed *logical data models* or *user views*; the models that describe physical storage of data are *physical data models* or *physical views*. The two data models reflect an ideal separation of how data is used from how data is stored and accessed. Ideally, changes in storage technology should be possible without affecting applications using data; changes in the logical data model should also be allowed without affecting physical storage. This separation of the physical and logical data models is termed *data independence*.

The logical data model aids users and designers to specify data requirements and relationships among data items. The logical model is conceptual, it mirrors the way users describe reality. The user or analyst is responsible for defining logical data requirements; the developer of the database system is responsible for defining the physical storage of data in such a way that the logical requirements can be met.

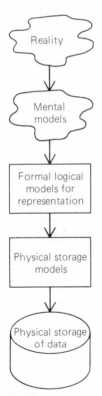

Figure 4-1
Relationship of reality, data models, and physical storage of data.

The overall flow from reality to logical views of data to physical storage models is shown in Figure 4-1. The complexity of reality is organized and simplified by mental models (that depend on users and user objectives). The mental model is likely to be imprecise, and it is necessary to describe data requirements by some type of formal, logical representation. This logical, user-oriented description of requirements is mapped into or related to a physical storage model that describes the structure of data for storage.

A knowledge of how data items are organized and stored in physical storage is not required for users; however, it is often helpful for users to have some knowledge of physical data storage in order to understand and respond to constraints in logical representation that may be imposed by physical storage.

This section has used the terms logical and physical data models. In the literature on database systems, other terms are also used. The term *schema* is often used as a synonym for view, model or diagram. Three major schemas are related to logical and physical data models as follows:

External schema or *user view* is the way the user of the data defines the data and data relationships. Also called a subschema since it is one part or one view of the larger conceptual schema.

Conceptual schema is the overall logical model of the database.

Internal schema is the physical storage data model

Using these terms, the user view is defined in an external schema that is then related to the conceptual schema that defines the entire database (the user schema being only a small part). The external schema is not the same as the user's mental view of the data; it is

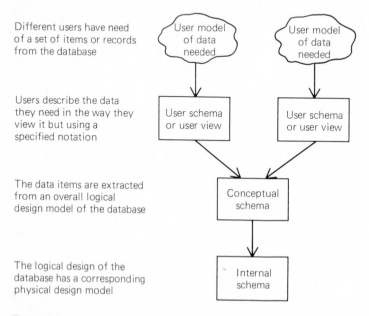

Figure 4-2
Relationship of user schema, conceptual schema, and internal schema.

formalized and probably simplified. The conceptual schema provides specifications that are met by the internal schema that establishes the physical storage (Figure 4-2).

LOGICAL DATA CONCEPTS AND DEFINITIONS

This section covers basic data concepts for files and databases. The emphasis is on logical data model concepts, but many of the concepts and definitions apply to both logical and physical models because of the relationship between them. A simple case situation will be used as an aid in explaining the concepts:

A professor needs to keep track of the students in his class. He wants background information about them (address, occupation, major, etc.) and a record of their grades on assignments and tests. He is accustomed to keeping an index card on each student, but thinks computer processing may be more efficient in keeping track of assignments, calculating grades, and producing class lists. He therefore investigates the construction of a computerized student file for his classes.

Entities, Attributes, and Relationships

An *entity* is any type of "thing" about which data is collected. Entities may be an object, person, abstract concept, or event. In the case situation cited, students in the professor's class are one type of thing about which data is collected. The class assignments are another entity. Doing an assignment is an event for a student.

An *attribute* is a characteristic of interest about an entity; the *values* of the attributes describe a particular entity. An *instance* of the entity is represented by a set of specific values for each of the attributes. For example, the professor is interested in the following attributes for the students in his class: name, student ID, address, major, and class status. The attributes are the same for each student, but the values of the attributes in each instance are different. He also wants grade attributes for each assignment. These concepts are illustrated in Figure 4-3.

A *relationship* is a correspondence or association between entities. For example, a student's grade performance associates a student with an assignment.

Data Items, Records, and Files

Each attribute of an entity is represented in storage by a *data item*. For example, there is a data item for student name, another data item for major, etc. A data item is assigned a name in order to refer to it in storage, retrieval, and processing operations. Associated with each data item is a set of possible values (domain of values). The set of possible values is defined in a general way by the value class from which they may be taken (such as numeric, alphanumeric, binary, etc.) The possible values may also be defined by enumeration, by limits, or by an algorithm. As an example, there are only five values for school class status (Frosh, Soph, Junior, Senior, and Grad). The data item may contain these values, or a code (such as 1 through 5) may be used in place of the five terms.

A data item is the elementary unit in data storage. Data items are usually grouped

Attributes of Student

Record address	Last name, First name	Student ID#	Address	Major	Class Status	Grades on Assignments 1	2	3	4	5
11	Jones, Tom	34313	316 Fitz Hall	Finance	Senior	B	B—	—	—	—
12	Gordon, Flint	36120	19 Eddy Hall	Accounting	Soph	A	B	—	—	—
13	Stanford, Clark	37666	214 Middlebrook	MIS	Junior	C	B+	—	—	—
14	Blake, Marie	38412	1919 Terrace	OB	Grad	A	A	—	—	—
15	Spencer, Sally	32714	1B Commonwealth	MIS	Grad	B	C	—	—	—

Entity instances

Value of attribute 'Major' for instance 'Sally Spencer' of entity 'student'

Figure 4-3
Concept of entity and attribute.

together to describe an entity; each data item in the group corresponds to an attribute of the entity. The data representation in storage of each instance of an entity is commonly termed a *record*. A collection of related records is called a *file*. The attributes for each student instance form a student record; all the student records form the student class file. Multiple values of the same attribute for an entity are represented by *repeating groups* of data items. The grades for each student in Figure 4-3 represent a *repeating group*, because there are multiple assignments and associated grades for each instance.

The level of subdivision for data items depends on how the user views the data (user schema). For example, NAME may be composed of the entire name, or it may be defined as being composed of two elementary data items—LAST NAME and FIRST NAME. A data item is sometimes referred to as a "field," but the term *field* is used more precisely to refer to the set of storage locations assigned to a data item (or the spaces on an input or output medium to be occupied by the data item values).

Record Identification and Location

One or more of the data items in a record is a unique identifier that differentiates that record from any other. For example, the student identification number is a unique identifier for the student record. Most data items cannot be record identifiers because they do not have unique values. The student name is not usually a unique identifier because more than one person may have the same first and last names. The unique identifier is also termed the *record key*.

In physical storage, a record has a physical storage location or address associated with it. (An exception is magnetic tape, to be discussed later in the chapter.) Usually record addresses are represented by sequential numbers indicating the record's position relative to the first record in the file. Relative record addresses are shown in Figure 4-3 at the far left of each record. The file organizations discussed in a later section are designed to associate a unique record key with the appropriate physical address, so that a record may be accessed on the basis of its key. Other methods permit records to be accessed on the basis of other attributes besides the record key. Two of these methods are indexes and pointers.

An *index* is a table associating attributes and physical addresses of records. In the class list example, the professor might have an index with the five values for the class status attribute and a list of record addresses for student records containing each value:

Attribute	Record Address
Frosh	—
Soph	12
Junior	13
Senior	11
Grad	14, 15

A *pointer* is a data item used to point to (identify) the location of another record. In the index above, the record addresses are pointers. Pointer data items can also be included in records to point to other records. For example, rather than keeping a list of all student ID numbers for each of the classes, the index could list the address of the first one. The first

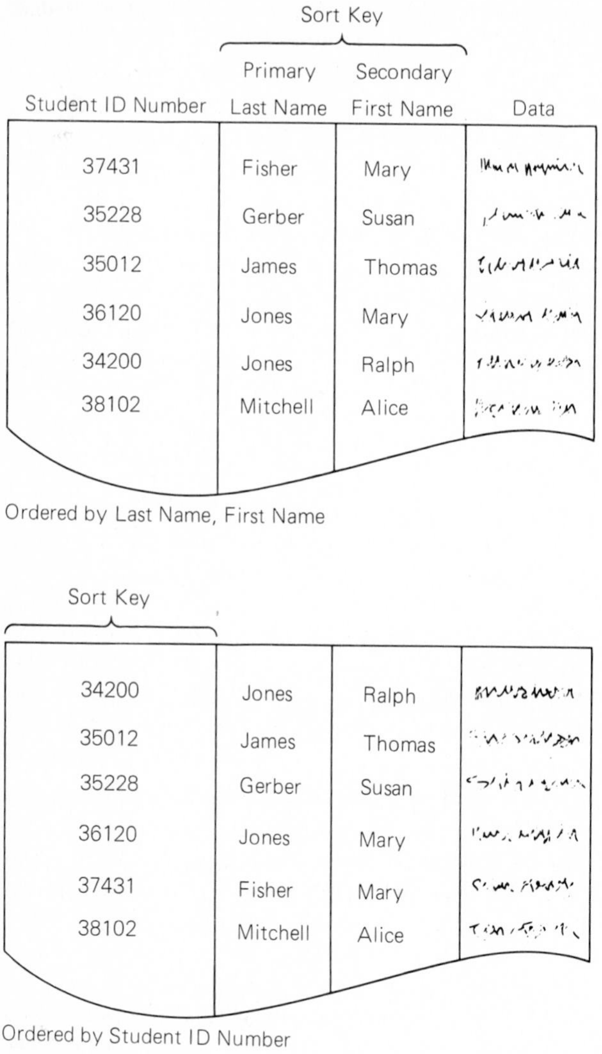

	Sort Key		
	Primary	Secondary	
Student ID Number	Last Name	First Name	Data
37431	Fisher	Mary	*IIwₐM Hₒₘᵢₐ·'ₗ*
35228	Gerber	Susan	*ₗ'ᵤₘ·ᵥᵏ·ₘ·ₐ*
35012	James	Thomas	*ₜ(ᵥᵣₐₗ'ᵣₗᵢₐ*
36120	Jones	Mary	*ᵥₜᵤᵥₘ ᵣ'ₘᵣ*
34200	Jones	Ralph	*ₜᵣₗₐᵥ'ₛ ᵥ'ₛ·ᵣₙ*
38102	Mitchell	Alice	*ᵣᵣₛ'ᵥᵣₘ 'ᵣₙ*

Ordered by Last Name, First Name

Sort Key			
34200	Jones	Ralph	*ₛᵥₗᵥₛₐᵥₘₗₛₐ*
35012	James	Thomas	*'ₐᵥᵣ ᵥ'ₐₗᵥᵣₙ*
35228	Gerber	Susan	*ₛᵣᵣᵢₜₗᵣₗ·ᵥᵣ'ᵥₛ*
36120	Jones	Mary	*ᵣ'ₐᵥ·ₗ ₕᵣ'ₐₗᵣ' ₗ*
37431	Fisher	Mary	*ₛ'ₐᵥᵣ ᵣₛᵣₐₛᵣᵣ*
38102	Mitchell	Alice	*ₜ'ₛₙ'ᵣₛᵣᵣ''ₛ*

Ordered by Student ID Number

Figure 4-4
File sequenced in two ways.

record for Junior would contain a pointer to the second; the second to the third, etc. There can be pointers going in both directions, so the third record will have a forward pointer to the fourth record and also a pointer back to the second record.

Sequencing of Data

There are a variety of logical sequences for presenting data. The logical sequences depend on the purpose of the report being prepared; they have no necessary relationship to the physical sequence in which the data records are stored. The sequencing of data into the logical sequence needed for the output is termed *sorting*, a significant activity in data processing. For sorting, one or more data items are designated as the *sort key*, the item whose values determine the sequence of records. By designating a primary sort key and a secondary sort key, the records may be sorted into groups and then each group also placed in sequence. The process may be continued with more sort keys. For example, employees may be first sorted into employees who work at different locations and then sequenced by name for each location. Within the name list for a given location, employees with the same last name are sequenced by first name.

For example, the professor may keep his class file of students in alphabetical order. However, when grades are posted at the end of the term he will print a class list ordered by student ID number without the name (so that grades are anonymous). These two situations require that the records in the file be sequenced in two different ways (Figure 4-4). In the first case, the file is sorted by two keys, a primary key (last name) and a secondary key (first name). This means records are sequenced by first name "within" last name when the value of last name is identical. In the second case, there is only a single key on which the file is sequenced, student ID number.

Traditional Types of Files

Creation and maintenance of stored data is a major part of the workload of an information processing system. In traditional data processing prior to database technology, the emphasis was on files and the relationships among files. Since many of the concepts and terminology still exist, the major types of files will be reviewed. These are master files, transaction files, and report files.

1 *Master file*. This is a file of relatively permanent information about entities. It contains identification, historical, and statistical information. Master files are used as a source of reference data for processing transactions and often hold accumulated information based on transaction data. For example, an employee master file will contain identification and pay rate data as well as gross and net pay to date. A customer master file will contain data about current balance and past due amounts. The professor's class-student master file will contain identification data about students as well as accumulated data about grades.

2 *Transaction file* (or detail file). This is a collection of records describing activities or transactions by the organization. It is developed as a result of processing transactions and preparing transaction documents; it is also used to update the accumulated data in the master file. A maintenance transaction file may contain special transactions to modify relatively permanent data in the master file and add new records or delete old ones. An example of a typical transaction file is a payroll file created by the preparation of a weekly payroll; it is also used to update the year-to-date data items in the employee master file. In the example, the professor prepares a transaction file of grades for each assignment, and this grade file is used to update the class-student master file. He prepares file maintenance transactions to add or delete student records and to correct existing data items.

3 *Report file*. This is a file created by extracting data to prepare a report. An example is a report of all customers, by name, with past due balances over a given amount. The professor's class lists, by name and by student ID number, are another example. The ease of handling special requests for reports depends on the availability of report generator software that efficiently extracts, sorts, and formats data for reports.

Databases

The logical concept of a file as a set of related records historically resulted in physically separate files with ''owners'' for each file. For example, there was a personnel records file with the personnel department being responsible for input and correctness of the personnel records, an accounts receivable file with responsibility (ownership) by the accounts receivable section of accounting, etc.

The ownership responsibility of separate files is a useful organizational control on the quality and use of data. However, it tends to restrict data access and results in duplication of data, lack of data sharing, and lack of data compatibility. If similar or identical data items are used in separate files, they are frequently updated separately at different updating intervals. There may be different quality control procedures, so that the data item values for identical entities may not agree. It is difficult to physically assemble data items when they exist on several separate files. It is also difficult to establish data security.

The solution to the problem is a single *database* which contains all related data files. A high uniform level of quality is obtained by quality assurance procedures applied consistently and by coordinated updating. All applications can access the data; all users of the data receive the same information with the same quality and same recency. The logical concept of a database requires software to manage it (a database management system) and a special organizational authority over it (database administration).

A *database management system* (DBMS) is a software system that manages the creation and use of databases. All access to the database is through the database management software; and access language facilities are provided for application programmer users and end users who formulate queries. Thus, application programmers define a user schema or user view as a logical model of the data to be processed by the application program. The programmer writes instructions using a programming language interface to the database management system, which handles the translation to internal schema of physical storage. All data validation and authorization checks of user authority to access a data item are handled through the DBMS. A person wishing to access the database for a query or special report uses a database query language to formulate the request and format the output. Thus, the database management system may be viewed as the only ''door'' to the physical storage of data in the database. The *database administrator* is the person who has authority over definition and use of the database. This is depicted in Figure 4-5.

PHYSICAL STORAGE DEVICES

Primary memory in the computer provides very fast access storage; programs or program segments being used and data records being processed by the computer are stored in it. Since primary storage is expensive and only a limited amount can be used efficiently by the computer, large files and databases are stored on secondary storage devices and moved into primary storage a small part at a time for processing.

The two types of secondary storage most widely used are magnetic disks and magnetic tapes. Both basic types are used on both large-scale computers and microcomputers, although they differ in speed, capacity, and specific technology.

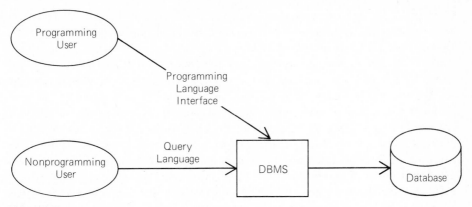

Figure 4-5
DBMS as the "door" to the physical database.

	Disk technology	**Tape technology**
Large-scale computer	Disk packs ● Removable ● Nonremovable ● Sealed disk (Winchester)	1/2-inch tape ● Reel tape ● Cassettes
Microcomputer	Nonremovable rigid disk (hard disk) Sealed disk (Winchester) Removable, flexible diskette	1/4-inch tape cassettes

Tape and disk technology represent two different types of physical access mechanisms—serial access and direct access. Direct access devices, such as disks, support a variety of physical storage and access structures. Magnetic tape will efficiently support only sequential file organization and sequential access (discussed in a later section of this chapter).

Although both disks and tapes are widely used, the trend is toward disk for storage of active files and magnetic tape for backup and archival storage. This reflects a general tradeoff between the low cost of tape and the faster direct access of disks. The relationship between primary memory, disk, and tape forms a storage hierarchy as discussed in Chapter 3.

Serial Access Devices

Magnetic tape is termed a serial access device because a given stored record cannot be read until the records preceding it on the storage medium have been read. Magnetic tapes for large-scale systems are typically 1/2-inch tapes of 2,400-foot length. Microcomputers sometimes use 1/4-inch tape cassettes. The density of storage on magnetic tape is the number of characters that can be stored per inch of tape.

With a magnetic tape, the average time required to access a particular record at random is approximately one-half the time required to read the entire file, because on average half the records need to be read. Accessing of records in random order is therefore very inefficient, and because of this, files stored on magnetic tape are normally organized and processed in sequential order. Thus, magnetic tape is acceptable for applications for which sequential ordering of records for processing is natural.

There are no physical addresses on a magnetic tape to identify the location of stored data. The records are stored in blocks on the tape (Figure 4-6); a block is the amount of data transferred at one time from secondary to primary storage. Each block on the tape is separated from the next by an interblock gap (gaps of 0.6 or 0.3 inches are common). The block may contain more than one record. The gap allows the magnetic tape drive to accelerate to reading speed before sensing the data and to sense the end of the data and decelerate. The start and stop times are very slow relative to read time. This means that overall reading time is significantly reduced by having large blocks of data. The limit on the block size is the amount of storage space available for the block when it is read into primary storage.

Magnetic tape may only be read or written in a single processing run. In other words, it is not possible to read a few records, then stop and write a record on the tape. A tape is assigned as "read" or "write" by the operating instructions setting up the processing run. In order to protect against inadvertently writing over a tape, a *write ring* is used. This is a simple plastic or rubber ring placed on the inner edge of the tape before it is mounted on the tape drive; the tape cannot be written on unless it has a write ring.

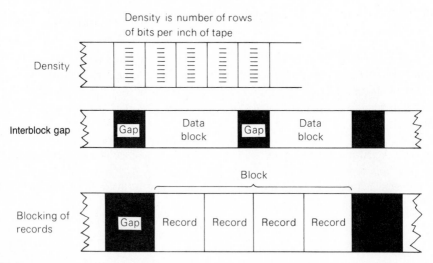

Figure 4-6
Magnetic tape characteristics.

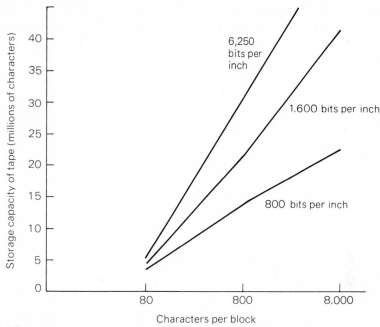

Figure 4-7
Storage capacity of magnetic tape as function of density and block size (2,400-foot reel and interblock gap of 0.6 inches).

The speed of access or data transfer rate for magnetic tape is based on three characteristics of the tape and the tape drive:

1 Tape density (characters per inch)
2 Tape speed (inches per second)
3 Size of interblock gap

The storage capacity of a reel of magnetic tape is based on tape density, interblock gap, and the length of the reel (normally 2,400 feet). Some concept of the range of performance is given in Table 4-1.

TABLE 4-1 TAPE STORAGE TYPICAL PERFORMANCE RANGE (1984)

	Low	Medium	High
Tape density (characters per inch)	800	1,600	6,250
Tape speed (inches per second)	75	125	200
Size of interblock gap (inches)	0.6	0.6	0.3
Transfer rate (thousands of characters per second)	60	200	1,250

Figure 4-7 shows graphically the effect of block size on storage capacity and illustrates why block size is an important processing consideration when using magnetic tape. A similar graph would show the effect of block size on transfer rates.

There are other tape unit designs. For example, tape units called streaming tape are designed for backup units that record continuously without blocking of records.

Direct Access Devices

A direct access storage device (DASD) can access any storage location without first accessing the location preceding it. The dominant direct access storage device is disk. The storage medium is a round disk with a substratum of metal or plastic covered by a coating that can be polarized in two directions to store binary coded data. The recording areas are concentric circles called *tracks* on the surface of the disk. Depending on the design of the disk storage device, the tracks may be further divided into sectors. Each disk surface has an address; each track on a disk surface has an address; and each sector (if used) has an address (see Figure 4-8). The address of a particular record in storage would thus be the surface, track, and sector addresses combined; these serve to locate the particular sector in which the record is stored.

The small diskettes used on microcomputers (8, 5 1/4, and 3 1/2 inches) are based on similar concepts of addressing and access. Hard sectored diskettes have predefined sectors. With soft sectored diskettes, the sectors are defined with software. A major difference between flexible disks and the hard disks is that the hard disks are constantly rotating; the flexible disks are started before each access and stopped after it is complete. Thus, access is significantly faster with hard disks than with diskettes.

Reading or writing of data is accomplished by an ''arm'' with a read-write head which moves back and forth across the surface of the disk to the track desired. The disk revolves to position a sector or other location on the track under the read-write head of the arm. Most removable disk pack units contain from one to eleven individual disks. A separate read-write arm accesses each pair of disk surfaces so that movement of the arm is in and out but not up and down. The arms generally move in and out together, so at any one time they are positioned over a cylinder consisting of the same track on each disk surface (Figure 4-8). Some disks use head-per-track arms which do not move at all; the result is that they are significantly faster than single-head disks but also considerably more expensive.

Direct access storage devices have been called ''random access devices,'' implying that the time to access any record at random is the same regardless of its location. This term is not completely accurate because the time required to access a storage location is somewhat dependent upon the current location of the read-write head. If the record immediately preceding (physically) the one desired has just been read, the read-write head is already positioned over the record to be read. But if the last record was on a different track, the arm may be required to move to obtain the next record. This is in contrast to primary storage where there is no difference in read time among different storage locations.

Unlike magnetic tape, magnetic disk storage may be read and written in the same processing run. A record may be accessed and read into primary memory, changed based on a transaction, and written back to the same location in storage. This read-write capability is the basis for online, realtime processing, since the processing of a single

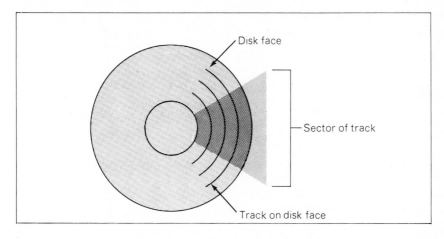

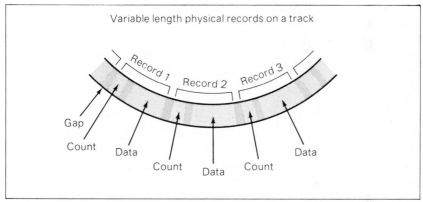

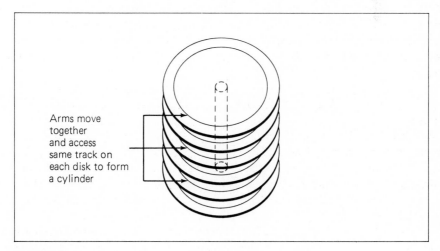

Figure 4-8
Disk file addressing.

transaction is instantly reflected in the data on the storage medium.

The time to read any location on a disk is composed of two elements:

    1 The *seek time* to position the read-write arm.

    2 The time for the disk to revolve so that the location to be read moves under the read-write head (*rotational delay*).

The technical specifications for disk files are beyond the scope of this overview.

FILE ORGANIZATIONS

Physical data models describe how to put data items into storage locations so that they can be retrieved. Traditional data processing has used file organizations; the trend is to a more complex physical organization required for databases. Efficiency in processing is a dominant factor in file organization, whereas database organization is also influenced by other factors such as availability, evolvability, and integrity.

Concerns in File Organization

The organization of data in a file is influenced by a number of factors, but by far the most significant factor is the very large difference between the time required to access a record and transfer the data to primary storage or to write a record compared with the time to do the processing once the record is in primary storage. The magnitude of this relative difference for disk drives is from one thousand to one up to one hundred thousand to one.

ANALOGIES TO ILLUSTRATE IMPORTANCE OF STORAGE ORGANIZATION

To understand the reason for the attention devoted to file organization and design of access paths for storing and retrieving data on disk drives, consider the following analogies that reflect the difference between internal processing times and secondary storage access times:

- The difference between going to the grocery store on the corner a block away to buy groceries versus flying from Minneapolis to Tokyo to obtain groceries
- The difference between doing something in five seconds versus taking one to ten days

---

Given the significant differences in these times, an important factor in information system file design is a physical organization that will support the kind of record access needed yet be efficient in terms of access times.

The following types of operations are required for processing records in files:

    1 File creation

    2 Locating a record

    3 Adding a record

    4 Deleting a record

    5 Modifying a record

Each file organization is more efficient at some operations than others. The choice of file organization will therefore be influenced by the physical storage device being used and the mix of operations.

The file storage organization determines how to access the record; it does not define the internal record structures. Internal record definition includes how the data will be encoded within the record, whether records are fixed or variable length, how the length of a variable length record is determined, and whether data compression is used to reduce file size. These issues will not be covered here. Four file organizations will be explained: sequential, hashed, indexed, and multikey.

Sequential File Organization

In a sequential file organization the records are stored in order by record key. There is a single access path for obtaining records which is the order in which they are physically stored. For example, if the key of the class-student file is student ID number, the record for student 35012 will precede the record for student 35013 in the record sequence. Sequential file organization is very common because it makes effective use of the least expensive secondary storage device (magnetic tape) and because sequential processing at periodic intervals using a batch of transactions (batch processing) is very efficient in many applications. It is also consistent with many periodic business processes such as weekly payroll, monthly billing, etc. A disk storage device can be used much like a magnetic tape with the data records stored and accessed in sequence.

When a file is organized sequentially by record key and is accessed in sequence, there is no need to know specifically where any record is stored, only that it is in order by the sequencing key. Locating any particular record is performed merely by starting at the beginning of the file, reading each record, and comparing its key to the record which is being sought. Efficiency of processing thus requires that all transactions to be processed using a sequential file should be organized in the same order as the file, so that the first record on the file to be sought will be found first and the transaction which needs that record will be processed first, the second transaction will find its corresponding file record next, etc. The entire master file is therefore read in a single processing run involving a group of transactions which require master file records in order to be processed, or which result in a change to master file records. This is one reason it is desirable to hold transactions until a reasonable sized batch can be processed. Since every master file record must be processed regardless of the number of transactions in a batch, a larger batch is more efficient for processing than a smaller one.

Since magnetic tape does not permit a record to be read and written in the same place, updating of records sequentially with magnetic tape requires that an entirely new record be written on a different tape (with changes if the record was updated). The nature of sequential processing in which the entire file is read and written thus results in a new master file being created at each run which is useful for backup and recovery. The old master file and the file of transactions can be saved and used to recreate the new master file in case it is destroyed or damaged.

The efficiency of a sequential organization in locating data specified by inquiries depends on the type of inquiry. If the inquiry is for a specific record identified by its key, the file is searched from the beginning until the record is found. On average, finding one record will require that one-half of the records in the file be read. If inquiries can be collected into a batch to be processed at one time and sorted by record key before processing, the efficiency of processing each inquiry will be improved. Requests involving multiple selection criteria based on data items (attributes) other than identifier key (such as "students with a major in MIS or accounting with an average grade of B + or better") are processed by reading the entire file and checking each record to see if it matches all the criteria.

The performance of a sequential file organization based on the five operations is summarized in Table 4-2.

TABLE 4-2   PERFORMANCE IN TERMS OF BASIC OPERATIONS
OF SEQUENTIAL FILE ORGANIZATION

Operation	Comments
Create a file	Very efficient if transaction records are ordered by record key.
Locate a record	Inefficient. On average, one-half of the records in the file must be processed.
Add or delete a record	Entire file must be read and written; more efficient with greater number of additions and deletions; both operations may be combined with modification transactions for greater efficiency.
Modify a record	If the number of records to be modified (activity rate) is high, very efficient. Transactions must be in order by record key.
List or process all records in sequence	Very efficient if the required sequence is the same as the file (key) sequence. A sort of the entire file is required for any other sequence.

Hashed File Organization

Since storage technology permits many external access paths to stored data, it is not necessary to read records sequentially. Records can be accessed in random order. The major difficulty is determining the storage location where a record is stored. Thus, some relationship must be established between the record key and the storage location; this will determine where an individual record is initially stored and subsequently accessed. It would be efficient for direct access if the record keys could be the same as the identification numbers for the disk storage locations, but this is rarely the case because identification numbers are usually based on other criteria. An alternative is to use the record key to determine the storage location. In other words, the task is to take a set of record keys and find a formula to map them into a set of disk storage location identifiers. If the record keys ran sequentially with no gaps, this might be a fairly simple matter, but this condition almost never exists. In addition to gaps, many identification codes are not sequential because they are designed to have some other significant meaning, such as showing territory or product line, or they are adapted from other uses, such as social security number.

Because of the infeasibility of making a simple transformation on the record key, other methods must be used. An arithmetic procedure to transform the record key into a storage address is termed *hashing* or *randomizing*. Transformation of the nonsequential numbers representing records to a range of storage addresses is based on the uniform distribution of random digits. If, for example, each storage location is capable of holding one or more record, 100,000 storage locations are to be assigned, and the occurrences of the digits 0 to 9 in each position of the storage addresses are tallied, there will be about 10,000 1s, 10,000 2s, etc. Therefore, a hashing procedure takes part or all of the record key and performs an arithmetic procedure to produce a random number falling somewhat uniformly in the range of the assigned storage identifiers. An example of a hashing procedure is to divide the key by a prime number close to the number of storage locations (in this case, a prime number near 100,000) and use the remainder as the storage location.

A major difficulty with a randomizing procedure is that some addresses will never be generated while two or more record keys may produce identical disk addresses or *synonyms*. In that event, one of the records is stored at the generated location and a mechanism is provided to store the synonym in an *overflow* location. Subsequently, when a record is retrieved there must be a method for finding it in the overflow location. There are several possible ways to handle overflow, such as using the next empty location, using a separate overflow area, or using a pointer in each record to point to the physical address of a synonym.

The advantages of the hashed file organization arise primarily in situations where the records need to be located quickly such as in online inquiry and online updating. There is no need to sequence transactions to be processed against the file. If a file using hashed organization is to be output in key sequence, either it is copied and sorted into sequential order or the keys are sorted and the records are retrieved one at a time in the sorted sequence using the hashing procedure.

TABLE 4-3   PERFORMANCE IN TERMS OF BASIC OPERATIONS
            OF HASHED FILE ORGANIZATION

Operation	Comments
Create a file	Each record stored in same way as additions to an existing file. A storage location is calculated using the key for each record and an overflow operation performed if necessary.
Add or delete a record	Becomes more inefficient as many records are added and storage begins to fill.
Locate or modify a record	Locating a particular record for inquiry or modification is efficient relative to sequential access if transactions cannot be put in sequence (as with online processing) or the number of records to be modified is low.
List or process all records in sequence	The file can be copied and sorted, or the keys are sorted and each record is located in sequence using the hashing algorithm. No meaningful sequence is directly available.

A difficulty with the hashed organization is that overflow becomes a severe problem if most of the storage locations are used. If, for instance, 50 percent of the locations are used, overflow is generally not a problem; but if 80 percent of the locations are used, overflow will usually become quite large. Allocating a large number of storage locations (many of which will be empty) reduces overflow but wastes storage space. To more fully utilize storage, the hashing address may refer to a *bucket*, or group of records, instead of a single record location. The group of records stored in the bucket is searched sequentially to find the appropriate record. The extra processing for sequential search of a bucket is offset by the increased use of storage and reduction in overflow records.

The performance of a hashed file organization in terms of the basic operations to be performed is summarized in Table 4-3.

Indexed File Organization

In the indexed file organization, determining the storage location is a separate operation from accessing the record. An index contains a list of record keys and the physical address of the record associated with each key (Figure 4-9). To find a particular record, the index is searched. This can be done by a sequential search, binary search, or multiple indexes.

If the index is in record key sequence, a *binary search* is an efficient procedure for locating a key. A binary search is performed by starting at the middle entry in the index and comparing the key in the index with the desired key. If the desired key is in the second half of the index, the search continues on only that half. The middle record of that half is examined, and the search then continues on the upper or lower half of that segment. This halving and comparison procedure continues until the desired key is located. The efficiency of a binary search procedure is shown by the fact that to locate a particular entry in an index of 2,000 entries requires examination of no more than eleven entries.

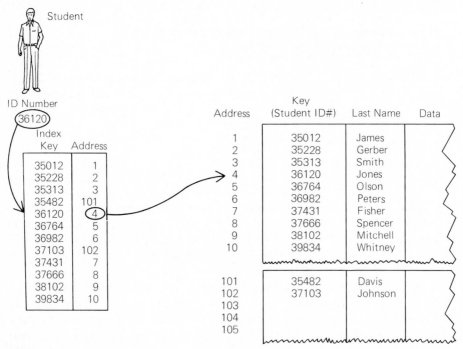

Figure 4-9
Indexed file organization.

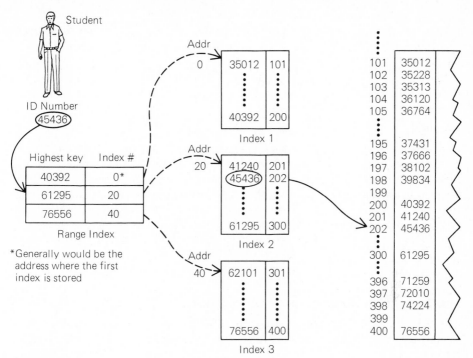

Figure 4-10
Searching an indexed sequential file using a range index.

Accessing records through the index may be especially efficient if the index can be kept in primary memory during processing. If the file is very large, the index has many items and finding a particular record even using a binary search may become inefficient. This problem may be eliminated by the use of multiple indexes and a *range index*, which is an index to the indexes. The sequential index is first divided into several indexes. The range index (which is small and can fit in primary memory) contains the address of each index on secondary storage and the highest key value contained in that index. The range index is searched for the proper index, which is then read into primary memory and searched for the particular key. The procedure is illustrated in Figure 4-10.

The indexed file organization may be modified slightly to assist in sequential ordering, yet allow for easy insertions into the file without frequent reorganization. As with hashing, records can be organized in buckets with the index referencing the bucket number. This reduces the size of the index but means that once the bucket is located, records in the bucket must be searched sequentially. Since the bucket is usually small, this is not serious. Buckets are organized with extra locations so that records may be added or deleted from the bucket without reorganizing the rest of the file.

A common indexed organization is the *indexed sequential* organization (often called ISAM for "indexed sequential access method"). With this method, records are stored on the disk sequentially by record key so that sequential processing may be performed, but indexes are also maintained to allow direct retrieval based on a key value. The indexed sequential organization allows records to be processed relatively efficiently in either sequential or random order, depending on the processing operations.

The performance of indexed file organization on the basic operations is summarized in Table 4-4.

TABLE 4-4 PERFORMANCE IN TERMS OF BASIC OPERATIONS
OF AN INDEXED FILE ORGANIZATION

Operation	Comments
Create a file	Requires extra procedures to create indexes.
Add or delete a record	Addition requires adding a record to storage, setting up pointers (to retain sequential order if ISAM), and modifying indexes.
Locate or modify a record	Locating a particular record for online inquiry or updating can be accomplished very efficiently through the index.
List or process all records in sequence	The file can be copied and sorted, or keys are sorted and records are retrieved in sequence. If index is in a sequence, records can be retrieved in that order.

File Organizations to Support Multiattribute Search

The three file organizations described so far are used for single-record, single-key files. In other words, they do not allow ready access to a record through multiple attributes or multiple keys.

The concept of using indexes for locating records in the file may be extended to the creation of indexes for many data items in the records. An index may contain all possible values for a particular data item (or ranges of values) and a record address (or pointer) for every record that contains that value for the data item. This concept is called an *inverted index*. It is illustrated in Figure 4-11.

Inverted indexes are very efficient for information retrieval by multiple attributes. The index is searched for the attribute values desired rather than having to search the file itself. Multiple indexes may be compared for retrieval on multiple fields. For instance, a retrieval of students who are MIS majors and have an average between 3.01 and 3.50 is a search of values in the indexes MAJOR and GRADE. Search routines find the appropriate value in the two indexes and select all record addresses that are common to both. The records meeting the criteria are accessed based on the addresses in the indexes.

A *list organization* may be used in place of inverted indexes to link together all fields with the same content. In the inverted index, a record address is stored which points to the appropriate record in the file. In a list organization, the pointers are moved to the records themselves and stored as separate data items. The pointers allow a logical retrieval and processing sequence to be imposed on the file regardless of the physical sequence of the records in the file. For example, all students with the same major may be logically linked together through a ''major'' pointer field. An index is established with each value for major and a corresponding entry to the first record in the file with that major. The first record contains a pointer to the second record with the same major, etc. A record may be part of several logical list files because there may be many pointers in the same record. Figure 4-12 illustrates the use of logical list files to accomplish the same function as the inverted indexes shown in Figure 4-11.

File Sequenced by Student ID #

Addr	Student ID #	Last Name	First Name	Major	Class in School	Grades 1	2	3	4	Avg.
51	34200	Jones	Ralph	MIS	Jr	A	B	A	A−	2.55
52	35012	James	Thomas	Acct	Sr	B	C	B−	C	3.05
53	35228	Gerber	Susan	Fin	Sr	B	C−	C	B	3.50
54	36120	Jones	Mary	MIS	Sr	A	B+	A	B	2.75
55	37431	Fisher	Mary	Fin	Fr	D	F	B	C	1.85
56	38102	Mitchell	Alice	MIS	Jr	C	D	C	B	3.95

Major Index

Major	Addresses
Acct	52
Fin	53, 55
Mgmt	
MIS	51, 54, 56
OR	
QA	

Class Index

Class	Addresses
Fr	55
So	
Jr	51, 56
Sr	52, 53, 54
Gr	

Average Index

0.00–1.00	
1.01–1.50	
1.51–2.00	55
2.01–2.50	
2.51–3.00	51, 54
3.01–3.50	52, 53
3.51–4.00	56

Figure 4-11
Use of inverted indexes for information retrieval.

DATABASE ORGANIZATIONS

Database organizations are more complex than file organizations because they provide more retrieval capabilities and perform more functions. They extend the information stored by establishing the relationships between records. It is important to again emphasize the distinction between a logical data model and its physical implementation.

Addr	Student ID #	Last Name	First Name	Major Value	Ptr	Class Value	Ptr	Average Value	Ptr
51	34200	Jones	Ralph	MIS	54	Jr	56	2.55	54
52	35012	James	Thomas	Acct	*	Sr	53	3.05	53
53	35228	Gerber	Susan	Fin	55	Sr	54	3.50	*
54	36120	Jones	Mary	MIS	56	Sr	*	2.75	*
55	37431	Fisher	Mary	Fin	*	Fr	*	1.85	*
56	38102	Mitchell	Alice	MIS	*	Jr	*	3.95	*

Major Index
Major Pointer

Acct	52
Fin	53
Mgmt	*
MIS	51
OR	*
QA	*

Class Index
Class Pointer

Fr	55
So	*
Jr	51
Sr	52
Gr	*

Average Index
Average Pointer

0.00−1.00	*
1.01−1.50	*
1.51−2.00	55
2.01−2.50	*
2.51−3.00	51
3.01−3.50	52
3.51−4.00	56

Figure 4-12
Use of logical list with pointers in records for information retrieval.

The user may be provided with programming and query facilities based on a logical database organization, but the actual storage organization need not mirror the logical model. In general, physical storage of a database will utilize methods already discussed, such as indexes and pointers. The following discussion refers only to logical data models; this is consistent with the approach that the user need not be concerned about the physical implementation of the logical data model.

Existing database management systems typically follow one of three logical models: hierarchical, network, and relational. However, a flat file (although technically a physical implementation) is frequently used and needs to be mentioned.

DATABASE SYSTEMS ARE ONLY AS GOOD AS THE DATA WITHIN THEM

The Illinois Department of Law Enforcement has a criminal history system to track the estimated 250,000 felony criminal cases filed each year in the state. According to a recent audit report, almost 59 percent of the 1.25 million arrest files in the database contain incomplete records of final disposition. This compromises the usefulness of the system.

Police officers tend to file every possible charge when making arrests; state attorneys tend to prosecute only the strongest charges without reporting back that they have dropped the other charges. A factor aggravating these problems is that two counties accounting for 50 to 60 percent of all dispositions have their own automated systems, and the two systems are incompatible. Also, there has been no uniform system of classifying criminal reports.

Extracted from Peter Bartolik, "Illinois System Loses Track of Half Its Data Base," *Computerworld*, December 12, 1983, p. 12.

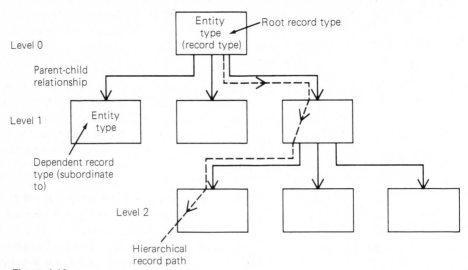

Figure 4-13
Schematic of a hierarchical tree structure.

Single Flat File

A flat file consists of records without repeating groups. Referring back to Figure 4-3, there is a repeating group for grades on assignments. To have a flat file, the repeating group would need to be removed and made into separate files for each of the assignments. The advantage of the flat file is that it can be viewed as a table with records for rows and attributes for columns. Establishing selection criteria for records is essentially setting selection values for one or more attributes (connected by AND and/or OR operators). For example, if we use the data in Figure 4-3 a selection instruction to find the records with MAJOR = MIS AND CLASS-STATUS = GRAD will return one record (for Sally Spencer). For microcomputers, a flat file is frequently the underlying physical implementation for relational models (to be described later).

Hierarchical Database Structure

Database management systems following a hierarchical model employ hierarchical or tree structures to represent the relationships among entities. A record may have multiple records subordinate to it, which in turn may have multiple records subordinate to them. In other words, multiple records of a particular type "belong to" (are subordinate to) a single record of another type higher in the hierarchy. "Parent" records can have several "children" records, but a "child" can have only one "parent." Figure 4-13 shows a simple schematic of a hierarchical tree structure.

In Figure 4-14, the course-student example is depicted as a hierarchical structure with STUDENT records subordinate to COURSE records. Each course (course number, section number) is described by a single record; the course "owns" students who are described by student records that are subordinate to the course record. An alternative method of representing the relationship between courses and students in a hierarchical structure is to have multiple course records subordinate to a student record, so that each student "owns" a record for each course he or she is taking. The choice of superior-subordinate records depends in part on storage efficiency as well as on the quantity and types of queries. The important point is that, even though both of these relationships occur in actuality, only one is usually represented in the hierarchical structure.

Many natural relationships among entities can be represented adequately in a hierarchical structure (e.g., multiple employees "belong to" a single department) and processing efficiency is often very high. The following examples relate to Figure 4-14 and illustrate the advantages and disadvantages of a hierarchical structure:

Query: Find ID numbers of students in MIS 5101 Section 2.
This query can be handled easily by accessing every record subordinate to COURSE MIS 5101 SECTION 2.

Query: Find courses taken by student 37431.
This query can only be answered by searching all subordinates of *every* course record for occurrences of 37431 as STUDENT ID#. Or, if the STUDENT relationship to STUDENT COURSE is maintained, this can be used.

Insert: Add student 36998.
A student record cannot be added unless (or until) it is assigned to a course. Then it is added to *every* course for which it is assigned.

Delete: Student 36120 drops MIS 5101 Section 1.
This can be handled fairly easily by searching all subordinates to the course record for an occurrence of 36120 as STUDENT ID#. However, another

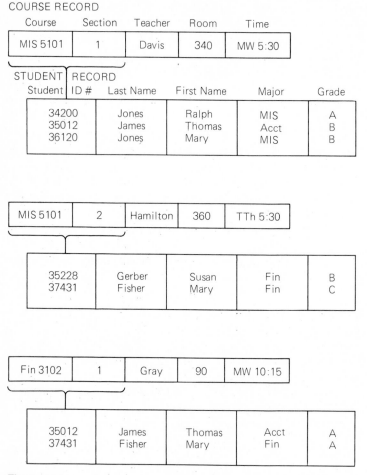

Figure 4-14
Example of a course-student relationship as a hierarchical tree structure.

problem occurs in that this is the only course in which the student was enrolled. When the student record for this course is deleted, all information about that student is deleted from the database.

Update: Student 35012 changes his major.
           This is a problem because, in order to avoid inconsistencies, the entire database must be searched for every occurrence of 35012 as STUDENT ID#.

Network Database Structure

Many of the problems encountered with a hierarchical data structure can be avoided with network structures. A hierarchical structure has one superior record for one or more subordinates. A network system allows a given entity to have any number of superiors as well as any number of subordinates. The relationships between entities must be represented. A common approach is multiple pointers, usually with a *link node* record representing the connection between the two entities. A network structure is depicted schematically in Figure 4-15.

Figure 4-16 shows the COURSE-STUDENT relationship depicted as a network structure. As opposed to the hierarchical structure, there is only one record for each student as well as one record for each course. Multiple pointers represent all the relationships between courses and students, with the link node record being the student's grade in each course (since it is unique to the relationship between a particular course and a particular student). Initially, these link node records will have no value but will exist to supply the linking function.

In Figure 4-16, there are multiple pointers represented by lines between the record occurrences. Each COURSE-SECTION record is linked to each STUDENT in the course through the GRADE link record (solid lines), and each STUDENT is also linked to all courses he or she has taken through the GRADE link record (dotted lines). These links would be represented by a series of pointers in the physical storage structure.

An examination of the same queries that were posed for the hierarchical structure illustrates differences:

Query: Find ID numbers of students in MIS 5101 Section 2.

First, the appropriate COURSE-SECTION record is accessed directly. The first student record it points to, through the grade link pointer, is STUDENT ID# 35228. Then the chain is followed to the next grade link pointer for that course, which points to student 37431. In the example, only the two students taking the course are shown. Accordingly, the course link through the grade records returns to the COURSE-SECTION record "MIS 5101 Section 2" after the second STUDENT ID# is accessed.

Query: Find classes taken by student 37431.

This query involves exactly the same process as the first query, except the appropriate student record is accessed and the other link (represented by dotted lines) is followed to pick up all courses taken by that student.

A query about a particular grade for a student in a course may be answered by either starting with the course and searching through the links

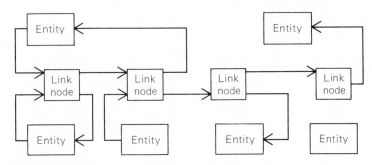

Figure 4-15
Schematic of a network data structure.

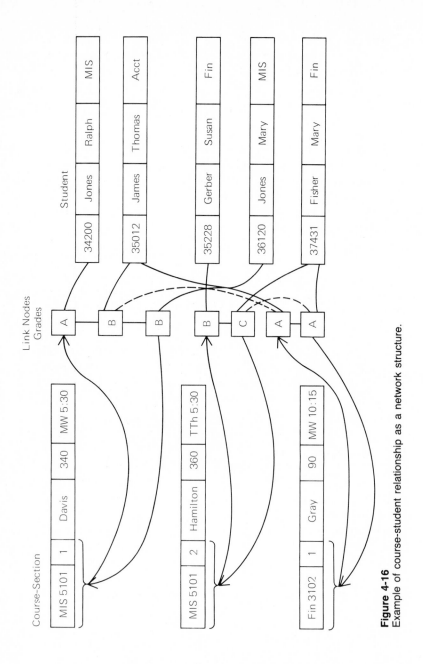

Figure 4-16
Example of course-student relationship as a network structure.

to the right student, or starting with the STUDENT ID# and searching through the other set of links to the right class.

Insert: Add student 36998. A student record can be added without requiring it to be assigned to a course. The links may be added later.

Delete: Student 36120 drops MIS 5101 Section 1. If a student drops a course, a simple readjustment of the pointer chains is required. No other information about the student is affected.

Update: Student 35012 changes his major. Since information about a student's major is only recorded in one place, a change can be made easily without introducing update inconsistencies.

Although many of the problems inherent in a hierarchical structure do not exist with a network database, a major disadvantage of a network structure is its complexity. A user of a network system must have explicit knowledge of the relationships represented, including the link nodes, in order to accomplish a query or an update. In addition, knowledge of the physical storage structure, including how links are physically represented, is required for efficient use of many network systems.

Relational Database Structure

A database employing a relational structure consists of a set of tables. In each table, the rows (called *tuples*) represent unique entities or records and columns represent attributes. Each table is a relation, and so a relational database can be thought of as a collection of tables. Relationships are represented by common data values in different relations (tables). Relational data structures are based on a formal theory of relational algebra which uses very specific terms to refer to the concepts underlying the structure. A discussion of relational systems in these terms is beyond the scope of this text.

The example of classes and students as they would appear in a relational structure is shown in Figure 4-17 with a brief explanation here. There are three tables or sets of relations. The COURSE-SECTION table contains values of attributes pertaining only to courses and sections: TEACHER, ROOM, and TIME. The first two columns (attributes), COURSE NUMBER and SECTION, uniquely identify each row in the table; they can therefore be thought of as the key for this relation. The STUDENT relation (Table 2) has as its key the first column, STUDENT ID#, which is also unique to each row. The attributes in Table 2 refer only to students. The third table represents the relation COURSE-SECTION-STUDENT. All three attributes make up the unique key for each row. Relationships are represented by the attributes. The attribute GRADE is also stored in this table because it is unique for each COURSE-SECTION-STUDENT relation.

In processing tables there are three fundamental operations:

Operation	Explanation
Projection	Select specified columns from a table to create a new table.
Selection	Create a new table by selecting rows that satisfy conditions.
Join	Create a new table from the rows in two tables that have attributes satisfying a condition.

Table 1 – Course-Section

Course Number	Section	Teacher	Room	Time
MIS 5101	1	Davis	340	MW 5:30
MIS 5101	2	Hamilton	360	TTh 5:30
Fin 3102	1	Gray	90	MW 10:15

Table 2 - Student

Student ID #	Last Name	First Name	Major
34200	Jones	Ralph	MIS
35012	James	Thomas	Acct
35228	Gerber	Susan	Fin
36120	Jones	Mary	MIS
37431	Fisher	Mary	Fin

Table 3 – Course-Section – Student

Course	Section	Student ID #	Grade
MIS 5101	1	34200	A
MIS 5101	1	35012	B
MIS 5101	1	36120	B
MIS 5101	2	35228	B
MIS 5101	2	37431	C
Fin 3102	1	35012	A
Fin 3102	1	37431	A

Figure 4-17
Example of course-student relationship as a relational structure.

The operations and activities described earlier illustrate the relational data structure.

Query: Find ID numbers of all students in MIS 5101 Section 2.

   This query is handled by a selection operation on the third table representing the COURSE-SECTION-STUDENT relation. The first two columns are searched for all occurrences of the value "MIS 5101" and "2". When the rows containing these are found, a project operation creates a relation (a table) by selecting only STUDENT ID# for MIS 5101 Section 2, which represents the answer to the query.

Query: Find all classes taken by student 37431.

   Using a selection operation, the third column in Table 3 is searched for all occurrences of the appropriate STUDENT ID#, and by means of a projection operation, a new table is created from the selected rows taking the first three columns.

Add: Add student 36998. A student or class may be added to the appropriate table without affecting the other relations.

Delete: Student 36120 drops MIS 5101 Section 1. If a student drops a class, the appropriate row is simply deleted from the COURSE-SECTION-STUDENT relation.

Update: Student 35012 changes his major. Since nonkey attributes are stored only with the proper key attributes, update inconsistencies should not arise. For instance, a student's MAJOR is only associated with the student relation, and so it is stored (and changed) only in that table. Similarly, a grade change would affect only the table representing the COURSE-SECTION-STUDENT relation.

Many updates and queries are accomplished by combining multiple tables in various ways, thus providing an extremely powerful access capability. For example, Table 1 and Table 3 can be "joined" along with select and project operations to find the student ID numbers for students in the class taught by Davis. Table 2 can be added to the join operation to find the names of the students taught by Davis.

The foregoing discussion of relational data structures is very simplified and meant only to provide an overview of their use. However, it should be clear that, conceptually, they are straightforward in design when compared to hierarchical and network structures. In addition, the underlying theory is elegant and precise, allowing for complex natural relations to be represented clearly.

In a hierarchical or network structure, the connections and relationships are in the data structure. The difference between the two structures is the type of relationship built in—hierarchical or network. If a new relationship is to be added, new connections and access paths must be established. In a relational database, access paths are not predetermined. Creating new relations simply requires a joining of tables. Relational databases are therefore the most flexible and useful for unplanned, ad hoc queries.

The preestablished relationships of the hierarchical or network structures require more complex data definition and data manipulation languages. Maintenance is more difficult. The relational model data definition and data manipulation languages are simple and user-oriented. Maintenance and physical storage are fairly simple.

Given these comparative advantages, why are all databases not relational? For many applications, the relationships are not ad hoc. If relationships can be preestablished, the access paths are much more efficient than general table operations. Therefore, if there are large numbers of records (say more than a million), and/or performance requirements are critical, or if transaction volumes are large, and ad hoc queries are very infrequent, the hierarchical or network models are more efficient than the relational model.

OPINIONS ON RELATIONAL DATABASE SYSTEMS IN PRACTICE

Some comments about the performance of relational systems:

"There is no intrinsic reason why a relational system should perform any worse than any other kind of system.

"One reason for the performance advantage of nonrelational systems is simply that those systems have been running for 10 or 15 years and have been constantly improved and tuned throughout that time. Relational systems will improve, too, over the next few years.

"Even if the nonrelational system provides superior run time performance, the value of that benefit has to be balanced against the amount of time it takes to get the system operational in the first place (not to mention the amount of time spent in subsequent maintenance)."

C. J. Date
Consultant in relational database
Computerworld February 13, 1984, pp. ID19–20

"There are signs that the DBMS is evolving from a full-function DBMS towards two types of DBMS—a high performance DBMS and a decision support DBMS. The evolution is shaped by the realization that high-performance DBMS do not a make good foundation for MIS and that decision support systems do not make a good foundation for operational systems.

"A high performance database environment is needed for 'high transaction arrival rates, large amounts of data, operational systems, very limited sequential capabilities, and high online availability.'

"A decision support database environment is identified with 'ease of use, ease of change, short development cycle, database scan capabilities, reporting capabilities, and batch orientation with online characteristics.'"

William Inmon
Director at Coopers & Lybrand, Denver
Computerworld, November 28, 1983, pp. 69, 76

SUMMARY

The database is a vital part of the management information system and technology for managing data is critical. There is a distinction between logical data models and physical data models. This chapter describes models for storing data; Chapter 16 describes conceptual models for defining the data to be stored and the relationships to be included.

The chapter presents basic data storage concepts and definitions. Entities are objects about which data is processed; the objects have attributes. Records are used to store data about entities; data items store attributes. Groups of records about similar entities may be combined into files. A record key is a data item used to order records in the file or to uniquely identify a record. Pointers are data items that specify the location of records; they can be used in indexes or as items in records to point to other associated records.

The type of file organization used is partially dependent on physical storage structures. Magnetic tape is inherently a serial access storage device. Magnetic disk has the capability to access any particular record by its address, and so can be used for file organizations using either direct access or sequential access.

The type of file organization chosen influences the efficiency of different operations. Sequential file organization is efficient when large numbers of records are read or processed as a batch in sequential order. Direct access is efficient for retrieval of any particular record by its identifying key. The most common methods of direct access use a hashed file organization or an indexed file organization. File organization for multiattribute search can use indexes or pointers to support searching on several attributes.

Four different organizations used with database management systems were described: single flat file, and hierarchical, network, and relational models.

MINICASES

1 THE SUBSCRIPTION DATABASE

Xenon Publications is developing a subscription system. They need to create and delete records of subscribers. Also, subscriber records must be updated when there is an address change, name change, or change in the expiration date (i.e., after a subscription is renewed). All issues sent are recorded on the individual's record.

One function of the system will be to print mailing labels. These should be printed in zip code order to facilitate bulk mailings. Also, management is concerned that the zip code length was recently expanded by the postal service.

There are 15 million subscribers. Some of these people telephone the subscription department for a variety of reasons: an issue has not been received, their payment check for subscription renewal has not cleared, there is a change in their personal information, etc. Mail inquiries are also received.

Questions

a What type of file organization would you select? Compare this file organization with one of the types that you would not select.

b Within a record how would you compensate for the zip code change?

2 CHURCH PLANNING DATABASE

Churches using a database to make decisions on where to market their services? Strange as it may seem, that is the purpose for which the Census Access for Planning in the Church (CAPC) system was designed. Family size, occupation(s), income, ages, and church contributions are some of the information items in the database located at Concordia Teachers College in River Forest, Illinois.

Twenty-five denominations pay an average of $1,500 each to utilize this service. The information is used to pinpoint a target location and congregation for a new church. For example, the user might seek a congregation with a certain set of characteristics, i.e., high income, managerial constituency, etc.

The database combines information provided by both the U.S. Bureau of Census and the member churches. The Census Bureau designates 100 organizations and universities as Summary Tape Processing Centers. The college is one such center. Following a census, the centers are provided with portions of the data. The centers are authorized to act as information distributors and provide the public with generalized versions.

Some of the member churches provide CAPC with specific details on the donation habits of their congregation as well as the number of children who attend parochial school. While church records are not public, the information provides insight when combined with census data.

Tim Scannell, "Service Finds Likely Locations for New Parishes," *Computerworld*, February 19, 1979, p. 21.

Questions

a What are the entities in this database? What are some of the attributes?

b In this case, what type of file organization is most appropriate for processing? What type of storage device would you use?

3 AUTHORING *TV GUIDE* MAGAZINE

There are 20 million subscribers to *TV Guide* who weekly receive one of 101 separate editions. Local program listings are obtained by the 1,369 staff members employed in 30 different field offices. VDTs are utilized for input at 25 remote offices.

TV Guide maintains a database of 120,000 to 200,000 brief synopses of movies released for television and synopses of syndicated shows. New descriptions are constantly being added while others are dropped when films are removed from the viewing pool. The synopses and other information are stored on 18 disk drives, each with a capacity of 500,000 words.

The synopses exist in one-, three-, five-, seven-, and nine-line versions, each a complete description with varying detail. Editors choose among the five lengths to fill the available space when composing a page. This eliminates the need for filler material and allows them to accommodate easily to size and location of the advertisements.

Marguerite Zientara, "DP Power Makes *TV Guide* Listings Possible," *Computerworld*, February 19, 1979, p. 15.

(handwritten annotations: "Yes, Shows in Alphabetical order", "Channel, Date, Time", "hierarchical", "Yes. Movies alphabetically ; Syndicated Shows")

Questions

a In what order would the editors want to sort the file of local program listing data? How would this be accomplished? Would you suggest using an index? Why or why not?

b What database structures would you suggest? Do they differ for the movies and syndicated shows?

EXERCISES

1 Define the following terms:
  a Entity
  b Attribute
  c Data item
  d Record
  e Block
  f File
  g Pointer
  h Index

2 Explain, compare, and contrast the following pairs of terms:
  a File and database
  b Sequential and indexed file organization
  c Indexed and hashed file organization
  d Tape and disk storage
  e Master file and transaction file

3 How is a record identified for retrieval? What are the criteria for selecting the identification?

4 Why should multiple record keys be needed? How can they be used in information retrieval?

5 Explain the organization of a sequential file on tape or disk. Summarize advantages and disadvantages. Give an example where it would be appropriate. Explain how it is used in:
  a Updating based on a transaction
  b Retrieval request
  c Preparing a report
    (1) in same sequence
    (2) in different sequence

6 Explain direct file organization using hashing of keys. Summarize advantages and disadvantages. Give an example where it would be appropriate. Explain:
  a How a record location is selected and overflow handled.
  b How a record is retrieved.
  c How records can be retrieved already sorted in a desired sequence.

7 Explain indexed organization. Summarize advantages and disadvantages. Give an example where it would be appropriate. Explain:
  a How a record is stored
  b How a record is retrieved
    (1) without use of buckets
    (2) with use of buckets
  c How selected records are obtained in sequence if:
    (1) entire file is to be output
    (2) selected records are in same order as file
    (3) selected records are in different order from file

8 If a file has 1 million records and an index is used to locate a record, how many accesses using a binary search would be required to locate a record? [Note that in practice there would probably be a range index and multiple indexes for such a large file.]

9 Calculate the effect of block size on effective transfer rate for magnetic tape. Use the following formula to complete a comparison table (byte = character).

$$
\begin{array}{l}
\text{Effective transfer} \\
\text{rate (in characters} \\
\text{per second)}
\end{array}
=
\left[
\begin{array}{l}
\text{Effective} \\
\text{characters} \\
\text{(bits) per inch}
\end{array}
\right]
\times
\left[
\begin{array}{l}
\text{tape speed} \\
\text{(in inches per} \\
\text{second)}
\end{array}
\right]
$$

$$
\begin{array}{l}
\text{Effective} \\
\text{characters} \\
\text{per inch}
\end{array}
=
\cfrac{\text{block size in characters}}{\left[\cfrac{\text{block size in characters}}{\text{characters per inch}}\right] + \text{gap in inches}}
$$

Density (characters per inch) and gap (in inches)

Block size	1600/0.6	6,250/0.3
100		
1,000		
10,000		

10 If primary memory could be made large enough to store all data, and access delays (such as rotational delays with disk storage) were eliminated, how would this affect storage organization?

11 Explain a flat file.

12 Explain a hierarchical database organization. Give an example of data that has a "natural" hierarchical order. What are the limitations of a hierarchical organization?

13 Explain a network organization. Give an example of data that has a "natural" network organization. What are the limitations of a network organization?

14 Explain a relational database organization. Why is it favored for ad hoc queries? Why is it not used for all databases?

15 Does a user of a database need to know anything about the data organization or physical storage? What insight might a user gain from this knowledge?

SELECTED REFERENCES

Canning Publications: "Relational Data Systems Are Here!" *EDP Analyzer*, October 1982.

Claybrooke, Billy: *File Management Techniques*, John Wiley, New York, 1983.

Date, C. J.: *An Introduction to Data Base Systems*, Third Edition, Addison-Wesley, Reading, MA, 1981.

Everest, G. C.: *Database Management: Objectives, System Functions, and Administration*, McGraw-Hill, New York, 1985.

Kim, W.: "Relational Database Systems," *Computing Surveys*, 11:3, September 1979, pp. 185-212.

Loomis, M.: *Data Management and File Processing*, Prentice-Hall, Englewood Cliffs, NJ, 1983.

Martin, James: *Computer Data Base Organization*, Second Edition, Prentice-Hall, Englewood Cliffs, NJ, 1977.

Sanberg, G.: "A Primer on Relational Data Base Concepts," *IBM Systems Journal*, 10, 1981.

Severance, D. G., and J. V. Carlis: "A Practical Approach to Selecting Record Access Paths," *ACM Computing Surveys*, 9:4 December 1977, pp. 259-272.

Special Report: "Real Benefits of Data Base Technology," *Computerworld*, October 25, 1982.

Stoeller, Willem, "Panacea or Pitfall? The Impact of Relational Databases on Your Environment," *Proceedings of the 1983 National Computer Conference*, AFIPS Press, Arlington, VA, 1983, pp. 309-315.

CHAPTER 5

TRANSACTION PROCESSING, OFFICE AUTOMATION, AND INFORMATION PROCESSING CONTROL FUNCTIONS

INFORMATION SYSTEMS AVAILABILITY CONTROLS
  Physical Facilities Control
  Terminal Access Control
  Backup and Recovery
SUMMARY
MINICASES
EXERCISES
SELECTED REFERENCES

This chapter completes the review of the basic technology and processes of information systems. It reviews transaction processing, office automation, and information processing control.

Transaction processing is a fundamental organizational activity. Although this text emphasizes the use of an information system to support management, control, and other knowledge work, this emphasis should not obscure the importance of transaction processing. Without transaction processing, normal organizational functioning would be impossible, and the data for management activities would not be available.

Office automation is a popular term for the application of computer and communications technology to office functions. It supports not only clerical office work but also the work of management and professionals. In this chapter, three office automation technologies will be explained: document preparation, message and document communications, and public data services.

Certain management and control procedures are required to control organizational information processing. The chapter provides a brief overview; the topics are amplified in Chapters 19 and 20.

TRANSACTION PROCESSING

In Chapter 2, transaction processing was defined as one of the basic processing functions, and transaction records were described as one of the outputs of an information system. The transaction processing system is vital to the operations of an organization. Without it, bills would not be paid, sales orders would not be filled, manufacturing parts would not be ordered, and so on. Prior to computers, transaction processing was performed manually or with mechanical machines; computer-based data processing has altered the speed and complexity of transaction processing, but not the basic function.

Transaction Processing Cycle

The transaction processing cycle begins with a transaction which is recorded in some way. Although hand-written forms are still very common, transactions are often recorded directly to a computer by the use of an online terminal. Recording of the transaction is generally the trigger to produce a transaction document (Figure 5-1). Data from the transaction is frequently required for the updating of master files; this updating

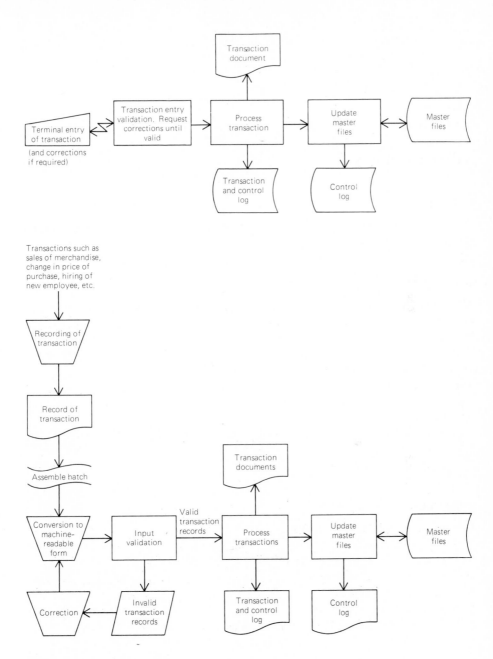

Figure 5-1
The transaction processing cycle.

may be performed concurrently with the processing of transaction documents or by a subsequent computer run. The alternatives of periodic batch and online processing of transactions are discussed in the next section.

The capturing of data on documents or by direct entry is a necessary first step preceding other activities in processing the transaction. Some examples of initial data capture are the following:

Transaction	Initial data capture method	Comments
A sales order taken during a sales visit	Manual recording	A sales order form is prepared by the salesperson.
A telephoned sales order	Terminal entry	Order taker at telephone enters order at terminal.
Purchase order	Manual recording or terminal entry	A purchase order is prepared manually and then typed for use, purchasing agent enters order data on visual display terminal using order form, or purchasing agent uses terminal to enter order directly into vendor's computer without use of a manual form.
Savings deposit (where online system is in use)	Manual recording or terminal entry	Customer makes out deposit slip manually; teller enters record of transaction via online terminal. Alternatively, customer enters transaction directly through an automated teller machine (ATM).
Airline reservation	Terminal entry	Reservation agent enters reservation information directly. No paper document is required.

When a transaction is recorded manually, a copy of the document is usually used for data preparation. Special data preparation equipment may be used offline to create machine-readable records for subsequent batch entry into the computer or the data from the document may be entered directly. Some examples of data preparation are:

Data preparation method	Explanation
Keydisk	Data is entered via a keyboard and stored on diskette, cassette, or fixed disk. Replaces data preparation using keypunch where the machine-readable record was on a card.
Optical character recognition (OCR)	Records data in machine-readable form using a special typewriter font or block lettering in a fixed format.
Magnetic ink character recognition (MICR)	Magnetically encoded characters are encoded on the document using a special MICR input device. Major application is checks and deposit slips.

Data validation is the testing of input data records to determine if they are correct and complete. This cannot be accomplished with complete assurance, but reasonable validation is usually possible. Validation tests applied against each data item or set of items may include the following:

Validation Test	Comments
Missing data	Test for existence of data item; there is an error if it is always required and is missing.
Valid size for item	There is an error if there are too few or too many characters.
Class or composition error	There is an error if data should be numeric and has alphabetic or special characters, or the reverse.
Range or reasonableness test	Test for values that fall in the acceptable range or are reasonable for the type of transaction (for example, negative pay amount is not reasonable).
Invalid value	If there are only a small number of valid values (such as class codes), an item can be checked to see if it is in the valid set.
Comparison with stored data	Compare with data in the file (for example, compare input of payment made with payment due from file).

Numeric codes such as identification numbers can be validated for size, range, and composition of characters. An additional validation technique for these codes, which is very effective in detecting input errors, is a check digit. A check digit is a redundant digit derived by computations on the identification number and then made a permanent part of the number. During data preparation and input validation, the check-digit derivation procedure is repeated. If the procedure results in a different check digit, there has been an error in recording or entering the identification number.

When input data items have been validated, the valid records are processed. Subsequently, two major activities occur during transaction processing: updating of machine-readable stored data (master file) related to or affected by the transaction and preparation of outputs such as transaction documents and reports. In both of these activities, control information is also produced.

Transaction data output can be classified as to its purpose. As explained in Chapter 2, there are three major reasons for producing transaction documents or other transaction output:

1 Informational: To report, confirm, or explain proposed or completed action
2 Action: To direct a transaction to take place
3 Investigational: For background information or reference by recipient

Action documents include shipping orders, purchase orders, manufacturing orders, checks, and customer statements. These documents instruct someone to do something. For example a purchase order instructs a vendor to ship, a check instructs a bank to pay, etc. When action is taken, the completed action (or lack of completion) is reported back to the organizational unit initiating the action. A sales order confirmation verifies receipt of an order. Lists of checks not paid by banks represent a confirmation of completed action (if not on list, checks have been paid) and lack of completed action (by being listed as unpaid). A single document or different copies of it may serve both action and informational purposes. For example, one copy of the sales order confirmation may be sent to the customer to confirm the order; a second copy may be used as an action document to initiate filling of the order.

A document designed to initiate action and then be returned to use in processing the completion of the transaction is known as a *turnaround document*. Examples are optically readable documents, stubs, or punched cards included with customer billings with the request that they be returned with payment (Figure 5-2). The turnaround document assists in positive identification and reduces errors because the document with the required feedback information is already prepared, often in machine-readable form.

WHY SHOULD I SEND BACK THE TURNAROUND DOCUMENT?

The customer who is billed is usually requested to enclose a turnaround document. Examples are the top part of the bill or a special slip. A return envelop is normally provided. In some cases, the turnaround document has the return address on it and must be placed in the return envelope so that it shows through the address window. The person making a payment is asked to perform data processing tasks, often without understanding why they are being done or what happens if they are not done.

The turnaround document identifies the payor and the account to which the payment should be applied. It reduces the risk of the payment being applied to the wrong account. If it is in machine-readable form, it also reduces the probability that the payment amount, if the account is paid in full, will be miscoded.

The use of the window envelop permits different return addresses for bills produced by the same processing run. For example, an oil company may process all bills at a central data processing center but have payments come to lock boxes at selected locations in order to speed up collections. Another use is a service center that processes bills for many customers. All bills can have the same return envelope, but the different addresses for the payments are specified on the turnaround slips.

Some transaction records are distributed to other departments in the organization to provide background information for recipients in the event that they need to respond to inquiries or need them for other reference. With online systems, a reference copy of the transaction can be stored in a computer file and may be retrieved via a terminal by anyone who is authorized and has need of the information. Transaction documents may also be used for managerial information or control scanning, as when a purchasing manager scans all purchase orders to spot unusual occurrences. In general, however, managerial information purposes are better met by reports or analyses which summarize transactions.

When transactions are processed, a listing of data about each transaction is usually prepared. The listing includes control totals for the number of transactions processed, total dollar amount of transactions, etc. The listing represents a batch of transactions or, for online processing, processing during a period of time. It provides a means of processing reference and error control.

Methods for Processing Transactions

There are three different methods commonly used for processing transactions and updating master files: periodic data preparation and periodic batch processing (usually termed *batch processing*), online entry with subsequent batch processing, and online entry with immediate processing (termed *online processing*). When computers were first used for transaction processing, technical limitations required that periodic data

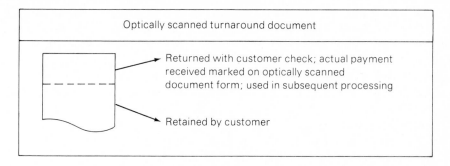

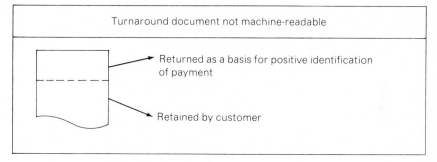

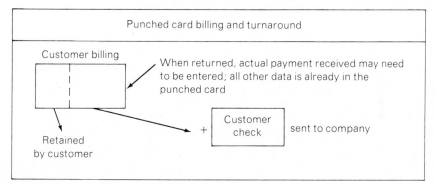

Figure 5-2
Turnaround documents for customer billing applications.

preparation and periodic batch processing be utilized. Online entry and immediate processing are now commonplace. The choice of methods should reflect the underlying process being supported. If the underlying process is transaction-oriented with immediate completion of the transaction desirable (as with order entry), online processing is indicated. If the process is periodic (as with payroll), batch processing is adequate.

Batch processing involves the accumulation of transactions until a sufficient number have been assembled to make processing efficient or until other considerations, such as a report cycle, initiate processing. The processing of batches can be daily, weekly, monthly, etc., depending on the volume of transactions and other considerations.

Batch processing of transactions can be very efficient in terms of data preparation and processing of transactions, especially when they are processed against a sequential file as described in Chapter 4. Control of processing may be enhanced by the use of batch controls, to be described later in this chapter. One major disadvantage of periodic batch processing is the delay in detecting and correcting errors. This is an especially serious problem for errors that can be found only when the transaction is compared against the master file. For example, if a transaction is coded with a valid but nonexistent customer number, the error will not be detected until processing is attempted against the customer file. The delay makes it difficult to trace the transaction back to the origination point and identify the correct customer.

When transactions are entered at an online terminal, the transaction is entered directly

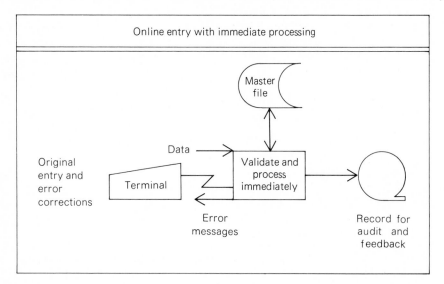

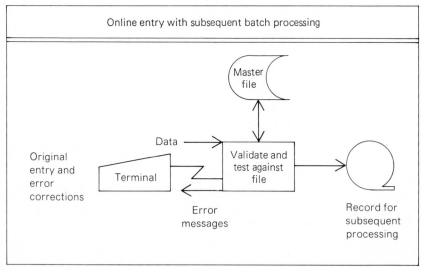

Figure 5-3
Two alternatives for online direct entry.

into the computer and validated immediately. The processing itself may be performed immediately or at a subsequent time as with periodic batch processing (Figure 5-3). One advantage of online entry over periodic data preparation and input is that most of the validation may be performed while the transaction is being recorded. Many errors can therefore be corrected immediately while the person entering the transaction is available for correction. Often the user or customer originating the transaction is still available to make appropriate changes. In addition, the master files can be accessed for the detection of errors such as nonexistent master file records. In *online entry with subsequent batch processing*, the computer is used for direct data entry and validation, but valid transactions are stored for later periodic batch processing.

In *online entry with immediate processing*, the transaction is validated online and then processed immediately if valid. A response with the result of processing or a confirmation of completion of processing is generally provided to the user at the input terminal. The advantages of this approach are the same as direct entry with subsequent processing (i.e., immediate validation with opportunity for immediate corrections by the person doing the input) plus the additional advantage of immediate processing with immediate results. The master files are always up to date. For instance, after an item is sold the inventory master file reflects the actual state of the inventory for that item. The disadvantages of immediate processing are the higher cost of online processing versus periodic batch processing (requires greater computer power and often data communications) and the extra procedures required to produce adequate control information and to safeguard the files against accidental or deliberate destruction during online updating.

SOMETIMES BATCH IS BEAUTIFUL

The new data processing manager was an advocate of online transaction processing. He had implemented major online systems for order entry and inventory control. The next application on his agenda was the payroll. It seemed to him that payroll processing as still in the dark ages, and he proposed to bring it into the 1980s mode of online processing.

The payroll manager argued that people were paid periodically and that therefore processing the payroll periodically in batch was adequate. Also, batch processing allowed the payroll personnel to establish processing controls over all payroll changes transmitted to data processing and to check the output batch controls with control totals maintained in the payroll department. There were almost no inquiries or analyses performed on payroll data that required up-to-date pay information; there were frequent inquiries about classification, pay rate, number of minorities, etc. The responses to these inquiries were always slightly incorrect because of unprocessed changes to the files.

After discussing the alternatives, the payroll personnel decided to enter all payroll master file changes daily through a terminal. Examples of these changes included new or terminated employees and revisions in classification, pay rate, name, or address. The processing of the paychecks was left as a periodic batch process.

Controls for Transaction Processing

The *audit trail* (or a processing reference trail) is the trail of references (document numbers, batch numbers, transaction references, etc.) which allows tracing of a transaction from the time it is recorded through to the reports in which it is aggregated with other transactions, or the reverse, tracing a total back to amounts on individual source documents. The processing trail is required for internal clerical, analytical, and management use because of the frequent need to examine the details behind a total or to trace what happened to a transaction. It is also needed by external auditors and is required by certain tax regulations for tax-related records.

An audit trail should always be present. Its form may change in response to computer technology, but three requirements should be met:

1 Any transaction can be traced from the source document through processing to outputs and to totals in which it is aggregated. For example, each purchase of goods for inventory can be traced to inclusion in the inventory totals.

2 Any output or summary data can be traced back to the transactions or computations used to arrive at the output or summary figures. For example, the total amount owed by a customer can be traced to the sales and payments that were used to arrive at the balance due.

3 Any triggered transaction (a transaction automatically triggered by an event or condition) can be traced to the event or condition. An example is a purchase order triggered by a sale that reduced inventory below an order point.

In general, audit trail references begin at the transaction level with one or more of the following:

- Preassigned document number
- Number assigned by document preparer at preparation
- Batch number assigned to a batch of documents
- Transaction number assigned by computer

These references are used as processing references in updating master file records, reports, etc.

Control of transaction processing begins with the design of the document for initially recording the transaction. If the document is manually prepared, it should be designed to minimize errors in completing it. This requires adequate space, unambiguous directions and labels, and a sequence of recording that is natural to the preparer. Boxes, lines, colors, labels and menus of alternatives are some of the methods to aid the preparer (to be discussed in detail in Chapter 17). One serious problem is how to make sure every transaction is recorded and entered into processing. Interruptions, carelessness, etc., may cause a transaction to not be recorded or the source document to be misplaced. To prevent or detect such errors and omissions, the transaction processing system may have one or more controls such as the following:

Source Document Control	Comment and Examples
Prenumbered source documents	All source documents can be accounted for.
Anticipation control	Certain transactions can be anticipated, such as a payment due on a certain date.
Document produced as by-product of transaction	Credit card payment produces document.
Transaction activity produces control report	Cash register produces list of all cash and all credit sales.
Related transaction produces control total	Cash receipts are a control total for cash sales and payments on accounts receivable transactions.

The use of a terminal to enter the original transaction has the advantage that a machine-readable record is produced at the same time as source documents needed for the transaction. If a source document is misplaced or lost, the computer record permits tracking or reconstructing the missing record. Accuracy and completeness considerations for source document design also apply to input screen design for the visual display terminal. Since online entry may also be performed without a source document (as with order entry by telephone), the machine record may be the only "document."

In the flow of control in batch processing, it is best to establish a control total of documents before data preparation. The control total can be one or more of the following:

- Record (document) count
- Financial total
- "Hash total" of numbers such as account numbers, which are not normally summed (hence the total is meaningless except for control purposes)

During the data preparation process, the control totals are checked to verify that no transactions are missing and that items used in control totals were entered correctly. The control total is input with the data and checked by computer as part of data validation, processing, and output. The control totals appear on batch reports and on other control reports. The output (after adjusting for rejected transactions) should match the control total for the input batch. Computer programs and control personnel make control total comparisons during processing; users check controls on output against control totals for data they submitted for processing. This checking provides a simple but powerful control procedure to ensure that all transactions in the document batch are processed.

In the case of online input from documents, there is no control total of transactions prior to entry. However, if there are reasonable control procedures to enforce entry of all transactions, control totals can be developed for logical batches of input (transactions that are logically grouped by some common feature). The logical batches provide a basis for listings for reference, follow-up, comparison with physical evidence, etc. For example, the log of all transactions entered is sorted, and logical batches of transactions are prepared by terminal, by operator, by type of transactions, etc.

There are special control considerations with online processing. The files change continuously, and therefore any error can disrupt a file and create additional errors as subsequent transactions are processed. The straightforward preprocessing batch control totals cannot be used to check batches before updating. Some examples of problems and controls will illustrate how control in online processing is handled.

Problem	Control procedure
Transaction is lost—never gets processed	Feedback to terminal to verify processing.
Computer system goes down when transactions are in process	Procedures to manually process transactions and introduce them into system when computer is again working. Restart procedures tell input personnel which transactions were lost when system went down and need to be reintroduced.

Problem	Control procedure
Errors in file updating may not be detected until later, making file correction difficult	A copy of the file is used for online updating. A separate backup copy is available for reconstruction. A log of all incoming transactions is used for reconstruction and error tracing.

A basic purpose of these online control procedures is the preservation of an adequate processing trail and reconstruction capability, including backup copies and transaction logs. There are, however, many other possible control procedures. For example, the file in use during the day may be a work file only. The transactions may be accumulated and processed again, at night for instance, to produce a daily updated file. In other words, the work file is used temporarily during the day for updated reference, but processing at night produces the necessary file control and reconstruction.

Retrieval in Transaction Processing

Many online systems use data retrieval software (described in Chapter 3) to support transaction processing. Even in applications where batch updating is appropriate, the capability to access related records during transaction preparation is often desired. For instance, a retail department store may want to perform a check on the account status of a customer when a charge transaction is made; the credit check requires an immediate retrieval even though the customer account is updated in batch. A bank may install online terminals so that customers may inquire about the status of their accounts. A customer complaint department in a retail catalog company may check the status of an order when a customer calls. In these examples, online inquiry into master files is required.

Inquiries associated with a transaction processing system tend to be fairly structured, so that they may be programmed to use a standard set of commands that can be mastered fairly easily. In some systems, commands can be assigned to special function keys on the keyboard so that the operator needs only to press a single key rather than type in a command. Terminals that are only to be used for inquiries, such as terminals for customer use on a bank floor, may be specially designed with only function keys. The design of commands and use of function keys for inquiry processing will be discussed in Chapter 17.

DOCUMENT PREPARATION

Document preparation facilities aid in the production of text (words) rather than processing of transactions. Typically, document preparation software is used on microcomputers or word processing systems (special purpose microcomputers), although document preparation software is also available on large mainframe computers with operation through a terminal.

Word and Text Processing

Word processing generally refers to the computer-assisted preparation of documents and correspondence. Hardware systems dedicated to word processing are of two types: a single workstation with a small amount of secondary storage or multiple workstations sharing a single secondary storage device. Text is entered via a keyboard (with keyboard layout similar to a traditional typewriter) and displayed on a visual display screen. Special commands are used to set the document to the appropriate formats. Error correction can be performed very easily on the screen, and edit functions such as searching for character strings or moving paragraphs (electronic "cut and paste") are provided. More sophisticated systems allow the user to work on two or more documents at the same time in different parts of the screen. For example, one document (or a portion of it) shows at the top of the screen and the other on the bottom, and the user can copy blocks of text from one to the other. Most systems optionally justify the right margin on a document, and the more sophisticated ones allow hyphenation of words based on a predefined logic or set of words. Many systems have an automatic spelling correction routine based on a predefined dictionary of words (say 50,000 or more) that can be easily augmented with a user-defined dictionary of special terms. A few have limited capabilities for checking grammar and usage.

Text editors are software packages which perform essentially the same functions as word processors. The difference in terminology is primarily historical. Word processing began as hardware and software dedicated support systems for typists, while text editing software was used for preparing documents on general purpose computers. Over time, the distinction has become less important, although word processing systems tend to have some commands especially suited to letters, memos, etc., and text editors have some special commands to format output for high-speed printers.

A PHASED INTRODUCTION OF OFFICE AUTOMATION AT CARNEGIE HALL

In October 1979, office automation made its debut at the prestigious performing arts center, which has showcased prominent musicians from Pablo Casals to Bessie Smith.

Before 1979, all aspects of Carnegie Hall's operations were based on manual systems, which were used to record donations, assign seats, and handle all accounting procedures.

Recently, Carnegie Hall began a program to increase its donor base and subscription ticket sales—its primary source of funds. Working with a limited budget, Herbert Weissenstein, director of development and strategic planning, devised a four-year growth plan for automating different areas of the hall's operations over several years, beginning with fund-raising. With virtually no experience in word processing or computer equipment on the part of Carnegie Hall, a major criterion was to develop a system that was easy to use. A second requirement was that the system would be able to grow modularly to accommodate gradual installation of a system. The system chosen was a multiuser system with a large disk drive, one workstation (to start), and a word processing printer.

The first application was a central customer file. Each of the then approximately 600 donors to Carnegie Hall was assigned a record with specific data, including a history of donations. This allowed Carnegie Hall to track donations and pledges accurately and respond quickly to contributors. Personalized letters were produced to acknowledge gifts.

The second phase of the installation involved the maintenance of subscription lists and seat assignments. The third phase was an inhouse mailing list. Weissenstein estimated Carnegie Hall saved over $20,000 per year in service bureau costs with this application.

The fourth and final phase of the installation involved computerizing financial records—accounting, accounts payable, accounts receivable and general ledger. During this period the system was upgraded with much more memory, another disk drive, three diskette drives, another word processing printer, three matrix printers, and seven workstations.

Adapted from "System Now in Full Swing at Carnegie Hall," *Computerworld*, June 13, 1983, p. 49.

Document Filing

If documents are coded in machine-readable form by word processing and stored in computer storage, it would seem to be a simple task to replace paper-based files with a computer-based filing system. This is not necessarily the case, however, either because many documents, both incoming and outgoing, are not in machine-readable form or because they were prepared using different word processing systems at different locations. In addition, correspondence filing systems tend to be highly personalized. Hence, computer-based filing systems generally fall in the domain of formal private systems (as discussed in Chapter 2).

Computer-based filing systems have the advantage, besides space savings, of permitting easily modifiable cross-reference indexes. For instance, a document may be stored by a unique identification number. The number may be added to the appropriate index entries for a ''subject'' index, a ''from'' index, a ''to'' index, and even a ''date'' index. These indexes contain pointers to the location of the document itself.

Computer Graphics

Graphic illustrations of numeric comparisons and trends, in the form of bar charts, line charts, pie charts, etc., have long been used in articles and presentations. However, their preparation has been costly and has usually required the services of a graphic arts department. Computer technology provides a low-cost method of graphics preparation.

The use of a computer for graphics requires a graphics software package and a *high-resolution* visual display terminal (VDT). A graphics picture is created by programming single bits of the screen called *pixels*. The greater the number of pixels on a screen, the higher its resolution and the clearer the picture. Many high resolution VDTs also support the use of color to enhance graphic presentation. For high quality hard copies of graphics, a special plotter-printer is required; lower quality graphics may be produced by some printers.

Figure 5-4 shows some types of graphics used to communicate business information that otherwise might be presented in tabular form. Each type of graph has appropriate and inappropriate uses. For instance, pie charts are appropriate for showing parts of a whole but not for time series or comparisons of two or more different items.

The primary justifications for using computer-based graphics rather than tabular reports are improved productivity and improved quality of analysis or decision making. Although limited, research results to date show little impact of graphics on decision-making performance; however, people prefer graphics and color over tabular reports. Therefore, proper design of graphics for information presentation is a significant issue.[1] Some effects of different uses of graphics on human information processing will be discussed in Chapter 8.

Computer graphics are used in many other applications. Computer-aided design is the use of graphics in engineering design; calculations and measurements are input to design software which presents and manipulates graphical representations that previously were

---

[1]B. Ives, "Graphical User Interfaces for Business Information Systems," *MIS Quarterly*, Special Issue, December 1982, pp. 15–47.

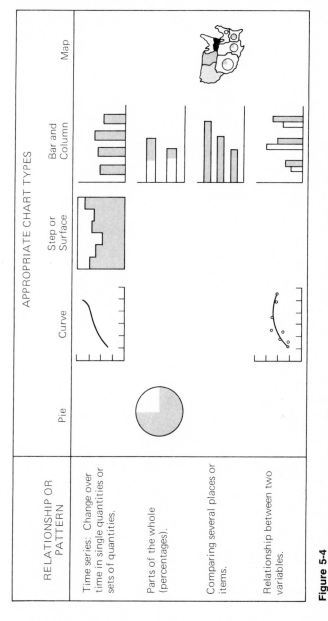

Figure 5-4
The right graphics chart for the right situation. (From A. Paller, K. Szoka, and N. Nelson, *Choosing the Right Chart*, USSCO Graphics, Integrated Software Systems Corporation, 10505 Sorrento Valley Road, San Diego, California 92121, 1980.)

drawn by hand. Computer graphics are also used in architecture to replace hand drafting of blueprints. These specialized graphics systems are more expensive than the general-purpose graphics applications described previously.

GRAPHICS AID SUPERMARKET DISPLAYS

Planning product displays on supermarket shelves is a tedious task if done by hand. Preparation time for fitting products onto each shelf has been pared down from one hour to 15 minutes by one distributor in Schiller Park, Illinois.

The planning is performed by Sales Force Companies, Inc. (SFC), a bulk-goods distributor located in Schiller Park that serves 23 central states from Indiana to Colorado to New Mexico. The company is also a manufacturer's representative with four major functions: to introduce, promote, service, and report on food products to the manufacturer of those products.

Each of the sales offices has a terminal that enables the sales staff to enter the statistics necessary to create the drawing of the shelf. These statistics include a product description, graphics code, the number of inches per item in facing size, dollar sales per product, percentage of total sales, the number of cases that sell per week, number of items per case, retail price, and number of shelves. These data items are collected in the grocery store by retail personnel.

The computer sequences items on the shelves, calculating placement by descending order of dollar sales per square foot. A plotter prints a multicolored shelf "planogram," which is submitted to retail store management for approval. Once approved, the planogram is reproduced for field personnel, who arrange the items on the shelves.

Shelf positions used to take an hour to draw manually. If there were changes, the shelf had to be redrawn. The plotter takes about 15 minutes to produce the first drawing, and changes can be made in seconds. Staff are more creative and experiment with various displays.

Adapted from "Graphics Helping Markets Plan Shelf Displays," *Computerworld,* June 13, 1983, p. 50.

Composition and Reproduction

The printers available with word processors range from matrix printers (with low to high resolution) to letter quality printers with output comparable to high quality electric typewriters. Two examples of high quality output methods illustrate this feature of office automation:

Output Method	Comments
Laser printer	This printer can be programmed to "draw" many different type fonts and to produce a high quality output. Multiple copies can be produced at low cost. Very high speed. Codes can be added to the text for features such as font, type size, justification, etc.
Compositor	Text in machine-readable form can be coded with simple instructions for photocomposition. The simple codes are replaced by compositor codes using computer search and replace operations.

This text was prepared in machine-readable form using a word processing package on a microcomputer. It was then transmitted using telecommunications to the automated compositor at a printer. The galleys were produced without any keying of the text by the printer.

MESSAGE AND DOCUMENT COMMUNICATION

In Chapter 3, facilities for data communication were discussed. Emphasis was placed on the use of communication facilities between remote computer sites for information processing. Communications networks such as local area networks and public packet switching can also be utilized for transmission of documents and messages from one location to another. Data communication facilities can replace much paper-based informal communication, such as memos and telephone calls. As the cost of data transmission decreases and the availability of alternative transmission media increases, these facilities are expected to find more use in office information processing. Several uses of data communication facilities in support of traditional office functions are described in this section.

Document Distribution

A single word processor may have communications capabilities added to it through a modem or local area network so that it can communicate with other word processors and so that documents can be transmitted from one location to another. Word processors can also be "clustered" around a single communications controller so that documents can be transmitted from one point to any other point. Other output devices such as high-quality printers and graphics plotters can also be connected for use by any word processor in the network; this is an example of *shared resources*. The obvious advantage of document distribution via a communication network is the speed of transmission across a widely dispersed geographic area. Although shared-resource communicating word processing systems are relatively expensive, the cost and speed of document transmission compared to mail service makes them cost-effective in many situations.

Facsimile Transmission

An alternative method for transmitting documents across geographically dispersed areas is facsimile transmission. While communicating word processors transmit characters, facsimile technology transmits the actual image on a page.

In facsimile transmission, a facsimile machine at the sending station scans a page from left to right, top to bottom, translating the areas of change from light to dark into coded signals that are transmitted. A similar machine at the receiving end, connected via communications facilities, reproduces the page image.

The advantage of facsimile transmission over data transmission is that graphics, signatures, and other images may be faithfully reproduced. Its primary disadvantage is slow transmission time. A great deal more coded data is required per character to code the image of a character than to code the character. As a result, it may take from two to six minutes to transmit a page of text via facsimile as compared to six to twenty seconds via data transmission through standard codes.[2] Although facsimile technology is improving transmission time through data compression techniques, the cost of transmission over long distances is still relatively high.

---

[2] R. Panko, ''Electronic Mail,'' in K. T. Quinn (ed.), *Advances in Office Automation*, 1, John Wiley, London, 1984.

Computer-Based Message Systems

Another use of computer and communications technology for office functions is *computer-based message systems*, also known as electronic message systems or electronic mail. Some commercial services compete directly with regular mail systems for distribution to points outside the organization. For internal messages, computer-based message systems are utilized primarily in place of internal memos and telephone conversations. They are generally used directly by the person initiating the communication rather than indirectly through an intermediary such as a secretary.

A computer-based message system is a simple but powerful software package for sending, reading, and forwarding messages. Figure 5-5 shows a list of available features for a typical system. A user types the message to be sent and then types a simple command to send it to one or more receivers. Predefined ''distribution lists'' can be used to distribute a message to many people without having to enter individual names each

Commands

ANSWER	Answers a message sent to you
COMPOSE	Composes a message
DELETE	Deletes a message
DISPLAY	Displays system information
EDIT	Edits parts of a message
FILE	Files a message
FORWARD	Forwards a message to another user
LOGOUT	Ends the COMET session
MOVE	Moves a message from one file to another
READ	Reads a message sent
RETRIEVE	Retrieves filed messages
SCAN	Scans messages in your files
SEND	Sends a message to someone
SET	Sets password or terminal attributes

In addition, the HELP command displays on your terminal a brief description of each of the COMET commands.

Example of ANSWER Command

The ANSWER command provides a convenient way of replying to a user who has sent you a message. After reading the message, type ANSWER in response to the command prompt. COMET asks you for the text of the reply and automatically addresses your reply message to the person(s) you are answering.

Examples	Typical Abbreviations
ANSWER	**ANS**
ANSWER 1	**ANS 1**
ANSWER ALL	**ANS ALL**
ANSWER 3 ADD	**ANS 3 ADD**

Figure 5-5
Features available on the COMET computer-based message system. (Source: *COMET-II Users Guide*, Computer Corporation of America, ©1981.)

time. Each user of a computer-based message system has an electronic "mailbox" in computer storage to hold the message.

Computer-based message systems are available through three different sources:

1 A software package may be purchased for use on an inhouse central computer. Any person with a valid account on the computer automatically has an electronic "mailbox" and can exchange messages with any other valid user.

2 A system may be utilized on a timeshared basis. The system resides in the computer of the vendor and may be supplied with other timesharing services. A company typically pays one fee for a timesharing account and an additional small fee for each "mailbox." A user may contact any other person with a mailbox on the system, whether or not they are in the same organization.

3 A system is provided as an additional service over a public packet-switching network. These services permit messages to be transferred from one mainframe computer to another and then to be distributed locally the same as internal messages.

Another alternative for message systems is electronic voice store-and-forward. Using a special device or set of codes entered into the telephone, the user speaks a message which is translated into a digital pattern and stored in a receiver's electronic mailbox in the central computer. Voice messages can then be distributed to prestored mailing lists, forwarded, etc., the same as text messages; however, a message cannot be printed.

The primary advantages of computer-based message systems are the speed of distribution and the low preparation cost. Another advantage over telephone and face-to-face exchanges is the asynchronous nature of computer-based message systems. Telephone and face-to-face interactions generally entail interruption of the receiver from another task; users of message systems have greater control over the flow of communication. In essence, they provide an electronic screening of demands on a person's time, thus replacing to some extent the "gatekeeping" role of a personal secretary.

Another potential advantage of computer-based message systems is that communications are independent of both time and location: a person can keep in touch from any location where there is access to a terminal and a telephone communications link to the central computer.

ELECTRONIC MAIL SAVES METROPOLITAN LIFE MORE THAN $100,000 EACH YEAR

Metropolitan Life Insurance Company describes its electronic mail system as a "general management tool for supplying information." Using this system helped to streamline its online message and reporting capabilities. It eliminated the need for duplicate hardware and helped save the company over $100,000 each year.

According to Vice President Bruce J. Goodman, Metropolitan Life had to ensure rapid communication within its firm after decentralizing its New York home office functions in 1970. By establishing nine head offices across the country, the $52 billion company gained an opportunity to enhance customer service and to tap diviersified labor markets. Because of cost considerations, these head offices serviced old policies whose historical paper records remained in the New York headquarters.

"It became the responsiblity of head offices to administer several million policies issued some 30 to 40 years ago," said Goodman. "Thus, rapid communication between the head offices and New York became crucial to providing a high level of service to our policyholders."

Before instituting its electronic mail service, the head offices requested policy information from New York via a Telex system. Even though the system met the company's basic business needs, It required additional staffing and was prone to mechanical failure and human error. For instance, a correspondent received a request and filled in a form, and someone else cut the Telex paper tape, which was clumsy and occasionally ripped. Others would keypunch and batch multiple messages, which could only be transmitted to the home office at specific times. A total of 39 separate paper-handling steps were required in the overall work flow for one inquiry under the old system.

Using an electronic mail system, Metropolitan's head offic customer service representatives send requests directly from their own terminals. As a result, each head office saved from one-half to one full-time clerk. At the home office, the previous 39 separate paper handling steps decreased to 22 steps, and the service time lapse improved by one to two days. Twelve clerical positions were no longer needed for processing message requests.

The system was first used to deliver daily operation a status reports to head office end users and corporate management from the computer centers located in four cities. Computer center employees previously called in such reports by telephone. Not only did it take time to contact all necessary offices but it usually took more than one phone call to reach the right person. One operator can now key a message, send it simultaneously to several offices, and not be restricted by multiple time zones.

Press release.

Public Data Services

One significant development for office automation is the use of public databanks or data services that can be purchased or accessed through timesharing. One example is COMPUSTAT, a databank of financial information about publicly owned companies; the files can be leased or the databank can be accessed through timesharing services. Various analytical routines to process and present the results are also provided.

Several low-cost information services offer a variety of types of information through timesharing. One example is The Source, which provides such commonly used information as airline schedules and stock market information. Figure 5-6 shows a partial index of subjects available through The Source. "Information providers" pay a fee to The Source for carrying their data, while users pay for connect time and an additional fee for data which is accessed. For instance, The Source has a division called electronic publishing in which an author creates a newsletter on the service and receives royalties from readers who access it. The Source also carries an electronic message system that can be utilized by any subscriber. The growth of The Source is attributed primarily to home users of personal computers.

A class of services, often called *videotex*, has a general objective of providing a large databank of general information to consumers in their homes. Videotex services are accessible through a telephone and television which utilize a special decoder; a personal computer or terminal and modem are not required. The price of a decoder is small, and users pay a fee per "page" (or screen) accessed; the price of a general videotex service is intended to be within the reach of most consumers. Since the service is interactive through the decoder (users select pages to be viewed and can send limited data to the central computer), potentially major services are electronic shopping and electronic banking. Videotex services are characterized by the use of graphics images as well as words.

I. COMMUNICATIONS

Source Mail
    To check mailbox . . . . MAILCK
    To read letters . . . . MAIL R
    To scan letters . . . . MAIL SC
Mailgram Message Service . . . . MGRAM
Chat . . . . HELP CHAT
Teleconferencing . . . . PART I
Post: Bulletin Board Classifieds
   . . . . .

II. NEWS AND INFORMATION SERVICES
   . . . . .

III. BUSINESS SERVICES

Business Programs
    Income Tax Calculation . . . . HELP TAX
   . . . . .
Employment Services
Information Management
Financial Markets
Stocks
    Daily Trading Activity . . . . UNISTOX
Research
   . . . . .

IV. CONSUMER SERVICES

Shopping & Transactions
Employment
Personal Finance . . . . HELP PERSFI
Taxes
    Taxes . . . . HELP TAX
    Computing Taxes . . . . TAX
    Balancing Checkbook . . . . HELP R CKBAL
    Amortization of Loan . . . . HELP R LAMORT
   . . . . .
Consumer Tips
    Home Design . . . . PUBLIC 182 DIRECT
    Be Your Own Lawyer . . . . PUBLIC 121 DIRECT
   . . . . .
Personal Computers & Software
   . . . . .

V. ENTERTAINMENT

Astrology
Biorhythm
Cards
Games (over 65 games) A few examples are:
    Checkers . . . . PLAY CHECKERS
    Horse Race . . . . PLAY HORSE
    Star Trek . . . . PLAY STARTREK
   . . . . .
Health & Medicine
Movie Reviews
New York City Entertainment Guide
Television Reviews

Figure 5-6
Example from index of subjects available on The Source. (Courtesy of Source Telecomputing, MacLean, Virginia.)

The most advanced videotex service to date is Great Britain's Prestel, sponsored by the British Postal Service. In the United States, limited experimental trials are being carried out, primarily by newspaper and television broadcasting companies. Although videotex services were originally conceived for the consumer in the home, today over 75 percent of usage of external information services in the United States and an even greater percentage of use of Prestel in Britain is business-related.[3]

INFORMATION PROCESSING CONTROL

Organizational control procedures are designed to ensure that information services conform to organizational objectives and policies and that information provided is complete and correct. This section surveys these control responsibilities and procedures; the next section reviews security and protection provisions for facilities and data.

Information Systems Management and Control

Information systems management has responsibility for management and control of the development and operation of the overall information system of the organization. The following are some examples of activities associated with this responsibility:

- Maintenance of qualified staff (selection, training, and evaluation).
- Acquisition of appropriate hardware and software.
- Scheduling and control of work of development staff.
- Control over software resources of the installation (documentation, program change controls, etc.).
- Control over maintenance (correction and revisions) of existing applications.
- Control over the database (definition, authorization for access, etc.).
- Establishment and enforcement of guidelines, standards, and technical support for user facilities.

The role of information systems management is evolving. While much of the activity continues to be based on centralized control over system operation and development, more responsibilities are shifting to support of user-developed systems and user-operated facilities. The role of information systems management is discussed in more detail in Chapter 20.

Control Functions for Information Processing

Three types of controls are associated with information processing: general control procedures for system operations, controls for a specific application, and application development controls. The latter are described in Chapter 18; the first two are surveyed here and explained in more detail in Chapter 19.

General control functions internal to information system operations ensure that

---

[3]J. Carey and M. Moss, "New Telecommunication Technologies and Public Broadcasting," Corporation for Public Broadcasting, 1984.

applications are run correctly and that the facilities are operational. These controls include the following:

- Scheduling control for online systems, internal timesharing, and production batch systems
- Library control for program and data files and documentation
- Database control for creation, updating, and use of databases
- Access control for physical access to computers through terminals
- Backup and recovery procedures

The general purpose of application control procedures is to ensure that processing is accurate and that no data is lost or mishandled during processing. Each application, whether developed by the systems development staff or by users, should contain a basic set of processing controls. Examples of application controls are the following:

1 Controls over offline data recording and preparation
2 Controls over data input, in the form of input validation
3 An adequate audit trail
4 Controls over access to the files or database
5 Controls over distribution and use of output
6 Controls over backup and recovery for the application
7 Controls over physical security for the application

The last two controls are primarily handled on a general basis, but are important at the application level when users control operation of the system.

Outside independent checks of applications processing procedures are important to the assurance of integrity and organizational control. User departments may perform independent checks of production runs processed by system operations. For example, the accounting department may keep a separate control total of all debits and credits to be posted by the computer processing the general ledger. Another outside check is provided by an independent quality control evaluation group in a user department where the volume of data to be controlled is large. As an example, a large corporation has a payroll processing control group responsible for evaluating the payroll data produced by the computer. Independent review of system operating procedures may also be carried out by a review staff such as the internal auditors.

Guidelines for End-User Computing Facilities

Users in an organization may obtain their own hardware and software. In essence, the organization may have many computer processing installations. One issue is the role of the central information services function in terms of organizational control over multiple operations facilities. It can have, for example, complete authority over user facilities or can have only an advisory and monitoring role. The latter is generally more consistent with the concept of end user computing.

The advisory and monitoring role may include obtaining agreement on and enforcement of standards for acquisition of equipment and services. For instance, instead of dictating hardware brands, the systems department may provide a set of standard guidelines for acquisition. Ideally, these guidelines are derived from an overall master plan for information resources and are designed to ease the transition to that plan. Users have choices within these limits.

The organizational standards for user installations will usually conform to standards for hardware, software, or communications already in place. For instance, a company may have invested in a network that only handles one type of communication protocol; any hardware acquired must adhere to that protocol in order to interface with the network. As another example, a company may choose a standard operating system for all personal computers in order to allow sharing of software. Only personal computers that utilize that operating system are approved for acquisition.

Another important support role is training. The responsibility for supplying training either internally or through access to outside resources is critical to effective user-controlled services. Training may be for a specific new language or package or for general user understanding of the information system resource. An ongoing training resource as a consulting service is effective for meeting user training requirements on an as-needed basis.

One strategy that combines ongoing training and other types of ad hoc technical support is the *information center*. This is a separate function, usually under the management of information systems, of trained experts specializing in very high level languages and personal computers. Users can make use of the information center facility, which also contains equipment resources, for training and consulting on their projects. They may also call on the information center experts to design short programs for meeting ad hoc requirements or do research on new products. The information center is discussed in detail in Chapter 20.

INFORMATION SYSTEMS AVAILABILITY CONTROLS

The information system represents a valuable asset of the organization. Its value is as a total system, and the loss of any of its parts can impair the value of the whole. Safeguarding availability of the information system hardware, software, and data is therefore an important organizational concern.

Physical Facilities Control

The equipment in a computer installation has a value ranging from a few thousand to several million dollars depending on the size of the installation. The equipment is concentrated in a small area and is easily damaged. In a civil commotion or riot, a centralized computer facility is a likely target for destruction. The magnetic tape and magnetic disk packs have only a modest intrinsic value, but the data they contain has a high value to the organization. In many cases, the data on the tapes and disks has a value to outsiders—for example, prospect lists, employee lists, and mailing lists.

Because of the risk of damage from unauthorized access and the potential loss from theft or destruction of data files, programs, procedures, etc., access to the computer facility is generally restricted. Organizational controls for security and protection include division of duties (so that a single person does not have complete control over the processing of an application), internal and external audit review, restricted access by operators to program documentation, and restricted access to data files and program files. This latter control is exercised through the use of a librarian who keeps track of the files and makes them available only to authorized personnel. Access to software may be controlled by the librarian and by library control software.

With distributed systems, it is harder to provide physical security around each installation. However, each site represents a smaller investment in hardware than a central site. Availability provisions in a distributed system should include authorization procedures for switching processing to alternate locations in case one local site is not functioning. The capability to continue processing at at all sites except the nonfunctioning one is called *fail-soft* protection and is a major advantage of distributed systems over centralized processing, where if the computer "goes down" all processing ceases.

Protection for physical facilities also includes fire and flood protection and fireproof vaults. Security procedures should be supplemented by insurance against loss of equipment, software, and data. A combination of careful employment screening plus fidelity insurance may be used to protect against employee dishonesty.

In the case of small computers or terminals located in user areas, there should still be some restrictions and controls over access to equipment, software, and data files.

Terminal Access Control

In systems using online processing and communications networks, there should be protection against illegal access. The terminals represent access to computer processing capabilities and stored data; therefore, there should be controls over access to the device itself, various locks to prevent unauthorized physical availability, and password control for authorization prior to actual use. Password control is included in the features of the computer's operating system or in special security software. The control usually consists of one or more access passwords which the user must accurately supply before access to the system programs and data is permitted. Password protection may also be placed on individual files and record types, so that only users knowing a file password may access or update records in that file or portion of the database.

Backup and Recovery

No matter how large and complex or how simple and small the computer system, provisions are required to recover from events such as fire, natural disaster, malicious damage, or accident that destroys equipment, software, or data. In addition to these major disasters, there need to be procedures to recover from errors or failures to follow correct procedures. The general approach to recovery is backup by creating copies of the files. Procedures are also established to recreate current processing status using the backup copy and all transactions made subsequent to the last backup. For example, if an error destroys records in a file, backup procedures permit a previous version of a file to be restored and the processing repeated. Examples of backup and recovery provisions are:

- Backup copies of data and software stored off premises
- Arrangements for backup site and facilities and backup supply of forms and other supplies
- Backup and recovery plan

With a microcomputer, backup is less complex but should still be performed. Diskettes or cassettes with data should be copied each night (or other appropriate frequency). The backup copies should be stored in a secure location.

BE PREPARED

A catastrophic fire consumed the facilities of General Computer Services (GSC), a data processing service bureau in Huntsville, Alabama. Items destroyed included all documentation, company records, and corporate information. How did the company manage to survive without losing a customer?

Nearly all the GSC software programs were accessible because a backup system was housed with a remote processing vendor in nearby Birmingham. The biggest losses were hardware items. Fortunately, within 10 days, GCS's hardware vendors had resupplied them with the needed equipment.

The day of the fire, which occurred around 6 a.m., GCS was scheduled to deliver 15 payrolls. At 10 a.m., operating units were established in four employees' homes. GCS customers were informed of the situation and told that work would continue despite the fact that GCS's payroll check stock had been destroyed.

A customer transferred use of his bank account and payroll checks to GCS. He had recently changed banks but had not yet closed his old account. During the next two weeks, payrolls for 40 companies were met through this account with the borrowed checks.

Relocation of employees was another inconvenience. Some worked in Birmingham in the office of the remote processing vendor, while others relocated to various customer sites.

Reinstalling the communications system and rebuilding have been difficult. The situation was summed up by President Tom Keown who stated, "Anything that can go wrong will," after the company's new sign was delivered with the word "computer" misspelled.

Bruce Hoard, "Software House Suffers $750,000 Loss in Blaze," *Computerworld*, March 24, 1980, p. 32.

SUMMARY

The chapter provides an overview of transaction processing, office automation, and information processing controls. Transaction processing is a fundamental procedure required for operations. Checks must be written, purchase orders prepared, orders processed, etc. The data from transaction processing results in transaction documents and also provides the data for managerial reports and analyses.

There are three major approaches to processing transactions: periodic data preparation and periodic processing of batches of data (batch processing), online data entry and immediate processing of individual transactions (online processing), and online data entry with periodic processing of batches of data. There are advantages and disadvantages of each, and the choice of method depends on the technology available and the characteristics of the applications. The controls that ensure correct and complete processing of transactions include an audit trail, data entry controls, data validation, and various types of control totals. Report processing includes preplanned reports and ad hoc reports.

Office automation includes a variety of capabilities. The chapter focuses on document preparation and message and document communication. The use of public data services is also surveyed in the context of office automation. Document preparation is performed using word processing or text processing software. The documents can be filed electronically. With many systems, computer graphics can be prepared using workstations and inserted in text. Composition and reproduction are extensions of the word and text processing facilities.

Message and document communication can be accomplished efficiently using computer-based message systems or voice store-and-forward systems. Facsimile is an alternative when the actual image of the document (including signatures, etc.) needs to be transmitted. Public data networks facilitate message and document transmission. Public data services provide general information or specific industry data through timesharing.

Control of information systems requires both general controls and application-level controls. Management of information systems has overall responsibilities for maintaining qualified staff and appropriate direction. There are specific control duties and functions that operate to ensure quality and completeness of processing. End user information processing facilities present special control problems. One approach is to have the central information system organization provide technical support, standards, and training.

Information systems need to be safeguarded, and availability of information processing needs to be ensured. Controls and safeguards include protection for physical facilities and access controls for terminals. Since no controls can prevent all errors, omissions, and disasters, alternative facilities and backup of data files provide a basis for recovery.

MINICASES
1 THE GUIDEPOSTS REMITTANCE PROCESSING SYSTEM

Guideposts Magazine recently purchased a separate hardware and software system for remittance processing. It allows an operator at a workstation to process as many as 1,200 payment and renewal transactions in an hour. *Guideposts'* staff processes 9 million mail items yearly. Their circulation is 3.5 million subscribers.

The system has its own minicomputer which makes it self-sufficient. *Guideposts* uses it to scan, verify, MICR-encode, and endorse payments, and to print audit trail information. An optional feature of the system is microfilming capability. In the near future the system will be used for order entry processing.

An operator can complete all processing at one workstation with minimal movement. The workstation consists of a keyboard, an easy to read screen (CRT), and an optical character recognition (OCR) reader. Users can easily scan different locations on a document by looking at the screen. The system features step-by-step procedures which simplify the correction of errors.

A custom software package available with the system facilitates programming. Two programmers from the *Guideposts* staff quickly and easily designed and programmed a second application. They anticipate easy completion of future programming projects also.

This system is appropriate for a variety of transaction processing applications. Examples include: banking, insurance, utilities, government, publishing, and fund raising.

"A Magazine's System Handles 1,200 Transactions Hourly," *Computerworld*, February 2, 1981, p. 33.

Questions
a One of the system's features is an audit trail. What is it, and why is it necessary?
b Management thinks this system is cost-effective and efficient. Based on this information, what methods may have been used for remittance processing prior to the installation of this system?

c An optional feature of *Guideposts'* system is its microfilming capabilities. Why would management want this capability? Would you recommend another method of accomplishing the same task? If so, describe it.

d What types of new applications might be provided through the programming facility?

2 A DEPARTMENT STORE INVENTORY SYSTEM

Hess's is a department store chain with a total of 15 stores in Pennsylvania and Maryland. Headquarters are in Allentown, Pennsylvania. While some of Hess's administrative processes were computerized in the past, the purchase order management system has only recently been automated.

The manual system required Hess's buyers to monitor order and inventory information utilizing unit control books. Accuracy and timeliness were often lacking since these factors depended on a variety of people with posting responsibilities.

Inventory of current orders and goods was taken monthly by buyers at the receiving and marking center. This was a time-consuming procedure in which the buyer's files were compared to the receiving center's files. Merchandise received on each order was checked. Existing inventory was counted and reviewed in light of the budget.

Errors occurred in the preparation of original handwritten purchase orders. Extensions were also calculated by hand. Since this procedure was performed by 100 buyers and assistants, there were numerous errors in both pricing and penmanship. Copies of orders sent to vendors were sometimes not intelligible. This caused confusion and discrepancies between items ordered and items delivered.

The manual system has now been replaced by a hardware and software system which links regionally located computers. Prior to entering data, buyers and assistants utilize worksheets to rough out orders. Once the data is entered, purchasing budgets are monitored by the computer. Data entry operators are immediately notified if the budget is exceeded by a buyer. Authorization is required to process an over-budget order. For in-budget orders, routine extensions are calculated automatically from the merchandise price. The vendor is sent a purchase order printed by the computer.

The computer provides two methods of data access to the receiving center. When data is entered, it is printed automatically at the receiving center. This paper copy is the backup in case of hardware failure. The second method is online access through visual display terminals in the warehouse.

A remote terminal is used at the receiving center to record information on goods after they have been shipped to the stores. Buyers have online access to current inventory information. Reports are on an exception basis and are received by buyers weekly if they have not requested them earlier. All inventory and budget information is included in the stock status reports sent regularly to the buyers. Currently six of the fifteen stores have online, interactive terminals. In the near future, merchandise tickets will be automatically read by the computer once terminals are equipped with optical scanning wands. Real-time inventory updates will be possible because the wands will transmit the transaction data to the computer.

"System Unites Scattered Stores," Courtesy of Hess's Department Stores, 1979.

Questions

a Describe the new system in terms of the components of the transaction processing cycle shown in Figure 5-1.

b Review the different forms of system output and identify the purpose of each.

c What control procedures should be utilized once all the inventory and order information is online?

d An optical scanning (OCR) wand is a hand-held optical scanning device. It is moved by the clerk over the price ticket that has a bar code for the merchandise item. Price may also be encoded or may be obtained from the computer. Why is this an appropriate input device? What are the advantages and disadvantages relative to keying?

3 A DISTRIBUTED PROCESSING SYSTEM

The XYZ bank has a dozen branch offices as well as its corporate headquarters in a large metropolitan area. A customer opens an account at a particular branch (typically the one closest to home or work) and carries out the majority of his or her banking at that branch. Recently the bank installed a distributed processing system for handling daily banking transactions. Each branch has its own minicomputer, and there is a large centralized computer at corporate headquarters. The minicomputers have communications with each other through message switching via the central computer. The objectives of the system are to have online updating of all accounts and a highly secure transaction control and audit system at minimum cost.

Each branch is sent each morning, from the central computer, a "clean" up-to-date copy of its file of accounts. During the day, all transactions on that branch's accounts are updated online on its file; a separate "log" file of transactions is also kept. Any transaction pertaining to an account at another branch is updated online at the appropriate minicomputer via the communications network.

At night, each branch's transaction log is transmitted to the central computer site which contains a master account file of all branch accounts. The same transactions are used to update the accounts in batch, and the results are compared to the results of the day's local processing at each branch. All discrepancies are recorded in an error log for follow-up and clarification. The central file is considered the correct, permanent record of all accounts. At the beginning of the next day, the clean copies of local files are again downloaded from the central site to the branch for the day's processing (along with requests to check on discrepancies).

Questions

a Why are multiple copies of the files kept? What are the costs of this procedure?

b Why would the centralized file be considered the correct, permanent file, even though the other files are updated as transactions occur?

c Can you think of situations where the online updating system could result in account discrepancies? Explain.

EXERCISES

1 Define the following terms:
   a Audit trail
   b Batch processing
   c Online processing
   d Transaction
   e Turnaround document

2 Explain the advantages and disadvantages of each of the following:
   a Periodic batch processing
   b Online entry and subsequent batch processing
   c Online entry and immediate processing

3 Consider an *Automatic Teller Machine* in banking.
   a Why are cash withdrawals debited instantly, while deposits are not credited to a person's account until the next day?
   b What kinds of inquiries can a customer make? How are the inquiries designed for ease of use?
   c If you have used an ATM, describe ways the interface could be improved.

4 What is the difference between a word processor and a personal computer workstation with word processing capabilities?

5 You are a member of a project team of five people which is developing an application system for inventory control for the Hess Department Store (see Minicase 2). Three of you are located in corporate headquarters in Allentown, Pennsylvania, and one each in two of their main department stores in Maryland. The primary users with inputs to the design are the inventory

managers of each of the two stores. Explain how you could use each of the following communication facilities in your work as a project team:

a Computer-based message system

b Facsimile transmission

6 Describe the control requirements for a human resources database application with an ad hoc inquiry facility purchased by the personnel department for execution on their own minicomputer.

7 Describe how a personal microcomputer system might be controlled and backup and recovery provided. (Hint: Keep it simple.)

8 How is a terminal protected so that it cannot be used by unauthorized access?

9 In the "Be Prepared" story on page XX, the data processing service company had backed up software and files, but the description of the recovery indicated that it had made a serious omission in recovery preparations. What was it? What should have been done?

10 The computer center was left unlocked and unguarded during change of night shift. The major equipment items were too large to steal in a short time. What was at risk?

SELECTED REFERENCES

No selected references are given because of the overview nature of the chapter. There are a number of elementary textbooks that cover transaction processing and management and control. Office automation is described with significant frequency in the popular and professional literature; both books and articles tend to become quickly obsolete in this area.

CONCEPTUAL FOUNDATIONS

What good are theories and concepts? Why not get to the part where we learn *how*? There is a very practical need for concepts and theory. They provide a framework for thinking about processes and problems. The framework assists in simplifying and structuring the problem for solution and in choosing among available alternatives. Theory and concepts are very valuable in education and training. They aid in generalizing past experience and condensing it for transmission to others.

The concepts and theories underlying information systems are sometimes imprecisely defined, and the relevance of the concepts to information system analysis and design ranges from weak to strong. However, the field of information systems is still embryonic, and the connection between the theoretical and the practical will certainly be strengthened as additional experience is gained and additional research is performed.

In many respects, the six chapters in this section are the core content of the book. An underlying thesis of the text is that users can specify their requirements more correctly and completely and use information systems more effectively if they conceptually understand the phenomena underlying their need for information and how these phenomena relate to information systems. The same applies to developers and managers of information systems. They can design better, develop better, and manage better if they understand the concepts that explain an organization's need for information and how it is used.

The section on conceptual foundations contains six chapters. A few comments about each chapter will aid in understanding the scope of the section.

Chapter number and title	Notes on content
6 The decision-making process	A survey of models and concepts of decision making and methods for deciding among alternatives. A discussion of their relevance to information system design.
7 Concepts of information	Describes various concepts relating to the meaning of information and explains attributes of information, such as age and quality.
8 Humans as information processors	Explains a model of the human information processing system and describes various factors affecting human information processing performance.
9 System concepts	A survey of system concepts with an emphasis on concepts significant to information systems.
10 Concepts of planning and control	Describes concepts and processes for planning and control and how information systems relate to them.
11 Organizational structure and management concepts	Highlights major concepts of organizational structure and management and their implication for information systems.

THE DECISION-MAKING PROCESS

How are decisions made? The answer affects the design of computer-based information systems to support the decision-making process. The purpose of this chapter is to summarize major concepts of decision making and to explain the relevance of these concepts to the design of information systems.

PHASES IN THE DECISION-MAKING PROCESS

The well-known model proposed by Herbert A. Simon[1] will be used as the basis for describing the decision-making process. The model consists of three major phases:

Phases of decision-making process	Explanation
Intelligence	Searching the environment for conditions calling for decisions. Data inputs are obtained, processed, and examined for clues that may identify problems or opportunities.
Design	Inventing, developing, and analyzing possible courses of action. This involves processes to understand the problem, to generate solutions, and to test solutions for feasibility.
Choice	Selecting an alternative or course of action from those available. A choice is made and implemented.

---

[1]Herbert A. Simon, *The New Science of Management Decision*, Harper and Brothers, New York, 1960, pp. 54ff.

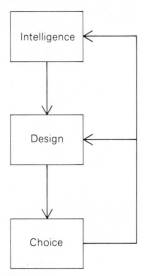

Figure 6-1
Flowchart of decision process.

There is a flow of activities from intelligence to design to choice, but at any phase there may be a return to a previous phase. For example, the decision maker in the choice phase may reject all alternatives and return to the design phase for generation of additional alternatives (Figure 6-1).

The intelligence phase of the model includes activities to identify problem situations or opportunity situations requiring design and choice. Intelligence entails scanning the environment, either intermittently or continuously, depending on the situation. For example:

- An air controller maintains continuous scanning to detect problems in the air space.
- Each time the user of an automobile starts the engine, there is a conscious or unconscious scanning (listening, checking gauges, etc.) to detect possible engine problems.
- A marketing executive makes periodic visits to key customers to review possible problems and identify new customer needs.
- A plant manager reviews the daily scrap report to check for quality control problems.
- A design engineer attends a trade show to observe new materials that may be incorporated in future product designs.

In other words, intelligence activities result in dissatisfaction with the current state or identification of potential rewards from a new state.

Simon's model does not go beyond the choice phase. Some models of decision making include implementation and feedback from the results of the decision. For example, Rubenstein and Haberstroh[2] proposed the following steps:

―――――――――――
[2]A. A. Rubenstein and C. J.Haberstroh (eds.), *Some Theories of Organization*, Richard D. Irwin, Homewood, IL, 1965.

1 Recognition of problem or need for decision
2 Analysis and statement of alternatives
3 Choice among the alternatives
4 Communication and implementation of decision
5 Follow-up and feedback of results of decisions

The next section reviews the intelligence and design phases. A later section reviews methods for choosing among alternatives.

INTELLIGENCE AND DESIGN PHASES

Three important aspects of the intelligence and design phases are problem finding, problem formulation, and development of alternatives.

Problem Finding

Problem finding, as part of the intelligence phase, is conceptually defined as finding a difference between some existing situation and some desired state. In other words, there is some model of what is desired that is selected by the problem finder. This is compared to reality, differences are identified, and the differences are evaluated as to whether they constitute a "problem."

Pounds[3] identifies four models which produce expectations against which reality is measured:

1 Historical models in which the expectation is based on an extrapolation of past experience
2 Planning models in which the plan is the expectation
3 Models of other people in the organization, such as superiors, subordinates, other departments, etc.
4 Extraorganizational models in which expectations are derived from competition, customers and professional organizations

An interesting concept from the Pounds formulation of problem finding is the necessity for the manager or other problem finder to have some model of the process or situation in order to find problems. If the manager's model of the situation is changed to a more complete or more sophisticated model, problem finding also changes.

Problem Formulation

There is always a significant danger, when a problem is identified, of solving the wrong problem. The purpose of problem formulation is to clarify the problem, so that design and choice activities operate on the "right" problem. Frequently, the process of clearly stating the problem is sufficient; in other cases, some reduction of complexity is needed. Four strategies[4] for reducing complexity and formulating a manageable problem are:

1 Determining the boundaries (i.e., clearly identifying what is included in the problem)
2 Examining changes that may have precipitated the problem
3 Factoring the problem into smaller subproblems
4 Focusing on the controllable elements

---

[3]William F. Pounds, "The Process of Problem Finding," *Sloan Management Review*, 1:2, Fall 1969, pp. 1–19.

[4]K. R. MacGrimmon and R. N. Taylor, "Decision Making and Problem Solving," in M. D. Dunnette (ed.), *Handbook of Industrial and Organizational Psychology*, Rand McNally, Chicago, 1976, Chapter 32.

In formulating a problem, it is often useful to establish an analogy or relationship to some previously solved problem or class of problems. For example, a recognition that a problem can be understood as a scheduling problem reduces the complexity of the problem. It is in establishing such analogies that past experience becomes important.

Development of Alternatives

A significant part of the process of decision making is the generation of alternatives to be considered in the choice phase.[5]

The act of generating alternatives is creative, and creativity may be taught. Basic creativity may also be enhanced by alternative-generation procedures and support mechanisms. The creative process requires that there be adequate knowledge of the problem area and its boundaries (domain knowledge) and motivation to solve the problem. Given these conditions, creativity can be enhanced by aids such as scenarios, analogies, brainstorming, checklists, templates of decision process, etc.

CONCEPTS OF DECISION MAKING

Decisions differ in a number of ways. These differences affect the formulation of alternatives and the choice among them. They also affect the design of information system support for decision activities. Four dimensions of decision types which are useful for information systems are level of knowledge of outcomes, level of programmability, criteria for the decision, and level of decision impact.

Knowledge of Outcomes

An outcome defines what will happen if a particular alternative or course of action is chosen. Knowledge of outcomes is important when there are multiple alternatives. In the analysis of decision making, three types of knowledge with respect to outcomes are usually distinguished.

Outcome state	Explanation
Certainty	Complete and accurate knowledge of the outcome of each alternative. There is only one outcome for each alternative.
Risk	Multiple possible outcomes of each alternative can be identified, and a probability of occurrence can be attached to each.
Uncertainty	Multiple outcomes for each alternative can be identified, but there is no knowledge of the probability to be attached to each.

If the outcomes are known and the values of the outcomes are certain, the task of the decision maker is to compute the optimal alternative or outcome. The optimizing criterion may be least cost. For instance, a shopper is considering two different brands of

---

[5]A. Arbel and R. M. Tong, "On the Generation of Alternatives in Decision Analysis Problems," *Journal of Operational Research Society*, 33:4, 1982, pp. 377–387.

a product which appear to be equal in value to the purchaser. However, one costs 20 percent less than the other. *All other things being equal*, the purchaser will choose the less expensive brand. (The example shows that decision making under certainty is rare because all other things are rarely equal.) In some cases, the computation for an optimal decision can be quite large and sometimes impractical without a computer. Linear programming is an example of a technique for locating an optimal solution under certainty. Without a computer, linear programming problems of any size are computationally infeasible. Even with the computer, some problems are too large for standard computational methods.

The making of decisions under risk, when only the probabilities of various outcomes are known, is similar to certainty; instead of optimizing outcomes, the general rule is to optimize the expected outcome. A basic assumption is that the decision maker is rational; this assumption will be examined later in the chapter. For example, faced with a choice between two actions, one offering a 1 percent probability of a gain of $10,000 and the other a 50 percent chance of a gain of $400, the rational decision maker will choose the second because it has the higher expected value.

Probability	×	outcome	=	expected value
.01	×	10,000	=	100
.50	×	400	=	200

Decisions under uncertainty (outcomes known, but not the probabilities) must be handled differently because, without probabilities, the optimization criteria cannot be applied. Most suggestions for handling uncertainty are designed to supply the unknown probabilities, so that the problem can be treated as a decision problem under risk. For example, one suggestion is to assign equal probabilities. Other decision rules that have been suggested are to minimize regret and to use the maximin and maximax criteria. These rules are explained later in this chapter.

Programmed versus Nonprogrammed Decisions

As explained in Chapter 2, decisions can be classified as programmed or nonprogrammed on the basis of the ability of the organization or individual to preplan the process of making the decision. *Programmed decisions* are those decisions that can be prespecified by a set of rules or decision procedures. Programmed decisions are reflected in rule books, decision tables (say, in a manual procedure), and regulations. Programmed decisions imply decision making under certainty because all outcomes must be known.

Nonprogrammed decisions have no preestablished decision rules or procedures. Nonprogrammed decisions may range from one-time decisions relating to a crisis (such as a civil war in a country where a plant is located) to decisions relating to recurring problems where conditions change so much that decision rules cannot be formulated.

Programmed decisions can be delegated to low levels in an organization or automated; nonprogrammed decisions generally cannot. One strategy for increasing the number of decisions which can be programmed is to specify rules for all normal conditions and let the programmed decision rules handle these normal cases. When conditions or actions do not fit the decision rules, the decision is considered nonprogrammed and is passed to a higher level of decision making. The dangers of applying methods for programmed decision making are rigid results and possible application of inappropriate rules.

Criteria for Decision Making

A model of decision making which tells the decision maker how to make a class of decisions is *normative* or *prescriptive*. A model which describes how decision makers actually make decisions is *descriptive*. Normative models have generally been developed by economists and management scientists. Linear programming, game theory, capital budgeting, and statistical decision theory are examples of normative models. Descriptive models attempt to explain actual behavior and therefore have been developed largely by behavioral scientists.

The criterion for selecting among alternatives in the normative model is maximization or optimization of either utility or expected value. The criterion, when stated in quantitative terms, is referred to as the objective function for a decision. It assumes a completely rational decision maker who will always choose the optimal alternative. Decision making under certainty will select maximum utility. For a business firm, utility is usually thought of as being profit, but it can also refer to such concepts as least cost or market share. The traditional view of the criterion for decision making under risk is to maximize expected value.

An alternative view of the criterion for decision making is *satisficing*. This view comes from the descriptive, behavioral model which says that decision makers are not completely informed about alternatives and must therefore search for them. They are neither completely rational nor completely thorough in their search. They simplify the factors to be considered. The assumption of the satisficing concept is therefore *bounded rationality* rather than complete rationality. Decision makers have limited cognitive ability to perceive alternatives and/or consequences. As one result of these constraints, decision makers limit the search for alternatives and accept the first alternative which satisfies all the problem constraints, rather than continue to search until the optimal alternative is found. Alternative models of decision makers are discussed further in the next section.

BEHAVIORAL MODELS OF THE DECISION MAKER

The way a person examines a problem and makes a decision can be described from several different viewpoints, depending on the assumptions made. Several models of the decision maker are described below.

Classical Economic Model of Decision Maker

A normative model of the decision maker in organizations is described by the classical economic model. It has the following assumptions:

1 All alternatives and all outcomes are completely known (decision making under certainty).

2 The decision maker seeks to maximize profit or utility.
3 The decision maker is infinitely sensitive to difference in utility among outcomes.

The first criterion can be relaxed to assume decision making under risk, i.e., probability can be attached to each outcome. It is then assumed that the decision maker will maximize expected value.

The classical economic model is a prescriptive model of the decision maker: completely rational, having complete information, always choosing the "best" alternative. It describes how a person *should* make a decision but, in fact, all criteria of the model are rarely met in a decision situation. Even so, the rational decision maker model is useful; many methods for selecting among alternatives assume complete rationality and provide mechanisms for identifying the optimal choice.

Administrative Model of Decision Maker

The administrative model of the decision maker is descriptive. It explains how decision making actually does take place. As first proposed by Simon,[6] the administrative model views the decision as taking place in a complex and partially unknown environment. The decision maker is assumed not to be completely rational but rather to display rationality only within limits imposed by background, perception of alternatives, ability to handle a decision model, etc. This is the concept of bounded rationality already described. Whereas the goal of the classical economic model is well defined, the goal of the administrative model may change as the decision maker receives evidence of success or failure. The administrative model assumes that the decision maker:

1 Does not know all alternatives and all outcomes.
2 Makes a limited search to discover a few satisfactory alternatives.
3 Makes a decision which satisfies his or her aspiration level (i.e., satisfices)

Simon suggests that most problem-solving strategies for satisficing are based on heuristics or rules of thumb rather than explicit decision rules. This has implications for the design of decision models; they should provide appropriate data and allow decision makers to explore alternatives using their own heuristics. The development of models to support the decision-making process under these assumptions is discussed in Chapter 12.

Human Expectations and Decision Making

Humans display a variety of responses in decision making. Some are related to individual differences, such as cognitive style; these are discussed in Chapter 8. Others are related to expectations. Some of these responses are summarized in this section. Responses that occur in decision making under psychological stress are described later in the chapter. The role of expectations in decision making can be partially explained by the theory of cognitive dissonance, commitment theory, and the theory of anticipatory regret.

Cognitive dissonance, a theory by Leon Festinger,[7] explains behavior after a choice

---

[6]Simon, *The New Science of Management Decision.*

[7]L. Festinger, *A Theory of Cognitive Dissonance*, Row & Peterson, Evanston, IL, 1957.

is made. An alternative that is selected has some negative features, and rejected alternatives have some positive characteristics. A decision maker will tend to have cognitive dissonance, feelings of mental discomfort following a decision because of the recognition of negative and positive elements of the alternatives. After a decision is made and announced, the decision maker reduces cognitive dissonance by increasing the perceived difference in the attractiveness of the alternatives. This is done by avoiding information that might be contrary to the decision and by interpreting dissonant information in a biased way. For example, people who have bought a certain make of car will tend to read the advertisements for that car and not read competitive ads. Sales procedures that follow up a sale with congratulatory information make use of the "bolstering" effect of cognitive dissonance reduction by decision makers.

Theories of commitment stress the effect on decision making of commitment to a decision. If a person knows that the decision is not revocable (there is a firm commitment following the decision), the decision time increases and decision processes are likely to be more careful. Having spent time on a decision and having announced it, a person is reluctant to change it. In fact, having made a fairly minor decision with respect to an issue, a decision maker tends to be more open to a bigger commitment.

Anticipatory regret is a psychological response to alternatives. The decision maker anticipates the regrets that may occur if a certain decision is made. The anticipatory regret inhibits the decision maker from making a decision without contemplating the consequences. Anticipatory regret can also be used as a means of lessening postdecision regret; thinking about consequences before they happen reduces the psychological impact when they happen.

BEHAVIORAL MODEL OF ORGANIZATIONAL DECISION MAKING

The behavioral theory of the firm has been described most fully by Cyert and March.[8] The ideas of Simon and others have also contributed to the material in this section. The theory begins with the assumptions of the administrative model of the decision maker and explains the behavior of decision makers in an organizational context. Major concepts used to explain organizational decision making are quasi-resolution of conflict, uncertainty avoidance, problemistic search, organizational learning, and incremental decision making.

Quasi-resolution of Conflict

An organization represents a coalition of members having different goals and unequal power to influence organizational objectives. The organizational goals change as new participants enter and old participants leave. There are conflicts among the various goals of the organizational members. Even if various personal goals are ignored, the goals of subunits, such as production (level production of standard items), sales (respond to what customer wants by having high inventories), and inventory control (low inventory), are contradictory. Such conflicts are resolved by three methods:

---

[8]Richard M. Cyert and James G. March, *A Behavioral Theory of the Firm*, Prentice-Hall, Englewood Cliffs, NJ, 1963.

Method of conflict resolution	Explanation
Local rationality	Subunits are allowed to set their own goals.
Acceptable-level decision rules	Within certain limits, units are allowed to make their own decisions using agreed-upon decision rules and decision procedures.
Sequential attention to goals	The organization responds first to one goal, then to another, so that each conflicting goal has a chance to influence organizational behavior. Giving sequential attention to conflicting goals means also that certain conflicts are never resolved because the conflicting goals are never handled at the same time.

Uncertainty Avoidance

Organizations live in uncertain environments. The behavior of the market, suppliers, shareholders, and government is uncertain. The behavioral theory of organizational decision making assumes that the organization will seek to avoid risk and uncertainty at the expense of expected value. In general, a decision maker will be willing to accept a reduction in the expected value of an outcome in exchange for an increase in the certainty of outcome. A person, for example, is more likely to choose a 90 percent chance of obtaining $10 than a 12 percent chance of obtaining $100 even though the expected value of the latter is higher. In some cases of collusion by sellers (such as in the assigning of markets), the profits of the conspirators do not appear to have been substantially increased. The major benefit was apparently a reduction in uncertainty. Some legal methods used to reduce or avoid uncertainty are the following:

Methods for avoiding uncertainty	Explanation
Short-run feedback and reaction cycle	A short feedback cycle allows frequent new decisions and thus reduces the need to be concerned about future uncertainty.
Negotiated environment	The organization seeks to control its environment by industry-wide conventional practices (sometimes just as restrictive as collusive behavior), by long-term supply or sales contracts, etc.

Problemistic Search

The search for solutions is problem-stimulated; there is very little planned search for solutions not motivated by problems. The behavioral theory postulates that search for solutions is based on rather simple rules:

 1 Search locally either close to the present symptom or close to the present solution. For example, a failure in achieving the sales goal will cause the search to start with the sales department and the sales program.

2 If local search fails, expand the search first to organizationally vulnerable areas before moving to other areas. Vulnerable areas are areas with slack resources (e.g., personnel overstaffing) or with goals that are difficult to calculate (e.g., research).

Organizational Learning

Organizations exhibit adaptive behavior over time. They change their goals and revise their problem search procedures on the basis of experience. Aspiration levels for goals are assumed to change in response to the results experienced. In the steady state, aspiration levels are a little above achievement; when there is increasing achievement, the aspiration level will lag behind achievements. Where there is a decreasing level of achievement, aspiration levels will decrease but tend to remain above achievement levels. These phenomena are important to planning and control because plans tend to reflect aspiration levels, and controls (with reports, etc.) can have positive or negative impacts on performance depending on aspiration levels of units being evaluated. The information system is therefore one factor in reconciling the achievement level and aspiration level.

Incremental Decision Making

A variation on the concept of satisficing is an incremental approach in which decision making in organizations is confined to small changes from existing policy and procedures. The emphasis is on correcting or improving existing policies and actions. The range of choices considered tends to be very narrow and reflect the consensus of groups in positions of influence and power. In fact, the satisficing criterion for this decision-making strategy is consensus. This approach has been termed ''muddling through'' by Lindblom,[9] who identifies it as a common strategy in governments and large organizations. It tends to be a reasonable strategy when consensus is important for changes and the changes needed are small. The incremental nature of the changes suggest that it is not a good strategy when there is need for significant shifts in policy and actions. Etzioni[10] has suggested that organizations use a mixed strategy (mixed scanning) for decision making in which minor decisions use an incremental approach, but major policy decisions require a complete consideration of alternatives.

DECISION MAKING UNDER PSYCHOLOGICAL STRESS

The models of decision making thus far in the chapter (except for the notes on expectations) have focused on the decision-making process as a calm, reasoned process, even when constrained by human limits that lead to satisficing instead of optimizing. There are many decisions in organizations and in personal life that are charged with emotion because of strong desires by the decision maker to achieve certain objectives or to avoid dangers or unpleasant consequences. There are strong opposing tendencies in

[9]C. E. Lindblom, ''The Science of Muddling Through,'' *Public Administration Review*, 19, 1959, pp. 79–88.

[10]A. Etzioni, ''Mixed Scanning: A Third Approach to Decision Making,'' *Public Administration Review*, 27, 1967, pp. 385–392.

the individual with respect to courses of action. The result is decisional conflict, a significant source of psychological stress. The stress from decisional conflict can lead to impaired decision-making processes. This concept is important to the design of information systems, because a decision support system to be used under conditions of decisional conflict may not be effective unless it is designed to take into account decision behavior under psychological stress. The concepts presented in this section are based on the conflict-theory model of Irving L. Janis and Leon Mann.[11]

Decisional Conflict and Psychological Stress

Decisional conflict arises when an important decision has to be made. The conflict is heightened if the decision maker becomes aware of the risk of serious losses from every alternative course of action. In other words, all decision making causes some decisional conflict, but the serious symptoms to be examined here occur in the case in which all courses of action appear to have serious undesirable outcomes. The symptoms of such serious decisional conflict are apprehensiveness, hesitation, vacillation, distress, etc. Decisions are still made, however, by using various coping patterns.

Coping Patterns

The conflict-theory model of decision making can be seen most directly in emergency situations, such as a fire or flood. However, it can be extended to almost any decision associated with threats or perceived threats to important goals of the decision maker. There are four questions that determine the typical coping pattern:

- Are the risks serious in the absence of a change?
- Are the risks serious if change is made?
- Is it realistic to hope for a better solution?
- Is there sufficient time to search and deliberate?

If the answer to the first question is no, then no change need be made; if yes, then the next question is relevant. If the consequences of change are perceived as not serious, then a change can be made without decision conflict; if the consequences are serious, the question of better solutions is relevant. If no better solution is perceived possible, defensive avoidance may be the coping pattern. If a better solution is thought possible and there is time, the coping strategy can be a vigilant process of search, appraisal, and contingency planning. If there is no time (as in a fire), the coping pattern may be hypervigilance. Hypervigilance and defensive avoidance will be explained because these patterns may result in incomplete search and appraisal. However, the one that is most of interest in terms of information systems and decision support systems is defensive avoidance.

Hypervigilance is typically a response to disasters. The person focuses on the expected unfavorable consequences and fails to process information indicating that they may not happen. The person feels a pressure to take immediate action, hastily choosing without considering the overall result or considering other possible actions.

---

[11]Irving L. Janis and Leon Mann, *Decision Making: A Psychological Analysis of Conflict, Choice, and Commitment*, Free Press, New York, 1977, p. 11.

Defensive Avoidance

Defensive avoidance as a dominant coping strategy is marked by the decision maker avoiding exposure to disturbing information, wishful thinking, distortion of information received, and selective inattention. If the decision maker feels the risk of postponing a decision is low, procrastination will be selected. If not, getting someone else to make the decision (buckpassing) might be tried. Prior to making a decision under a defensive avoidance pattern, the decision maker may perform bolstering tactics if no more information about alternatives is expected. After the decision is made, bolstering is used to reduce cognitive dissonance about the decision. The following are examples of bolstering tactics:

- Exaggeration of favorable consequences
- Minimizing of unfavorable consequences
- Denial of adverse feelings
- Exaggeration of remoteness of action that will be required following decision
- Assuming lack of concern by society (it is a private decision)
- Minimizing of personal responsibility (social pressure or "orders")

The pattern of defensive avoidance associated with a single decision maker can also be observed under certain conditions in groups. The group may be a management group, a labor union, a religious body, etc. Janis has coined the term *groupthink* for collective defensive avoidance.[12] The conditions he has identified are illustrated by an industry that is failing to react to vigorous price, quality, and design competition by foreign competitors.

Symptoms of groupthink	Example for industry faced with serious foreign competition
1 Illusion of invulnerability	The company is large and powerful and has customer loyalty.
2 Collective rationalization	No one can match our research.
3 Belief in the inherent morality of the group	The managers are the best trained and preserve "the traditional" values.
4 Stereotypes of outgroups	The competitor products are inferior. They cannot provide service.
5 Direct pressure on dissenters	Demotion or firing of managers who disagree about the danger.
6 Self-censorship	The subject of foreign competition is never put on the agenda by anyone.
7 Illusion of unanimity	No one is objecting, and so everyone must agree that foreign competition is not serious.
8 Self-appointed mind guards	Evidence that contradicts the thinking of the group is removed as it moves up the organization.

---

[12]Janis and Mann, *Decision Making: A Psychological Analysis of Conflict, Choice, and Commitment*, pp. 129–133.

METHODS FOR DECIDING AMONG ALTERNATIVES

Numerous methods help one decide among alternatives. The methods generally assume that all alternatives are known or can be known even though the search process often stops well before all feasible alternatives have been examined. This section reviews a number of methods. The classes of methods to be reviewed are optimization techniques, payoff matrices, decision trees, decisional balance sheets, elimination by aspects, game theory, and statistical inference. Methods for handling a problem when it is difficult to estimate probabilities are also discussed. The explanations provide an idea of the range of methods but are not detailed.

Optimization Techniques Under Certainty

The techniques for optimization assume that all alternatives and their outcomes are known (decision making under certainty). The computational problem is to calculate which alternative is optimal for a given objective function. Some of the techniques are listed below to illustrate the variety of techniques used, but an explanation of how to use these techniques is beyond the scope of this text:

Systems of equations
Linear programming
Integer programming
Dynamic programming
Queuing models
Inventory models
Capital budgeting analysis
Break-even analysis

Payoff Matrices in Statistical Decision Theory

The term *statistical decision theory* is used to refer to techniques for mathematically evaluating potential outcomes of alternative actions in a given decision situation. All alternatives and outcomes are assumed to be known, and the decision maker has an objective such as maximization of profit. The methods of presenting the data in decision theory are a payoff matrix and a decision tree. The payoff matrix will also be used in Chapter 7 in the discussion of the value of information.

The payoff matrix consists of rows for the alternatives or strategies available to the decision maker and columns for the conditions ("states of nature" in decision theory terminology) that affect the outcomes of the strategies. (Figure 6-2 shows the general model.) It is, of course, possible to make the rows stand for states, events, or conditions and the columns for alternatives or strategies. Each cell (intersection of a strategy and a state of nature) contains the payoff (the consequences, say, in dollars) if that strategy is chosen and that state of nature occurs. If there is certainty as to which condition or state of nature will prevail, the decision maker need only select the strategy that provides the highest payoff.

States of nature				
Strategies	n_1	n_2	n_3	n_4
S_1				
S_2				
S_3				

Contains conse-
quences (payoff)
if strategy S_1
is chosen and state
n_2 occurs

Figure 6-2
General payoff matrix.

Strategies	Conditions or events (states of nature) with probability of occurrence		
	Same .50	New competitor .20	Highway rerouting .30
Do nothing	2	0	−1
Refurbish	4	3	−3
Rebuild	7	2	−10

Figure 6-3
Payoff matrix for owner of quick-service restaurant (payoff in thousands of dollars).

The payoff matrix is best explained by an example. Assume the data shown in Figure 6-3. An entrepreneur is deciding among three alternatives for a fast-service restaurant that she owns: (1) leave as is; (2) refurbish it to improve the layout; or (3) rebuild completely to add capacity and improve layout. There are three significant, independent conditions (assume only one may occur) that affect the possible profit (payoff) from each of the alternative strategies. These conditions are: (1) a competitor may open on a nearby property, (2) a proposed highway rerouting will change traffic passing by, or (3) conditions will stay approximately as they are. The entry in each cell of the matrix indicates the profit (or loss) from the combination of a strategy and a condition. The decision to refurbish will yield a profit of $4,000 under a continuation of existing conditions, a profit of $3,000 with new competition, and a loss of $3,000 if there is a highway change. If we assume that conditions will stay the same, rebuilding is the best alternative. Assume also, however, that probabilities are assigned to each possible state of nature—the same conditions given a probability of .50, a new competitor a probability of .20, and a highway rerouting a probability of .30. The expected value of each strategy is computed by multiplying each payoff by the probability for the column and summing across the row. The results are:

Strategy	Arithmetic	Expected value
Do nothing	(.50)(2) + (.20)(0) + (.30)(– 1) = .70	.70 or $ 700
Refurbish	(.50)(4) + (.20)(3) + (.30)(– 3) = 1.70	1.70 or $1,700
Rebuild	(.50)(7) + (.20)(2) + (.30)(–10) = .90	.90 or $ 900

The maximum expected value is to refurbish, and this should be chosen under the criterion of maximizing expected value.

The probabilities of various conditions or states of nature are assumed to be known with reasonable exactness in the above analysis, but what if the decision maker is very uncertain about the probabilities of the various conditions which may occur? Some rules for deciding are minimize regret, maximin, and maximax. The ways they would be applied in the case of the payoff matrix shown in Figure 6-3 are summarized below:

Decision rule	Explanation
Minimize regret	The rule is to select the action or strategy which minimizes the sum of the regrets for the strategy. The regrets are the differences between the best payoff for a state of nature and the other outcomes. To compute a matrix of regret, subtract the value in each entry in the column from the highest value in the column. Sum the rows to compute the regret for each action. (If the payoff matrix has columns for actions and rows to show states, the instructions would be reversed.) The regret matrix based on Figure 6-3 is the following:

Do nothing	5	3	0	= 8
Refurbish	3	0	2	= 5
Rebuild	0	1	9	= 10

	The action which minimizes regret is therefore the action to refurbish. The above assumes equal probabilities for outcomes. An expected regret for each strategy can also be computed by multiplying each regret by its probability.
Maximin rule	Select the strategy which will have the highest utility payoff (max) if the worst state of nature (min) occurs. Stated differently, identify the state of nature with the worst payoff and choose the strategy with the least unfavorable payoff, given that state. Essentially a pessimistic view, this would result in choosing to do nothing because the worst case occurs with rerouting and do nothing is the best strategy for this worst case.
Maximax rule	Select the strategy or alternative which provides greatest (max) utility payoff if the most favorable state of nature (max) occurs. An optimistic view, this rule would result in the strategy of rebuilding because the payoff of 7 is the best.

Each of these decision rules has been criticized as having some disadvantages when applied as a general decision rule.[13]

---

[13]W. Edwards, "The Theory of Decision Making," *Psychological Review*, 51:1, 1954, pp. 380–417.

Utility and Indifference Curves

The examples of decisions in statistical decision theory have used monetary value (dollars) or expected monetary value. The case of dollars, sales, or other such measures works reasonably well for a narrow range of values, but not at the extreme values. Also it is often desirable to weight nonmonetary considerations.

For these reasons, a measure called *utility* is frequently used in place of monetary or other value. The units are called *utiles*. Figure 6-4 shows a possible utility function for money. The shape of the curve says that the relation is linear ($1 = 1 utile, $2 = 2 utiles, etc.) over a certain range but then rises rapidly. This means that the utility of getting a fairly large sum is larger than the utility computed from a set of small amounts. In other words, $1 = 1 utile, but $100,000 in one payment is larger than 100,000 utiles for $1. This helps to explain attitudes toward insurance, and it may partially explain gambling (but is certainly not a complete explanation). After rising steeply, the curve flattens out because the utility of substantially more money is not great; $2 million has not much greater utility for the average individual than $1 million.

The loss side of the curve has a different behavior than the gain side. A large loss has significantly greater negative utility than merely the sum of disutilities for smaller losses. The loss of $10,000 is greater than the quantity: (1,000 × the disutility of losing $10). This phenomenon is relevant to insurance. Assume an insurance problem with the following payoff matrix:

	Fire .003	No fire .997	
Insurance	−$240	−$240	= −$240 expected value
No insurance	−$50,000	0	= −$150 expected value

Insurance costs $240, potential loss is $50,000, and expected value of the insurance policy is $150 (.003 probability of loss by $50,000 loss). Therefore, the insurance is

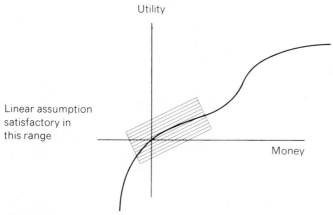

Figure 6-4
Estimated utility function for money.

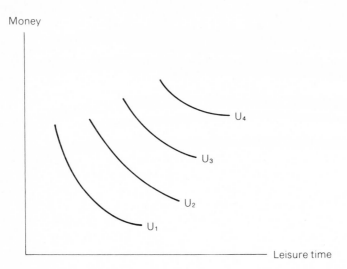

Figure 6-5
Utility indifference curves.

uneconomic. However, assume a utility function as shown in Figure 6-4 and that a loss of $50,000 will have disasterous consequences (say –150,000 utiles) while the insurance has –240 utiles. The payoff matrix with utiles instead of dollars is now:

	Fire .003	No fire .997	
Insurance	–240 utiles	–240	= –240 expected value in utiles
No insurance	–150,000 utiles	0	= –450 expected value in utiles

For the utilities in this example, it appears the decision maker would pay up to $450 for insurance (utile = $1).

The above example of utility used only one value property—money. In many cases, however, there is more than one value property, and various combinations of the properties may yield the same total utility. For example, a person may be interested in both leisure time and money and will trade off one for the other. This trade off can be represented by indifference curves for each level of total utility (Figure 6-5).

Decision Trees

When the decision maker must make a sequence of decisions, a decision tree is a useful method for presenting the analysis. The analysis is named a decision tree because the different alternatives form branches from an initial decision point. The analogy with a tree suggests that the initial decision should be at the bottom of the page and that the branches stretch upward to the top. However, it is more common to arrange the presentation from left to right or top to bottom (Figure 6-6).

The decision tree is best explained by an example. A hotel chain with hotels in major cities around the world is analyzing the decisions in building a hotel in a newly independent, developing country. The decisions are whether to build or lease and whether to have local shareholders. Figure 6-7 shows the decision tree. The states of nature (events) are government decisions to either have free enterprise or expropriate foreign-owned properties (but not locally owned properties), to encourage economic activity which is the major determinant of occupancy and thus income, and to set the results of appraisal for compensation to the company for expropriated properties—either fair or low.

The steps in using a decision tree in the analysis of alternatives are the following (Figure 6-7):

   1 Build the tree, starting with decision points and adding branches for external states of nature (events) that may occur. Include the probability of each state of nature.
   2 For each unique branch (end point) or outcome, assign a value.
   3 Work backward to analyze the consequences of each alternative at each "node" of the tree.

To analyze the decision tree in Figure 6-7, start at the tips or ends of the branches (the right side of the figure). Compute the expected value for each set of end branches, and write the expected value in the circle (node). Work back to the next node and compute the probabilities, taking into account the probabilities already calculated plus the new probabilities. At the decision point, write the highest expected value coming into the decision point in the rectangle. In Figure 6-7, the value resulting from this process is the expected value of the decision to enter the hotel business in the country. For example, starting at the top right, we compute the first node as:

Probability		Value of outcome		Expected value
.20	×	100	=	20
.50	×	80	=	40
.30	×	50	=	15
				75

Moving down the tree to the second set of branches from the second node, we calculate as follows: $(.25 \times 10) + (.75 \times -100) = -72.5$. These two nodes are the data to calculate the expected value from which they stem:

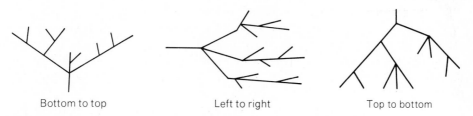

Bottom to top   Left to right   Top to bottom

Figure 6-6
Alternative representations of decision trees.

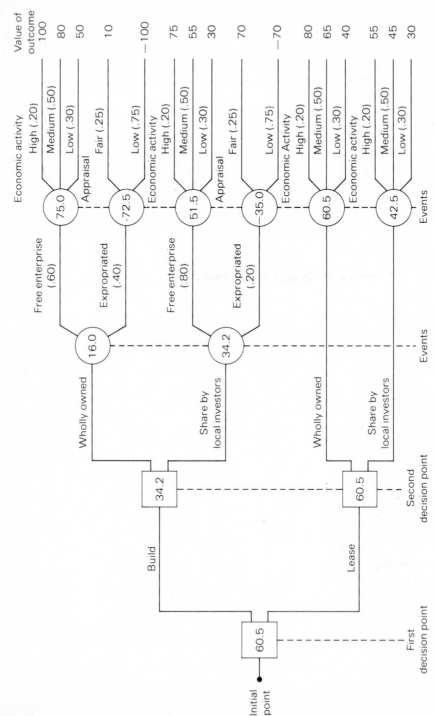

Figure 6-7
Decision tree for decision to invest in hotel in a newly developing country.

75 × .60 (probability of free enterprise)	45.0
−72.5 × .40 (probability of expropriation)	−29.0
Expected value of decision to build a wholly owned hotel	16.0

The decision point to build or lease shows an expected profit of 34.2 if the build policy is coupled with a "share by local investors" policy, etc. The expected profit of 60.5 from a lease policy is coupled with a policy of having a wholly owned hotel. Thus, the decision is to lease and to have the hotel wholly owned.

The use of both payoff matrices and decision trees requires the use of probability estimates. Objective probabilities based on measurement of like situations are not generally available, so the probabilities used are subjective. The advantage of the technique is that it requires the explicit use of the subjective probabilities rather than using them without making them explicit.

Ranking, Weighting, or Elimination by Aspects

In decisions involving a number of factors or aspects, each factor is assigned a relative importance or weight by the decision makers. The degree to which the alternatives meet the decision factor is weighted by the importance (or rank). The sum of the weighted factors or ranks is used to rank or compare the alternatives. For example, in a computer selection process, software may be given an importance weight of 40 (out of 100 points). A vendor meeting 90 percent of the software requirements would be given a weighted software factor of 36 (.90 × 40); a vendor meeting only 70 percent of requirements (or ranked as a 70 compared to 90 for the first vendor) would receive a software decision factor of 28 (.70 × 40).

Tversky[14] describes a procedure for elimination by aspects instead of weighting. The requirements to be met are identified and ranked in terms of importance or value. Starting with the most important requirement, all alternatives that do not contain that aspect are eliminated. This process continues through all aspects. For example, a major aspect for microcomputer selection may be IBM compatibility; alternatives that do not meet this aspect are eliminated from further consideration.

Game Theory

Game theory is another means of analyzing a decision in a competitive situation such that when one decision unit (player) gains, the other loses. In a two-person zero-sum game, there is equality of gains and losses; what one person gains, the other loses. Game theory is useful in understanding conflict bargaining situations but appears to have limited utility in organizational decision making.

---

[14]A. Tversky, "Elimination by Aspects: A Theory of Choice," *Psychological Review*, 79, 1972, pp. 281–299.

Classical Statistical Inference

Statistical inference is termed "classical" or "objective" as opposed to the Bayesian approach which uses subjective probabilities. The techniques of classical statistics can be very useful in preparing information for decision making. Some techniques are listed to remind the reader of the variety of tools available.

Statistical technique	Comment
Sampling	A small portion of the population is sampled in order to estimate parameters—mean, variance, etc.
Probability distributions	There are a number of distributions (e.g., normal, Poisson, exponential, Weibull). If the data approximates one of these distributions, the theoretical distribution can be used for decision purposes. The Chi-square goodness-of-fit test is one of the most common methods for determining how well a theoretical distribution approximates the real data.
Regression and correlation analysis	The relation between a dependent variable and one or more independent variables is determined by correlation analysis. The correlation coefficient is a summary measure to explain the degree to which changes in the dependent variables are explained by changes in the independent variables.
Testing of hypotheses	Hypotheses can be tested to judge whether they are true or false.

Decisional Balance Sheet for Decision Making under Stress

Janis and Mann[15] propose a schema for decision making under conditions of stress. For each alternative, positive and negative anticipations are elicited for four categories of gains and losses and placed on a grid.

	Anticipations	
Category of gains or losses	Positive	Negative
1 Tangible gains and losses for *Self*		
2 Tangible gains and losses for *Others*		
3 Self-approval or self-disapproval		
4 Social approval or social disapproval		

[15]Janis and Mann, *Decision Making: A Psychological Analysis of Conflict, Choice, and Commitment*, pp. 135–169.

Having filled in the grid, the decision maker can evaluate the strength of the various gains and losses and rank the alternatives.

In addition to the decisional balance sheet, Janis and Mann also advocate decision counseling to stimulate evaluation of alternatives, role playing exercises (psychodrama) to stimulate awareness of anticipations, emotional inoculation against postdecisional setbacks, and procedures to avoid the collusive behavior of groupthink.

DOCUMENTING AND COMMUNICATING DECISION RULES

An important element of organizational learning is documenting decision rules and procedures so that they can be retrieved by persons who have to make the decision and communicated to new personnel. The documentation is in procedures manuals, forms, instructions, training materials, report formats, etc. In the case of decision procedures that are coded into computer programs, the decision procedures are documented by the program narrative, program code, and other program documentation plus user manuals. Documentation of decision rules is therefore an important matter for both information system designers and users. This section will survey various layouts by which procedures can be documented.[16]

A procedure may be a completely determined sequence of actions, or it may incorporate decision making based on alternative conditions. Methods for documentation of decision logic are given below and illustrated in Figure 6-8.

Method	Comment
Matrix	A matrix can be used to present pairs of conditions and a resulting action (decision).
Decision table	The decision table documents rules that select one or more actions based on one or more conditions from a set of possible conditions. It is precise and compact.
Flowchart	A flowchart is the equivalent of a decision table with each separate path through a flowchart representing one decision rule. It is less compact than a decision table but easy to follow.
Decision tree	This is a flowchart without decision symbols or processing boxes. It is oriented to show decision paths that may be taken rather than the criteria for selecting a given path. It is convenient for showing probabilities for outcomes.
Pseudocode	This shows the decision logic in the IF-THEN format of a computer program. It is a precise description, but may be too concise and formal for those not familiar with computer programming.

A narrative format is commonly used in documentation, yet a narrative format tends to be inadequate for documenting decision procedures. The selection of one of the above methods depends on the context and the users. Simple pairs of conditions are best documented by a matrix while multiple sets of conditions and actions require a decision table or flowchart. If the main objective is to show the decision paths, a decision tree

---

[16]C. Haga, ''Procedure Manuals,'' *Ideas for Management*, Systems and Procedures Association, Cleveland, OH: 1968, pp. 127–154.

works well. Pseudocode that is oriented to program code is probably not suitable for readers not conditioned to formal program logic statements; the use of a structured English form in pseudocode is often satisfactory.

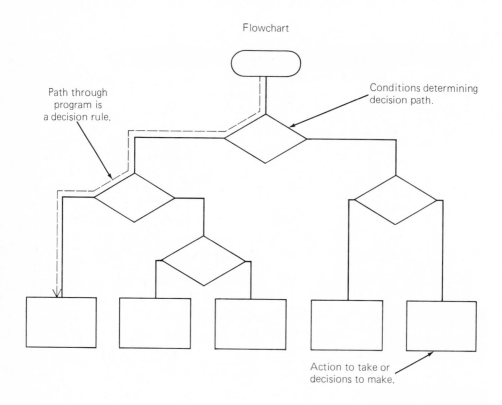

Flowchart

Path through program is a decision rule.

Conditions determining decision path.

Action to take or decisions to make.

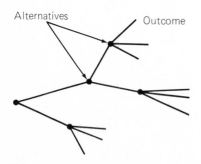

Decision Tree

Alternatives

Outcome

Figure 6-8
Alternatives for documenting and communicating decision procedures: matrix, decision table, flowchart, decision tree, and pseudocode.

Matrix

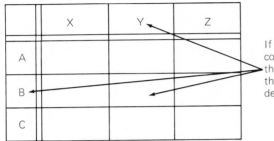

	X	Y	Z
A			
B			
C			

If condition B and condition Y apply, then perform (choose) the action or decision described in intersection.

Decision Table

		Rules				
		1	2	3	4	5
Conditions	A		T			
	B		T			
	C		F			
Actions	R					
	S		X			
	T		X			

Rule 2 says: *If* condition A is true and condition B is true and condition C is false, then perform actions S and T.

Pseudocode

DO for all departments
  Select department number in order
  For each employee PRINT detail
  IF net pay is outside limits
    (negative or > 300) PRINT
    error code on same line
End of DO

Mostly Nouns & Verbs
Make Clear, precise, condensed
easily interpreted
Purpose:
Very simply tell someone what to do

RELEVANCE OF DECISION-MAKING CONCEPTS FOR INFORMATION SYSTEM DESIGN

The decision-making concepts presented in this chapter should be understood by both the designer and user of systems to support decision making. Some concepts should be explicitly considered in support system design; others provide limits on what a decision model should be expected to accomplish. The relevance of these decision concepts for decision support system design are summarized below; explicit considerations for decision support systems are discussed in Chapter 12.

Support for Decision-Making Phases

The Simon model is relevant to the design of information support for decision making within a management information system. This relevance is summarized for the three phases of the Simon model. The use of these concepts in design of reports to aid decision-making are described in Chapter 12.

Phase of decision-making process	Relevance to support systems for decision-making
Intelligence	The search process involves an examination of data both in predefined and in ad hoc ways. Information systems support should provide both capabilities. The information system itself should scan all data and trigger a request for human examination of situations apparently calling for attention. Various models should be incorporated in the scanning and report layouts. Examples are historical, planning, other units, and extraorganizational models. Either the system or the organization should provide communication channels for perceived problems to be moved up the organization until they can be acted upon.
Design	The information system should contain decision models to process data and generate alternative solutions. It should assist with checklists, templates of decision processes, scenarios, etc. The models should assist in analyzing the alternatives.
Choice	An information system is most effective if the results of design are presented in a decision-impelling format. When the choice is made, the role of the system changes to the collection of data for further feedback and assessment.

Support for Programmed versus Nonprogrammed Decisions

The distinction between programmed and nonprogrammed decisions (also termed structured and unstructured) affects information processing support. This was introduced in Chapter 2.

Nonprogrammed decisions are ill structured, not repeated frequently, or the conditions are so different at each repetition that no general model can be developed as a basis for programming them. Decision support systems are designed for these (as explained in Chapter 12).

The decision activities for both establishing rules for a programmed decision and making a nonprogrammed decision can follow the decision-making process involving intelligence, design, and choice. The decision rules for a programmed decision must provide a general solution which takes into account a variety of conditions, whereas the nonprogrammed decision need relate to only a specific situation.

Although the rules for a programmed decision conserve scarce managerial time and energy, there is a very significant problem in their use in information and decision systems. The problem is the application of the decision rule to a problem situation for which they are not suitable. The lack of applicability may occur in their use on problems for which the rules were not designed, in the existence of conditions not contemplated or in changes in the characteristics or objectives for the decision. For example, an inventory reorder model for fast-moving items is generally not appropriate for slow-moving items. An inventory model which assumes ready availability of items to be ordered is not suitable if there is scarcity or rationing. A capital investment model to maximize rate of return may not be appropriate for a company faced with minimizing expected losses from nationalization by an unfriendly government. The problem of applying the right decision model to the right problem suggests that decision support models for programmed decision making should be designed to facilitate human review.

Relevance of Models of the Decision Maker

Where appropriate, the computer can be used as a computational device to apply optimization techniques under the assumption of complete information and rational decision making. However, such models are limited to extremely constrained conditions. Efforts to apply optimization techniques under conditions which are inappropriate (incomplete information about alternatives, political constraints preventing optimization, personal characteristics of the decision maker, etc.) have been a major cause of failure of the use of computerized models to aid decision makers.

An alternative approach is to aid the decision maker under the assumptions that information is incomplete and costly, satisficing is the goal, and decision making has psychological effects. In the decision support approach, the computer essentially acts as an adjunct to the human decision maker in such tasks as computing, storing, retrieving, and analyzing data. The design allows decision makers to allocate tasks to themselves or to the computer and to iterate with proposed solutions (discussed further in Chapter 12).

Application of the Behavioral Model of Organizational Decision Making

The behavioral theory of organizational decision making alerts the system designer to the organizational constraints on a decision maker. The designer may be interested in rationality, but the decision maker may want uncertainty avoidance. The behavioral theory defines the methods for uncertainty avoidance which may need to be supported by information. The information system design should recognize the practical, behavioral limitations of organization wide optimization models because these models assume consistent organization goals, whereas the behavioral theory emphasizes the existence of inconsistent goals. Recognition of problem-stimulated local search will provide guidance in designing information and decision models that provide an adequate search space and assist the decision maker in recognizing the value of expanded search if such value appears to exist. Organizational learning and adaptive behavior is important in the design of information procedures for planning and control systems because of the need to recognize changing goals and aspirations. Information system support can aid decision makers to avoid incremental decision making for policy decisions (where inappropriate) by presenting information in forms that stimulate more complete analysis.

Support for Decision Making under Stress

The design of information systems to support decision making can include preprogrammed decision modules to be invoked when certain crises occur. The model can provide immediate prespecified responses or interaction with the decision maker to explore options. Models such as the decisional balance sheet can be interactively built to provide a basis for the decision.

Support for Alternative Techniques

Methods for deciding among alternative decision procedures should be available as part of decision support systems. For some problems, the appropriate technique should be provided automatically; for others, two or more techniques may be provided. The information system should be supportive of decision makers in their search for the best approach.

Where probabilities and other estimates must be provided, a user-machine dialogue is helpful. The user should be able to alter conditions or probabilities easily and quickly and see the effects of the changes on outcomes. For example, a decision support system may require a best estimate of the sales for a new product. The decision maker may be asked to provide greater-than or less-than estimates of finer and finer limits until he or she indicates an inability to continue. The results are converted to probability statements which are used in the decision process. Various checks for consistency are used to assist the decision maker in arriving at the final estimate.

Support for Quality of Decision Making

It is frequently difficult to evaluate the quality of a decision that has been made; it is possible, however, to evaluate the quality of the process by which the decision was made. Janis and Mann[17] have identified seven major criteria for judging the quality of

---

[17]Janis and Mann, *Decision Making: A Psychological Analysis of Conflict, Choice, and Commitment.*

the decision-making procedures. Quality of a decision process consists of a decision maker who, ''to the best of his ability and within his information processing capabilities:

1 Thoroughly canvasses a wide range of alternative courses of action

2 Surveys the full range of objectives to be fulfilled and the values implied by the choice

3 Carefully weighs whatever he knows about the cost and risks of negative consequences, as well as the positive consequences, that could flow from each alternative

4 Intensively searches for new information relevant to further evaluation of the alternatives

5 Correctly assimilates and takes account of any new information or expert judgment to which he is exposed, even when the information or judgment does not support the course of action he initially prefers

6 Reexamines the positive and negative consequences of all known alternatives, including those originally regarded as unacceptable, before making a final choice

7 Makes detailed provisions for implementing or executing the chosen course of action, with special attention to contingency plans that might be required if various known risks were to materialize.''

The information system can be designed to reinforce decision procedures that meet these criteria. The decision criteria relate to information processing, so the decision support system can prompt the decision maker to do the processing and, by interactive dialog, can prompt the decision maker to evaluate adherence to procedures that satisfy the quality criteria.

SUMMARY

The process of decision making can be described as consisting of three major phases: (1) intelligence to search out problems or opportunities, (2) design to analyze problems or opportunities and generate feasible solutions, and (3) choice to select among alternatives and implement the chosen one. Decision making may be based on outcomes that are known with certainty, outcomes with known probabilities of occurrence (risk), or outcomes with unknown or very uncertain probabilities (uncertainty). Decision response may consist of a preprogrammed application of decision rules and procedures or nonprogrammed procedure to look for a solution.

The descriptions of decision making that indicate how decisions should be made are termed normative or prescriptive; the descriptions that explain actual human decision behavior are termed descriptive. The classical economic model of the decision maker is a prescriptive model which assumes complete information about alternatives, complete rationality of the decision maker, and optimization of expected value as the goal. The administrative model is descriptive; it assumes that information is incomplete and that search is limited and costly. The decision maker exhibits bounded rationality and uses satisficing as a goal. A behavioral model of organizational decision making is descriptive; it focuses on quasi-resolution of conflict, avoidance of uncertainty, problemistic search, organizational learning, and incremental decision making.

Decision making frequently occurs in stress situations where all outcomes appear unfavorable. Under these conditions individuals use various coping methods which may yield unsatisfactory results.

When alternatives are known and their values can be determined, various methods for deciding among alternatives are available; some methods were explained briefly.

The orientation of information systems to both information and decision making means that the system designer should be well-versed in decision theory and decision techniques. Moreover, the designer should understand the nature of the decision-making process, which imposes limits on the usefulness of many techniques and introduces new requirements for decision support.

Review Cases

MINICASES

1 THE ROBOT SUICIDE

Isaac Asimov's science fiction mystery *The Naked Sun* (Fawcett, New York, 1957) takes place on a planet served by robots. In order to protect the humans on the planet, the robots are programmed with the Laws of Robotics. The first two laws are:

1 A robot may not injure a human being or, through inaction, allow a human being to come to harm.

2 A robot must obey the orders given it by a human being except where such orders conflict with the first law.

In one episode, a robot serves a glass of water to a man. The man is poisoned. The robot short circuits because it brought harm to the man, although it did not know the water was poisoned.

Questions

a Using this illustration, describe the problem(s) of programmed decision making.

b Why wasn't the robot programmed to recognize that giving a normally noninjurious substance or object to a human that turns out to do injury does not violate the first law (or does it)?

c What would be the implications of a decision rule that required human decisions when no other decision rule applied?

2 SOLAR ENERGY DECISION

The leasing of solar energy equipment for industrial use is a potential alternative to federally subsidized programs for encouraging use of solar technology. The factors encouraging the leasing of solar equipment include rising fuel costs, decreasing cost of solar technology, and the Business Energy Property Tax Credit. The latter measure, passed by Congress in 1980, added an incentive credit of 15 percent for energy savings on top of the already existing 10 percent business investment tax credit.

Planned Energy International (PEI) is perhaps the first company to have formalized a lease for solar equipment. According to PEI's president, Billie Jolson, the company leased 52 solar panels to a California laundromat. She estimated the savings to the business would be $165,000 over the seven-year lease, including $720 in the first year.

Under a typical arrangement, PEI conducts extensive energy audits of the potential client company and estimates the potential savings on utility bills each year under a lease agreement. Once the lease is signed, PEI assumes all responsibility for purchasing, delivering, installing, and maintaining the solar equipment.

"Solar Energy: Leasing Cuts High Cost of Providing 'Harness' for the Sun," *Christian Science Monitor*, July 20, 1981.

Questions

a What appears to be the goal of each organization in relation to solar energy? (Hint: Examples are maximizing, minimizing regret, satisficing, avoiding uncertainty, and resolving conflict.)

b What are the information requirements for each goal?

c Which decision model fits each organization?

3 EXCELLENCE IN MANAGEMENT

Recently, the management consulting firm of McKinsey and Company conducted an in-depth study of 37 firms considered to be examples of well-managed companies. The study revealed eight attributes that the firms had in common. The most significant attributes were concentration on one key business value, simple form and lean staff, a bias toward action, and emphasis on doing what they know best.

Some of the companies used modern management tools such as decision support systems and strategic planning. Rather than a perfect overall plan, they preferred controlled experiments. The general attitude was "get some data; do it; adjust it.'

Both new ideas and problems were handled quickly. Ideas were implemented quickly on a small scale, with the results leading to rapid expansion or to the idea being discarded. Problems were put into the hands of a task force or a person with temporary but extraordinary power. Action, not reports, were expected. A later follow-up would evaluate the action taken; rewards or criticism would then result. Most problem handlers preferred to find solutions expeditiously and return to their interrupted work.

"Putting Excellence into Management," *Business Week*, July 21, 1980, p. 196.

Questions

a What form of decision making is illustrated in these "well-run" companies?
b What are the decision attributes?
c What information is of greatest interest to those who are assigned problems?

4 DECIDING WHERE TO SEND CHECKS

One way a bank can improve its performance is to speed up collection of out-of-town checks. When a bank accepts an out-of-town check, it must clear the check by sending it to the bank on which it was drawn. There are several ways this can be done, each having a cost and a time. In increasing order of cost, typical options are:

- Clear through the Federal Reserve System
- Send the check to a private clearing bank which transports the check
- Use direct courier service

The time each option takes will depend on the time of day and day of week. The decision must be made for each check.

The Maryland National Bank, averaging over 500,000 transit checks per day, developed an integer linear program for decision making as to the clearing option. The bank has saved over $100,000 per year using the linear program analysis.

Reprinted by permission of Robert E. Markland and Robert M. Nauss, "Improving Transit Check Clearing Operations at Maryland National Bank," *Interfaces*, 13:1, February 1983, pp. 1–9, ©1983 The Institute of Management Sciences.

Questions

a How does this application fit into the categories of decision making?
b What kind of decision rules might be prepared if the criterion were satisficing?

EXERCISES

1 Identify, for the following decisions, the activities which may have preceded the choice. Classify each activity as either intelligence or design:
  a Market a new product.
  b Hire Bill Smith as controller.
  c Cancel development of a new product.

d Enter into licensing agreement with a firm holding a patent.

e Lower prices on widget from $1.15 to $1.

2 Explain how the Rubenstein and Haberstroh model can be described by the Simon model. Illustrate with an example of the problem of a production process that is high in cost, but apparently can be reduced in cost by new machinery.

3 Human expectations affect motivation to make a decision and also affect postdecision behavior. Using expectancy theory, anticipatory regret, commitment, and cognitive dissonance, trace the effect of each on behavior in making each of the following decisions:

a Personal decision to purchase a house (major purchase).

b Business organization decision on where to locate a new plant (president's behavior).

c Purchase of land to locate the new plant.

d Purchase of a microcomputer for a personal work station.

4 Identify problem situations where outcomes are known with:

a Certainty

b Risk

c Uncertainty

5 Identify the following techniques as being *most* relevant to decisions under (**a**) certainty, (**b**) risk, or (**c**) uncertainty.

(1) Linear programming

(2) Payoff matrix

(3) Capital budgeting

(4) Integer programming

(5) Game theory

(6) Set of simultaneous equations

(7) Decisional balance sheet

(8) Elimination by aspects

6 What is the difference between maximizing expected value and maximizing expected utility?

7 Using the concept of expected value, show why it is not generally rational to buy insurance. Using the concept of maximizing utility, explain why insurance is purchased.

8 Gambling cannot be explained by use of expected value concepts. Attempt to explain it using utility concepts. Can the utility concept include nonmonetary satisfaction associated with taking risks?

9 Under what conditions is defensive avoidance a coping strategy? How is bolstering related to cognitive dissonance?

10 Define programmed and nonprogrammed decisions. Identify each of the following with the type of decision to which it is *most* likely to apply:

a Computer program

b Ad hoc decision

c Judgment

d Regulations

11 Define *normative* and *descriptive* as they apply to decision making. Identify each of the following with the one to which it is *most* applicable:

a Management science

b Game theory

c Microeconomic theory

d Behavioral science

e Scientific management

f Risk avoidance concept

g Operations research

h Satisficing concept

i Incremental decision making

12 What is the objective function for a decision? State an objective function for each of the following decisions:
a To introduce new product
b To increase advertising
c To replace unsafe machines
d To buy a new automobile for personal use
e To drop a course in which a failing grade is probable

13 Explain the difference in decision-making procedures if the criteria are satisficing versus optimizing. Explain the use of the two criteria for the following decisions:
a Purchase new automobile for personal use.
b Decide on quantity of inventory to order.
c Decide on new plant site.
d Decide on feed mix formulation.

14 Explain the implications for organizational behavior of the following pairs of differing assumptions:
a Single organizational goal versus a coalition of members with different goals.
b Uncertainty avoidance versus risk taking.
c Restricted search versus unrestricted search for solution.
d Single aspiration level versus adaptive, changing aspiration level.

15 Decision making under psychological stress is observed in a variety of situations in which many or all of the outcomes can be serious. Give examples of possible ways defensive avoidance may be used by local management and employees of a plant that is so inefficient and expensive to operate that it will be shut down unless drastic changes are made in procedures, productivity, pay rates, etc.

16 Using the concept of decision making under psychological stress and groupthink behavior, do a short analysis of the Professional Air Traffic Controllers strike of August 1981. Give examples for each of the groupthink symptoms.

17 Read newspapers or news magazines at the time of the United States action in Grenada (week of October 21, 1983). Identify evidence of bolstering.

18 What is problem finding? How does it relate to the Simon model? What models are used by problem finders in identifying problems?

19 Assume that the vice president for academic affairs says, "We have a problem of decreasing enrollment." Formulate one or more manageable problems by following the four strategies for reducing complexity and formulating problems.

20 Using the example of selecting a personal computer, show the elimination by aspects decision procedure.

21 Select and sketch a documentation model for the following decisions and explain why it was chosen:
a Given a value for height and one of four bone structure classes, an ideal weight is established.
b The admission decision using multiple combinations of criteria.
c A scenario of treatment decisions and outcomes for handling a complex medical case.
d Validation of an input data item.

22 A difficult and often stressful personal decision is whether to move to a different region of the country because of lack of job opportunities in one's current location. Use the decisional balance sheet to show how a person might fill in the balance sheet if he or she:
a Has a large family with school-age children and has skills which are in great demand elsewhere.
b Is single and has skills which are in questionable demand elsewhere.

23 A decision problem involves three alternative strategies called alpha, beta, and gamma. There are four possible events or states of nature. The following is the payoff matrix:

	W	X	Y	Z
Strategies	.10	.25	.35	.30
Alpha	0	15	30	10
Beta	25	10	10	20
Gamma	45	10	25	−10

Make the decision and indicate payoff using each of the following decision rules:
a Maximax
b Expected value with equal probabilities
c Maximin
d Minimize regret (equal probabilities)
e Expected value
f Minimize expected regret

24 Draw indifference curves for money and prestige as two alternative forms of compensation using the following data (**P** = prestige, $ = money):

	P	$	P	$	P	$
Curve 1	2	6	4	3	6	2
Curve 2	4	6	6	3	8	2
Curve 3	6	6	8	4	10	3

25 Draw a decision tree and prepare an analysis for the following problem. A company must make a decision whether to market a new product. The success of the venture depends on the success of a competitor in bringing out a competing product (.60 probability) and the relationship of the competitor's price to the firm's price. Because the firm expects to be able to differentiate its product somewhat, there will be sales even if the competitor's price is lower. Traditional pricing in the industry suggests $.99, $1.29, and $1.59 as the prices that are at issue. The table contains the conditional profit for each set of prices by the company and its competitor.

Company's price	Competitor's price			Profit if no competitor
	$.99	$1.29	$1.59	
.99	30	40	45	$50
1.29	21	42	45	70
1.59	10	30	53	90

The probability of the competitor's price being one of these three is influenced by the company's price which must be set first because its product will be out first. If the company's price is specified, the probability of a competitor's price is shown below:

If company sets price of	Competitor's price will be		
	$.99	$1.29	$1.59
$ .99	.80	.15	.05
$1.29	.20	.70	.10
$1.59	.05	.35	.60

Probabilities of given competitor price if company sets a stated price

SELECTED REFERENCES

Arbel, A., and R. M. Tong: "On the Generation of Alternatives in Decision Analysis Problems," *Journal of the Operational Research Society*, 33:4, 1982, pp. 377–387.

Cyert, R. M., and J. G. March: *A Behavioral Theory of the Firm*, Prentice-Hall, Englewood Cliffs, NJ, 1963.

Edwards, W.: "The Theory of Decision Making," *Psychological Review*, 51:1, 1954, pp. 380–417.

Etzioni, A.: "Mixed Scanning: A Third Approach to Decision Making," *Public Administration Review*, 27, 1967, pp. 385–392.

Hammond, John S., III: "Better Decisions with Preference Theory," *Harvard Business Review*, November–December 1967, pp. 123–141.

Holloway, C. A.: *Decision Making under Uncertainty*, Prentice-Hall, Englewood Cliffs, NJ, 1979.

Huber, George P.: *Managerial Decision Making*, Scott Foresman, Glenview, IL, 1980.

Janis, I. L., and L. Mann: *Decision Making: A Psychological Analysis of Conflict, Choice, and Commitment*, Free Press, New York, 1977.

Keen, Peter G. W., and Michael Scott-Morton: *Decision Support Systems: An Organizational Perspective*, Addison-Wesley, Reading, MA, 1978.

Lindblom, C. E.: "The Science of Muddling Through," *Public Administration Review*, 19, 1959, pp. 79–88.

MacGrimmon, K. R., and R. N. Taylor: "Decision Making and Problem Solving," in M. D. Dunnette (ed.), *Handbook of Industrial and Organizational Psychology*, Rand McNally, Chicago, 1976, Chapter 32.

Magee, John F.: "Decision Trees for Decision Making," *Harvard Business Review*, July–August 1964, pp. 126–138.

Mintzberg, H., D. Raisinghani, and A. Theoret: "The Structure of 'Unstructured' Decision Processes," *Administrative Science Quarterly*, 21, 1976, pp. 246–275.

Polya, G.: *How to Solve It*, Princeton University Press, 1973.

Pounds, William F.: "The Process of Problem Finding," *Sloan Management Review*, 1:2, Fall 1969, pp. 1–19.

Raiffa, H.: *Decision Analysis: Choice Under Uncertainty*, Addison-Wesley, Reading, MA, 1974.

Simon, Herbert A.: *The New Science of Management Decision*, Harper and Row, New York, 1960.

Tversky, A.: "Elimination by Aspects: A Theory of Choice," *Psychological Review*, 79, 1972, pp. 281–299.

Tversky, A., and D. Kahneman: "The Framing of Decisions and the Psychology of Choice," *Science*, 211, 1981, pp. 453–458.

Van Gundy, Arthur B.: *Techniques of Structured Problem Solving*, Van Nostrand Reinhold, New York, 1981. A review of 60 methods of problem definition, idea generation, evaluation, and implementation.

CONCEPTS OF INFORMATION

Management information systems deal with information, but what is "information"? How much information does an information system provide, and how much is provided by more informal organizational information channels? Is there no adequate method for measuring the information from an information system? Is it possible to use a formula or algorithm for computing information content? Several theoretical concepts are useful in partially answering these questions. This chapter describes several concepts related to the meaning of information, the value of information, and various attributes of information. (Chapter 8 also deals with concepts of information because it explores the capabilities of humans as information processors.)

DEFINITION OF INFORMATION

Information is an imprecise term as commonly used. However, underlying the use of the term in information systems are several common ideas: information adds to a representation, corrects or confirms previous information, or has "surprise" value in that it tells something the receiver did not know or could not predict. Information reduces uncertainty. It has value in the decision-making process in that it changes the probabilities attached to expected outcomes in a decision situation.

A useful general definition of *information* for the purpose of information systems is the following: *Information is data that has been processed into a form that is meaningful to the recipient and is of real or perceived value in current or prospective actions or decisions.* This definition recognizes both the value of information in a specific decision

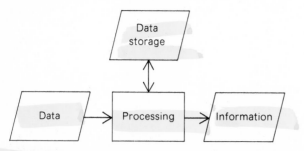

Figure 7-1
Transformation of data into information in an information system.

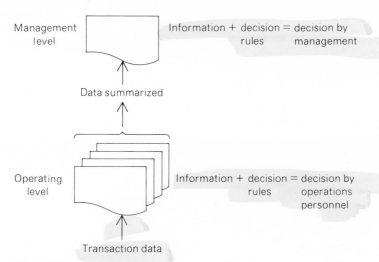

Figure 7-2
Data for one level of an organization may be information for another.

and the value of information in motivation, model building, and background building affecting future decisions and actions.

The relation of data to information is that of raw material to finished product (Figure 7-1). In other words, an information processing system processes data into information. More precisely, the information system processes data in unusable form into a usable form that is information to the intended recipient. The analogy of raw material to finished product illustrates the concept that information for one person may be raw data for another—just as the finished product from one manufacturing division may be the raw material for another division. For example, shipping orders are information for the shipping room staff, but they are raw data for the vice president in charge of inventory (Figure 7-2). Because of this relationship between data and information, the two words are often used interchangeably.

Information resources (in the sense of stored data of all types) are reusable. When information is retrieved and used, it does not lose value; in fact, it may gain value through the credibility added by use. This characteristic of stored data makes it different from other resources.

The value of information is described most meaningfully in the context of a decision. For example, the characters 3109.49 cannot be judged as to value unless the decision affected by them is known. If there were no current or future choices or decisions, information would be unnecessary. Theoretically, then, information has value only as it affects the decision or action to be taken.

Data, the raw material for information, is defined as groups of nonrandom symbols which represent quantities, actions, objects, etc. Data items in information systems are formed from characters. These may be alphabetic, numeric, or special symbols such as * and $. Data items are organized for processing purposes into data structures, file structures, and databases. Data relevant to information processing and decision making may also be in the form of text, images, or voice. These concepts were reviewed in Chapter 4.

In summary, then, the terms "data" and "information" are often used interchangeably, but the distinction lies in the fact that data items are the raw material processed to provide information. Information has value within a specific decision-making context; it also has value within the context of future decisions and actions.

INFORMATION IN THE MATHEMATICAL THEORY OF COMMUNICATION

The term *information theory* is often used to refer to the mathematical theory of communication. The mathematical theory has direct application in mechanical and electronic communication systems. It is limited in its practical use for management information systems, but it does provide insight into the nature of information.

The problems of information communication in information systems can be considered in terms of three levels:

1 Technical level. How accurately can information be transmitted?
2 Semantic level (presentation). How precisely do the transmitted symbols convey the desired meaning?
3 Effectiveness level (quality). How suitable is the message as a motivator of human action?

The mathematical theory of communication as discussed in this section deals with the technical level. The next two sections deal with aspects of the semantic and effectiveness levels.

Historical Development

Information theory was developed by Norbert Weiner, a well-known mathematician, as a result of his study of cybernetics.[1] Weiner's contention was that any organism is held together by the possession of means for acquisition, use, retention, and transmission of information. Claude Shannon of Bell Laboratories developed and applied these concepts to explain communications systems such as telephone systems.[2] In the context of Shannon's work and most subsequent research, information theory has developed primarily as a mathematical theory of communication.

Model of a Communication System

A general model of a communication system was discussed in Chapter 3 and is repeated in Figure 7-3. The purpose of a communication system is to reproduce at the destination a message selected at the source. A transmitter provides coded symbols to be sent through a channel to a receiver. The message which comes from a source to the transmitter is

---

[1] Norbert Weiner, *Cybernetics, or Control and Communication in the Animal and the Machine*, Wiley, New York, 1948.

[2] Claude E. Shannon, "A Mathematical Theory of Communication," *Bell System Technical Journal*, 1948, pp. 370–432, 623–659.

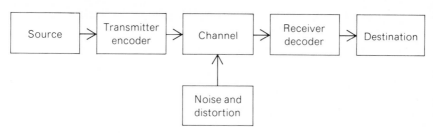

Figure 7-3
General model of a communication system.

generally encoded there before it can be sent through the communications channel and must be decoded by a receiver before it can be understood by the destination. The channel is not usually a perfect conduit for the coded message because of noise and distortion. Distortion is caused by a known (even intentional) operation and can be corrected by an inverse operation. Noise is random or unpredictable interference.

There is a finite set of possible messages to be transmitted. For example, each of the letters and numerals is a possible message to be transmitted by a Telex system. Each sound, inflection, pitch, etc., of the human voice is a message in the telephone system. Suppose a message, "Now is the time for all good men to pray," is spoken over the telephone and also transmitted over a Telex. The meaning is essentially the same, but the information transmission capacity required is substantially different. Considerably more messages are required to relay the voice than the coded letters and numbers (probably by a factor of over 500 to 1). The meaning of information in the theory of communication will help explain this difference.

Mathematical Definition of Information

As used in the mathematical theory of communication, information has a very precise meaning. It is the average number of binary digits which must be transmitted to identify a given message from the set of all possible messages to which it belongs. If there are a limited number of possible messages which may need to be transmitted, it is possible to devise a different code to identify each message. The message to be transmitted is encoded, the codes are sent over the channel, and the decoder identifies the message intended by the codes. Messages can be defined in a variety of ways. For example, each alphanumeric character may be a message, or complete sentences may be messages if there are a limited, predefined number of possible sentences to be transmitted.

The size of the code is dependent on the coding scheme and the number of possible messages. The coding scheme for information theory is assumed to be binary. In other words, if the communication system is required to respond to only two responses, "yes" or "no," then the system needs to transmit one of only two possible signals; they are represented by 1 and 0, the two values in the binary system. In this communication system, the information content of the message to be sent is said to be one bit. As another example, assume a system is used to transmit only birthday greetings. However, senders may not write their own greetings—they may only select from several standard messages such as "Wishing you happiness on your birthday." Assuming there are eight such messages, the information content required to identify the selected message for the receiver is three bits. The codes for each of the eight messages are:

Message no.	Bits
1	000
2	001
3	010
4	011
5	100
6	101
7	110
8	111

Note that a separate unique code of a combination of three 0s and 1s identifies each message and distinguishes it from the other seven.

The information content (or code size in bits) may be generalized as:

$$I = \log_2 n$$

where n = the total number of possible messages, all equally likely.

To understand the application of this formula, consider some examples where $n = 8, 2, 1,$ and 27.

$$n = 8 \qquad I = \log_2 8 = 3$$

This is the same as the example of eight birthday greetings where it was shown that three bits would be needed.

$$n = 2 \qquad I = \log_2 2 = 1$$

If there are only two outcomes, a single bit (0 or 1) value can identify which of the two is intended.

$$n = 1 \qquad I = \log_2 1 = 0$$

If there is only one message to select from, there is no need to transmit anything because the answer is already known.

$$n = 27 \qquad I = \log_2 27 = 4.75$$

If the set of messages is the alphabet plus a space symbol, the number of bits required will average 4.75 per letter, assuming all letters to be equally probable.

The last example of the information content of a code for the alphabet illustrates the effect on the code when the messages to be transmitted (alphabetic characters plus space in this case) are not equally likely. If each of the 27 characters were equally likely, each would appear 1/27 of the time (a probability of .037). But letters do not occur with equal frequency. The probability of occurrence for a few letters illustrates the wide difference in English text:

Letter	Probability
A	.0642
B	.0127
E	.1031
J	.0008
Space	.1859

The use of short codes for common letters and the space and longer codes for the letters occurring less frequently (much like the Morse code) reduces the average code size (average information) required to transmit alphabetic text. The information required to identify a message will also be different for each one—short codes for messages with many common characters and long codes for messages with many uncommon characters. The information content (average) is the sum of the probability times the $\log_2$ of 1/probability for each item (character). This is stated as:

$$I = \sum_{i=1}^{n} p_i \log_2 \frac{1}{p_i}$$

A computationally equivalent form is $I = -\sum_{i=1}^{n} p_i \log_2 p_i$. As an example, assume four messages. If they were all equally likely, the formula $\log_2 n$ would yield an average of two bits. If the probabilities were unequal (say, .50, .25, .15, and .10), the computation would be as follows:

Message number	Probability of the message	$\log_2 p_i$	$p_i \log_2 p_i$
1	.50	−1.00	−.50
2	.25	−2.00	−.50
3	.15	−2.74	−.41
4	.10	−3.32	−.33
		=	−1.74

$I = -\Sigma p_i \log_2 p_i = 1.74$ for set of messages

Even though there are still four messages, the average number of bits needed (the average information content) is less than if they were equally probable.

Reduction of Uncertainty

The emphasis so far has been on the coding scheme, but notice that the formula for information specifies how much information is required to tell the receiver something not already known or not predicted with certainty. Information in this sense might be termed as having "surprise" or "news" value.

I COULD NEVER HAVE GUESSED IT!

The following headline appeared in the University of Minnesota Daily, the student newspaper:
MANY STUDENTS AND BAR OWNERS SAY NO TO BILL RAISING LEGAL DRINKING AGE TO 21.
Based on information theory, the information value of this headline is zero because the statement could have been predicted with complete certainty.

Information reduces uncertainty. Given a set of messages, the receiver does not know which one will be selected (is uncertain) until information is received. Partial information will reduce the uncertainty but not eliminate it. For example, in the case of the eight birthday messages, three bits are required to eliminate uncertainty completely by identifying the exact message. However, transmitting a single bit reduces the number of possible messages to be considered and therefore reduces uncertainty. In the case of eight 3-bit codes, if four of the codes start with a 0-bit and four with a 1-bit, transmitting a single bit selects one of the two groups and reduces the possibilities from eight to four, as shown below.

Start with 0-bit			Start with 1-bit		
0	0	0	1	0	0
0	0	1	1	0	1
0	1	0	1	1	0
0	1	1	1	1	1

Another example may assist in understanding the effect of partial information. If a decision maker has 10 possible actions (say, 10 job applicants to choose from) and they all appear to be equally qualified, the probability that a single individual is more qualified is 1/10, or .10. Information which positively identifies the best candidates has a value of 3.32 bits ($\log_2 10$). However, a message such as an aptitude test which reduces the selection from ten candidates to four has an information value of 1.32. This is computed as the difference between the information needed to select from ten candidates (3.32) and the information needed to select from four (2.0).

Redundancy

A communication is rarely if ever completely composed of information. There are usually redundant elements. Redundancy reduces the efficiency of a particular transmission because more codes are transmitted than are strictly required to encode the message. However, some redundancy is very useful for error control purposes. A message may not be received as sent because of noise in the communication channel. The transmission of redundant data allows the receiver to check whether the received message is correct and may allow the original message to be reconstructed. Suppose, for example, a message dealing with the history of the United States was partially intermixed with noise so that only the following came through to the receiver (* stands for an undetermined character):

T** F**ST PR***DE*T O* THE UN***D S**T** *E**** **SH*NG***

The fact that the reader immediately perceives the sentence as reading ''The first president of the United States George Washington'' indicates that the original message was highly redundant. In fact, the garbled message is still redundant. The redundancy means that the listener need not read and decode every letter in order to understand the message.

Redundancy is usually built into data communications systems through the transmission of *parity bits*. The use of parity bits to detect and correct errors in data transmission is illustrated in Figure 7-4.

Redundancy in coding is computed as the percentage of the information coding capability not being used.

$$R = 1 - \frac{In}{Im}$$

where In = Information capacity needed

Im = Information capacity of code

For example, a code using six bits, which can code 64 possibilities, might be used in a particular situation that has only 16 possibilities to differentiate. The redundancy in this

Case 1 Simple parity bit to detect errors

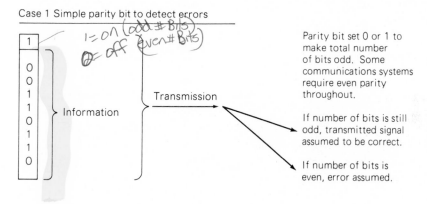

Parity bit set 0 or 1 to make total number of bits odd. Some communications systems require even parity throughout.

If number of bits is still odd, transmitted signal assumed to be correct.

If number of bits is even, error assumed.

Case 2 Row and column parity to detect and correct errors

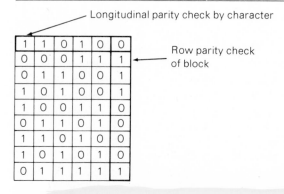

Longitudinal parity check by character

Row parity check of block

Combination of row and longitudinal parity. This allows specific error bit to be isolated and corrected.

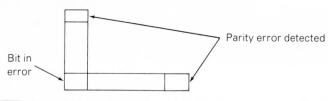

Parity error detected

Bit in error

Figure 7-4
Use of parity bits in error detection and correction.

case is computed as follows:

$$In = \log_2 16 = 4$$
$$Im = \log_2 64 = 6$$
$$R = 1 - \frac{4}{6} = \frac{1}{3} \text{ or } .33 \text{ redundancy}$$

The information capacity needed and redundancy are affected by the probability of each message being transmitted. Suppose there are four equally likely possibilities. A selection requires an average of two bits ($\log_2 4 = 2$). However, if the four possibilities are not equally likely, a two-bit code is slightly redundant.

Outcome	p_i	$\log p_i$	$p_i \log_2 p_i$
1	.20	−2.32	−.46
2	.30	−1.74	−.53
3	.40	−1.32	−.53
4	.10	−3.3	−.33
			−1.85 | = 1.85

$$R = 1 - \frac{1.85}{2.00} = .08 \text{ or 8 percent redundancy in use of a 2-bit code for this data.}$$

INFORMATION PRESENTATION

The mathematical theory of communication deals with information content of messages which are assumed to be objective. However, the richness of language by which humans communicate and the constraints on humans and organizations as information processors means that the interpretation of received messages are subject to misunderstanding. Communication of information for human use is affected by methods of transmission and message handling. These methods can be classified as those which increase system sending or receiving efficiency and those which permit content or distribution discretion on the part of the organizational unit or individual handling the message.[3]

Methods that Increase the Sending and Receiving Efficiency of a System

The limits on the capacity of humans to process information and limits on the capacity of the information system to generate it require that various methods be used to reduce the quantity of data stored and presented for human use. Two methods for more efficiently providing information are summarization and message routing. Within organizations, *message summarization* is commonly utilized to reduce the amount of data transmission required without changing the essential meaning of the original message. Formal

---

[3] George Huber, "Organizational Information Systems: Determinants of Their Performance and Behavior," *Management Science*, 28:2, February 1982, pp. 138–155.

summarization is illustrated by accounting classifications. The president of an organization cannot normally review each sale to get information for decisions. Instead, the accounting system summarizes all sales into a "sales for the period" total. The system may provide more meaningful information for decision purposes by summarizing sales by product group, geographical area, or other classification.

The level of summarization is dependent on the organizational level of the decision maker. For example, the president may need only the total sales by area, but the sales manager for the area may need sales by sales representative and sales by product. This is consistent with the classifications of information by management level discussed in Chapter 2.

Another method of increasing the efficiency of the system is *message routing*. Any particular message is only distributed to those individuals or organizational units which require the information for some action or decision. This is illustrated by the transmission of copies of purchase orders to only those departments (production, distribution, billing) which take direct action based on the information on the order. The marketing department does not require the particular information on the order but may require summarized information on a periodic basis as described previously. The efficiency of message routing is often thwarted by individuals who have little or no use for information but require their own record of it "just in case." (This phenomenon will be explained in Chapter 8).

Methods to Exercise Information Content or Distribution Discretion

Individuals or organizational units exercise some discretion over the content and distribution of messages to control their workloads, to control distribution of information that may have perceived undesirable effects to the individual or unit handling the message, or as part of the preparation of information in a presentation format. The methods through which this discretion is demonstrated are message delay, message modification or filtering, inference or uncertainty absorption, and presentation bias. The methods are summarized below and described briefly in this section.

Method	Reasons for use
Message delay	To avoid overload To distort, inhibit, or suppress transmission
Message modification or filtering	To modify by summarization To block certain data by filtering
Uncertainty absorption	To reduce data transmission (by removing recipient from contact with detail data)
Presentation bias	To bias by order and grouping in data presentation To bias by selection of limits that determine whether items are presented To bias by selection of graphics layout

In *message delay*, transmission is delayed because a message does not require immediate action, and the message receiver might experience information overload (a problem discussed in Chapter 8). In other cases, message delay can be utilized to distort, inhibit, or suppress transmission. An example of suppressing a transmission is a subordinate who seeks to inhibit the discovery of an error in a transaction by simply placing it aside.

THE MISSING DATA FOR A DECISION

This is an actual conversation between an agent for an airline and a person seeking a seat:

Agent: Flight 462 at 1:40 p.m. that we confirmed earlier today when our computers were down is full. I can waitlist you on that flight and confirm you on flight 55 at 11:45.

Traveler: How many people are waitlisted on flight 462?

Agent: We don't have that information.

Traveler: But that is the information that is critical to my decision. If I am first on the waitlist, I will still plan on flight 462; if not, I will go on flight 55 or take an alternate airline.

Agent: We don't have that information.

Traveler: (Under breath) Why not? The system knows it!

A common method of exercising discretion over message transmission is *message modification* or *filtering*. Unlike summarization, the meaning of the message is altered prior to transmission. Customer attitudes as perceived by the salespeople, changing policies of government regulatory agencies, and financial condition of major suppliers are examples. These "messages" are summarized in various ways as they move up the organization; the efficiency and accuracy of communication depends on the organizational methods for eliciting the data and the communication channel provided for them (Figure 7-5). Unless there is a formal procedure to classify, summarize, and transmit them to the decision maker, the signals may be filtered out by intermediate organizational elements. For example, customer complaints of tactics of salespeople in a particular sales district may be blocked by the district sales manager, who does not wish the criticism to reach the corporate level because it reflects personally on his or her performance. The manager may also feel that the situation can best be remedied at the district level.

March and Simon[4] use the term *uncertainty absorption* for the form of message modification that occurs when *inferences* are drawn from a body of data and the inferences instead of the data itself are communicated in the organization. This results in substantial data reduction (Figure 7-5). The inference may be based on quantitative data such as statistical inference or may be more subjective, reflecting a set of nonreproducible inputs to the inferential process. An example of the latter might be an inferential message regarding the anticipated role of the Federal Antitrust Division in mergers during the coming period. The reason for terming this "absorption of uncertainty" is that the data has uncertainty associated with it, but the recipient of the inference information is removed from the original data and must, for practical purposes, rely on the inference itself. However, he or she may have a subjective estimate of the confidence to be placed in the inference as well as its source.

---

[4] James G. March and Herbert A. Simon, *Organizations*, Wiley, New York, 1958, pp. 164–169.

Message modification or filtering

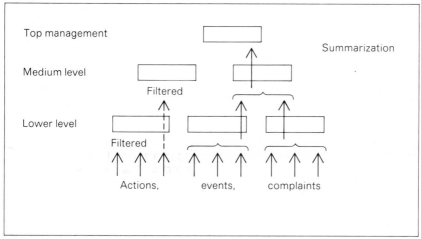

Inference

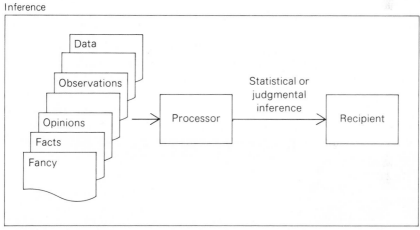

Figure 7-5
Discretion over information transmission by message modification or filtering and inference.

Discretion is manifest in information transmission by *presentation bias*. The way that data is presented will influence or bias the way it is used and the interpretation of its meaning. Bias is not used in the sense of good or bad; it specifies influence, intentional or unintentional. Three examples of presentation bias are order and grouping in presentation, exception selection limits, and selection of graphics layout.

Order and grouping of data influence the perception of importance and affect the comparisons a user is likely to make. For example, if a portfolio manager requests lists of stocks with rates of return greater than 5 percent, the stocks may be presented in different ways. The manager's approach to decision making is likely to be influenced by the presentation. To illustrate, consider three alternative listings and possible biases to decision making.

Forms of presentation	Decision bias caused by data presentation
Alphabetical order	In an alphabetical list of any length, the first items will tend to receive more attention than later items.
Order by rate of return	The items with the highest rate of return will be emphasized with less regard for industry, size, etc.
Order by rate of return within industry	Rate of return and industry will be emphasized. Size, etc., will have less influence.

The selection of exceptions to report also causes presentation bias. In exception reporting, only those items that vary from an "acceptable level" by a fixed deviation are presented to the decision maker. The choice of a limit which selects an "exception" automatically introduces presentation bias. For instance, in an inventory system, exceptions are items whose inventory levels are too low. The limit may be set too narrow, so that many exceptions print out and the decision maker must search for the items needing immediate attention. On the other hand, it may be set too wide so that too many items with dangerously low inventory levels are assumed not to require attention and, therefore, are not listed.

A third example of potential presentation bias is the layout of graphics. Figure 7-6 shows the presentation of the same information by means of a line graph versus a report. The graphical presentation encourages the decision maker to look at relative trends while the report probably triggers a focus on total volumes and individual discrete amounts. It was pointed out in Chapter 5 that a positive relationship between use of graphics and decision quality has not been established, but there is evidence that graphics can introduce significant bias. Examples of ways in which bias is introduced are:

- Choice of scale. This affects the perception of differences in trend charts.
- Choice of graphic. Visual comparison of difference is difficult with bar charts, relatively easy with superimposed lines, and between these two for bar charts.
- Choice of size. By making a chart or graphic small, differences are minimized. If graphs to be compared are of different size, visual comparison is more difficult.
- Choice of color. Use of certain colors draws attention (when, for example, red is used to show deficits).

In the cases in which presentation bias is inadvertent or attributable to poor system design, such bias may be reduced by building flexibility into the reporting system and by allowing the recipient to select presentation format, etc. For instance, the decision maker should be allowed to choose different exception limits (including percentages and actual amounts), alternative groupings, alternative graphics, etc. On the other hand, such system flexibility may increase the discretionary judgment of the individual presenting the information and reduce objectivity in reporting (objectivity = a consistent bias).

USING CHARTS REDUCES DECISION TIME

According to one General Motors manager, meetings that used to last longer than two hours have been trimmed to 20 minutes due to the use of computer graphics. "In charts you see the relationship vividly displayed" says another user, noting that the interpretations of columns and

XYZ Corporation
Sales for Last 12 Months (000)
Period Ended September 1984

	Product 1	Product 2	Product 3	Total
October 1983	103	146	13	262
November 1983	110	150	12	272
December 1983	101	149	13	263
January 1984	96	158	14	268
February 1984	112	160	11	283
March 1984	88	151	12	251
April 1984	102	160	13	275
May 1984	114	162	13	289
June 1984	109	158	14	281
July 1984	116	166	12	294
August 1984	115	164	11	290
September 1984	110	168	12	290

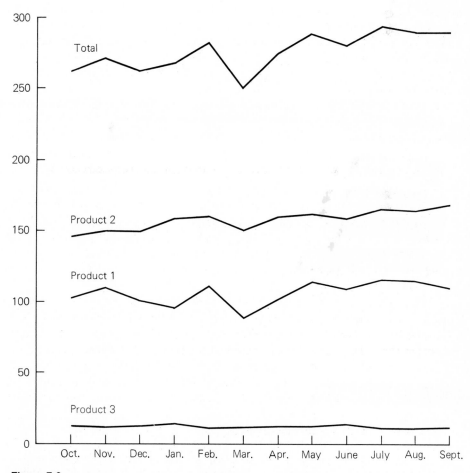

Figure 7-6
Comparison of graphical and report presentations of information.

rows of traditional reports are more difficult because they must be done mentally. In the past, of course, managers have had in-house artists make up charts and graphs, but the time required to produce them often made extensive use impractical. It used to take GM two years to manually produce maps with dots locating current and potential customers. Now Cadillac's computer link system allows them to access vehicle registration data. Consequently, they produce 75 maps a year showing locations of their dealers, their competitors, and high income households. This information has led to the relocation of over 100 Cadillac dealerships.
"The Spurt in Computer Graphics," *Business Week,* June 16, 1980.

QUALITY OF INFORMATION

Even if information is presented in such a way as to be transmitted efficiently and interpreted correctly, it may not be used effectively. The quality of information is determined by how it motivates human action and contributes to effective decision making.

The value of information may be theoretically determined by the value of a change in decision-making behavior. This concept will be discussed in the next section. In this section, some aspects of information quality in terms of the perceptions of the decision maker are discussed: utility of information, information satisfaction, and error and bias.

Utility of Information

Andrus[5] suggests that information may be evaluated in terms of *utilities* which, besides accuracy of the information, may facilitate or retard its use. He identifies four information utilities:

  1 Form utility. As the form of information more closely matches the requirements of the decision maker, its value increases.
  2 Time utility. Information has greater value to the decision maker if it is available when needed.
  3 Place utility (physical accessibility). Information has greater value if it can be accessed or delivered easily. Online systems maximize both time and place utility.
  4 Possession utility (organizational location). The possessor of information strongly affects its value by controlling its dissemination to others.

Andrus points out that information has a cost as well as a value associated with it, in terms of both accuracy and utilities. If the cost of acquiring information exceeds its value, there are two alternatives:

  1 Increase its value by increasing accuracy and/or increasing utilities
  2 Reduce its cost by decreasing accuracy and/or reducing utilities

Information Satisfaction

The contribution of a particular item of information to improvement in decision-making quality is difficult or impossible to determine in an organizational context. One

---

[5] Roman R. Andrus, "Approaches to Information Evaluation," *MSU Business Topics,* Summer 1971, pp. 40–46.

substitute measure for the utility of information in decision making is *information satisfaction*, the degree to which the decision maker is satisfied with the output of the formal information system. An approach to determining information satisfaction is provided by Seward;[6] based on a concept of Cyert and March.

If the decision maker perceives that a formal information system should be available to provide required information, he or she will first query that source. If the information is readily available, satisfaction with the information system is reinforced. If it is not, the decision maker must conduct an expanded search for the required information; frustration or dissatisfaction with the formal information system is reinforced. Information satisfaction can be used as one basis for evaluating formal information systems. Methods for measuring information satisfaction and important factors that affect it are discussed in Chapter 19.

Errors and Bias

Given a choice, managers have a strong preference for improvement in quality of information over an increase in quantity. Information varies in quality because of bias or errors. Bias, as already discussed, is caused by the ability of individuals to exercise discretion in information presentation. If the bias of the presenter is known to the receiver of the information, he or she can make adjustments. The problem is to detect the bias; the adjustment is generally fairly simple.

Error is a more serious problem because there is no simple adjustment for it. Errors may be a result of:

1 Incorrect data measurement and collection methods
2 Failure to follow correct processing procedures
3 Loss or nonprocessing of data
4 Wrong recording or correcting of data
5 Incorrect history (master) file (or use of wrong history file)
6 Mistakes in processing procedure (such as computer program errors)
7 Deliberate falsification

In most information systems, the receiver of information has no knowledge of either bias or errors that may affect its quality. The measurement processes which produce reports and the precision of data in the reports imply an underlying accuracy that is not warranted. For example, an inventory report may indicate that there are 347 widgets in stock. However, this figure is probably based on a perpetual, book inventory; various errors in recording inventory issues, receipts, etc., mean that in a significant number of cases there is small error, and in a few cases, large error. This is the reason for periodic physical counts to correct the book inventory.

The difficulties due to bias may be handled in information processing by procedures

---

[6] Henry H. Seward, "Evaluating Information Systems," in F. W. McFarlan and R. L. Nolan (eds.), *Information Systems Handbook*, Dow Jones-Richard D. Irwin, Homewood, IL, 1975.

[7] Richard Cyert and James March, *A Behavioral Theory of the Firm*, Prentice-Hall, Englewood Cliffs, NJ, 1963, p. 126.

to detect and measure bias and to adjust for it. The difficulties with errors may be overcome by:

1 Internal controls to detect errors
2 Internal and external auditing
3 Addition of ''confidence limits'' to data
4 User instruction in measurement and processing procedures, so users can evaluate possible errors

There is a difference in the effect of the first two and the last two error remedies. The last two remedies attempt to provide the user with confidence limits, whereas the first two methods attempt to reduce the uncertainty about the data and therefore increase the information content. Internal controls and auditing can be thought of in this context as adding value to the information being provided by the information system by reducing the uncertainty about the existence of most errors.

AN ERROR CAUSES PROBLEMS AND LOSSES

The following quotation is an excerpt from a letter from a stock broker to clients eight days after informing them that one of their stocks had gone bankrupt.

As you know, as of July 1, 1981, your account held securities of Transcontinental Energy Corporation, a Delaware corporation. On July 8, 1981, we inadvertently mailed to you a copy of a bankruptcy court document with reference to a different corporation with the same name but a different state of incorporation; Transcontinental Energy Corporation, a Nevada corporation.

Transcontinental Energy Corporation, a Delaware corporation, is not involved in bankruptcy proceedings.

Transcontinental Energy Corporation of Delaware had recently changed its name from Continental Oil Corporation. In updating our files, certain of our customers' records of the two corporations were erroneously merged for a period of several days, during which the mailing was prepared. Please be assured that our records have been corrected.

We apologize for this error and regret any inconvenience to you or to Transcontinental Energy Corporation, a Delaware corporation.

During the same period the account statements that were sent out showed that the current value of the stock was N.A. (Not Available), thereby lowering the reported values of the portfolios which held it.

VALUE OF INFORMATION IN DECISION MAKING

Decision theory provides approaches for making decisions under certainty, risk, and uncertainty, as discussed in Chapter 6. Decision making under certainty assumes perfect information as to outcomes; risk assumes information as to the probability of each outcome but not which outcome will occur in any given case; and uncertainty assumes a knowledge of possible outcomes but no information as to probabilities. A value of information can be computed for decisions which fit these frameworks of analysis.

In decision theory, the value of information is the value of the change in decision behavior caused by the information less the cost of obtaining the information.[8] In other

---

[8] For a rather complete exposition on this concept, see James C. Emery, *Organizational Planning and Control Systems*, Macmillan, New York, 1969, Chapter 4.

words, given a set of possible decisions, a decision maker will select one on the basis of the information at hand. If new information causes a different decision to be made, the value of the new information is the difference in value between the outcome of the old decision and that of the new decision, less the cost of obtaining the new information. If new information does not cause a different decision to be made the value of the new information is zero.

Cost avoidance

Value of Perfect Information

A very simple example will illustrate the value of perfect information in a decision with only one future condition or state of nature. Assume that there are only three alternatives called A, B, and C. The decision maker, on the basis of prior knowledge (imperfect information), estimates that the outcome (payoff) from A will be $20, B $30, and C $15, and is therefore ready to choose B. Perfect information is then provided which establishes without doubt that the payoff of C is $30 and the payoff from B is only $22. The information causes the decision maker to select C instead of B, thereby increasing the payoff from $22 to $30. The value of the perfect information is therefore $8 minus the cost of obtaining it.

Payoff matrix #1			Payoff matrix #2		
A	20		A	20	
B	30	Decision = B	B	22	Decision = C
C	15		C	30	

The value of perfect information is computed as the difference between the optimal policy without perfect information and the optimal policy with perfect information. The value of perfect information in this example involves only one state of nature, so that once an alternative is chosen, the choice is the one that has the highest outcome.

Suppose that there are two conditions or states of nature, x_1 and x_2 (e.g., corresponding to government contract obtained (x_1) and government contract not obtained (x_2)). Each of these has a probability attached to it by the decision maker; assume .60 for x_1 and .40 for x_2. The payoff matrix might then appears as follows:

	x_1	x_2	
	Probabilities		
Strategies	.60	.40	Expected value
A	20	18	A = $19.20
B	30	0	B = $18.00
C	15	8	C = $12.20

This says that if A is chosen and x_1 (contract received) occurs, the payoff will be $20; if A is chosen and x_2 occurs, the payoff is $18. The expected value or average payoff is the sum of the payoff for each decision times the probabilities for each outcome. The expected value for decision strategy A is .60 (20) + .40 (18) = $19.20.

The value of information for more than one condition is the difference between the maximum value in the absence of additional information and the maximum expected value with additional information, minus the cost of obtaining it. Note that the maximum expected value can change by a change either in the probabilities for the conditions x_1 and x_2 or in the payoffs associated with them.

The payoff matrix presented in Chapter 6 for the decision to rebuild, refurbish, or do nothing to a roadside restaurant will be used to further illustrate the concept of perfect information with more than one condition (Figure 7-7). The optimal policy is to refurbish the restaurant because that policy has the highest expected value. In other words, if the investor had many investments with exactly the same decisions to be made, the average result of always choosing "refurbish" would be $1,700 per decision. Not knowing which event will occur, the policy of choosing "refurbish" provides the highest results on the average.

Policy	Computation of expected value	Expected value
Do nothing	2(.50) + 0(.20) + −1 (.30) =	.70 ($700)
Refurbish	4(.50) + 3(.20) + −3 (.30) =	1.70($1,700)
Rebuild	7(.50) + 2(.20) + −10 (.20) =	.90 ($900)

If information could be obtained on the actual event to occur in each case, the investor would not choose "refurbish" in every case, but would choose the optimal decision for the event that is certain to happen. Since the different states of nature or events occur with the frequency of .50, .20, and .30, the average result when the condition is known and all decisions are optimal is as follows:

Condition	Optimal strategy	Payoff	Percentage of occurrences	Average payoff from optimal decision
Same traffic and competition	Rebuild	$7,000	.50	$3,500
New competitor	Refurbish	$3,000	.20	$ 600
Highway rerouting	Do nothing	−$1,000	.30	−$ 300
		Expected payoff with perfect information =		$3,800

The average or expected payoff per decision with perfect information as to each condition is $3,800, whereas the maximum expected value without the knowledge of the future condition other than its probability is $1,700. The difference of $2,100 ($3,800 − $1,700) is the expected value of perfect information. In other words, a decision maker could pay up to $2,100 for information which identified with perfect foresight the event or condition affecting this decision.

The value of perfect information may also be defined as the expected value of opportunity losses. In other words, there is a difference between the optimal, perfect-foresight policy and the other strategies for a given event. The difference from not taking the optimal decision is the opportunity loss. The matrix of opportunity losses is given by

Strategies	Conditions or events (states of nature) with probability of occurrence		
	Same .50	New competitor .20	Highway rerouting .30
Do nothing	2	0	− 1
Refurbish	4	3	− 3
Rebuild	7	2	−10

Figure 7-7
Payoff matrix for owner of quick-service restaurant (payoffs in thousands of dollars) (same as Figure 6-3).

Figure 7-8. Note that this is the same as the regret matrix in Chapter 6. The expected value of any strategy under risk is the expected value of the optimal set of decisions under certainty less the expected opportunity losses. As presented in Chapter 6, the opportunity loss is the difference between the best decision and the decision being evaluated. The opportunity loss for ''refurbish'' for the ''same'' future condition is the difference of 3 between the highest payoff of 7 for rebuild and the payoff of 4 for refurbish. The expected opportunity loss for refurbish is thus $(.50)(.3) + (.20)(0) + (.30)(.20) =$ $2,100, which is the same as the value of perfect information. By use of these figures, the expected value of the optimal policy under risk is obtained as follows:

Expected value under certainty	$3,800
Expected opportunity loss (same as value of information)	−2,100
Expected value of optimal policy under risk	1,700

Almost no decisions are made with perfect information because obtaining it would require being able to foresee or control future events. The concept of the value of perfect information is useful, however, because it demonstrates how information has value as it

Strategies	Condition, event, or state		
	Same	New competitor	Highway rerouting
Do nothing	5	3*	0
Refurbish	3	0	2
Rebuild	0	1	9

*For a new competitor event, a do nothing strategy is 3 worse than the optimal strategy of refurbish.

Figure 7-8
Matrix of opportunity losses (in thousands of dollars) (based on Figure 7-7).

influences (i.e., changes) decisions. The discussion explains why information from market research can be assigned a value. Most such research is imperfect information but similar principles (beyond the scope of this chapter) can be applied. The quantitative approach suggests the value of searching for better information, but decisions are usually made without the "right" information. Some reasons[9] are:

1 The needed information is unavailable.
2 The effort to acquire the information is too great or too costly.
3 There is no knowledge of the availability of the information.
4 The information is not available in the form needed.

INFORMATION FOR SHOPPING

Polls by Rowe Furniture Corporation show customers desire clearer and more honest information about home furnishings. They also need reasonable and believable assurances in making their purchases. Their shopping methods are changing due to the rising cost of gasoline and the dwindling shopping time among women who have entered the work force. Nonstore methods such as catalog shopping have become important time-saving conveniences.

Teleshopping and computerization are two methods that may become more widespread for furniture shopping. Teleshopping includes the present use of toll-free numbers and credit card combinations. It could eventually mean keying questions in a home computer and getting a response on a television screen (as a replacement for catalogs). Computers can also be used to assist in furniture selection within a store. An entire room can be designed by computer selection and then shown to the customer from several angles including colors. Computers are also being used to calculate the correct stereo equipment required for any given room and to place it properly for optimum effect.

"Computer Technology Enters Interior Design Through Home Communications," *Christian Science Monitor*, July 20, 1981.

Value of Information and Sensitivity Analysis

Sensitivity analysis consists of analytical procedures to determine the degree of impact on a solution algorithm or model of changes in one or more variables. The following questions illustrate the reasons for sensitivity analysis:

- What is the effect on profit of a 10 percent increase in sales or a 10 percent decrease in sales (from the best estimate)?
- What is the effect on rate of return from extending the useful life to 12 years instead of 10?
- Will the project still be justified if costs increase 10 percent?

Sensitivity analysis can be used to determine the changes in such factors as estimated costs, revenues, and obsolescence that are large enough to cause a change in a decision. In doing so, it identifies variables for which more information will be valuable.

---

[9] Rudolf E. Hirsch, "The Value of Information," *The Journal of Accountancy*, 125:6, June 1968, pp. 41–45.

- If the decision is not sensitive to the value of a variable over a wide range of values, additional information on the future value of the variable (if it is already within the decision range) will have no effect on the decision (have no value).
- If the decision is highly sensitive to changes in the future value of a variable, sensitivity analysis also indicates the degree of sensitivity. The effect of the variable on decision making shows the value of more information to reduce uncertainty as to the future value of the variable.

THE RATIO OF DATA DIFFICULT TO ESTIMATE

The XYZ Company was designing a supplies reordering system using a traditional economic order quantity formula for computing a suggested order quantity. The formula is:

$$EOQ = \sqrt{\frac{24MP}{UH}}$$

where EOQ is in units to reorder
- M = monthly usage in units
- P = cost of placing an order
- U = cost per unit
- H = cost of holding inventory expressed as a yearly percentage of inventory value

In examining the formula, the analyst doing the application observed that there were two costs to be estimated; all other variables were specific to the item being analyzed. It is difficult to estimate with any accuracy a cost of placing an order and also difficult to estimate the cost of holding inventory. In fact, it is the ratio of ordering cost to holding cost that affects the order quantity. Using a typical item with a monthly usage of 25 and a cost of $5, the analyst constructed a graph to show the effect (sensitivity) on the order quantity of the estimated cost of ordering (from $10 to $15) and the cost of holding (from 18 to 24 percent). The graph, shown in Figure 7-9, was used to obtain a decision from executives as to the ratio to include in the formula.

VALUE OF INFORMATION OTHER THAN IN A DECISION

If the value of information were based only on identified decisions, much of the data that organizations and individuals prepare would not have value. Since the market for information suggests that it does have value, there must be other bases for the value of information. Some other reasons for value of information are motivation, model building, and background building.

Motivation

Some information is motivational; it provides the persons receiving the information with a report on how well they are doing. This feedback information may motivate decisions, but its connection is often indirect. The information may reinforce an existing understanding or model of the organization. It may provide comforting confirmation that results are within allowable limits. It also aids in learning as individuals receive feedback on the consequences of actions.

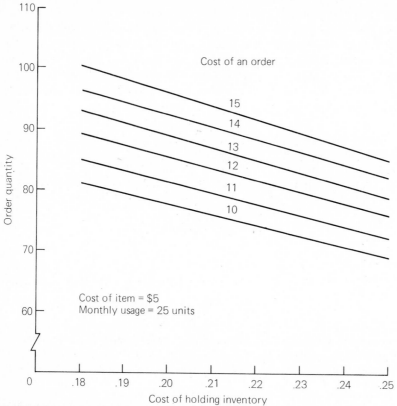

Figure 7-9
Sensitivity analysis for order quantity for typical item.

Model Building

The management and operation of an enterprise function with models of the enterprise within the minds of the managers and operations personnel. The models may be simple or complex, correct or incorrect, etc. Information that is received by these individuals may result in change or reinforcement in their models. This process is a form of organizational learning and expertise building. Since the models are used in problem finding to identify problems, a change in the models will have an influence on identification of problems.

Background Building

In decision theory, the value of information is the value of the change in decision behavior (less its cost), but the information has value only to those who have the background knowledge to use it in a decision. The most qualified person generally uses information most effectively but may need less information since experience has already reduced uncertainty when compared with the less-experienced decision maker. Thus, the more experienced decision maker may make the same decision for less cost, or a better decision for the same cost, as the less experienced person.

The value of the specific information utilized in a decision cannot be easily separated from the accumulated knowledge of the decision maker. In other words, much of the knowledge that individuals accumulate and store (or internalize) is not earmarked for any particular decision or problem. A set of accumulated knowledge allows a person to make a better decision, or the same decision at less immediate cost, than one who lacks this expertise. An imperfect market value of expert information is reflected in the cost of hiring the expert to give advice.

Much of the success of problem finding and problem formulation is dependent on the person having a rich background of knowledge from which analogies, similar situations, problem solutions, and models may be drawn. Background building allows construction of this background knowledge. It is expected to have future use rather than immediate use. It can be far removed from the current problem environment. This argues for the value of a broad education.

AGE OF INFORMATION

This section explores the attribute of age of information with respect to information contained in periodic reports,[10] such as the monthly operating report and the statement of financial position at the end of a period. Two types of data are defined:

1 *Condition data* which pertains to a point in time such as December 31. An example is the inventory at 12/31/84 as reported on the balance sheet.

2 *Operating data* which reflects changes over a period of time. Examples are inventory used during a month or sales for a week.

An *information interval* (i) is defined as the interval between reports. For weekly reports, the information interval is one week; for monthly reports, one month. The *processing delay* (d) is defined as the processing delay between the end of the information interval and the issuance of the report for use. By use of these two variables, the maximum, average, and minimum age of information in management reports is defined as follows and in Figure 7-10:

	Condition information	Operating information
Maximum age	$d + i$	$d + 1\ 1/2\ i$
Average age	$d + 1/2\ i$	$d + i$
Minimum age	d	$d + 1/2\ i$

where i = information interval between reports

$\quad\ d$ = processing delay

For condition information the minimum age is the processing delay. For example, if the processing delay is five days, the inventory figure for September 15 will be at least

[10] This section is based on an article by Robert H. Gregory and Thomas V. V. Atwater, Jr., "Cost of Value of Management as Functions of Age," *Accounting Research*, 8:1, January 1957, pp. 42–70. (The journal is no longer published.)

five days old before it is received on September 20. If inventory reports are issued weekly ($i = 7$ days), the age of the information on hand just prior to receiving a new report is $7 + 5$ days. The average age of the report during the period of its use is $5 + (7/2) = 8\ 1/2$ days ($d + 1/2i$).

The operating information is accumulated over a period of time. The average age of operating information accumulated during an interval is therefore one-half the interval. Since it will be d days (the processing delay) after the end of the period until the information is available, the minimum age is $d + 1/2i$. The age of operating data under these assumptions is always half an interval greater than the age of condition information.

The age of information available to management can be altered by changing i, d, or both. In practice, d depends somewhat on the type of processing used: batch or online. For batch processing, a significant part of the processing delay is the batch preparation time, the period during which a batch is prepared for processing. It may be possible to

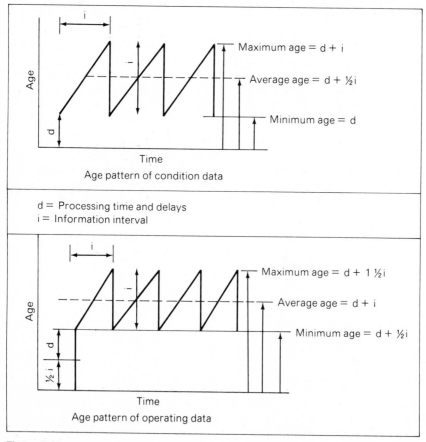

Figure 7-10
Patterns for age of information. (Adapted from Robert H. Gregory and Thomas V. V. Atwater, Jr., "Cost and Value of Management Information as Functions of Age," *Accounting Research*, 8:1, January 1957, pp. 49, 51.)

obtain condition data very quickly after the batch run, but it is already out of date; i.e., it has an age equal to the processing delay to prepare and run the batch. For inquiry rather than regular reports, the information interval (i) is the batch updating interval during which a batch is accumulated (but not prepared for running). If online inquiry is used to access condition data prepared by batch processing, the average age will be one-half the batch interval (assuming no online inquiry processing delay). A system of immediate access to condition data in a database updated weekly, when compared to batch processing of inquiries with one day turnaround, reduces average age of retieval data from 4 ½ days to 3 ½ days.

For online processing, data is processed as received, so that the processing delay is zero. An inquiry for condition data can be processed with very little delay so that i is also very small. Technically, the system should allow i to be varied for operating data and allow condition data to be available at any point in time, subject only to very small processing delays. However, there is some tendency to continue to use traditional intervals of week, month, and quarter.

The impacts of both the information interval and the processing delay are important for information system design. Much attention has been focused on the minimum age of information, but the average age is probably more significant. Computer data processing has concentrated to a great extent on reducing the processing delay by online processing, while not much emphasis has been placed on the impact of the information interval. Moreover, flexible online inquiry provides the capability to vary information intervals to fit particular circumstances.

THE MACHINE GIVES BETTER THAN IT TAKES

A Citibank official was asked why the lines seemed to form at the automated teller machines even when the people-staffed windows were open. "Our research shows people prefer to deal with the automated teller machines when they are withdrawing money," he answered. He also observed that the withdrawals at the machine are posted immediately whereas withdrawals from a teller and deposits to either a machine or a teller are not posted until a batch processing run each night. Customers received a report of their current, updated balance with each machine withdrawal (deposits made at the machine are not handled until later). With teller withdrawal, there is no such report.

The average information interval and processing delay for a machine withdrawal are therefore zero; a teller withdrawal results in an average condition age based on an information interval of 15 days (with monthly statements) plus several days processing delay.

APPLICATION OF INFORMATION CONCEPTS TO INFORMATION SYSTEM DESIGN

The mathematics of information theory has been applied to the design of communication systems. The insights provided by the theory are useful in design:

1 Information has surprise value.
2 Information reduces uncertainty.
3 Redundancy is useful for error control of communication.
4 Information only has value if it changes a decision.
5 Not all data that is communicated has information value.

In decision theory, information is associated with uncertainty because there is a choice to be made and the correct choice is uncertain. The reason for obtaining information is to reduce uncertainty so the correct choice can be made. If there were no uncertainty, there would be no need for information to influence the choice. Information received will modify the choice by altering the subjective estimate of the probability of success. The decision theory approach focuses the attention of the information system designer not only on the value of information in decision making but also on the fact that the cost of obtaining more information may not be worthwhile.

Much data is received and stored without reference to decisions being made. Mathematical information theory has no explanation for data not related to a choice. Two views are possible: (1) there is no information content until there is a choice, or (2) there is information content if there is expected use for potential choice. The second view is close to the information system view that information is data that is meaningful to the recipient and is of real or perceived value in current or prospective decisions. Sensitivity analysis is a practical procedure for identifying the value of more information for a particular variable. The value of background information and experience in experts as compared to novices supports the concept that information is valuable only to those who have the expertise to use it. Systems that demonstrate expertise, called expert systems, are described in Chapter 12.

The existence of noise is explicitly defined in communication theory. Redundancy is used to ensure correct receipt of the transmitted message. In management information systems, there is substantial noise due to unknown but differing backgrounds of humans, differing frames of reference, varying prejudices, varying level of attention, physical differences in ability to hear and see, and other random causes. Redundancy can be effectively used to overcome noise and improve the probability of messages being received and interpreted correctly.

Concepts of information presentation suggest two ways to improve sending and receiving efficiency, both of which are relevant to the design of information systems— summarization and message routing. Concepts of information content and distribution discretion are reflected in introduction of delays, message modification or filtering, inference, and presentation bias. Both the system designer and the decision maker should be especially aware of bias in perception, particularly since systems can be designed to provide alternative forms of presentation.

The quality of information received is not directly measurable. However, the decision maker's perceptions of quality, such as information satisfaction, can provide useful guidelines to the designer in "fine-tuning" a system to meet information requirements in an efficient manner.

The idea that information has value only in that it alters a decision provides a useful guideline for parsimony of information. A common mistake in information system design is to produce volumes of data in the form of reports because they are easy to produce. In many cases, the actual value of the additional information is zero. On the other hand, information systems may be designed to accumulate data for later utilization in decisions; the value of the information cannot be determined at the time it is collected and stored. These are both important factors in the process of cost justifying information system applications for storage and retrieval of data.

The concepts relating to age of information introduce the idea of condition data measured at a point in time and operating data for a period of time. The concepts of an information interval plus a processing delay are important to information system design because the age of information is related to both factors and not just to the processing delay. The concept of information interval is also useful in information system design of flexible reporting systems.

SUMMARY

This chapter has been devoted to exploring concepts of information. Information theory is more properly termed the mathematical theory of communication, but it does provide some useful insights for management information systems. It emphasizes the fact that the need for information arises from uncertainty and choice, and the role of information is to reduce uncertainty.

Concepts of information presentation were explained in terms of sending or receiving efficiency and content or distribution discretion. Efficiency methods are message summarization and routing. Methods for content or distribution discretion are delay, modification or filtering, inference, and presentation bias. Some user-defined measures of information quality, information utilities and information satisfaction, were described. Methods for designing information systems to improve information quality by detecting and adjusting for bias and controlling for errors were discussed.

The decision theory approach to measuring the value of information was discussed. When payoff matrices are available, the expected value of perfect information can be computed. The concepts provide insight, but in practice the value of information is difficult to determine at the time a decision is made. Sensitivity analysis may be used to identify value of additional information about decision-sensitive variables.

Information value also can be traced to data items that have value in motivation, model building, and background building. These are expected to affect future decision and action, but the relationship may be undefined.

The concepts of age of information point out the relationship of information interval, condition or operating data, and the processing delay in determining the age of information.

MINICASES

1 INCREASING COMMUNICATIONS CHANNELS

"What is the use of sending 6.3 million bits of information from one place to another (in one second), if we can't do anything with them when they get there?" asked one executive from a company considering the use of Satellite Business Systems (SBS). The company provides users with a big pipeline for transmitting large quantities of data, voice, and video information from one dedicated satellite ground station to another, as an alternative to land-based lines originally developed for voice communications. Its president, Robert C. Hall, sees SBS's slow growth as a problem of introducing a new product. "We think we've got a headstart. Many advanced applications have not been developed because no network has been available. We plan to provide that network and we're not a bit concerned that we're limited to a few customers at present."

One customer is ISA Communications Services Inc., which resells the service to smaller companies. Their customers include insurance companies that need communications links for claims transfer between their headquarters and their databases in other cities. SBS has also fostered AM International's efforts to develop an extremely high speed communication copier system.

SBS will expand its product offerings to other forms of communication. Since they also have satellite channels for voice and video transmission, they are finding customers for these channels. Telephone services are projected to account for 40 percent of their 1984 revenue or $325 million. The three SBS owners (IBM, Aetna Life and Casualty, and Comsat General Corp.) will supply another 40 percent.

An official of AT&T, which became SBS's primary competition when they entered voice communications, commented, "SBS is simply doing what other specialized communications common carriers have done before them. It is going after the MTS and WATS long-distance telephone services. After all, that's where the money is."

"SBS Casts a Wider Customer Net," *Business Week*, July 21, 1980, p. 155.

Questions

a Why do you think the demand for SBS data communications services has not been as great as they had predicted?

b What changes in organizational operations could occur because of the availability of such network services?

2 ENTREPRENEURIAL SPIRIT

Almost any IBM employee can tell you a story about personally solving a customer's problem. Customer service is a dominant value in IBM's organizational culture. Top managers at IBM spend a minimum of 30 days a year conferring with their best customers. IBM leaves managers in staff positions for no more than three years because managers thus removed from the mainstream do not meet customers regularly. IBM also assigns assistants to senior managers of customers. Their function is to process customer complaints within 24 hours.

IBM finds new ideas and then explores them through its Fellows Program. This group maintains communications with thousands of IBM technical people. The final decision to adopt a product is not made on market potential only, however; the product must find a champion among management. This entrepreneurial spirit once caused expensive difficulties when promises for one IBM product outran their ability to deliver. IBM's reaction was to set up stringent checks and balances to prevent recurrences. IBM president Frank T. Cary soon realized that the constraints would also impede new systems development by preventing the kind of thinking that leads to new ventures. He removed the constraints.

Feedback on the success of new products also comes from customers. Management's compensation is partially based on the results of consumer satisfaction surveys.

"Putting Excellence into Management," *Business Week*, July 21, 1980, p. 196.

Questions

a How is information about new products gathered at IBM?

b How is this information disseminated throughout the organization? What methods are used to alter its presentation?

c How is the value of this information determined?

EXERCISES

1 The code of Paul Revere was "One if by land and two if by sea." Changing the conditions slightly, assume that Paul Revere had lanterns which could display either red *or* green. He would then have used only one lantern with the instruction "Red if by land and green if by sea." If the British could have taken *many* routes, tell how many lanterns (each with red and green) Paul Revere would have needed to signal the route taken if there were:
  a 4 routes
  b 20 routes
  c 30 routes

2 Assume the same facts as in question 1 but that Paul Revere and the receiver agree to include some redundancy in the message so that the receiver could make sure he or she has received it properly. Indicate how an additional lantern could serve this purpose. (Hint: This can be a parity type of code.)

3 Assume a set of six possible messages identified by the letters A, B, C, D, E, and F.
  a Assuming that the six messages are equally probable, use the formula $H = \log_2 n$ to determine the average information required. The $\log_2$ for 1 to 8 are given below for your use.

No.	log$_2$	No.	log$_2$
1	0.2	5	2.32
2	1	6	2.58
3	1.585	7	2.81
4	2.0	8	3.0

  b Assume that the probabilities of the different messages are not the same. Apply the formula for unequal probabilities to compute the average information required to identify the messages:

$$I = -\sum_{i=1}^{n} p_i \log_2 p_i$$

Message	Probability	Log$_2$
A	.10	−3.32
B	.25	−2.00
C	.40	−1.32
D	.20	−2.32
E	.03	−5.06
F	.02	−5.64

Account for differences between the answer obtained for **a** and the answer in **b**.

4 Define the following terms as used in information theory:
  a Information
  b Channel
  c Noise
  d Redundancy

5 Explain how information reduces uncertainty.

6 How can a transmission of a set of random digits contain more information than a transmission of text from a book?

7 A message consisting of random alphabetic characters contains more information than an English text because the set of random characters is completely unpredictable (I = 4.75) and the English text is somewhat predictable. Shannon estimated that the average number of bits required to encode English text would average only one bit per letter if each code was based on groups of letters rather than single letters. Explain Shannon's estimate.

8 Assume a parlor game in which you are trying to guess the content of a short English language sentence. The sentence is not gibberish but neither is it a well-known sentence. Just pick sentences from a textbook or a novel. You are allowed to ask questions that can be answered with only "yes" or "no." For **a** and **b** the letters should be mixed up rather than being asked in word order. Play the game with three different strategies:

   a Attempt to learn each letter without regard to the context. In effect, assume that the letters are random and all occur with the same probability. (Hint: Ask questions such as "Is the letter before M and after G?")

   b Assume that the letters occur randomly but with the probability found in English given below. Alter the questioning to take this into account.

		Total
Over 8%	Space, E	29%
5 to 8%	A, I, N, O, S, T	38%
3 to 4.9%	D, H, L, R	16%
Less than 3%	15 others	17%

   c Assume the frequencies in **b** above plus a meaningful text.

    (1) Write down the questions you should ask (in order of use) for each of **a**, **b**, and **c**.

    (2) Keep statistics on the number of questions required to obtain an answer.

    (3) What is the theoretical average number of questions for **a** and **b** assuming that probabilities and logs are:

	Probability	$\log_2$
Space	.18	−2.5
E	.10	−3.3
A, I, N, O, S, T	.07 each	−3.8
D, H, L, R	.04 each	−4.7
Others	.01 each	−6.6

9 The game of Twenty Questions is based on "yes" and "no" answers. Assuming equal probability, how many different items can there be for which 20 questions will allow one of the items to be identified?

10 Compute redundancy in the following cases:

   a An 8-bit code is used to encode 58 alphanumerics ($\log_2 58 = 5.86$).

   b A 3-bit code is used to encode five possibilities with the following probabilities. The logs of the probabilities are also given.

Outcome	p	$\log_2 p$
A	.10	−3.32
B	.25	−2.00
C	.40	−1.32
D	.15	−2.74
E	.10	−3.32

11 The double-entry system of accounting records the dual effect of transactions. It is said to be quite redundant. If it is really redundant, what kind of system performance would be expected with regard to error detection and ability to reconstruct results from partial records? How do the expected characteristics compare with actual characteristics of accounting?

12 What are the advantages and disadvantages of the following activities associated with distribution of information across departments and upwards in the organizational hierarchy?

a Message summarization
b Message routing
c Message delay
d Message modification

13 A detailed examination was made of 1,000 credit histories. The analysis of the data is reported to management in the following statements: "There is a 95 percent probability of a credit applicant becoming a delinquent account if he receives less than a score of 50 on the credit application rating. Only 1 percent of those scoring 64 or above become delinquent." Explain why these inferences constitute uncertainty absorption.

14 A decision maker has four alternatives with payoffs and estimates as follows. Additional information changes the estimated payoffs. What is the value of the information?

Alternative	Payoff	Revised payoff
S	7	18
T	19	19
R	12	15
N	13	16

15 A decision maker has the following prior probabilities and payoffs:

Action	Probability of success	Payoff if successful
Z	.30	$100
Y	.10	350
X	.20	200
W	.40	150

The decision rule followed by the decision maker is to choose the action with the highest expected value. The decision maker receives a message revising the probabilities or payoffs. What is the value of the information in each of the following messages?

a $Z = .50$; $Y = .10$; $X = .15$; $W = .25$; payoff the same.
b Payoff $Z = 200$; $Y = 150$; $X = 200$; $W = 80$; probabilities the same as problem.
c Payoff $Z = 150$; $Y = 525$; $X = 300$; $W = 225$; probabilities the same as problem.

16 A decision maker has four alternatives which have varying payoffs based on different conditions that may occur.

	Conditions			
	1	2	3	4
	Probabilities			
Alternatives	.10	.30	.25	.35
B	15	8	-3	5
L	10	10	-5	6
M	12	5	-10	7
P	6	7	-1	5

a Calculate expected value.
b Calculate value of perfect information.
c Show that the expected value is equal to the expected value with perfect information less the opportunities lost.

17 The principle of information hiding (used in programming) is that modules should be written as if they did not have knowledge of some parameters that the programmer really knows when writing the modules. The result is more independent modules not affected by changes in other modules. Can you think of instances in which "hiding information" will cause better decisions to be made? Explain how making reservations for the same travel with different carriers may benefit from information hiding.

18 How can sensitivity analysis aid in identifying the value of more information?

19 What assumption about flow of data is necessary to have the age of operating data equal $\frac{1}{2}i$ at the end of the information interval?

20 Write formulas for minimum, average, and maximum age of inquiry data obtained from a file that is updated by periodic batch processing. The inquiry may specify either operating or condition data and may specify the information interval for operating data.

21 How does online updating affect age of information for monthly reports?

22 Explain how the concepts of this chapter apply to or explain the following situations:
   a A decision maker who says, "Don't bother me with the facts; my mind is made up."
   b A decision maker who will not make a decision without more information.
   c The president of a company who feels the need to go out and mingle with customers and suppliers in order to make good decisions.
   d The president who complains that he is receiving much data from his government intelligence office which does not make sense; the data does not seem to apply to him and his company.

23 Using the nondecision value of information, specify the value of the following:
   a A performance report that establishes how well you are doing.
   b A performance variance report that highlights areas of concern.
   c A report on international production trends.

24 Mock (see bibliography) suggests that information systems should be designed such that "learned" views-of-the-world and their underlying assumptions are continually challenged (p. 778). What information would do this? How does it fit into the value of information?

25 If information value comes from providing data for building an enterprise model and a background model within a manager's mind, the value of the information decreases as the model and backgrounds are built. If true, what implications does it have for information systems?

SELECTED REFERENCES

Bello, Francis: "The Information Theory," *Fortune*, 48:6, December 1953, pp. 136–141.

Cherry, Colin: *On Human Communication*, MIT Press, Cambridge, 1957. Discusses information concepts in broader context.

Emery, James C.: *Organizational Planning and Control Systems*, Macmillan, New York, 1969.

Feltham, Gerald A.: "The Value of Information," *The Accounting Review*, October 1968, pp. 684–696.

Feltham, Gerald A., and Joel S. Demski: "The Use of Models in Information Evaluation," *The Accounting Review*, October 1970, pp. 623–640.

Gilbert, E. N.: "Information Theory after Eighteen Years," *Science*, 152, April 1966, pp. 320ff.

Huber, George: "Organizational Information Systems: Determinants of Their Performance and Behavior," *Management Science*, 28:2, February 1982, pp. 138–155.

Jackson, Barbara Bund: *The Value of Information: Course Moduli*, The Division of Research, Harvard Business School, Cambridge, 1979.

Levitan, Karen B.: "Information Resources as 'Goods' in the Life Cycle of Information Production," *Journal of the American Society for Information Science*, 33:1, January 1982, pp. 44–54.

Mock, Theodore J.: "Concepts of Information Value and Accounting," *The Accounting Review*, October 1971, pp. 765–778.

Raisbeck, Gordon: *Information Theory*, MIT Press, Cambridge, 1964. Good, short coverage. Moderately mathematical.

Shannon, Claude E., and Warren Weaver: *The Mathematical Theory of Communication*, University of Illinois Press, Urbana, 1962.

Taylor, Robert J.: "Value-Added Processes in the Information Life Cycle," *Journal of the American Society for Information Science,* September 1982, pp. 341–346.

Weiner, Norbert: *Cybernetics, or Control and Communication in the Animal and the Machine*, Wiley, New York, 1948.

West, Charles K.: *The Social and Psychological Distortion of Information*, Nelson-Hall, Chicago, 1981. Focuses on the social psychology of the distortion of information.

HUMANS AS
INFORMATION PROCESSORS

Probably the most critical component of a management information system is the interface between the system and its users. For the user, the system-user interface is the only part of the system which is meaningful; the rest is invisible. Many systems which support planning and decision making (to be discussed in Chapter 12) require that the decision maker have an interactive dialogue with the system. Many clerical functions are performed in a manner dictated by computer requirements. Since the design of a system-user interface is thus critical to good information system design, an understanding of humans as information processors will provide useful guidance for interface design.

This chapter describes both a general model and the Newell-Simon model of the human as an information processor. It describes some tentative limits on human information processing and some of the effects of information on human performance. It also describes concepts and research from other fields, such as cognition theory and industrial psychology, that help explain how humans process information and how this affects information system design. Chapter 17 will provide specific guidelines for user interface design based on the concepts in this chapter.

GENERAL MODEL OF THE HUMAN AS AN INFORMATION PROCESSOR

A simple model of the human as an information processor consists of sensory receptors (eyes, ears, nose, etc.) that pick up signals and transmit them to the processing unit (brain with storage). The results of the processing are output responses (physical, spoken, written, etc.). This model is diagrammed in Figure 8-1.

The capacity of the human to accept inputs and produce outputs (responses) is limited. When the human capacity for processing information is surpassed, information overload can cause the response rate to decrease and performance is degraded. A simple experiment of human ability to respond to musical tones resulted in performance shown in Figure 8-2. Note that up to the information overload point, each input resulted in an output. For example, 10 inputs resulted in 10 outputs during the time allowed. When overload was reached, performance began to decrease. If the overload point, for example, was 40 inputs (with 40 outputs), then 45 inputs resulted in fewer than 45 outputs. In assessing input overload, it is important to keep in mind the fact that humans have multiple input channels and these can operate together (sight, hearing, touch, etc.) to increase input capacity.

The world provides more input than the human processing system is able to accept. In order to prevent information overload, the human reduces input to a manageable quantity by a filtering or selection process in which some inputs are blocked and prevented from

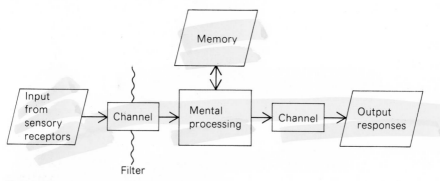

Figure 8-1
Model of a human as information processor.

entering processing (Figure 8-3). The filter may result from:

1 Frame of reference of the individual, based on prior knowledge and experience
2 Normal decision procedure
3 Decision making under stress

Individuals establish filters based on their experience, background, customs, etc. Decision procedures identify relevant data and therefore provide a filter to screen factors considered unnecessary to the decision. The filtering mechanism may be changed by decision-making stress. The stress of making decisions under time pressure will cause filtering to increase, thereby reducing the amount of data to be processed by the decision maker. For example, a production line supervisor will, during a period of crisis and stress, concentrate on the most important problems and will not accept stimuli that are related to less important problems.

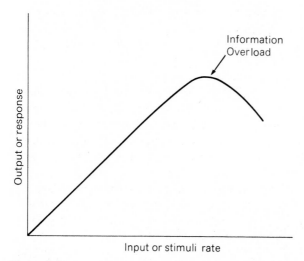

Figure 8-2
Performance of human as information processor. (Adapted from Harry H. Good, "Greenhouse of Science for Management," *Management Science*, July 1958, p. 3.)

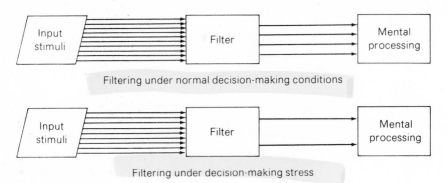

Filtering under normal decision-making conditions

Filtering under decision-making stress

Figure 8-3
Filtering of information to reduce processing requirements.

The concept of frame of reference applies to both input and processing. To develop a new processing routine for each new stimulus would use processing capacity and reduce the stimuli that could be processed. Over an extended period of time, and on a continuing basis, the brain establishes patterns or categories of data which define the human understanding of the nature of the environment. These patterns or frames of reference are called into use in processing the input (Figure 8-4), thereby reducing processing requirements. Effective use of relevant frames of reference which have been accumulated over a long period is one characteristic of expertise in a particular field.

Besides blocking unwanted data, filtering may work to block data that is inconsistent with an established frame of reference. This factor and the natural limits on the human sense receptors may lead to information perception errors such as omissions, distortions, and inferences. The writer of a report may mean one thing; the reader may perceive another. These errors of perception increase uncertainty as to the message being transmitted which, as explained in Chapter 7, reduces the information content.

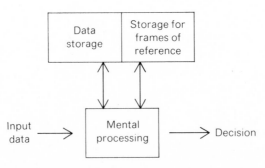

Figure 8-4
Use of input data, stored data, and frame of reference to process a decision.

THE NEWELL-SIMON MODEL

Allen Newell and Herbert A. Simon[1] proposed a model of human problem solving which makes use of the analogy between computer processing and human information processing. This is not to say that humans solve problems like computers, but the analogy is very useful in understanding human information processing. Figure 8-5 compares the Newell-Simon model of information processing with a general model of a computer system.

The Human Information Processing System

The human information processing system consists of a processor, sensory input, motor output, and three different memories: long-term memory (LTM), short-term memory (STM), and external memory (EM). The system operates in serial fashion rather than in parallel. This means that the human can perform only one information processing task at a time, whereas a computer may operate in either serial or parallel design. A good

---

[1]Allen Newell and Herbert A. Simon, *Human Problem Solving*, Prentice-Hall, Englewood Cliffs, NJ, 1972. See also Herbert A. Simon and Allen Newell, "Human Problem Solving: The State of the Theory in 1970," *American Psychologist*, February 1971, pp. 145–159.

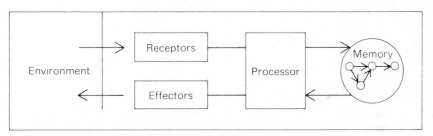

General structure of a human information processing system *(Allen Newell and Herbert A. Simon , Human Problem Solving, Prentice-Hall, Inc., Englewood Cliffs, N. J., 1972, p. 20)*

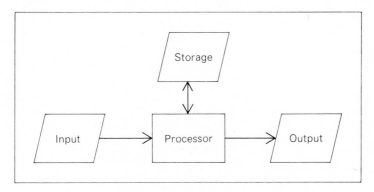

General model of computer information processing system

Figure 8-5
Comparison of Newell-Simon model and model of computer system.

example of computer parallel processing is the simultaneous addition of all pairs of bits in two computer data words. Normally, humans add serially a pair of digits at a time from right to left. Three processing operations to be described in the following list are also illustrated in Figure 8-6.

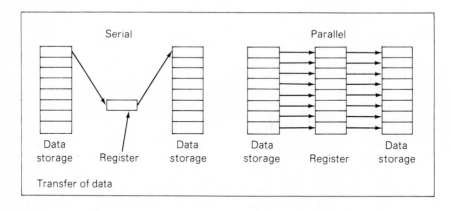

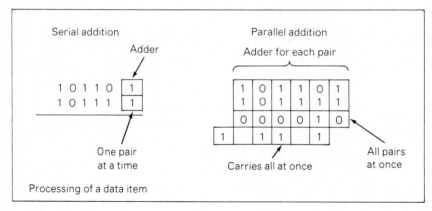

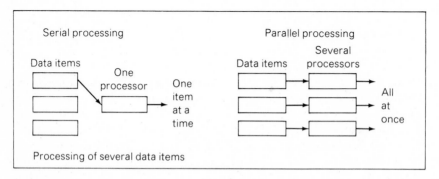

Figure 8-6
Examples of serial and parallel processing in computers.

Operation	Serial design	Parallel design
Data transfer	Data transferred a bit at a time.	Data transferred a word at a time (e.g., 32 bits).
Arithmetic on one data item	One adder-comparator. Operations on pairs of bits from right to left.	One adder-comparator for each set of bits. Operations on all pairs of bits simultaneously.
Processing of several data items	One processor. Processing of one item at a time.	CPU consists of several small processors. Several items processed concurrently.

The fact that a human is a serial processor does not mean that he or she cannot work on more than one task concurrently. Although this is not described by the Newell-Simon model, the human probably does it by rapid switching from one task to another with short bursts of processing for each. This is analogous to time-sharing in which a computer works on several programs at once by switching from one to another. Also, the human processor utilizes pattern matching; this is not well explained by the computer analogy.

The three memories of the Newell-Simon model are shown in Figure 8-7. The long-term memory has essentially unlimited capacity. Its content consists of symbols and structures of *chunks*. A chunk is a unit of stored information—it can be a digit, a word, an image, etc. Storage may be quite compact so that an entire configuration of stimuli may be designated by a single symbol. It requires only a few hundred milliseconds to read (recall) from long-term memory, but the write time (commit to memory) is fairly long (say, 5K to 10K seconds for K symbols). This means that it requires an average of 50 to 100 seconds to memorize a 10-digit member, but once stored, one can recall it for use in a few hundred milliseconds.

The short-term memory is part of the processor and it is quite small. It holds only five to seven symbols. However, only about two can be retained while another task is being performed, which suggests that part of the short-term memory is used for input and output processing. Read and write time are very fast. A typical example is the ability to rehearse an unfamiliar telephone number long enough to dial it, but no longer. A computer analogy is the storage of data in registers during processing, as shown in Figure 8-6. Registers have very fast read and write times, but hold data only temporarily while the contents are being acted upon.

The external memory in the human processing system consists of external media such as a pad of paper or a chalkboard. The access time for the eye to locate the symbols at a known location is quite fast (say, 100 milliseconds), and read times are estimated at about 50 milliseconds. The write times (say, one second per symbol) are much less than the write times for long-term memory, which accounts for the efficiency of using external memory in problem-solving procedures. It also eases the constraints of short term memory. For example, if two 10-digit numbers are to be added, the following approximate times are required by long-term and external memories.

	Seconds using long-term memory	Seconds using external memory
Accept numbers	Same	Same
Write numbers to memory	50.0 to 100.0	10.0
Read numbers to add	1.0 to 2.0	0.6
Process (add digits a pair at a time)	Same	Same
Write result to memory	50.0 to 100.0	10.0
Total	101.0 to 202.0	20.6

Even if large errors are assumed in the estimated times for reading and writing, the point about the operating efficiency of external memory is easily seen. By way of contrast, the retrieval, processing, and storage of results by computer would require a few millionths of a second.

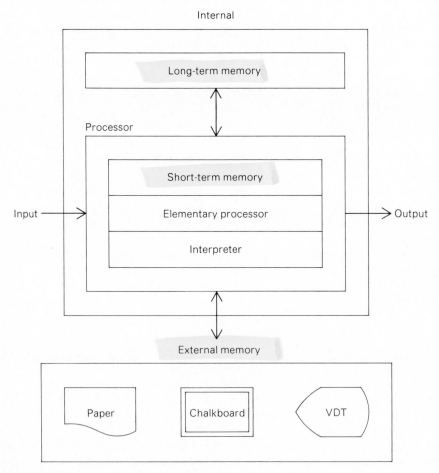

Figure 8-7
The three memories of the Newell-Simon model.

The processor of the information processing system contains three parts: the elementary processor, the short-term memory, and the interpreter which interprets part or all the program of instructions for problem solving (Figure 8-7). The program used by an individual will depend on a number of variables such as the task and the intelligence of the problem solver.

Task Environment and Problem Space

Another Newell-Simon concept useful in understanding human information and decision processing is that of task environment and problem space. The *task environment* is the problem as it exists; the *problem space* is the way a particular decision maker represents the task in order to work on it. In other words, confronted by a problem, the problem solver formulates a representation to use in working on the problem. This representation is the conceptual space where problem solving takes place. The problem space is determined by the task environment, but is not identical to it.

The structure of the problem space (how the problem solver represents the task) determines the processes to be used for problem solving. The problem space can be thought of as a network of knowledge state nodes; each node describes what the problem solver knows at a moment in time. A knowledge state will consist of a few dozen or perhaps a few hundred symbols. Problem solving takes place by a search process in the problem space until a desired knowledge state is reached. Problem solving thus consists of constructing a problem space and processing in the problem space until a solution is found.

Structure in a problem space is equivalent to redundancy. This means that information in one part of the problem space is, by means of the structure, predictive of properties in another part of the space. It thus permits a more efficient search process.

LOST IN PARIS AND THE PROBLEM SPACE

The professor was lost; there was no doubt of it. He had started walking from his hotel in the direction he understood would get him to his destination, but the streets had become unfamiliar. The task environment was essentially a geometric one—the directional vector that extended from his location to the target location. Under the circumstances, the lost traveler represented the task as moving along a set of streets in the right direction. Given this problem space, the knowledge state nodes consist of information about current location, directional information, or information on how to employ alternatives (taxi or the subway).

- Using a taxi knowledge state, he tried to hail a taxi. If he had succeeded, the problem would have been solved.
- Using his limited French, he could have progressed a few streets at a time (because he couldn't process the entire set of directions in French).
- Going to the subway knowledge state required one request for directions. Once in the subway, the subway map was processed to locate the line, direction, and stop. Once off the stop, one more set of directions were sufficient to lead to the address (the desired knowledge state).

Heuristics

In Chapter 6, a normative model of decision making was presented. According to this model, humans act with complete rationality, utilizing all the information available to them in making decisions. There is substantial evidence to the contrary, however, which indicates that the descriptive model of the decision maker, also given in Chapter 6, is more accurate. Humans utilize past experience, inductive inference, and intuition. The process of decision making does not follow an algorithmic, "brute force" reasoning process, by which all possible alternatives in the search space are analyzed and an optimal solution is guaranteed. Instead, the decision maker utilizes *heuristics*, judgmental rules of thumb which eliminate alternatives without explaining them and thus reduce the search space.

The use of heuristics in decision making may be an efficient as well as effective method if the individual has adequate experience and judgment to make appropriate choices. A good example is a master chess player who drastically reduces the number of alternatives on a single move through rules of thumb developed by past experience. On the other hand, there is some evidence that individuals utilize heuristics in such a way as to reduce the quality of a decision. Limits on human judgment that inhibit adequate use of heuristics are discussed in the next section.

A concept related to the use of heuristics is bounded rationality. The method of satisficing in searching for alternatives as a result of bounded rationality was explained in Chapter 6. Humans have a limited capacity for rational thinking; they generally construct a simplified model of the real situation in order to deal with it. Their behavior with respect to the simplified model may be rational. However, it does not follow that the rational solution for the simplified model is rational in the real situation. Rationality is restricted or bounded not only by limitations on human processing capacities but also by individual differences such as age, education, and attitudes. The effect of individual differences on human information processing is discussed in a later section of this chapter.

The importance of bounded rationality with respect to the problem space is illustrated by the research of Vitalari.[2] He found that a characteristic of proficient system analysts is that they have learned to use a general model to bound the problem space and aid in efficient search for requirements. Poorly rated analysts have a poorly developed model and have difficulty in adequately bounding the problem space.

TENTATIVE LIMITS ON HUMAN INFORMATION PROCESSING

The Newell-Simon model suggests that there are limitations on the ability of humans as information processors. There is some empirical evidence relating to these limits and their relationship to heuristic problem solving. One set of limits concerns the processing of data and is directly related to short-term memory. Another set of limits is the ability of

---

[2]N. P. Vitalari, "An Investigation of the Problem Solving Behavior of System Analysts," unpublished doctoral Dissertation, University of Minnesota, Minneapolis, 1981; see also N. P. Vitalari and G. W. Dickson, "Problem Solving for Effective Systems Analysis: An Exploration," *Communications of the ACM*, 26:11, November 1983, pp. 948–956.

humans to detect differences. Humans are also limited in their ability to generate, integrate, and interpret probabilistic data.

Limits to Short-Term Memory

Miller coined the phrase "the magical number seven, plus or minus two"[3] to describe human capability for processing information. His survey, supported by empirical research, shows in essence that the number of symbols or "chunks" humans can hold in short-term memory and process effectively is from five to nine, with a common limit of seven. (Some researchers believe the mean number is about five.)

The limits of 7 ± 2 are most easily observed in human information processing of codes, quantities, and other data composed of single symbols. The application of the limits to codes is important because information processing depends heavily on the use of codes and coded data. The following summary of some studies indicates the validity of the limits Miller proposed:

Study	Object of study and results
Crannell and Parish[4]	Immediate oral recall of orally presented numeric data. Span for immediate recall slightly better than seven digits.
Conrad[5]	Telephone operators memorizing telephone numbers and then recalling them. Error rates on recall were:
	<table><tr><td>Digit length</td><td>Percent in error</td></tr><tr><td>8</td><td>30</td></tr><tr><td>9</td><td>44</td></tr><tr><td>10</td><td>54</td></tr></table>
Chapdelain[6]	Error rate for transcribing coded data from one form to another for codes from 5 to 15 digits in length. The frequency of errors from least to highest was 5, 6, 7, 8, 10, 11, 13, 9, 14, 12, 15. The differences were significant. Note that 9 and 12 are out of order. A 12-digit code had almost double the error rate of a 13-digit code.
Owsowitz and Sweetland[7]	Error rates for codes composed of mixed alphabetic and numeric characters. Error rates increase when alphabetic characters are mixed with numeric characters. Codes with one part (say, half) alpha and the other part numeric had lower error rates than codes with alpha, numeric, alpha, etc.

---

[3]George A. Miller, "The Magical Number Seven, Plus or Minus Two: Some Limits on Our Capability for Processing Information," *The Psychological Review*, 63:2, March 1956, pp. 81–97.

[4]C. W. Crannell and J. M. Parrish, "A Comparison of Immediate Memory Span for Digits, Letters and Words," *The Journal of Psychology*, 44, October 1957, pp. 319–327.

[5]R. Conrad, "Errors of Immediate Memory," *The British Journal of Psychology*, 50:4, November 1959, pp. 349–359.

[6]P. A. Chapdelain, "Accuracy Control in Source Data Collection," Headquarters, Air Force Logistics Command, Wright-Patterson Air Force Base, Ohio, 1963.

[7]S. Owsowitz and A. Sweetland, "Factors Affecting Coding Errors," Rand Memorandum RM-4346-PR, The Rand Corporation, Santa Monica, CA, 1965.

Graphic representation is another method for increasing the input to human processing. A graph is a "chunk," yet it may provide the same input of data as a large number of data items that would each use one chunk of capacity. For users who have hardware and software to process them, graphics are especially efficient in showing trends, relationships, and relative sizes.

Recent research in cognitive psychology reports some success by individuals in extending the limits of short-term memory through spatial analogies. One method is to associate objects to be memorized (say, a list of numbers) with other objects that are well-known and easily recalled through a visual image (e.g., furniture in a room). People frequently use space on desks and shelves as an organizing strategy; this aids in remembering where things are. The visual image becomes an index to information already stored away and easily retrievable. Some startling results have been shown in particular cases where, after training and practice, an individual can recall as many as 75 digits.[8]

THE POSTAL LOCATION CODE AND LIMITS TO SHORT-TERM MEMORY

The United States postal location code (zip code) consists of five numeric digits. It is well within the limits of short-term memory. However, an extended code is being implemented consisting of four additional numeric digits to identify small areas within a zip code. The four digits are separated from the rest of the code by a hyphen. There has been opposition to the implementation timetable because of the necessity for modification of computer programs and reformatting of files. There has been no discussion of increased input errors from human operators.

The Canadian postal location code is more error-prone than the United States code. It consists of two sets of three characters of the format: ANA NAN where A = alphabetic and N = numeric.

Just Noticeable Differences

The ability of human information processors to identify differences may be important in detecting errors (i.e., noticing differences between correct and incorrect data) and also in their reactions to variations in data they receive. In other words, how do humans evaluate the significance of differences such as profit differences and cost differences? Weber's law[9] of just noticeable differences is a theory in the field of cognitive psychology with respect to judgments of physical stimuli such as the brightness of light, the loudness of sounds, and the heaviness of weights. The law says that the difference that is noticeable is a constant proportion of the physical dimensions of the stimulus. In other words, if C denotes a criterion and $\triangle C$ is the just noticeable difference, then:

$$\frac{\triangle C}{C} = k \text{ for all } C$$

---

[8]Experiments by William G. Chase, Carnegie-Mellon, described in Chris Welles, "Teaching the Brain New Tricks," *Esquire*, March 1983, pp. 49–61.

[9]Weber's law of just noticeable differences is explained in many experimental psychology texts.

This means that as C changes, $\triangle C$ changes in order to hold k a constant. If, for example, a variation of 1/5 pound is sufficient difference to distinguish between two 5-pound weights, then:

$$\frac{1/5}{5} = \frac{1}{25}$$

For two 20-pound weights, the difference must be 4/5 pound to hold the ratio constant.

$$\frac{4/5}{20} = \frac{1}{25}$$

In other words, a larger difference is required to distinguish between two heavy objects than between two light ones, but the relative difference is the same.

There is some evidence to suggest that Weber's law also holds for processing of data. For example, the reader of a financial report considers differences to be significant as judged by their size relative to the base rather than the absolute amount. A 10 percent variation in budgeted sales of $100,000 (variance of $10,000) has the same significance in terms of noticeable difference as a 10 percent variation in selling expense of $10,000 (variance of $1,000). Although comparisons of numeric data seem to follow Weber's law, numeric differences are not the same as physical differences. Experiments by Dickhaut and Eggleton[10] suggest that subjects follow simple decision rules such as constant percentage difference that give the same pattern as Weber's law. The results of another experiment[11] indicate that decision makers use past experience and judgment to judge the importance of a variance, using not just its percentage or absolute difference but a combination of the two via a complex weighting scheme.

WEBER'S LAW AND THE DEMISE OF THE ANTHONY DOLLAR

The U.S. treasury introduced a new coin in 1980—a dollar coin honoring Susan B. Anthony. In spite of heavy publicity and a large inventory of coins, the public refused to use it.

When a Treasury official was asked about it, he responded to an objection about the closeness of the Anthony dollar to the size of a quarter (a common objection to it) by saying there was as much difference as between a dime and a nickel. The public obviously was applying a different standard for differences (Weber's law?).

| Anthony dollar | Quarter | Nickel | Dime |

---

[10]John W. Dickhaut and Ian R. C. Eggleton, "An Examination of the Processes Underlying Comparative Judgments in Numerical Stimuli," *Journal of Accounting Research*, 13:1, Spring 1975, pp. 38–72.

[11]P. Judd, C. Paddock, and J. Wetherbe, "Decision Impelling Differences: An Investigation of Management by Exception Reporting," *Information and Management*, 4, 1981, pp. 259–267.

Handling Probabilistic Data

Decision makers are frequently required to perceive, process, and evaluate the probabilities of uncertain events. There is evidence of serious deficiencies in performance of humans as intuitive statisticians.[12] Some of the deficiencies identified by research are:

1 Lack of intuitive understanding of the impact of sample size on sampling variance
2 Lack of intuitive ability to identify correlation and causality
3 Biasing heuristics for probability estimation
4 Lack of capability for integrating information

Sampling variance decreases in proportion to sample size. In other words, if a sample of 10 manufactured parts is examined for defects and 2 are found defective, the meaning is different from 20 defects in a sample of 100. In a study of the practices of psychology researchers, Tversky and Kahneman[13] found that the investigators did not seem to perceive correctly the error and unreliability inherent in small samples. Other studies with students suggest humans do not understand random error effects in small samples, and this results in unwarranted conclusions.

It is important in decision making to identify correlation and causality because this allows a prediction of the value of one variable from the value of another. Research suggests that causality is frequently intuitively identified with joint occurrence, although there is no basis for this inference.[14] For example, a common finding in research in social psychology is that people are more inclined to see a causal relationship between their own failings and external factors (e.g., luck), while they ascribe the failings of others to internal factors (e.g., competence).[15] Another related phenomenon that has been observed is "illusory correlation."[16] Individuals who expect to observe causality will often observe dependencies between two variables and make a judgment of observed association where none in fact exists.

As pointed out earlier, humans operate with bounded rationality. Estimation of probabilities is influenced by a variety of biasing factors, for example, the availability of data. Events that are easily remembered or imagined are assigned a higher probability (an availability bias). Related to this is a recency bias in which recent results are given a greater weight.

---

[12]William F. Wright, "Cognitive Information Processing Biases: Implications for Producers and Users of Financial Information," *Decision Sciences*, 11, 1980, pp. 284–298.

[13]A. Tversky and D. Kahneman, "The Belief in the Law of Small Numbers," *Psychological Bulletin*, 76, 1971, pp. 105–110.

[14]A. Tversky and D. Kahneman, "Causal Schemata in Judgments under Uncertainty," in M. Fishbein (ed.), *Progress in Social Psychology*, Earlbaum, Hillsdale, NJ, 1977.

[15]H. H. Kelley, *Attributions in Social Interaction*, General Learning Press, Morristown, NJ, 1972.

[16]Wright, "Cognitive Information Processing Biases: Implications for Producers and Users of Financial Information," L. J. Chapman and J. P. Chapman, "The Illusory Correlation As an Obstacle to Valid Psychodiagnostic Signs," *Journal of Abnormal Psychology*, 74:3, 1969, pp. 271–280; S. L. Golding and L. G. Rorer, "Illusory Correlation and Subjective Judgment," *Journal of Abnormal Psychology*, 80:3, 1972, pp. 249–260; and P. Slovic, "From Shakespeare to Simon: Speculations—and Some Evidence—About Man's Ability to Process Information," Research Monograph, Oregon Research Institute, 12:12, 1972.

There is evidence[17] that when individuals are told that a specific outcome has occurred in the past, they assign a significantly higher probability estimate of the outcome occurring in the future than do those who have no information about past occurrence. This phenomenon, called "hindsight bias," may inhibit learning over time because expectations based on past events inhibit evaluations of current experience.

BIAS IN WHERE TO BET

Spain has a lottery called LaGorda (the fat one). Spaniards buying lottery tickets tend to purchase them from establishments that have sold winning lottery tickets in the past. This suggests hindsight bias, since there is no logical connection between future winning numbers and past winning numbers.

Humans are not usually consistent in patterns of choice when faced with different types of information and values. Researchers have demonstrated a "cue-response interaction" in that cues which are measured in the same units as a variable to be judged are weighted more heavily in the judgment than other cues measured in different units.[18] Cue-response effects are important for information systems and information use. Changing the units in which information is presented or presenting other data in different units may alter user judgment. For example, a result stated in financial terms has a greater impact in financial decisions than nonfinancial data. A report that 10 sales were lost in district D this month has less weight than the statement that $110,000 in sales (or $35,000 in gross margin) were lost beause of sales force problems.

Human Information Processing Strategies

Humans adopt strategies for dealing with their limitations as information processors and for easing the strain of integrating information. Two examples are concreteness and also anchoring and adjustment.

The concept of *concreteness* is that the decision maker tends to use only information that is readily available and only in the form in which it is displayed. There will be a tendency not to search for data stored in memory or to transform or manipulate the data that is presented. Explicit, available information thus has an advantage over data that must be obtained or manipulated before use. In particular, individuals rely on concrete observable characteristics of evidence and neglect other information related to the process or context of evidence, leading to possible errors in judgment.

---

[17]B. Fischhoff and R. Beyth, "'I Knew It Would Happen'—Remembered Probabilities of Once-Future Things," *Organizational Behavior and Human Performance*, 13:1, 1975, pp. 1–16.

[18]P. Slovic and S. Lichtenstein, "The Relative Importance of Probabilities and Payoffs in Risk Taking," *Journal of Experimental Psychology*, Monograph Supplement 79, No. 3, Part 2, 1968; Lichtenstein and Slovic, "Response-Induced Reversals of Preference in Gambling: An Extended Replication in Las Vegas," *Journal of Experimental Psychology*, 101:1, 1973, pp. 16–20.

POWER IN THE CHALK

In conferences to discuss problems, one of the participants always sat near the chalkboard. After the discussion had developed to a reasonable extent, he would go to the board and, depending on the problem or issue, would write a list of issues, sets of alternatives, or steps to be followed. He would then summarize his comments. When asked why he did this, he replied that the "concreteness" of his outline or list dominated the discussion and often caused other items to be ignored. There was "power in the chalk."

The idea of *anchoring and adjustment* is that humans tend to make judgments by establishing an anchor point and making adjustments from this point. The anchoring and adjustment behavior reduces information processing requirements. It is a common phenomenon in budgeting, planning, and pricing. The anchoring and adjustment process can have a negative effect on judgment in two ways. First, individuals may use inappropriate criteria for choosing an anchor. One common criterion is past experience, and due to the phenomenon of cue-response interaction already described, they may tend to use a scale or unit of measure which is the same as the value to be judged. Second, when a value is compared to the anchor, the adjustment process tends to undervalue the importance of the new evidence since it is only considered relative to a somewhat arbitrary anchor point.

CONCEPTS OF HUMAN COGNITION AND LEARNING

Much of the research in human cognition and learning is important for information system design in that it explains how human capabilities can be enhanced or supplemented by information systems. Some relevant topics are cognition theory, cognitive style, and learning theory.

Cognition Theory

Cognition refers to "the activities by which an individual resolves differences between an internalized view of the environment and what is actually perceived in that same environment."[19] *Cognitive models* are attempts to explain or understand various human cognitive processes. For instance, the Newell-Simon model is a cognitive model of human problem solving. Another well-known cognitive model is the theory of *cognitive dissonance*,[20] discussed in Chapter 6, which explains how individuals revise previous opinions in order to conform with a particular choice after they have made that choice.

An example of a cognitive model relevant to information systems is Shneiderman's model of programmer behavior.[21] According to this model, an experienced programmer has developed a complex body of knowledge about programming concepts and

---

[19]Robert W. Zmud, "Individual Differences and MIS Success: A Review of the Empirical Literature," *Management Science*, 25, October 1979, pp. 966–979.

[20]L. Festinger, *A Theory of Cognitive Dissonance*, Row & Peterson, Evanston, IL, 1957.

[21]Ben Shneiderman, *Software, Psychology: Human Factors in Computer and Information Systems*, Winthrop, Cambridge, MA, 1980, pp. 46–49.

techniques that is stored in long-term memory. This body of knowledge can be divided into semantic knowledge and syntactic knowledge. *Semantic knowledge* refers to general functional concepts (e.g., a subscripted array, an assignment statement, a sort or merge algorithm) which are important for programming in general but independent of any specific programming language. *Syntactic knowledge* includes the specific grammar, syntax, and format of a particular language. Shneiderman argues that internalizing models and constructs as semantic knowledge is more important to developing good programming skill than syntactic knowledge, which primarily involves memorization of grammatical rules. Experienced programmers learn new languages relatively easily, indicating that semantic knowledge is generalizable. Shneiderman has performed a number of experiments with experienced and novice programmers to validate this cognitive model. The model explains that such programming techniques as top-down design, stepwise refinement, and structured programming (to be discussed in Chapter 18) are important productivity aids because they encourage the development of semantic knowledge.

Cognitive Style

Two individuals rarely follow the same decision-making process, even if they make the same choice. One aspect of individual decision-making style that has received much research attention is *cognitive style*. This refers to the process through which individuals organize and change information during the decision-making process.

One model of cognitive style classifies individual styles along two continuums (Figure 8-8).[22] The *information gathering* dimension relates to the perceptual processes by which the mind organizes verbal and visual stimuli. At one extreme of this dimension, *preceptive* individuals focus on relationships among data items and attempt to generalize from them about the environment. At the other extreme, *receptive* individuals focus on details and attempt to derive specific knowledge about the environment from the available data.

The other dimension, *information evaluation*, refers to the sequence by which the individual analyzes that data. At one extreme, *systematic* individuals (also referred to as *analytics*) follow a structured, deductive approach which, if followed through, leads to a likely solution. *Intuitive* (or *heuristic*) individuals use trial-and-error strategies, act spontaneously on the basis of new information, and respond to and incorporate nonverbal cues.

The research on cognitive style is directly relevant to the design of management information systems. Computer-based systems tend to be designed by individuals who perceive the decision-making process to be systematic. Systematic managers are generally willing to use such systems; they are typically looking for a technique and view the system designer as an expert with a catalog of methods. However, such systems do not conform to the natural style of a heuristic decision maker. For this individual, a system should allow for exploration of a wide range of alternatives, should permit changes in order of processing, should allow the user to shift easily between levels of

---

[22]James L. McKenney and Peter G. W. Keen, "How Managers' Minds Work," *Harvard Business Review*, May–June 1974, pp. 79–90.

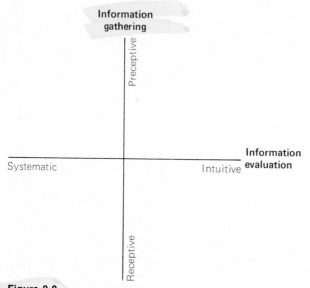

Figure 8-8
Model of cognitive style (Reprinted by permission of *Havard Business Review*. Exhibit 1 from article by J. L. McKenney and P. G. W. Keen, "How Managers' Minds Work," May-June, pp. 79-90. Copyright © 1974 by the President and Fellows of Harvard College; all rights reserved.)

detail and generality, and should permit some user control over output form (e.g., visual, verbal, graphical, etc.).

Although cognitive style is a useful concept, it may be overemphasized in the MIS literature. There are difficulties in applying it to information systems and decision making.[23] For one thing, cognitive style is a continuous variable. For example, a person is not heuristic or analytic but is more or less heuristic. Furthermore, the task to be performed frequently has more influence on the decision style selected than the preferred style of the decision maker. Finally, humans have a high capacity to adapt. A person with heuristic bias may adapt fairly easily to an analytic decision-making procedure. Education and training may have a greater effect on cognitive style in a given situation than natural tendencies.

THE MAP TEST

A couple applied the concept of heuristic and analytic decision styles to a problem in their marriage. When traveling to a specific site, the exact location of which they were unsure, they differed significantly in their approach to finding it, leading to marital conflict. The husband tended to be heuristic and preferred to drive to the approximate location to see if he could find it; if not, he would look at the map. The wife preferred to look at the map before leaving and trace the route, an analytic approach. When they perceived the conflict as a result of decision-making style differences, he agreed to use the analytic approach to location finding, reasoning it was easier (and perhaps more efficient) for a heuristic to adapt to the analytic approach in this situation. End of conflict.

---

[23]George P. Huber, "Cognitive Style As a Basis for MIS and DSS Designs: Much Ado about Nothing?" *Management Science*, 29:5, May 1983, pp. 567–597.

Left Brain-Right Brain

Recent research suggests a biological explanation for individual differences in problem solving.[24] The brain exhibits *hemispheric specialization*, as shown in Figure 8-9. The left side of the brain favors rational, analytic processing, while the right side utilizes intuitive, spatial, creative processing. Although, theoretically, individuals should be equally adept at both kinds of processing, experience and education leads us to favor one over the other. Thus a person's approach to a particular problem is conditioned by past experience as well as by the task itself.

Proponents of "dual dominance" of both sides of the brain in problem solving see cognitive style as being a characteristic of the left brain only. In other words, even an extreme heuristic individual utilizes the rational-analytic left brain to the extent possible. Decision support systems for heuristic problem solving are not usually designed to take advantage of the intuitive capabilities of the right side of the brain. A decision support system for intuitive right-brain processing would have a highly flexible system-user interface utilizing graphics, natural language, color, visual images, and possibly randomly generated "surprise" alternatives for consideration. The left brain-right brain

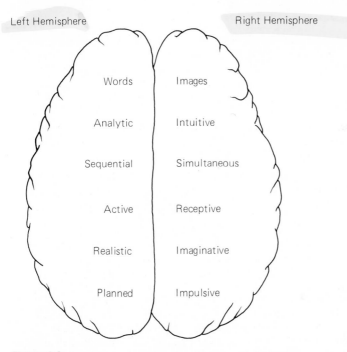

Left Hemisphere   Right Hemisphere

Words   Images

Analytic   Intuitive

Sequential   Simultaneous

Active   Receptive

Realistic   Imaginative

Planned   Impulsive

Figure 8-9
Summary of clinical and experimental evidence about hemispheric specialization of the brain (from Robey and Taggart, "Human Information Processing in Information and Decision Support Systems," *MIS Quarterly* 6:2, June 1982).

[24]D. Robey and W. Taggart, "Human Information Processing in Information and Decision Support Systems," *MIS Quarterly* 6:2, June 1982, pp. 61–73.

concept is useful in considering individual differences; there are, however, researchers who discount the predictive power of the theory.[25] The discussion of decision support systems in Chapter 12 will show that such an approach to decision support is technically feasible.

Learning Theory

Information and information systems can aid individual learning. The learning process has four important elements: drive, cue, response, and reinforcement. The drive to learn in an infant is primarily associated with physiological processes; in an adult, the drives to learn beyond innate curiosity are acquired. Cues are stimuli that guide and determine responses. Reinforcement consists of the reward or punishment or praise that follows a response. The reinforcement causes responses to be "learned."

At a higher level of mental processes, some responses are actions; others produce cues. For example, cues may be received relative to a problem. A cue-producing response is to label the problem such as a "rate of return problem" or a "modification problem." These labels serve as cues to further responses based on the problem label. Information systems aid in the learning process by providing cues, responses, opportunities for classifying and labeling, etc.

Artificial intelligence is concerned with using computers to perform tasks that would be called "intelligent" if people did them. The objectives are two fold: to improve understanding of human cognition and to improve the potential of the computer as a tool for problem solving. One significant area of research concerns how people acquire and organize expert knowledge; the goal is to be able to simulate, with a computer, expert knowledge and its use in problem-solving behavior. Developments in "expert systems" will be discussed in greater detail in Chapter 12.

CHARACTERISTICS OF HUMAN INFORMATION PROCESSING PERFORMANCE

Earlier in this chapter it was explained that humans have constraints on their information processing abilities, and individual characteristics such as cognitive style affect their decision-making processes. In this section, other characteristics of individuals that affect their cognitive processes and the effectiveness of their decision making will be discussed.

Need for Feedback

In computer systems, various mechanisms are used to determine that output has been received. The printer returns a signal to the central processor to indicate that it has been activated. A data terminal returns a signal to indicate receipt of a block of data. Similar feedback mechanisms must be provided in human processing situations not only for error control but also to meet the psychological needs of human processors for assurance that output was received.

---

[25]M. S. Gazzmga and J. E. Ledoux, *The Integrated Mind*, Plenum, New York, 1978.

THE IMPORTANCE OF THE NEED FOR FEEDBACK IN A USER INTERFACE

A system used a source data recorder for entering work performed plus start and stop times.[26] The employee entered data which was transmitted to a central location, but the device returned no response (such as a light, hum, or buzz) to indicate that the input was recorded. The result was duplicate entry of data by frustrated employees who were not sure the first entry was received.

Another illustration was an incident connected with the installation of one of the first nationwide online airline reservation systems using typewriter terminal input and output.[27] The computer load was estimated at 85 percent of capacity, but it was immediately overloaded. An analysis revealed that the reservation operators did not trust the computer. After entering reservation data, they immediately entered an inquiry to see if the system had received the data. This effectively doubled the load on the computer system. The solution was to provide a feedback signal confirming that the message had been received. In this case, the feedback was to wiggle the typewriter ball.

In an online system, an important aspect of feedback is response time: the time between the user entering a message and some response being returned. In the design of online transaction processing systems, an important design goal is to achieve response times which maximize the speed of entry and minimize error rates. The most common problem is too long a response time, so that the user becomes restless and loses concentration. However, response times can also be too short, so that the user feels "driven" by the system and errors increase. For systems which are heavily oriented to data entry, a response time of two or three seconds is reasonable; for more complex tasks, longer response times are acceptable. If response times need to exceed, say, 10 seconds, a message should be sent periodically to show the user the system is processing. Another design goal related to response time is to keep it as consistent as possible.

IT SEEMS LONGER IF THERE IS NO RESPONSE

A manager using an online financial planning package was very dissatisfied with its operations. He complained to the package designer that the response time at initialization of the system was inordinately long. The designer looked at the program and found that several files were opened when the program began. He modified the program so that, for each file opened, a message printed on the screen indicating that the file was ready for execution. The reaction of the manager was that the initialization time was reduced, even though in fact it was slightly longer because of the overhead to print the messages!

---

[26]J. Anderson, G. Dickson, and J. Simmons, "Behavioral Reactions to the Introduction of a Management Information System at the U.S. Post Office: Some Empirical Observations," in D. Sanders (ed.), *Computers and Management*, Second Edition, McGraw-Hill, New York, 1974.

[27]Reported by C. Dudley Warner, "System Performance and Evaluation—Past, Present, and Future," *Proceedings of the Fall Joint Computer Conference*, American Federation of Information Processing Societies, 1972, p. 962.

Psychological Value of Unused Data

A common phenomenon in organizations is the accumulation and storage of data that has very little probability of being used. There are several explanations for uneconomic accumulation and storage of data. One explanation may be the increased confidence decision makers appear to obtain from added data, even if unnecessary. Two other useful explanations are the concept of the value of unused opportunities and information as a symbol.

The basic theory of the value of unused opportunities is that people attach a significant value to opportunities even though they are not used. This phenomenon was demonstrated in an investigation into the reasons people liked living in the New York City area. The responses typically included a substantial listing of cultural facilities such as museums, art galleries, and theaters. Yet the people who listed these factors did not, in general, use them—they did not go to the theater, art galleries, or museums. The value of the cultural facilities was not related to actual use. Having them there in case they ever did want to go appeared to be the significant value.

The theory of unused opportunities may be applied to explain the phenomenon of apparent uneconomic accumulation and storage of data. The value is not the actual use, given any expected frequency of access, but is a psychological value assigned by the recipients to having data available. In cases where this theory is applicable, it has implications for information system design. Users can be provided with data access mechanisms rather than individual (unused) copies of outputs.

Feldman and March[28] propose other explanations for the conspicuous overconsumption of information.

  1 Organizations are designed with incentives for gathering extra information. Examples are the separation of information gathering function from information using.
  2 Much of the information gathered by organizations is for surveillance and not for decision making.
  3 Information is often gathered and communicated to persuade and even to misrepresent.
  4 Information use is a symbol of commitment to rational choice.

The researchers conclude that the last reason is the most significant of the four. Within the organizational culture, having information available is a symbol of competence and inspires confidence in decision-making abilities, regardless of whether the information is used. Information is thus a symbol of rational choice as much as a contributor to it. This has interesting consequences for terminal-oriented systems. Access to a terminal and password authority to access information may play the same symbolic role as receiving reports.

Information Overload

It has already been noted that the human capacity to accept inputs from the environment is limited. In addition, humans have built-in filtering or selection processes to handle information overload. In his popular book *Future Shock*, Alvin Toffler argues that the speed of change in our environment today, and the consequent information overload to

---

[28]Martha S. Feldman and James G. March, "Information in Organizations As Signal and Symbol," *Administrative Science Quarterly*, 26, June 1981, pp. 171–186.

which humans are subjected, is a major cultural and societal problem.[29] According to Toffler, our natural capacity to filter and select information is overworked; we are constantly required to operate in "crisis mode," resulting in higher stress and its accompanying physical problems. Toffler even suggests that government policies are needed to control the rapid pace of technological change.

A more immediate implication of the problem of information overload is in the design of information systems. The decreasing cost of computers, increasing capacity of data storage, and availability of communications technology permit organizations to process, transmit, and store greater amounts of data than were ever possible before. Managers have traditionally responded to increased information capabilities by requesting more and more information. Ackoff[30] argues that many managers assume they lack relevant information and therefore ask for more; however, the real problem is "overabundance of irrelevant information." It is possible to include in information system design various mechanisms to summarize, filter, and otherwise reduce the quantity of information.

Individual Differences

Cognitive style described earlier is one example of individual differences that may affect use of and satisfaction with information systems. There has been research on other individual differences to identify those critical to successful use of information systems and to determine how to design systems to accommodate them.[31]

Even though many individual differences affect information system use and satisfaction, it is frequently not possible to design individually tailored systems. The systems have to be general enough to cover more than one user. The results shown here give indications of the dimensions that should be considered when designing information systems. The systems can be designed to reflect the dominant individual differences or designed with options to respond to the range of differences.

The following table summarizes major research results regarding personality, demographic, and situational differences as they affect the use of information in decision making. See the selected references at end of the chapter for research by authors cited below.

Individual differences	Explanation	Effect on information processing
Locus of control (internal-external)	Extent to which events are perceived to be controlled by internal processes (with low task uncertainty) versus controlled by external forces (with high task uncertainty).	Internal locus of control related to more information search activity than external locus of control (Lefcourt; Phares).

---

[29]Alvin Toffler, *Future Shock*, Bantam Books, New York, 1970.

[30]Russell L. Ackoff, "Management Misinformation Systems," *Management Science*, 14:4, December 1967, pp. B.147–B.156.

[31]An excellent review of research on individual differences and MIS can be found in Zmud, "Individual Differences and MIS Success: A Review of the Empirical Literature," *Management Science*, 25, October 1979, pp. 966–979. The research cited in this discussion is summarized from that review.

Individual differences	Explanation	Effect on information processing
Dogmatism (low-high)	Extent to which person is positive about beliefs and opinions.	Low dogmatism related to more information search activity, more deliberation, and less confidence in decisions (Lambert and Durand; Long and Ziller; Taylor and Dunnette).
Risk-taking propensity (low-high)	Extent to which person is willing to take risks.	High risk-taking propensity related to more information search activity than low risk-taking propensity (Taylor and Dunnette).
Extroversion-introversion	Extent to which person is concerned with external physical and social environment versus own feelings and thoughts.	Extroverts have quicker retrieval from long-term memory, better retention over short intervals, and less retention over long intervals as compared to introverts (Eysenck).
Tolerance for ambiguity (low-high)	Extent to which person needs clarity and specificity versus vague, unclear rules, directions, procedures, etc.	Lower tolerance for ambiguity related to preference for concrete information and perception that more information will be valuable (Dermer).
Intelligence (low-high)	Measured by ability to perform well on intelligence tests.	High intelligence related to faster information processing, more effective information selection, better retention, faster decisions, and better internal organization of information (Taylor and Dunnette; Hunt and Lansman).
Quantitative abilities (low-high)	Extent of ability to perform computations, formulate algorithms, and use numeric reasoning.	High quantitative abilities related to more use of short-term memory and less use of long-term memory compared to low quantitative abilities (Hunt and Lansman).
Verbal abilities (low-high)	Extent of vocabulary development and use in expressing thoughts.	High verbal abilities related to more effective short-term memory (Hunt, Frost, and Lunnebourg).
Experience in decision making	Extent of experience in formal decision making.	Experience related to more effective information selection, less effective integration, greater flexibility, and less confidence (Taylor and Dunnette).
Task knowledge (low-high)	Extent of knowledge of how to perform the task.	High task knowledge related to less information search compared to low task knowledge (Benbasat and Schroeder).
Age	Chronological age.	Older subjects use more information search, select information more effectively, are more flexible, and require more decision time than younger subjects (Taylor; Taylor and Dunnette; Eysenck).
Management level	Expressed in terms of operational-level management, middle management, and top management.	High management level related to less decision time than low management level (Taylor).

Nonverbal Information Input

Information input to human processing is usually described in terms of written or verbal input. Another significant input of information comes from nonverbal human communication (as contrasted with verbal communication). In face-to-face communication, more than half of the information may be communicated by nonverbal body language. An understanding of "body language" is important to analysts who interview users to obtain information requirements, evaluate satisfaction, etc. In system design, the extent to which humans communicate through body language in certain contexts may be a constraint on substitutes for face-to-face communication (such as electronic mail and teleconferencing).

The following examples illustrate the effect of nonverbal communication on the meaning of the verbal message.

- "I am angry with how you handled that customer" (accompanied by a smile)
- "I am angry with how you handled that customer" (accompanied by a scowl)
- "I am angry with how you handled that customer" (accompanied by a wink)

In other words, the verbal meaning is altered or reinforced by the body language which accompanies it. A more complete discussion of body language and its relevance to information analysis activity can be found in Jenkins and Johnson.[32] The overview in this section is based on that discussion.

There are seven major subsystems in the body language or non-verbal human communication system:

Subsystem	Description
Hand movements	There are three types of hand movements: 1 *Emblems* are hand movements that are understood in a specific culture or occupation. An example is a thumbs-up gesture. 2 *Illustrators* are gestures that relate to what is being said, such as pointing or accentuating. 3 *Adaptors* are touching of oneself or other objects. Self-adaptors are often associated with anxiety, guilt, hostility, and suspicion.
Facial expression	When used, these are generally understood. Examples are smiling and frowning. Even when people suppress facial expressions, they may make very short expressions lasting only a fraction of a second that reflect their true feelings.
Eye contact	Eye contact is a major regulator of conversation. Although there are individual differences, eye contact suggests understanding and interest.
Posture	Posture is the way people position their bodies with regard to other people. This can be a closed position with arms folded to reflect exclusion or the opposite to show inclusion. Having congruent positioning reflects agreement or acceptance.
Proxemics	How people use interpersonal space can express intimacy, social distance, and public distance. For example, standing close indicates intimacy, and sitting at the head of a table indicates

[32]A. Milton Jenkins and Randall D. Johnson, "What the Information Analyst Should Know about Body Language," *MIS Quarterly*, 1:3, September 1977, pp. 33–47.

Subsystem	Description
	status. Sitting alongside a desk indicates openness; sitting behind the desk while the other person is in front indicates a superior-subordinate relationship.
Body rhythms	How people move in relation to others, frequency of speaking, and speaking turns provide clues to meaning being conveyed.
Speech	Choice of words can reflect involvement or distance, or enthusiasm or lack of it.

This overview should provide insight into the fact that nonverbal communication has a variety of forms. Although body language clues are fairly well understood implicitly, individuals will differ in how they use them. Also, cultural differences will change the meaning of body language. For example, in some cultures, nodding in agreement is considered polite, even though there is no agreement; in other cultures, this would not be done.

The importance of nonverbal information may be a major factor in explaining preference for face-to-face discussion. In a set of experiments, Alphonse Chapanis[33] and his colleagues studied how people communicate in the exchange of factual information to solve problems. Their goal was to determine how communication and problem-solving processes are affected by the communication procedures used. They studied two-person teams solving problems for which a computer could be used. Four modes of communication were studied: face-to-face, voice-only, handwriting, and typing.

The consistent finding over a variety of experiments was that problem solving with a voice link was faster. Face-to-face communication was slightly faster than voice-only, but both were significantly faster than either handwriting or typing. In terms of information content, the two voice modes contained more messages (delivering eight times as many messages) and were more redundant than handwriting or typing. The significance of these findings is that communication through electronic media may be less efficient than direct interaction with another person in situations with high affective (emotive) content because of the need for nonverbal clues, etc.

MANAGERS AS INFORMATION PROCESSORS

The organizational position of a person may have a significant effect on performance as an information processor. This section will examine information processing by one organizational position or role—a manager.

A study by Henry Mintzberg[34] of managers in their jobs characterizes managerial work as follows:

   1 Much work at an unrelenting pace. Managers seldom stop thinking about their jobs; during the regular work day the pace of activity is high and constant.

---

[33]A. Chapanis, R. N. Parrish, R. B. Ochsman, and G. D. Weeks, "Studies in Interactive Communications: II. The Effects of Four Communication Modes on the Linguistic Performance of Teams During Cooperative Problem Solving," *Human Factors*, 19:2, 1977, pp. 101–126.

[34]Henry Mintzberg, *The Nature of Managerial Work*, Harper & Row, New York, 1973.

2 Activity characterized by brevity, variety, and fragmentation. Half of the acivities of chief executives took less than nine minutes and only one-tenth took more than an hour. In a study of factory foremen, Guest[35] found that the average activity took 48 seconds, and in a study of MIS executives, Ives and Olson[36] found that the average duration of an activity was 10.3 minutes (with 70 percent lasting less than 9 minutes).

3 Preference for live action. According to Mintzberg, there is strong indication that the manager gravitates toward the more active elements of work—activities that are current, specific, concrete, and nonroutine.

4 Attraction to the verbal media. Mintzberg estimated that managers spend up to 80 percent of their time in verbal communication, a result which was also found in the study of MIS executives. Figure 8-10 shows the breakdown of activities found in Mintzberg's study and corresponding results of the study of MIS executives.

5 Network of contacts. Managers maintain a complex network of relationships with a variety of contacts outside the organization, comprising as much as 50 percent of all contacts. In the study of MIS executives, there were fewer contacts outside of the organization but many with other departments within it. The remaining contacts are primarily with superiors and subordinates of which the former is as little as 10 percent of all contacts.

6 The manager's job is a blend of rights and duties. Managers can exert control over their activities through proper manipulation of these rights and duties.

Ives and Olson noted that managers are likely to pass on rather soft information while their subordinates provide them with factual information. They also found that managers make more requests for information than subordinates.

The relevance of these findings to information systems is that not only are many managerial decisions unstructured, the environmental context in which the decision-making process takes place is also highly unstructured. Given these characteristics of a manager's activities, an information system that requires long uninterrupted periods of concentration is difficult to use regardless of a manager's cognitive style. Decision support systems need to be easily interruptable and easily combined with other forms of information gathering and evaluation (such as informal contacts with outsiders) in order to be effective. The need for integration of multiple functions (including analysis, text processing, and communications) in an intelligent workstation is motivated partly by an understanding of the nature of managerial work. Managers operate in an interruption-driven environment and have very little actual control over the flow of events. Electronic communications systems, such as computer-based message systems and voice mail, are advantageous in removing the interruption component when they replace verbal communication.

Since humans have limits to their processing capabilities, the question arises as to the effect of compressed data (summarized data) on human performance, especially management decision making. In the "Minnesota Experiments,"[37] one of the variables studied was the effect of summarized data versus raw transaction data on decision performance. The group with summarized data made better decisions but were less

[35]R. H. Guest, "Of Time and the Foreman," *Personnel*, 32, 1955–56, pp. 478–486.

[36]B. Ives and M. H. Olson, "Manager or Technician? The Nature of the Information Systems Manager's Job," *MIS Quarterly*, 5:4, December 1981, pp. 49–62.

[37]G. W. Dickson, J. A. Senn, and N. L. Chervany, "Research in Management Information Systems: The Minnesota Experiments," *Management Science*, 23:9, May 1977, pp. 913–923.

Ives and Olson: Information Systems Managers

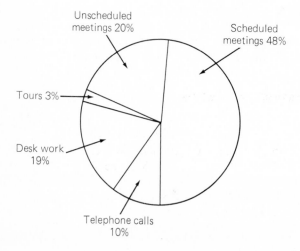

Mintzberg: Chief Executive Officers

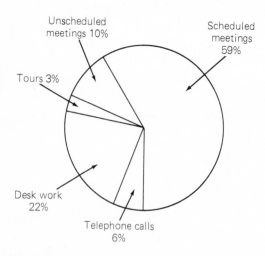

Figure 8-10
Distribution of time by managers. (From Henry Mintzberg, *The Nature of Managerial Work*, Harper & Row, New York, 1973, and B. Ives and M. Olson, "Manager or Technician? The Nature of the Information Systems Manager's Job," *MIS Quarterly* 5:4, December 1981, pp. 49-62.)

confident of their decisions. This may explain the reluctance of some managers to eliminate detailed transaction listings. Scanning the raw data may not improve a manager's decision performance, but it will strengthen confidence.

A related study performed by Anderson[38] investigated decision maker response to probabilistic information. Decision makers were presented with one, two, or three types of data for a series of capital budgeting decisions:

1 Mean value
2 Mean value plus ranges
3 Probability distributions

Decision makers provided with all three items were less consistent in decision making than those receiving only the first, but they were more confident of their decisions.

IMPLICATIONS FOR INFORMATION SYSTEMS DESIGN

The material presented in this chapter provides useful background for information systems designers. Some of these concepts have direct relevance to system design, others to the relationships between the system designer and the user.

Some of the limits on humans as information processors should be directly addressed in system design. Examples are:

Concept	Implications for information system design
Filtering	Information systems should be designed to filter irrelevant data and to provide increased filtering for stress decisions. Systems should attempt to override undesirable frame-of-reference filters by reinforced display of relevant data.
Newell-Simon model	Information systems should assist in defining problem space and in the search process for a solution. The information format should attempt to expand the limits of bounded rationality. Systems should utilize the user memory that is suited to the task.
Magical number 7 ± 2	Codes for human use should not exceed five to seven symbols or be divided into segments of five or less. Systems should not have humans do significant, unaided processing. Graphics may be used to present "chunks" of data in an efficient way.
Just noticeable differences	Systems should highlight significant differences rather than assuming humans will notice them.
Humans as intuitive statisticians	The information system should provide statistical analysis of data: sample variance, correlation, probability estimates, etc. Decision algorithms should provide a consistency check of various information sources. Data generation procedures should be designed to assist in eliminating bias such as recency of events.

[38]John C. Anderson, ''Decision-Maker Response to Probabilistic Information in the Capital Investment Decision Process,'' unpublished doctoral dissertation, University of Minnesota, Minneapolis, 1973.

Concept	Implications for information system design
Concreteness	The information needed should be presented in the form needed. No added processing should be required.
Anchoring and adjustment	Information and decision systems should be designed to assist in selecting a suitable anchor point and for prompting adequate adjustments from it.
Cognitive style: right brain-left brain	Systems should allow selection of alternatives for order of processing and forms of information presentation in order to accommodate different styles.
Learning theory	System interface should be comprehensible to the novice user as well as efficient for the skilled user, and should facilitate a normal progression of learning.
Feedback	Systems should provide feedback to indicate that data has been received, processing is taking place, etc. Response times should be such that throughput is meaningful and errors are minimized.
Value of unused data	Explains some of pressure for data with no apparent utility. Suggests storage and retrieval strategies and terminal access to increase availability without individual storage.
Information overload	Input should be kept below the overload point. System use should not involve managing or processing amounts of data beyond overload.
Individual differences	Those which are critical to system use should be identified and explicitly accommodated, whenever possible, through a flexible interface.
Nonverbal input	System design and training in use should consider the effect of absence of nonverbal clues in electronic communication.
Processing timing	Managers need short bursts of information processing to support their mode of operation.
Amount of information compression	Information systems should present summarized data in a decision-impelling format, but the system should also allow browsing through the raw data.

Many of the concepts discussed in this chapter should be explicitly considered during the system design process. The description of managerial activities suggests that a designer should observe and understand the work environment of a manager. The use of prototype systems aids in observing the task environment because managers can use, experiment with, and adapt systems to their work patterns during development. This approach to system design will be discussed in Chapter 18.

SUMMARY

The basic model of the human as an information processor consists of input from sensors, a processing unit, and output responses. Since inputs are too numerous for all to be accepted, a filtering or selection mechanism is applied to input. The Newell-Simon model focuses on three types of memory used in human information processing: short-term, long-term, and external storage. The varying read-and-write speeds for the different storages plus the differences in capacity explain many characteristics of human processing.

Some tentative limits on humans as information processors are expressed by the "magical number seven, plus or minus two." Another limit is the amount of difference that is noticed or considered significant by a receiver. Humans are also not good as intuitive statisticians.

The area of cognition theory, especially the study of cognitive style, permits useful insights into how individuals approach the problem solving process. The difference between left-brain and right-brain processing suggests that systems can be designed to take advantage of the more intuitive right-brain functions. Other individual differences also affect human problem solving and use of information systems. Need for feedback and psychological value of unused data are characteristics of human processing that should be accommodated by the system. Information overload is an increasing danger as system and communication capacities increase. Individual differences affect information search and use; an understanding of these differences may aid a system designer. Since nonverbal communication is eliminated in many systems, system design must be changed to reflect this reduction in input. The task being performed affects information processing. This is seen in managers. Characteristics of managerial activity important to use of information systems are fragmentation, brevity, frequent interruptions, and a preference for face-to-face communication. Decision making performance of managers tends to improve with summarized data but confidence in decisions is enhanced by the use of raw data.

MINICASES
1 NEED TO KNOW AND AVAILABLE INFORMATION

Employee preferences regarding the sources of information they use in their work are quite different from the sources they usually depend on outside of work. That was the conclusion of the International Association of Business Communicators after they surveyed work communication in 40 companies.

Ninety percent of those surveyed preferred to get news from their immediate supervisors. The next most favored sources were small group meetings, the top executive, and handbooks —in that order. Fifty-five percent get their information from supervisors. The next most available source, however, was the least favored of all 15 surveyed in the study: the grapevine. The employee handbook and the bulletin board ranked third and fourth as the most available sources.

The survey also asked what it was the employees wished to know. The three subjects which ranked highest were the organization's future plans, personnel policies, and productivity improvement information—in that order.

Source: A joint survey by the International Association of Business Communicators, San Francisco, CA, and Towers, Perrin, Forster, & Crosby, Inc., New York, 1980.

Questions
a Mintzberg's study shows that executives prefer an oral means of communication. How does that compare with this study of workers? *the same*
b What do their choices indicate about their locus of control?
c Identify the frame of reference and the filters that appear to be operating in these workers.
d How is their problem space probably defined?

pg 243

2 DAYDREAMS IN MANHATTAN

"A penny for your thoughts" was the inducement some psychology graduate students gave pedestrians on Fifth Avenue when they wanted to study what passersby had on their minds.

Two tables were set up on a fine Friday lunch hour to sample people's thoughts at Fifth Avenue near 57th Street and at 14th Street. The results showed that the two environments produced quite different thoughts. At fashionable Fifth Avenue, the most common thoughts were about the environment, the misfortune of having to return to work, and members of the opposite sex—in that order. In the open market area of 14th Street, the most common thoughts were of money and shopping. Those were followed in frequency by thoughts of the future and thoughts about a particular member of the opposite sex. In addition, men were more likely to be thinking about themselves while women were more likely to be thinking about another person.

"Daydreams in Manhattan," *Psychology Today*, August 1981.

Questions

a How do you feel about this story as a source of information? Would you be likely to base a business decision on it?

b If you did decide that it might be a useful study, what additional information would you want to have about the study?

c What do your answers say about your limitations as an intuitive statistician?

Need to resist impulse to draw inferences from the Sampling

EXERCISES

1 Describe the Newell-Simon model of the human as an information processor.
2 Explain the effect of too much input on performance.
3 Explain the filtering process. How is it affected by stress? What are the implications for information system design?
4 Why do people use heuristics in information processing? Give an example of both good and bad heuristics.
5 Compare the access, read, and write speeds estimated for the Newell-Simon model to the speeds of any modern computer system.
6 What are the implications for information system design of the statement that humans are serial rather than parallel processors?
7 Explain multiprogramming. How might this concept be used by humans in processing?
8 What is problem space? Illustrate the relationship of task environment and problem space by an example from your experience.
9 Explain the implications of "the magical number seven, plus or minus two" for information processing system design.
10 Explain Weber's law of just noticeable differences. Describe its implication for information processing.
11 What type of feedback mechanisms are built into the following?
   a Computer-based message system
   b Word processor
   c Keyboard of a CRT terminal
   d Voice store-and-forward message system
12 What are the implications for information system design of the psychological need for feedback?
13 Explain the value of unused opportunities. What are the implications for information system design?
14 How does the model of human processing assist in explaining the decision maker who makes decisions more easily under stress, apparently with very little information?
15 Given our understanding of managerial activities, how can computer-based information systems best be utilized to improve managerial performance?
16 What are some advantages and disadvantages of the use of computer-based message systems in organizations?

17 Assuming the following are true, explain the possible implications for information system design of the following:

a Most analysts are analytic rather than heuristic.

b Heuristics can adapt easily to analytic analysis; analytics cannot adapt easily to a heuristic approach.

c The concept of analytic-heuristic is a continuous variable. A person is not either-or but is more inclined to one or the other.

d Analytic or heuristic reasoning both use the rational analytic left brain. Neither draws in the right side of the brain.

e The more you know, the less you need to find out.

f Executives prefer face-to-face communication.

g Nonverbal messages may communicate as much information as verbal messages.

18 Information systems used in a task not only perform processing required for the task; they are part of the task learning process. Comment on this concept and its implications for information system design for novices and for experts.

19 An analyst responded to the table of personality, demographic, and situational differences affecting information use with the statement: "I don't know what to do with it!" Explain some information system design implications in the following cases:

a A data entry system for 150 data entry personnel.

b An executive information system for the president.

c Differences of opinion relative to sales analysis and marketing system design features between a group of sales managers and the system analyst (each having different personalities).

20 Explain some tendencies with respect to information requirements:

a Type and availability of information for a young executive with low tolerance for ambiguity and a high task knowledge.

b Response time requirements for a bright, quantitative introvert.

c Type of information capabilities for a young stock market analyst with high risk taking propensities.

d Type of information capabilities for a planner with external locus of control, low dogmatism, and high risk propensity.

SELECTED REFERENCES

Ashton, R.: *Human Information Processing in Accounting*, Studies in Accounting Research, American Accounting Association, 1982.

Benbasat, Izak, and R. G. Schroeder: "An Experimental Investigation of Some MIS Design Variables," *MIS Quarterly*, 2:2, 1978, pp. 43–54.

Conrad, R.: "Errors of Immediate Memory," *The British Journal of Psychology*, November 1959, pp. 349–359.

Crannell, C. W., and J. M. Parrish: "A Comparison of Immediate Memory Span for Digits, Letters and Words," *The Journal of Psychology*, 44, October 1957, pp. 319–327.

Dermer, J D.: "Cognitive Characteristics and the Perceived Importance of Information," *The Accounting Review*, 48, 1973, pp. 511–519.

Dickson, G. W., J. A. Senn, and N. L. Chervany: "Research in Management Information Systems: The Minnesota Experiments," *Management Science*, 23:9, May 1977, pp. 913–923.

Eysenck, M. W.: "Human Memory: Theory, Research and Differences," Pergamon, Oxford, 1977.

Gul, Ferdinand A.: "The Joint and Moderating Role of Personality and Cognitive Style on Decision Making," *The Accounting Review*, 59:2, April 1984, pp. 264–277.

Huber, George P.: "Cognitive Style as a Basis for MIS and DSS Designs: Much Ado About Nothing?" *Management Science*, 29:5, May 1983, pp. 567–597.

Hunt, E., N. Frost, and C. Lunnebourg: "Individual Differences in Cognition: A New Approach to Intelligence," in G. H. Bower (ed.), *The Psychology of Learning and Memory*, Academic Press, New York, 1973.

Hunt, E., and M. Lansman: "Cognitive Theory Applied to Individual Differences," in W. H. Estes (ed.), *Handbook of Learning and Cognitive Processes*, Earlbaum, Hillsdale, NJ, 1975.

Jenkins, A. Milton, and Randall D. Johnson: "What the Information Analyst Should Know about Body Language," *MIS Quarterly*, 1:3, September 1977, pp. 33–47.

Lambert, Z. V., and R.M. Durand: "Purchase Information Acquisition and Cognitive Style," *Journal of Psychology*, 97, 1977, pp. 3–13.

Lefcourt, H.M.: "Recent Developments in the Study of Locus of Control," in B. A. Maher (ed.), *Progress in Experimental Psychological Research*, Academic Press, New York, 1972.

Libby, R.: *Accounting and Human Information Processing: Theory and Applications*, Prentice-Hall, Englewood Cliffs, NJ, 1981.

Long, B. H., and R. Z. Ziller: "Dogmatism and Predecision Information Search," *Journal of Applied Psychology*, 49, 1965, pp. 376–378.

McKenney, James L., and Peter G. W. Keen: "How Managers' Minds Work," *Harvard Business Review*, May–June 1974, pp. 79–90.

Miller, George A.: "The Magical Number Seven, Plus or Minus Two: Some Limits on Our Capability for Processing Information," *The Psychological Review*, 63:2, March 1956, pp. 81–97.

Mintzberg, Henry: *The Nature of Managerial Work*, Harper & Row, New York, 1973.

Newell, Allen, and Herbert A. Simon: *Human Problem Solving*, Prentice-Hall, Englewood Cliffs, NJ, 1972.

Phares, B. J.: *Locus of Control in Personality*, General Learning Press, Morristown, NJ, 1976.

Robey, D., and W. Taggart: "Human Information Processing in Information and Decision Support Systems," *MIS Quarterly*, 6:2, June 1982, pp. 61–73.

Shneiderman, Ben: *Software Psychology: Human Factors in Computer and Information Systems*, Winthrop, Cambridge, MA, 1980.

Simon, Herbert A., and Allen Newell: "Human Problem Solving: The State of the Theory in 1970," *American Psychologist*, 26, February 1971, pp. 145–159.

Slovic, Paul: "From Shakespeare to Simon: Speculations—and Some Evidence—about Man's Ability to Process Information," Research Monograph, 12:12, Oregon Research Institute, University of Oregon, April 1972.

Taylor, R. N.: "Age and Experience as Determinants of Managerial Information Processing and Decision Making Performance," *Academy of Management Journal*, 18, 1975, pp. 74–81.

Taylor, R. N., and M. D. Dunnette: "Relative Contribution of Decision Maker Attributes to Decision Process," *Organizational Behavior and Human Performance*, 12, 1974, pp. 286–298.

Tversky, A., and D. Kahneman: "The Framing of Decisions and the Psychology of Choice," *Science*, 211, January 1981, pp. 453–458.

Zmud, Robert W.: "Individual Differences and MIS Success: A Review of the Empirical Literature," *Management Science*, 25, October 1979, pp. 966–979.

SYSTEM CONCEPTS

The term "system" is in common use. One speaks of an educational system, computer system, solar system, system of theology, and many others. System concepts provide a useful framework for describing and understanding many organizational phenomena including features of information systems.

DEFINITION OF A SYSTEM

Systems can be abstract or physical. An *abstract system* is an orderly arrangement of interdependent ideas or constructs. For example, a system of theology is an orderly arrangement of ideas about God and the relationship of humans to God. A *physical system* is a set of elements which operate together to accomplish an objective. A physical system may be further defined by examples:

Physical system	Description
Circulatory system	The heart and blood vessels which move blood through the body.
Transportation system	The personnel, machines, and organizations which transport goods.
Weapons system	The equipment, procedures, and personnel which make it possible to use a weapon.
School system	The buildings, teachers, administrators, and textbooks that function together to provide instruction for students.
Computer system	The equipment which functions together to accomplish computer processing.
Accounting system	The records, rules, procedures, equipment, and personnel which operate to record data, measure income, and prepare reports.

The examples illustrate that a system is not a randomly assembled set of elements; it consists of elements which can be identified as belonging together because of a common purpose, goal, or objective. Physical systems are more than conceptual constructs; they display activity or behavior. The parts interact to achieve an objective.

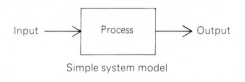

Simple system model

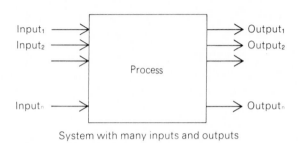

System with many inputs and outputs

Figure 9-1
General models of a system.

GENERAL MODEL OF A SYSTEM

A general model of a physical system is input, process, and output. This is, of course, very simplified because a system may have several inputs and outputs (Figure 9-1). The features which define and delineate a system form its *boundary*. The system is inside the boundary; the *environment* is outside the boundary. In some cases, it is fairly simple to define what is part of the system and what is not; in other cases, the person studying the system may arbitrarily define the boundaries. Some examples of boundaries are:

System	Boundary
Human	Skin, hair, nails, and all parts contained inside form the system; all things outside are environment.
Automobile	The automobile body plus tires and all parts contained within form the system.
Production	Production machines, production inventory of work in process, production employees, production procedures, etc., form the system. The rest of the company is in the environment.

The production system example illustrates the problem of the boundary concept. Is raw material inventory included in the production system? One definition of the production system may include raw material because it is necessary for the purpose being studied; another use may exclude it.

Each system is composed of *subsystems* which in turn are made up of other subsystems, each subsystem being delineated by its boundaries. The interconnections and interactions between the subsystems are termed *interfaces*. Interfaces occur at the

Computer configuration as system

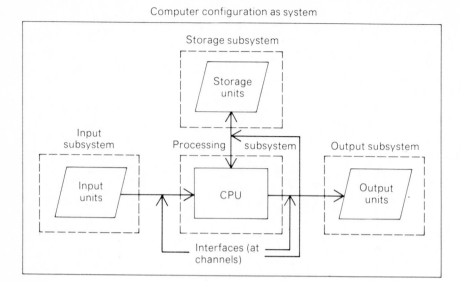

Central processing unit as system

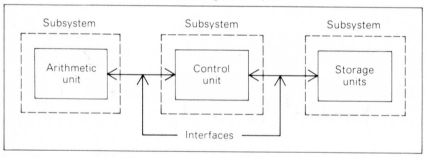

Figure 9-2
Above and facing page: Examples of subsystems and interfaces.

boundary and take the form of inputs and outputs. Figure 9-2 shows examples of subsystems and interfaces at boundaries.

A subsystem at the lowest level (input, process, output) is often not defined as to the process. This system is termed a *black box*, since the inputs and outputs are known but not the actual transformation from one to the other. The major system concepts of boundary, interface, subsystem, and black box are illustrated in Figure 9-3. Another major system concept, feedback for system control, will be described in Chapter 10.

TYPES OF SYSTEMS

Although many phenomena as different as a human and a computer program can be described in systems terms, they are still quite different. There are several ways of classifying systems that emphasize these differences. Two such classifications are deterministic versus probabilistic and closed versus open systems.

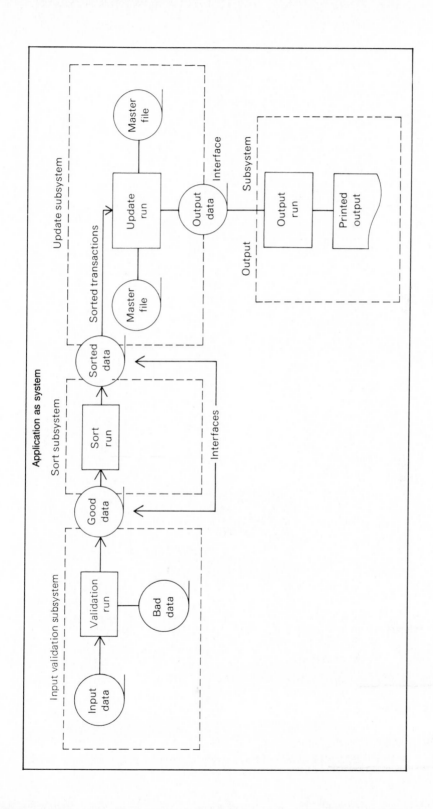

Application as system

Input validation subsystem

Input data

Validation run

Bad data

Good data

Sort subsystem

Sort run

Sorted data

Interfaces

Update subsystem

Sorted transactions

Master file

Update run

Master file

Output data

Interface

Subsystem

Output run

Printed output

Output

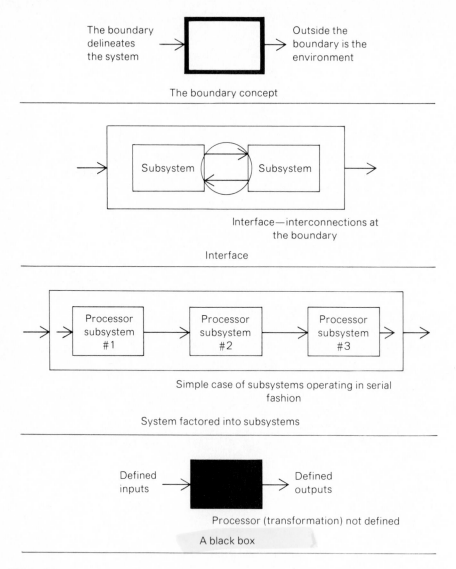

Figure 9-3
System concepts.

Deterministic and Probabilistic Systems

A *deterministic system* operates in a predictable manner. The interaction among the parts is known with certainty. If one has a description of the state of the system at a given point in time plus a description of its operation, the next state of the system may be given exactly, without error. An example is a correct computer program which performs exactly according to a set of instructions.

The *probabilistic system* can be described in terms of probable behavior, but a certain degree of error is always attached to the prediction of what the system will do. An inventory system is an example of a probabilistic system. The average demand, average time for replenishment, etc., may be defined, but the exact value at any given time is not known. Another example is a set of instructions given to a human who, for a variety of reasons, may not follow the instructions exactly as given.

Closed and Open Systems

A *closed system* is defined in physics as a system which is self-contained. It does not exchange material, information, or energy with its environment. An example is a chemical reaction in a sealed, insulated container. Such closed systems will finally run down or become disorganized. This movement to disorder is termed an *increase in entropy*.

In organizations and in information processing, there are systems that are relatively isolated from the environment but not completely closed in the physics sense. These will be termed closed systems, meaning relatively closed. For example, systems in manufacturing are often designed to minimize unwanted exchanges with the environment outside the system. Such systems are designed to be as closed as possible, so the manufacturing process can operate without disturbances from suppliers, customers, etc. A computer program is a relatively closed system because it accepts only previously defined inputs, processes them, and provides previously defined outputs. In summary, the relatively closed system is one that has only controlled and well defined inputs and outputs. It is not subject to disturbances from outside the system (Figure 9-4).

Open systems exchange information, material, or energy with the environment, including random and undefined inputs. Examples of open systems are biological systems (such as humans) and organizational systems. Open systems tend to have form and structure to allow them to adapt to changes in their environment in such a way as to continue their existence. They are "self-organizing" in the sense that they change their organization in response to changing conditions. Living systems (cells, plants, humans, etc.) are open systems. They attempt to maintain equilibrium by *homeostasis*, the process of adjusting to keep the system operating within prescribed limits. An example is the body which maintains its temperature within very narrow limits.

Organizations are open systems; a critical feature of their existence is their capability to adapt in the face of changing competition, changing markets, etc. Organizations illustrate the system concept of *equifinality*: more than one system structure and process may achieve the same result (but not necessarily at the same cost). Characteristics of organizations as open systems are discussed in a later section of this chapter.

Artificial systems are systems that are created rather than occurring in nature. Organizations, information systems, and computer programs are all examples of artificial systems. The artificial systems are designed to support the objectives of the designers and users. They exhibit, therefore, characteristics of the system that they support. Principles that apply to living systems are also applicable to artificial systems that support human or other living systems.

In Chapter 6 two models of the decision maker were described—a classical economic model and an administrative model. They correspond to closed and open systems. A

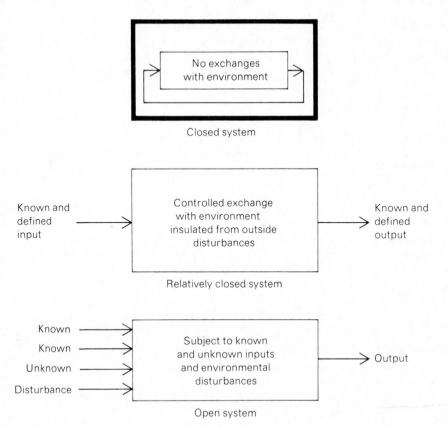

Figure 9-4
Concept of open and closed systems.

closed decision system is represented by the classical economic model. The decision maker logically examines all alternatives (which are completely known), preference-orders the consequences, and selects the alternative which leads to the best (optimizing) consequences. The quantitative models of decision making are typically closed decision system models.

An *open decision system* is represented by the administrative model of the decision maker. The decision takes place in a complex and partially unknown environment. The decision maker is influenced by the environment. Whereas the goal of the closed model is well defined, the goal of the open model is similar to an aspiration level in that it may change as the decision maker receives evidence of success or failure.

Human-Machine Systems

Information systems are generally human-machine systems (or user-machine systems) in that both perform some of the activities in the accomplishments of a goal (e.g., making a decision). The machine elements (computer hardware and software) are relatively closed and deterministic, whereas the human elements of the system are open and probabilistic. Various combinations of human and machine are possible. For instance, the computer can be emphasized and the human simply monitor the machine operation. At the other extreme, the machine performs a supporting role by doing computation or searching for data while the user performs the significant work. A typical compromise system is one where the machine is used for regular, ''programmed'' decisions and alerts the human to exceptions for processing as ''unprogrammed'' decisions. An appropriate balance in division of functions is critical to the successful performance of each component in accomplishing its objective; the division between human and machine will thus vary from application to application.

A HUMAN-MACHINE SYSTEM FOR BABY CARE

Isolettes are environments for newborn high-risk babies. Their purpose is to monitor the child's vital signs and to keep the temperature stable. Cincinnati General Hospital uses a computer system named Alcyon and the thermal environment of Isolettes to monitor and record the baby's vital signs. In the nurse-computer system, the nurses have three responsibilities:

1 See that each of four skin thermistors (temperature probes) are in their proper places; one must be taped to the infant, one each to the front and the top of the Isolette and one suspended in the air of the enclosure to properly measure the temperature. The other end of each thermistor is plugged into an input box which transmits the information to the computer. There is also a visual alert on a screen near the ceiling level to call for human evaluation of a particular Isolette.

2 Examine the information collected by the computer and use it in making care decisions and problem solving. Each nursery has terminals for the input of initial information on the baby and for requesting data on its current status.

3 Fill the infant's needs to be turned, fed, have diapers changed, and to bond with its parents. In other words, the nurses must recognize the importance of the therapeutic nurse-patient relationship. They must never feel that the child is on "automatic pilot." A skilled nurse can see the infant "doesn't look right" before the computer notes the changes in vital signs. "Using Computers in Newborn Intensive Care Settings," *American Journal of Nursing*, July 1981, p. 1336. ©1981 by the American Journal of Nursing Company; Reproduced by permission.

SUBSYSTEMS

Smaller boundary than system decomposition is useful for analysis

The use of subsystems as building blocks is basic to analysis and development of systems. This requires an understanding of the principles which dictate how systems are built from subsystems.

Decomposition

A complex system is difficult to comprehend when considered as a whole. Therefore, the system is decomposed or factored into subsystems. The boundaries and interfaces are defined, so that the sum of the subsystems constitutes the entire system. This process of decomposition is continued with subsystems divided into smaller subsystems until the smallest subsystems are of manageable size. The subsystems resulting from this process generally form hierarchical structures (Figure 9-5). In the hierarchy, a subsystem is one element of a *suprasystem* (the system above it).

An example of decomposition is the factoring of an information processing system into subsystems. One approach to decomposition might proceed as follows:

1 Information system divided into subsystems such as:
a Sales and order entry
b Inventory
c Production
d Personnel and payroll
e Purchasing
f Accounting and control
g Planning
h Environmental intelligence

2 Each subsystem is divided further into subsystems. For example, the personnel and payroll subsystem might be divided into the following smaller subsystems:
a Creation and update of personnel-payroll records
b Personnel reports
c Payroll data entry and validation
d Hourly payroll processing
e Salaried payroll processing
f Payroll reports for management
g Payroll reports for government

3 If the task is to design and program a new system, the subsystems (major applications) defined in (2) might be further subdivided into smaller subsystems or modules. For example, the hourly payroll processing subsystem might be factored into modules for the calculation of deductions and net pay, payroll register and audit controls preparation, check printing, and register and controls output (Figure 9-6).

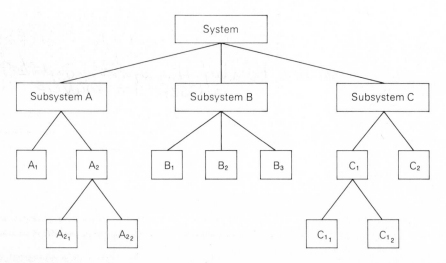

Figure 9-5
Hierarchical relations of subsystems.

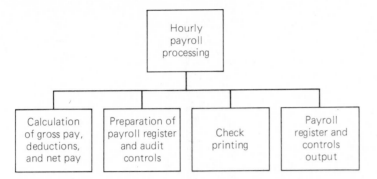

Figure 9-6
Hierarchical structure of subsystems of a payroll system.

Decomposition into subsystems is used both to analyze an existing system and to design and implement a new system. In both cases, the investigator or designer must decide how to factor, i.e., where to draw the boundaries. The decisions will depend on the objectives of the decomposition and also on individual differences among designers; the latter should be minimized.

The general principle in decomposition which assumes that system objectives dictate the process is *functional cohesion*. Components are considered to be part of the same subsystem if they perform or are related to the same function. As an example, an application program to be divided into modules (subsystems) will divide along major program functions such as accumulating hours worked, calculating deductions, printing a check, etc. In design, the identification of functionally cohesive subsystems is the first step. The boundary then needs to be clearly specified, interfaces simplified, and appropriate connections established among the subsystems.

Simplification

The process of decomposition could lead to a large number of subsystem interfaces to define. For example, four subsystems which all interact with each other will have six interconnections; a system with 20 subsystems all interacting will have 190 interconnections. The number can rise quite quickly as the number of subsystems increases. The number of interconnections if all subsystems interact is in general $1/2n(n-1)$, where $n =$ the number of subsystems. Each interconnection is a potential interface for communication among subsystems. Each interface implies a definition of a communication path (Figure 9-7).

Simplification is the process of organizing subsystems so as to reduce the number of interconnections. Some methods of simplification are:

1 Clusters of subsystems are established which interact with each other, then a single interface path is defined from the cluster to other subsystems or clusters of subsystems (Figure 9-7). An example is a database which is accessed by many programs, but the interconnection is only through a database management interface.

2 Methods are established for decoupling systems (see below) so that the need for interconnection is reduced.

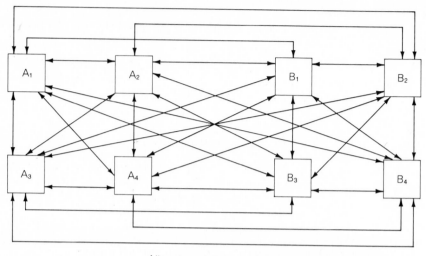

All systems interconnected

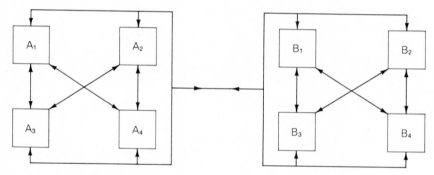

Systems connected within cluster, and clusters interconnected
with single interface

Figure 9-7
Clustering of subsystems to simplify interface patterns.

Decoupling

If two different subsystems are connected very tightly, very close coordination between them is required. For example, if the raw material is put directly into production the moment it arrives at the factory, the raw materials system can be said to be tightly coupled. Under these conditions, raw material delivery (input to production system and output from raw material system) must be precisely timed in order to avoid delays in production or to prevent new material from arriving too soon with no place to be stored.

Such tight coupling places a heavy coordination and timing requirement on the two systems. Because they are somewhat independent, it is difficult to make them operate completely in synchronized fashion. Since random events make delivery times uncertain, expected arrival times vary. Likewise, the production process can experience random or unplanned delays. The solution is to _decouple_ or loosen the connection so that the two systems can operate in the short run with some measure of independence. Some means of decoupling are (Figure 9-8):

   1 _Inventories, buffers, or waiting lines._ In the example of the raw material subsystem and production subsystem, a raw material inventory allows the two subsystems to operate somewhat independently (in the short run). Data buffers are used in some computer systems and some communications systems to compensate for different rates of input and output of data.

   2 _Slack and flexible resources._ When the output of one subsystem is the input to another, the existence of slack resources allows subsystems to be somewhat independent and yet allows each to respond to the demands of the other subsystem. For example, most data processing systems can provide an extra report or extra analysis because they have slack resources. The ability of an organization to respond to variations in demand by the use of slack resources is enhanced if the available resources can be employed for a variety of purposes. An information systems organization that uses the concept of a combination of systems analyst-programmer has more flexibility in meeting variations in demand between analysis and programming than an organization with the same number of personnel that uses systems analysts only for analysis and design and programmers only for programming. (But, of course, this is only one consideration in the choice of separate or combined jobs.)

   3 _Standards._ Standards specifications, standard costs, and other standards allow a subsystem to plan and organize with reduced need to communicate with other subsystems. If, for example, the production department wishes to design a data processing module involving finished goods and a standard product code is used throughout the organization, there is no need to communicate and negotiate with other departments about the codes to be used. A standard

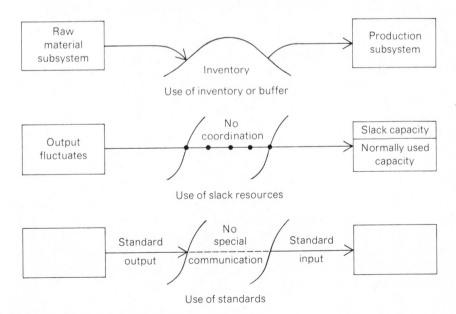

Figure 9-8
Decoupling mechanisms to reduce need for communication and close connection among subsystems.

database description maintained by the data administrator (the data dictionary) allows use of the database without tedious and time-consuming checking with other subsystems also using the database.

A FLEXIBLE PROGRAM AND SLACK RESOURCES

"We simply wanted to know where the ash would be going, so we used the National Weather Service forecast as an input to our own trajectory model to tell us where the ash would be and when," explained research meteorologist Nick Heffter. He was referring to the tracking of debris from the eruption of Mount Saint Helens in the spring of 1980.

The model had been developed five years previously to track any type of tracer including nuclear fallout. Its purpose was to alert key government agencies to changing conditions during an alert. Variables included wind speed and direction, air temperature, height, pressure, and humidity. It predicted as far as 84 hours into the future.

The Meteorological Center in Maryland used its three computers for the complex calculations in the days immediately following the eruption. The results were reported twice daily to the Federal Aviation Administration for airplane schedules and the Environmental Protection Agency for radiation levels. As the cloud of ashes grew more diffuse, the Center's computers were returned to their normal use of weather analysis and forecasting. ("Weather Models Turn to Tracking Volcanic Ash," *Computerworld*, June 2, 1980.)

The problems of tight coupling stem not only from the physical problems of coordinating movement of resources but also from the problem of communication. The various methods for decoupling reduce the need for communication and allow the subsystems to communicate on an exception basis. Only if the subsystem begins to operate out of certain limits do the other subsystems with which it interconnects need to be informed. For example, the processing of vendor payments may be handled by a subsystem in accounting and data processing. It may be able to handle an average of 200 payments per day and by using slack resources handle up to 300 payments per day. The purchasing subsystem initiates the orders which result in the processing load in the payments subsystem. Because the payments subsystem can handle up to 300 payments, the purchasing subsystem need not communicate variations in orders placed unless there is an increase beyond 300 per day. The use of decoupling mechanisms may therefore be viewed as an alternative to increased communications. This implies that an improved information or communication system may increase the opportunity for tight coupling and may reduce the need for decoupling mechanisms.

The process of decoupling and allowing each subsystem some independence in managing its affairs has many benefits, but it is not without its costs. One of these is the cost of the decoupling mechanism itself (inventory, buffer, waiting line, slack resource, standards, etc.). Another cost stems from the fact that each subsystem may act in the best possible way as a subsystem, but the sum of their actions may not be optimal for the organization. This is the problem of suboptimization. For example, the production may be organized to make use of production equipment by scheduling several weeks in advance; this prevents the sales subsystem from meeting urgent customer requests.

THE JAPANESE SOLUTION OF NO INVENTORY

Observers at Japanese automobile factories note the lack of inventories of parts for assembly. The American manufacturers had the practice of selecting suppliers without regard for distance from the plant and then using the in-plant inventory to handle any disturbances in delivery. Instead, the Japanese located the supplier plants adjacent to the assembly plant. Parts flowed from supplier to assembly location "just in time." The suppliers were given long-term contracts.

In system terms, the Japanese had coupled the systems more tightly and thereby reduced inventory, a costly decoupling mechanism. The tighter coupling increased the need for parts movement communication. On the other hand, longer-term contracts reduced communications regarding product specifications, quality control, etc.

PREVENTING SYSTEMS ENTROPY

Entropy - decline or decay

Systems can run down and decay or can become disordered or disorganized. Stated in system terminology, an increase in entropy takes place. Preventing or offsetting the increase in entropy requires inputs of matter and energy to repair, replenish, and maintain the system. This maintenance input is termed *negative entropy*. Open systems require more negative entropy than relatively closed systems for keeping at a steady state of organization and operation, but all the systems described in the text require it. Examples of system maintenance through negative entropy by inputs of matter and energy are:

System	Manifestations of entropy	Negative entropy
Automobile	Engine won't start Tires too thin	Tune up engine Replace tires
Organization	Employees retire Procedures not followed	Hire new employees Training and improved supervision, motivation procedures
Computer program	User dissatisfaction with features Errors	Program enhancements Repair program
Computer data files	Errors and omissions in data field Not all relevant entities included	Review and correct procedures Procedure to identify omission and obtain data

APPLICATION PROGRAM MAINTENANCE AS NEGATIVE ENTROPY

It is estimated that 70 percent of programmer and analyst resources are being devoted to maintenance of existing programs. Corrections of bugs will be virtually complete after the first year (although there may still be latent errors). Enhancements continue to be done on a fairly regular basis. Over a five year period, bug correction plus enhancement may average about 50 percent of original development cost.

SYSTEM STRESS AND SYSTEM CHANGE[1]

Systems, whether they be living or artificial systems, organizational systems, information systems, or systems of controls, change because they undergo stress. A stress is a force transmitted by a system's suprasystem that causes a system to change, so that the suprasystem can better achieve its goals. In trying to accommodate the stress, the system may impose stress on its subsystems, and so on.

Types of Stress

There are two basic forms of stresses which can be imposed on a system, separately or concurrently:

1 A change in the goal set of the system. New goals may be created or old goals may be eliminated.

2 A change in the achievement levels desired for existing goals. The level of desired acheievement may be increased or decreased.

For example, the goal set for a computer system may change if a requirement is imposed by management (the suprasystem) for system data to be shared among multiple users rather than be available only to a single user.

Consequences of Stress

When a suprasystem exerts stress on a system, the system will change to accommodate the stress, or it will become pathological; that is, it will decay and terminate. A suprasystem enforces compliance by the system through its control over the supply of resources (matter-energy) and information input to the system. If the system does not accommodate the stress, the suprasystem decreases or terminates the supply of matter-energy and information input. A positive correlation exists between the supply of resources and information and the extent to which the system facilitates the suprasystem meeting its goals. For example, in a computer environment, if a computer application system does not meet user requirements, it will fall into disuse. Users will not supply input to the system and the system files will become outdated, or the data supplied will contain errors because the users have little interest in maintaining the integrity of the data input.

Process of Adaptation

Systems accommodate stress through a change in *form*; there can be *structural* changes or *process* changes. For example, a computer system under stress for more shareability

---

[1]Material in this section is adapted from Gordon B. Davis and Ron Weber, *Auditing Advanced EDP Systems: A Survey of Practice and Development of a Theory*, The Management Information Systems Research Center, Minneapolis, 1983, pp. 20–22. A research report for the Limperg Institute of The Netherlands, the report is available through the Institute of Internal Auditors, Altamonte Springs, Florida.

of data may be changed by the installation of terminals in remote locations—a structural change. Demands for greater efficiency may be met by changing the way in which it sorts data—a process change.

It is very unlikely that system changes to accommodate stress will be *global* change to its structure and processes. Instead, those responsible for the change will attempt to *localize* it by confining the adjustment processes to only one or some of its subsystems. This principle of *stress localization* exists for two reasons:

1 The process of accommodating stress often places abnormal demands on system performance. If a global change has to be made, it is more likely that the system will become pathological than if changes can be limited.

2 One of the defining characteristics of complex systems that survive is that they have relatively independent subsystems.[2] This enables one subsystem to remain stable even though another subsystem may be undergoing change. Thus, the disruption caused by change is minimized.

The principle of stress localization has important implications for understanding how systems can be adapted to accommodate stress. It implies that not all subsystems in the system have to be examined to understand the effects of stress. Instead, only those subsystems that adjust to accommodate the stress need to be examined.

As a general rule, the subsystems closest to the stress will change the most. Closeness to stress is usually functional; the subsystem that performs the function most similar to the function needed to alleviate the stress is the subsystem closest to the stress. As an example, in the case of a stress because of unauthorized updating of records in an online system, the subdivision closest to the stress is the input subsystem which has the authorization function.

The concept of stress aids in explaining some of the dynamics which cause information systems to change. The process of information system change follows a general conceptual model of adaptation to system stress:

1 The organization places a stress on the information systems function to better meet organizational needs. The organizational needs may be new and stem from new environmental stresses or may be long-standing needs that have not been met because of technology, cost, or other constraints. The stress may be to conform information systems more closely to organizational processes.

2 The information systems function seeks to respond to the stress for improvement or changes from the organization. If new technology or new system designs are available, a more advanced system may be installed to better respond to the needs of the organization.

3 Information system subsystems that are closest to the stress are the ones that have the greatest influence on the design of the revised system.

As an example of this concept, an organization has received orders from customers in the mail. After the orders are transcribed into machine-readable form, a batch processing run each night has determined whether stock is available for shipment. The customer has been informed by mail. The organization has wanted to provide instant response to

[2]Herbert A. Simon, *The Sciences of the Artificial*, Second Edition, MIT Press, Cambridge, 1981.

customer inquiry about availability, but has been constrained by information processing technology. The availability of online technology has increased the stress being applied to information systems to meet the organizational needs. As a result, an online processing system has been installed with terminals at customer sites and online entry of orders. The entire information system did not change to meet the immediate response to customer stress, only those systems closest to the stress—the order entry, input of order, and availability response subsystems.

SYSTEM CONCEPTS AND ORGANIZATIONS

Chapter 11 will describe concepts of organizational structure and organizational dynamics. However, two system-organization concepts will be described here—organizations as open systems and organizational efficiency and effectiveness.

Organizations as Open Systems

Organizations are open systems, since they receive unplanned and unscheduled inputs from their environment and adapt in such a way as to continue their existence. Katz and Kahn have identified nine common characteristics of open systems which are particularly applicable to organizations:[3]

1 *The importation of energy.* New supplies of energy are brought into the organization in the form of people and materials.

2 *Throughput.* Inputs are altered in some way as materials are processed or as people are served.

3 *Output.* The organization produces something which interacts with the environment.

4 *Systems as cycles of events.* Products sent into the environment are the basis for the source of energy for the repeating of the event. A business organization uses labor and materials to produce a product, and the income from the sale of the product is used to buy more materials and labor. A voluntary professional organization does something for its members which leads them to continue to contribute energy to it.

5 *Negative entropy.* An organization attempts to import more energy than it expends in the process, in order to maintain the system and to ensure its ongoing existence.

6 *Information input, negative feedback, and the coding process.* The information coming into the organization is coded and selected so that it does not inundate the organization. Information provides negative feedback from the environment, providing a control mechanism to indicate and correct for negative deviation from environmental demands.

7 *The steady state and dynamic homeostasis.* Systems tend to maintain their basic character, attempting to control threatening external factors. As growth and expansion occur, basic system characteristics tend to remain constant.

8 *Differentiation.* There is a tendency toward elaboration of roles and specialization of function.

9 *Equifinality.* The organization has more than one way of accomplishing organizational objectives.

---

[3]D. Katz and R. L. Kahn, *The Social Psychology of Organizations*, Second Edition, Wiley, New York 1978.

The concept of the organization as a system provides a framework for an information systems analyst to understand the organization and to study its subsystems.

Organizational Efficiency and Effectiveness

One common organizational problem is how to evaluate an organizational unit or activity. Systems concepts suggest two major classes of performance measurement:

Measurement	Explanation
Effectiveness	Outputs from the system. These represent the reason the system exists. Being effective implies doing the "right" thing (producing the desired result).
Efficiency	The use of inputs to produce outputs, i.e., the use of system resources to achieve results. Being efficient implies the system is operating the "right" way.

The relationship between effectiveness and efficiency is that effectiveness is a measure of "goodness" of output, while efficiency is a measure of the resources required to achieve the output. This relationship is diagrammed in Figure 9-9.

The importance of the efficiency-effectiveness dichotomy is that organizations tend to measure and control efficiency more than effectiveness. The reason is that efficiency measurements tend to be easier to obtain and more precise in formulation. This often leads to producing the wrong output efficiently. For example:

- Information system development for applications may be measured by adherence to budget and development standards (efficiency) with no attention to how well the applications meet needs of the customers (effectiveness).
- A public school measures performance by cost per credit hour (efficiency), but does not measure the effect of the credit hours on the students.
- A word processing center monitors keystrokes, errors, and lines produced (efficiency), but not whether the documents produced have higher quality than typewritten documents (effectiveness).

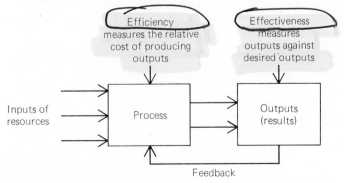

Figure 9-9
Relationship of efficiency and effectiveness.

SYSTEMS CONCEPTS APPLIED TO MANAGEMENT INFORMATION SYSTEMS

Management information systems may be understood in terms of the systems concepts described in this chapter. In addition, many of the concepts are directly applicable to the process of information system design. Concepts of system control through feedback are also relevant and will be discussed in the next chapter.

Information System as a System

The information system receives inputs of data and instructions, processes the data according to the instructions, and outputs the results. The basic system model of input, process, and output is suitable in the simplest case of an information processing system in which all inputs come in at the same time, but this is rarely true. The information processing function frequently needs data collected and processed in a prior period. Data storage is therefore added to the information system model, so that the processing activity has available both current data and data collected and stored previously (Figure 9-10). When data storage is added, the information processing function includes not only the transformation of data into information but also the storing of data for subsequent use. This basic information processing model is useful in understanding not only the overall information processing system but also the individual information processing applications. Each application may be analyzed in terms of input, storage, processing, and output.

The information processing system has functional subsystems such as the hardware system, the operating system, the communication system, and the database system. It

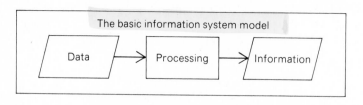

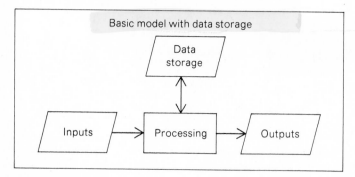

Figure 9-10
Basic information systems model.

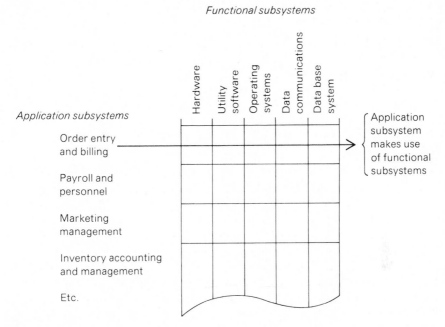

Figure 9-11
Functional subsystems and application subsystems in information system.

also has application subsystems such as order entry and billing, payroll, and personnel. The application subsystems make use of the functional subsystems (Figure 9-11).

The information system can be divided into five major subsystems, each of which can be further divided.[4] The five major subsystems are:

Subsystem	Description
Hardware and system software	The computer hardware and the system software necessary for hardware operation.
Management and administration	Planning, budgeting, staffing, training evaluation and related management functions.
Operations	Operation of the computer facilities in processing applications.
Application system development and maintenance	The development of new application systems and the maintenance of existing systems.
Application systems	The systems which perform activities necessary to process transactions, update data, produce output, etc.

The further subdivision of these five major systems is shown in Figure 9-12. Note that the subdivision of the system into five major subsystems and the smaller subsystems is not the only way the system can be factored.

---

[4]Davis and Weber, *Auditing Advanced EDP Systems*, p. 30.

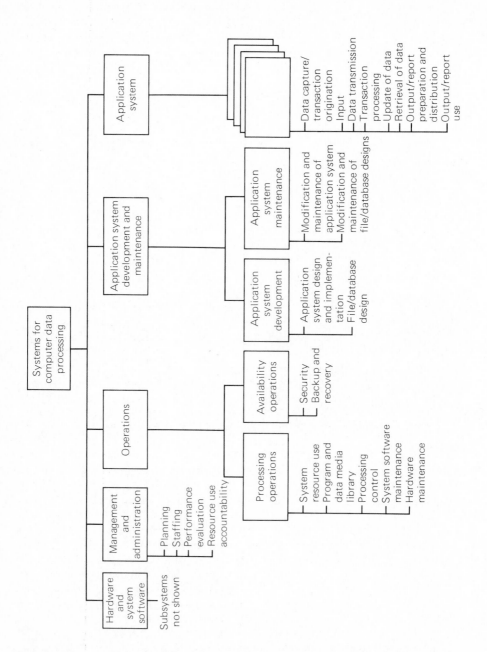

Figure 9-12
Subsystems for information systems. (From Gordon B. Davis and Ron Weber, *Auditing Advanced EDP Systems: A Survey of Practice and Development of a Theory*, Management Information Systems Research Center, Minneapolis, MN, 1983, p. 31.)

Information systems and other artificial systems are human artifacts; the systems exist only because humans design and build them. The fact that they are human artifacts means that they reflect characteristics and objectives of human systems. The design and operation of living systems allows them to adapt and survive. Likewise, there is an objective of survivability in artifical systems.[5] In order to achieve this survivability objective, the systems are designed with characteristics such as functionally cohesive subsystems, hierarchical organization of subsystems, and loose coupling among subsystems.

Systems Analysis and Design

The essence of systems analysis is to look at an entire problem in context, to systematically investigate the objectives of the system and the criteria for system effectiveness, and to evaluate the alternatives in terms of effectiveness and cost. The results of the analysis is a requestioning of the objectives and criteria, formulation of new alternatives, etc., until the problem, the objectives, the assumptions, and the cost-effectiveness of alternatives are clarified.

The principles of systems analysis are applied when an information system or application is first proposed. An analysis of the existing and proposed systems, including a cost-effectiveness analysis, is carried out (a feasibility study). The concept of system stress aids in identifying requirements for information systems support and suggesting applications.

Once there is an agreed-upon plan for an information system or application, development of the system can begin. The following systems concepts can be applied in the development of information system projects:

1 The information system is defined and overall responsibility assigned.
2 Major information processing subsystems are defined. Boundaries and interfaces are carefully specified.
3 A development schedule is prepared.
4 Each subsystem, when ready for development, is assigned to a project. The project leader factors the job into subsystems and assigns responsibility for each.
5 The control system is used to monitor the development process.

The use of systems concepts to decompose the information system and define the boundaries and interfaces of each subsystem is generally called *structured design*.

Use of Subsystems in Information System Design

It was already shown (Figure 9-6) that an information system can be described as a hierarchy of subsystems. The structured design approach encourages definition of subsystems from the top down; at each "level" of the hierarchy, the interfaces between the lower level subsystems are clearly defined. This allows development personnel to

---

[5]Ron Weber, "Toward a Theory of Artifacts: A Paradigmatic Basis for Information Systems Research," Working Paper, University of Queensland, St. Lucia, Queensland, Australia, 1984.

clearly define the objectives of each subsystem and provide checkpoints for its accomplishments.

The concept of black box is also useful when subsystems, boundaries, and interfaces are being defined: lower-level subsystems can be defined as black boxes while the higher-level subsystems are being designed. (In some methods, higher-level subsystems or modules are also coded and tested before lower-level subsystems). For example, when designing an order entry system, credit checking may be viewed as a black box and not defined in terms of the rules for deciding whether a customer can be given credit. It is defined only as to input and output. Later in the development process a systems analyst is provided with the defined inputs and required outputs and assigned to work with the credit department as it defines the rules inside the black box.

Decoupling of Information Systems

In information system design, emphasis is placed on the decoupling of subsystems, so that each subsystem is as independent as possible. This enhances the adaptability of the system by permitting isolation of the impact of potential changes on the system. In other words, the more decoupled (or loosely coupled) the system, the easier it is to modify a subsystem without affecting the rest of the system. Ease of maintenance and assurance of error-free code are important goals of design.

Decoupling can be achieved by defining subsystems so that each performs a single complete function; thus, connections between subsystems are minimized. For instance, in order entry, credit checking is done in only one subsystem and credit information is only required by that module. Another method of decoupling is minimizing the degree of interconnection. This means the number of assumptions a module needs to make about the internal workings of another module (e.g., the value of a data item) should be minimized. Methods for achieving minimal degrees of interconnectedness among modules are well defined; their explanation, however, is beyond the scope of this text.

The concept of decoupling is also useful to the overall design of information systems and the human-machine interface. Examples of the use of inventories or buffers, slack resources, and standards are described below:

Decoupling mechanism	Application to information system design
Inventory, buffer or waiting line	In computer processing, the input-output systems operate at different rates from those of the processor. A buffer memory is used to hold data to compensate for the different rates. In human-machine systems, it is not possible for the person to receive or send whenever the computer sends or asks for a response. The computer is not always available to accept messages. This means that there must be a buffer in which to store messages to allow for this difference.
	In cases where prompt service is expected but there are variations in arrival rates of people or messages, etc., to be serviced, a waiting line provides a decoupling mechanism. For example, in a telephone information service, a waiting line is established by asking the person on the telephone to wait until an information operator is free to process the call.

Slack resources	Computer hardware systems are generally designed with slack resources. A computer system is rarely fully loaded with work—some hours are not scheduled. This allows the system to handle fluctuations in processing load. The accounts receivable department does not need to inform data processing that the number of receivables for processing will be 25 percent above normal. The slack resources of the computer will normally handle this input variation without strain. In human-machine systems, human processors will be able to respond to significant short-term variations in activity. For example, a clerk receiving payments may be able to handle an average of 15 per hour. However, the clerk can temporarily increase processing to handle an increased demand—say, of a doubled rate for up to one hour.
Standards	The use of standards can eliminate or reduce the need for communication among information subsystems. For instance, the use of documentation standards reduces the need for communication among programmers and systems analysts working on a project. A database normally represents a simplification of the relations of the program to the data. A programmer does not have to consider all the other programs communicating with the database. A standard method is provided for accessing the database, thereby eliminating the need for close coordination with other subsystems.

Project Management

The systems approach may be applied to project management. Each subsystem of the overall system to be developed is carefully defined as to its objectives, interfaces to other subsystems, and time for delivery. Since each subsystem is defined to be relatively independent, its development can also be monitored relatively independently. Subsystems can be assigned to different members of a project team. Usually, however, a single project manager is responsible for the entire project.

A project planning and control system monitors each subsystem. The progress of each subsystem is followed with respect to such factors as time schedule and performance of completed system components. As changes are made in specifications or time schedules are altered, the project management system communicates the necessary information to each subsystem that is affected. Planning and control are guided by system objectives. Performance for the project is measured by overall system performance rather than by the performance of the separate subsystems.

SUMMARY

This chapter highlights those concepts of systems and organizations that are particularly relevant to information system design.

A system consists of elements which operate together to accomplish an objective. The basic model is input, process, and output. Systems can be deterministic or probabilistic and open or closed. An information system is a human-machine system, with the machine elements relatively closed and deterministic, the human elements open and probabilistic.

The decomposition of systems into subsystems is an important step in simplifying the design of systems. The use of subsystems usually requires some decoupling mechanisms to reduce the complexities of coordination and communication among them. Some methods of decoupling are inventories or buffers, slack and flexible resources, and standards. Systems are maintained and kept from decay by negative entropy. Changes in goals set externally to a system create stresses to which the system must adapt. Systems concepts apply to organizations which are open systems. The concepts explain the relationship between organizational effectiveness and efficiency.

The systems approach is especially relevant to information systems, which can be viewed as systems in the environment of the organization. Subsystems and decoupling concepts are used in the definition of specific applications, program modules, and design features to ensure that systems are flexible and maintainable. These concepts also are relevant to system operations, such as the use of slack resources in computer hardware. Systems concepts are also applied in project management.

MINICASES
1 THE MYTHICAL MAN MONTH

A well-known book describes the problems of project scheduling. Among other things, the author suggests that adding people to a late project is successful only if the project is completely partitionable and requires no communication among those working on it. In such a case, the same project that one person can perform in 10 months can be completed by 10 people in one month. The author points out that in systems projects this perfect interchangeability is rarely the case. He goes on to assert that, "Adding manpower to a late project only makes it later." (From Frederick Brooks, *The Mythical Man Month: Essays on Software Engineering*, Addison-Wesley, Reading, MA, 1975.)

Learning curves problems, Coupling process inadequate

Questions

Project manager S/B a user

a Explain the assertion in systems terms.
b What are alternatives in project management to correct or prevent the problems of late project completion? *More Decoupling; realistic design time; better utilization of slack resources (people, supplies)* *review subsystems individually*

2 THE VIRTUAL COMPANY

Coupled Environment

When two or more companies share resources via computer, traditional relationships are redefined. The result has been termed a "virtual company" because a logical company is created, even though no physical, legal organization is formed. Some examples illustrate this trend:

- American Hospital Supply provides customers with an online terminal for directly entering orders to the company's order entry system.
- Hartford Fire Insurance Company markets to independent insurance agents software packages to support insurance agent operations.
- Airline companies make reservations by accessing the reservation computers of other airlines.

Based on Robert Benjamin, "When Companies Share, It's Virtually a New Game," *Information Systems News*, December 26, 1983.

Virtual Memory = Phantom Memory; Looks like its there, but its really not.

Questions

a Explain the virtual company in terms of systems concepts.
b What are the system advantages of this sharing of computer resources?

Eliminates need for large salesstaff, for customers quicker response time, lower inventory requirement

3 SYSTEMS THEORY AND CONTINGENCY THEORY

Contingency theories about organizations have high face validity (they appear to be correct to knowledgeable observers) but very poor evidence to prove them. For example, a contingency theory for development of computer applications may describe the best approach to develop an application given a set of conditions for that application. When a set of applications is studied to see if the contingency theory is supported, the various possible outcomes for the applications are evaluated, development methods are examined, and contingency factors (the set of conditions affecting choice of methods) are documented. The results are analyzed statistically to see how results are correlated against using the correct method (based on the contingency theory). The results of such analysis are generally supportive of the contingency theories, but are not strong in terms of correlation.

Equifinality => You can have a bad system w/ good results and a good system w/ bad results

Questions

a How can the adaptive nature of open systems explain how a poor method can sometimes result in a satisfactory result? *An open system is adaptive*
b How does the principle of equifinality apply to alternative methods?
c If two methods yield identical results, but one causes more adaptive behavior and system stress, which one is preferred? Why? *The one w/ less stress w/absorbs more inputs*

4 SOVIET MANAGEMENT AS A TIGHTLY COUPLED SYSTEM

It is sometimes a puzzle to the casual observer why the Russian economy can put complex rockets into space but has difficulty producing acceptable consumer products. Each factory is given a production quota and instructed as to the suppliers of inputs to the production process. If a shipment of material is defective, it cannot be rejected and another supplier obtained. A report must be filed with a government bureau that investigates and makes a decision.

Questions

a What requirements does the system impose for communication to support tight coupling?
b Each subsystem can be operating as instructed, yet the results will not be acceptable to the consumer. Explain this in terms of systems theory.

EXERCISES

1 Define:
   a System
   b Subsystem
   c Interface
   d Boundary
   e Black box
   f System stress
2 Differentiate between:
   a Open and closed systems
   b Deterministic and probabilistic systems
   c Subsystem and suprasystem

3 Define the inputs, process, and outputs for the following systems:
  a Operating system (software)
  b Accounting system
  c Heating system (for home)
  d School system

4 Define the boundaries and interfaces for the following subsystems:
  a Disk storage subsystem
  b Accounts payable subsystem
  c Administrative subsystem (of school system)
  d Error analysis subsystem (of operating system)

5 **a** If there are 21 subsystems and each subsystem must be able to communicate with each other subsystem, how many interconnections must there be?
  b Suppose the 21 subsystems are arranged in three clusters of seven subsystems, each communicating with the others in the cluster and clusters communicating with each other. How many interconnections are required?

6 A student may be considered a subsystem. Each course may be viewed as a subsystem which provides input and asks for output from the student subsystem. The course work subsystems are not coordinated to level the student subsystem load. How does a student decouple?

7 How have the following systems handled the problem of decoupling:
  a The telephone system
  b The computer center at a university
  c The construction industry

8 What are the essential features of systems analysis?

9 Describe the systems approach to project management using the example of preparing a group project for a course in systems analysis.

10 Explain how systems concepts are applied (or are not applied) to information systems in the following cases:
  a Executive wants to see all sales over $50,000.
  b Company insists programmers use modules in programming job.
  c A data administrator controls all access and changes to database.
  d Programming group issues standard programming practices manual.
  e A total integrated system is to be implemented. All files and processing are to be interrelated. There is immediate input, immediate response, immediate updating of all files, etc.

11 Explain the system objectives and effectiveness and efficiency measures for:
  a A course subsystem (in a university).
  b A police system (in a community).
  c An information system for marketing.
  d An information system for an executive.

12 An analysis of a manufacturing company shows each subsystem operating well but the company as a whole is operating very poorly as evidenced by:
  a Long delays between receipt of order and delivery.
  b Large inventories of raw material.
  c Large inventories in process.
  Explain this phenomenon in terms of systems concepts.

13 Explain how the concept of system stress can assist an analyst in deciding where to concentrate systems analysis activities.

14 The telephone is a technology that tightly couples the two parties even though, for many conversations, there is no need. Explain in systems theory terms how electronic mail decouples the communication.

15 Deterministic, relatively closed systems are relatively easy to study and to provide algorithms for operations. Computer science researchers express surprise at the lack of algorithms in the study of information systems. Explain why there are more experiments and field studies in information systems and less algorithmic research.

SELECTED REFERENCES

Ackoff, R. I.: "Towards a System of System Concepts," *Management Science*, July 1971, pp. 661–671.

Boulding, Kenneth: "General Systems Theory—The Skeleton of Science," *Management Science*, April 1956, pp. 197–208. Widely reprinted.

Buckley, Walter (ed.): *Modern Systems Research for the Behavioral Scientist*, Aldine, Chicago, 1968. Collection of articles.

Checkland, Peter: *Systems Thinking, Systems Practice*, Wiley, New York, 1981.

Churchman, C. W.: *The Design of Inquiring Systems*, Basic Books, New York, 1971.

Churchman, C. W.: *The Systems Approach*, Dell, New York, 1968.

Cleland, David I., and William R. King: *Systems Analysis and Project Management*, McGraw-Hill, New York, 1968.

DeGreen, Kenyon B. (ed.): *Systems Psychology*, McGraw-Hill, New York, 1970.

Emery, F. E. (ed.): *Systems Thinking*, Penguin, Baltimore, 1969.

Emery, James C.: *Organizational Planning and Control Systems*, Macmillan, New York, 1969.

Hare, VanCourt, Jr.: *Systems Analysis: A Diagnostic Approach*, Harcourt, Brace, New York, 1969.

Katz, Daniel, and Robert L. Kahn: *The Social Psychology of Organizations*, Second Edition, Wiley, New York, 1978.

Markus, M. Lynne: *Systems in Organizations: Bugs and Features*, Pitman, Boston, 1984.

Miller, James G.: *Living Systems*, Wiley, New York, 1978.

Miller, James G.: "Living Systems: The Organization," *Behavioral Science*, January 1972, pp. 1–182.

Sayles, Leonard R., and Margaret K. Chandler: *Managing Large Systems*, Harper & Row, New York, 1971.

Simon, Herbert A.: *The Science of the Artificial*, Second Edition, MIT Press, Cambridge, 1981.

Von Bertalanffy, Ludwig: *General Systems Theory: Foundations, Development, Applications*, George Braziller, New York, 1968.

Weinberg, Gerald: *An Introduction to General Systems Theory*, Wiley, New York, 1975.

Yourdon, E., and L. L. Constantine: *Structured Design: Fundamentals of a Discipline of Computer Program and System Design*, Prentice-Hall, Englewood Cliffs, NJ, 1979.

CONCEPTS OF PLANNING
AND CONTROL

INFORMATION SYSTEM SUPPORT FOR CONTROL

SUMMARY

MINICASES

EXERCISES

SELECTED REFERENCES

A plan is a predetermined course of action. It represents goals and the activities necessary to achieve those goals. Control is the activity which measures deviations from planned performance and initiates corrective action. In this chapter, the processes of planning and control in organizations are discussed. Approaches to development of organizational plans are described. In Chapter 12, elements of support systems which extend the capabilities of management to perform planning and control are discussed.

CONCEPTS OF ORGANIZATIONAL PLANNING

Planning is an ongoing organizational function that provides the framework for operational activities and decision making. The organizational mission is translated into operational objectives through an organizational hierarchy of planning activities.

There is planning in organizations even though there may not be a formal organizational plan; however, informal planning is usually inconsistent and incomplete. The reasons for formal organizational planning are to focus the energies and activities of the organization on achievement of its objectives, to reconcile differences in objectives and plans of subareas and individuals within the organization, and to remove ambiguities about what the organization should do. The formal plan not only guides activities; it provides a basis for evaluating results. The planning process can result in significant motivation for individual and organizational achievement, but there are also individual and organizational forces opposed to planning.

Setting of Goals and Objectives

There is general agreement on the meaning of terms used in planning, but they tend to be used imprecisely and interchangeably. As used in this text, planning terms have the following meanings (Figure 10-1). The examples are from the service operations of a computer vendor.

Term	Definition and example
Mission	Broad statement of the purpose of the organization. "To provide a high-quality product and convenient customer service."
Goals	General statement of what is to be accomplished. "Reduce time to respond to service request without increasing number of service personnel."
Strategies	General approaches to achieving goals. "Improve procedures for handling service requests; provide procedures for reducing time required at each site."

Objectives	Statement of measurable results to be achieved. "Reduce average time from request to completion of service call."
Plans and budgets	Schedule of specific activities and actions to achieve objectives. "Revise service call request procedures; revise servicing procedures to improve use of diagnostic tools."
Policy	Limits to acceptable behavior express ethical and moral values, decision limits, and standards. "System interfaces shall be designed to enhance and enrich the job performed by users."

PLANNING IN RESPONSE TO COMPETITIVE PRESSURES

In 1978 Esmark Inc.'s CEO Donald P. Kelly warned its subsidiary, Swift and Company, that there must be improvements in its earnings. Although sales of the meat packing company rose afterward, its earnings declined by one-third. In June 1980, Kelly sold off nine plants and, after a thwarted attempt to salvage plants by turning them over to employee ownership, closed three others. Escalating labor costs were felt to be the obstacle that Swift could not overcome. Since Swift's competition used new automated meat-cutting and packaging techniques in highly efficient and nonunion plants, they had lower costs with which Swift could not effectively compete. Esmark retained Swift's line of processed food which fitted its goals of concentration on consumer name-brand products. ("Swift Gets an Order: No More Fresh Meat," *Business Week*, July 14, 1980, p. 100.)

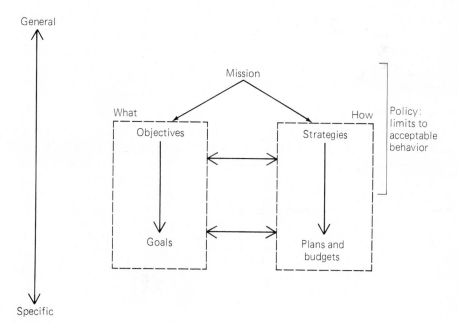

Figure 10-1
Relationship of terms used in planning.

- Strategic Planning (5 years and beyond)

  Which businesses should the firm be in?
  How should they be financed?
  How should scarce resources be allocated across business sectors?

- Tactical Planning (1 - 5 years)

  What are the optimal patterns of capital investment and divestment for implementing some longer-range plan?
  What decisions about facility location, expansion, or shut-down will maximize profitability?
  What products should be added to or deleted from the product line?
  What is the optimal product pricing pattern?

- Operations Planning (1 - 12 months)

  What is the optimal operating plan (raw material acquisition, product sources, inventory levels, distribution system configuration, route and mode of distribution, etc.) to meet specified system objectives, consistent with some longer-term plan, with existing facilities in the next planning period (for example, month, quarter, year)?
  What is the best operating plan on which to base plans for production and dispatch?

- Scheduling and Dispatching (right now)

  What specific operations or sequences of operations should be performed with which existing facilities, or meet specified output requirements in the next operational period (for example, hour, day, week)?

Increasing Scope ↑ ↓ *Increasing Detail*

Figure 10-2
Hierarchy of planning. Reprinted by permission of David S. Hirshfield, "From the Shadows," *Interfaces*, 13:2, April 1983, p. 74. ©1983 The Institute of Management Sciences.

It is customary to talk of the goals of an organization as if the organization existed apart from its members. As Cyert and March[1] point out, people have goals; collections of people do not. The goals of an organization represent, in effect, a series of constraints imposed on the organization by its participants. If the organization is viewed as a coalition of individuals, each of which has goals, the goals arrived at for the coalition represent bargaining among its members. The goals change in response to changes in the coalition membership and to changes in the goals of the participants.

Bargaining is in general very constrained by the existing organizational structure. Through mechanisms such as operating procedures, decision rules, and budgets, coalition agreements are made semipermanent. The individuals in an organization have limited time to devote to the bargaining process, so that bargaining tends to start, not

---

[1]Richard M. Cyert and James G. March, *A Behavioral Theory of the Firm*, Prentice-Hall, Englewood Cliffs, NJ, 1963, pp. 26–45.

fresh each time, but from the current state of affairs. Attention is not focused on all matters at once, but in a sequential fashion as the demand arises. Goals in an organization tend to have inherent contradictions, but devices such as organizational slack are used to "absorb" the inconsistency.

The goals of business firms are generally stated in terms of goals for profit, market share, sales, inventory, and production. These are expressed in operational terms. The goal "to be a pleasant place to work" is nonoperational. "To reduce turnover to 4 percent" is more meaningful in operational terms. When objectives are clearly and operationally stated, they form the basis for a plan to achieve goals.

Hierarchy of Planning

Four conceptual levels of planning in an organization can be identified, differing in the organizational level of responsibility identified, the scope of planning issues addressed, and the planning horizon.[2] The characterization corresponds to the framework of Anthony[3] described in Chapter 2 with the addition of scheduling and dispatching. These are the following (Figure 10-2):

Level of management	Anthony framework	Definition
Strategic planning	Same	What function will the organization serve and what will it be like in future (five years and beyond)? Strategic plan should include business to be in, market it should sell to, etc.
Tactical planning	Management control	Physical implementation of strategic plans (one to five years). Reflected in capital expenditure budget and long-range staffing plan.
Operations planning	Operational control	Allocation of tasks to each organizational unit in order to achieve objectives of tactical plan (one to twelve months). Yearly budget.
Scheduling and dispatching	—	Assign specific units of organizational activity to achieve operational objectives (immediately).

See Graph pg 48 & 36

THE PLANNING PROCESS

Planning is a significant activity for management and many other positions in the organization, but it is frequently neglected. The reasons for the neglect of an activity

---

[2]D. S. Hirshfield, "From the Shadows," *Interfaces*, 13:2, April 1983, pp. 72–76.

[3]R. N. Anthony, *Planning and Control Systems: A Framework for Analysis*, Harvard University Press, Cambridge, 1965.

recognized as very important center around four characteristics of planning as a human
activity.

[handwritten left margin: Why Planning Isn't Done]

[handwritten right margin: Prefer to do, not Plan]

1 Planning is a very difficult cognitive activity. It is hard mental work. Because of the
cognitive strain involved in doing planning work, people avoid planning.

2 Planning makes evident the uncertainty of future events. By making explicit the various
uncertainties, the future may appear more uncertain after planning than before. There is a
human tendency to avoid uncertainty, and this may be reflected in planning avoidance.

3 Planning reduces perceived freedom of action. When plans are made, individuals are
committed to a narrower range of actions than when no formal plans are made.

4 Planning is a very intensive effort, and it is difficult, given the nature of managerial work
(see Chapter 8), to take the time for planning. This is one reason that organizations have retreats
where all other activities are shut out in order to concentrate on planning.

[handwritten left margin: Why managers Don't like Planning]

5 Planning is computationally tedious. Each change in planning assumptions affects other
figures in the plans. Analysis of past data and current expectations requires significant
computational work. The popularity of planning software reflects the need for computational
assistance in planning.

6 Plans are often made and then ignored. One reason they may be ignored is that they don't
represent real agreement. However, if they are ignored, people become reluctant to be involved
in planning.

[handwritten: 7. Managers may be held accountable for fulfilling the plan]

The high cost of preparing data for planning and of manually examining alternative
plans places severe limitations on planning activities. The use of planning support
systems to remove some of these constraints and to enhance the planning process will be
discussed in Chapter 12.

The plans of an organization reflect expectations about the environment, expectations
about the capabilities of the organization, and decisions and bargains on such matters as
allocation of resources and direction of effort. The quantified expectations are input to
models used in planning. In this section, methods for quantifying and classifying
expectations, obtaining planning data, and developing quantitative models to support the
planning process are described.

Quantifying and Classifying Expectations

The analysis to formulate and quantify expectations for planning may use three methods:

1 *Statistical methods.* Trends, projections, correlation analysis, and sampling provide
expectations based on statistical analysis of historical data. These methods are surveyed later in
the chapter.

2 *Objective analysis of value and priority.* Where quantitative measures of value are
available, they can often be applied to alternatives to arrive at priorities for use in planning.
Examples are rate of return computation for revenue-producing or expense-saving expenditures and marginal revenue-marginal cost analysis for expenditures such as advertising.

3 *Judgment.* Judgment is used to formulate expectations in cases where there are no
statistical or other quantitative bases for forecasting.

The reliability of data is important to the planning process. The reliability of statistical
data is measured by the consistency of data resulting from a repetition of the same
measurements under identical conditions. According to this concept, planning data have

high reliability if the planning procedure yields identical results for several different planners. The reliability of planning data is influenced by such factors as the following:

1 *Source of data.* Data from outside sources will receive different evaluations by different planners because of uncertainty as to its quality, etc.

2 *Influence of plan on outcome.* Some plans, such as an appropriation type of budget, have a strong determining influence on the outcome itself, i.e., units spend whatever is budgeted.

3 *Intended accuracy.* Planning estimates do not require a uniform standard of accuracy since certain figures are more critical than others. For example, an error of 50 percent in the calculation of the cost of office pencils for the budget period is not nearly so serious as a 50 percent error in the cost of raw materials.

4 *Time.* The predictability of future events generally decreases with the prediction time span. When the forecast period is extended, the planning data tends to become less accurate as an expression of what is to be expected. Different planners will tend to have greater variation in their long-term projections than in their short-term estimates.

The classifications of expectations is dependent on the type of plan for which they are being classified. Data may be organized in a variety of ways. For example, expenditures in a budget plan may be classified in one or more of the following ways:

Expenditure classification	Examples
Object of expenditure	The classes of items being purchased, e.g., salaries, supplies, travel.
Reason for expenditure (functions, activities, or programs)	Examples of functions are manufacturing or marketing. Examples of programs (say, for a government) are health care, sanitation, and protection.
Outputs	Output classification for, say, an appliance manufacturer might be based on end products such as refrigerators and washing machines.
Organizational unit	Departments and other organizational units.
Cost behavior	Classification by variability with changes in activity and by controllability by management.

This brief summary of expenditure classifications illustrates the variety of planning structures and the need to select an appropriate classification. The way data items are classified affects the value of the data for analyzing past behavior and generating future expectations. Classifications differ in their objectives; the following examples provide some indication of the variety of their uses:

Classification	Possible purpose
Object of expenditure	Control over what is being purchased.
Function	Control over the functions for which expenditures are made.
Program	Control over expenditures for programs.

Classification	Possible purpose
Output	Control over results to be achieved with a level of expenditures.
Organizational unit	Control by person making decision to spend.
Cost behavior	Estimation of planned costs under different levels of activity.

Subject	Explanation
Marketing	
Consumer credit	Credit ratings of individuals for banks, retailers, and credit card companies.
Business credit	Credit ratings of businesses for potential creditors.
Marketing and demographic statistics	Location of customers and estimated buying power for makers of industrial and consumer products.
Business and Finance	
Econometric statistics	Planning data for marketers and for strategic planners in government, industry, and education.
Stock, bond, and commodity prices and trading information	Timely price and volume data for making buy-and-sell decisions and for valuing assets in portfolios.
Corporation statistics and news	Historical financial statistics and news of business events including corporations.
Bibliographic	
General news abstracts	Abstracted articles from newspapers and the popular press for analyzing current events and political climate.
Scientific and technical abstracts	Summaries of technical writing and meetings, prepared by experts for use in scientific investigations.
Legal	Statutes, decisions, administrative rulings, trademarks, and patents for use by lawyers in advising clients and preparing for litigation.
Library	Filing and cataloging systems for library administration.

Figure 10-3
Examples of databank products offered in ten major subject areas. (Reprinted by permission of *Havard Business Review*. Excerpted from Exhibit 1 from article by J. W. Darrow and J. R. Belilove, "The Growth of Databank Sharing," November-December, pp. 180-194. Copyright © 1978 by the President and Fellows of Harvard College; all rights reserved.)

Sources of Planning Data

The sources of planning data are internal data organized and processed for planning purposes, external data from various sources, and environmental scanning. The internal data reflects the historical performance of the organization. It is usually very accessible, and its accuracy is known. However, it should not be the sole input to planning because external factors may invalidate historical performance for projections. For example, projecting past sales of computers without considering the impact of microcomputers (a new technology) would yield misleading results.

External data can be obtained from traditional sources such as published reports, government documents, or services that provide industry data. Some trade associations provide industry data and projections. As an example, one company obtains information about competitors from regularly published financial reports and from government SEC filings by competitors which are publicly held companies.

External data can also be obtained from databanks covering a wide variety of economic activity. Generally, databanks should be considered instead of direct data collection when the following conditions apply (assuming the appropriate databank is available):[4]

1 The body of information is large and expensive to collect.

2 The databank requires frequent, expert updating.

3 A large databank, or an unpredictable subset of one, is needed only on an infrequent or ad hoc basis.

4 No competitive advantage will be lost, nor any significant security risk incurred, by relying on an outside source.

Figure 10-3 contains a few examples of subjects on which information is typically available from databank vendors.

Another alternative for obtaining planning data is the use of various environmental scanning techniques. These are methods for analyzing the environment and generating planning data. The following are some examples:

Technique	Description
Scenario writing	Individuals are asked to write scenarios of events they think may occur. These represent a set of plausible future events that the organization should consider in its planning.
Simulation	The effect of external events is simulated. Examples are the effect of a change in age distribution of the population, the effect of changes in worldwide interest rates, etc.
Cross impact analysis	The impact on the organization of events in one of the environments is estimated. Environments are social, political, physical, technological, and

[4]Joel W. Darrow and James R. Belilove, "The Growth of Databank Sharing," *Harvard Business Review,* November-December 1978.

Technique	Description
	institutional-legal. For example, estimate the impact of a change in import policy in the Common Market on demand for company products.
Econometric model	If the organization has an econometric model that estimates demand for its products or services and costs, environmental scanning will look for environmental changes affecting the factors in the model. For example, if construction activity is an important variable, then factors affecting interest rates are of concern (assuming interest rates are part of the model).
Input-output analysis	The effects of activities or changes in one sector of the economy are traced to other sectors. For example, if the price of oil is increased, the cost effect can be traced to all sectors using oil or oil-based products.
Delphi projection	Those concerned with estimating the future are asked to specify their projections. The projections are summarized, and participants are asked whether they wish to revise their estimates based on the average estimate. The process may go through several iterations in order to find areas of consensus or reasons for differences in projections.

Development of Planning Models

A planning model is a method for structuring, manipulating, and communicating future plans. The model describes the process by which plans are developed from input data and internal calculations. For example, a very simple profit model of a business organization might consist of the following statements describing how a profit plan is to be implemented.

```
Sales = input variable
Cost of sales = 0.40 × sales
Gross margin = sales − cost of sales
Operating expenses = input variable
Profit before taxes = gross margin − operating expenses
Taxes = 0.48 × profit before taxes − taxes
Net profit = profit before taxes − taxes
```

The profit model requires two inputs—sales and operating expenses. For example, an input of $100,000 for sales and $52,000 for operating expenses would allow the model to produce the following simplified income plan. A different set of values for the two input variables would yield a different profit plan.

XYZ Company	
Profit Plan for Year Ended 198X	
Sales	100,000
Less cost of sales	40,000
Gross profit	60,000

Less operating expenses	52,000
Profit before taxes	8,000
Less taxes	3,840
Net profit	4,160

This simple example illustrates the nature of a planning model. The model provides for the following:

1 A format for presenting the results from processing the model (the profit plan statement in the example).

2 A set of input data (sales and operating expenses in the example).

3 A set of processing statements (formulas, logic statements, etc.) to operate on the input data.

Model building for a planning model can begin with simple models calling for inputs of major, high-level items. Subsequent model development can expand the details of the model to calculate the high-level items from more basic input. For example, in the simple model just given, the operating expenses were an input variable. An expansion of the model might provide a set of statements such as the following for computation of operating expenses:

```
Selling expenses = 0.10 × sales
Advertising expenses = 0.05 × sales
Interest expenses = 0.10 × average long-term debt + 0.12 × average short-term loans
Bad debt expense = 0.01 × accounts receivable balance at beginning of period
Administrative expense = input variable
Operating expense = selling + advertising + interest + bad debt + administrative expenses
```

Note that the more detailed model for operating expenses requires input data on average long-term debt, average short-term debt, and accounts receivable balance at the beginning of the month. These are from another related model—the balance sheet model. Administrative expense is still an input item; another level of detail in the model might provide for the calculation of that expense.

In this simple model, the sales estimate is a key variable since many other variables are computed from it. This is a common pattern in organizational models because expenditures depend to a great extent on the activity which drives the organization. However, sales are not completely under the control of the organization, and estimates of sales must take into account a variety of external factors. Examples of such factors are:

Disposable income (available to customers)
Consumer demand for product
Level of advertising, prior year
Level of advertising, current year
Level of competitive advertising, prior year
Level of competitive advertising, current year
Prior-year level of sales
Prior-year level of sales of competitors
Level of price for product
Level of competitors' price for product

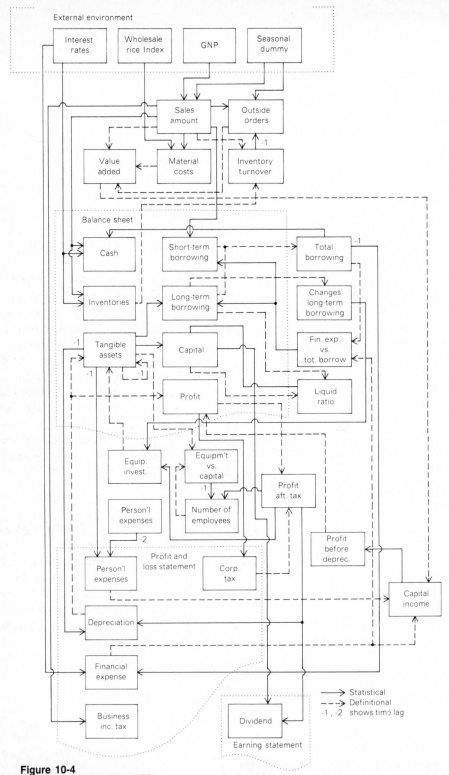

Figure 10-4
A financial forecasting model. (M. Aiso, "Forecasting Technique," *IBM Systems Journal*, 12:2, 1973, p. 206. Reprinted by permission from the *IBM Systems Journal*, Copyright 1973 by International Business Machines Corporation.)

By the use of such factors, an estimating equation might be developed to yield a sales estimate based on the underlying causal factors for sales. These estimates require estimates of environmental factors such as disposable income and the level of consumer demand for the product.

Certain variables may have a lag relation in which the level of a variable in the prior period will be the estimator for the level of another variable in the current period. For example, the accounts receivable for month n is related to the sales in month $n-1$ (for 30-day accounts) and to the preceding months for delayed payment plans or slow-paying accounts.

When an estimate for a period such as a year is used to develop estimates for shorter periods such as a month, it is necessary to calculate seasonal patterns. The monthly sales are rarely one-twelfth of the yearly sales. The months vary as percentages of the yearly activity based on seasonal patterns. For example, while the sales of new automobiles by the manufacturer are nil during the model changeover period in July-August, they are high during September. These seasonal patterns tend to persist year after year.

Although individual planning models can be built for separate functions, the plans themselves are interrelated; more sophisticated planning models are integrated to represent the interrelationships. Figure 10-4 is an example of a financial planning model showing interrelated flows among balance sheet and income statement items.

The model and the output from the model should assist planners to understand the nature of the process and the effect of changes in variables. For example, one of the important objectives of planning for business organizations is a satisfactory return on investment (return on assets employed). The focus on this single figure may obscure the component ratios that affect it. A model that shows these relationships is shown in Figure 10-5. It is sometimes referred to as the DuPont model because of its use in that organization. The planning model output should focus the attention of planners on the components as well as the summary ratio.

Ratios may be used to estimate various items within the plan (such as product returns as a percent of sales). They are also useful outputs which allow comparison with other firms. The following are examples of the types of financial ratios that are used in estimating or that are used as outputs from planning:

Current ratio (current assets to current liabilities)
Quick ratio (cash, marketable securities, and current receivables to current liabilities)
Day's sales in receivables
Day's sales in inventory
Net working capital
Total asset turnover
Interest coverage
Debt to (debt plus equity)
Gross margin percentage [(sales minus cost of sales)/sales]
Earnings as a percent of sales
Return on assets employed
Return on common stock equity
Earnings per share
Expected value of a share of common stock (using expected price earnings multiple)
Growth in earnings per share

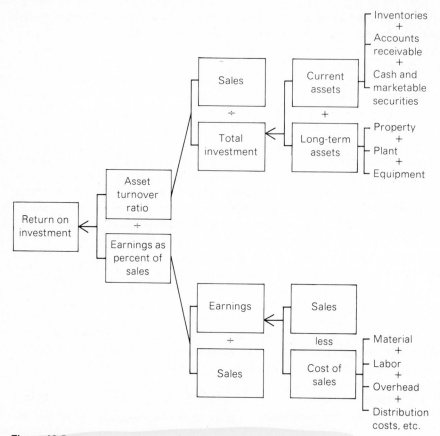

Figure 10-5
The DuPont model showing composition of return of investment.

Relate's earnings to the use of assets

COMPUTATIONAL SUPPORT FOR PLANNING

There are four types of computational support needed for the analysis preparatory to planning, the preparation of the plans, and the output of the results:

1 An analysis of historical data to obtain relationships useful for projections
2 Various projection and forecasting techniques to estimate future values
3 Computations internal to the plan and computations required for outputs
4 Output of the results in a meaningful planning format

This computational support can range from sophisticated statistical techniques to a fairly simple spread sheet computational procedure.

Historical Data Analysis Techniques

Historical data is analyzed to discover patterns or relations that will be useful in projecting the future values of significant variables. Even when quantitative relations are not sufficiently stable to use in forecasting, data analysis is useful for input into the judgmental forecast. The major techniques are summarized below.

Data generation techniques	Comments
Time trend or growth rate	Computation of rate of change or growth over a specified period. For example, sales grew at a rate of 19.1 percent during the years 1980 to 1984.
Data smoothing	Raw data generally contains random variations or other irregularities which make the normal level difficult to observe. Data smoothing techniques are used to smooth the irregularities.
Seasonal analysis	Economic activity varies with the time of year. For example, sales of turkeys are especially high in November and December. Seasonal analysis is used to obtain the seasonal pattern and to adjust for it in the overall pattern.
Autocorrelation analysis	Certain variables have a time delay relation with each other. For example, sales of repair parts in period n is a function of the sales of new units in period $n-1$. Autocorrelation analysis assists in discovering these relations.
Cross-correlation analysis	The degree of association between two sets of data is calculated.
Data description and dispersion analysis	It is useful to understand data in terms of measures such as mean, median, mode, intervals, and standard deviations. For example, the analysis that identifies daily sales as being 100,000 units with a standard deviation of 12,000 units is useful in understanding the nature of the sales activity being planned. Among the most useful statistics are measures of central tendency (mean, median, mode) and measures of dispersion (standard deviation). Graphs and histograms may be prepared for visual analysis.

Historical Extrapolation Techniques

Historical data describes the past, but planning involves the future. Estimating is generally based on analysis of past history combined with various techniques to generate data for planning purposes. Some of the common estimation techniques for planning are:

Data generation techniques	Comments
Extrapolation of time series or growth rate	Time series and growth rates can be extrapolated from historical data analysis. If the past growth rate has been 10 percent, the

Data generation techniques	Comments
	rate is assumed to continue (unless modified by judgment).
Extrapolation based on regression analysis	Past patterns of activity obtained by regression analysis can be used if they are expected to continue. The patterns may be based on time and a growth rate or on causal relationships among variables.
Interpolation	If historical data exists, but not for the values related to planning, the needed value can often be interpolated. If cost is known for 12,000 and 14,000 units, a cost can be interpolated for 13,000 units.
Formula or relation	Many planning figures are derived from computations on other figures. For example, sales returns may be computed as a percentage of gross sales. Sales for the month may be computed from yearly sales multiplied by the seasonal factor for the month.

USING THE WRONG STATISTICAL FORECASTING TECHNIQUE GIVES THE WRONG ANSWER

The company sold earth moving equipment. Regression analysis was used to analyze past sales; they were found to fit a pattern of constant percent of growth. The company extrapolated the growth percentage forward and built a new plant to handle the growth in sales. The plant was opened and almost immediately closed because sales lagged far behind projections.

In reviewing the planning, the statistical fit of past sales to the growth curve was very good; it was, however, the wrong technique to use. The sales of earth moving equipment are not associated with time; they are associated with replacement of existing equipment and demand derived from changes in construction and mining activity. The regression technique had therefore been the wrong basis for forecasting.

Financial Planning Computations

Models that involve financial plans need to provide for various computations and analyses commonly required for measuring or evaluating profitability. Examples are depreciation computation, rate of return analysis, and break-even analysis.

Depreciation is a significant computation in most financial planning. It affects profit computations because it is an expense, and it affects cash flow because of its impact on taxes. There are several methods for computing depreciation, all of which should be available to the planner. These methods are straight-line, double-declining-balance, sum-of-the-year's-digits, and production or use-basis.

Rate of return analysis is a method for computing the profitability of an investment, taking into account the timing of the investment and the cash flows stemming from the investment. There are several methods for computing the rate of return which should be a part of the planning model.

Break-even analysis is a fairly simple but very useful computation for determining the volume of activity at which there is no loss or profit. In evaluating alternatives, two situations may have identical expected profits, but the one with a lower break-even point is to be preferred (all other factors being equal).

Output of Planning Results

The output of the planning process will be plans in a format suited to the needs of their various users. It is common to have the major financial plans (projected income statement, balance sheet, statement of cash flow, etc.) in the same form as the actual results are reported. They are often termed pro forma statements (in the form as if they had happened). Other outputs will be prepared in a form suitable for the function, project, organizational unit, etc., receiving their part of the plan.

One of the problems of planning is preparing outputs, because each change in any variable has an effect that may ripple through the entire output. The outputs may not be complex or long, but the constant changes during the planning process cause a substantial clerical cost to redo the outputs, unless there is computer modeling support.

The planning models discussed in this chapter are much more effective if used with a computer. Computer-based planning models provide facilities for developing and validating analytical models, flexible access to data in the database, and facilities for manipulating the model and posing "what if" questions. Using an interactive computer-based model, a number of combinations of values for variables can be used in trial-and-error planning iterations, and the effects of a change of one variable on others can be seen quickly. Computer-based planning models are described in Chapter 12.

THE DEMAND FOR PLANNING AIDS FOR MANAGEMENT

"Electronic spread-sheet packages are the most popular business application programs for microcomputers. More than one million spread-sheet packages have been sold since VisiCalc was introduced in 1979, one for every five microcomputers sold to date. More than 50 VisiCalc clones are on the market...."

Alan Hirsch, "New Spread-Sheet Packages Do More Than Model," *Mini-Micro Systems*, June 1983, pp. 205–212.

CHARACTERISTICS OF CONTROL PROCESSES

Control consists of procedures to determine deviations from plans and indicate corrective action. Every major organizational function has a set of controls associated with it. In Chapter 9, the concept of a system was explained. In this section, specific characteristics of control in systems are discussed. In the next section, control processes in organizations are described.

Control in Systems

The basic model of a system as inputs, process, and outputs, presented in Chapter 9, did not include regulation and control of the system. For control purposes, a feedback loop is added to the basic model (Figure 10-6). In its simplest form, outputs from the system are

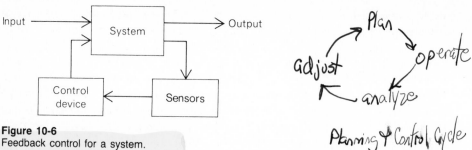

Figure 10-6
Feedback control for a system.

compared with the desired output (standard), and any difference causes an input to be sent to the process to adjust the operations so that output will be closer to the standard.

Feedback which seeks to dampen and reduce fluctuations around the standard is termed *negative feedback*. It is used in feedback control loops. *Positive feedback* reinforces the direction in which the system is moving. In other words, positive feedback causes the system to repeat or amplify an adjustment or action. For example, a programming supervisor may have learned about the use of modular program structure. After trying it on a small project with good results (positive feedback), the supervisor tries it on a larger project, again with good results. The supervisor may continue this until all programming is done in that way (a steady state) or until projects are found for which it does not work.

Feedback in which the system changes its operation is not the only adjustment an organizational system may make. In response to feedback, the organization may change its standards (objectives, goals, purposes, etc.). In the example above, the positive results from use of modular program structure may result in an adjustment of the standard for programmer performance. Since organizations are goal-directed and self-organizing, a change in goals may often lead to changes in the system to achieve the new goals.

Negative Feedback Control

Negative feedback control in a system means keeping the system operating within certain limits of performance. For example, an automated production system is in control if inputs of material and energy are converted to output of produced items using a standard amount of material and energy and with the percentage of defective items falling within allowable limits. A system which is out of control functions outside the allowable limits because the regulatory mechanisms are not operative. Control using negative feedback normally involves four elements.

    1 A characteristic or condition to be controlled. The characteristic or condition must be measurable from some output.

    2 A sensor for measuring the characteristic or condition.

    3 A control unit which compares the measurements with a standard for that characteristic or condition.

    4 An activating unit which generates a corrective input signal to the process.

These elements are diagrammed in Figure 10-7. A very common example is the thermostat in a heating system. The thermostat measures the temperature of the air (a result of the heating system) and compares it with the thermostat setting. If the temperature drops below the setting (standard), the thermostat switches on the furnace, causing the production of more heat. An organizational example is the use of a budget as a standard and the application of various organizational pressures (including the termination of employees) to keep income and expenditures close to the budget. The supervision and operation of a system may become more and more expert so that the system achieves a steady state in which it shows only small, random variations around the standard. However, soon some disturbance (change of personnel, change of supervisor, new pay policy, new types of documents) will cause the system to fluctuate again. If the negative feedback and adjustment systems are working, the system will soon stabilize.

Feedback control loops are frequently classified as closed or open. A *closed control loop* is an automated control such as a thermostat or computer-controlled process. In much the same way that a closed system is insulated from disturbances in the environment, a closed feedback loop is insulated from disturbances in the control loop. An *open control loop* is one with random disturbances, such as those associated with human control elements. There are variations between the two extremes. A human-machine system is thus an attempt to use the best characteristics of both open and closed controls to make the system as closed as possible.

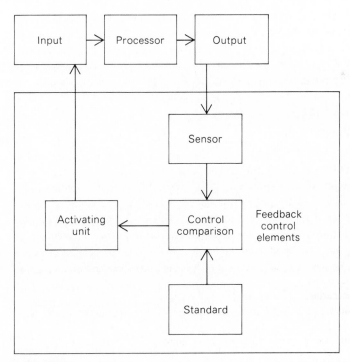

Figure 10-7
Negative feedback control elements.

State of variable	Control response
S_1	C_1
S_2	C_2
S_3	C_3
.	.
.	.
.	.
S_n	C_n

Enumeration

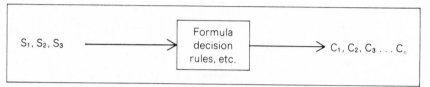

S_1, S_2, S_3 ⟶ Formula decision rules, etc. ⟶ $C_1, C_2, C_3 \ldots C_n$

Deterministic control response generator

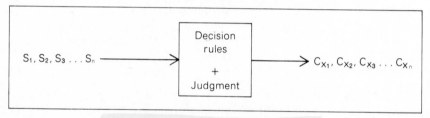

$S_1, S_2, S_3 \ldots S_n$ ⟶ Decision rules + Judgment ⟶ $C_{X_1}, C_{X_2}, C_{X_3} \ldots C_{X_n}$

Self-organizing response system

Figure 10-8
Methods for providing sufficient system control responses.

Law of Requisite Variety

One of the basic notions of system control theory is the *law of requisite variety* to obtain control. This has various rigorous formulations, but a common-sense understanding is that to control each possible state of the system elements, there must be a corresponding control state; to control a hundred states of the system elements, there must be a hundred different states of controls. To view it another way, there must be at least as many variations of control to be applied as there are ways for the system to get out of control. This means also that the controller for a system must be able to determine variations of the control variables and send system change instructions for each change. In human or organizational terms, a manager who wishes to control an inventory of 10,000 stockkeeping units needs to have available detailed information on each stockkeeping unit and to generate a control response for each possible variation in the state of each stockkeeping unit. This is beyond the capabilities of one person—in terms of channel capacity to receive and transmit the data and in processing capability to generate the variety of control responses. The manager handles this by assigning standard control procedures that can be applied to all units and furnishing a subordinate with decision rules for generating the variety of responses required to control the inventory assigned.

The law of requisite variety means that for a system to be controlled, every controller (human or machine) must be provided with (1) enough control responses (what to do in each case) to cover all possible conditions the system may face, (2) decision rules for generating all possible control responses, or (3) the authority to become a self-organizing system in order to generate control responses (Figure 10-8). Enumerating all responses is possible only in simple cases. Providing decision rules works well, but it is difficult to be all-encompassing when open systems are involved. Computer-controlled open systems are not feasible because of the law of requisite variety. The solution is the use of human-machine systems in which the computer applies decision rules to generate control responses for all expected situations and a human decision maker is used to generate control responses for the unexpected.

A SYSTEM WITHOUT REQUISITE VARIETY

A company making heavy equipment suddenly found its raw materials and in-process inventory climbing, but, at the same time, it was experiencing reduced sales and reduced production. The system was out of control. The cause was traced to the materials analysts who made the detailed inventory decisions. They had been furnished with decision rules for ordering, canceling, etc., under normal conditions, but they had no rules governing how to handle the inventory when production was decreasing and production lots were being canceled. In other words, the system did not provide the requisite variety of control responses. In this case, the urgency of remedy did not allow new rules to be formulated and validated. Instead, each materials analyst was treated as a self-organizing system, given a target inventory, and told to achieve it. With the analysts given the freedom to generate control responses, the inventory was reduced in a few months.

THE NATURE OF CONTROL IN ORGANIZATIONS

The control process requires measurement of performance and a standard for comparison. Measurement is basic to human experience; we think, move, and act in terms of measured amounts of time, distance, and value. Performance is expressed as measured units of input, activity, and output. Management evaluates performance, but it requires a standard against which an object, activity, or result may be placed to decide whether performance is satisfactory. Are oranges at 79 cents per pound expensive? The answer is dependent on having a standard or customary price for oranges. The standard may be vague or precise, written or not written, but for evaluation to take place there must be a standard.

Performance Standards

For control purposes, the standard can be a budget or plan that was previously arrived at following consideration of alternatives and surrounding conditions. The planned performance is usually the best that can realistically be expected rather than what is desired. A loss may be budgeted by a business. If the actual loss is the same as the budgeted loss, performance must be evaluated as acceptable. In other words, it is any deviation from the budget or plan that calls for corrective action. Information support for control purposes is therefore based on the comparison of actual performance with the plan and the analysis of reasons for any deviations (Figure 10-9). Interpretive comments are often included on control reports to explain deviations from the planned or budget standard.

The control report issued to management represents a comparison of actual performance with planned performance. Use of the term ''control'' to refer to such a report does not refer to the performance being reported; the activity presented has already taken place. It is no longer subject to control. An activity can be controlled before it takes place or while it is taking place, but it cannot be controlled after it has been completed. A report summarizing past activity is an evaluation report. Only if the report of past performance is the basis for control of future action may it be considered to be a control report.

When the object of a control system is individual performance, it is important that personnel connected with the activity being evaluated should regard the standard or plan as being fair. Experiments indicate that individuals reject standards that are too easy or too hard. The acceptance of goals and their use as a motivator to improve performance are enhanced by their being set within the limits that the individuals involved consider feasible. Therefore, it is considered desirable for the individuals themselves to participate in setting the budget or standard by which they may judge themselves and by which they know they will be judged by others. This is a basic principle of *management by objectives*.

A COMPLIANCE CONTROL SYSTEM

"Legal fallout" is the label given to court battles over who should bear the responsibility for the effects of toxic waste. Courts in Pennsylvania, Colorado and Washington have adopted the rule of absolute liability. This means that if a company markets an inherently dangerous product, the company is assumed to know of any hazards associated with the product's use, even if those hazards were unknown at the time of sale. In most states, manufacturers are liable to consumers for injuries caused by hazards which they should have known about and for which they failed to provide warnings.

A number of companies such as Standard Oil of Indiana, Monsanto, DuPont, and Allied Chemical have built monitoring systems to accumulate data on dangerous substances and their effects on humans. These systems collect data based on periodic personnel examinations, including those of high-risk workers. Other databases contain information on hazardous substances and workplace environment.

The correlations from these databases may help rebut claims that exposure of a worker to an environmental hazard caused a specific ailment. There is no doubt that it will increase scientific knowledge. The data may also, however, be subpoenaed to show that a company "willfully" allowed a hazard to continue. As yet, it has not been legally established when a company is required to act on the information it collects. Hence, a monitoring system established to comply with the law's demand for executive knowledge may wind up as evidence against those same executives. ("A Legal Time Bomb for Corporations," *Business Week*, June 16, 1980, p. 150.)

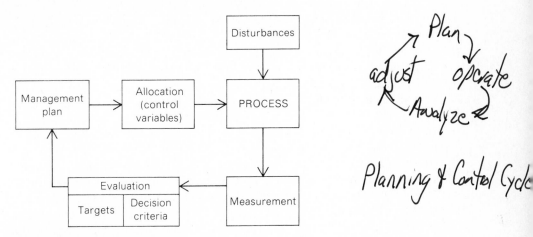

Figure 10-9
The management control cycle. (Bartow Hodge and Robert N. Hodgson, *Management and the Computer in Information and Control Systems*, McGraw-Hill, New York, 1969, p. 116.)

The Avoidance of Uncertainty

The purpose of organization and control is to reduce uncertainty regarding the task to be performed, how it is to be performed, and when it will be performed. The opposite of organization and control is disorganization and entropy. As noted in earlier chapters, a major purpose of information is to reduce uncertainty.

The problem of avoidance of uncertainty with respect to planning and control is that it may manifest itself in an avoidance of planning or in excessive control. As noted earlier in the chapter, the avoidance of planning may be explained in part by an avoidance of explicit recognition of uncertainty. In the case of control, attempts to avoid uncertainty may result in excessive rules and regulations, thereby stifling individual initiative and self-organization. The problems of control are especially relevant to information system design since many organizational systems are designed to use information acquisition and information processing to achieve control.

There is a basic conflict between the desire to control and thereby reduce uncertainty and the desire of individuals for the opportunity to self-organize (self-control) and exercise initiative (Figure 10-10). Different organizations and different parts of the same organization may have differing need for certainty, so the mechanisms for control may vary.

The Behavior of Control Personnel

There are a number of control positions in organizations. Their primary function is verification that organizational policies and procedures are being followed. Examples are budget officers, performance review personnel, and auditors. While these control tasks are a necessary and useful organizational function, the tendency is to make the reward structure for personnel performing them dependent upon discovering and pointing out errors. In other words, the person in a control position tends to receive

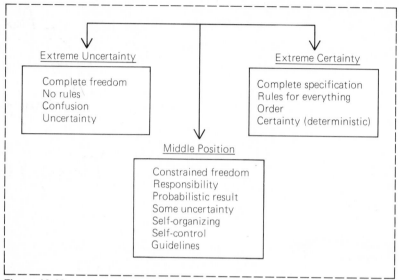

Figure 10-10
Extreme uncertainty, extreme certainty, and a middle position.

organizational rewards for finding the mistakes and failures of other members of the organization. This may lead to a tendency on the part of persons being evaluated to manipulate the information being provided. The integrity of the information system may be affected by data items that are misclassified or otherwise misreported.

INFORMATION SYSTEM SUPPORT FOR CONTROL

Information systems are used extensively for control purposes, primarily in reporting variances from a standard. System corrections can be performed by programmable decision rules, but information systems mainly serve the purpose of notifying a human decision maker when corrective action is required.

The control feedback loop is basic to systems design. The computer can improve the control process in several ways.

1 The standard can be more complex. Computational simplifications are not necessary. (However, people will generally object to using a standard that they are unable to compute easily.)

2 The computation of deviation and identification of cause can be more sophisticated.

3 Reporting with computers can use irregular time intervals (which is very difficult with manual processing), and can be done more frequently.

Information system support for control begins with the planning model, which can be used to set standards of performance. Computational support for control includes variance analysis plus other analyses which might assist in understanding both the reasons for variances and the course of action that will correct future performance.

Another use of information system support in control is continuous monitoring of performance rather than simple periodic reporting. Monitoring makes use of the planning model plus the concept of control limits to track performance. When performance falls outside the control limits, a message is provided to the proper control unit. The control limits are set so that random variations do not trigger control actions. The concept may be visualized by a control chart showing one process in control, even though it has random variations, and a second process that has gotten out of control (Figure 10-11).

Some concerns have been expressed that information technology can be used to continuously monitor performance of employees using computer terminals.[5] Evaluation may take place automatically, without the knowledge of the employee, and management has greater access to subordinates' information related to their work. Such "overcontrol" can lead to increased resistance, reduced initiative, and increased stress on the part of employees.

Some executives have viewed the online database as a means to access data for evaluation purposes directly without having it filtered through the people being evaluated. The result of such direct access is the ability to centralize control through the use of an online database rather than having it decentralized to self-organizing

---

[5]S. Zuboff, "New Worlds of Computer-Mediated Work," *Harvard Business Review*, September–October 1982, pp. 142–152.

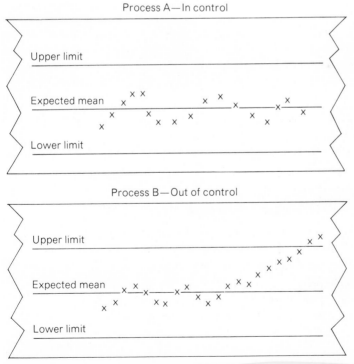

Figure 10-11
Control charts to illustrate use of control limits and continous monitoring.

subsystems. Whether information systems actually permit control to be more centralized in organizations is an issue of ongoing debate, which will be discussed in Chapter 11.

SUMMARY

Planning sets the course of action an organization will take; control causes events and activities to conform to plans. An important element of management, and the basis for planning, is the process of setting goals and objectives. One theory is that such goals are a result of bargaining among the individuals in the group, each one having individual goals. Planning takes place at the strategic, tactical (management control) and operational levels of the organization.

The planning process requires future expectations to be quantified and classified. A planning model is prepared as a method of structuring, manipulating, and communicating expectations and plans. Planning data items are derived from internal historical data as well as a variety of external sources. Computational support for the planning process consists of historical data analysis techniques, estimating and forecasting techniques, financial planning computations, and output formatting.

Control consists of activities which measure deviations from planned performance and initiate corrective action. Systems concepts relevant to control systems are negative feedback control and law of requisite variety. The control process utilizes the planning model to generate the performance standards. Controls may be viewed as methods of avoiding uncertainty. This may have negative implications in either the avoidance of planning (avoiding recognition of uncertainty) or excessive controls. Personnel responsible for maintaining control systems tend to be rewarded for finding errors, which may lead to manipulation of input to the control system by those being evaluated.

Information systems provide the capability to extend the manager's planning activities and allow iterative trial-and-error analysis of alternative plans. For control purposes, comparative advantages of computer-based information systems are the capability to monitor performance continuously rather than periodically and to make comprehensive analysis of performance.

MINICASES
1 FUEL SHORTAGES AND THE AIRLINES

In February 1979 (during a general fuel shortage), several oil companies asked the airlines at Kennedy Airport in New York to cut back their fuel consumption by as much as 50 percent. These fuel cutbacks, as well as distribution problems and rising prices, caused a number of airlines to cancel flights. It also caused them to reexamine their flight planning models.

The flight planning models utilized by the airlines at that time optimized the cost of fuel and determined where to buy it. They analyzed the fuel required for a particular flight considering weather and passenger load. They allowed extra fuel up to the point when it became too expensive to carry it. What most models did not deal with was fuel shortages. National Airlines kept cancellations in this period to a minimum by using a fuel management model which also dealt with fuel scarcity. It mapped out a complex system which balanced the cost of carrying fuel over the entire airplane route to achieve the lowest overall purchase price.

United Airlines used a different model which tracked existing fuel supplies. Previously used in the 1973–1974 fuel crisis, it depended on an officer onboard relaying information on the

[handwritten top margin: Levels (strategic Tactical operations scheduling) of Planning]

amount of fuel on the plane to flight operations. Based on this and the station fuel supply, United could predict when the station would run low on fuel. Gordon McKinzie, manager of fuel performance control, noted "It's kind of crude... a beads-sorting type of thing, but it works." ("Airlines Dig Up Models to Cope with Fuel Cuts," *Computerworld*, March 12, 1979.")

Questions

[handwritten: operational and tactical]

a What hierarchical level of planning do these models represent? Is this level adequate? Why or why not?
b What definitional elements and computations would be used in each model?
c What are the advantages of each of these approaches?
d Are these models adequate to deal with cutbacks in fuel consumption? Why or why not?

[handwritten: NO, Need models to measure more fuel availability]

2 THE HERD MASTER MANAGEMENT SYSTEM

In 1981, farmers anticipated that Congress would reduce price supports for dairy products from 85 percent to 75 percent. The parity system relies on government purchases of surplus dairy products to prevent oversupply from reducing prices below the parity level set by Congress. The narrower profit margins meant farmers had to increase productivity and efficiency in order to stay in business. The Kessler family of St. Louis, for instance, installed a Herd Master Management System, hoping this modernization would increase their return on investment. Their 330 cows, worth $660,000, were only part of this investment.

The Herd Master Management System cost $70,000 but would soon pay for itself in saving expensive feed by regulating the grain fed to the cows. Each cow had a plastic responder hung around her neck. As she ducked into one of the farm's grain feeding stations, her consumption of hay was recorded. Since Tom Kessler knew each cow by name and number, he could figure, by reading the midnight printout sheet, which cows had not eaten the amount they needed. This provision for "more tender loving care" was projected to a milk yield increase: the average daily production per cow was running at 50 pounds but would, hopefully, soon approach the yield of their best milker of the past decade, 140 pounds per day, or close to 20 gallons. ("Milk Producers Turn to Technology to Boost Efficiency," *Christian Science Monitor*, July 1, 1981.)

Questions

a What expectations are cited as causing the Kesslers to modernize? *[handwritten: Cutback in parity funds]*
b What were the sources of their data? *[handwritten: - Rumbling in Congress]*
c What time factors may have entered in? *[handwritten: Cost of operations,]*
d What models have the Kesslers built in by which to measure and control the business? *[handwritten: cows would eat a optimum mix of feed]*
e Are there any ordinary but uncontrollable factors which could still disrupt the plan?

[handwritten: disease, grazing disrupts eating habits, disaster, system failure] *[handwritten boxed: optimum Milk is trial & Error]*

3 PLANNING PAPER PRODUCTION

In 1979, International Paper Company (IP) had the world's largest paper production capacity as well as resources to feed that capacity. They could produce the whole range of paper products except tissues. Cardboard and container shipping were also a major part of their business. In 1979, while other forest product producers gained 32 percent in their operating earnings, IP lost 2.2 percent.

Referring to IP's management strategies at this time, one newly hired officer stated: "Many companies fail to manage change. They ride a successful pattern but the pattern wears out and they haven't perceived that change is needed."

J. Stanford Smith, IP's CEO in 1978, recognized IP's reputation as the industry's "dinosaur" and set in motion strategic organizational changes. They were based on the notion that paper products should be treated as commodities, where the highest profits go to the lowest cost producer. Smith also put new emphasis on research and product development.

Edwin A. Gee, who succeeded Smith as president the following year, continued Smith's strategy to turn the company around. He chose to undo some of the diversification of the 1970s which had protected IP from takeover attempts. For example, he sold General Crude Oil, a fuel exploration company, and replaced it with Bodcaw Company, a Louisiana board mill with more than 300,000 acres of prime timberland.

Some of the other areas in which Gee sought possible alternatives were the following:

- Narrowing the total product line
- Modernizing or discontinuing the remaining old-fashioned and inefficient plants
- Changing plants from multiproduct manufacture to specialized manufacture that would provide economies of scale
- Harvesting timber from the larger trees, like those in Louisiana, and using the "scraps" for paper as many other forest product manufacturers do
- Keeping strategy in long-term perspective which would mean long-term growth and modernization but low stock dividends in the short term

In the action to turn the company around, many top managers were replaced. The new management team put more emphasis on specialized management functions where the older personnel had emphasized knowing the paper business. The new organizational structure, based on separate profit centers and a strong corporate staff, replaced a centralized hierarchy oriented toward function and geographic region. This aggravated the normally different points of view among the IP divisions and reinforced a legacy of skepticism about corporate strategy. A former IP corporate planner summed up the situation by pointing to a lack of objective analysis and planning. He saw the planning process as "so incredibly political that it just destroys any sort of objective analysis." ("International Paper Tries Managing for the Long Run," *Business Week*, July 28, 1980, p. 94.)

Questions

a How would IP's mission statement have been changed?
b How would this change translate into strategies, objectives, and operational goals?
c Under the old and the new organizational structures, what is the relationship between planning and control?
d Was the "former IP corporate planner" correct in his observations? Why or why not?

4 PROFESSOR CHALLENGES BASIC ASSUMPTION ABOUT PLANNING AND CONTROL

Professor A. Van Cauwenbergh of Antwerp University, in a paper presented at the Tenth Anniversary Conference of the European Institute for Advanced Studies in Management, May 1982, presented four revisions to traditional management theory. In summary, the revisions are:

(1) The initiative for the renewal and adjustment of the activities of a firm should come from the different levels in the management hierarchy. "Strategy is not a privilege of top management."

(2) Firms, especially big firms, are incoherent systems (goals of the different component systems are not simply subdivisions of an overall goal; there are individual, conflicting goals as well). Some of these differences are manifestations of organizational initiative and vitality. Using information systems and central planning and rule making to suppress all differences is destructive to organizations.

(3) The most vital "fluid" of an enterprise is the aggregate of its entrepreneurial values. The most fundamental motivation and control comes through these shared values relative to work, quality, efficiency, etc. Management often neglects these values and assumes that the collection and dissemination of information will provide sufficient motivation and control.

(4) Enterprises are open systems; their structure and operating processes are determined by their environment. This means organizations must be designed to continually adjust to the environment.

Questions

a If these revisions are correct, how should planning be organized? How should the information system support this planning organization?
b Can the information system aid in achieving shared values?
c How might a comprehensive information system be used to stifle initiative?

EXERCISES

1 Explain the relationship between organizational planning and control.
2 A computer vendor has a mission to provide a highly reliable computer system. Translate this mission into:
　a Goals
　b Strategies
　c Objectives
3 What are the factors that influence the reliability of planning data?
4 Explain reasons why a profit plan might classify expenditures by:
　a Function
　b Organizational unit
　c Cost variability
5 Explain the usefulness of each of the historical data analysis techniques.
6 Explain the importance of depreciation in financial modeling.
7 Explain the relation of asset turnover to earnings as a percentage of sales. (Hint: See the DuPont model in Figure 10-5.)
8 Using the simple model described in this chapter, prepare a profit plan for 1985, 1986, 1987, and 1988 with the following input variables (all in thousands):

Variable	1985	1986	1987	1988
Sales	110	120	130	150
Average long-term debt	100	100	100	100
Average short-term debt	10	15	10	20
Accounts receivable at beginning of period	30	35	35	40
Administrative expense	40	45	45	55

9 This question is adapted from Paul D. Payollat.[6] Not only does a hospital need financial planning for its own financial management, it has federal and state requirements for medium-term and short-term budgets. Given the following data and relations, prepare a financial plan.

	Revenues
Daily hospital services	Occupied beds × billing rate
Ancillary	Ancillary procedures × billing rate
Outpatient revenue	Outpatient visits × billing rate
Total revenue	Daily hospital service through outpatient revenue
Deductions	Five percent of total revenue
Net revenue	Total revenue less deductions

---

[6]Paul D. Payollat, "HOSPLAN: A Financial Model for Hospitals," *The Arthur Young Journal*, Winter 1972, pp. 1–9.

	Expenses
Salaries	15,000 fixed + 1.50 × occupied beds
Benefits	25 percent of salaries
Supplies	200 fixed + 8 percent of total revenue
Fees	2,150 fixed
Depreciation	1,000 fixed
Total expenses	All the above plus interest
Net income	Net revenue less total expenses

Input data

	Period 1	Period 2	Period 3	Period 4	Period 5
Beds	360	440	440	440	440
Daily occupancy, %	83	84	82	80	81
Ancillary procedures	300	350	400	450	500
Outpatient visits	8,000	8,000	8,000	8,000	9,000
Daily rate, $	76	77	78	79	80
Ancillary rate, $	31	32	33	34	35
Outpatient rate, $	15	17	19	20	22
Interest	600	550	500	450	400

The plan is best done by using a spreadsheet processor of planning language. What is the effect on net revenue of increasing salaries 10 percent and increasing daily rate by $3?

10 Describe the basic control elements for each of the following:
a A thermostat
b Warehouse inventory
c Effectiveness of advertising for a new product
d Shoplifting in a department store
e Number of calls handled by an airline reservations operator
f Performance of a programmer on a large system development project

11 Explain the application of negative feedback in the following:
a A management reporting system using budgets.
b A management reporting system using standard costs.
c A management reporting system reporting actual figures with no comparison.

12 An inventory decision rule is stated as:

$$Q = \sqrt{\frac{24SC_O}{C_uC_h}}$$

where S = monthly usage in units
C_O = cost of ordering
C_u = cost per unit
C_h = cost of holding inventory as a yearly percentage of inventory value

a Does this have requisite variety?
b Suppose the rule is supplemented by:
(1) No order greater than 12 months supply.
(2) No order less than 2 weeks supply.
Is there requisite variety now?

13 Explain how the law of requisite variety can be applied to the following system design activities:

a Design of an input validation routine

b System testing

14 An inventory decision rule is stated as:

Average usage per month	Order quantity
1–5	5
6–10	10
11–15	30
16–25	45

Does this have requisite variety? Explain.

15 Explain the following organizational incidents in terms of system control principles:

a Clerk cannot complete unusual transaction. The clerk's instructions are to send the customer to the assistant manager.

b The program documentation for a job for several error codes says: "can't happen." They did happen, but the operator does not know what to do.

c Hours lost due to computer hardware failure are summarized for management. There is no agreed-upon acceptable level.

16 Explain the following organizational behavior in terms of concepts of planning and control:

a The president explains the importance of planning, but the company has no strategic plan.

b The department heads are reluctant to provide budget figures for the next year's budget.

c The department head always talks about individual initiative, yet she insists on a rule for everything.

d A supervisor's monitoring responsibilities on an assembly line are replaced by an automatic control device with a red light that flashes every time there is a quality control problem. The employees go on strike.

17 According to Drucker (*Managing in Turbulent Times*, Pan Books, London, 1981), planning that starts with the trends of yesterday and projects them into the future will not work in turbulent times. Environmental analysis becomes very important in planning. Six environmental sectors included in the analysis are social, political, economic, physical, technological, and institutional-legal environments. Describe the information system requirements to support environmental analysis for planning in turbulent times.

18 The directing unit for an organization seeks to have all units of the organization direct their efforts toward organizational goals. Individual units may use some of their resources for alternative goals set by the persons within them (security, quality of work life, leisure on the job, etc.). The directing unit needs information in order to enforce the use of resources for organizational goals, but the information may cost more than the misdirected resources. Explain how an improved, computer-based planning and control system might affect these dynamics.

19 Designing an organization with self-organizing systems (relatively autonomous units) provides members of these units with more local control but reduces the control exercised by higher levels in the organization. Explain this in terms of systems control theory.

20 Frederick Taylor introduced "Scientific Management" in the 1920s. He believed in a system of management based on simple tasks, standard tools and equipment, and fixed work rules. This approach was very effective in improving production efficiency in the production line industries in the 1920s and 1930s. Now there is a trend toward participation in self-governed work groups. Explain these alternatives in terms of systems control theory. Ignoring motivation and cost of participation, what are the advantages and disadvantages of participation?

SELECTED REFERENCES

Anthony, R. N.: *Planning and Control Systems: A Framework for Analysis*, Harvard University Press, Cambridge, 1965.

Cyert, Richard M., and James G. March: *A Behavioral Theory of the Firm*, Prentice-Hall, Englewood Cliffs, NJ, 1963.

Drucker, Peter: *Managing in Turbulent Times*, Pan Books, London, 1981.

Fahey, L., and R. King: "Environmental Scanning for Corporate Planning," *Business Horizons*, 20:4, August 1977.

Hofstede, G. H.: *The Game of Budgetary Control*, Royal van Gorcum, Assen, The Netherlands, 1967.

Mason, R. O., and I. I. Mitroff: *Challenging Strategic Planning Assumptions*, Wiley, New York, 1981.

Thomas, P.: "Environmental Scanning: The State of the Art," *Long Range Planning*, 13, February 1980.

ORGANIZATIONAL STRUCTURE AND MANAGEMENT CONCEPTS

Given the organizational context for management information systems, organizational design, behavior, and management are important underlying concepts. These subjects are too large in scope for an in-depth treatment in this book. Each topic requires one or more books to describe adequately. Therefore, this chapter will briefly survey a number of topics in organizational structure and management with emphasis on the relevance of each topic area to management information system design and operation.

THE BASIC MODEL OF ORGANIZATIONAL STRUCTURE

Organizational structure is the arrangement of organizational subsystems (or subunits) and the accompanying division of labor and hierarchy of authority relations.[1] Organizations differ in their structures for a variety of reasons. To illustrate, one major theory relevant to information systems is that organizations differ in their need for information interchange based on the degree of internal and external task uncertainty; they therefore select organizational structures with adequate information processing capabilities. (This theory is described further later in the chapter.) In this section, common dimensions of organizational structure are reviewed: hierarchy of authority, specialization, formalization, and centralization.

---

[1]Richard H. Hall, *Organizations: Structure and Process*, Third Edition, Prentice-Hall, Englewood Cliffs, NJ, 1982, pp. 53–54.

Hierarchy of Authority

The traditional organizational structure can be depicted as a hierarchical or pyramidal structure of positions (Figure 11-1). Each position has authority or right to "command" associated with it. Authority is evidenced by control over resources, rewards, and tasks, and authorization to make decisions regarding them. As a rule, authority is distributed according to the level in the hierarchy; i.e., the higher the level of a position, the greater its authority.

Each position has a *span of control*. This describes the number of immediate subordinates that a manager is to supervise. For example, the director of data processing may be one of six managers reporting to the vice president of administration; the director in turn may have seven people reporting directly. In the first case, the span of control is six; in the second case, it is seven.

The "shape" of the hierarchy of authority is affected at all levels by spans of control. Two extremes are shown in Figure 11-2. On the top, a "tall" hierarchy results from narrow spans of control at each level. On the bottom, a "flat" hierarchical structure is shown with the chief executive having a very wide span of control. An organization may have very narrow spans of control at some levels and very wide at others, depending on the nature of the work to be performed, the amount of direct supervision required, and the number of rules and procedures in place regarding decision making at each level.

Specialization

Specialization refers to the division of labor within the organization. A typical organization is divided along functional lines (e.g., marketing, production, accounting, etc.), which encourages specialization within each function (refer to Figure 11-1). Generally, there are two different ways in which tasks can be divided and assigned. The first is to give broadly trained specialists a comprehensive range of activities to

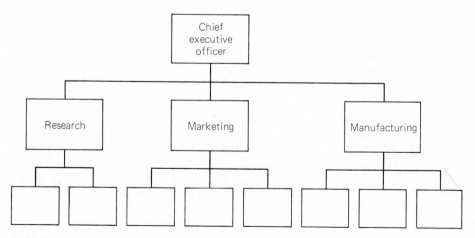

Figure 11-1
Basic hierarchical organization with functional specialization.

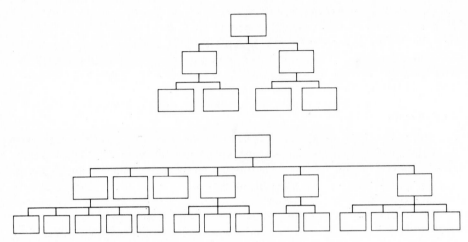

Figure 11-2
Effect of span of control on structure.

perform; the second is to subdivide the activities into small, well-specified tasks that nonspecialists can be easily trained to perform. Examples of the former are professionals and craft workers; the latter is exemplified by an assembly-line occupation.

Organizations may be more or less specialized, depending not only on the products or services they provide but also on the organizational philosophy of management. Some parts of the organization may be more specialized than others; research and development may contain only highly trained professionals while production utilizes narrowly defined tasks and nonspecialist workers.

The concept of specialization at the function and task level is illustrated by the information systems function. The development of applications is generally separated from information systems operations. There are several important reasons for this functional specialization:

> **1** The two functions require different training and expertise. An analyst needs different skills and training than an operator.
> **2** Segregating the two functions improves internal control because the design of procedures is separated from their execution. If the person who designs and implements an application also operates it, there is more opportunity for fraud or unauthorized changes in executing the procedures.

Formalization

The degree of formalization is the extent to which rules and procedures exist to handle organizational activities.[2] One indication of formalization is the degree to which decisions for handling various situations are programmed, i.e., decision rules are specified in advance. The more formalized the organization, the less discretion

---

[2]Hall, *Organizations: Structure and Process*, pp. 95–96.

individual organization members have in making decisions. Degree of formalization is illustrated in the information systems department by the contrast between an organization that has formal procedures for development of computer applications and an organization that lets each analyst establish the development procedures and development documentation.

Centralization

Organizational centralization generally refers to the level in the organization where decision making occurs.[3] In a highly centralized organization, most decision making occurs at the top of the hierarchy; the more decision-making authority is delegated to lower levels, the greater the decentralization.

There tends to be an association between centralization and hierarchy. A flat hierarchy with a wide span of control is more likely to be associated with decentralization of authority and decision making; a tall hierarchy with narrow span of control is likely to be associated with centralization.

Centralization is also related to formalization. In a highly formalized organization, operating personnel at low levels make decisions based on rules and procedures provided to them; exceptions are referred to higher levels for decisions.

---

[3]Hall, *Organizations: Structure and Process*, pp. 114–115.

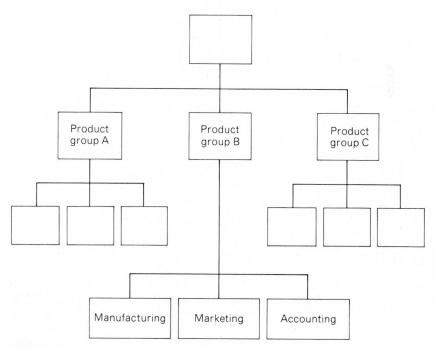

Figure 11-3
Product organization.

MODIFICATIONS OF BASIC ORGANIZATIONAL STRUCTURE

The basic organizational model emphasizes hierarchy of authority, span of control, unity of command (each subordinate has only one superior), and functional specialization. However, other structures are also found in practice that are variations on the basic model. This section surveys organization by product or service, organization by project, use of lateral relations, and matrix organizations.

Organization by Product or Service

Instead of being structured by functions such as manufacturing or marketing, the organization may be structured first by product (or service). Each product or service group will have its own functions for manufacturing, marketing, accounting, etc. This results in an organizational structure focused on output rather than the processes. It seeks to bring under a unified command all decisions affecting each group of outputs. Figure 11-3 illustrates this type of organization. Examples would be a consumer product organization with product groups such as household supplies, appliances, and industrial solvents. A service or governmental organization might have service groupings. A computer software firm might be organized by custom software, package software, and computer time-sharing sales.

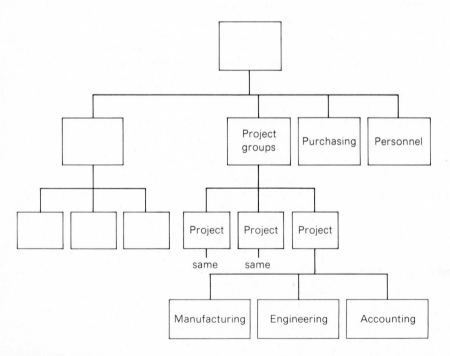

Figure 11-4
Project organization.

Project Organization

In project organization, resources are assigned to projects, each headed by a project director (Figure 11-4). A construction company might be organized in this way. Aerospace concerns have used the method for research and development projects. Information systems departments often use the project organization for management of the work of systems analysts and programmers. One might view a project organization as a dynamic form of organization by product or service. The temporary nature of the projects necessitates special organizational responses to obtain, coordinate, and reassign resources among different projects. A project manager has considerable authority for the duration of a project.

Lateral Relations

It is efficient to combine similar activities into a single function (such as marketing or manufacturing). The fact that different products and services make use of the functions creates a need for coordination and conflict resolution since the objectives of the organization are the products or services, but the basic organizational structure is by function. Organizational methods for reconciling the functional organization with product or service objectives are termed *lateral relations*. Some important methods for providing lateral relations are described below with information system examples:

1 *Direct contact among managers.* Managers initiate contacts with other managers to resolve conflicts. For example, the information systems manager contacts the controller to resolve conflicts regarding the processing of accounting applications.

2 *Liaison roles.* Responsibility for coordinating lateral flow of a product or service is assigned to an individual. For example, an individual is assigned responsibility for coordinating the efforts of production and information systems in the preparation of daily production schedules.

3 *Task force.* A formal group with representation from each department or function is established to resolve conflicts. For example, a task force with representation from several functions may be formed to investigate office automation and make recommendations.

4 *Teams.* Teams are formed around frequently occurring problems. For example, a team might be formed to handle certain groups of clients, regions, functions, or products. For information systems, this might be a database quality assurance team.

5 *Integrating personnel.* Examples are product manager, project manager, and brand manager. They do not supervise actual work, but are responsible for the integration of the independent subunits. An information systems example is an information systems manager responsible for integrating the use of data communication services.

6 *Matrix organization.* See discussion below.

Matrix Organization

The matrix organization represents formalized use of integrating, lateral relations. For each product or service grouping there is a separate integrating department which has lateral relations with each level of the functional organization. Each level of the organization affected has a vertical authority relation for the function, such as manufacturing, and a lateral authority relation with the corresponding level of the integrating product or service department, such as consumer products. A matrix

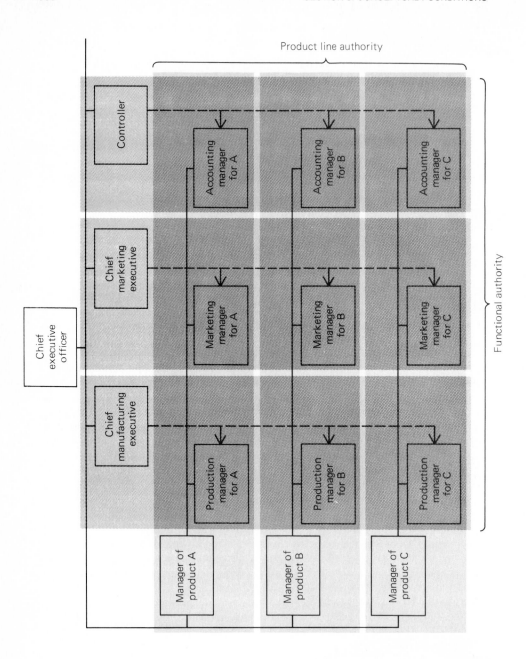

Figure 11-5
Matrix organization with three product lines. Drawn to emphasize matrix.

organization is illustrated in Figure 11-5. It can be described by a matrix with the rows being integrating departments and the columns the functional departments.

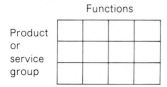

The matrix organization is often used in large, diversified companies. In typical matrix organizations, business units are organized around product or service lines; functional specialists in each business unit report through the hierarchy to the head of the business unit and also have ''dotted line'' responsibility to the corporate functional head. The corporate functional organization provides standards, training, and supervision for

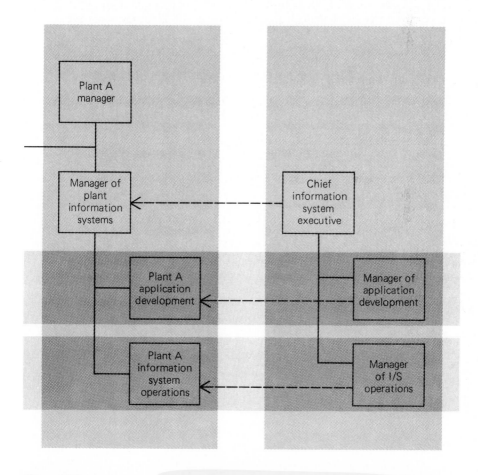

Figure 11-6
Lateral relationships drawn in matrix format for decentralized information systems.

the technical performance of the function in the business unit. This form is often used for decentralized information systems with the decentralized facility reporting to the unit it serves but receiving technical standards, training, and supervision from the corporate MIS group. This is illustrated in Figure 11-6.

INFORMATION PROCESSING MODEL OF ORGANIZATION STRUCTURE

Throughout the discussion of organizational structure, it has been implied that there is no ''one best way'' to organize. A relevant question is the appropriate criteria for determining which structure is most appropriate. An approach to this question which has particular significance for information systems is a contingency approach to organizational design based on the information processing and communication requirements experienced by an organization.[4] The basic premise is that the need for variations in organizational structure is explained by differences in task uncertainty and the ability of different structures to process and communicate information to deal with task uncertainty.

Amount of Information Processing by Organizations

The need for an organization to process information (i.e., the amount of information exchanged within the organization) is a function of the following factors:

Factor	Comments
Task uncertainty	The greater the task uncertainty, the greater the amount of information that must be processed to ensure effective performance. If an activity is well understood, it can be preplanned; if it is not well understood, there will be many changes during task performance.
Number of units relevant for decision	The number of units is related to number of departments, products, clients, etc. The greater the number of units, the greater the need to process information.
Interdependence of organizational units	If organizational units are not interdependent or interrelated, the amount of communication for conflict resolution will be small; if they are highly interrelated, the amount of information processing required to handle coordination will be high.

---

[4]The information processing model is developed by Jay R. Galbraith in *Organizational Design: An Information Processing View*, Addison-Wesley, Reading, MA, 1973. This section reflects many of the ideas in this study.

Organizational Structure to Achieve Information Processing Requirements

Given that the amount of information processing required by an organization is a function of task uncertainty, number of units relevant for decision making, and interdependence, the next step is to identify the organizational responses that allow it to handle the information processing load. These responses include:

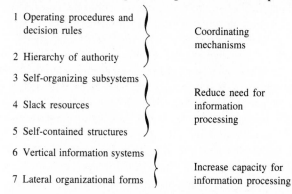

1 Operating procedures and
   decision rules

2 Hierarchy of authority

   Coordinating
   mechanisms

3 Self-organizing subsystems

4 Slack resources

5 Self-contained structures

   Reduce need for
   information
   processing

6 Vertical information systems

7 Lateral organizational forms

   Increase capacity for
   information processing

These responses are not independent—several or even all may be used by the same organization. Of special relevance to the information system designer is the fact that the use of a computer to process and transmit information faster is only one of many possible ways to handle the problem of information processing and communication in an organization.

Operating Procedures and Decision Rules. Coordination is simplified if organizational behavior can be specified in advance (programmed) by operating procedures and decision rules (increase in formalization). This provides partial decoupling of organizational units. Different parts of the organization can operate without communication because the behavior of the parts is known. There will, however, always be many situations that cannot be covered by operating procedures or decision rules.

Hierarchy of Authority. A hierarchy of authority is used for handling unusual situations that are not covered by decision rules and operating procedures. Exceptions are passed up to higher levels in the organization. Conflict involving two organizational units is moved up to the executive who has responsibility for both. For example, a conflict involving inventory at two plants, if not resolved by the plant managers, is referred to the vice president for manufacturing to whom both plants report. The information processing load imposed on an executive by these and other activities is the major element affecting the span of control that an executive can effectively exercise.

Self-organizing Subsystems. Increasing uncertainty of organizational tasks limits the use of decision rules and operating procedures. It also limits the use of a hierarchy of authority because of the processing load imposed by the number of responses required from higher levels. One organizational response to these conditions is to define various parts of the organization as self-organizing subsystems and decentralize decision-making authority to them. In other words, the organizational unit is given goals plus output and interface specifications and then allowed to exercise discretion as to use of resources to meet the goals. This is also termed *local rationality*.

Slack Resources. The interdependencies that cause organizational communication and information processing can be reduced by relaxing the specifications under which each organizational unit operates or by providing more resources. Each unit operates under time, resource (budget, manpower, etc.), and product specification constraints. Relaxing one or more of these constraints provides slack resources and tends to reduce the necessity for coordination because one major reason for interaction is to attempt to resolve conflicts caused by the inability of subunits to perform within the constraints.

Self-contained Structures. Product group organization is an example of self-contained structures. It is an extension of the concept of self-organizing subsystems. In addition to decision-making authority, segments of the organization are furnished with the resources needed to stand alone for operations. Each product group has its own facilities for manufacturing, marketing, accounting, and other functions. This reduces the number of levels through which decisions must pass that affect two functions such as manufacturing and marketing. However, this occurs at the expense of duplication in facilities and loss of economies of scale and specialization.

Vertical Information Systems. The ability of the organization to provide direction under conditions of uncertainty is limited by the time and resources that are required for planning and replanning. The planning and replanning time cycle may be reduced by adding staff (assistants), adding scheduling staffs, using computer processing, and providing better access to databases with planning data. Computers also increase formalization because more complex decision rules may be handled with the use of the computer. Thus, formal information systems increase the capacity of the organization to pass information for planning and coordinating activities up and down the hierarchy.

Lateral Organizational Forms. The lateral organizational forms reviewed earlier in the chapter are means for increasing the communication and information processing capacity of the organization, particularly laterally:

1 Direct contact
2 Liaison
3 Task force
4 Teams
5 Integrating personnel
6 Matrix organization

The forms are listed in approximate order of use when there are situations of task uncertainty. An organization with very uncertain tasks will tend to use more and more of the methods, whereas an organization with less uncertainty may use only the first two methods.

Computer databases may be used for lateral communications. If an interfacing subunit can interrogate a database to learn about factors generated by another subunit which affect its performance, the need for lateral relations may be reduced or the efficiency of lateral relations improved.

ORGANIZATIONAL CULTURE AND POWER

The classical descriptions of organizations and organizational structure do not explain many significant organizational behaviors. The information system designer who looks only at the organization chart will miss factors that may be vital to an understanding of the organization and to the design of an appropriate information system. Two areas of significance are organizational culture and organizational power.

Organizational Culture

Organizations have a culture and subunits within an organization have a culture. It may be well-articulated or relatively obscure. For example, one large organization has a culture that emphasizes service. The company training emphasizes service and the "tales" that are told in the organization reinforce it. Employees who do not conform to this service culture leave the organization. Another organization puts a high value on being on the leading edge of technology. The culture may reflect the dominant ideas of the founders or subsequent strong leaders. An example was the low-cost, single-style car philosophy of Henry Ford that dominated Ford Motor Company until a change was forced by very aggressive competition. Other causes are history, stage in technology, perceived reasons for past success, etc. Some extremes of perception of culture for an organization are:

High technology	Low technology
Price leader	Price follower
High quality, high price	Low quality, low price
High service	Low service
Innovator	Follower-copier
Selective marketer	Mass marketer
Risk taker	Risk averse

The cultures of different organizations differ with respect to the value attached to data and information; they also differ with respect to data discipline (the degree to which personnel are willing to develop and apply prescribed procedures for obtaining and providing timely, accurate data). For example, a financial institution expects a high level of data accuracy and completeness based on the basic objectives and operations of the organization; the culture of a merchandising organization accepts a lower level of data accuracy. The cash and securities inventory figure of the financial institution is very precise; the accounts receivable and goods-for-sale inventory figures of the merchandiser will have a lower level of accuracy.

Differences in accuracy can also be observed within organizations. Accounting has a higher level of accuracy than sales which reflects not only the data processing systems but also training and culture of the function. Accountants have a culture which emphasises accuracy (reinforced by training and "tales of finding the three cent error"); salespersons have a culture that focuses on the sale, without concern for a few cents (or dollars). The "tales" that reinforce this sales culture may include the use of large expense accounts to help achieve results. Such culture differences within an organization may create culture clashes as accountants with their culture of accuracy conflict with the sales area and their culture of results, not expenses.

The information system function within an organization tends to have its own culture based on the professional values, training, and beliefs of information systems professionals. This culture is reinforced by computer jargon. There are frequent culture clashes because the design of computer applications frequently reflects the cultural values of designers (e.g., precise, rational logic with no exceptions and detailed logging for monitoring purposes), but these cultural values may be inappropriate for its users. Failures in system implementations resulting from such problems are discussed in Chapter 18.

Organizational Power

Power in organizations refers to the ability to obtain and utilize human and material resources to accomplish objectives. This power is not distributed uniformly across the organization. Some organizational units are more powerful than others; some positions have more power; and some people seem to have more power than others in comparable positions. A recognition of power differences and their causes can aid in the design and development of information systems that support the organization, its functions, and individuals within it.

There are three contributors to the power of an organizational subunit:[5]

1 *Workflow pervasiveness.* The number of tasks in the organization which are dependent on the unit activities.

2 *Immediacy.* The speed at which the loss of the subunit activities would affect other organizational units and the severity of the loss.

3 *Substitutability.* The ability of another unit to perform the activity or to find alternative suppliers.

An effective information system requires organizational resources. These must be obtained in competition with other parts of the organization. In this competition, both organizational power and personal power are often critical variables. Personal power in an organization is partly a function of style and skill but, for the most part, is derived from a person's position in the organization (job definition and activities) and connections to other powerful people in the organization. The job that promotes individual power is one that is relevant to important organizational problems, is visible to the rest of the organization, and allows for discretion and creativity in its performance.

It has been observed that information systems executives often do not have the amount of organizational power that is required to acquire the resources to develop adequate information systems. There are two fundamental steps that an information system executive may take in acquiring requisite power:

1 Develop a personal understanding (a personal vision) of the role of information and the information system as a key competitive strategy for the organization. This is obtained by understanding why information resources are critical to the organizational mission and to the strategic direction of the organization. It also comes from an analysis of the ways in which the information system is critical to the operation and success of other organizational units.

2 Persuade others in the organization as to the critical role of the information system in the organization. The personal vision must be shared by others in the organization. Various activities can aid in achieving this shared vision of the importance of the information system.

---

[5]D. J. Hickson, C. R. Hinings, J. M. Pennings, and R. E. Schenk, "Structural Conditions of Intraorganizational Power," *Administrative Science Quarterly*, 19:1 March 1974, pp. 22–24.

One example is the process of organizational information requirements analysis. In performing the analysis, information requirements are linked to organizational strategy and organizational objectives thereby making the connection specific. Another example is the performance of a study of information system backup and recovery in the event of a disaster. The study will identify the consequences of failure in the information system and thus make clear the importance of the information system.

ORGANIZATIONAL CHANGE

One of the central system concepts described in Chapter 9 is that a system will decay and disorganize if it does not change in response to changes in the environment. Change is important, yet there are significant problems with organizational change. This section describes organizational change as a natural growth and decline process. Systems and their goals are not stable; they change because of goal displacement, organizational learning, or specific project change procedures. The section also presents the case for stable systems and describes systems that promote organizational change.

Organizational Growth Cycle

In nature, there is a cycle of growth and decay starting with birth and ending with death. In general terms, organizations and products do the same. The basic description for the growth phenomenon in organizations, organizational activities, and products is the sigmoid or S curve. It has been widely applied to the marketing of products (Figure 11-7) but, less frequently, to the organization and other activities.[6]

The stages in the cycle of growth represent major changes. Some typical stages for product sales are given below:

Stage	Comments
Introduction	The activity or product is new, and there is initial experimentation and gradual acceptance.
Growth	There is a rapid growth of the activity or rapid increase in sales.
Maturity	The activity or sales remain high, but there is no increase.
Decline	Competition and other forces cause a decline.

The growth curve is also applicable to the introduction and growth of internal organizational functions. Such a growth curve will look somewhat different from the curve shown in Figure 11-7 if the function becomes well integrated into the organization. In its ''mature'' stage (rather than in its ''declining'' stage) it will show slow but steady growth and acceptance within the organization.

A well-known explanation of information system organizational change (Nolan's stage theory) also uses an S curve. This will be described in Chapter 14.

---

[6]Larry E. Greiner, ''Evolution and Revolution as Organizations Grow,'' *Harvard Business Review*, July–August 1972.

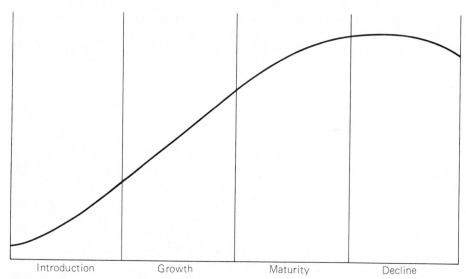

| Introduction | Growth | Maturity | Decline |

Figure 11-7
Sigmoid or S curve with stages of growth.

Goal Displacement

It is customary to talk of the goals of an organization as if the organization existed apart from its members. As discussed in Chapter 10, the organization can be viewed as a coalition of individuals, each of which has goals, and the goals arrived at for the coalition represent bargaining among the members. The goals change in response to changes in the coalition membership and changes in the goals of the participants as the environment changes. Goal changes cause changes in the structure of the system.

One of the problems with system goal changes relevant to information systems is *goal displacement* in which the goals of those operating the system displace the output goals as the primary goals of the system. Examples are offices with hours designed for the convenience of the staff rather than meeting the objective of servicing clientele, government agencies designed to regulate business that instead protect business firms from competition, and computer centers whose primary goal of providing computing services is displaced by a goal of providing a technologically interesting environment for staff experimentation. Based on systems theory as discussed in Chapter 9, the system is no longer functioning in response to its environment and may decline or decrease in effectiveness.

THE UNIVERSITY TRAVEL SERVICE WITH DISPLACED GOALS

The student association at a university organized a travel service to advise students and faculty on study and travel abroad, especially in Europe. The service was staffed by students and arranged summer charter flights. Over the years, the services changed, primarily in response to the desires of the staff rather than the needs of the student and faculty.

- The staff wanted to travel free of charge, so tour groups were arranged to cover the staff's travel costs.

- The employees did not want to leave when they graduated, so full time, nonstudent jobs were created.
- The full-time employees wanted the "perks" afforded to regular travel agents (free tickets, free hotels, complimentary familiarization tours, etc.), and so the student travel service was changed to a regular travel agency.

The three changes, beneficial only to the staff, were based on goals that displaced the goals for which the service was established.

Organizational Learning

Organizational learning is the process by which an organization identifies action-outcome relationships, identifies and corrects errors, stores the experience in organizational personnel who teach new employees, and stores the experience in procedures, forms, systems, rules, computer programs, and other forms for transferring experience. In other words, it exhibits adaptive behavior. For example, a new employee in the data entry function is instructed in entry procedures plus error control and error handling procedures. Forms, screen formats, report formats, and instruction manuals contain the formal organizational experience on how to do the job. The supervisor and other data entry employees have additional verbal instructions and tell stories that assist the new employee to learn quickly. As the neophyte makes typical learner mistakes, the organizational experience is incorporated in the individual who carries forward the unwritten rules, tips, and guidelines.

Organizational learning may be facilitated and encouraged by management practices and organizational culture, the social and cultural environment in which the organization exists, or from learning mechanisms designed into the organization. The latter include committees, planning systems, information systems, and procedures and regulations.

Organizational learning is often prevented or inhibited by the behavior of individuals based on their models of how management should work or on self-interest, such as preventing discovery and correction of errors because doing so would be threatening.

Individuals within organizations have assumptions about the goals to be achieved and ways to achieve the goals. For example, a manager's assumptions about motivation will affect the choice of data collected for control purposes. One difficulty with learning from feedback is that the learning may be concentrated on adjustments to correct performance without examination of the assumptions and theories that underlie performance deviations. A manager may "learn" how to use variance reports in supervising subordinates and getting explanations from them; this expertise is codified in the organization by manuals, reports, experience, etc. However, the performance feedback may not cause any learning with respect to the assumptions underlying the use of the variance reports to achieve organizational goals in that organizational setting. Argyris has termed the learning that takes place within the context of a theory the manager has adopted (implicitly and explicitly) as *single loop learning*, and learning that focuses on the underlying assumptions and theories being used as *double loop learning*.[7] Single

---

[7]Chris Argyris, "Organizational Learning and Management Information Systems," *Database*, 13:2–3, Winter–Spring, 1982, pp. 3–11. Reprinted from *Accounting Organizations and Society*, 2:2, 1977, pp. 113–121. See also Chris Argyris, "The Executive Mind and Double-Loop Learning," *Organizational Dynamics*, Autumn 1982, pp. 5–22.

loop learning from feedback is important because it focuses on the operational performance of the system. However, double loop learning should also occur in order to have relevant, useful assumptions. Management information systems tend to focus on outputs such as variance reports that support single loop learning, but it is possible to have reports that aid in double loop learning.

Model of Organizational Change

There is general consensus on the difficulty of organizational change. Unless the organization is experiencing a crisis, change is likely to be incremental rather than radical. Change is not simply a rational process of demonstrating that the new method is better for the organization. Change that appears to be desirable to one group may be perceived as a bad idea by others. Innovation can threaten the established interests of individuals and groups. Even if the end result looks good, there is uncertainty about what will ''really happen.''

New information systems represent major organizational change. The most commonly used model for system change is the three-stage model of Kurt Lewin.[8]

Stage	Description
Unfreezing	Create a climate for change and get contracts with users.
Change	Analysis, design, development, and installation.
Refreeze	Institutionalize the new system.

This model emphasizes the fact that stable organizational systems with supporting political coalitions need to be disturbed before change begins. The parties involved need to want the changes. A contract for change must be achieved. After the change is complete, it is important to institutionalize the change (refreeze) by procedures, training, and evaluations.

The effects of organizational change are particularly important for information system design because the introduction of a new information system represents a significant organizational change, often crossing boundaries between organizational units. System designers are usually external ''change agents'' to the organizational units where the change will occur. They may not be aware of the expectations of those who will be affected by the change or of the existing power balance, culture, and conflicts of interest. Thus a new system may be introduced into an environment where ''unfreezing'' has not taken place. One method of unfreezing that is especially applicable to information systems, called sociotechnical design, is introduced later in this chapter.

The Case for Stable Systems

Even though change may be necessary and desirable, a high, uncontrolled rate of change is difficult for organizations to handle. This is especially true of changes that affect many

---

[8]K. Lewin, ''Frontiers in Group Dynamics,'' *Human Relations*, 1, 1947, pp. 5–41.

organizational units; information system changes usually have a multiple system effect.

In the case of information systems, a significant part of the cost of a new system is the cost of training users and developing user proficiency in the application. There are new protocols for accessing the system, new commands to use the system, new screen and report formats, new terminology, and new procedures. Learning the set of procedures and other features is a cost of change. Once the application has been learned and the procedures become habitual, each change in the inputs, processes, or outputs will disturb the users and increase the difficulty and time for use. Changes in one system require communication and coordination with the systems to which it interfaces.

THE UNSTABLE SYSTEM AND A USER AND PROGRAMMER DIALOGUE

User: Why didn't the cash management program work right this morning? The codes for the banks where we deposit funds were all fouled up.

Programmer: Didn't you notice how fast it ran. The table lookup function for depositories was very slow. I made the lookup five times faster, and made the program run in one-tenth the time. I had to rearrange some codes to do it.

User: I can't tell if it runs faster. Most of my time is spent on input; I haven't noticed any excessive running time. It worked just fine. I wasted two hours this morning because of the code changes, and I'll have to rerun this afternoon. I don't want to learn new codes. Besides, all the old data will now be inconsistent with the new.

Programmer: No problem. I'll write a program to convert the old data to the new codes.

User: That's fine, but I don't know from day to day whether I am using the application correctly. I spent a lot of time manually checking the results.

Programmer: No need to do that. I always test my changes.

User: I have to test if I am uncertain as to changes. In any case, I don't want to start each day learning about your changes. Starting today, I will accept enhancements to this program only once a quarter—the first scheduled date is three months from today.

Information to Promote Organizational Change

Some authorities on information systems suggest that regular reports contribute to organizational rigidity and hamper organizational search for problems and opportunities. Regular reports in standard format are efficient for monitoring clearly specified performance criteria. However, readers may overlook significant problems because the data describing them does not appear on the report or because the data is not analyzed to bring out the problem.

The information system can have elements which promote exploration and problem finding and identify the need for change in organizational systems. Many of these features will be discussed in later chapters. Three concepts can be utilized in the design of information system features to promote organizational change. The idea underlying each of them is that appropriate information will assist the organization to unfreeze and to be amenable to change.

1 Identification of significant internal or external variables that may signal a basic change in conditions for the organization. For example, a company selling baby products should be interested in the rate of family formations, average number of children, etc. Units affected by technology changes should keep track of technology innovation.

2 Identification of significant relationships among internal and external variables where a change in the relationships may signal a change in conditions affecting the organization. For example, the relationship between college-age students and students enrolling in college is important in forecasting demand for higher education. If this relationship changes significantly (or there is a surge of older people returning to school), this affects the university.

3 Use of (and providing reports from) multiple information channels, multiple evaluation criteria, and incompatible reporting dimensions. This has been termed a "semiconfusing" information system by Hedberg and Jonsson.[9] The idea is that many information systems homogenize and eliminate all noise from information before it is reported. For some applications, this is appropriate. For applications to alert the organization to the possible need for change, the reporting of somewhat conflicting, semiconfusing data provides managers with a better picture of the uncertainty that really exists. Also, some of the clues that are very important may be removed unless multiple, somewhat conflicting channels are provided.

GETTING SOFTWARE GROUPS TO ACCEPT INNOVATION

Since the early 1970s, there have been significant improvements in software methodologies, yet these innovations have had only modest adoption. There are several explanations for this slow rate of adoption: lack of recognition of need, low top-management support, individual differences, and lack of information about software innovations. The latter point was the subject of a research study by Zmud. He studied 49 software development groups to find out the effect on adoption of modern software practices of information channels linking software group members with external information about innovations in software development methodology. His findings are interesting for information systems:

1 Innovation of software is facilitated by linkages to outside information.

2 The effect of external information in promoting software innovation is contingent on the internal environment of the software group.

3 Some channels to external information were associated with adoption of innovation; others were not. For example, dues payments, subscriptions, a library, and internal training were associated with adoption; professional meetings, tuition payments, and internal training as a secondary work role were not.

Robert W. Zmud, "The Effectiveness of External Information Channels in Facilitating Innovation within Software Development Groups," *MIS Quarterly*, 7:2, June 1983, pp. 43–58.

MANAGEMENT THEORIES

The discussion of organizations has dealt so far with their structures and has not focused on the behavior of individual organization members. In this section, theories of human motivation, leadership style, and job design will be surveyed, especially as they relate to information system design.

---

[9]Bo Hedberg and Sten Jonsson, "Designing Semiconfusing Information Systems for Change Organizations," *Database*, 13:2–3, Winter–Spring, 1982, pp. 12–24. Reprinted from *Accounting, Organizations and Society*, 3:1, 1978, pp. 47–63.

Human Motivation

Early management theory was somewhat mechanistic in its view of human motivation. The goals of the members of an organization were assumed to be consistent with, or at least sublimated to, organization goals. Employees were assumed to respond positively to authority and to be motivated by monetary rewards. The most well-known proponent of early management theory was Frederick Taylor,[10] often called the "father of scientific management." Taylor's principles of scientific management involved careful scrutiny of a task to be performed and minute division of labor so as to achieve maximum productivity of a worker in "harmony" with a machine. Scientific management also implied removal of control over the pace of the work from the person performing it, to be set by the "experts" who studied the task.

The human relations movement, which began with the Hawthorne studies between 1927 and 1932, established the concept of the organization as a social system. Motivation was found to be based on more than economic reward. Work groups, coworkers, etc., were found to be important. Leadership styles were suggested which would increase the satisfaction of workers with the organization.

Motivation is the reason a person carries out certain activities; it is usually explained in terms of the person's drives or needs. The needs of a person are not fixed; they change over time with the stage of his or her career, and as certain needs receive more satisfaction. A useful classification of general human needs is a hierarchy developed by Abraham Maslow.[11] It cites five basic needs, but the higher needs become activated only to the extent that lower needs have been somewhat satisfied.

Level	Need	Explanation
Lowest	Physiological	Physical needs such as satisfaction of hunger or thirst, and activity need.
	Safety	Protection against danger, threat, deprivation.
	Love	Satisfactory associations with others, belonging to groups, giving and receiving friendship and affection.
	Esteem	Self-respect and respect of others.
Highest	Self-actualization	Self-fulfillment. Achieving one's potential. Creativity. Self-development. Self-expression.

The work of Maslow and also of Frederick Herzberg[12] have contributed to an understanding of organizational rewards. Essentially, such rewards as high pay and safe working conditions only motivate employees up to a point. Other job factors affect employees' satisfaction with their jobs, which presumably leads to superior perfor-

---

[10]F. W. Taylor, *The Principles of Scientific Management*, Harper, New York, 1911.

[11]A. H. Maslow, "A Theory of Human Motivation," *Psychological Review*, July 1943, pp. 370–396.

[12]Frederick Herzberg, *Work and the Nature of Man*, World, Cleveland, OH, 1966.

mance. Primary among these factors are a sense of achievement, recognition, interesting and challenging work, responsibility, and advancement.[13]

It should be noted that there is controversy over the validity of the theories of Herzberg and, to a lesser extent, of Maslow. However, even though they may be oversimplifications, they do provide useful descriptive categories and insight into the motivation of organizational personnel.

More recently, a theory of motivation called *expectancy theory* has received considerable attention.[14] Expectancy theory is an explanation of motivation to make a decision. As defined by Lewin, Vroom, and others, it states that the course of action chosen by a person depends upon the relative strength of three sets of psychological forces. First is the individual's belief that the course of action will lead to a certain outcome. Second is the "valence" (value or worth) of that outcome to the indivdual. Third is the individual's expectation that he or she can perform at the desired level. Given multiple alternatives, the individual will choose the one for which the combination of these three psychological forces is highest.

Leadership Style

Leadership is interpersonal influence which persuades or motivates a group toward the attainment of a specified goal or goals. There are numerous theories about leadership and much empirical data regarding conditions under which different leadership styles are appropriate.[15] The purpose here is only to point out the relevance of leadership style to information system design; for this purpose, two extremes of leadership style are defined:

Type	Explanation
Autocratic	The leader determines policy and directs the activities required to carry it out. He or she seldom gives reasons for orders. The leader's commands are enforced by the power to reward or punish.
Supportive	This type is called participative, consultative, or democratic leadership. The leader solicits suggestions and consults with his or her subordinates about decisions affecting them or decisions they will have to carry out. Supervision is general, and subordinates are encouraged to use initiative.

The autocratic style implies a mechanistic view of human motivation affected primarily by economic rewards. The supportive style, on the other hand, assumes job

---

[13]For a summary of research on these theories, see A. C. Filley, R. J. House, and S. Kerr, *Managerial Process and Organizational Behavior*, Second Edition, Scott, Foresman, Glenview, IL, 1976.

[14]K. Lewin, *The Conceptual Representation and the Measurement of Psychological Forces*, Duke University Press, Durham, NC, 1938; see also V. H. Vroom, *Work and Motivation*, Wiley, New York, 1964.

[15]Douglas M. McGregor, *The Human Side of Enterprise*, McGraw-Hill, New York, 1960; Rensis Likert, *The Human Organization*, McGraw-Hill, New York, 1967; and Filley, House, and Kerr, *Managerial Process and Organizational Behavior*.

satisfaction to be an important motivation and that all individuals have the capacity to assume responsibility.

The path-goal theory of leadership[16] is based on expectancy theory. According to path-goal theory, the appropriate leadership behavior (style) depends on the extent to which subordinates see their behavior as either an immediate source of satisfaction or as leading to future satisfaction. Furthermore, the leader's behavior will motivate subordinates to the extent that it makes satisfaction of their needs contingent on their performance as well as provides the necessary support environment to achieve high performance (through training, guidance, rewards, etc.).

LEADERSHIP STYLES AND ORGANIZATONAL STRUCTURE

In 1981, a *Business Week* article contrasted Japanese and American management to illustrate how trust could increase low-cost productivity. It stated that Japanese companies assume personnel at all levels to be competent and trustworthy and to have the company's best interest at heart; more people are in profit-related jobs than in American firms. American business, by contrast, has a large number of "reviewers," desk people who monitor other people's work. One result of this is a much more complex managerial hierarchy in the American firms. Ford, for example, has eleven levels of management while the Japanese company Toyota has only six.

American branches of Japanese companies such as Quasar Company and Matsushita Industrial Company seem to be able to manage in the same way. Design engineers, production engineers, and marketing directors meet together and resolve differences before passing their recommendations to a higher level. Since employees learn the intricacies of other departments before they are permitted to specialize, they have sympathy for, rather than suspicion of, their managerial counterparts. There may be some "sibling rivalry" in the organization but the overall family consciousness is greater. ("Trust: The New Ingredient in Management," *Business Week*, July 6, 1981, p. 104.)

Job Design

Job design, or "job enrichment," is an approach to improving motivation and satisfaction of employees through the diagnosis and design of specific characteristics of their jobs. Through research,[17] five job dimensions that affect the motivation of employees have been identified.

1 *Skill variety*—the degree to which a job requires employees to perform activities that challenge their skill and abilities.

2 *Task identity*—the degree to which the job requires completion of a "whole" and identifiable piece of work.

3 *Task significance*—the degree to which the job has a substantial and perceivable impact on the lives of other people, either within or outside of the organization.

4 *Autonomy*—the degree to which the job gives the worker freedom, independence, and discretion in scheduling work and determining how it will be done.

5 *Feedback from the job*—the degree to which an employee gets direct information about the effectiveness of his or her efforts.

---

[16]R. J. House and T. R. Mitchell, "Path-Goal Theory of Leadership," *Journal of Contemporary Business*, Autumn 1974, pp. 81–97.

[17]J. R. Hackman and G. R. Oldham, *Work Redesign*, Addison-Wesley, Reading, MA, 1980.

The job design concept is very significant to information systems because of two job design effects:

1 Introduction of new information system support for a task frequently causes a change in the design of jobs.
2 Information systems create new jobs.

ORGANIZATIONS AS SOCIOTECHNICAL SYSTEMS

Most of the discussion in this chapter has focused on organizations as systems and on formal organizational structure. The previous section was concerned with the roles of individuals as organization members. Each employee has needs which, if congruent with the goals and objectives of the organization, should lead to high levels of performance and job satisfaction. When individual needs and organizational goals are not congruent, poor performance, resistance, and other dysfunctional consequences can result.

The introduction of an information system can alter the relationship between individual needs and organizational objectives. This section describes an approach to viewing organizations from both the individual and overall organizational perspective. Called the sociotechnical approach, it is useful for dealing with the effects of new information systems.

The Leavitt Model of Organizational Subsystems

The Leavitt model[18] describes the organization as consisting of four interrelated components:

1 Task
2 Technology
3 Structure
4 People

Many management theorists add organizational culture as a fifth element. Figure 11-8 shows a model of the interrelated components, including culture. The significance of Leavitt's model for understanding organizational change is that, because of the strong interdependence, a change in one component inevitably has effects, planned or unplanned, on the others.

The implicit approach of most systems designers is to focus on the task and technology subsystems and completely ignore their effects on people and structure. Technology refers here generally to all tools used in task accomplishment. Changes in technology such as new information systems inevitably affect the way individuals relate to the tasks they are responsible for performing, as well as the organizational structure and culture which act to facilitate task accomplishment.

---

[18]H. J. Leavitt, "Applying Organizational Change in Industry: Structural, Technological and Humanistic Approaches," in J. G. March (ed.), *Handbook of Organizations*, Rand McNally, Chicago, 1965.

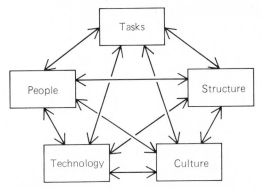

Figure 11-8
An alternate model of organizational subsystems modified from the Leavitt model to include culture.

Concepts of Sociotechnical Design

A sociotechnical approach to organizational change has been defined as one which recognizes organizations as purposive entities which have a variety of goals and which, in order to survive, have to interact successfully with their surrounding social and business environments. Viewing organizations as sociotechnical systems requires making explicit the interrelationships between the subsystems in the Leavitt model. Specifically, it focuses on human as well as technical and organizational objectives in effecting organizational change.

Several researchers, primarily Enid Mumford and her colleagues,[19] have developed a sociotechnical approach to systems design. The approach recognizes the interaction of technology and people; its goal is to produce systems which not only are technically efficient but also lead to high job satisfaction.[20] The sociotechnical approach to systems design emphasizes participation by those who are to be affected by the new system as well as the technical experts (systems designers). The sociotechnical design process, shown in Figure 11-9, can be applied to information system requirements determination and system design procedures (to be described in Chapters 15 and 18).

The first step in the process is to assess the existing social system, primarily by measuring the job satisfaction of the work group and reporting the results in a group feedback session. The job satisfaction data is then used as a basis for setting human (social) objectives directed at increasing job satisfaction. This can be the responsibility of the work group. Social alternatives will deal with different work group structures, allocation of tasks, and design of individual jobs. The technical experts examine alternatives for meeting the technical objectives of the system (usually set prior to initiating the design effort).

Once technical and social alternatives have been identified, the next step is for the entire design team to select those alternatives that meet *both* social and technical

---

[19]Enid Mumford and Mary Weir, *Computer Systems in Work Design: The ETHICS Method*, Wiley, New York, 1979.
[20]Mumford and Weir, *Computer Systems in Work Design: The ETHICS Method*, p. 6.

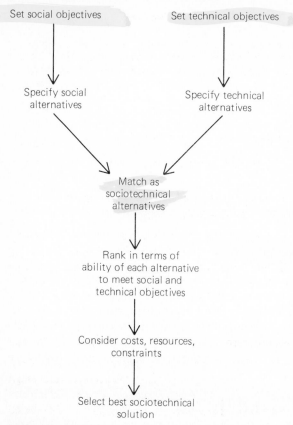

Figure 11-9
Sociotechnical systems design (from E. Mumford and M. Weir, *Computer Systems in Work Design: The ETHICS Method*, Wiley, New York, 1979).

objectives. The result should be a system design which improves task efficiency *and* job satisfaction.

The sociotechnical design approach is especially suitable for clerical systems where a large number of operating personnel will be affected. There are constraints on its use: applying it to systems design can be time-consuming, and it requires training of systems designers in work redesign and group communications skills.

APPLYING THE LEAVITT MODEL AND SOCIOTECHNICAL DESIGN

The manufacturing and engineering division of Corning Glass was given a mandate to decrease its budget by 15 percent. Operations manager Dorothy McConnell studied the problem of installing automated office equipment through interviews with 800 employees. The interviewing process was unusual in that peers interviewed peers to find out how they spent their time and what their needs were. The questionnaire was carefully prepared and revised, with each question accompanied by a stated objective so the respondent would understand the line of questioning. Questions included what people thought they should be doing and what they would do if available work time were cut in half. The interviews lasted two and a half hours each.

McConnell insisted that management take the results seriously. When managers disagreed with workers on certain issues, she pointed out that the workers' perception of their situation was reality and must be dealt with as such. She also pointed out that ergonomic considerations, such as skylight and window space, could go a long way in easing the stress period which would accompany the change to an automated environment.

Part of the survey was designed to reveal the sections of the company which were most overworked and in need of help. These sections became prime candidates for pilot projects.

"Corning Glass Combines Automation, Ergonomics, to Bolster Productivity," *Computerworld*, October 13, 1980.

IMPLICATIONS OF ORGANIZATIONAL STRUCTURE AND MANAGEMENT THEORY FOR MANAGEMENT INFORMATION SYSTEMS

The influence of information system and organization structure is reciprocal. Management information systems can affect future organizational structure. The existing organizational structure can influence how information systems are designed, whether they are implemented successfully, and how they are used. Management theory and sociotechnical theory suggest choices to be made in information system design.

MIS and Formal Organizational Structure

It has been predicted that information systems lead to increasing centralization; improved access to relevant information allows top management to act on a wider range of problems and thus retain centralized control of decision making. This prediction was first made by Leavitt and Whisler in 1958.[21] There has been some evidence of increased centralization, primarily reported by Whisler in a study of insurance companies.[22] Other studies have shown no change in centralization as a result of the computer.[23] In a study of eight organizations reported by Robey,[24] five of the organizations had no change in formal structures. Where changes did occur, the existing organizational structure was usually reinforced. Today, it is generally accepted that

1 Information systems do not *cause* structural changes

2 Information systems can be designed to support increasing centralization or decentralization, depending on the objectives, strategies, and goals of the organization. Factors other than the use of information systems are more crucial to the decision to centralize or decentralize.

---

[21]Harold J. Leavitt and Thomas L. Whisler, "Management in the 1980's," *Harvard Business Review*, November–December 1958, pp. 41–48.

[22]Thomas L. Whisler, *Information Technology and Organizational Change*, Wadsworth, Belmont, CA, 1970.

[23]George E. Delehanty, "Computers and the Organizational Structure in Life Insurance Firms: The External and Internal Economic Environment," in Charles A. Myers (ed.), *The Impact of Computers on Management*, MIT Press, Cambridge, 1967, pp. 61–106; and Rosemary Stewart, *How Computers Affect Management*, MIT Press, Cambridge, 1971.

[24]Daniel Robey, "Computer Information Systems and Organizational Structure," *Communications of the ACM*, 24:10, October 1981, pp. 679–687.

Leavitt and Whisler also predicted a restructuring of middle management jobs. They expected many jobs to become more structured or formalized, with reduced individual discretion. Others (such as research and programming) would become less structured and move up in the organizational hierarchy. The net result would be an organizational hierarchy which was heavy at the top and bottom with few middle management positions. Trends in management so far have contradicted this prediction. Several studies have shown that implementation of computer systems is associated with an increase in the number of levels in the organizational hierarchy.[25] Although there are insufficient results to be conclusive, it is generally assumed that information systems can support either increased or decreased spans of control.

The evidence is strong that computer-based information systems are associated with greater horizontal differentiation in organizations, i.e., subdivision of functions.[26] The information system may also be used to coordinate lateral activities. Computer-based techniques such as material requirements planning (MRP) are used to coordinate such activities as purchasing, production, and inventory management.

**INFORMATION SYSTEMS PLUS LATERAL RELATIONS
FOR PERSONNEL SCHEDULING**

An airline must schedule flight crews and flight attendant crews. By using a computer-based information system, a central crew scheduling office gained access to local data and could determine the most effective adjustments in schedule from an overall workforce perspective. Flight attendants scheduling used the same computer software system, but a different organizational unit did the scheduling.

Although flight crews and flight attendants were scheduled by separate units, there was need to coordinate. The schedulers for flight crews and flight attendants (plus aircraft routing) worked together as a team (a lateral relation) with each using a separate scheduling application to provide input and evaluation.

Reported by Daniel Robey in "Computer Information Systems and Organizational Structure," *Communications of the ACM*, 24:10, October 1981, pp. 679-687.

Organizational Structure Implications
for Information System Design

The different characteristics of organizational structures have implications for the design of information systems.

Concept	Implications for information systems
Hierarchy of authority	A tall hierarchy with narrow span of control may mean that more formal control information is needed by upper levels than a flat hierarchy with wide span of control.

---

[25]P. M. Blau, C. M. Falbe, W. McKinley, and P. K. Tracy, "Technology and Organization in Manufacturing," *Administration Science Quarterly*, 21:1, March 1976; and Marshall W. Meyer, "Automation and Bureaucratic Structure," *American Journal of Sociology*, 74:3, November 1968, pp. 256–264.

[26]Robey, "Computer Information Systems and Organizational Structure."

Specialization	Information system applications are specialized to fit the specialization of the organization.
Formalization	Information systems are a major method for increasing formalization.
Centralization	Information systems can be designed to suit any level of centralization.
Modification of basic model	Information systems can be designed to support product or service organization, project organization, lateral relations, and matrix organization.
Information model of organization	Organizational mechanisms reduce the need for information processing and communication. Vertical information systems are an alternative to lateral relations. Information systems are used to coordinate lateral activities.
Organizational culture	Organizational culture affects information requirements and system acceptance.
Organizational power	Organizational power affects organizational behavior during information system planning, resource allocation, and implementation. Computer systems can be an instrument of organizational power through access to information.
Organizational growth cycle	Information systems may need to change for different stages of growth.
Goal displacement	When identifying goals during requirements determination, care should be taken to avoid displaced goals.
Organizational learning	Suggests need for information system design for both efficiency measures to promote single loop learning and effectiveness measures for double loop learning.
Project model of organizational change	Describes general concept for managing change with information system projects.
Case for stable systems	Establish control over frequency of information system changes.
Systems that promote organizational change	Reporting critical change variables or relationships and use of multiple channels in a semiconfusing system may be useful for promoting responses to a changing environment.
Organizations as sociotechnical systems	Provides approach to requirements determination and job design when both social and technical considerations are involved.

Management Theory and Information System Design

Designers of computer-based information and decision systems are frequently guilty of the mechanistic view of the human in the human-machine system. For example, a proposed online system designed for the loan officers of a bank was intended to automate a large number of functions formerly performed manually. The system appeared feasible and very advantageous. However, when the job content which the designers proposed for the loan officer was examined, it was found to have insufficient variety to make an interesting job environment. The system was restructured to enrich the job of the loan officer at the cost of a small reduction in some of the automated functions.

If an autocratic, nonparticipative style of leadership and a mechanistic, economic motivation are assumed, information system design is less complicated. Functions can be allocated between humans and machines on the basis of relative efficiency. Computer-based decision rules provide instant decisions with little participation. However, the following factors suggest difficulties in pursuing this view for applications:

Problem	Comments
Not all managers have the same leadership style.	This may mean that a system designed for a nonparticipative leader will not suit a participative leadership style.
Not all work groups have the same need for participation.	For example, where decisions must be made quickly, there will be little demand for participation. But where the technical ability of subordinates is equal to or even greater than the leader (such as in a research group), participation is likely to be important.
Computerizing some activities may reduce task variety and make a job less interesting.	Computers do not need variety; humans do. Computers make possible assembly-line style pacing for many clerical and managerial activities, but if the job is reduced in variety, it may cause boredom and decreased job satisfaction.

Extending the last point, information systems tend to change job content and frequently change the social system in the organization. This change in job characteristics provides an opportunity to redesign jobs to enhance motivation.

SUMMARY

This text emphasizes information systems within the context of an organization. An understanding of organizational structure and processes is necessary for the analysis and design of even the lowest level information processing systems; this understanding is vital to the design of a management information system.

This chapter surveys concepts of organizations and management as they relate to information system design. No single, comprehensive theory of organizations can be described in a few pages. The student is assumed to have already studied management theory; those areas considered particularly relevant for information systems are highlighted. The focus is primarily on organizational structure and concepts of management.

The organization consists of a relatively permanent structure exhibiting a hierarchy of authority, specialization, and some degree of formalization and centralization. Variations in organizational structure depend in part on the goals and environment of the organization. A survey of organization power and culture and a look at organizational change provides additional background for the information system designer. A model of an organization as an information processing system helps illustrate the complexity of factors impacting organizational structure, communications, and information requirements.

Several theories related to management, including human motivation, leadership style, and job design were briefly reviewed. The implication for information systems of the concepts of organization structure and management were noted. Information systems can have an impact on organizational structure; and organizational structure can affect system design.

The sociotechnical approach to system design illustrates an approach to improve job satisfaction and human or social characteristics as well as to improve task performance.

UPS => Uninterrupted Power Supply

MINICASES

1 THE DATA ACCESSIBLE HOSPITAL

Can a hospital with only 214 beds support 4,500 admissions and 50,000 outpatients annually? Not if the data is handled by paper shuffling according to the City of Hope National Medical Center in San Antonio, Texas.

By slowly increasing their data processing expertise over five years, the hospital has developed an integrated information system. Now each division of the organization feeds a common database of information in a form which is meaningful to managers in other divisions. Several departments receive scheduled reports or can request them as needed. All patient data is entered by patient number and assigned to the proper cumulative record file. All patient-care personnel can access laboratory and clinical data immediately following patient examination through the terminals available in treatment areas. This leads to more timely and accurate patient data and gives the patients faster turnaround time and less frustration.

The system also provides statistical, operating and management reports, including appointment scheduling and room availability. This permits better staff and facility utilization while using less administrative time. In order to record cost-incurred expenses, the system also identifies all patient charges and assigns them the proper expense code even though the care is free to the patients.

"Texas Medical Center Integrates Systems," *Computerworld*, August 4, 1980, p. 51.

Questions

a Identify and describe the organizational structure mechanism(s) used to facilitate communication between the hospital's subsystems. *Coordination, Common data base,*
b Identify the risks built into this form of communication. *Common accessibility*

—> Control of information; heavy reliance on data base; Possible error in system

2 TROUBLE AT PBS

In the spring of 1981 the nonprofit Public Broadcasting Service (PBS) was having difficulty finding its position in the marketplace. The commercial networks were planning to present opera, ballet, and symphonies which had been the cornerstone of PBS's alternative programming. Moreover, PBS's funding had been reduced 10 percent because of cutbacks in federal grants for the arts.

PBS was established in 1970 to distribute programming and channel funds to its member stations. Among the 270 members, many wanted freedom to select and produce their own programs. Independence was a hallmark of a public broadcasting system. Political pressure, however, caused PBS to relinquish some authority over programming and major funding decisions in 1973.

Stations such as WNET (New York), WGBH (Boston), and KCET (Los Angeles) produced their own high-quality programs. Among the wide variety of owners, however, some suffered from lack of direction. Many stations allowed PBS to handle prime-time scheduling in order to benefit from the national promotion and advertising. Over half of the members also paid PBS dues to participate in scheduled fund-raising events.

Lawrence Grossman, PBS's president since 1976, proposed the strategy of setting up a paid television service called Public Subscriber Network (PSN). PSN would allow supporting corporations to run institutional messages. (PBS currently only acknowledges institutional funding.) Some stations opposed the messages because they would usurp the member's role in searching for funds. Others objected that since commercial television would get there first, PSN would not have found an alternative niche.

Business Week, March 9, 1981, p. 104.

Questions
a How is work specialized between PBS and the member stations?
b Discuss the amount of centralization that PBS has and whether this is functional or dysfunctional.
c How are goals changing?

EXERCISES
1 Describe the basic model of organizational structure. What are the principles underlying this model?
2 Explain how each of the different organizational variations differs in form from the basic model.
3 Using the information processing model, explain why each of the organizational forms is used. Define the conditions which suggest the use of each model.
4 Describe the information processing model of organizations in terms of systems concepts presented in Chapter 9.
5 Explain the Maslow hierarchy of needs. How is it relevant to organization and management?
6 Compare scientific management to job design as two approaches to implementing an online transaction processing system.
7 Identify leadership styles. If leadership style does not affect performance (evidence not clear), what difference does it make?
8 Cyert and March argue that only individuals can have goals. Does their theory mean that no organizational goals can be identified?
9 Explain and contrast how organizational culture might affect the process of collecting information and the way decisions are made for the following two situations:
a A high-technology research and development organization
b A highly formalized organization producing a standardized product
10 Analyze the potential organizational power of information systems for:
a A university administrative information system.
b A bank with online terminals and cash machines.
c A small specialty store (bridal clothes).
11 Write up a short case description of goal displacement you have observed.

12 The XYZ Company uses a budget for planning and control. Top management intended that planning be the major objective. The budget officer requests detailed explanations of every variance. The departments have started to miscode data to make the expenditures fit the budget. Discuss this situation in terms of goals (who has goals) and goal displacement.

13 There is general concern that computer-based information systems have perpetuated (and perhaps made worse) reporting systems that are rigid and do not alert management to effectiveness issues or to a need to change goals and objectives. Explain the role of organizational learning concepts and semiconfusing systems in addressing the problem. Why does it help the problem to have information that is not consistent, not in same form, etc.?

14 Summarize the case for and against stable systems. Divide your answer into short-run stability (six months or less) and long-run stability (about five to ten years).

15 Analyze the effect of the deregulation and breakup on the AT&T company's culture, goals, organizational learning, and stability.

16 Compare the need for sociotechnical design for two applications:
  a Order entry with 50 clerks
  b A financial planning application for three financial analysts

17 Apply the criteria of job design to the following jobs:
  a Student teaching assistant
  b Application programmer
  c Data entry operator

18 Assume that you are starting a 30-person firm to develop and market software. Explain the choices you would make and the reasons for them for the following:
  a Hierarchy of authority
  b Specialization
  c Formalization
  d Degree of centralization
  e Leadership style

19 For question 18, what kind of a culture would you like to achieve and how would you achieve it?

20 For the company in question, how would you expect the organization to change as it matured and reached a level of 300 employees?

SELECTED REFERENCES

*Anthony, Robert N.: *Planning and Control Systems: A Framework for Analysis*, Harvard University Press, Cambridge, MA, 1965.

Argyris, Chris: "Double Loop Learning in Organizations," *Harvard Business Review*, September–October, 1977.

Argyris, Chris: *Increasing Leadership Effectiveness*, Wiley-Interscience, New York, 1976.

Argyris, Chris: *Reasoning, Learning and Action: Individual and Organizational*, Jossey-Bass, San Francisco, 1982.

Argyris, Chris: "The Executive Mind and Double-Loop Learning," *Organizational Dynamics*, Autumn 1982, pp. 5–22.

Bariff, Martin L., and Jay R. Galbraith: "Intraorganizational Power Considerations for Designing Information Systems," *Accounting, Organizations, and Society*, 3:1, 1978, pp. 15–17.

Barnes, Louis B.: "Managing the Paradox of Organizational Trust," *Harvard Business Review*, March–April 1981.

Bjorn-Anderson, N., and P. H. Pederson: "Computer Facilitated Changes in the Management Power Structure," *Accounting, Organizations, and Society*, 5:2, 1980, pp. 203–216.

Cummings, L. L.: "Organizational Behavior in the 1980s," *Decision Sciences*, 21, 1981, pp. 365–377. See also comments on the paper.

*Cyert, Richard M., and James G. March: *A Behavioral Theory of the Firm*, Prentice-Hall, Englewood Cliffs, NJ, 1963.

Drucker, Peter F.: *The Practice of Management*, Harper & Row, New York, 1954.

Filley, Alan C., Robert J. House, and Steven Kerr: *Managerial Process and Organizational Behavior*, Second Edition, Scott, Foresman, Glenview, IL, 1976. Excellent for understanding the evidence which supports management and organizational theory.

*Galbraith, Jay R.: *Organizational Design: An Information Processing View*, Addison-Wesley, Reading, MA, 1973.

Hackman, J. R., and G. R. Oldham: *Work Redesign*, Addison-Wesley, Reading, MA, 1980.

Hall, Richard H.: *Organizations: Structure and Process*, Third Edition, Prentice-Hall, Englewood Cliffs, NJ, 1982.

Herzberg, F.: "One More Time: How Do You Motivate Employees?" *Harvard Business Review*, January–February 1968, pp. 53–62.

Hunt, J. G., and P. F. Newell: "Management in the 1980's Revisited," *Personnel Journal*, 50, 1971, pp. 35–43.

*Hofstede, G. H.: *The Game of Budgetary Control*, Royal Van Gorcum, Assen, The Netherlands, 1967. An excellent text for understanding the human problems of budgeting.

Kanter, Rosabeth Moss: "Power Failure in Management Circuits," *Harvard Business Review*, July–August 1979, pp. 65–75.

Kling, R.: "Automated Welfare Client-Tracking and Service Integration: The Political Economy of Computing," *Communications of the ACM*, 21:6, June 1978, pp. 484–493.

Kling, R.: "Social Analyses of Computing: Theoretical Perspectives in Recent Empirical Research," *Computing Surveys*, 21:1, March 1980, pp. 61–110.

Koontz, Harold, and Cyril O'Donnell: *Principles of Management*, Fourth Edition, McGraw-Hill, New York, 1968. A good survey of management.

*Leavitt, H. J., and T. L. Whisler: "Management in the 1980's," *Harvard Business Review*, November–December 1958, pp. 41–48.

Likert, Rensis: *The Human Organization: Its Management and Value*, McGraw-Hill, New York, 1967. Describes management system called System Four.

McGregor, Douglas: *The Human Side of Enterprise*, McGraw-Hill, New York, 1960. Describes Theory X and Theory Y.

*March, James, and Herbert A. Simon: *Organizations*, Wiley, New York, 1958.

*Mintzberg, Henry: *The Structuring of Organizations*, Prentice-Hall, Englewood Cliffs, NJ, 1979.

Pugh, D. S., D. J. Hickson, and C. R. Hinings: *Writers on Organization*, Second Edition, Penguin Books, Harmondsworth, England, 1971. A brief but useful summary of major writers and researchers.

Reich, Robert B.: "Regulation by Confrontation or Negotiation," *Harvard Business Review*, May–June 1981.

Starr, Martin K.: *Management: A Modern Approach*, Harcourt Brace Jovanovich, New York, 1971. An unusual management text taking a modeling, management science approach.

Whisler, T. L.: *The Impact of Computers on Organizations*, Praeger, New York, 1970.

Weick, K.: *The Social Psychology of Organizing*, Second Edition, Addison-Wesley, Reading, MA, 1979.

*These references are especially relevant to the background knowledge of information systems specialists.

INFORMATION-BASED SUPPORT SYSTEMS

Information systems do not operate independently of the organization; they exist because they support organizational processes and the acheivement of organizational goals. Information systems are therefore properly termed ''support systems.'' There are a number of information-based systems which support major organizational functions:

- Transaction processing support system
- Office support systems
- Operational control support systems
- Management control support system
- Decision support systems
- Strategic planning support system

The information-based support systems include support for planning, control, and decision making associated with the above functions. These support systems are knowledge work support systems (as contrasted with manual work support technology).

The first chapter in this section will emphasize the planning, control, and decision making support components (Chapter 12). This relects the management orientation of the text. Also, these support components represent an active area of new system development and academic research. The second chapter (Chapter 13) discusses the broader topic of support for knowledge work, whether in transaction processing, office functions, or management activities. The chapter covers the nature of knowledge work, technology for performing it, and system facilities to support it.

essentially
application of
chapters 6-10

CHAPTER 12

SUPPORT SYSTEMS FOR PLANNING, CONTROL, AND DECISION MAKING

Information systems provide support for management at all levels: operational control, management control, and strategic planning. Each of these classes of management activity includes planning, control, and decision making. This chapter focuses on support operations for these three functions. In terms of a support system, all of the systems described in the chapter are decision support systems; planning and control support systems are subsets of the broad concept of DSS. The chapter first explains the design of systems which support decision making. A special class of support systems called expert systems is described. This is followed by a discussion of approaches to development of DSS. The chapter also explores the elements of a planning support system and notes features that may be included in a control support system.

DECISION SUPPORT SYSTEMS

The term *decision support system* (DSS) refers to a class of systems which support the process of making decisions. The emphasis is on "support" rather than on automation of decisions.[1] Decision support systems allow the decision maker to retrieve data and test alternative solutions during the process of problem solving.

Characteristics of Decision Support Systems

The concept of decision support systems is based on several assumptions about the role of the computer in effective decision making:[2]

    1 The computer must *support* the manager but not replace his or her judgment. It should therefore neither try to provide the "answers" nor impose a predefined sequence of analysis.

    2 The main payoff of computer support is for *semistructured* problems, where parts of the analysis can be systematized for the computer, but where the decision maker's insight and judgment are needed to control the process.

---

[1]Steven L. Alter, *Decision Support Systems: Current Practice and Continuing Challenges*, Addison-Wesley, Reading, MA, 1980, p. 1.

[2]P. G. W. Keen, "'Interactive' Computer Systems for Managers: A Modest Proposal," *Sloan Management Review*, Fall 1976.

3 Effective problem solving is *interactive* and is enhanced by a dialog between the user and the system. The user explores the problem situation using the analytic and information-providing capabilities of the system as well as human experience and insights.

The decision support system should provide ease of access to the database containing relevant data and interactive testing of solutions. The designer must understand the process of decision making for each situation in order to design a system to support it. This design problem will be discussed in subsequent sections of this chapter.

SUPPORTING PLANNING DECISIONS

A very large multinational consumer products company has two main reasons for using a planning model for new product projections—to provide an information storage bank and, more important, to answer "what if" questions.

Using the model, the company can accumulate data in a central unit, with each alternative spelled out and noted. This feature is especially helpful in developing income statements using varying product formulas, sales volumes, and marketing programs. The other key aspect of the model is the speedy manipulation of alternatives. Here is an illustration:

The company had envisioned launching a new product that would sell three million units nationally, with a marketing cost during the first year of $6 million. The estimated payout was less than three years and the rate of return was estimated at 20 percent. Through the model, marketing management defined the risk to cash flow, the inventory assumptions, and the investment spending exposure. The project was approved, and plans to introduce the product proceeded.

A competitor unexpectedly entered the market with a lower-quality, lower-priced product and a different marketing mix. The marketing research and brand operations departments responded with a new plan for marketing, but the new variable, when added to the information already in the model system, produced discouraging prospects: an eight-year payout and a 5.1% return. The company scrapped the product.

Reprinted by permission of the *Harvard Business Review*. Excerpts from "Computer-Based Planning Models Come of Age" by Ephraim R. McLean and Gary L. Neale, July-August, 1980, pp. 46-48. Copyright © 1980 by the President and Fellows of Harvard College; all rights reserved.

Decision Support and Structure of Decision Making

Although decision support systems can be used for a wide variety of decisions, the decision support concept applies better to some types of decisions than to others. In Chapter 2 decisions were classified as structured or unstructured, with an intermediate category called "semistructured." Gorry and Scott Morton[3] classified information systems by these categories on one dimension and by level of management activity on the other. The result is the framework, including examples, shown in Figure 12-1 (reproduced from Table 2-2).

---

[3]G. A. Gorry and M. S. Scott Morton, "A Framework for Management Information Systems," *Sloan Management Review*, 13:1, Fall 1971, pp. 55–70.

Management activity

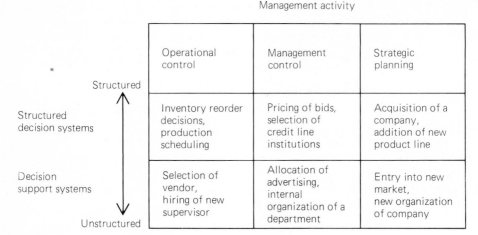

Figure 12-1
Types of decision by management activity.

SCHEDULING IN OPERATIONAL DECISION MAKING

Airlines use automatic call distributors (ACDs) to distribute incoming calls to available agents and to maintain queues of calls waiting for service. The operational management problem is to collect data on calls, monitor network traffic, and plan for availability of agents (and schedule individual agents).

A software package called Employee Management and Planning System has been developed by Cybernetics Systems International to summarize activity data from ACDs, estimate a near-optimal number of agents for each shift of a projected volume, and provide a suggested daily work schedule.

Extracted from *Honeywell Consultant's Communicator*, April 1984.

When information systems were first developed for semistructured and unstructured decisions, emphasis was placed on finding the structure and programming as much of the decision as possible. The results were often inefficient, inflexible systems that were ignored or sabotaged by decision makers because of their ineffectiveness.

Decision support systems (DSS) represent a different approach to information system support for semistructured and unstructured decisions. The approach is not to find the structure and automate it; rather it is to support a variety of unstructured decision processes. This has several important implications for the design and use of these systems:[4]

    1 The designer of decision support systems applies a different set of skills than the designer of structured, operational systems. DSS designers must not only be technically competent but also able to observe, understand, and identify with the decision maker's world.

---

[4]P. G. W. Keen and M. S. Scott Morton, *Decision Support Systems: An Organizational Perspective*, Addison-Wesley, Reading, MA, 1978, pp. 92–93.

2 The technology required for DSS is based on the need for flexible access. Reliable communication networks, availability of terminals, and even stand-alone personal computers are more important than large-scale data processing centers.

3 There is an emphasis on small, simple models that are easily understood and implemented rather than complex, integrated models. A good example is the trend to replace sophisticated integrated (and expensive) corporate planning models with planning model generators for ad hoc analyses.

4 The process of development of decision support systems is evolutionary and requires extensive participation by the end user (the decision maker). The development of a working prototype system that is changed with use is common. The process of system development by prototyping will be discussed in Chapter 18.

Some problems which appear to be highly unstructured exhibit a ''deep structure'' when examined more closely.[5] Such problems may be partly or fully automated once their structure is identified. One example is *material requirements planning* (MRP), a highly complex interaction of raw materials ordering, production scheduling, and inventory control. This problem used to be viewed as highly unstructured, requiring the skill and knowledge of an experienced production manager. Material requirements planning (MRP) systems support requirements planning, scheduling and inventory control, and have proved effective in reducing inventory costs and improving production scheduling.

The degree of structure of a decision may also vary with the phase in decision making: intelligence, design, or choice. Types of decision support for each phase will be discussed in a later section of this chapter.

Decision Support and Repetitiveness of Decisions

Highly repetitive decisions (whether structured, semistructured, or unstructured) can frequently benefit from decision support systems. If the decision process is basically the same each time, a model can be tailored to fit the process, even for a single decision maker. Demonstrable benefits of such systems are faster decision making, improved consistency and accuracy, and improved methods for analyzing and solving problems.[6]

At the other extreme, nonrepetitive, one-time decisions require decision support of a very different nature. The primary requirement of systems to support one-time decisions is flexible access to a database and other forms of information such as external databanks. Emphasis tends to be on the search phase of decision making, where different kinds of data in different forms are needed for each decision process.

Classes of Decision Support Systems

In an extensive investigation of 56 decision support systems in use in organizations, Alter[7] developed a taxonomy of decision support systems based on the ''degree of action implication of system outputs,'' that is, the degree to which the system outputs can

---

[5]Keen and Scott Morton, *Decision Support Systems: An Organizational Perspective*, p. 94.
[6]Alter, *Decision Support System*, Chapter 1.
[7]Alter, *Decision Support Systems*, Chapter 2.

directly determine the decision. The resulting classification of system types is summarized in Figure 12-2 and described on the following page.

1 *File drawer systems.* These allow immediate access to data items. They are basically online mechanized versions of manual filing systems. Examples are status inquiries for inventory information, airline reservations requests, and shop floor monitoring.

2 *Data analysis systems.* These allow the manipulation of data by means of either analysis operations tailored to the task and setting or general analysis operations. They are typically used by nonmanagerial personnel to analyze files containing current or historical data. Examples are a budget analysis system and a financial system for analyzing alternative investment opportunities.

3 *Analysis information systems.* These provide access to a series of databases and small models. An example is a marketing decision support system containing internal sales data, promotion and pricing data plus access to external databases. Another example is a sales analysis system containing detailed sales data, customer information, forecast data, and models.

4 *Accounting models.* These calculate the consequences of planned actions on the basis of accounting definitions. They typically generate estimates of income, balance sheets, etc., based on variations in input values to the definitional formulas. Examples are monthly budgeting systems for operational decision making and short-term financial planning.

5 *Representational models.* These estimate the consequences of actions on the basis of models that represent some nondefinitional characteristics of the system such as probabilities of occurrence. They include all simulation models that contain elements beyond accounting definitions. An example is a risk analysis model using estimated probability distributions for each of the key factors.

6 *Optimization models.* These provide guidelines for action by generating the optimal solution consistent with a series of constraints. They are used for repetitive decisions that can be described mathematically and where a specific objective, such as minimizing cost, is the goal. Examples are a system for scheduling training classes under a complex set of constraints and a material usage optimization system.

7 *Suggestion models.* These compute a specific suggested decision for a fairly structured and repetitive decision. Their purpose is to bypass other (less efficient) procedures for generating the suggestion. Examples are an insurance renewal rate calculation system and a model to price cardboard boxes based on a standard set of dimensions and decision rules.

The taxonomy illustrates that decision support systems can vary across a wide number of situations and a variety of users. There are many different ways decisions can be supported; moreover, there are unique implementation problems related to each type.

DECISION SUPPORT FOR PARTICULAR PROBLEMS

Dillingham Corporation has used DSS successfully to improve the profitability of management service, according to Robert Vierk, director of information services. The corporation utilizes Boeing Executive Services timesharing system to develop and run decision support systems for particular problems. The results are displayed on Dillingham's graphics terminal.

In one example, a study involving condominium management, internal data used in the relatively simple model included the costs and revenues of each condominium and the internal administrative costs. External data were also used: the market size, the economy, and competitive sales. Company information about pricing philosophy and marketing policies were also included. The model compared the policies of the organization with what was actually happening and showed that the corporation should probably get out of the condominium management business.

"Decision Support Guidelines Advised," *MIS Week*, June 17, 1981.

System type	Type of operation	Type of task	User	Usage pattern	Time frame
File drawer systems	Access of data items	Operational	Nonmanagerial line personnel	Simple inquiries	Irregular
Data analysis systems	Ad hoc analysis of files of data	Operational or analysis	Staff analyst or managerial line personnel	Manipulation and display of data	Irregular or periodic
Analysis information systems	Ad hoc analysis involving multiple database and small models	Analysis, planning	Staff analyst	Programming of special reports, development of small models	Irregular, on request
Accounting models	Standard calculations that estimate future results on the basis of accounting definitions	Planning, budgeting	Analyst or manager	Input estimates of activity; receive estimated monetary results as output	Periodic, e.g., weekly, monthly, yearly
Representational models	Estimating consequences of particular actions	Planning, budgeting	Staff analyst	Input possible decisions; receive estimated results as output	Periodic or irregular (ad hoc analysis)
Optimization models	Calculating an optimal solution to a combinatoric problem	Planning, resource allocation	Staff analyst	Input constraints and objectives; receive answer	Periodic or irregular (ad hoc analysis)
Suggestion models	Performing calculations that generate a suggested decision	Operational	Nonmanagerial line personnel	Input a structured description of the decision situation; receive a suggested decision as output	Daily or periodic

Figure 12-2
Characteristics of different classes of decision support systems. (Adapted from S. L. Alter, *Decision Support Systems: Current Practices and Continuing Challenges*, Addison-Wesley, Reading, MA, 1980, pp. 90-91.)

Decision Support System Users

The ultimate "user" of a decision support system is the decision maker. However, he or she may not actually run the system. Based on his research on 56 decision support systems, Alter[8] identified four distinct usage patterns (Figure 12-3):

1 *Subscription mode.* The decision maker receives reports that are generated automatically on a regular basis. This is the typical mode of usage for management reporting systems. Although some data analysis systems or accounting models might be used in this way, it is not typical for decision support systems.

2 *Terminal mode.* The decision maker is the direct user of the system through online access.

3 *Clerk mode.* The decision maker uses the system directly but offline, preparing input on a coding form. The primary difference between this mode and the terminal mode is in the technology employed (batch versus online).

4 *Intermediary mode.* The decision maker uses the system through intermediaries, who perform the analysis and interpret and report the results. The decision maker does not need to know how the intermediary used the system to arrive at the requested information.

The role of an intermediary is common in the use of decision support systems and merits separate attention. It has typically been argued that decision support systems will be resisted because managers will refuse to use terminals. As noted earlier in the text, the jobs of chief executives are highly fragmented with frequent interruptions. Such a pattern of activity is a major constraint on the use of a system requiring concentration

---

[8]Alter, *Decision Support System*, p. 110.

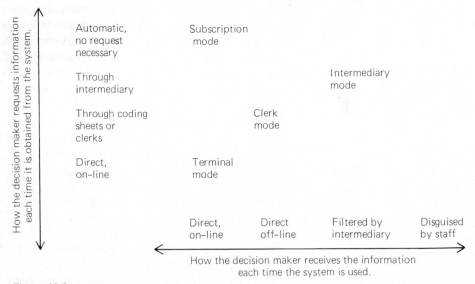

Figure 12-3
Patterns of system usage from the decision maker's viewpoint. (From S. A. Alter, *Decision Support Systems: Current Practices and Continuing Challenges*, Addison-Wesley, Reading, MA, 1980, p. 111.)

over a period of time. The use of an intermediary allows the manager to benefit from the decision support system without actually having to execute it.

There are two types of intermediaries that reflect different types of support for the manager:[9]

    1 Staff assistant or staff analyst. This person has specialized knowledge about problems and some experience with the decision support technology. The staff assistant essentially extends the manager's capabilities by taking over many of the tasks of problem solving such as setting up the problem, obtaining data, and building the initial model. The manager can concentrate on the more unstructured portions of the problem solving task. The staff assistant performs work the manager could do if time were available.

    2 Expert tool user. This person is skilled in the application of one or more types of specialized problem solving tools. The expert tool user performs tasks which the problem solver does not have the skills or training to perform.

Although most intermediaries are staff assistants, there is also frequent need for the expert tool user. The use of intermediaries permits the systems to be more sophisticated and powerful. Online, interactive systems are still desirable with intermediaries because they allow them to work more quickly and efficiently.

Although an interactive system has advantages, it is not the critical factor in whether decision support systems improve decision-making effectiveness. Rather, the critical factor may be *responsiveness*,[10] which is defined as a combination of the following characteristics:

    1 *Power*—the degree to which the system (including its human element) can answer the most important questions.

    2 *Accessibility*—the degree to which the system can provide these answers in a timely and consistent manner.

    3 *Flexibility*—the degree to which the system can adapt to changing needs and situations.

EXPERT SYSTEMS

An *expert system* is a computer application that guides the performance of ill-structured tasks which usually require experience and specialized knowledge (i.e., expertise). Using an expert system, a non-expert can achieve performance comparable to an expert in that particular problem domain.[11] Expert systems can be considered an instance of a decision support system. The unique, distinguishing feature of an expert system is the *knowledge base*, the data and decision rules which represent the expertise.

As an example, a user of a medical diagnosis expert system provides the system with a particular set of symptoms. The program searches its knowledge base of symptoms and possible causes; it might begin an interactive dialog with the user to elicit more information or to suggest a strategy of further tests. The problem is unstructured in that information may be incomplete or inaccurate.[12] Various strategies are being imple-

    [9]John A. Lehman, ''A Manager's Guide to Selection of Decision Support System Alternatives,'' Management Information Systems Research Center Working Paper 84-07, Minneapolis, 1984.

    [10]Alter, *Decision Support System*, p. 114.

    [11]D. S. Nau, ''Expert Computer Systems,'' *Computer*, February 1983.

    [12]R. Davis, ''A DSS for Diagnosis and Therapy,'' *Data Base*, 8:3, Winter 1977, pp. 58–72.

mented for restructuring and searching the knowledge base of an expert system. Research on expert systems is often associated with the field of artificial intelligence.

There are a number of significant problems with expert systems. They are costly to develop. Some large experimental systems have required from 10 to 25 work years of effort and millions of dollars. Eliciting knowledge from an ''expert'' to incorporate in an expert system is costly and difficult. One reason is that experts establish heuristics to reduce the problem space (within their own knowledge domain) and aid their search for a solution. Often, to merely ask experts how they reason is not adequate; to ask them to ''think aloud'' as they respond to a problem situation may be useful but results are not certain of completeness. Another problem with the development of expert systems is the need for a simple but flexible user interface with a nonexpert user. Some issues related to the design of user interfaces are discussed in Chapter 17.

The development of expert systems represents a very active area of ongoing research. Despite the difficulties in designing such systems, a few are in limited use. Some examples of expert systems in experimental or practical use illustrate the variety of applications.[13]

Task domain	Expert system
Hypothesizes molecular structure from mass spectograms	DENDRAL
Oil exploration	DIPMETER ADVISOR
Medical consulting	CADEUCIUS
Medical consulting	MYCIN
Mineral exploration	PROSPECTOR
Computer configuration	R1

SUPPORT FOR DECISION-MAKING PHASES

In Chapter 6, the Simon model of decision making was presented. This model has three phases: intelligence, design, and choice. This section of the chapter describes the types of information system support that can be provided for each phase of decision making.

Support for the Intelligence Phase

The intelligence phase of the decision making process consists of problem finding activities related to searching the environment for conditions calling for decisions. Analysis and choice cannot proceed until the problem has been identified and formulated. The intelligence phase, therefore, consists of searching or scanning the internal and external environment for conditions which suggest an opportunity or a problem (Figure 12-4). The existence of an opportunity or a problem initiates the design and choice phases of decision making.

---

[13]Nau, ''Expert Computer Systems.'

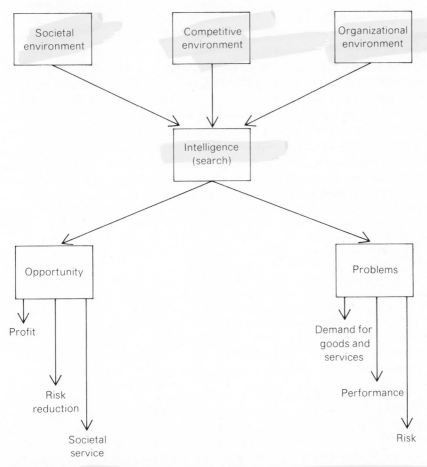

Figure 12-4
Search for opportunity and problems in intelligence phase of decision making.

The database needed in the intelligence phase is very comprehensive. In general, it should cover three environments:

Environments	Description
Societal	The economic, social, and legal environment in which the organization operates
Competitive	The characteristics and behavior of the marketplace in which the organization operates
Internal	The capabilities, strengths, weaknesses, constraints, and other factors affecting the ability of the organization to perform its functions

The data on the internal environment is generally available through processing of operational data. Some societal and competitive data is available through published databanks such as those described in Chapter 10.

The concept of decision support systems does not imply that all the data is in computerized databases. It does imply, however, that the data is systematically collected and stored and is accessible to the user of the system. In some cases, the database can store a pointer to the data such as a reference to a government statistical report.

The primary requirement of decision support for intelligence is the ability to search the database for opportunities and problems. The search process has different characteristics depending on whether it can be structured and whether it is continuous or ad hoc. These differences are summarized in three types of search:

1 *Structured, continuous search.* Some problem areas, such as inventory balances and product prices relative to competitors, are relatively structured and can be examined regularly. Periodic reporting systems providing condition data support this type of search. Decision support systems permit the scope, number, and frequency of information outputs to be extended with scanning of all known indicators of potential problems or opportunities. Output can be produced on a periodic basis or whenever a problem or opportunity is detected. Data analysis systems and suggestion systems can support this type of search.

2 *Structured ad hoc search.* Many problems and opportunities do not occur frequently enough to be handled by regular search. However, the search process can be structured. For example, plant location may be a problem for an expanding company, but it may not occur with sufficient frequency to justify a database and regular scanning for plant location sites. Instead, the intelligence process is structured, but it is applied only when other indicators suggest the need for it. System support for structured ad hoc search involves intelligence algorithms (preestablished logic for scanning and search) or expert systems and report formats. Analysis information systems and representational models may be used.

3 *Unstructured search.* In many cases, the search or intelligence algorithms cannot be specified; the decision support system must allow the user to approach the task heuristically through trial and error rather than by preestablished, fixed logical steps. Support for unstructured search is primarily based on flexible access to the database. The user needs to be able to perform such functions as retrieval, presentation, scanning, analysis, and comparison on data in order to discover new relations and new conclusions that have not previously been defined. Interactive systems enhance the performance of unstructured search by allowing the user to change parameters of the problem and quickly see their effect. In some cases, system support may include analysis information systems and representational models; in other cases, system support may be a file drawer system with fast access to the database.

ASSESSING SALES POTENTIAL USING ELECTRONIC SPREADSHEETS

Account managers must ask many strategic questions: Are we calling too often on an account? Should we pay more attention to existing accounts or try to develop new accounts? Are we getting equal penetration in all departments of an account? How can we increase our share of the account potential? Answers to these questions require a forecast of account potential. A simple spreadsheet model can be used for assessing sales potential.

The spread sheet model contains data and assumptions often used in forecasting the potential of an account: account requirements for the previous period, estimated growth rates per period, sales for the previous period, estimated share points for the next period, and an estimate of the number of calls necessary to achieve these share points. The computer estimates total requirements for the forecast period, share points for the previous period, company sales, and sales per call.

This analysis should raise many intelligence phase and design phase questions in the mind of the account manager, including: What can we do to increase our share of this business? Are we making too many or too few calls on a customer? Should we drop some accounts?

Reprinted by permission of the *Harvard Business Review*. Excerpts from "Computerized Sales Management" by G. David Hughes, March-April 1983, pp. 102-112. Copyright © 1983 by the President and Fellows of Harvard College; all rights reserved.

Decision support systems generally focus on systems other than the regular reporting system. However, regular reports can be designed to assist in the problem finding activity of comparing expectations with current and projected performance. The following are report elements that assist in problem finding:[14]

Report element	Problem finding use
Summarization	Current performance is summarized but expectations are provided by the user of the report. Any projections are made by the user.
Comparison	The report has explicit comparisons with current performance expectations: • Comparison with plans, budgets or standards. Variance reports. • Comparison with competitors, industry averages, and other extraorganizational models.
Prediction	Forecasts of future performance and explicit or implicit comparison with expectations: • Prediction based on budget or planning model or historical ratios. • Prediction based on seasonally adjusted (or other method) forecast of current performance to the end of the planning period.
Confirmation	Data items that allow the user to validate or audit the report to provide assurance that the report corresponds to underlying detail or other data available to user. Confirmation may use historical data, planning data, or data from elsewhere in the organization.

A PROBLEM FINDING REPORT FOR NEW EQUIPMENT SALES

The manager of new equipment sales for the Falcon Dealership has a report prepared each month which not only reports activity, but also highlights possible problems to be investigated. There is a summary sheet for each facet of analysis; detailed analysis is available on request. Figure 12-5 shows an outline of the format of the summary sheet for gross margin on sales analysis. The problem finding reasons for the lines and columns on the report are:

• There are three divisions in the report: gross margin, units sold and unit margin (average gross margin per unit). Gross margin is the difference between the sales price to the

---

[14]Based on C. H. P. Brookes, "A Framework for DSS Development," Information Systems Forum Research Report, Department of Information Systems, University of New South Wales, Sydney, Australia, 1984.

customer and the dealer cost. The total amount is the product of two components: units sold and unit gross margin.

- For each of the three divisions, there is a data point for the month, a year to date figure, and a projected amount to the end of the year (based on past seasonal patterns of activity). The projected figure is a dynamic "what if" report.
- Thre are variances from planned performance based on projected economic activity and planned performance as adjusted for actual economic activity
- The actual figure is reported.
- There are comparison with industry averages, averages for all dealers for the company, and comparison of dealers in the market area. These represent a gross comparison, a comparison reflecting the product being sold, and a comparison reflecting the activity in the market area.

THE FALCON DEALERSHIP
GROSS MARGIN ANALYSIS
November 1985

| | Variance | | | Comparison Averages | | |
	From Plan	Adj Plan	Actual	Industry	Company	Mkt Area
Gross Margin (000)						
This month						
Model year to date						
Model year projected						
Unit Sales:						
This month						
Model year to date						
Model year projected						
Unit Margin:						
This month						
Model year to date						
Model year projected						

Figure 12-5
A problem finding report: gross margin analysis for equipment dealer.

Support for the Design Phase

Following the intelligence phase which results in problem or opportunity recognition, the design phase involves inventing, developing, and analyzing possible courses of action. Support for the design phase should provide for iterative procedures in considering alternatives. The following iterative steps are typical:

1 Support in understanding the problem. A correct model of the situation needs to be applied or created, and the assumptions of the model tested.

2 Support for generating solutions. The generation of possible courses of action is aided by:

- The model itself. The manipulation of the model frequently provides insight leading to generation of solution ideas.
- The database retrieval system. The retrieval capabilities yield data useful in generating solution ideas.

In many cases, the decision model will provide a suggested solution. For example, an inventory reorder model may suggest a solution to the problem of how much to order. This quantity is a suggestion that can be modified, but it represents a feasible solution (and perhaps an optimal solution based on the factors in the model).

Often the decision support system will lead the user in a rational search strategy for solutions. For example, the solution search procedure might begin with a set of questions relating to common solutions. These questions might be followed by a series of questions which assist the decision maker to consider all alternatives. The advantage of structured approaches is that they assist in systematically exploring the normal decision space; the disadvantage is the tendency to suppress search outside the normal decision space.

3 Support for testing feasibility of solutions. A solution is tested for feasibility by analyzing it in terms of the environments it affects—problem area, entire organization, competitors, and society. The analysis may be performed judgmentally against broad measures of these environments. Another approach is to analyze the proposed solutions using models of the different environments. These models will generally involve computer programs and a database. The model base in a comprehensive MIS will have a number of such models that can be used in testing solutions. The following are examples:

Model	Comment
Overall organization model	This might be a budget model, a comprehensive planning model, or a simple model such as a cash flow model.
Competitor	A model of the market for the goods and services offered by the organization with competitor characteristics and competitive behavior included where feasible.
Society model	Probably not a complete, formal model but essentially a set of societal considerations such as legal, safety, and pollution.

As an example of the use of these models, one solution to a problem of increasing scrap might be acquisition of a new machine. This would be tested against the budget model or cash flow model to determine if the acquisition is feasible from a cash resources standpoint. This solution might also be evaluated against organizational factors related to employment and against societal factors relating to pollution standards.

The requirements for the design phase can be met by a variety of models. Using the Alter classification explained earlier (Figure 12-2), the types of decision support systems that are most likely to be useful in the design phase are the following:

System type	Design phase support	Example
Data analysis	Understanding the problem	Analysis of factual data. Budget variance analysis to identify reasons for variance.
Analysis information system	Understanding the problem and generating solutions	Causal models for analysis and presentation of causal relationships and inferential data analysis. Sales analysis model to identify sales problems

System type	Design phase support	Example
		and to suggest alternatives for solutions. Machine load analysis to identify bottleneck facilities.
Accounting models	Understanding the problem, generating solutions, and testing feasibility	Deterministic models. Budget planning model to show effect on financial statements of various factors being examined.
Representational models	Understanding the problem and generating solutions and testing feasibility	Deterministic and probabilistic models. Material requirements planning (MRP) model to understand the nature of scheduling problems and to generate and test solutions for feasibility.

FINDING ALTERNATIVE SOLUTIONS

A 1980 article in the *Harvard Business Review* tells how a number of companies have found ways to turn their pollution problems into economic opportunities. Here are four examples.

  1 Minnesota Mining and Manufacturing reduced all its wastes in the four years following 1976. Liquid effluents went from 47 tons to 2.6, gas from 3,000 tons to 2,400 tons, and solid waste from 6,000 tons to 2,400. At the same time the cleanup saved $2.4 million a year. The cleanup at 3M followed a realization of the increasing costs of pollution control. Its slogan was "Pollution Prevention Pays"; pollution came to be viewed as an indicator of waste. A program was initiated to collect pollution abatement programs from all corporate personnel. Programs could be proposed to eliminate or reduce pollutants, to conserve water, energy or raw materials, and to increase profit through increased sales, deferred controls, or decreased manufacturing cost.

  2 Ciba-Geigy, a chemical company, changed its manufacturing process to recycle water and solvents. It saved $400,000 a year and used less energy while eliminating 50 percent of its annual pollution from operations. It now markets its environmental expertise to other companies.

  3 In 1974, Japan used strict control legislation to boost construction and engineering and thus stimulate the economy. One Japanese propylene factory now sells its waste for $140 a ton. It gets a tidy profit over the $100 a ton costs of waste recovery.

  4 North British Distilleries turns its highly polluting still bottoms into nutritious animal feed.

Support for the Choice Phase

Software support for the intelligence and design phases assists in providing alternatives. The choice phase requires the application of a choice procedure and the implementation of the chosen alternative. Methods for deciding among alternatives were surveyed in Chapter 6.

  A decision support system, by definition, does not make a choice. However, optimization models and suggestion models can be used to rank the alternatives and otherwise apply decision choice procedures to support the choice of the decision maker. For example, a decision to acquire a machine from among several alternatives may be structured by one or more criteria such as the following:

Rate of return
Years to payback
Minimum cash outlay
Executive preference
Employee preference
Minimum risk

These criteria can be applied by use of decision software. The choice is then made by a decision maker and communicated to persons who can implement the result.

An important consideration in evaluating alternatives is the sensitivity of the solutions to changes in the assumptions on which the decision is to be made or in the conditions which are expected to occur. Sensitivity analysis is performed most easily when a quantitative model is available for manipulation.

Decision Support and Alternative Concepts of Decision Making

In Chapter 6, several concepts of decision making were described. The rational, quantitative decision making model was said to apply only in some situations. Some characteristics of information system support for decision making were noted in that chapter. The concept of a decision support system is flexible enough to fit a variety of decision-making concepts.

Decision concept	Application of decision support system
Programmed versus nonprogrammed decisions	Decision support systems can support both types of decisions; the tendency is to use DSS in an interactive mode, so that all results including programmed decision-making outputs are displayed for human review. The DSS should provide support for establishing programmed decision rules, executing programmed rules, and making nonprogrammed decisions.
Satisficing behavior	The interactive and evolutionary nature of DSS development and use allows a search for solutions and a stopping short of optimality if costs of further search are excessive. It also may facilitate expansion of search beyond the satisficing level.
Behavioral model of organizational decision making	DSS should provide for adequate search space for problem solutions. It should stimulate adequate analysis (to avoid incremental decision making) and stimulate recognition of effects of changing goals and aspirations on decision making.
Decision making under stress	A DSS may provide programmed decision modules to be invoked in crises allowing little time for analysis or, if time is available, prespecified interactive

Decision concept	Application of decision support system
	dialog for exploring alternatives. Methods such as the decisional balance sheet may be applied interactively.
Alternative approaches	DSS software should provide alternative decision procedures and provide guidance in selection. For example, alternatives might be the use of a deterministic simulation or a simulation using probabilities.
Quality of decision making	A DSS can provide decision procedure checklists and checklists for assessing quality of decision-making processes.

APPROACHES TO DEVELOPMENT OF DECISION SUPPORT SYSTEMS

A decision maker faced with a problem must first decide if it justifies the development of a computer-based decision support system. In some cases, a manual approach to decision support may be satisfactory and more cost-effective. The conditions that suggest the need for a computer-based modeling approach are:

1 Complex manipulation of data
2 Several iterations before an acceptable result is achieved
3 Frequent need for reanalysis

The ability to ask "what if" questions and quickly see the consequences of changes in input variables is perhaps the most important advantage of the computer-based modeling approach. Once the model is available, the cost of iterations is small. Sensitivity analysis to discover how sensitive the results are to changes in the input variables can be easily performed. Questions can be posed to ascertain what inputs will be required to obtain a specified output, e.g., what level of sales will be required to achieve a profit of $100,000? If there is frequent reanalysis, the computer model reduces the time required to generate new plans.

There is general agreement that decision support systems are developed most successfully by an iterative, prototyping approach. The designer of the support system model (a systems analyst, specially trained user analyst, or the end user) examines the decision situation and builds a simple, rough initial model. The model may contain only a few simple functions and may be thought of as "Version 0";[15] the important objective is to provide the user with a working system. The design process then proceeds iteratively, with interaction between the user and the designer. This alternating process of change, use, change then continues until an acceptable system is developed. Development may continue even after the user successfully applies the model to one specific situation in order to adapt the model to other problems.

The model itself may be one of the types described earlier (such as accounting model or representational model). The programming of the model may be done using one of four general approaches:

---

[15]P. G. W. Keen, "Decision Support Systems: Lessons for the 80's," *EDUCOM Bulletin*, Fall 1982.

1 Programming language
2 Spreadsheet processor
3 Analysis package
4 Model generator

Each of these will be described briefly.

CITY-WIDE MAP OF UTILITIES AND OTHER FEATURES

The Windy City has been developing a detailed interactive computer graphics map to give decision support capabilities to city agencies and utilities. Chicago's Bureau of Maps and Plots is providing a detailed utility map as part of the model. "Just in preventing a street from being dug up twice (by two different utilities) in a season, we'll save the city the cost of the computer equipment," according to Danielle Barcilon, deputy director of data processing. For the utility companies, use of the equipment will preclude the necessity of going through 1,800 80-acre maps to make repair decisions.

Chicago's Planning Department is adding block-by-block information to be used in the statistical planning of the fire and police departments as well as streets, sanitation, water, and sewer departments. Currently, for example, the police department analyzes districts beat by beat, drawing maps, recording crimes, and recommending changes. Each suggestion causes a delay of several weeks as new maps are drawn by city drafters. The thematic map is designed to give graphic displays of statistical information on request. A major advantage to the Planning Board will be the ability to play "what if" games producing several maps for the police to examine.

The map project is incomplete after three years of development. According to Barcilon, "Adding the information has been simple. Checking [it]... has been the hardest part." The first map is expected to be accurate to eight decimal places with all "ghost" pipes eliminated and an error margin of less than a foot per mile.

When the system is completed, each department will retain control of its own information but respond to requests for it. Barcilon notes that the project has already resulted in increased information sharing across departmental lines and better overall perceptions of the city's work.

Projected as future additions to the model are records of hookups of utilities to private residences and pipe diameters, age, and deterioration rates. The forestry department is investigating the possibility of adding the city's trees to the map.

"Windy City Is Mapping Its Future Graphically," *MIS Week*, June 10, 1981, p. 10.

Programming Language

Programming languages designed for algorithmic processes or procedural logic are better adapted to programming decision support systems than data processing languages. Two examples of widely used algorithmic languages that may be appropriate are FORTRAN and BASIC. Two advantages in their use are the high level of vendor support for the languages and the high level of programming expertise in these languages among analysts. In the case of BASIC, many users may be able to program it themselves. The disadvantages are the number of statements to program the computational procedures of the support system and the time required to write and debug them. Two alternatives to these traditional procedural languages are a higher level, more compact algebraic language and a very high level fourth generation language.

One high level, compact algebraic language often used as a tool for DSS development is APL (*A Programming Language*). APL is a very powerful language because complex

```
DYADIC FUNCTIONS

X * Y        X TO THE YTH POWER
X ● Y        BASE-X LOGARITHM OF Y
X Γ Y        MAXIMUM OF X AND Y
X L Y        MINIMUM OF X AND Y
X ∧ Y        X AND Y
X ∨ Y        X OR Y


MONADIC FUNCTIONS

× Y          SIGNUM Y (RETURNS 0 IF Y=0,  -1 IF Y<0,  1 IF Y>0))
÷ Y          RECIPROCAL OF Y
● Y          NATURAL LOGARITHM OF Y
! Y          FACTORIAL Y
? Y          RANDOM NUMBER ≤ Y
○ Y          PI TIMES Y


MIXED FUNCTIONS

X [Y]        YTH ELEMENT OF X
X ι Y        FIRST LOCATIONS OF Y WITHIN THE VECTOR (MATRIX) X
X ? Y        X INTEGERS SELECTED RANDOMLY FROM Y WITHOUT REPETITION
X ← Y        X ASSIGNED THE VALUE OF Y
X ⊟ Y        MATRIX DIVISION
```

```
    ∇   PROGRAM
[1]   A THIS APL PROGRAM IS A LINEAR LEAST SQUARES MODEL
[2]   A THE Y VECTOR REPRESENTS SALES, THE X VECTOR INVENTORY
[3]     Y← 25000 100000 150000 200000 250000 300000
[4]     X← 16500 18000 19500 21000 22500 24000
[5]     Y⊟X∘.* 0 1
```

```
     PROGRAM
¯552380.9524 35.71428571
```

Figure 12-6
Examples of APL statements and an APL program.

mathematical operations can be performed using very few statements. It can also be learned relatively quickly, at least for simple operations.

APL utilizes special symbols and therefore requires a special keyboard for input. (Many terminals have an alternative APL character set built in.) Some typical APL statements and their meanings are shown in Figure 12-6. One very powerful feature is the capability to input and perform operations on entire matrices of numbers through a single command. Since APL statements are powerful, an APL program can be written very quickly to support a particular decision problem. In many organizations, APL specialists write programs on request for specific problems; the programs may be discarded after being used once (this is often called "throw-away code"). There are enthusiastic supporters of APL for this environment; others point out that it has poor documentation characteristics and that it is error prone for occasional users because its rules do not match the natural way that novice users expect to do procedures.

Very high level fourth generation languages have been introduced in Chapter 3. They will receive further explanation in Chapter 13. They provide powerful facilities for programming a decision support system. A few statements perform the procedures that require many FORTRAN or BASIC statements.

If the developers choose to use a programming language approach to programming a decision support system, the selection of a language depends on factors such as:

- Availability of language and support for it
- Experience of developers with various languages
- Amount of manipulation versus presentation of data
- Need to document and maintain the program
- Frequency of use and number of users

Spreadsheet Processor

The spreadsheet processor is the most available and commonly used model building and programming facility. Spreadsheet processors are available for use on most personal computers. The first (and best known) of these is VisiCalc, but there are many products (commonly referred to as Calcs) that perform similar functions. Similar capabilities are available with more complex modeling facilities and planning languages on larger computers.

Because of the general availability and power of spreadsheet processors, they are described here in more detail than other modeling facilities. The description will be a useful overview for a reader with experience in their use and background for those who have not yet had an opportunity to use them. Some very simple problems to provide opportunities for developing models with a spreadsheet processor are included in the exercises at the end of the chapter.

The spreadsheet processor defines an output in the form of a worksheet traditionally used to develop plans, budgets, and other analyses. There are columns and rows with labels on each. The statements that define the model indicate what value each cell on the electronic worksheet is to receive or how the value is to be computed. Statements also define the computational operations such as summing across a row to provide a row total and summing down a column to produce a column total. Figure 12-7 shows the spreadsheet output for a simple example.

An explanation of how the example in Figure 12-7 was produced will provide insight into the basic capabilities of the spreadsheet processor; additional capabilities are available for more complex models. The steps in building the model are the following:

1 Define the objective of the model and sources of data. The objective of the model in Figure 12-7 is to project the profitability of a new product for its expected five years of life. The model also provides some diagnostic percentages such as percent of projected five-year sales for each year and percent of five-year profit estimated for each year. The sources of data for this planning model are the sales executives for sales estimates, engineering for estimates of costs, and past experience for life cycle percentages.

2 Determine the format of the output. In this case, there are columns for 1984, 1985, 1986, 1987, 1988, and total. The rows are labelled unit sales, unit price, sales, cost of sales, gross

	1984	1985	1986	1987	1988	Total
Unit sales	5500	11500	16000	10500	6500	50000
Unit price	5.50	5.78	6.07	6.37	6.69	
Sales	30250	66470	97120	66885	43485	304210
Cost of sales	19663	41909	59397	39679	25023	185671
Gross margin	10587	24561	37723	27206	18462	118539
Promotion	5060	10580	14720	9660	5980	46000
Other expense	2000	2100	205	2315	2431	11051
Profit	3527	11881	20798	15231	10051	51488
Profit %	11.7	17.9	21.4	22.8	23.0	20.2

Figure 12-7
Output from a simple budget planning model.

margin, promotion, other expense, profit, and profit percent. There are no decimal places in the financial data; there is one decimal place in the percentage figures.

3 Determine how a value is to be obtained for each cell in the spreadsheet. In this case, sales are a percent of total five-year sales (an overall estimate). The percentage for each year is based on a life cycle for products of this type 10, 22, 32, 22, 14. Unit price is based on the initial price with an increase of five percent per year for inflation. Cost of sales is a decreasing percent of sales starting at 65 percent with a two percent reduction per year reflecting efficiencies of production. Gross margin is computed from sales and cost of sales. Promotion is a percentage of total based on a life cycle for a product of this type; the percentage varies for each year (same as sales). Other expenses are based on an initial amount adjusted upward each year by five percent for inflation.

4 Write statements to create the worksheet model. The procedures and instructions differ somewhat among spreadsheet processors. For the software used in this case, the following actions were taken:

- The cursor was moved to each column and the year was entered as the column heading. Using an alphabetic command, total was entered for the last column.
- The space for row labels was reset from the default option of 5 spaces to 14 spaces by using the format command.
- The formatting of data in the spreadsheet was set, using the format command, to integers for financial data (except for unit price) and one decimal place for percentage data.
- The first row was labeled unit sales. The cursor was moved to the column position for each year and the unit sales defined by a formula as a percent of total sales.
- The second row was defined as unit price. The cursor was moved to the cell for the first year and unit price was entered. The cursor was moved to the second year and a formula was entered to make unit price equal to the five percent increase. The formula was then copied for each subsequent column.
- Sales was defined as unit sales times unit price.
- Cost of sales was defined as a percentage of sales for each entry in the next row, decreasing by two percent per year.
- Gross margin was made equal to sales minus cost of sales.
- Promotion was defined as a specified percentage of sales for each year.

- Other expense was specified by an initial amount for the first period and a formula for subsequent periods that increased the prior year amount by five percent.
- Profit and profit percent were defined by formulas.

5 Write statements to run the model. Check the results. Make changes until it is correct.

6 Make changes in the model and rerun it to evaluate alternative values of the variables in the model. For example, in the simple example, what is the effect of an initial price of $6.00 instead of $5.50? One simple change was made, the model was rerun, and the total five-year profit was $72,238.

The power of the spreadsheet processor should be apparent with a simple example. It conforms to the common and familiar representation of data as rows and columns. It performs the error-prone work of computing figures and preparing sums, totals, subtotals, percentages, etc. Once the model is debugged, it is easy to make changes to enhance the model or to run it with alternative estimates.

NATIONAL CAR RENTAL USES ELECTRONIC SPREADSHEET

National Car Rental has three main uses for spreadsheet processors. Most of the spreadsheet analysis is performed on microcomputers, but much of the data is downloaded from the large mainframe computer.

1 In financial planning, spreadsheet models are used to help determine future corporate financing needs, methods, and timing.

2 The company's rental car division uses spreadsheet analysis with such factors as car costs, interest rates, rate of growth, and customer driving habits to set prices.

3 The truck leasing division compares full service leasing rates among competitors (when such rates are based on different formulas) for dealing with inflation.

Ron Salmela, "Electronic Spreadsheets," *IBM Computer User*, 3:1, January 1984, p. 7.

Analysis Package

In some DSS applications, the significant elements are statistical analysis or use of standard computational models. For example, a DSS may be needed to perform linear programming analysis to compute an optimal mix for product ingredients or compute sample statistics as part of making projections. In the case of forecasting, there are a number of procedures that are available in analysis packages. The packages assist in the preparation of a file of input data and in performing the analysis. The package may provide output only in a standard format (requiring a separate report preparation for the DSS report) or may have facilities for formatting the output. Graphic output is often supported.

Model Generator

A model generator (or decision support system generator) is a software package which facilitates the development of models and decision support systems. It is a comprehensive package incorporating the capabilities of the first three approaches to DSS development (programming language, spreadsheet processor, and statistical package). Ideally it contains facilities to define models, to perform statistical analysis, to link models to a database, and to create appropriate user dialog. In practice, it may be limited in one or more of these capabilities. For example, one model generator may have a convenient language for usability and access to data but limited modeling capability; another may not have database access, but may be very flexible and adaptive in terms of modeling.

Two basic objectives of a model generator are:[16]

- To permit quick and easy development of a wide variety of models
- To be flexible and adaptive enough to facilitate interactive design of systems and simple modifications.

In order to satisfy these objectives a model generator should have the following capabilities:[17]

1 *Usability*. The model generator should create models which are easy and convenient for non-technical people to use. It should also be easy and convenient to build and modify a model.

2 *Data*. The model generator should provide access to a wide variety of internal and external data sources.

3 *Analysis*. The model generator should have analysis capability to support a wide variety of users, problems, and contexts.

A number of packages have the significant elements of a model generator approach to support decision making. The most significant existing packages (in terms of widespread use) are those oriented to planning support, but which have capabilities for a broad range of decision support system development. A short description of three of these modeling packages illustrates the capabilities that may be obtained:[18]

Language	Description
ADR/EMPIRE (Applied Data Research Inc.)	Modeling, analysis, and reporting system; provides full computational capabilities, automatic solving of linear and nonlinear simultaneous equations and a library of financial, statistical, and mathematical functions. Additional features: data manager; report writer; graphics facilities supporting both conventional and graphics terminals; interactive analysis features; data analysis and forecasting for interactively using various regression, smoothing, moving average, seasonal, or advanced statistical techniques to develop relationships from time series information.

---

[16]R. Sprague, Jr., and R. Panko, "Criteria for a DSS Generator," *Proceedings, 13th Annual Meeting of the American Institute of Decision Sciences*, Atlanta, Georgia, 1981.

[17]Sprague and Panko, "Criteria for a DSS Generator."

[18]Ellen Benoit, "Financial Modelers Add Might to Minis," *Business Computer Systems*, October 1983, pp. 107–122.

EXPRESS (Management Decision Systems Inc.)	Database management system to support reporting, analysis and modeling requirements; integrates ad hoc and formal reporting, preprogrammed financial and statistical routines, color graphics, and financial modeling capabilities.
IFPS (EXECUCOM)	"What if" capabilities; report generator; consolidation from detailed models, sensitivity-impact analysis and goal seeking; Monte Carlo simulation for risk analysis; financial, data smoothing and projection functions.

Examples from a comprehensive, integrated package for interactive information analysis and decision support system building will illustrate the capabilities of model generators and the procedures required to use such development systems. The system used for the examples is Analect, a product of OR/MS Dialogue, Inc. The system provides a wide range of specialized functions for marketing and sales analysis, financial and corporate planning, and forecasting for production planning. The system tools include analysis, graphics, retrieval and reporting, and data management. Two figures

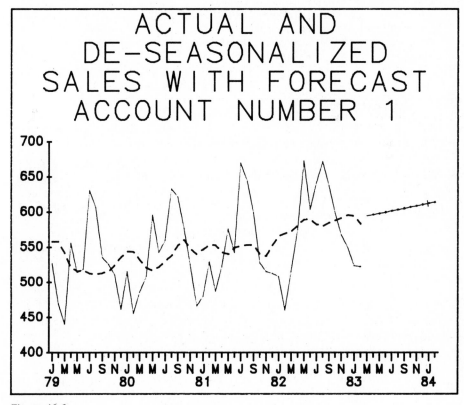

Figure 12-8
Graphics output from model generator illustrating plotting of actual data, de-seasonalized data, and forecast. (Courtesy of OR/MS Dialogue Inc.)

illustrate the concepts explained in the chapter relative to a model generator. The first (Figure 12-8) shows a combination of analysis and graphics with three data analyses on one graph: actual data, deseasonalized data, and deseasonalized forecast data. The second (Figure 12-9) is graphic output in simple bar chart form. The instructions to the model generator to produce the bar chart illustrate the high-level instructions used.

GENERATING ALTERNATIVE GEOGRAPHIC ASSIGNMENTS

An example of a decision support system for a specific application is the police beat allocation system developed by a police officer and used on an experimental basis by the city of San Jose, California. This system allowed a police officer to display a map outline and call up data by geographical zone, showing police calls for service, activity levels, service time, etc. The interactive graphic capability of the system allowed an officer to manipulate the maps, zones, and data for a variety of police beat alternatives quickly and easily. In effect, the system provided tools to amplify a manager's judgment. In a later experiment, a traditional linear programming model was applied to the problem. The solution was less satisfactory than the one designed by the police officer.

The system was built from the Geodata Analysis and Display System (GADS), an experimental system developed at the IBM Research Laboratory in San Jose. By loading different maps, data, menu choices, and procedure command strings, GADS was later used to build a DSS to support the routing of IBM copier repair personnel. The development of this new "application" required less than one month.

R. Sprague, Jr., "A Framework for the Development of Decision Support Systems," *MIS Quarterly*, 4:4, December, 1980, pp 1-26.

Model Base Management

Conceptually, an information system should contain a *Model Base Management System* (MBMS) that manages models and analysis programs in much the same way that the database management system manages data. Besides providing access to a variety of models for flexible use, the MBMS should contain the following:[19]

- the ability to catalog and maintain a wide range of models
- the ability to interrelate these models and link them to the database
- the ability to integrate model "building blocks"
- the ability to manage the model base with functions analogous to database management

Although there is a direct analogy between the idea of a database management system and a model base management system, the model base management system concept is at the experimental stage. Some of the desired capabilities are included in model generators and in comprehensive statistical-analysis packages.

---

[19]R. Sprague, Jr., "A Framework for the Development of Decision Support Systems," *MIS Quarterly*, 4:4, December 1980, pp. 1–26.

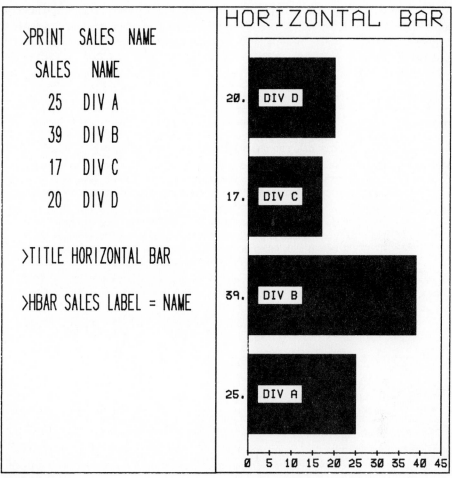

Figure 12-9
Graphics output in bar chart form (right) and instructions to model generator (left). (Courtesy of OR/MS Dialogue Inc.)

SUMMARY OF A PLANNING SUPPORT SYSTEM

As noted in Chapter 10, planning is difficult cognitive work, and there is evidence that humans avoid planning activity. Planning support systems are important both in aiding the performance of difficult work and in overcoming the phenomenon of avoidance of planning. Performance is aided through the capabilities of planning support systems; humans are aided in overcoming planning avoidance through the procedures implemented with a planning support system.

Models and Facilities Used in Planning Support

Planning support systems are part of the broad concept of a DSS; they tend to use DSS software and design concepts. They will be explained as a separate instance of a DSS in order to clarify and illustrate the use of support systems in planning. Using the Alter taxonomy presented earlier in the chapter, planning support can utilize the following types of systems:

Classification	Application to planning support
Data analysis system	Planning requires analysis of past data in order to project future relationships and to extrapolate past performance. This analysis of past data can use standard analysis and forecasting modules.
Analysis information	Access to databases and to small models is important to system planning. The databases provide data for planning analysis; the models provide planning analysis specific to organizational planning.
Accounting models	A significant part of a planning effort is in the context of the accounting model of the organization. Future plans can be summarized in pro forma financial statements. These require the use of accounting decision rules to make the planned results consistent with accounting for actual results.
Representational models	These models estimate the consequences of various actions using techniques such as simulation and scenario building. They extend beyond the limits of accounting models. They are important components of planning support, since probable consequences not contained in accounting models should be considered and simulated.

Planning Software Systems

A number of planning languages or planning software systems are designed especially for financial planning. Although they may be used in other planning, simulation, and decision support settings, the major orientation of these packages is financial planning. The languages may be obtained through use of a timesharing service, by lease for use on an in-house computer, or by purchase for use on a microcomputer. The modeling packages described earlier in the chapter are primarily financial packages for use on large computers or through timesharing.

The specific capabilities of a planning package needed by an organization will vary with the type of planning problems and the planning approach taken. Some general capabilities that are likely to be found are the following:

Planning support feature	Comments
Report layout	Defining the headings, column and row labels, subtotals, etc., for a planning document.
Graphics	Plotting of data for graphs and diagrams.
Modeling	Building a model, editing and altering the model, and executing the model.
Housekeeping	Saving models and files. Retrieving models and files.

Building data files	Creating and editing data files needed for running the models.
Statistical analysis and forecasting	Various statistical routines to analyze data and to produce forecasts using statistical methods.
"What if" analysis and sensitivity analysis	Determining the sensitivity of the model to changes in selected variables.
Monte Carlo simulation	Simulation using probability distributions to select values for variables.
Goal setting analysis	Analysis to determine the values that variables must have to achieve a stated goal.

A comprehensive example will be used to illustrate the development and use of a planning model. The model is written in the IFPS language; it was run using several options.

PLANNING SOFTWARE SUPPORT FOR DIET DRINK

The Quick Diet Company produces a diet drink in cans. People drink one can in place of each regular meal. The formula contains soy protein, vitamins, minerals, flavoring, etc. Sales of the drink vary from month to month because people tend to be seasonal in their dieting habits; consumers tend to be very serious about dieting after the December holidays and just before summer. The company gets orders and ships the diet drink one to two months in advance of consumer demand. Although there are different flavors, the planning for all cans is essentially the same. The drink is sold in cases of 24 cans and planning is by case. The company has been concerned with the fact that production has been closely tied to sales in order to minimize inventory, but this has led to considerable overtime expense. In fact, overtime sometimes became so excessive that workers called in sick to avoid it. A planning model is to be developed to project staffing, inventory, profit, etc., under different production and staffing assumptions. In particular, the model is to investigate the effect of having a consistent ending inventory with the current workforce of 126, the effect of changing to a larger workforce and letting inventory vary to avoid overtime, and monthly case price to achieve a monthly gross margin of $3.5 million. The assumptions for planning are taken from historical analysis and engineering studies:

- Average production is 2,000 cases per employee per month. This includes mixing, canning, labeling, packing, and shipping. Even though a single additional employee does not do all of these tasks, the balancing of staff makes this average production assumption satisfactory for planning.
- Workers are paid an average of $7.50 per hour plus fringes for a total labor cost of $1,584 per month. Overtime is 150 percent of regular time.
- The ending month's inventory should be 60,000 cases in order to allow for normal fluctuations in demand. The initial inventory for planning is 60,000 cases on January 1.
- Revenue is $14.40 per case (60 percent of selling price of $1 per can). Material costs are $2.20 per case. Fixed production costs are $150,000 per month.
- Estimated sales are 3,600,000 cases per year. November, December, March, April, and May sales are respectively 12, 10, 9, 11, 9 percent of annual sales; other months are approximately 7 percent of annual sales.

Figures 12-10 through 12-13 illustrate the use of planning software, IFPS, for the Quick Diet Company.

- Figure 12-10 is a simple planning model to produce a forecast by month and a yearly total. Workforce is 126 and inventory is constant at 60,000 cases. Note that the statements are simple and clearly document the logic of the model.
- Figure 12-11 is the output from the model in Figure 12-10. Note that overtime is excessive. In November, there must be 90 work months of overtime and there are only 126 regular workers. On average, each worker would have 71 percent overtime.
- Figure 12-12 is a "what if" analysis changing workforce to 150 and allowing inventory to vary. To focus analysis, only three lines are printed.
- Figure 12-13 is goal seeking to get data for a variable pricing analysis. The goal is to achieve a gross margin of $3.5 million per month by varying price.

The model in IFPS

```
MODEL QUICK  VERSION OF  02/02/84  16:25
20 *       QUICK DIET COMPANY -- AGGREGATE PLANNING MODEL
30 *
40 COLUMNS JAN,FEB,MAR,APR,MAY,JUN,JUL,AUG,SEP,OCT,NOV,DEC,TOTAL
90 WORK FORCE = PRODUCTION/2000
91 OT WORK FORCE = WORK FORCE - REG WORK FORCE
92 REG WORK FORCE = 126
94 CASE PRICE = 14.40
97 SALARY RATE = 1584
98 MATERIAL COST = 2.20
110 *
120 PRODUCTION = SALES FORECAST
130 *
140 SALES FORECAST = 252000,252000,324000,396000,324000,252000,252000,´
150 252000,252000,252000,432000,360000
160 END INVENTORY=60000+PRODUCTION-SALES FORECAST,´
170 PREVIOUS END INVENTORY+PRODUCTION-SALES FORECAST
240 REGULAR TIME=WORK FORCE*SALARY RATE
241 OVER TIME = OT WORK FORCE*SALARY RATE * 1.50
280 MATERIAL = PRODUCTION*MATERIAL COST
286 FIXED COST = 150000
290 *
300 TOTAL COST = REGULAR TIME + OVER TIME + MATERIAL + FIXED COST
370 REVENUE = SALES FORECAST * CASE PRICE
380 *
420 GROSS MARGIN=REVENUE-TOTAL COST
430 COLUMN TOTAL FOR PRODUCTION THRU SALES FORECAST=SUM(C1 THRU C12)
440 COLUMN TOTAL FOR REGULAR TIME THRU GROSS MARGIN=SUM(C1 THRU C12)
END OF MODEL
```

The IFPS statements to run the model

```
INPUT: SOLVE
MODEL QUICK  VERSION OF  02/02/84  16:25 -- 13 COLUMNS 16 VARIABLES
ENTER SOLVE OPTIONS
INPUT: WIDTH 132,14,9,-1
INPUT: ALL
```

Figure 12-10
The statements in IFPS to build planning model for Quick Diet Company.

QUICK DIET COMPANY -- AGGREGATE PLANNING MODEL

	JAN	FEB	MAR	APR	MAY	JUN	JUL	AUG	SEP	OCT	NOV	DEC	TOTAL
WORK FORCE	126	126	162	198	162	126	126	126	126	126	216	180	
OT WORK FORCE	0	0	36	72	36	0	0	0	0	0	90	54	
REG WORK FORCE	126	126	126	126	126	126	126	126	126	126	126	126	
CASE PRICE	14.40	14.40	14.40	14.40	14.40	14.40	14.40	14.40	14.40	14.40	14.40	14.40	
SALARY RATE	1584	1584	1584	1584	1584	1584	1584	1584	1584	1584	1584	1584	
MATERIAL COST	2.200	2.200	2.200	2.200	2.200	2.200	2.200	2.200	2.200	2.200	2.200	2.200	
PRODUCTION	252000	252000	324000	396000	324000	252000	252000	252000	252000	252000	432000	360000	3600000
SALES FORECAST	252000	252000	324000	396000	324000	252000	252000	252000	252000	252000	432000	360000	3600000
END INVENTORY	60000	60000	60000	60000	60000	60000	60000	60000	60000	60000	60000	60000	3600000
REGULAR TIME	199584	199584	256608	313632	256608	199584	199584	199584	199584	199584	342144	285120	2851200
OVER TIME	0	0	85536	171072	85536	0	0	0	0	0	213840	128304	684288
MATERIAL	554400	554400	712800	871200	712800	554400	554400	554400	554400	554400	950400	792000	7920000
FIXED COST	150000	150000	150000	150000	150000	150000	150000	150000	150000	150000	150000	150000	1800000
TOTAL COST	903984	903984	1204944	1505904	1204944	903984	903984	903984	903984	903984	1656384	1355424	13255488
REVENUE	3628800	3628800	4665600	5702400	4665600	3628800	3628800	3628800	3628800	3628800	6220800	5184000	51840000
GROSS MARGIN	2724816	2724816	3460656	4196496	3460656	2724816	2724816	2724816	2724816	2724816	4564416	3828576	38584512

Figure 12-11
The output of the planning model in Figure 12-10 using the current policy of overtime with constant work force of 126.

```
ENTER SOLVE OPTIONS
INPUT: WHAT IF
WHAT IF CASE 1
ENTER STATEMENTS
INPUT: PRODUCTION = 300000
INPUT: REG WORK FORCE = 150
INPUT: SOLVE
ENTER SOLVE OPTIONS
INPUT: WORK FORCE, PRODUCTION, END INVENTORY

***** WHAT IF CASE 1 *****
2 WHAT IF STATEMENTS PROCESSED
```

User/system dialog to change assumptions and print three lines containing workforce, production, and ending inventory

	JAN	FEB	MAR	APR	MAY	JUN	JUL	AUG	SEP	OCT	NOV	DEC	TOTAL
WORK FORCE	150	150	150	150	150	150	150	150	150	150	150	150	
PRODUCTION	300000	300000	300000	300000	300000	300000	300000	300000	300000	300000	300000	300000	3600000
END INVENTORY	108000	156000	132000	36000	12000	60000	108000	156000	204000	252000	120000	60000	

Figure 12-12
Output from a revised model to eliminate overtime by staffing at 150 and allowing inventory to vary.

```
ENTER SOLVE OPTIONS
INPUT: GOAL SEEKING
GOAL SEEKING CASE 1
ENTER NAME OF VARIABLE(S) TO BE ADJUSTED TO ACHIEVE PERFORMANCE
INPUT: CASE PRICE
ENTER 1 COMPUTATIONAL STATEMENT(S) FOR PERFORMANCE
INPUT: GROSS MARGIN = 3500000

***** GOAL SEEKING CASE 1 *****
```

User/system dialog to execute goal seeking -- altering price each month to achieve monthly gross margin goal of $3,500,000

	JAN	FEB	MAR	APR	MAY	JUN	JUL	AUG	SEP	OCT	NOV	DEC	TOTAL
CASE PRICE	18.05	18.05	14.04	11.48	14.04	18.05	18.05	18.05	18.05	18.05	10.53	12.63	

Figure 12-13
Goal seeking to find the price per case that will provide a monthly gross margin of $300,000 (using assumptions of model in Figure 12-11).

Database and Database Query System for Planning

Planning requires the ability to browse through the database to check various planning assumptions and to obtain data for the planning model. Regular management reports typically will not have all data needed for planning, so the planning activity requires independent access to the database. Access to the database via a query language allows the planner to test hypotheses using historical data.

As explained earlier, planning requires access to external data sources as well as historical internal data. This is why there should be access to databanks of external data (usually maintained by outside vendors such as timesharing services).

In addition to internal data and external databanks, the planning support system may have support facilities for generating planning data (described in Chapter 10). These methods include scenario writing, simulation, cross impact analysis, econometric models, input-output analysis and Delphi projections.

Advantages of a Planning Support System

Within the context of organizational difficulties and constraints on planning and the use of the different support models, there are several advantages to using computer-based planning models:[20]

1 *Reduced information overload.* Planning involves a large number of variables which must be simultaneously considered. Computer-based models aid the decision maker by processing information quickly and efficiently.

2 *Information selection.* Key variables, identified within the model-building process, can assist in defining information to be included in the database.

3 *Economic solutions.* By enabling managers to experiment, planning systems can provide answers at low cost and with a minimum of human resources.

4 *Fast turnaround.* An interactive system allows decision models to be explicitly incorporated into the managerial planning process without delays.

5 *Interrelation of operations and planning systems.* Computer-based models facilitate the incorporation of operating results explicitly into the planning process.

6 *Communication aid.* An integrated model, encompassing the functional areas of the business, can provide a common language between functions and can improve communication of plans.

7 *Direct involvement.* Interactive modeling capability can be used directly by decision makers, bypassing such obstacles as communicating planning needs to programmers.

SUMMARY OF A CONTROL SUPPORT SYSTEM

Control systems in organizations tend to use predefined, periodic reports for monitoring performance and identifying conditions requiring intervention. Traditional performance reports and variance reports, produced from data in the internal database, are of this type. The use of computer-based systems can permit more complex variance analysis and some variations in the way reports are produced.

The information component of a control system should therefore have capabilities to:

1 Produce regular control reports

2 Produce ad hoc control analyses

3 Monitor and produce reports only if the system is going "out of control"

---

[20]Ronald A. Seaburg and Charlotte Seaburg, "Computer Based Decision Systems in Xerox Corporate Planning," *Management Science*, 20:4, Part II, December 1973.

4 Aid in forecasting the effect of current control policies
5 Access the database in order to discover relationships important to control
6 Analyze the consequences of alternative control responses

Control support systems should be designed in accordance with the principle of requisite variety. This means that there is a system control response for every out-of-control condition encountered. There is a tendency to attempt to automate all control responses, but organizational systems are open systems and subject to unknown inputs from the environment. The control system should therefore be designed to track deviations from standard or planned performance and to suggest control responses, but there should be well-defined procedures for handling exceptions by transmitting data to a supervisor or some other person who is given responsibility to generate a response. For example, the granting of credit by a department store is kept in control by the provision of a set of rules. The rules may be based on points granted for each of several characteristics. The problem is that there are exceptions. Rather than building in the exceptions at the first level of the credit granting process, the control system sends applications that are denied on for a higher-level review. Supervisors can overrule the point system and use a common sense rule.

SUMMARY

Decision support systems (DSS) are a class of subsystems of the management information system which support analysts, planners, and managers in the decision-making process. Planning support systems and control support systems are specific instances of the broad concept of a DSS. Expert systems are a type of decision support system that incorporate the knowledge base and heuristics of an expert with a flexible interface so that a novice can use the system to solve problems. Decision support systems are especially useful for semistructured or unstructured problems where problem solving is enhanced by an interactive dialog between the system and the user. Emphasis is on small, simple models that can be easily understood and implemented rather than complex, integrated models. The process of decision model development is usually iterative, requiring interaction between the designer and the system user.

Decision support systems may be classified on a continuum ranging from those which primarily allow easy data access to systems which suggest a decision. Decision support systems may be used directly by the decision maker, indirectly by the decision maker with clerical assistance, or through an intermediary. Intermediaries such as staff analysts with specialized expertise frequently perform the analysis and interpret the results for the decision maker. Interactive capability is not as essential to the decision making process as ''responsiveness''—meaning a system which is powerful, accessible, and flexible.

Different models may be used to support each of the phases of decision making: intelligence, design, and choice. For the intelligence phase, emphasis is on flexible access to internal and external databases, both computerized and manual. Systems may need to support structured continuous search, structured ad hoc search, and unstructured search. Decision support for the design phase emphasizes interactive analysis for understanding the problem, generating alternative solutions, and testing the feasibility of solutions. Decision support for choice helps to rank alternatives and otherwise apply decision procedures to support the choice made by the decision maker. A decision support system can be designed to reflect different concepts of decision making and different decision situations.

Decision support systems can be developed with a variety of tools—a programming language, spreadsheet processor, statistical-analysis package, or a model generator. The model generator software packages contain features for developing a flexible and usable interface, linking to databases, and accessing or generating appropriate models. Models may be stored through a model base management system and used or modified for other decision situations.

A planning support system will typically contain facilities to build models, perform planning analyses, and obtain data from internal databases and external databanks. A control support system will have regular reports, ad hoc reports, aids to forecasting, and aids for monitoring systems.

MINICASES

1 PREDICTING ENERGY USAGE

A forecast of electrical energy usage up to and including the year 2000 was undertaken in 1979 by the New England Power Pool. The researchers for this group gathered weather records, records of past electrical use and demographic data for their model. Statistical analyses identified weather effects and immigration patterns which affect electrical usage. The market was differentiated among domestic, commercial, and industrial usage. Different measures were used to predict electrical usage in each. The number of electrical appliances in use predicted home volume. Usage in commerce and industry were based on number of employees and industrial demand forecasts respectively.

The 73 New England electrical companies that pooled their resources to build the computer model can use the system interactively through terminals and a timesharing service. The hourly demand and peak load time projections can be modified by asking "what if" questions such as:

"What if electrical prices fluctuate?"

"What if there are changes in oil prices, in conservation policies, or in appliance efficiency?"

"What if electric cars become popular?"

"Utilities Build Model to Forecast Energy Needs," *Computerworld*, February 26, 1979, p. 16.

Questions

a What is the source of the data for this model? — *historical*

b What kind of accuracy can the model results be expected to have? — *Short-term fairly good*

c What are some of the data analysis techniques that would probably be used in this model? *Statistical progression*

2 PLANNING IN THE BOOK INDUSTRY

When John Murabito was hired by McGraw-Hill Book Company to help develop a functional budgeting system, he used the EMPIRE financial modeling language, a product of Applied Data Research (ADR). EMPIRE provides the facility to transform a matrix of data from rows and columns into reports, charts and graphs, as well as providing a "what if" questioning capacity. He used the language to generate projected income statements, profit and loss statements, and projections of assets and cash flow over the next three years.

By the following year, Murabito was looking for more complex models which would more closely reflect the corporate structure in which he worked. The overall sales forecasting for the company appeared fairly accurate, but the picture for each of 17 revenue divisions was not.

The revenue divisions were headed by editors, each representing a specialized book market. Murabito surveyed the revenue division controllers regarding what three factors were most important in the market areas. Some research showed that the knowledge of these veterans of the book business was highly accurate. Models were developed from the factors for each editor's market.

Because of the organization of revenue divisions, McGraw-Hill Books needed a third dimension added to their time and financial item matrix. Data Resources Inc. (DRI), another of McGraw-Hill's subsidiaries, helped develop the three-dimensional database in a form that enabled any two dimensions to be read. These dimensions could then be used in EMPIRE to check for regressions and correlations. Based on McGraw-Hill's specifications, DRI created utilities to link internal budget or financial databases with external databases (such as GNP, Title I funds available, or competitor sales) and an Econometric Programming System (EPS).

[An interview with Mr. John Murabito, Profit Planning Department, McGraw-Hill Book Company, July 1981.]

Questions

a What types of models were in place when Murabito arrived? What new types did he produce?

b Do the models appear flexible? Are they understandable to the managing editors of the divisions? When might the decision space need to be broadened? How often or under what circumstances should their key factors be rechecked?

c Is there any difference between Murabito's role and the role of the corporate information system?

3 AN EXECUTIVE INFORMATION SYSTEM

The chairman and the president of a large regional bankng system were frustrated with the information system of the bank. They observed that there were computer-based systems for transaction processing, operational reports, and control reports. There was, however, no systematic information system to support strategic management.

The two executives formed a task group to develop an Executive Information System (EIS) to support top level strategic management.

Questions

a What are the information requirements for a strategic management information system?

b What hardware and software support might be used to develop the system and operate it?

c What alternatives would you suggest to the two executives in terms of how they might use the system?

EXERCISES

1 Can a computer make decisions? Discuss.

2 What is the difference between a set of structured decision rules and a decision support system?

3 Give examples of types of problems for which each of the seven classes of decision support systems would be appropriate. For each, specify who would operate the system.

4 Define the three phases of the decision process and describe the decision support for each.

5 What is the difference between planning and decision making? How do the models supporting them differ?

6 Explain the differences in the three types of problem search and the decision support for each.

7 How can unstructured search locate problems and opportunities?

8 What is the difference between heuristic search and algorithmic search?

9 What is a model generator? What are its major components?

10 What are some considerations in deciding whether to develop a DSS using a procedural programming language, a spreadsheet processor, or a model generator?

11 What is the role of an intermediary in DSS operation?

12 What are the usage patterns that are typical for a decision support system? What are the advantages of each?

13 a Program the profit model given in exercise 8 of Chapter 10. Run the model for the base case then vary factors in the model such as the following:

Sales of 105, 115, 125, and 135 for 1985–1988
Selling expense 15 percent of sales

 b Program the hospital financial planning model given in exercise 9 of Chapter 10. Vary the input data to observe their effects on expenses and revenues.

14 What is the difference between ''interactiveness'' and ''responsiveness'' in a decision support system?

15 What is an expert system? How does it differ from other decision support systems?

16 Use a spreadsheet processor or planning software to do the following:

 a Prepare a plan for an individual who desires to avoid the use of loans or revolving credit plans by establishing a budget leveling account. Since some expenses (and some income) do not occur at the same level each month, the individual will pay all these nonlevel expenditures from a special fund; a level amount will be paid into the fund each month. The question is how much needs to be paid into the fund each month. Prepare a model in the following format. Generate expense titles and amounts (examples are insurance, taxes, tuition, vacation, Christmas presents, etc.) and test the model.

	Months	
Jan	....	Dec. Total

Irregular expenses

—

—

Total by month
Averaged amount
Net amount into
  or out of
    leveling account
Cumulative amount
  in leveling
    account

 b It has suddenly hit the father of four children that he should plan for college and marriage expenses. The rule he has in mind is that the children will earn (during the summer and during the school year) about 30 percent of their college expenses (in addition to covering their summer living). He is committed to providing a modest car for each of them at the beginning of the sophomore year. For planning purposes, he assumes that each one will be married the year after they graduate from college. He anticipates that the first and third child will also do two years of graduate work, and he expects to pay for 50 percent of those expenses. Prepare an education-marriage resource requirements plan for the next 10 years assuming the following:

Children: Girl, age 18, boy, age 16, girl, age 15, boy, age 12

Cost of undergraduate education: Currently at $8,000 per year and increasing at the rate of seven percent per year

Current cost of graduate education is $12,000 per year and increasing at the rate of eight percent per year

Current cost of a marriage for a girl is $6,000 and for a boy is $3,000 with an annual increase of five percent

Current cost of a modest, fairly new used automobile is $3,500 with an annual increase in price of six percent

17 How does a spreadsheet processor or planning language provide structure for planning? How do they aid in planning tasks?

18 Most examples of decision support systems are for use in planning. Why is this? Explain the difference between a support system for planning and a support system for control.

19 How can a DSS support decision making under stress?

20 Contrast the requirements of an executive's DSS with a DSS suitable for a staff analyst.

SELECTED REFERENCES

Alter, S.: "A Taxonomy of Decision Support Systems," *Sloan Management Review*, 19:1, Fall 1977, pp. 39–56.

Alter, Steven L.: *Decision Support Systems: Current Practice and Continuing Challenges*, Addison-Wesley, Reading, MA, 1980.

Bouwman, Marinus J.: "Human Diagnostic Reasoning by Computer: An Illustration from Financial Analysis," *Management Science*, 29:6, June 1983, pp. 653–672.

Carlson, Eric D.: "An Approach for Designing Decision Support Systems," *Data Base*, 10:3, 1979, pp. 3–15.

Elam, J., J. Henderson, and L. Miller: "Model Management Systems: An Approach to Decision Support in Complex Organizations," *Proceedings, Conference on Management Information Systems*, Philadelphia, PA, December 1980.

Ginzberg, M. J., W. Reitman, and E. A. Stohr (eds.): *Decision Support Systems*, Elsevier, New York, 1982.

Keen, P. G. W.: "'Interactive' Computer Systems for Managers: A Modest Proposal," *Sloan Management Review*, Fall 1976.

Keen, P. G. W., and M. S. Scott Morton: *Decision Support Systems: An Organizational Perspective*, Addison-Wesley, Reading, MA, 1978.

King, William R., and Jamie I. Rodriguez: "Participative Design of Strategic Decision Support Systems: An Empirical Assessment," *Management Science*, 27:6, June 1981, pp. 717–726.

Kroeber, H. W., H. J. Watson, and R. H. Sprague, Jr.: "An Empirical Investigation of Information Systems Evolution," *Journal of Information and Management*, 3:1, February 1980, pp. 35–43.

Little, J. D. C.: "Models and Managers: The Concept of a Decision Calculus," *Management Science*, 16:8, April 1970, pp. B466–B485.

Nau, Dana S.: "Expert Computer Systems," *Computer*, February 1983.

Sherwood, Dennis: *Financial Modeling: A Practical Guide*, Gee & Co., London, 1983.

Simon, H.: "Cognitive Science: The Newest Science of the Artificial," *Cognitive Science*, 4, 1980, pp. 33–46.

Sol, H. G. (ed.): *Processes/Tools for Decision Support Systems*, Elsevier, New York, 1983.

Sprague, R., Jr.: "A Framework for the Development of Decision Support Systems," *MIS Quarterly*, 4:4, December 1980, pp. 1–26.

Sprague, Ralph J., Jr. (ed.): "Selected Papers on Decision Support Systems," *SIGOA Newsletter*, 1:4–5, September–November 1980 (a special issue of *Data Base*, 12:1–2, Fall 1980, containing nine papers on decision support systems).

Sprague, Ralph J., Jr., and Eric D. Carlson: *Building Effective Decision Support Systems*, Prentice-Hall, Inc., Englewood Cliffs, NJ, 1982.

Sprague R. H., and H. J. Watson: "Model Management in MIS," *Proceedings, Seventh Annual Meeting of the American Institute of Decision Sciences*, Cincinnati, OH, November 5, 1975, pp. 213–215.

Sprague, R. H., and H. Watson: "A Decision Support System for Banks," *Omega—International Journal of Management Science*, 4:6, 1976, pp. 657–671.

Wagner, G. R.: "DSS: Hypotheses and Inferences," Internal Report, EXECUCOM Systems Corporation, Austin, TX, 1980.

Will, Hart J.: "Model Management Systems," in *Information Systems and Organizational Structure*, E. Grochla and H. Szyperski (eds.), Walter de Gruyter, New York, 1975, pp. 467–483.

CHAPTER 13

SUPPORT SYSTEMS FOR MANAGEMENT OF KNOWLEDGE WORK

END-USER COMPUTING
  End Users Classified by Support Requirements
  End-User Applications
  Very High Level Development Languages
  Expert Assistance
  Information Centers to Support End Users
ORGANIZATIONAL CONSIDERATIONS WHEN USERS ARE DEVELOPERS
  Advantages of User-developed Systems
  Organizational Risks from User-developed Systems
  Organizational Policies and Procedures for User System Quality Assurance
DEVELOPMENT SUPPORT FOR INFORMATION SYSTEM PROFESSIONALS
IMPACT OF TECHNOLOGY ON THE NATURE OF KNOWLEDGE WORK
  Changes in Work Roles
  Changes in Supervision
  The Information Mediator
SUMMARY
MINICASES
EXERCISES
SELECTED REFERENCES

Chapter 12 described information system support for decision making, planning, and control. This chapter covers support for the entire range of knowledge work. The objective of the chapter is to explain how knowledge work can be supported by information system technology. The potential benefits to an organization are significant. Poppel estimates U.S. 1982 expenditures for office work to be in the area of $1 trillion; $600 billion of it is for knowledge work. He estimates that better information support for knowledge work could result in a potential savings of 15 percent of an average knowledge worker's time.[1]

In this chapter, the concept of knowledge work is clarified, and the technology and support facilities for knowledge work are explained. A major development in connection with support for knowledge work is end-user computing. Facilities for end-user system development are described, and organizational functions to support end-user computing are explained. Examples are presented of specialized knowledge work support facilities which support the work of information system professionals. The chapter also includes a section on the impact of information systems on the nature of knowledge work.

---

[1] Harvey L. Poppel, "Who Needs the Office of the Future," *Harvard Business Review*, November–December 1982, pp. 146–167.

DEFINITION OF KNOWLEDGE WORK

The definition of knowledge work is not precise. The term contrasts with manual work, physical production work, or physical service work. Knowledge work is based on the knowledge possessed by the worker; not on ability to perform physical tasks. The outputs of knowledge work are diagnoses, descriptions, instructions, schedules, plans, memoranda, position papers, decisions, etc.; by way of contrast, the output of physical production work is a physical product (packaged cereal, computer hardware, etc.) or a physical service (lawn mowed, gasoline put in car, etc.).

A useful definition of *knowledge work* is work that involves thinking, processing information, and formulating analyses, recommendations, and procedures. Knowledge work may use verbal or written inputs and outputs. Knowledge work tasks involve the use of information. Some information derives from the knowledge and expertise of the knowledge worker; some derives from organizational and external data to which the knowledge worker has access. A task may require that the appropriate information be given structure and organization; support systems for knowledge work aid in that structure.

Knowledge work is a relative concept with respect to jobs. There are knowledge work components in many tasks, and probably no jobs are composed only of knowledge work or lack knowledge work. A person in a clerical position with highly structured, routine tasks may have relatively little knowledge work, but some clerical jobs involve significant amounts of knowledge work; most managerial activities have a high level of knowledge work, but managers perform some routine tasks that have little.

The theme of this chapter is that computer and communications technology can be used to support knowledge work and thus improve the productivity of knowledge workers. Many of the support facilities already exist individually and have been discussed in Chapters 3, 5, and 12. For example, decision support facilities, discussed in Chapter 12, represent one type of system support for knowledge work. The maximum benefit is obtained from these technologies by having them all readily available to the user in a knowledge work support system, i.e., through a consistent interface and directly under the user's control. One model for accomplishing this integration of functions is an *intelligent workstation*. The idea of an intelligent workstation and its primary functional components are discussed in this chapter. The chapter also describes strategies for end-user development of their own support systems for knowledge work. In Chapter 17, specific considerations in the design of user interfaces for support of knowledge work will be discussed.

TYPES OF KNOWLEDGE WORK

In this section, knowledge work is classified into basic generic activities. Each of these classes of activity require somewhat different types of system support, to be discussed later in the chapter. The knowledge work activities are:

Diagnosis and problem finding
Planning and decision making
Monitoring and control
Organizing and scheduling

Authoring and presentation
Communication
System development

This list is not meant to be all-inclusive; it merely provides a set of activities that characterize knowledge work and illustrates the features required for knowledge work support.

Diagnosis and Problem Finding

Diagnosis and problem finding were included in the previous discussions of decision making; they are identified separately here in order to emphasize that these activities are part of knowledge work. Diagnosis and problem finding are well illustrated by the work of a physician. Faced with a set of symptoms, the physician seeks to diagnose the cause of the conditions by applying diagnostic reasoning. The clues represented by the symptoms and preliminary test results provide the basis for making a diagnosis or for seeking more information through additional questions or tests.

The concept of diagnosis and problem finding can be applied to organizational problems. Symptoms such as the results of financial analyses provide clues to problems. Once problems are identified, decision making processes can be applied.

Diagnosis and problem finding are knowledge work because they depend heavily on the knowledge and expertise of the analyst or diagnostician. The work of diagnosis tends to be semistructured or unstructured.

Planning and Decision Making

The activities involved in planning and decision making and systems to support them have been described in Chapters 6, 10, and 12. Many people who engage in knowledge work may contribute to the decision-making process. Staff professionals such as financial analysts or market researchers are responsible for collecting and analyzing data before results are presented to the person responsible for making the decision. Planning analysts structure and analyze data to aid planning by managers.

Planning and decision making are knowledge work because they depend on the knowledge and expertise of the decision maker and the manipulation of data using a decision model. The level of knowledge work in planning tends to increase with the level of planning; tactical planning is more constrained and more structured than strategic planning. The strategic planner must establish a structure for the plan and map environmental estimates into the plan, whereas lower level planning already has significant structure. The same principle holds for decision making. Highly structured, programmed decision making has less knowledge work content than unstructured decision making.

Monitoring and Control

The concepts of monitoring and control were described in Chapter 10; some information system support facilities for control were explained in Chapter 12. Many monitoring and control activities can be structured and made fairly routine. However, there are significant portions of the monitoring and control function that cannot be defined by preestablished rules. Analysis of the meaning of monitoring reports and analysis of variances often require expertise and judgment on the part of the reviewer; these monitoring and control activities are knowledge work.

Organizing and Scheduling

In the context of knowledge work, organizing refers to personal organizing activity rather than to the establishment of rules and procedures for a work unit. The latter is system design, to be discussed later in this section. Within the context of organizing one's own work, the structuring of personal files, the number of piles of documents on a person's desk, and the person's method of keeping track of names and addresses are all part of highly individualized personal organizing activity. Organizing is a critical component of knowledge worker productivity.

Scheduling is a structuring activity which establishes a time sequence to other activities, including personal activities and meetings. It requires a significant amount of time and effort. For example, a recent study[2] showed that an average of 12 percent of MIS managers' verbal contacts involved scheduling of future activities.

Much of the inefficiency associated with scheduling meetings is caused by the media used to communicate scheduling needs and to record the appointed event. A meeting of 10 people is inefficiently handled by telephone, a one-on-one medium which is slowed down by ''telephone tag'' and the need for changes which require recontacting those already scheduled. Furthermore, most managers are dependent on a personal appointment book which must be accessible when they are contacted. One method of increasing the efficiency of scheduling is to have it handled by a secretary, but most knowledge workers do not have this support, and even when available, there is difficulty in coordinating one's personal book with the secretary's book.

Authoring and Presentation

Many professionals have as some component of their work the preparation of letters, memoranda, reports and presentations. The most common tools for authoring are pen and paper, but other methods such as dictating and direct keying while composing are also common. Presentations might involve graphics, elaborate printing, or even artwork. In general, the objective of this class of knowledge work is to progress from an idea through multiple media transformations to a final presentable form, whether a document, a diagram, or a set of visual aids for a presentation. Thus, one presentation progression is from idea to a handwritten draft to a typewritten draft to a revised final typewritten draft. Each medium in the transformation takes time and may introduce new errors into the document.[3] Thus, a goal of technological support is to reduce the number of media transformations while improving the quality of the final output.

---

[2]B. Ives and M. H. Olson, ''Manager or Technician? The Nature of the Information System Manager's Job,'' *MIS Quarterly*, 6:4, December 1982, pp. 49–63.

[3]J. Bair, ''Communications in the Office of the Future: Where the Real Payoff May Be,'' *Proceedings, International Computer Communications Conference*, Kyoto, Japan, September 1978.

Communication

Studies of managerial work have shown that managers spend as much as 85 percent of their time communicating, most of it face to face.[4] Managers seem to have an overwhelming preference for face-to-face contact. This reflects, in part, a preference for the richness of the combination of verbal and nonverbal communication as well as a preference for unfiltered messages. By way of contrast, managerial reports represent a filtered, compressed information source.

The flow of communications is determined by both job and personal style. Managerial work is a series of brief, overlapping, interactive activities. Much of the managerial pace is set by the uncontrolled flow of communications. They are interrupted by the telephone as well as by other people "dropping in" for a specific purpose or just to "keep in touch." Many nonmanagerial knowledge workers may have longer periods of uninterrupted work time, but they also have frequent interruptions for communications.

The two primary traditional media for unfiltered, direct communication are face-to-face conversation and telephone conversation. Alternative communication technology such as electronic mail and teleconferencing give the receiver more control over the flow of unfiltered communication, but there is a loss of nonverbal message content.

System Development

System development refers to the development of information systems to provide structure and support for the performance of organizational work. The analysis, design, and implementation of a system may be performed by systems analysts or directly by the end users of the system. The development of formal public information systems will be explained in later chapters; this section will emphasize the development of private systems as an important activity that most knowledge workers perform. System development may involve the use of technology (such as a programmer creating a personal work environment using an online system), or it may employ only manual procedures and tools.

Knowledge workers may design their own filing systems, design systems to obtain data for monitoring and planning, and develop forms and reports, etc. In one study of office activities,[5] it was found that the work of secretaries fell into two categories: work initiated by others and work initiated by themselves in response to general instructions to achieve a result or meet a particular need. While many of the former activities were highly structured, the latter activities were semistructured or unstructured. Furthermore, many of them constituted application development of an internal nature: create an inventory control system for office supplies, develop a label system to process multiple mailing lists, develop a system to monitor department expenditures, etc.

---

[4]Ives and Olson, "Manager or Technician?"; H. Mintzberg, *The Nature of Managerial Work*, Harper & Row, New York, 1973.

[5]C. V. Bullen, J. L. Bennett, and E. D. Carlson, "A Case Study of Office Workstation Use," *IBM Systems Journal*, 21:3, 1982.

TECHNOLOGY IN SUPPORT OF KNOWLEDGE WORK

Many elements of computer and communications technology provide direct technological support for knowledge work. Before discussing specific support facilities and how they may be integrated into a knowledge work support system, it is useful to survey trends in technology that have provided the capability to support knowledge work. Technological trends were generally explained in Chapter 3; only highlights specific to knowledge work will be reviewed in this chapter. Two significant developments are the personal computer and communication networks. The merging of these two technologies is the basis for the *intelligent workstation*.

Personal Computers

The first personal computers were introduced in 1975 by new companies not part of the traditional computer industry. Starting in 1977, sales of personal computers increased dramatically with models such as Apple II, Commodore Pet, and Radio Shack TRS-80. In 1982, IBM introduced the IBM PC. This personal computer not only achieved a significant market share; it also firmly established the personal computer as business equipment. All major computer manufacturers now market personal computers as part of their product line.

The strong acceptance of personal computers was based on four factors:

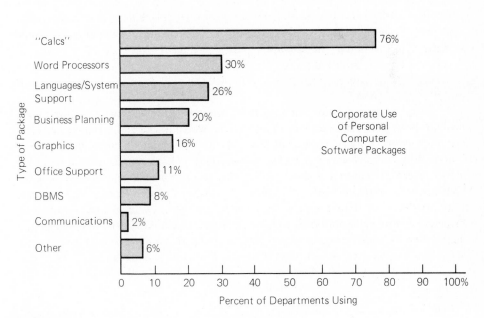

Figure 13-1
Corporate use of personal computer software packages. (Source: F. W. Miller, "Here, There." Reprinted from INFOSYSTEMS, April 1983. Copyright Hitchcock Publishing Company.)

- A complete hardware system that could be cost-justified for acquisition by individuals
- Software that made creation of new programs relatively easy
- Rapid diffusion of knowledge of small computer capabilities and requirements for use
- Tools to improve personal productivity

Although the first purchasers of personal computers were hobbyists, the market soon shifted to include technical and business professional users. As explained in Chapter 12, the most popular software packages, and the one most utilized by business and professional users, are spreadsheet processors. A survey of corporate uses of personal computer software is shown in Figure 13-1.

Communications Networks

Significant developments in communications technology were also discussed in Chapter 3. Since a large part of a knowledge worker's time is spent in communication, technological developments affecting the communication process can result in significant productivity gains. The cost of transmitting data, voice, and images has decreased and communications systems have become an important factor in knowledge work support.

In order for communications technology to significantly affect knowledge work, comprehensive communications networks are required. For example, electronic message systems are only effective when a fairly high proportion of others with whom one communicates have access to the network and use the system regularly. The communications network can also connect a user to the main computer and its database and to public databanks maintained by timesharing services.

Intelligent Workstations

The concept of an intelligent workstation (also termed a professional workstation or a personal workstation) is a combination of a personal computer and access to local and wide-area networks. It has been predicted that by 1990 an intelligent workstation will cost as little as 4 percent of a professional's salary, which approaches the cost of a telephone today; thus workstations will be easily accessible by all knowledge workers.[6] "Families" of workstations with modular components can be tailored to individual needs while remaining compatible with other machines. For example, a secretarial workstation may have powerful word processing capabilities while the managerial workstation may emphasize audio voice message facilities (through automatic dialing and voice message recording), but the two stations can communicate.

Although personal workstations may vary, the key physical components available for configuring a workstation are the following:

---

[6]R. I. Benjamin, "Information Technology in the 1990's: A Long-Range Planning Scenario," *MIS Quarterly*, 6:2, June 1982, pp. 11–32.

Workstation Requirements

Workstation component	Description
CPU	The processor is relatively small and often incorporated into the same box as secondary storage.
Visual display terminal	May be a color monitor, usually with graphics capabilities.
Keyboard and numeric keypad	Detachable from VDT. A numeric keypad may be separate or part of the keyboard.
Screen manipulation device	Typically a mouse or joystick for manipulating the cursor on the screen.
Printer	For creating a hard copy of text or images on the screen. May require "letter quality" output.
Secondary storage	Typically floppy disk or hard "Winchester-type" disk (if speed of data access is critical).
Communications capabilities	Interface to local area network and remote communication through wide-area network and modem.

Software capabilities for support of knowledge work functions may be "packaged" with the hardware; programming languages and other development tools are also available for developing application software. These are discussed in a later section of the chapter.

Integration of Facilities

A key concept in the design of workstations for knowledge work is integration of facilities. Rather than separate hardware, software, and communications for each of the components, these components are integrated into one facility. There are two types of integration: functional and physical.

Functional integration implies that the different software support functions for knowledge work are provided as a single system. For instance, electronic mail, word processing, storage of data, and access to external databanks can all be accomplished at the same workstation. Functional integration also means that the user can access these facilities through a single consistent interface and can switch from one task to another and back again (much as one does when working without the support of a workstation). For instance, a user may be preparing a document and be interrupted by a mail message, read the message, and then go back to the document. Ideally, functional integration also allows a user to create a graphical representation using data from an external databank and/or internal historical data and merge it with a document.

Physical integration refers to packaging of the hardware, software, and communications features required to accomplish functional integration. There are several elements of physical integration:[7]

---

[7]W. Newman, *Integrated Systems and the Office Environment*, McGraw-Hill, New York, 1985.

Elements of physical integration	Explanation
The user interface	The software should allow for several workspaces to be accessed concurrently, so that the user may combine elements from each and switch easily from one to the other. This feature is often called *multitasking*. It is commonly implemented by having multiple *windows* displayed on the screen at the same time, each representing an active task. Figure 13-2 illustrates a multiple window display. The design of user interfaces to support multitasking is discussed in more detail in Chapter 17.
Multiple media	The system should permit the creation and editing of documents from different media: text, graphics, databases, and voice.
Access to outside services	Through the network component, the user should be able to access external databanks and information retrieval services, public electronic mail services or services unrelated to the current task such as electronic banking.
Physical interconnection	Even when multiple products from multiple manufacturers are used, it should be easy to interconnect them to exchange information.

It should be noted that the concepts of functional and physical integration described here represent an ideal rather than the current state. It is particularly difficult to meet the requirements for integration that require some degree of consistency or standardization across vendors, i.e., access to outside services and physical interconnection among different types of equipment. Thus the concept of integration should be viewed as a widely accepted but ideal goal toward which new technology is moving.

SOFTWARE SUPPORT FACILITIES FOR KNOWLEDGE WORK

Many of the information processing functions that may be included in an intelligent workstation were described in Chapter 5. In this section, some of these functional capabilities will be described in the context of an integrated knowledge work support facility:

- Word and text processing
- Storage and retrieval of data
- Communications
- Decision support
- Graphics
- End-user application development facilities

Word and Text Processing

The workstation supporting knowledge work will normally have word and text processing capabilities. Capabilities may differ depending on the amount and type of

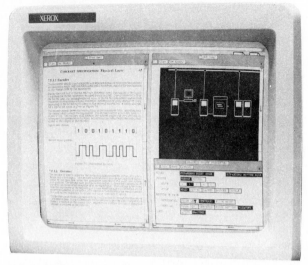

Figure 13-2
Illustration of multiwindow display. (Xerox Star courtesy of Xerox Corporation.)

word processing being performed. For instance, an author who is originating a manuscript tends to type slowly, use function keys for editing, and switch back and forth between documents or sections within documents performing electronic "cutting and pasting." A typist transcribing text from another medium emphasizes speed and accuracy and may require a keyboard of a different design. With a family of intelligent workstations, systems can be tailored and still be compatible, so that documents can be passed between them. It is common, for instance, for a manager to compose a first draft of a memo on his or her workstation and transmit it to the secretary's workstation with an electronic "message" attached requesting that it be formatted properly and distributed to a particular mailing list.

One question relative to word and text processing is whether managers and professionals will utilize intelligent workstations for drafting letters, memos, and documents in place of handwriting or dictating. The issue is more complex because intelligent workstations can accommodate many personal styles. In one example, a voice message capability allows an author to store annotations to a document in speech. Typing a draft directly onto a terminal can have advantages in terms of writing style and speed, because the author does not have to wait for someone else to transcribe a handwritten or dictated document. In addition, keying speed is not a critical factor when composing at a terminal because the thought process is generally slower than keying speed. Research has shown that, when composing text messages at a keyboard, lack of typing skills does not seem to be a major drawback.[8] Amy Wohl, a consultant on advanced office systems, reports: "We have never found...that someone didn't ultimately use the system because he or she couldn't keyboard."[9]

---

[8]A. Chapanis, "Interactive Human Communication," *Scientific American*, 32:3, 1975, pp. 36–42.

[9]E. F. Tunison and T. Moran, "Forum–Executive Productivity," *Today's Office*, November 1982, p. 49.

Storage and Retrieval of Data

Workstation storage facilities handle two types of files: data and text. For the management of data files, there are microcomputer database management systems. Some of these are provided in conjunction with fourth generation languages for data retrieval; these are discussed in a later section of the chapter. For text storage and retrieval, a flexible keyword filing facility with cross-reference indexes is required. The system should be able to store and retrieve documents, memos, mailing lists, etc. Computer storage need not contain all text to be retrieved; hard-copy documents can be located by stored references to the location where they are physically stored.

A key aspect of flexible use of an intelligent workstation is access to internal corporate databases. There may be several hierarchical levels of organization-wide data which are accessible to users with proper authorization. An authorized user has access to the centralized corporate database for one of two functions: to query the database with the workstation acting as a terminal, or to *download* (copy) a portion of the database onto the user's local storage facility. In the latter case, additional controls are required in order to keep the "memo" copy of the data accurate and current. Controls for operating in an intelligent workstation environment are discussed in a later section of this chapter.

There may also be intermediate file storage facilities. In a local area network, a large, fixed disk facility or file server may be shared by many workstations for file backup or temporary storage of large files.

The workstation should also have access to external databanks and information on retrieval services. The network component of the workstation connects the user to a wide-area network, either a public packet-switched network or telephone lines. The workstation then acts as a terminal device. Whether or not the data accessed can be downloaded onto the workstation for local processing depends on the type of databank service and restrictions placed on it by the service providers.

Communication Facilities

The primary communication facilities with an intelligent workstation are computer-based message systems and voice store-and-forward message systems (discussed in Chapter 5). In an integrated workstation the message system is interrelated to the word

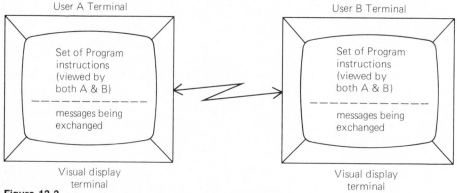

Figure 13-3
Diagram of a multi-window display with communications window.

and text processing function. A user may prepare a message via the word processing function and distribute it with a simple command via the message system. A formal document may also be prepared, formatted, and then distributed using the two functions.

Workstations with communication facilities provide capabilities for different users in physically separate locations to work on joint projects. One capability facilitating "remote group work" is a visual display screen showing two windows simultaneously combined with a "talk" feature for the two users to send messages to one of the windows. For instance, two programmers working on separate modules of a large program wish to discuss the program. They access the program file and show a portion of the program code on the top part of each of their screens; at the same time, a smaller window at the bottom of their screens is used for typing messages to each other. (Figure 13-3). Another ideal feature of remote group work is the ability to annotate a document electronically "in the margins" without making changes to it.

A type of "electronic meeting" support called *computer conferencing* can be provided by intelligent workstations. Computer conferencing systems are similar to computer-based message systems except that messages are focused on a particular conference topic. A conference may be restricted to an invited group of participants; other conferences are open to any users and tend to be "bulletin boards" of general information or tips. For instance, an open conference might be run for any users of a particular application package; users share experiences and suggestions on how to use the package.

Restricted conferences are run on a particular topic and may have a specific agenda. Participants read the discussion already on the system and add their contributions; the entire conference is stored centrally and entries are added in time order so that a transcript of the conference is produced. Figure 13-4 shows a transcript of part of a conference in a computer conferencing system.

One feature of computer conferencing systems is the ability to call a vote. A participant may "call" a question and request all others to vote; the system automatically tabulates the votes and can produce frequency tables. Computer conferencing systems have been used successfully in Delphi surveys.

One advantage of computer conferencing systems is that no user is hindered by physical appearance, disabilities, or personality traits such as verbal shyness. A disadvantage of computer-based conferencing is the loss of information normally transmitted through body language and other nonverbal cues.

Decision Support Systems

Decision support systems and model generators were discussed in detail in Chapter 12. In the ideal intelligent workstation environment, the model base management system is readily available to the user and models can be easily generated and stored locally. Functional integration permits final results produced from a decision support system to be incorporated into a report in the appropriate format.

Graphics

There are three general types of uses for computer graphics in organizational applications: analysis, presentation of stored data, and preparation of visual aids. In order for the

```
@notepad:note

NOTEPAD is ready.
Last Name: olson
Password:

The following activities are available to you:

                    Open Membership

* 1    The Open Forum
* 2    Micro-Scope
* 3    ITP Electronic Newsletter
* 4    THE SUGGESTION BOX

                  Assigned Membership

* 5    COMMUNICATIONS LAB FORUM
* 6    OFFICE AUTOMATION PILOT.
Please type the number of the activity you wish to join.

# 6

The Title of the Activity is:
OFFICE AUTOMATION PILOT.

[5]  BLOOMFIELD (SUZAN)   2-May-84 11:40AM-EDT
The following tasks need to be performed to successfully complete
the office automation needs assessment of the MIS department
office:
1.   Interview department chairman
2.   Interview secretaries
3.   Develop and distribute questionnaire
Please volunteer for which task you would like to be responsible.

Note  5  From BLOOMFIELD (SUZAN) To OLSON (MARGI)   2-May-84 11:42AM-EDT
Do you have access to word processing facilities where you
work?  If so, it might be best if you volunteer to draft
the questionnaire.  Thanks for your help.

[6]  KEINAN (EMILY)   2-May-84 11:47AM-EDT
I will volunteer to interview the department secretaries.
 I should be able to do the interviews Monday and Tuesday
of next week.

You are up to date.

ACTION:  Write Note 6 To: bloomfield SUZAN)
- Yes, I can use the word processing at my office.  I will
- volunteer to draft the questionnaire, but I will need some
- help.
-
ACTION:  Quit

Leaving NOTEPAD.

Thank you.
```

Figure 13-4
Transcript of a portion of a computer-based conference in NOTEPAD.

professional workstation to support graphics, it should be equipped with a high-resolution visual display terminal. Color is useful but optional. A graphics printer-plotter is frequently a shared facility on the local area network. In terms of integrated features, the most common requirement is that graphics be easily incorporated into document preparation. Some systems provide a free-form graphics capability for drawing diagrams as well as producing them automatically.

Other uses of graphics in combination with organizational applications are the following:

- *Forms generation*: a family of integrated workstations can support processing and transmission of standardized forms. Forms (complete with logo) may be easily created and altered through a graphics-based forms generation package.
- *Scheduling*: results of scheduling applications using critical path models can be presented using graphics.
- *User interface*: use of icons or symbols to replace words in a screen interface or to access a database. The use of icons in interface design is discussed in more detail in Chapter 17.

End-User Application Development Facilities

The intelligent workstation is a personal support facility under the direct control of the knowledge worker. One important capability that extends the power of the user to tailor a workstation to his or her own requirements is access to end-user application development facilities. These include not only access to application system development tools but also technical support, training, etc. The remainder of this chapter focuses on end-user application development tools and support facilities.

END-USER COMPUTING

The support facilities for knowledge work described above are available directly to end users without the need for intervention of a professional systems analyst or programmer. The capability of users to have direct control of their own computing needs has come to be referred to as *end-user computing*. As discussed above, one of the most powerful capabilities supplied directly to users is the facility to develop their own applications. This section describes current trends in end-user computing and end-user application development facilities.

The intelligent workstation with communications capabilities represents an ideal toward which organizations are moving. Currently, knowledge workers with access to their own computer facilities utilize one of three general types: terminals with timesharing access to a larger computer, personal computers, and personal computers with data communications so that they also access a larger computer. The trend is to the latter so users can download portions of the database and process locally.

End Users Classified by Support Requirements

Rockart and Flannery studied 200 end users of timesharing services in seven organizations.[10] Although the study did not include users of personal computers, the results are useful in understanding end-user computing. The researchers noted six types of users of timesharing facilities.

Type of user	Description
Nonprogramming end user	Accesses the system through a highly structured interface. Does not program applications.
Command level end user	Some application programming using high-level commands.
End-user programmer	More sophisticated user. Knows and uses programming language for solving problems specific to own job.
Functional support person	Sophisticated user. Writes programs and uses other facilities in support of users in a functional area.
End-user computer support person	A centralized information system specialist whose function is to utilize facilities to support the needs of end users.
Data processing programmer	Employs end-user facilities as an alternative to regular data processing development tools.

In the sample of 200 users, 271 timesharing applications were identified. The persons who programmed these were frequently not the ones who used them. The most common developer (48 percent of the systems) was a functional support person; the most common user (55 percent of the systems) was a nonprogramming end user. In this sample, end users themselves (the first three categories) used 93 percent of the applications, but programmed only 35 percent. However, almost all of the programs developed by end-user programmers were for their own use. The trend with very high level languages (discussed in the next section) is toward more user programming of their own applications.

AN END USER'S STORY

The vice president for management services at Florida Power and Light, B. L. Dady, is one of the major users of an end-user facility that includes color graphics. He cites an experience to demonstrate the value of the system to him.

"I had a telephone call about a quarter of five on a Tuesday afternoon relative to some information I was going to need at a meeting the next morning. The staff had just left for the evening. I was able to go to the terminal and compare some payroll information from Florida Power and Light with several other companies. From the COMPUSTAT database I had access to 20 years of payroll data from all utilities. I was able to put in parameters on what I wanted to look at—companies with nuclear plants (as we have) and companies that are over a certain size by number of customers and kilowatt hours produced annually. In a few seconds I had a list of 23 utility companies that met the criteria. There was one other company I also wanted to include, so I keyed that company in.

---

[10]J. Rockart and L. Flannery, ''The Management of End User Computing,'' *Communications of the ACM*, 26:10, October 1983, pp. 776–784.

"I asked the terminal to do a calculation: I wanted to know what the average payroll was per employee among those utility companies. It takes longer to tell about it than it took to do it. I got back the average figures for as many years as COMPUSTAT had data from the companies. I had the information in my hands in 20 minutes and was able to go home and look it over quietly that evening. There I added the numbers together and produced some averages, which took me another 30 minutes.

"The next morning it took me 25 minutes with the manual and interactive facility to produce a new graph of the data. I decided then to plot the data for only five years. On one graph I was able to show Florida Power and Light compared to the average of 24 selected companies, to the average of 8 selected companies, as well as to the high and low companies.

"Developing this kind of information would have taken weeks without the system. Moreover, it allowed me to refine my own thinking as I proceeded, depending on the significance of the numbers I generated."

"Graphic Systems Aid Executive Fact Finding," *IBM Information Processing*, 1:3, June–July 1982, pp. 5–6.

End-User Applications

End-user computing is expected to be the fastest growing area of computer use. Rockart and Flannery project annual growth rates of 50 to 100 percent compared to 15 to 20 percent for traditional applications.[11] Benjamin projects that end-user computing will represent one-third of information system spending by 1990 (compared to 14 percent in 1980).[12]

The survey by Rockart and Flannery showed that two-thirds of the applications were run on an ''as-needed'' basis, demonstrating that users took advantage of the flexibility provided by having control over their own computing. Twenty-eight percent of the applications were used on a periodic schedule and six percent were used one time only. The same survey classified applications (Table 13-1). The table shows that systems to perform analysis are dominant (71 percent).

TABLE 13-1: CLASSIFICATION OF SAMPLE OF TIMESHARING END-USER APPLICATIONS

Purpose	Number	Percent
Operational systems	24	9
Report generation	39	14
Inquiry/simple analysis	58	21
Complex analysis	135	50
Miscellaneous	15	6
Total	271	100

[Source: J. Rockart and L. Flannery, "The Management of End User Computing," *Communications of the ACM*, 26:10, October 1983, p. 779. ©1983, Association for Computing Machinery, Inc. By permission.]

[11]Rockart and Flannery, ''The Management of End User Computing.'

[12]R. I. Benjamin, ''Information Technology in the 1990s: A Long Range Planning Scenario,'' *MIS Quarterly*, 6:2, June 1982, pp. 11–31.

The sources of data for users in the above study indicate a problem. Many systems (31 percent) require users to key in data from reports, which means the data is already in the main computer data files but users cannot easily access it or do not know how. Rekeying the data is not only time-consuming, but creates problems of redundancy and lack of sufficient control over the accuracy and integrity of data. In other words, there is inadequate integration.

Very High Level Development Languages

The trend toward end-user application development is based on the availability of very high level languages or fourth generation languages (described briefly in Chapter 3). There may be disagreement about whether a specific language is fourth generation, but there is general agreement on the concepts governing the functionality and use of the languages.

The concept of "generation" was first applied to hardware; the term is still loosely applied to new hardware development. In the case of application development languages, the generation labels reflect a shift in level of detail at which the programmer must write instructions.

Software generation	Description
0 Machine language	Coding using machine-level codes and addresses.
1 Assembly language	A symbolic language at the same level as machine language, i.e., one assembly language instruction equals one machine language instruction.
2 Procedure-oriented language	Examples are COBOL and FORTRAN. The language instructions describe processing procedures. Each instruction is translated into multiple machine-level instructions.
3 Languages and development aids for different processing environments	Examples are online programming systems, database management systems, data dictionaries, and program generators
4 Integrated user-oriented development facilities	Integration of prior development facilities with relatively simple languages for writing queries and programming solutions.

The idea of a fourth generation is thus a natural progression of software development. Some features of an ideal very high level development language are:

- Interactive dialog to guide application development
- Powerful nonprocedural verbs with natural language syntax (English or other language)
- Simple to learn, helpful error messages, and use of defaults (most common option automatically applies unless changed)
- Relational database management
- High-level query language for direct access to the database

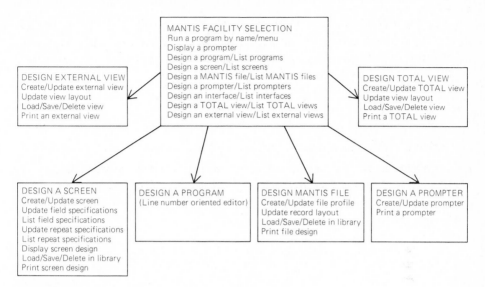

Figure 13-5
Overview of MANTIS screens. (Courtesy of Cincom, Inc.)

- Integrated data dictionaries
- Graphics capabilities
- Interactive editor for interactive update and retrieval
- High-level instructions that reduce number of program instructions required (say to ten percent of instructions in comparable COBOL program)
- Interfaces to other programming languages such as COBOL and FORTRAN

An overview of the VDT screens used by a very high level language (MANTIS) provides some insight into how a high-level language is used in development. Starting from a menu of major tasks, a developer selects from a menu of "task screens" (Figure 13-5).

The concepts inherent in fourth generation application development software are also commonly applied to software support for personal computers. The user is "online," there is interactive, relatively simple dialog, etc. Several microcomputer software vendors provide integrated, consistent, high-level development facilities for defining and processing files, queries, updates, reports, data screens, menus, texts, images, graphs, etc. In many respects, the microcomputer software equals or exceeds mainframe software in terms of its coherence, completeness, and user-oriented characteristics.

PRODUCTIVITY IMPROVEMENT WITH A FOURTH GENERATION LANGUAGE

The American Bankers Association (ABA) provides extensive services to its member banks. It handles government relations, runs about 60 conferences, and provides 4,000 products. It also keeps records on almost 900,000 bank employees who have attended educational courses of the American Institute of Banking.

The director of information systems reports they are doing work with a staff of seven that outside consultants said would require a staff of 60 to 75. He credits the productivity to the use of a fourth generation language. "It lets you sit at a terminal and think you are playing with a simple inquiry language, but it does everything COBOL does...with things like new reports, the user expectation becomes three hours instead of three weeks."

DP professionals always ask about efficiency of the fourth generation software. The director admits he uses more equipment but also a lot less people. He claims the total cost is lower.

Lois Paul, "MIS Managers, Staff of Seven Hike Output from 75 to 6,900 Programs in Seven Years," *Computerworld*, May 9, 1983, p. 11.

The advantages of a fourth generation language are impressive: faster, cheaper development of applications that are easier to maintain. The savings in development time

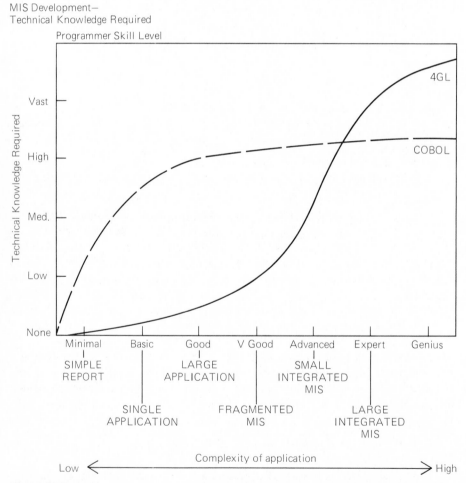

Figure 13-6
Developer knowledge level rises with increase in complexity of application. (Adapted from Nigel S. Read and Douglas L. Harmon, "Assuring MIS Success," *Datamation*, February 1981.)

are very significant. Some possible drawbacks have been reported based on one company's experience:[13]

    1 Computer resource usage is high. One application required up to 50 percent more resources (and five or six times more with poor database design), but on average their experience was 10 to 30 percent more.
    2 Program transportability is poor.
    3 Computation intensive work (scientific processing) is not efficient.

Nonprogrammers with fairly little training can use fourth generation software for report generation using single files. More complex usage requires a programmer with a relatively high skill level. The programmer skill level required for simple to complex applications is estimated in Figure 13-6.

On balance, however, very high level languages offer a significant advantage at every level of programming—from average user to expert professional. They also provide the capabilities needed to build and maintain a management information system containing reporting, applications, support system applications, and end-user development.

Expert Assistance

End users can perform much of their development and use without assistance. However, there need to be people who can provide assistance with difficult problems and guide or chauffeur users. These experts tend to be of two types:

    1 Local experts. Individuals in an organizational unit who have acquired knowledge and experience and aid newer users. A few users will tend to dominate as local experts.
    2 Information system personnel.

The concept of expert assistance is applicable also to end-user access to external databases. Research by Culnan[14] indicates that chauffeured access is most effective for nonrecurring requirements, probably because an individual with a one-time need does not wish to invest effort in learning the system for only one retrieval. More frequent users are willing to make the learning investment in order to directly access the system and eliminate an intermediary.

Information Centers to Support End Users

The concept of an information center for support of end users as developers was briefly described in Chapter 5 and is discussed in detail here. The information center (the term was first used by IBM) is based on a concept of providing end users with direct, ready access to computation and information processing resources through a central facility. Hardware, software, training, and consulting assist users to apply information resources to their problems. Specific support includes:

---

[13]N. S. Read and D. L. Harmon, "Assuring MIS Success," *Datamation*, February 1981, pp. 109–120.
    [14]M. J. Culnan, "Chauffeured Versus End-User Access to Commercial Databases: The Effects of Tasks and Individual Differences," *MIS Quarterly*, 7:1, March 1983, pp. 56–67.

- Technical assistance in writing instructions in a very high level language
- Education in the use of high level languages and development tools
- Assistance in accessing data
- Assistance in debugging
- Access to reference material on facilities, databases, etc.
- Administrative support with various computing procedures

Information center personnel generally act as teachers and consultants to users but usually do not program applications themselves. Thus, there can be a fairly small staff with a strong knowledge of the hardware, software, and databases to be utilized and who can teach and counsel users. The information center is a centralized support organization with all the advantages of having a centralized staff and facilities but with the disadvantage of lacking support tailored to particular applications or user functions.

Providing appropriate software for users of the information center is a key element in the concept of aiding users to do their own applications. The typical software in an information center will usually include the following:

- Query software to answer nonroutine information requests. It should allow questions to be formulated in familiar user terms.
- Graphics software to display data in graphic formats.
- Editor to compose, store, retrieve, and print documents.
- Report generator software to produce customized reports easily.
- A financial modeling and planning language.
- A very high level language for programming.
- One or more programming languages useful for end-user programming (such as APL or BASIC).

EXAMPLES OF INFORMATION CENTERS

North American Philips has a Solutions Center at its New York headquarters. It serves as a demonstration site for new equipment and new procedures, provides training sessions to groups from various divisions, and provides tools for non-DP people to perform their functions.

GTE Laboratories in Waltham, Massachusetts, has an information center with a large computer serving 250 visual display terminals located in the lab and in corporate offices. Users employ the terminals to access programs for text processing, financial planning, report analysis, query processing, and modeling. The system also includes graphics. About 100 individuals attend regular information center classes.

Blue Cross and Blue Shield of Michigan have a walk-in facility with two color graphics terminals and printer terminals online to a computer installed to support the center. Two full-time staff members provide training and assistance.

Alyeska Pipeline Service Company had a two- to four-year backlog of work in application development. After an information center was implemented, the backlog was cut in half. In one area, the financial department, it went from five years to zero. One of the first software products installed was an easy-to-use report writer package for professionals. A financial planning language and APL, BASIC, and FORTRAN were added. The center now has 200 users and a staff of two people. The center uses the existing computer systems, but added minicomputers for word processing.

Excerpt from "The Information Center," *IBM Information Processing*, 2:1, March 1983, pp. 12–27.

ORGANIZATIONAL CONSIDERATIONS WHEN USERS ARE DEVELOPERS

Although there are significant advantages to user-developed systems, there are also significant problems. The fundamental problem is the low development discipline of users. Information systems personnel generally accept and follow procedures and rules (a development discipline) that represent a codification of experience in application development. Users as new developers do not easily adopt this development discipline; they must obtain it through training, experience, and policies and procedures.

Advantages of User-developed Systems

There are three advantages to an organization in having users develop their own information system applications:

1 *Relieves shortage of system development personnel.* A common user complaint is that there are not enough analysts and programmers to keep up with the demand for new systems. There are several alternative solutions to this problem:

- Make analysts and programmers more productive
- Use more software packages
- Transfer development function to users

The latter alternative is appropriate when users can do the task satisfactorily and have adequate application development facilities.

2 *Eliminates the problem of information requirements determination by information systems personnel.* One of the major problems in information systems development is the need to elicit a complete and correct set of requirements (to be discussed in Chapter 15). Various methodologies have been proposed but it still remains a difficult process. The problem is made more difficult because the analyst is an outsider who must communicate with a user in eliciting the requirements. Having users develop their own systems eliminates the problems of inadequate communication between analyst and user. It does not eliminate the problem of obtaining requirements, but it places an "insider" in the role of requirements problem solver.

3 *Transfers the information system implementation process to users.* Poor implementation is one of the major reasons systems are not utilized. Difficulties arise from the interaction of the "expert" analysts and the nontechnical users who are providing requirements for the system. Users may develop less sophisticated systems when they do their own design and development, but they are more likely to use them.

A HYPOTHETICAL EXAMPLE OF PROBLEMS WITH A USER-DEVELOPED SYSTEM

The rapid decline and collapse of the XY Corporation has had financial analysts puzzled. In reconstructing the events that led to the bankruptcy, a reporter was able to identify some key decisions and actions that precipitated the rapid decline.

1 The XY Corporation was in negotiations to acquire the Kando Company. Thomas Lonnasen, financial vice president, was in charge of the proposal. Using a personal computer in his office, he constructed a model of the XY Corporation before and after the acquisition. Based on his model, he arrived at a purchase offer using stock in XY. Unfortunately, the acquisition model was faulty, so that the offer was excessive by 150 percent.

2 The owners of Kando Company immediately accepted the offer with the provision that there be no restrictions on their sale of the XY stock received.

3 The Kando holders of XY stock sold out immediately, depressing the price of XY stock by 40 percent.

4 XY delayed a large planned stock offering and added to its bank borrowing but was unable to borrow enough to carry out the integration of Kando. Planned savings were not achieved.

5 Due to a drop in profits, the bank demanded immediate payment of loans. The result was involuntary bankruptcy.

Organizational Risks from User-developed Systems

The advantages of user-developed systems are impressive. However, there are serious risks in the elimination of the analyst as a developer. Some major risks are:

1 *The risk from elimination of separation of the functions of user and analyst.* It is not sufficient to merely build and use support systems; they must meet organizational objectives and meet a level of quality and completeness that is appropriate to the organizational unit and decision activity. The analyst, in eliciting requirements and analyzing needs from a user, provides an "outside" review. User needs are questioned and alternatives suggested and discussed. Organizational experience with independent review suggests that this is often an important function. The use of an analyst in the development process also provides an organizational mechanism for enforcing appropriate standards and practices for documentation, controls, testing, interfaces with other systems, etc.

2 *The risk from limits on user ability to identify correct and complete requirements for an application.* The frequently observed difficulty of users in identifying a correct and complete set of requirements are described further in Chapter 15. Essentially, they result from:

- Human cognitive limits affecting requirements. The net effect of these limits is a significant bias toward requirements based on current procedures, currently available information, recent events, and inferences from small samples of events.
- Errors in selection of models for the problem. A characteristic of good analysis is the selection and use of an appropriate model for the problem to be solved.

3 *The risk from lack of user knowledge and acceptance of application quality assurance procedures for development and operation.* These risks occur as a result of reluctance to apply adequate procedures for:

- Testing
- Documentation
- Validation and other programmed assurance processes
- Audit trails
- Operating controls

Users developing their own systems may significantly underestimate the probability of errors and discount the need for and value of quality assurance and testing procedures, particularly if the systems are designed primarily for their own use.

4 *The risk from unstable user systems.* Most organizational processes depend on stable systems. This is especially true when tasks are pooled or are sequentially independent. Communication among subsystems will increase dramatically without stable interfaces such as standard procedures and decision rules. Users writing their own systems may tend to ignore this organizational need in writing for their own changing requirements.

5 *The risk from encouraging private information systems.* The complete information system of an organization is composed of systems that are formal or informal and public or private (see Chapter 2). User-developed systems, by promoting private formal systems, encourage information hiding by individuals. It is also difficult to transfer private systems to new persons taking over a position.

6 *The risk from permitting undesirable information behavior.* Uses can accumulate unused information, use information as a symbol, etc. (see Chapter 8) without the constraints imposed by formal application development.

Organizational Policies and Procedures for
User System Quality Assurance

The rapid growth in end-user computing has several implications for organizational policy. Rockart and Flannery[15] point out that despite the rapid growth in end-user computing in the organizations they studied, there was a noticeable lack of organizational strategies for promoting, managing, or controlling it. In order to take full advantage of the trend to end-user computing, organizations need to enforce a reasonable level of development discipline:

1 By the software development system. The software used to develop applications can either perform or enforce the performance of quality control procedures.

2 By organizational policies regarding review and quality assurance.

3 By training.

The trend in fourth generation software is to automatically generate some standard controls and quality assurance procedures. For example, a query to a database to retrieve records based on selection criteria may display not only the selected records but also the number of records that were utilized in the search process. The latter count is a control total to ensure that the complete database was searched. A second trend is to enforce data integrity by defining the criteria for integrity when data items are defined. The criteria are the basis for automatic generation of data validation procedures. For example, development software may request data specifications such as the following:

- Name for the data item
- Type (character, numeric, or a date)
- Length (maximum number of characters)
- Default value if no value is input
- Range of allowable values
- Input pattern or format in which data must be input

Because of the advantages of user-developed systems, organizational policy should normally encourage this approach. However, policies should also establish guidelines and responsibilities for quality assurance. Some examples of quality assurance policies are the following:

1 Each user has responsibility for appropriate quality assurance and review.

---

[15]Rockart and Flannery, ''The Management of End User Computing.''

2 Quality assurance and review procedures should be based on the intended use of the model and the importance of the decisions from its use.

3 Alternative levels of review are:

   a No outside review

   b Colleague in same function

   c Outside analyst review

   d Review group

Issues requiring training include several quality assurance procedures frequently omitted by users:

1 Testing. Testing is a difficult and time consuming process and users are likely to ignore the range of testing that is desirable because of their confidence in the system and in simple, cursory testing.

2 Documentation. User-developed systems may need less formal documentation than large applications, but some documentation is usually desirable. The extent of documentation may depend on the use of the application. Documentation is important for quality assurance procedures such as reviews. It is also important to future modification. The tendency is to avoid documentation, and user development software should enforce minimum documentation.

The idea of "throw away" code has been proposed. The suggestion is that a program written for a single use needs no documentation. Experience suggests that a large number of "throw away" programs are saved and thus need documentation.

3 Validation of data. All input data should be validated and echoed back to the person doing the input. There should be record counts, control counts, crossfooting tests, tests for reasonableness, etc. As explained earlier, these assurance procedures need to be enforced by the software development system.

4 Audit trails. Users will frequently omit audit trails because they do not appreciate the need for them. Any report figure should be traceable back to its constituent data items or any data item should be traceable forward to its impact on results and its inclusion in result figures. The output from a model should provide tracing pointers and intermediate outputs, so that any recipient can evaluate the assumptions of the model and the processing flow.

5 Operating control. A model should include quality assurance procedures to make sure the results at execution time are correct, i.e., all input data items have been entered and are valid, all records are processed, and results are compared to independent control figures.

6 Backup and recovery. Backup and recovery should be enforced by the software development systems, but the user should evaluate whether backup is adequate and recovery procedures can be applied.

DEVELOPMENT SUPPORT FOR INFORMATION SYSTEM PROFESSIONALS

A major area of knowledge work in organizations is the work of information systems analysts and programmers in developing and maintaining applications. A knowledge work support system tailored to information system application development has been called a *programmer's workbench*.

The value of a programmer's workbench is illustrated by contrasting it with a more traditional approach to systems analysis and programming without good development support. The traditional work support tools for analysts and programmers in a development group consist of pens, pencils, pads, and coding sheets. Program code (say in COBOL) is written in pencil on coding sheets, and the sheets are key-entered by the data entry personnel. The coded programs are compiled as special jobs in between regular data processing runs. A programmer may have to wait an hour or as long as a day for output in order to debug a program. All documentation is written by hand and typed by the typing pool. The development staff proofread the drafts and send them back for correction. One document cycle may take a week. Considerable work is involved in maintaining files of printouts, drafts of documentation, etc. Documentation is usually not up to date because it is so time consuming to have corrections done. In order to accommodate the delays in compilation and test runs of programs, programmers usually work on several programs at once. This causes extra mental effort to switch from one job to another.

Contrast the above lack of productivity support with development support designed to maximize productivity of development personnel. The facilities include:

1 Hardware for development tasks:

- A computer dedicated to development so there is no conflict with the data processing production computer.
- An online terminal (for every professional) connected to the development computer.

2 Software tools for development:

- Interactive programming software to allow online programming (write, edit, store, and test programs online) from the terminal and instant turnaround.
- Programming language facilities suited to the type of applications being developed. This includes preprocessors to reduce coding.
- Application generators to simplify programming of applications for which they apply. Examples are interactive programs to build application programs from screen specifications and processing rules.
- Report generator for report jobs.
- Query language for query jobs.
- Online documentation software to allow the programmer and analyst to prepare documentation online in parallel with development and to make changes easily.
- Data dictionary for keeping track of data definitions.

3 Methodologies to support development, such as scheduling, prototyping, etc.

The hardware and software support listed above can improve productivity of analysts and programmers significantly. This is an example of an important trade off: as the cost of technology decreases and the cost of personnel increases, it makes sense to increase the capacity of the former in order to improve the performance of the latter. Methodologies to support development are discussed further in Chapter 18.

IMPACT OF TECHNOLOGY ON THE NATURE OF KNOWLEDGE WORK

There has been some speculation that heavy utilization of computer and communications technology in the performance of knowledge work will have subtle but profound effects on the nature of work itself. Some potential effects are discussed in this section.

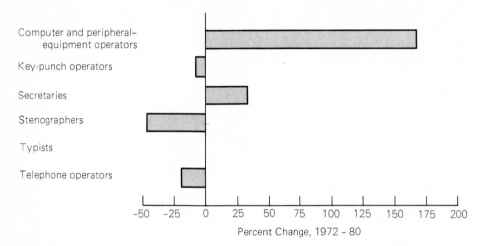

Figure 13-7
Changing nature of clerical office work, 1972-1980. (Source: Presentation by Capers Jones.)

Changes in Work Roles

A relatively arbitrary but useful distinction can be made between three different roles in white-collar or office work:
—Clerical-secretarial
—Professional
—Managerial

It should be clear from the foregoing discussion that although there are components of knowledge work in all three roles, emphasis in technological support has been on professional and managerial roles. However, the potential impacts on these two job types affect clerical roles as well.

Two different scenarios can be described of the impact of technology on clerical work. Generally, both are based on the assumption that clerical work will become more technology-intensive, more specialized, and more centrally controlled through an administrative hierarchy. Figure 13-7 shows the shift in clerical jobs between 1972 and 1980, clearly demonstrating increasing reliance on computer-based technology.

In one scenario, the difference between clerical and professional jobs will become more pronounced. Clerical jobs will become "deskilled, fragmented, routinized."[16] Division of labor will occur in such a way that each remaining job requires minimal training, little career potential, and easy replaceability. There is also, in some views, increased potential for differential treatment of clerical employees; work can be rewarded through piece rates and differential pay and benefits.

An alternative scenario is based on a blurring of the boundaries between clerical and professional jobs rather than a greater separation. In this view, clerical work evolves into

---

[16]J. Gregory and K. Nussbaum, "Race against Time: Automation of the Office," *Office: Technology and People*, 1:2–3, September 1982.

an administrative hierarchy of "information specialists," with opportunity for skill enhancement and increased career potential. Work can be organized to provide "job enrichment" (discussed in Chapter 11) where each worker performs a greater variety of tasks and has basic responsibility for all support requirements for a single work unit or principal.

The technological facilities discussed in this chapter and elsewhere in the book can be designed to support either scenario of clerical work. The nature of the implementation of the technology determines whether new clerical jobs are deskilled or enriched. Strategies for implementation of technology which encourage the positive scenario will be discussed in Chapter 18.

The impacts of technological support on professional and managerial roles are more subtle. Much of the "busy work" of a clerical nature is streamlined. Technology-based communications is under greater control of the individual because of its asynchronous nature; to some extent this replaces a critical "gatekeeping" function traditionally supplied by a personal secretary.

Another change for professionals is that most of the tools they need to perform their jobs are available via the nearest telephone line and terminal. Employees may work remotely from each other. This means they may be assigned to work groups without being relocated, increasing organizational flexibility in project assignments.

Changes in Supervision

The fact that employee work is performed online and stored electronically introduces the possibility for greater "electronic supervision." For clerical work, this can mean short-term, external pacing of work as well as close monitoring of key strokes, number of lines typed, etc. Many word processing systems now have the capability for electronic monitoring of work with results recorded at a supervisory workstation.

For professional employees whose work is often measured by completion of long-term deliverables, "remote supervision" implies greater emphasis on deliverables and less on face-to-face contact. This is especially true if employees work in geographically dispersed locations away from their supervisors. In general, the supervisory process may become more formalized, with greater reliance on procedures and measurable outputs than informal processes.

The Information Mediator

An interesting, potential side impact of the intelligent workstation concept is the relationship between the organization and the consumer. It has been proposed that through an integration of many functions that traditionally were specialized, the role of an "information mediator" is created.[17] The customer is presented with a single organizational contact who has access through a workstation to all administrative functions. This arrangement results in a decrease in total communications required to respond to customers and increased efficiency in dealing with them.

---

[17] Paul Strassman, Xerox Corporation

SUMMARY

The chapter explains how computer-based facilities can support knowledge work. Knowledge work involves thinking; using and processing information; and formulating analyses, recommendations, and procedures. Knowledge work tasks are diagnosis and problem finding, planning and decision making, monitoring and control, organizing and scheduling, authoring and presentation, communication, and system development. The technology affecting knowledge work includes personal computers, communications networks, and intelligent workstations. The different technological components are most effective when they are integrated.

Support facilities for knowledge work include text and word processing, data storage and retrieval, communication facilities, decision support systems, graphics, and end-user application development facilities. End-user computing refers to a major shift toward having users directly control their own application development and operation. It represents an evolving trend in information systems in organizations. Very high level (fourth generation) software development systems provide improved software support for end-user development; an organizational aid is the information center. End-user development of applications has many advantages, but there are some disadvantages. An organization should have policies that encourage end-user development but result in adequate quality assurance. One special area of knowledge work support is a development support system for information system professionals.

The use of support systems for knowledge work is one of the very important developments affecting individual work roles and organizational behavior. It may change roles in organizations, provide possibilities for changing patterns of supervision, and result in roles such as the information mediator to interface between the organization and its customers.

MINICASES

1 EXECUTIVE WORKSTATIONS AND MANAGERIAL PRODUCTIVITY

In 1980 TRW, a Fortune 500 manufacturer of electronic components and computer systems, decided to see if "executive workstations" really deliver what they promise.

Before the project was implemented, a study was conducted to determine how much time managers actually spend on various office activities. The research staff found the following uses of managers' time:

Meetings	34%
Supervisory activities	24%
Preparing reports	8%
Telephone calls	6%
Research and planning projects	6%
Travel	4%
Miscellaneous activities	17%

Forty employees located at four TRW sites within a 10-mile radius participated in the project. They included managers, senior professionals, and secretaries. An integrated office management system was chosen. Its capabilities included electronic mail, word processing, calendar management, telephone directories, personal computing and computer-based instruction. TRW programmers added other features, including a user's personal menu, a "suggestion box," and a remote-dial capability that allows users to dial into the company's timesharing system.

Preliminary findings show that the system can potentially save managers and professionals approximately an hour a day by cutting out certain routine tasks and paperwork and improving communications via electronic mail. Communication by electronic mail has eliminated some meetings but, more important, it is cutting down on missed telephone calls, message writing and the numerous other frustrations that are associated with telephone tag. In addition, the calendar function eliminates the telephone chores and paperwork normally required to arrange meetings. A survey showed that managers were utilizing electronic mail 65 percent of the time they were using the system. Other frequently used features included the calendar, word processing, and the telephone directory.

Based on a random sampling of employees' computer files, the TRW staff anticipated that employees using electronic mail as a substitute for telephone calls and meetings would spend an average of 4.8 hours a day communicating, a decrease from the 5.5 hours previously needed for that purpose. Other predicted savings were seen in reducing the time spent on paperwork from 2.5 to 2 hours per day through automatic filing, retrieval, and word processing procedures.

Based on Guy Talbott, "In Search of Management Productivity," *Today's Office*, Hearst Business Communications, Inc., May 1983, pp. 65–69.

Questions

a How would such a system be cost-justified to executive management?
b How can the system be evaluated? Can time savings be translated directly into productivity gains?

2 APPLYING THE WRONG MODEL

Refer back to the vignette on page 314, "Using the Wrong Statistical Forecasting Technique Gives the Wrong Answer." A staff person did a least squares regression on the logs of historical sales.

Questions

a What was the role of the user-developed system in the failure?
b Would the failure have been perceived differently if the analysis had been done by a systems analyst?
c Would a policy of quality assurance of user-developed systems have an effect in this case?
d What else would have prevented the error?

EXERCISES

1 What types of knowledge work activities would you expect to be performed by the following:
  a A salesperson of large mainframe computers
  b A retail department store buyer
  c An external auditor
  d An accounts payable clerk
  e A market research analyst
  f A regional sales manager of industrial goods
  g A bank loan officer
2 What technological support facilities would be most important in the intelligent workstations of those employees listed in question 1?

3 What is the difference between an intelligent workstation and the following:
  a A visual display terminal with modem
  b A personal computer
  c A word processor

4 What is the significance of integration of facilities in the workstation environment?

5 How are physical and functional integration related in a workstation environment?

6 Why would an end user not do the programming for his or her applications?

7 Why would an end user key in data from company reports?

8 What is a fourth generation language (4GL)? One author listed the four generations as:

Generation	Description
1	Machine language
2	Assembly language
3	Procedure-oriented language
4	Nonprocedural language

Comment on the difference between the above and the explanation in the text.

9 Suppose you are programming in a very high-level language and come to a part of the problem that you know would be handled inefficiently by the 4GL. Comment on the following alternatives:

a Use the 4GL and take the inefficiency.

b Use the exit facilities of the 4GL to attach a COBOL routine to do the processing in question.

c Do the entire project in COBOL.

10 Why do end users find fourth generation languages easy to use even if they contain very complex facilities?

11 Why can microcomputer software vendors very quickly provide very high level integrated development systems for the personal computer, yet these facilities have taken many years to implement for mainframes?

12 The information center is a centralized concept. How can it be implemented in a decentralized environment?

13 One installation described the service they provided for financial planning as: users get four hours access to the system—two in the morning and two in the evening. Discuss the pros and cons of this policy.

14 If a programmer's workbench improves programmer productivity, why don't all installations have them?

15 "No end user is going to access my database," said the controller. Comment on her reasons and on opposing views that might be presented to the president for resolution.

16 Estimate the percent of time you spend on various knowledge work activities and then explain how a knowledge work support system could aid you.

17 Keyboarding is not managerial work. Does this limit the use of personal workstations by managers?

18 Estimate the productivity improvement necessary to justify workstations costing $10,000 each. Assume pay rates for managerial and clerical users and a three-year life for equipment.

19 One large company is reported to require a notice "Prepared on a microcomputer" on all analysis prepared on personal computers. Comment on possible reasons for the policy and the effectiveness of the notice.

20 Knowledge work often requires access to external databases. How can "internal experts" aid a user in locating external data? What is the role of an information expert (such as reference librarian) in searching for external data?

SELECTED REFERENCES

Abbey, Scott G.: "COBOL Dumped," *Datamation*, January 1984, pp. 108–114.

Alloway, Robert M., and Judith A. Quillard: "User Managers' Systems Needs," *MIS Quarterly*, 7:2, June 1983, pp. 27–41.

Bechhoefer, Arthur: "Electronic Publishing: The New Newsletter," *Byte*, May 1983, pp. 124–129.

Culnan, Mary J.: "Chauffeured Versus End-User Access to Commercial Databases: The Effects of Task and Individual Differences," *MIS Quarterly*, 7:1, March 1983, pp. 55–67.

Gremillion, Lee L., and Phillip Pyburn: "Breaking the Systems Development Bottleneck," *Harvard Business Review*, March–April 1983, pp. 130–137.

Hammond, L. W.: "Management Considerations for an Information Center," *IBM Systems Journal*, 21:2, 1982, pp. 131–161.

"How Work Will Change," *EDP Analyzer*, 21:4 and 21:5, April and May, 1983.

Johnson, Richard T.: "The Infocenter Experience," *Datamation*, January 1984, pp. 137–142.

Kiechel, W.: "Everything You Always Wanted to Know May Soon Be On-line," *Fortune*, May 5, 1980, pp. 226–240.

Lucas, H. C.: "The Use of an Interactive Information Storage and Retrieval System in Medical Research," *Communications of the ACM*, 21:3, March 1978.

Martin, James: *Application Development without Programmers*, Prentice-Hall, Englewood Cliffs, NJ, 1982.

McCartney, Laton: "The New Information Centers," *Datamation*, July 1983, pp. 30–46.

McLean, E. R.: "End Users as Application Developers," *MIS Quarterly*, 3:4, December 1979, pp. 37–46.

Mintzberg, Henry: *The Nature of Managerial Work*, Harper & Row, New York, 1973.

Olson, M. H.: "New Information Technology and Organizational Culture," *MIS Quarterly*, 6:5, Special Issue 1982, pp. 71–92.

Olson, M. H., and H. C. Lucas, Jr.: "The Impact of Office Automation on the Organization: Some Implications for Research and Practice," *Communications of the ACM*, 25:11, November 1982, pp. 838–847.

Papageorgiou, John C.: "Decision Making in the Year 2000," *Interfaces*, 13:2, April 1983, pp. 77–86.

"Plan Now for Work Stations," *EDP Analyzer*, 21:2, February 1983.

Poppel, Harvey L.: "Who Needs the Office of the Future?" *Harvard Business Review*, November–December 1982, pp. 146–167.

Rockart, J. R., and L. Flannery: "The Management of End User Computing," *Communications of the ACM*, 26:10, October 1983, pp. 776–784.

Rockart, J. R., and M. E. Treacy: "The CEO Goes On-line," *Harvard Business Review*, 16:1, January–February 1982, pp. 82–88.

Ulrich, Walter: "Current Issues in Electronic Mail—Heralding a New Era," *AFIPS Conference Proceedings*, 1983, pp. 361–365.

INFORMATION SYSTEM
REQUIREMENTS

Correct and complete information requirements are key ingredients in planning organizational information systems, in implementing information systems applications, and in building databases. Despite trends to provide direct support to users as described in Section Four, major information system applications integrated with databases require careful planning and significant cooperative effort between users and information system professionals. Information requirements determination is a vital part of this cooperative activity. Users are the fundamental source of requirements, but it is difficult for users to define them. Inexperienced analysts often feel that users should tell them what the information requirements are so they can get on with the design and implementation of the system. Experienced analysts know that eliciting correct and complete requirements is one of their most challenging tasks. This section covers a range of topics related to information requirements determination. It should aid both users and analysts to understand better the process of the determination of information requirements and to improve their performance in this task.

There are four chapters in the section each covering a different area of information requirements.

Chapter	Title	Notes on content
14	Developing a Long-Range Information System Plan.	High-level requirements describe the overall structure of the information system and define and assign priorities to the portfolio of proposed applications.

Chapter	Title	Notes on content
15	Strategies for the Determination of Information Requirements.	Depending on the situation, the user or analyst may select a different strategy for obtaining information requirements. This chapter outlines the strategies and gives examples of methods that fit each strategy.
16	Database Requirements.	If a database is to contain the data items needed for most queries, there must be a method for eliciting the set of data items to be included and their relationships. Data modeling is a general approach to this problem.
17	User Interface Requirements	Having an overall architecture, defining information requirements, and defining database content are not sufficient if the system is not usable. User interface requirements for a well-designed system are described in this chapter.

The set of chapters thus provides strategies, methods, and concepts to aid users and analysts to define four sets of requirements: the overall plan, application information requirements, database content, and user interface requirements.

CHAPTER 14

DEVELOPING A LONG-RANGE INFORMATION SYSTEM PLAN

RESOURCE ALLOCATION
  Comparative Cost or Benefit
  Portfolio Approach
  Chargeout
  Steering Committee Ranking
SUMMARY
MINICASES
EXERCISES
SELECTED REFERENCES

The complexity of the information resources environment suggests that planning is vital to success. This chapter surveys the development of an information system plan and outlines the contents of the plan. A stage model of information system growth, which may aid in the development of a plan, is described. There are a variety of methodologies for information system planning; these are classified using a three-stage model. The three stages of strategic planning, organizational information requirements analysis, and resource allocation are then described in more detail.

   The type of plan assumed in the chapter is a comprehensive information resources plan which includes all areas of information handling assigned to the chief information executive. The plan will be referred to as an information system plan, master development plan, or information resources plan. The terms are used interchangeably to refer to the comprehensive plan for use of information technology to support organizational strategies, goals, and processes.

PLANNING FOR INFORMATION SYSTEMS

The value of planning is well understood. Companies that plan tend to achieve better results than companies that do not, yet many organizations do not plan or do it poorly.

PLANNING SHORTFALLS

"A 1980 Diebold Research Program survey of 150 major corporations...revealed that fully two-thirds (of MIS departments) had a formal planning process with published plans. However, a closer look at these findings shows that 63% of the plans are for three years or less. In other words, only one-fourth of all departments have plans that extend beyond their current backlogs of work.

   "A July 1981 sampling of 40 major corporations...revealed how serious the shortfall is in communications planning. Fully 62.5%—25 companies—had either just started planning in the past year or had no plans whatsoever."

   The Diebold Group, Inc., "Information Processing—An Action Plan for the '80s," *Newsweek*, Special Advertising Section, September 21, 1981.

   An information system is complex and therefore needs an overall plan to guide its initial development and subsequent change. The plan describes the structure and content

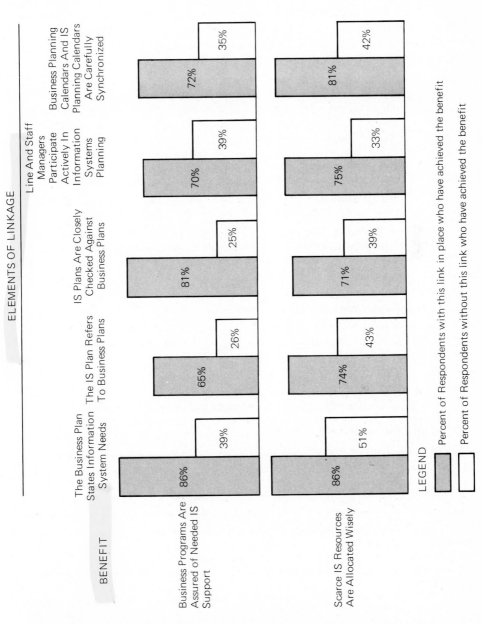

Figure 14-1
Impact of linkage on achievement of information system planning benefits. (Source: *Information Systems Planning to Meet Business Objectives: A Survey of Practice*, Cresap, McCormick and Paget, New York, 1983, p. 7)

of the information system and how it is to be developed. Since all projects cannot be developed and implemented concurrently, priorities must be set. As with other resources in an organization, information resources are scarce. In a dynamic organization there are more opportunities for information system applications than can be handled at one time, and therefore an allocation process must be worked out. The master plan, once developed, does not remain constant but must be updated as new developments occur.

A very important fundamental concept of information system planning is that the organization's strategic plan should be the basis for the MIS strategic plan. Alignment of MIS strategy with organizational strategy is one of the central problems of MIS planning. Methods for achieving this alignment will be discussed later in the chapter.

SURVEY RESULTS: INFORMATION SYSTEMS PLANNING STANDS A GREATER CHANCE OF SUCCESS IF...

A survey of 334 corporations by Cresap, McCormick and Paget, Inc., a management consulting firm, provided evidence that information systems planning stands a greater chance of achieving desired benefits if it is closely linked to the organization's overall business plan. The benefits to be achieved from planning are:

   1 Ensure that overall business programs receive the information systems support they need
   2 Allocate information systems resources wisely

The survey indicated that the planning success of firms using a methodology with links between business and information systems planning surpassed the firms that did not (Figure 14-1). Linkage elements were:

   1 The business plan states information needs
   2 The information system plan refers to business plans
   3 Information system plans are closely checked against business plans
   4 Line and staff managers actively participate in information systems planning
   5 Information systems and business planning calendars are synchronized.

Information Systems Planning to Meet Business Objectives: A Survey of Practices, Cresap, McCormick and Paget, New York, 1983.

There are different approaches to organizing and supervising the information system planning effort. The overall responsibility for MIS planning should be the overall responsibility of the chief information officer (CIO). For the development of a plan, the staffing alternatives are:

Organization for development of plan	Comments on effectiveness
Planning staff within information systems function	There are benefits from use of planning specialists, and completion of the plan is likely because it is a primary assignment of the planning staff. A disadvantage is the separation of planning from the operating level, and so planners "lose touch."

| Ad hoc planning groups within information systems | Working-level experience is valuable in planning, but planning expertise may be low. It may be difficult to allocate appropriate time for planning. |
| Planning group with representatives from various functions | The plan reflects the views of the organization being served by it. This approach aids in developing a political coalition in support of the plan. However, diversity of views and lack of interest by some participants may make it difficult to complete the plan. |

Review and approval of the plan by the functions being served by the information system is important, especially in negotiating project priorities and obtaining high-level support for the plan. In some companies, the review is performed by an information systems steering committee composed of executives from major functional areas plus the information systems executive. The steering committee reviews and approves the master development plan and also periodically reviews progress against the plan. When the information system plan has been completed, it can be presented to the organization's top planning committee for review, approval, and integration with other company plans.

It is desirable to define information system planning policies and procedures. These establish the information roles of various organizational units, the coordination and integration required by different functions planning for new or revised information resources, and the planning cycle. The allocation of tasks and the assignment of responsibilities to the information systems function should reflect the overall organizational philosophy, culture, and structure. The planning cycle for information systems should conform to the cycle for the organization plan, so that the information system plan can support and be merged into the overall plan.

CONTENT OF THE INFORMATION SYSTEM MASTER PLAN   *3-5yr Plan*

The master plan typically has two components—a long-range plan for three to five years (or longer) and a short-range plan for one year. The plan provides a basis for resource allocation and control. The long-range portion provides general guidelines for direction, and the short-range portion provides a basis for specific accountability as to operational and financial performance.

The master development plan establishes a framework for all detailed information system planning. In general, it contains four major sections:

1 Information system goals, objectives, and architecture
2 Inventory of current capabilities
3 Forecast of developments affecting the plan
4 The specific plan

Although a particular plan may not be organized this way, it should generally cover these topics. Each of these sections of the master development plan is described in more detail in the remainder of this section.

Information System Goals, Objectives, and Architecture

This section of the plan might contain descriptions of the following:

1 Organizational goals, objectives, and strategies
2 External environment (industry, government regulations, customers, and suppliers)
3 Internal organizational constraints such as management philosophy
4 Assumptions about business risks and potential consequences
5 Overall goals, objectives, and strategy for the information system
6 Architecture of the information system

Within the context of overall organizational goals, policy, objectives, strategies, and plans, there should be policy, goals, objectives, strategies, and plans for the information system. The general goals provide guidelines for the direction in which the information system effort should be directed. The objectives are more specific and should be stated so that performance or nonperformance may be measured. For example, a goal might be "to provide information resources on a timely basis to all organizational units." An objective might be "to provide periodic financial reports no later than 36 hours after the end of the period."

The overall architecture or structure of the information system provides a framework for detailed planning. The information architecture defines major categories of information and the major information subsystems or applications.

Current Capabilities

This is a summary of the current status of an information system. It includes such items as the following:

1 Inventory of:
   a Hardware
   b Generalized software (system software, database management system, etc.)
   c Application systems
   d Personnel
2 Analysis of:
   a Expense
   b Hardware utilization
   c Software utilization
   d Personnel utilization
3 Status of projects in process
4 Assessment of strengths and weaknesses

The purpose of the inventory is to clearly identify the current status of all systems. Applications may be classified by:

1 Major functional systems (such as accounting, marketing, human resources)
2 Organizational strategies (e.g., provide online ordering by customers)
3 Need for maintenance or revision:
   a Applications which are working reasonably well
   b Applications which require revised implementation or improvement
   c Applications which need to be substantially revised or completely replaced by new systems

In the case of personnel, useful classifications might include:

1 Job classification (programmer, operator, etc.)
2 Skill categories (COBOL programming, data communications, etc.)
3 Functional area experience (finance, accounting, manufacturing, etc.)

In each case, the classification should reflect planning concerns. For example, in planning for a shift to facilities for end-user computing, software might be classified with respect to users:

1 System software
   a For operations
   b For trained programmers
   c For both programmers and end users
   d For end users
2 Application software
   a Purchased or developed and supported by information systems personnel
   b Purchased or developed by users and supported by information systems personnel
   c Developed and supported only by users

Forecast of Developments Affecting the Plan

Planning is affected by current and anticipated technology. The impact of such developments as personal computers, local area networks, database management systems, and office automation should be reflected in the long-range plan. It is difficult to estimate technology far into the future, but most developments are announced one or more years before they become generally available. Broad technological changes can be perceived several years before they are implemented. For example, it was known for several years before business-quality personal computers became widely used that this technological development was imminent and that it would have a substantial impact on the design of future systems. Visual display terminals were available for several years before they became widely used. The technological advantages of using visual display were such that it was reasonably obvious they would be an important factor in future systems.

Software availability should also be forecast and the impact on future systems anticipated. For example, in 1965 when IBM announced the System 360, the software trend to COBOL as the dominant business procedural language was under way. Installations that perceived that trend correctly made better decisions than those which chose to ignore COBOL (and other procedure-oriented languages). In 1984, the trend in development software is to fourth generation languages. They are likely to have significant impact on future staffing, provisions for end-user computing, etc.

Methodology changes may also be forecast. As will be explained in Chapter 18, alternative development methodologies should be considered in place of or in addition to traditional life cycle methods. As another example, automated development tools are likely to have an impact and should be examined in the plan.

Environmental developments such as government regulations, tax laws, and competitor actions can also be included insofar as they affect information systems.

The Specific Plan

The plan should cover several years (say three to five) with the upcoming periods (say, the next one or two years) being reasonably specific. The next year should have sufficient detail to contain a budget. The plan should include:

1 Hardware acquisition schedule
2 Purchased software schedule:

- System software
- Applications software

3 Application development schedule
4 Software maintenance and conversion schedule
5 Personnel resources required and schedule of hiring and training
6 Financial resources required by object of expenditure (hardware, software, personnel, etc.) and by purpose (operations, maintenance, new development, etc.). Other classifications may also be useful.

Maintenance of the Master Plan

As each year passes, the information system plan requires updating. For example, the current status is updated with new equipment and changing personnel figures. Future plans are affected by changes in technology, experience with systems that have been developed, changing needs for new systems, and changes in the organization. For example, an organization may have acquired a new division; as a result, the necessity for common information processing, common codes, installation of common systems, etc., may affect the entire plan. A new hardware-software announcement may also affect future plans. Such developments should be assessed, and their impacts should be put into the revision of the plan. Pressures for changes in plans may come from internal events outside of information systems such as changing financial constraints. The master plan is also updated to reflect the status of systems installed and the progress of new systems.

Events in the external environment may also cause revisions of plans. Examples are government regulations, actions by competitors, etc.

THE NOLAN STAGE MODEL

Some computer-based information systems are relatively young; others are mature. The Nolan stage model is a framework for information system planning that matches various features of information systems to stages of growth. It is a contingency theory which states: IF these features exist THEN the information system is in this stage. The basic theme is that an organization must go through each stage of growth before it can progress to the next one; it thus provides a set of limits to planning if the organization's current stage of growth can be diagnosed.

Stages of Information System Growth

The basic stage model was described by Nolan in 1973–1974 in several articles, the most comprehensive being in the *Harvard Business Review* in 1974.[1] These articles identified four stages of information system growth (Figure 14-2**a**):

Stage of growth	Description
Initiation	Early use of computers by small number of users to meet basic organizational needs. Decentralized control and minimal planning.
Expansion (or contagion)	Experimentation with and adoption of computers by many users. Proliferation of applications. Crisis due to rapid rise in costs.
Formalization (or control)	Organizational controls established to contain growth in use and apply cost-effectiveness criteria. Centralization. Controls often prevent attainment of potential benefits.
Maturity (or integration)	Integration of applications. Controls adjusted. Planning well established. Alignment of information system to organization.

The growth curve of the Nolan model is the familiar sigmoid or S curve described in Chapter 11 as a general organizational growth cycle. In a subsequent 1979 *Harvard Business Review* article,[2] Nolan expanded the model to six stages (Figure 14-2**b**). He also proposed an alternative model in which major changes in technology eliminate the maturity stage. With the introduction of new hardware, software, and system designs, the organization starts on a new growth curve (Figure 14-2**c**).

Management responses to growth in computing are reflected in different levels of control or slack with each stage. Control is characterized by management systems and policies which ensure efficiency of computing use. Slack is the lack of controls and the availability of resources to experiment with application features not required to perform basic processing.

Stage	Levels of control or slack
I	Low control. Some slack. Little or no information system planning.
II	Greater slack in order to encourage use. Lack of planning. Costs rise and costs from lack of integration become visible.
III	High level of controls. Information system planning is given increased emphasis.
IV	Emphasis on integration. More emphasis on user control of information system costs. Use of databases.

---

[1]Cyrus F. Gibson and Richard L. Nolan, ''Managing the Four Stages of EDP Growth,'' *Harvard Business Review*, January–February 1974, pp. 76–88.

[2]Richard L. Nolan, ''Managing the Crises in Data Processing,'' *Harvard Business Review*, March–April 1979, pp. 115–126.

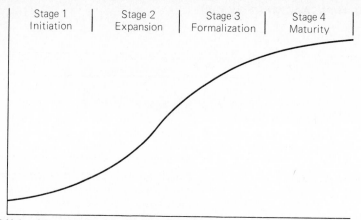

a The initial Nolan four-stage model of information system growth.

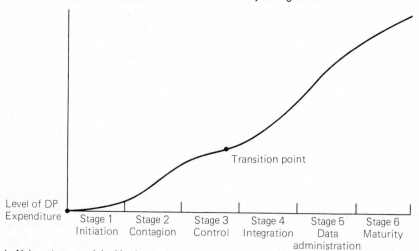

b Nolan stage model with six stages.

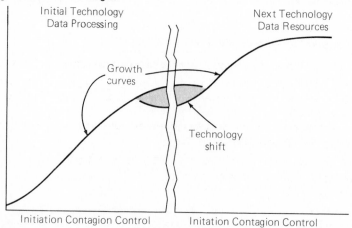

c Nolan stages of growth as three repeating stages after technology shift.

Figure 14-2
Nolan stage model.

Stage	Levels of control or slack
V	Focus on data administration. Some slack to encourage development of systems which contribute to strategic advantage of the organization.
VI	Application portfolio is complete and matches the organizational objectives.

Nolan makes certain assumptions about the growth dynamics of movement through the stages:

1 Organizational learning (as explained in Chapter 11) permits movement through stages. The limited experimentation of stage I is the basis for the contagion of stage II, and the contagious use allows diffusion of the technology before controls are applied.

2 Stages cannot be skipped because experience is necessary before the organization is ready for the next stage. If experimentation is not performed, there are no early users to promote contagion. If the organization goes from initiation to control, diffusion does not occur because controls stifle widespread trial-and-error use.

3 Although there are certain "natural" growth processes involved, the four growth processes can be planned, coordinated, and managed to move through the stages effectively and efficiently. Leadership styles and coalition building shift to meet the needs of each stage. The stages thus represent a sequence for planned and managed change.

Using the Stage Theory in Planning

The stage theory can be used both in diagnosis of current stage of growth and in planning changes to move in a controlled way to the next stage. Not all application subsystems grow at the same rate; accounting may be in stage III with controlled growth, while marketing should be encouraged to look for new applications (needs slack). Diagnosis and planning focus on a set of features associated with each growth process at each stage of growth (Figure 14-3).

An Evaluation of the Stage Theory

There is ample evidence of significant practitioner acceptance of the stage model:

1 Practitioners generally report it to have high explanatory value, or "face validity."

2 The model has had wide readership. It is one of the "classics" in the field based on frequency of citation.[3]

3 Over 200 studies of stages of growth in organizations have been performed by the consulting firm of Nolan and Norton, Inc.

The research evidence to date does not support the contingency relationship between stages and features associated with the four growth processes at each stage.[4] There may be several explanations for the lack of research evidence:

---

[3]B. Ives and S. Hamilton, "Knowledge Utilization among MIS Researchers," *MIS Quarterly*, 6:4, December, 1982, p. 67.

[4]I. Benbasat, A. S. Dexter, D. H. Drury, and R. C. Goldstein: "A Critique of the 'Stage Hypothesis': Theory and Empirical Evidence," *Communications of the ACM*, May 1984, pp. 476–485.

Growth Process \ Stage	I	II	III	IV	V	VI
Applications portfolio	Functional cost reduction applications	Proliferation	Upgrade documentation and restructure existing applications	Retrofit existing applications using database technology	Organization integration of applications	Application integration "mirroring" information flows
DP organization	Specialization for technological learning	User-oriented programmers	Middle management	Establish computer utility and user account teams	Data administration	Data resource management
DP planning and control	Lax	More lax	Formalized planning and control	Tailored planning and control systems	Shared data and common systems	Data resource strategic planning
User awareness	"Hands off"	Superficially enthusiastic	Arbitrarily held accountable	Accountability learning	Effectively accountable	Acceptance of joint user and data processing accountability

Figure 14-3
Matrix of features for growth processes at each stage of growth. (Reprinted by permission of *Harvard Business Review.* Excerpted from Exhibit 1 from Richard L. Nolan, "Managing the Crises in Data Processing," *Harvard Business Review,* March-April, pp. 115-126. Copyright © 1979 by the President and Fellows of Harvard College; all rights reserved.)

1 The research designs may not have been adequate.

2 Organizational contingency theories are difficult to "prove" by research because there are so many intervening variables and compensating behaviors.

3 The phenomenon of growth is continuous, yet the stages are discrete. In practice, shifts in stages and their accompanying features occur gradually and at different paces.

King and Kraemer[5] describe the Nolan model as an evolutionist model (a model that characterizes change by the direction the change is taking). The model describes the logic of change and the destination that is to be achieved. The strength of an evolutionist model and thus the strength of the Nolan model is its explanation of the logic of development. The weakness of an evolutionist model is lack of specificity; it does not define the mechanisms of change.

On balance, the Nolan stage model is a useful conceptual model to understand the general directions of change. At a conceptual level, it aids the planning process by providing a framework for understanding change. The diagnostic measurements and prescriptive elements of the model should be viewed as general guidelines for information system planning.

THE THREE-STAGE MODEL OF THE PLANNING PROCESS

A number of techniques have been proposed for information systems planning. A problem is to evaluate the place of a technique in the flow of activities for developing a long-range information plan and long-range information architecture. The three-stage model of information system planning developed by Bowman, Davis and Wetherbe[6] clarifies the generic planning activities, the order of the activities, and the alternative techniques and methodologies that apply (Figure 14-4).

Practical guidance for information system planning can be gained from the three-stage model. It can aid in recognizing the nature of the planning problems and in selecting the appropriate stage of planning. For example, an organization may view its information system function as not making an adequate contribution to organizational objectives. In seeking to resolve this problem, there may be a proposal to install a chargeout system (located in the resource allocation stage) to make information systems pay their own way. Another organization may conduct a business systems planning study (a type of organization information requirements analysis activity) to resolve the same problem of insufficient MIS contribution to organizational objectives. While these activities may result in improved information system services, the planning model suggests that they are probably not the appropriate methodologies in this situation. If the information system function is not responsive to the organization, the three-stage planning model indicates that a strategic alignment planning effort should precede organizational information requirements and resource allocation.

---

[5]John Leslie King and Kenneth L. Kraemer, "Evolution of Organizational Information Systems: An Assessment of Nolan's Stage Model," *Communications of the ACM*, May 1984, pp. 466–475.

[6]B. Bowman, G. B. Davis, and J. C. Wetherbe, "Modeling for MIS," *Datamation*, July 1980, pp. 155–162; and B. Bowman, G. B. Davis, and J. C. Wetherbe, "Three Stage Model of MIS Planning," *Information and Management*, 6:1, February 1983, pp. 11–25.

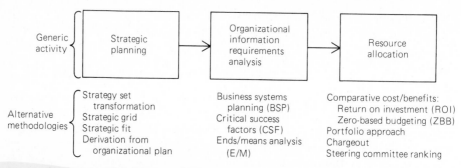

Figure 14-4
Three stage model of the information system planning process.

The three-stage planning model provides insight into the planning process and reduces confusion as to the position of competing planning methodologies. The next three sections will describe the stages in more detail and survey selected methodologies for each planning stage.

STRATEGIC PLANNING STAGE

The objective of the strategic planning stage of information system planning is to create objectives, goals, and strategies that align with (are derived from) the organization's objectives, goals, and strategies. Four techniques useful in this strategic alignment are derivation from the organizational plan, use of the strategic grid, fit with organizational culture, and strategy set transformation.

Derivation of Information System Strategy from Organizational Plan

If the organization has a plan that reflects organization goals, objectives, and strategies, information system goals, objectives, and strategy can be derived from it. Each objective, goal, and strategy in the plan is analyzed for required information system support. These can then be organized into information system goals, objectives, and strategies. Some examples illustrate the process:

	Organization plan	Derivation for information system plan
Goal	Provide high-quality widgets to the automotive industry	Provide information support for sales of quality widgets
Strategy	Establish quality control program for widgets	Establish quality control database for widgets
Objective	Implement quality circles in Detroit plant by 12/31/XX	1 Implement quality control report suitable for quality circles by 12/31/XX
		2 Design access procedures for quality circle to obtained data from quality control database by 6/15/XX

The McFarlan-McKenney Strategic Grid

One contingency approach to deciding on the information systems planning effort is the McFarlan-McKenney *strategic grid*.[7] The grid defines four types of information systems planning situations depending on the strategic impact of the existing information systems applications portfolio and the strategic impact of the portfolio of applications planned for development (Figure 14-5). The cells define the position of the information systems activity relative to the organization.

Strategic. Information system activities are critical to the current competitive strategy and to future strategic directions of the enterprise. Information systems applications are part of new strategic directions.

Factory. Information system applications are vital to the successful functioning of well-defined, well-accepted activities. However, information systems are not part of future strategic operations.

Support. Information system applications are useful in supporting the activities of the organization. A portfolio weighted to the support cell emphasizes traditional data processing applications. Information system activities are not "vital" to critical operations and are not included as part of future strategic directions.

Turnaround. This is a transition state from "support" to "strategic." The organization has had support-type applications, but is now planning for applications vital to strategic success of the organization.

An analysis of the current and planned portfolio is diagnostic of current status; it can

---

[7]F. W. McFarlan and J. L. McKenney, *Corporate Information Systems Management: The Issues Facing Senior Executives*, Richard D. Irwin, Homewood, IL, 1983.

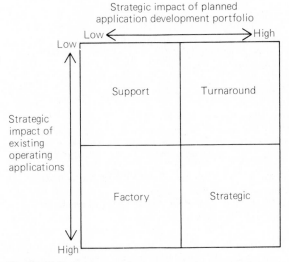

Figure 14-5
The strategic grid. (Adapted from F. W. McFarlan and J. L. McKenney, *Corporate Information Systems Management: The Issues Facing Senior Executives*, p. 15, ©1983, Irwin, Homewood, IL.)

also be used to change directions. The cell can then be used to suggest organization and management of information systems planning.

Position in grid	Organization and management of information systems planning
Strategic	Significant general management guidance Integration of corporate planning and information systems planning Need for smooth functioning of information systems activity
Turnaround	Same as strategic
Factory	Less involvement from top management Guidance from corporate plan to maintain information systems alignment Detailed operational and capacity planning by information system function
Support	Little top management involvement Little or no guidance from corporate plan

The strategic information system grid is a diagnostic tool to understand the role of information systems in an organization. The position in the grid explains the needed level of top management involvement and the relationship of the information system plan and organizational plan. The disadvantage of the grid is that it explains what is happening rather than what should happen. If an organization desires to be more strategic in its use of information systems, the grid provides no basis for deciding whether it can be.

Strategic Fit with Organizational Culture

As explained in Chapter 11, each organization has a culture which reinforces values, norms, and beliefs about the organization. Goals, objectives, and strategy for information systems should fit with the culture in order to avoid high resistance and high risk of failure. If the culture is not clear to information systems planners, clues can be obtained from sources such as the following:

1 *Stories*. Particular stories or incidents are repeated in an organization. An analyst seeking insight into organizational culture should listen to a number of stories. A pattern of meanings will tend to emerge. As an example, a company that emphasizes service may repeat incidents such as "the time we chartered a plane to get an expert here to help a customer get a system running."

2 *Meetings*. The subjects and order of agenda as well as attendees may provide clues as to the items considered important in the organization as well as which key managers support or block them.

3 *Top management behavior*. The behavior of top management generally influences the behavior of lower levels of management and other organization members. The way executives spend their time and the questions they ask demonstrate value systems that are likely to be emulated by others in the organization. Thomas J. Watson of IBM spent significant time on the

issue of customer service and wrote frequent memoranda on the subject. His concern was reflected throughout IBM.

4 *Physical layout.* The location of activities and the relative position and size of facilities, offices, etc., provide clues as to importance.

5 *Ritual.* Banquets, parties, orientations, frequently reflect significant organizational values.

6 *Documents.* What is written and to whom, and frequency of correspondence may indicate important beliefs about the ends and means for the organization.

These clues can be organized into "rules of the game" and classified into organizational tasks and relationships. The fit between the culture and the proposed information system plan can be assessed. Explicit decisions can be made to ignore the culture (usually dangerous), drop the strategy, seek a better fitting strategy, or (most difficult) plan actions to change the culture.

Strategy Set Transformation

It is very possible that there is no organizational plan to use in deriving information system goals, objectives, and strategy, and the information system planner must attempt to formulate necessary plans in a void. The strategic grid can be used to estimate the general strategic position of information systems, and organizational culture analysis can help to understand general values and directions, but neither is sufficient to develop information system goals and strategy. A more complete method is strategy set transformation as described by King.[8]

Strategy set transformation is used to produce goals and strategy for the information system by the following steps:

1 Explicate the organization's strategy set.
    a Delineate the organization's claimant structure. The clients, claimants, or stakeholders in the organization are identified. Examples are owners, customers, suppliers, and employees.
    b Identify goals for the claimants.
    c Identify organizational goals and strategies for each claimant group.
2 Validate the organizational goals and strategies by asking management to critique the statements. The organizational objectives, strategies, and strategic organizational attributes form the organizational strategy set.
3 Transform the organizational strategy set into the information system strategy set.
    a Identify one or more information system objectives for each organizational strategy and for each relevant organizational objective and attribute.
    b Identify information system constraints from organization strategy set and from information system objectives.
    c Identify information system design strategies based on organizational attributes, information system objectives and information system constraints.

As an example of this process, an organizational objective of improving cash flow may be derived from the profitability goals of shareholders and creditors. An

---

[8]W. R. King, "Strategic Planning for Management Information Systems," *MIS Quarterly*, 2:1, March 1978, pp. 27–37.

organizational strategy to achieve profitability may be an improvement in credit practices. An information system objective may be to improve speed of billing. Strategic organizational attributes relative to sophistication in use of computers and decision models will be reflected in information system constraints affecting the billing system. These can be expressed in system design strategies such as pilot projects for training, prototyping for development, etc.

ANALYSIS OF ORGANIZATIONAL INFORMATION REQUIREMENTS

Once goals and strategy have been delineated, the next stage is to obtain organizational information requirements. Information requirements are required at the organization-wide level for information system planning, identifying applications, and planning an information architecture. More detailed information requirements are required for design of applications. Although the level of specification is different for the organization and application, many of the methods for obtaining requirements are the same.

The discussion of methods for the determination of information requirements for both organization and applications will be combined in Chapter 15. However, to provide insight into the process of obtaining organizational information requirements, an example of an approach used by Wetherbe and Davis[9] that utilizes interviews with key management personnel is described in this section. The method is a synthesis of several existing approaches. In this method, obtaining organizational information requirements consists of several steps:

1 Define underlying organizational subsystems
2 Develop manager by subsystem matrix
3 Define and evaluate information requirements for organizational subsystems

A case study is used to illustrate the method. The company manages leasing of single-family dwellings.

Define Underlying Organizational Subsystems

The first phase of analysis is to define underlying organizational subsystems. The purpose of activity subsystem identification is to subdivide requirements determination by major organizational activity and make the process more manageable. For the home leasing company, the major subsystems are:

Credit	Client reporting
Leasing	Appraisal
Maintenance	Insurance
Evictions and delinquency	Sales
Marketing	Personnel administration
Advertising	Inspections
Accounts receivable and collections	Audit
Corporate accounting	Inventory
Market and product analysis	Legal

---

[9]J. C. Wetherbe and G. B. Davis, "Developing a Long-Range Information Architecture," *Proceedings of the National Computer Conference*, Anaheim, CA, May 1983, AFIPS Press, 52, pp. 261–269.

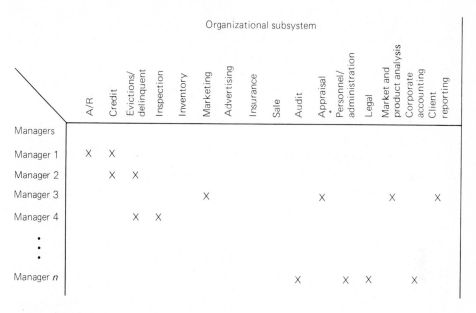

Figure 14-6
Manager by subsystem matrix.

These subsystems are obtained by an iterative process of discussing all organizational activities with managers and defining the activities as belonging to broad categories of subsystems. As new activities are considered, they are placed in previously defined categories, or a new category is created.

Develop Subsystem-Manager Matrix

Once the underlying organizational subsystems are defined, the next phase of the organizational information requirements analysis is to relate specific managers to organizational subsystems. The resulting manager-subsystem matrix for the home leasing firm is illustrated in Figure 14-6. Note that the subsystems across the top of the matrix are the same as those identified above.

The matrix is prepared by reviewing the major decision responsibilities of each middle- to top-level manager and associating decision making with specific subsystems. The matrix documents who has major decision-making responsibility for each subsystem. The purpose of this step is to clarify responsibilities and identify those managers to be interviewed relative to each subsystem.

Define and Evaluate Information Requirements for Organizational Subsystems

This step obtains the information requirements of each organizational subsystem by group interviews of those managers having major decision-making responsibility for the subsystem. Merely asking managers to define their information requirements is frequently not satisfactory because of the limitations on humans as information processors (see Chapter 8). It is therefore necessary to provide some structure to aid managers in thinking about information requirements.

The questions used in eliciting information requirements are derived from three approaches to be described in Chapter 15 (Business Systems Planning, Critical Success Factors, and Ends-Means Analysis). The questions reflect three ways of thinking about requirements, but each question also elicits unique requirements. The use of the three types of questions therefore increases the probability of obtaining a complete set of requirements. The three sets of questions are:

- What problems do you have and what information is needed for solving them? What decisions do you make and what information do you need for decision making?
- What factors are critical to the success of your activity and what information do you need to achieve success in them or monitor progress?
- What are the outputs (the ends) from your activities and what information do you need to measure effectiveness in achieving the outputs? What resources are used in producing the outputs and what information is needed to measure efficiency in use of the resources?

Interviews typically take two to four hours per subsystem. The maintenance subsystem at the leasing company illustrates the steps of the structured interview.

1 *Statement of purpose.* The first step of the interview is to get the managers to define a statement of purpose for the subsystem under consideration. For example, the purpose of *maintenance* was defined as: Maintain rental property at satisfactory level with minimal cost and process vendor payments.

2 *Subsystem mapping.* The second step of the group interview is to define the relationship of the subsystem to all other subsystems internal to the organization or entities external to the organization. It is constructed by drawing the subsystems under consideration in the center of a chalkboard or flip chart pad and by drawing around it the subsystems and entities with which it interacts. Next, labeled directional arrows are used to define the types of transactions or information flow that occur (Figure 14-7). The subsystem mapping makes the managers aware of the full scope of the subsystem under consideration.

3 *Questions to elicit requirements.* After the subsystem mapping is complete, information requirements are elicited using the three sets of questions.

4 *Define major information categories and classify information requirements.* The grouping of information requirements into broad general categories provides an overall profile of the information needs of the organization.

5 *Develop information-subsystem matrix.* The information categories are used to create a matrix showing which subsystem uses an information category. Rough measures of importance and current availability are specified (Figure 14-8). The matrix is used to define an information architecture for categories of information. It also indicates the subsystems that need to be involved in information system applications and relative priority for development.

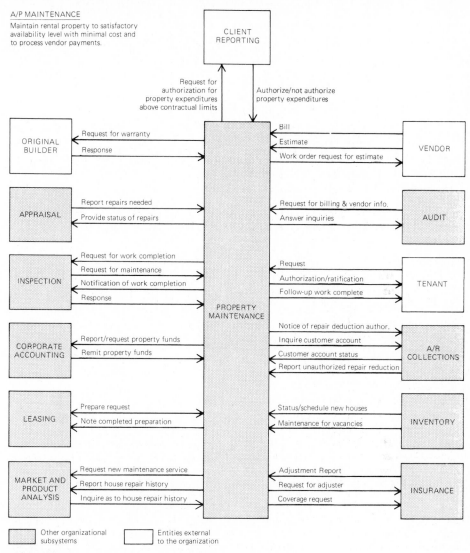

Figure 14-7
Subsystem mapping for maintenance subsystem.

RESOURCE ALLOCATION

The last stage of the three-stage model of MIS planning is the allocation of resources to determine which applications shall be implemented and in what order. Information system resources are limited, and not all projects can be done at once. Each project should be analyzed in terms of four factors.

1 *The expected cost savings or profit improvement resulting from the project.* This is an analysis of quantitative factors.

2 *Cost savings or increased profit which cannot easily be quantified.* These are judgmental factors which are expected to have a favorable result, but are difficult to measure. Examples are

ORGANIZATIONAL SUBSYSTEMS

Information Categories	Leasing	Maintenance	Accounts/Receivable	Credit	Evictions/Delinquent	Inspection	Inventory	Marketing	Advertising	Insurance	Sales	Audit	Appraisal	Personnel/Administration	Legal	Market and Product Analysis	Corporate Accounting	Client Reporting
Contract	1/3	1/3	1/3	1/2	1/3	1/2	2/3	1/3	2/1	2/3	1/3	1/3	1/3		1/3	1/3	2/3	2/3
Policy/Training	3/3	3/3	3/2	3/3	3/3	3/3		3/3		2/3	2/3	3/3	3/3	2/3	2/2	3/2	3/2	3/2
Customer Financial	2/3		2/3	1/3	2/3		2/3		2/3		1/3	3/2				2/3		
Customer Demographics	2/3		3/2	3/2	3/2		2/3		2/3		2/3					2/3		
Complaint	2/2	2/3	2/2		2/2	3/3	3/3			2/2	3/3	2/3	2/2	3/2	2/2	2/3	2/2	2/2
Leasing/Transactions	2/2		2/3	2/3								1/2	1/3		2/2		2/3	2/3
Vendor		2/3	3/2		2/3	3/3	2/3		2/3	2/2	2/3	1/2			2/3		2/3	
Accounts/Payable		2/2	2/1		2/2				2/3		2/2	1/3	2/3	2/3	1/2		1/3	2/3
Accounts/Receivable	2/1	2/1	1/3	1/3	1/3		2/3			1/3	2/3	1/3	2/3		1/3		1/3	2/3
Maintenance		1/3	2/3			1/3	1/3			1/3	2/3	1/3	2/2		1/1	2/2	1/2	2/2
Warranty		2/2				2/2	2/3			1/3	2/2	2/2					1/2	
Inventory	1/3	1/2	1/2		1/3	2/3	3/3	1/3	2/2		2/3				1/1	2/3	1/3	2/2

Key: Availability/value

Availability   Value
Very = 1   Low = 1
Medium = 2   Medium = 2
Low = 3   High = 3

Figure 14-8
Information categories by organizational subsystems matrix.

improved customer satisfaction for which no specific sales can be estimated or increased employee motivation for which no dollar impact can be preassessed.

3 *Institutional factors such as the need to have the development proceed in an orderly fashion or the need to have the entire organization involved in a new information system.* For example, a fairly low payout project in a department that would not otherwise be involved in an information system development effort might receive high priority.

4 *System management factors.* Some systems need to be prepared before others. Certain software packages must be developed so that there can be suitable interfaces. Personnel may be in short supply which affects the scheduling of projects, particularly those requiring specialized expertise.

Using the four factors as input, a number of methods have been proposed for allocating scarce development resources with different underlying criteria for decision making. The methods surveyed in this section illustrate some alternatives. The methods may be used singly or in combination.

Method	Underlying criteria
Comparative cost or benefit	Economic rationality
Portfolio approach	Project risk and extent to which project fits information system stage or strategic direction
Chargeout	Value to user (local rationality)
Steering committee ranking	Organizational power, politics, and coalitions

Comparative Cost or Benefit

Projects do not all have the same cost-benefit ratio. Some have a high economic value if successful; others have low payoff. Two methods of rational, economic decision making illustrate the use of economic rationality for allocating resources: return on investment and zero-based budgeting.

Return on investment (ROI) is a classic decision-making approach. In the case of information system projects, each one has quantifiable economic costs and quantifiable economic benefits. Using the streams of costs and benefits, the return on the investment can be calculated. A decision rule based on ROI is to choose projects (among those that are optional) that have the highest ROI. There are three difficulties with this approach:

1 Many benefits may be difficult to quantify, yet the project is understood to have a high priority.

2 Projects based on ROI alone may not provide a balanced portfolio along other dimensions such as risk.

3 The ROI technique is incremental; it does not cause reconsideration of current applications.

Zero-based budgeting is a procedure to reevaluate all programs, activities, and expenditures in terms of cost or benefits. The steps are:

1 Develop decision packages—documents that describe each activity that can be separately added or dropped. Examples are programs, projects, services, and personnel.

2 Rank packages in order of importance.

3 Allocate available resources to decision packages.

In the case of information systems, zero-based budgeting causes the existing portfolio to be examined along with the proposed portfolio. Each function or area for computer applications starts with a zero base of applications and indicates the priority they assign to applications if they were to add them incrementally. The method appears to be useful for examining the entire allocation of resources; it tends to be very time consuming for regular decision making on projects.

Portfolio Approach

The basic idea of the portfolio approach is that projects should be evaluated not only individually but as part of a portfolio of projects that have an overall impact. The portfolio should have an appropriate mixture of risk, support for strategic directions, and applications that fit the stages of growth of the various organizational subsystems.

The portfolio approach has been described by McFarlan[10] with respect to risk; he also applies the approach to project management, to be discussed in Chapter 18. Other criteria for building a portfolio are implied by the strategic grid[11] and the stage theory of Nolan.[12]

Portfolio-based risk assessment recognizes that projects differ relative to risk of various failures such as schedule failure, cost overrun, performance shortfall, and abandonment. McFarlan identifies three dimensions that contribute to the uncertainty of the success of the project:

1 Project size. Large projects are riskier than small ones.

2 Experience with the technology. Risk is reduced to the extent that the development team has experience with the technology being used and the development team and users are knowledgeable in the application area.

3 Project structure. Risk is reduced to the extent the application fits existing structure for performing the task and the organization demonstrates commitment to the change.

After the risk of each proposed project has been evaluated, the overall riskiness of the portfolio can be assessed. An appropriate balance of risk will depend on factors such as the organizational culture with respect to risk taking, the importance of risk taking to support major shifts in information system strategy, etc.

The portfolio concept can be applied along other dimensions such as the following to achieve balance in development:

- A balance between support and strategic applications
- A balance between centralized systems and end-user facilities
- A balance between high risk/high payoff and low risk/low payoff
- A balance between applications for aggressive, mature users and timid, initial users

---

[10]F. W. McFarlan, "Portfolio Approach to Information Systems," *Harvard Business Review*, September–October 1981, pp. 142–150.

[11]McFarlan and McKenney, *Corporate Information Systems Management*.

[12]Nolan, "Managing the Crises in Data Processing."

Chargeout

Chargeout is an accounting mechanism for allocating the costs of information system resources to their users. There are two methods of chargeout. The first is a straightforward allocation of costs to different users in order to give them some idea of how resources are being used. The user has no control over the costs. The primary purpose of this method is to aid in internal control of information system costs. In the second method, users are charged for information services, but they can control costs by reducing services or by choosing alternative methods or suppliers. The latter is consistent with a profit or cost center concept of local responsibility for costs or profit of the unit. For new system development, the allocation rule is therefore based on whether users are willing to ''buy'' the application. If the user is willing to pay for development (e.g., a fixed price), the information systems function must allocate necessary personnel resources to accomplish it.

There are significant advantages to the chargeout method (if it fits the organization), but it tends to promote local rationality rather than rationality for the entire organization, and it does not resolve allocation if there are more projects being ''bought'' than information systems can develop. A detailed description of chargeout as a resource allocation mechanism is given in Chapter 20.

Steering Committee Ranking

In spite of all attempts at rationality and balanced portfolios, significant allocation decisions usually remain to be made. These may be made by a single executive (such as the information system executive); an alternative is a steering committee composed of executives from major functions in the organization. The important point is that project selection should not fall to lower-level systems planning personnel who have neither appropriate authority nor the broad knowledge of business needs to do it correctly.

An advantage of the steering committee is that it allows for exercise of organizational power and politics. Ideally, it arrives at a plan which is the optimal allocation of resources organization-wide. It facilitates coalitions and builds support for the allocations and the resulting plan. Disadvantages are the time required for the negotiation of a steering committee and the possibility that ''information needy'' but less powerful groups will be overlooked.

SUMMARY

The development of an information plan for information system resources is a vital part of good management. There are a variety of approaches to organizing for planning; the approach chosen should include appropriate participation and review by the organization to ensure that the plan meets organizational needs and that it has organizational support. A fundamental principle for the plan is that it should be derived from and conform with the organization's plan. The contents of the plan demonstrate this conformance and describe how the plan is to be executed.

There are several models that are useful in the planning process and the positioning of an organization with respect to planning. The Nolan stage model describes the direction of change as organizations adopt information technology and develop organizational mechanisms to benefit from it. The three stage model of MIS planning is a useful framework for describing the stages of planning and the role of methodologies in strategic planning, organizational information requirements analysis, and resource allocation.

Within the information system strategic planning stage, several techniques are available for ensuring strategic alignment with the organizational plan: derivation from the organizational plan, use of the strategic grid, fit with organizational culture, and strategy set formation. Approaches to the information requirements stage will be explained in Chapter 15; this chapter explained an approach to eliciting high level requirements for planning an information architecture through interviews with managers. For the resource allocation stage, four approaches were explained: comparative cost-benefit, portfolio, chargeout, and steering committee ranking.

MINICASES

1 TEN GUIDELINES FOR STRATEGIC MIS PLANNING

Robert V. Head, a consultant on MIS planning, provided ten guidelines to help MIS executives who are on the threshold of experimenting with strategic MIS planning:

1 Make provisions in the systems plan for taking small steps rapidly. "Don't have a plan with goals extending so far into the future that there is no way of tracking it."

2 Develop alternative plans when significant contradictory trends are discerned in business objectives or technology.

3 Interface the systems plan with the corporate plan, modifying both appropriately.

4 Document the systems plan in a format intelligible to top management and arrange for personal presentation.

5 Establish a formal mechanism for review and reiteration of the systems plan.

6 Develop a system for tabulating and forecasting utilization of installed data processing (DP) equipment.

7 Fix the organizational responsibility for systems planning. This may involve modifying the job description of the person who is charged with the planning activity.

8 Rotate the assignment of technical personnel to the planning staff in order to avoid an "ivory tower aura."

9 Budget for research and development.

10 Set up a comparative systems intelligence activity.

Phil Hirsch, "Analyst: IS Planning Key for Future MIS Execs," *Computerworld*, October 3, 1981, p. 22.

Questions

a For each guideline, note the topic or page number where discussed in the text.

b Note any differences, additions, or omissions between the text and these guidelines.

2 ALTERNATIVE DESCRIPTION OF THE MIS PLAN

In an article on MIS planning (Jerry Kanter, "MIS Long Range Planning," *Infosystems*, June 1982, pp. 66-70) the following structure for an MIS plan is explained:

Contents of MIS plan	Answers the question
Corporate guidelines Environment Current operations	Where are we?
Mission/direction statement Objectives/goals Assumptions/risks	Where do we want to go?
Strategies Policies Programs/projects Management control Transition	How do we get there
Priorities and schedules Organization and delegation	When will it be done and who will do it?
Resources Budget	How muct will it cost?

Questions

a What are the differences between the above structure and the contents described in the chapter?

b If plans for management control of the process and the organization and delegation are not included in the MIS plan, where would they be found

3 THE MICROCOMPUTER DECISION

The Dean of the School of Management was upset. He was just about to make a decision to purchase microcomputers for the faculty and staff of the School. A vendor and model number had been selected. Then a new product announcement was made for a better, faster, cheaper computer. He had seen similar announcements every few months. How was he to make a decision on equipment when the "leading edge" where he wanted to be was a moving target?

Questions

a Explain how this decision can be made within the context of an information system plan.

b The replacement period for the microcomputers was never specified. If the plan calls for a three year life before replacement, aid the Dean by explaining the dynamics of product announcement, availability of initial software, availability of significant amounts of software, and hardware obsolescence.

EXERCISES

1 Humor often expresses deep feelings. What can you say about planning based on the following comments (from Kanter, "MIS Long-Range Planning," p. 70):

a "The trouble with planning is that it has a tendency to deteriorate into work."

b The company's planning style is "ready, fire, and aim."

2 A large company with a a strong, decentralized profit center structure and culture has centralized data processing. A high-level decision is to have all organizational support functions conform to the decentralized structure. Prepare a short statement for the information system plan expressing:

a Information systems goals relative to the decentralization.

b Information system strategies.

c Information system objectives.

3 Based on the Nolan stage theory, why can't an organization just skip over the first two stages?

4 Apply the Nolan's stage theory concept to a newly formed business venture when:

a All executives and supervisors have had extensive experience using sophisticated information systems.

b The executives and supervisors are history professors turned entrepreneurs. They have previously used computers for statistical analysis of research data.

5 If Nolan is right, why don't the research studies demonstrate the connections he describes in the stage model?

6 There is evidence that innovation comes primarily from trial and error investigating by small groups and not from large, well-organized, planned research. If so, what type of resource allocation strategy fits best with innovation?

7 Take a small unit in a company (or a university) and do strategy set transformation.

8 Organizational culture represents the informal organization and unwritten policies and taboos. Using methods listed in the chapter, describe the organizational culture of a company (or a university) with respect to:

a Distribution of information about decisions, activities, etc.

b Quality of accounting data and management reports.

c Use of formal reports for decision making.

9 Three information system executives heard about the strategic grid for information systems. They were in the support quadrant and decided to do something about moving to the strategic quadrant. Describe a few ways that information could be strategic (perhaps as part of a strategic growth move by the organization).

a Life insurance company. Current support is primarily accounting, billing, policy record keeping, etc.

b Grocery store chain. Current support is traditional accounting, purchasing, payables, receivables, inventory, bookkeeping, etc.

c Large law firm. Current support is personnel and payroll plus timekeeping and billing.

10 Describe how organizational culture may constrain information system strategies. Use a company you know or a hospital or university.

11 Why should a manager need a cognitive framework for getting at information requirements (remember Chapter 8)? Why might the use of more than one framework yield additional requirements?

12 How does the information-subsystem matrix relate to an information architecture (structure of the information system and overall structure for data)?

13 The portfolio idea is essentially that there should be a balance between different kinds of projects. Since a project can be classified according to several characteristics, the portfolio analysis can be very simple (one characteristic) or complex (many characteristics). For the following projects, define possible characteristics (risk, payoff, etc.) that might be used for portfolio selection.

a Revised accounting system

b New online order entry system

c Model for scheduling assembly line

d Competitor intelligence system (data collection and analysis)

14 The resource allocation methods can be used in combination. Define three logical combinations and comment on why they make sense.

15 Explain the role of a steering committee in the political process of planning and resource allocation.

SELECTED REFERENCES

Bowman, B., G. B. Davis, and J. C. Wetherbe: "Modeling for MIS," *Datamation*, July 1980, pp. 166–162.

Bowman, B., G. B. Davis, and J. C. Wetherbe: "Three Stage Model of MIS Planning," *Information and Management*, 6:1, February, 1983, pp. 11–25.

Ein-Dor, P., and E. Segev: "Strategic Planning for MIS," *Management Science*, 24:15, November 1978.

Hax, Arnoldo C., and Nicolas S. Majluf: "The Use of the Growth-Share Matrix in Strategic Planning," *Interfaces*, 13:1, February 1983, pp. 46–65.

Hax, Arnoldo C., and Nicolas S. Majluf: "The Use of the Industry Attractiveness-Business Strength Matrix in Strategic Planning," *Interfaces*, 13:2, April 1983, pp. 53–71.

Highsmith, J.: "Structural Systems Planning," *MIS Quarterly*, 5:3, September 1981, pp. 35–54.

Kanter, Jerry: "MIS Long-Range Planning," *Infosystems*, June 1982, pp. 66–70.

King, W. R.: "Strategic Planning for Management Information Systems," *MIS Quarterly*, 2:1, March 1978, pp. 27–37.

Lientz, P. B., and M. Chen: "Long Range Planning for Information Services," *Long Range Planning* February 1980.

Long, Larry: *Design and Strategy for Corporate Information Services: MIS Long-Range Planning*, Prentice-Hall, Englewood Cliffs, NJ, 1982.

McFarlan, F. W.: "Portfolio Approach to Information Systems," *Harvard Business Review*, September–October 1981, pp. 142–150.

McFarlan, F. W., and J. L. McKenney: *Corporate Information Systems Management: The Issues Facing Senior Executives*, Richard D. Irwin, Homewood, IL, 1983.

McFarlan, F. W., and J. L. McKenney: "The Information Archipelago—Maps and Bridges," *Harvard Business Review*, 60:5, September–October 1982, pp.109–119.

McFarlan, F. W., J. L. McKenney, and P. J. Pyburn: "The Information Archipelago—Plotting a Course," *Harvard Business Review*, 61:1, January–February 1983, pp. 145–156.

McLean, E., and J. Soden: *Strategic Planning for MIS*, Wiley, New York, 1977.

Nolan, Richard L.: "Managing Information Systems by Committee," *Harvard Business Review*, July–August 1982.

Pyburn, Philip J.: "Linking the MIS Plan with Corporate Strategy: An Exploratory Study," *MIS Quarterly*, 7:2, June 1983, pp. 1–14.

Schwartz, M. H.: "MIS Planning," *Datamation*, 16:4, September 1970, pp. 28–31.

Wetherbe, J. C., and G. B. Davis: "Developing a Long-Range Information Architecture," *Proceedings of the National Computer Conference*, Anaheim, CA, May 1983, AFIPS Press, 52, pp. 261–269.

Wind, Yoram, and Vijay Mahayan: "Designing Product and Business Portfolios," *Harvard Business Review*, January–February 1981, pp. 155–165.

Zani, William M.: "Blueprint for MIS," *Harvard Business Review*, November–December 1970, pp. 95–100.

The Nolan Stage Model

Benbasat, I., A. S. Dexter, D. H. Drury, and R. C. Goldstein: "A Critique of the 'Stage Hypothesis': Theory and Empirical Evidence," *Communications of the ACM*, 27:5, May 1984, pp. 476–485.

Drury, D. H.: "An Empirical Assessment of the Stages of DP Growth," *MIS Quarterly*, 7:2, June 1983, pp. 59–70.

Gibson, Cyrus F., and Richard L. Nolan: "Managing the Four Stages of EDP Growth," *Harvard Business Review*, January–February, 1974, pp. 76–88.

King, J. L., and K. L. Kraemer: "Evolution and Organizational Information Systems: An Assessment of Nolan's Stage Model," *Communications of the ACM*, 27:5, May 1984, pp. 466–475.

Lucas, H. C., and J. A. Sutton: "The Stage Hypothesis and S-Curve: Some Contradictory Evidence," *Communications of the ACM*, 20:4, April 1977, pp. 254–259.

Nolan, Richard L.: "Managing the Computer Resource: A Stage Hypothesis," *Communications of the ACM*, 16:3, March 1973, pp. 399–405.

Nolan, Richard L.: "Managing the Crises in Data Processing," *Harvard Business Review*, March–April 1979, pp. 115–126.

CHAPTER 15

STRATEGIES FOR THE DETERMINATION OF INFORMATION REQUIREMENTS

An information system should meet the needs of the organization it serves, and applications should meet the needs of their users. The requirements for the information system are therefore determined by the strategies, goals, procedures, and behavior of individuals within the organization acting individually and collectively. Since this is so, why not ask the participants to describe the requirements for the information system? This chapter will explain why this simple strategy may not be adequate. It will then describe alternative strategies and some criteria for selecting among them.[1]

A STRATEGY APPROACH TO THE DETERMINATION OF INFORMATION REQUIREMENTS

There are four major reasons it is difficult to obtain a correct and complete set of requirements:

1 The constraints on humans as information processors and problem solvers.
2 The variety and complexity of information requirements.
3 The complex patterns of interaction among users and analysts in defining requirements.
4 Unwillingness of some users to provide requirements (for political or behavioral reasons).

The four reasons for difficulty in arriving at correct and complete requirements for information systems suggest that there should be several general strategies for requirements determination. The selection of a strategy is based on the conditions (contingencies) that apply in a specific case.

An information requirements determination strategy is a general approach to obtaining requirements. The specific procedures are information requirements determination methods. A set of related methods is a methodology (although the terms method and methodology are frequently used interchangeably). Within the broad outlines of a strategy, methods may be used singly or in combination to elicit

---

[1]The chapter is based on G. B. Davis, "Strategies for Information Requirements Determination," *IBM Systems Journal*, 21:1, 1982, pp. 4–30.

requirements and to document the results. The distinction between methods of determination and methods of documentation is important because methods of documentation frequently contain the implicit assumption that the requirements are known and must only be documented. This chapter will emphasize methods of determination.

THE THREE LEVELS OF INFORMATION REQUIREMENTS

There are three levels at which information requirements need to be established in order to design and implement computer-based information systems:

1 The organizational information requirements to define an overall information system structure and to specify a portfolio of applications and databases.
2 The requirements for each database defined by data models and other specifications.
3 The detailed information requirements for an application.

Some methods of requirements determination are more suitable for the less-detailed, broader-scope, organization-level information requirements, whereas other methods may be more suitable for the more detailed application information requirements. Some methods can be applied to requirements determination at both levels. The process of organizational information requirements determination was introduced in Chapter 14; this chapter will explain specific techniques for information requirements at the level of the organization and application. The methods for determining database requirements will be explained in Chapter 16.

Organization-Level Information Requirements

Information requirements determination at the organization or enterprise level is a key element in developing an information system master plan. Often termed enterprise analysis, the process of organization-level information requirements determination obtains, organizes, and documents a complete set of high-level requirements (described in Chapter 14). The requirements are factored into databases and subsystems (a portfolio of applications) that can be scheduled for development. The overall information architecture is defined, and the boundaries and interfaces of the individual application subsystems are specified.

Database Requirements

Database requirements arise both from applications and ad hoc queries. The overall architecture for the databases to meet these requirements can be defined as part of organizational information requirements. Major classes of data are defined and associated with organizational processes that require them. There is very little detail in the requirements at this level.

The process of obtaining and organizing more detailed database requirements can be divided into defining data requirements as perceived by the users (programs or ad hoc queries) and defining requirements for physical design of the databases. User requirements are referred to as conceptual or logical requirements because the user views of data are separated from the organization of data in physical storage. User requirements may be derived from existing applications or by data modeling (to be explained in Chapter 16).

The requirements for physical database design are derived from the conceptual requirements, the hardware and software environments, and specifications related to use of the database. Physical database design is beyond the scope of this text.

Application-Level Information Requirements

An application is a subsystem of the overall information system structure; it provides information processing for an organizational unit or organizational activity. The process for the determination of information requirements at the application level defines and documents specific information content plus design and implementation requirements.

There are essentially two types of information system application requirements: social and technical. The social or behavioral requirements, based on job design, specify objectives and assumptions such as the following:

- Work organization design objectives
- Individual role assumptions
- Responsibility assumptions
- Organizational policies

The technical requirements are based on the information needed for the job or task to be performed. They specify outputs, inputs, stored data, and information processes. A significant part of the technical requirements are associated with the structure and format of data. The formulation of data models is described in the next chapter.

The technical requirements include interface requirements between the user system and the application system. The interface requirements include data presentation format, screen design, user language structure, feedback and assistance provisions, error control, and response time. These interface requirements are explained in Chapter 17.

CONSTRAINTS ON HUMANS AS SPECIFIERS OF INFORMATION REQUIREMENTS

Humans appear to be so versatile with respect to information use that human constraints or limitations are frequently ignored. Yet "asking" users to define their information requirements will not necessarily yield a complete and correct set of requirements. These limitations, explained in Chapter 8, are humans as information processors, human bias in selection and use of data, and human problem-solving behavior. The relevance of these limitations to the specification of information requirements will be summarized.

Humans as Information Processors

Humans make use of three memories in information processing: external, long-term, and short-term. The limits of short-term memory affect the information requirements obtained whenever the process being used to elicit requirements uses only short-term memory (e.g., an interview in which there is no use of external storage such as notes, reports, or documents). The user being interviewed cannot hold a large number of items in short-term memory for discussion or analysis purposes and is therefore limited in processing responses. The short-term memory limitation may also affect the number of requirements that users define as important. In various processing activities using short-term memory, the user may have selectively emphasized a few items of information and recorded these in long-term memory as being the most important. These few requirements may be the only ones recalled when a question is asked.

Short-term memory limitations can be significantly reduced by the use of external memory to store data being processed and by the use of methodologies that systematically elicit and record small numbers of data chunks.

Human Bias in Selection and Use of Data

There is substantial evidence to show that humans are biased in their selection and use of data.[2] Behavior resulting in bias was discussed in Chapter 8. The effects of biases on information requirements determination are summarized below. The net effect on the determination of information requirements is a significant bias toward requirements based on current procedures, currently available information, recent events, and inferences from small samples of events. The analyst and user who understand these biases may compensate for them; a significant method of compensation is to provide a structure for eliciting of requirements.

Human biasing behavior	Effect on information requirements determination
Anchoring and adjustment	Information requirements from users will tend to be the result of an adjustment from an anchor of the information currently available.
Concreteness	Requirements provided by users will be biased by the information they already have about their requirements and the form of this information.
Recency	An information need that was experienced recently will be given greater weight than a need based on a less recent event.
Intuitive statistical analysis	Human lack of understanding of the effects of sample size of variance is an important limitation because many organizational phenomena occur at a fairly low rate. Also, tendency to identifying causality with joint occurrence and assign cause where none exists may result in misjudging the need for information.
Placing value on unused data	Humans bias toward obtaining and storing information may result in requirements for information "just in case" it is needed or information to use as a symbol of rationality.

[2]G. A. Miller, "The Magical Number Seven, Plus or Minus Two: Some Limits on Our Capacity for Processing Information," *The Psychological Review*, 63:2, March 1956, pp. 81–97.

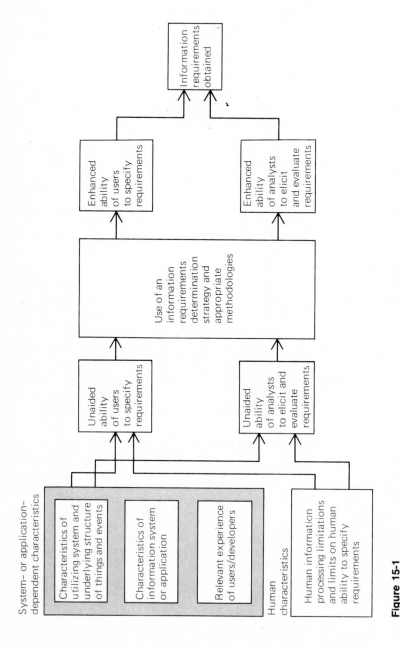

Figure 15-1
Effect of application characteristics, human characteristics, and information determination strategies and methodologies on information requirements obtained.

Human Problem-Solving Behavior

The problem space for information requirements determination is how a particular analyst or user formulates a representation to use in working on information requirements. Methods for the determination of information requirements provide such a structure for the problem space (Figure 15-1).

The users and analysts involved in the process apply bounded rationality using a somewhat simplified model of the organization and its information requirements. The completeness and correctness of the requirements obtained are thus limited by the model as well as by the training, prejudice, custom, and attitudes of users and analysts involved in the process. The effect of bounded rationality in analyzing information requirements is demonstrated in the behavior of systems analysts. A characteristic of proficient systems analysts is that they have learned to use a general model to bound the problem space and aid in an efficient search for requirements; low-rated analysts have a poorly developed model and, therefore, a poorly developed search procedure in the problem space.[3] Also, higher-rated analysts consider organizational and policy issues in establishing requirements; low-rated analysts do not.

PURPOSES OF A METHOD FOR THE DETERMINATION OF INFORMATION REQUIREMENTS

Based on human limitations, a method for determining information requirements should be able to accomplish the following:

1 Assist an analyst to constrain and structure the problem space. It is estimated that analysts spend 75 percent of their time on this activity.[4]

2 Assist in searching efficiently within the problem space by aiding in discovering requirements and in overcoming short-term memory limitations in human information processing.

3 Assist in overcoming biasing factors such as recency, concreteness, small samples, and placing value on unused data.

4 Aid in overcoming user or analyst training, prejudice, custom, and attitudes.

5 Provide assurance that requirements are complete and correct.

Methods differ in the amount of structure provided. Some provide conceptual structure but little process and documentation structure; others provide detailed structure for all tasks and all documentation. The importance of detailed structure may vary depending on the circumstances. For example, analysts and users with little experience and expertise may find detailed structure very useful; analysts and users experienced in the application area and able to define requirements may find detailed structure to be inhibiting and frustrating.

---

[3] N. P. Vitalari, ''An Investigation of the Problem Solving Behavior of Systems Analysts,'' unpublished doctoral dissertation, University of Minnesota, Minneapolis, 1981. Summarized in N. P. Vitalari and G. W. Dickson, ''Problem Solving for Effective Systems Analysis,'' *Communications of the ACM*, 26:11, November 1983, pp. 948–956.

[4] Vitalari, ''An Investigation of the Problem Solving Behavior of Systems Analysts.''

THE VALUE OF A REQUIREMENTS STUDY

Perhaps the best way to illustrate the value of an organization's having an organizational information architecture for MIS is to quote the president of EPIC a year after he personally led the development of their architecture:

I had worked in top management in one of our other subsidiaries and experienced the disappointment that comes from developing systems in the traditional FIFO, piecemeal way with the consequences of redundant, non-integrated and inaccessible information.

When I took over a new subsidiary, I decided there must be a better way. There was. By developing an information architecture before developing systems we have been able to pull all our systems together. Our short-run system decisions are dovetailing into our long-range systems. We know where we are going and getting there.

Beyond that, just the process of going through an organizational information requirements analysis gave me and my management invaluable insight into our business.

Source: J. C. Wetherbe and G. B. Davis, "Developing a Long-Range Information Architecture," *Proceedings of the National Computer Conference*, Anaheim, California, May 1983, AFIPS Press, p. 268.

STRATEGIES FOR DETERMINING INFORMATION REQUIREMENTS

A strategy was defined earlier as an approach for achieving an objective. There are four strategies for determining information requirements:

1 asking directly
2 deriving from an existing information system
3 synthesizing from characteristics of the utlizing system
4 discovering from experimentation with an evolving information system

---

USERS TEND TO USE MIXED STRATEGIES TO IDENTIFY REQUIREMENTS

In a research project, information requirements were elicited from executives using two alternative methods:

1 Data analysis (i.e., deriving from data in existing application). Existing reports were examined and data items were dropped or added.

2 Decision analysis (i.e., synthesizing from characteristics of the utilizing system). Using a decision flowchart, decisions were analyzed and informal requirements derived.

The objective was to compare the two approaches. One interesting result was that it was difficult for users to follow a pure strategy; they wanted to use a mixed strategy. Those doing decision analysis kept referring to existing reports and those doing data analysis often analyzed the existing data in terms of decisions.

Source: M. C. Munro and G. B. Davis, "Determining Management Information Needs: A Comparison of Methods," *MIS Quarterly*, June 1977, pp. 55–67.

Asking Directly

In an asking directly strategy, the analyst obtains information requirements from persons in the utilizing system solely by asking them what their requirements are. From a conceptual standpoint, the asking directly strategy assumes that users can structure their problem space and overcome or compensate for biases due to concreteness, recency, small sample size, and unused data. Anchoring by users in formulating responses is assumed to yield satisfactory results. These conditions may hold in very stable systems for which a well-defined structure exists or in systems whose structure is established by law, regulation, or other outside authority. There are a variety of methods for carrying out an asking strategy. Some asking methods are listed below with comments on conditions that suggest their use.

Asking method	Description	Conditions suggesting use
Closed questions	Each question has a defined set of possible answers from which the respondent selects.	When set of factual responses are known or respondent may not be able to recall all possibilities. Analyst must know all possible responses.
Open questions	No answers provided. Respondent is allowed to formulate response.	When feelings or opinions are important or when respondent has knowledge and ability to formulate responses.
Brainstorming	Group method for eliciting wide variety of suggestions by open flow of ideas.	Used to extend boundaries of problem spaces of participants and elicit nonconventional solutions.
Guided brainstorming	Participants are asked to define ideal solutions and then select the best feasible ideal solution. The IDEALS method[5] is an example.	Used to guide brainstorming to "ideal" solutions. Useful where participants have system knowledge, but may be locked into an anchoring and adjustment behavior.
Group consensus	The participants are asked for their estimates or expectations regarding significant variables. Delphi method and group norming are examples.	Used to arrive at "best" judgmental estimate of variables that are difficult or impossible to estimate quantitatively.

If a pure asking directly strategy is followed, one or more asking methods are used to elicit requirements, and analysis is limited to consistency checks as requirements are documented. The asking methods can also be used in conjunction with other strategies.

---

[5]G. Nadler, *Work Design: A Systems Concept*, Revised Edition, Richard D. Irwin, Homewood, IL, 1970.

Deriving from an Existing Information System

Existing information systems that have an operational history can be used to derive requirements for a proposed information system for the same type of organization or application. The types of existing information systems that are useful in deriving requirements for future systems are:

1 Existing system that will be replaced by the new system
2 Existing system in another, similar organization
3 Proprietary system or package
4 Descriptions in textbooks, handbooks, industry studies, etc.

With regard to human problem-solving behavior, deriving from an existing information system is an explicit use of anchoring and adjustment. Users and analysts explicitly choose an existing system as an anchor and adjust the requirements from it. Deriving information requirements from an existing information system has also been termed a data analysis approach[6] since the data inputs and outputs of the existing system are the focus of analysis.

If the information system is performing fairly standard operations and providing fairly standard information for utilizing systems that are stable, the use of an existing system as an anchor is appropriate. In application systems for some well-defined functions such as payroll, data analysis of an existing system can be a useful primary method. In the early application of computers to organizational transaction processing and accounting systems, derivation of requirements from the processing performed on the data provided by the existing system was widely used.

Some analysts use data analysis of the existing system as a secondary method for deriving requirements. To avoid being overly influenced by the concreteness of the existing system, they may delay its use until after their primary analysis method has provided an initial set of requirements.

Synthesis from Characteristics of the Utilizing System

Information systems provide information services to facilitate the operation of object systems, those that utilize the information. Requirements for information thus stem from the activities of the object system. This suggests that the most logical and complete method for obtaining information requirements is from an analysis of the characteristics of the utilizing system. This approach may overcome biases by providing an analytical structure for the problem space of the user or analyst. The object system analysis is therefore appropriate when the utilizing system is changing or the proposed information system is different from existing patterns (in its content, form, complexity, etc.), so that anchoring on an existing information system or existing observations of information needs will not yield a complete and correct set of requirements.

Several methods have been proposed for implementing a strategy for determining information requirements from object system analysis. Eight general methods described

---

[6]M. C. Munro and G. B. Davis, "Determining Management Information Needs: A Comparison of Methods," *MIS Quarterly*, 1:2, June 1977, pp. 55–67.

in this section illustrate the alternatives. Although useful at both organizational level and application level, each method has a primary orientation as shown in Table 15–1.

TABLE 15–1: CHARACTERISTICS OF METHODS FOR DETERMINING INFORMATION REQUIREMENTS

	Primary requirements orientation	
Method	Organization	Application
1 Normative analysis	X	
2 Strategy set transformation	X	
3 Critical factors analysis	X	
4 Process analysis	X	
5 Ends-means analysis	X	
6 Decision analysis		X
7 Sociotechnical analysis		X
8 Input-process-output analysis		X

The descriptions of these methods are very short and provide only an idea of the central focus of each approach. The objective of this section is not to explain these methods in detail, but to illustrate how the strategy of synthesis from characteristics of a utilizing system may be implemented. The common feature of all the methods is that requirements for the information system are obtained from a study of the object or utilizing system. The questioning or analysis process in each case begins with the needs, structure, objectives, etc., of the utilizing system. When these components are established, they are the basis for deriving the information system requirements.

Normative analysis methods are based on the fundamental similarity of classes of object systems. For example, all billing applications perform a set of basic functions that can be prescribed in advance. These fundamental characteristics are the basis for a prescribed or normative set of requirements. Analysis then concentrates on tailoring the normative requirements to meet nonstandard needs of a specific organization or application.

Strategy set transformation is a methodology primarily for describing organization-level information requirements[7] from the objectives of the organization. For example, if an organizational objective is to improve profits and the selected strategy is to change the sales mix to a larger proportion of higher gross margin products, the information system requirement derived from this objective is a gross margin analysis application. Strategy set transformation was described in more detail in Chaper 14 as a method for alignment of the information system plan with organizational objectives.

In the *critical factors analysis* approach, information requirements are derived from the critical factors for operating and managing an enterprise. There is therefore a two step process of eliciting the critical factors and then deriving information requirements. An

---

[7]W. R. King, "Strategic Planning for Management Information Systems," *MIS Quarterly*, 2:1, March 1978, pp. 27–37.

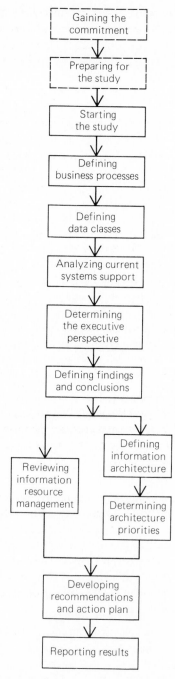

Figure 15-2
Steps in defining a proposed information architecture in Business Systems Planning. (Source: *Business Systems Planning—Information Systems Planning Guide*, Third Edition, GE20-0527, IBM Corporation, 983, p. 25.)

example of critical factors analysis is the Critical Success Factors (CSF) method.[8] The analyst asks users to define the factors that are critical to success in performing their functions or making decisions. A small number of critical factors usually emerges from this eliciting process. Information requirements can then be derived. It can be used at both the organization and application level.

Process analysis is another approach to the synthesis of requirements. The idea underlying this approach is that business processes (groups of decisions and activities required to manage the resources of the organization) are the basis for information system support. Processes remain relatively constant over time, and the requirements derived from the process will reflect the nontransient needs of the organization. An example of a process-based methodology is Business Systems Planning (BSP). The method is primarily appropriate for developing an information system master plan.

BSP is a comprehensive IBM methodology[9] well supported by materials and instruction. Information requirements are derived from the object system in a top-down fashion by starting with business objectives and then defining business processes. Business processes are used as the basis for data collection and analysis. In interviews to clarify processes, executives are also asked to specify key success factors and to identify decisions and problems. Logically related categories of data are identified and related to business processes. This information is used in defining a proposed information architecture. The steps in this top-down process of determining requirements are illustrated in Figure 15–2. Based on the current system and proposed information architecture, application priorities are established and migration to databases planned.

Ends-means analysis is a technique for determining requirements based on systems theory.[10] The technique can be used to determine information requirements at the organizational, departmental, or individual manager level.

The technique separates the definition of ends or outputs (goods, services, and information) generated by an organizational process from the means (inputs and processes) used to accomplish them. The ends or output from one process (whether the process be viewed as an oganizational, departmental, or individual process) is the input to some other process. For example, the inventory process provides a part to the production process, the accounting process provides budget information for other organizational processes, and the marketing process provides products to customer processes.

A model of ends-means analysis is provided in Figure 15–3. Managers are first asked to define both ends and means for their unit. They are then asked to describe measurements for effectiveness and efficiency. Effectiveness information requirements are based upon what constitutes effectiveness for outputs and what information or

---

[8]J. F. Rockart, "Critical Success Factors," *Harvard Business Review*, March–April 1979, pp. 81–91.

[9]*Business Systems Planning—Information Systems Planning Guide*, Application Manual, GE20-0527-3, Third Edition, IBM Corporation, July 1981; available through IBM branch offices.

[10]J. C. Wetherbe and G. B. Davis, "Strategic MIS Planning Through Ends/Means Analysis," University of Minnesota, Management Information Systems Research Center Working Paper Series.

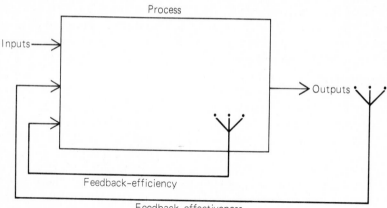

Figure 15-3
Model of ends-means analysis.

feedback is needed to evaluate effectiveness. Efficiency information requirements are based upon what constitutes efficiency in an input and transformation process and upon what information or feedback is needed to evaluate efficiency.

Ends-means analysis has been used in diverse industrial settings with positive results. Information requirements are determined that are often more far-reaching than requirements generated using other techniques. A problem with many information requirements methods is that they result primarily in efficiency-oriented information. However, managers agree that it is more important to be effective than to be efficient. Ends-means analysis brings out the effectiveness information requirements.

ASK ME IN MORE THAN ONE WAY

Wetherbe and Davis report experience in eliciting requirements using a group eliciting session. Participants include all managers having decision responsibility affecting a subsystem. Three sets of questions guide the sessions:

- Questions based on information needed for problems and decisions derived from Business Systems Planning (BSP)
- Questions based on concept of Critical Success Factors (CSF)
- Questions based on Ends-Means Analysis

The participants in the eliciting sessions have different preferences for the three questioning methods, but there is general agreement that the use of three methods elicits a more complete set of requirements. Each method adds to the requirements and further clarifies the need for data.

Source: J. C. Wetherbe and G. B. Davis, "Developing a Long-Range Information Architecture," *Proceedings of the National Computer Conference*, Anaheim, California, May 1983, pp. 261–269.

The *decision analysis* method for information requirements determination is performed by the following steps:[11]

---

[11]R. L. Ackoff, "Management Misinformation Systems," *Management Science*, 14:4, December 1967, pp. B147–B156.

1 Identify and prescribe the decision.

2 Define the decision algorithm or decision process. Various documentation methods may be used. Examples are decision flowcharts, decision tables, and decision trees.

3 Define information needed for the decision process.

Decision analysis has been shown to be very useful in clarifying information requirements with users in cases where the decision process is fairly well defined. For unstructured, poorly understood decision processes, decision analysis does not appear to perform any better than other approaches. Also, decision analysis does not apply to all applications or all information included in applications.[12]

The *sociotechnical analysis* approach[13] consists of two parts: social analysis and technical analysis. The social analysis determines system requirements relative to the social, human interaction system of the organization. These requirements include system design features and implementation procedures. The social analysis is performed by studying patterns of social interaction and group behavior in the current system. Technical analysis is an analysis of variances and control loops that require information. The sequences of steps in sociotechnical analysis was discussed in Chapter 11 (see Figure 11-9 on page 356).

Requirements for sociotechnical design are usually obtained from participative methods and are oriented to application-level analysis. It is especially appropriate for applications that involve many users, particularly secondary users (such as data preparation personnel), or where the application will significantly change the work environment, social interaction, or job design.

Input-process-output analysis is a system approach. A system is defined in terms of its inputs, outputs, and transformation processes for receiving inputs and producing outputs. The approach starts in a top-down fashion on an object system. Subsystems of the object system are analyzed to subdivide them into smaller subsystems, etc., until information processing activities are defined as separate activities within a subsystem. The advantage of analysis based on inputs, processes, and outputs of systems is that it is systematic and comprehensive. By starting at a high level and factoring into subsystems, there is reasonable assurance of completeness. Analysis can be carried to as low a level of detail as desired.

One example of the input-process-output approach is data flow diagrams.[14] When used at a high level of analysis, data flow diagrams are a graphic method for defining inputs, processes, and outputs and for factoring systems into subsystems. The factoring process is top-down and can be carried to the level of program module specification. An

---

[12]Munro and Davis, ''Determining Management Information Needs.''

[13]R. P. Bostrom and J. S. Heinen, ''MIS Problems and Failures: A Socio-Technical Perspective; Part I: The Causes,'' *MIS Quarterly*, 1:3, September, 1977, pp. 17–32; and ''Part II: The Application of Socio-Technical Theory,'' *MIS Quarterly*, 1:4, December 1977, pp. 11–28.

[14]The literature on data flow diagrams and structured analysis is fairly extensive. For example, see T. DeMarco, *Structured Analysis and System Specification*, Yourdon, New York, 1978; D. T. Ross and K. E. Schoman, Jr., ''Structured Analysis for Requirements Definition,'' *IEEE Transactions on Software Engineering* SE-3, 1, January 1977, pp. 6–15.

example of the use of data flow diagrams is shown in Chapter 18 (Figure 18-5). Other useful methods based on a system approach are SADT (Structured Analysis and Design Technique)[15] and ISAC (Information Systems work and Analysis of Changes).[16]

Discovering from Experimentation with an Evolving Information System

Traditional procedures for determining information requirements are designed to establish a complete and correct set of requirements before the information system is designed and built. In a significant percentage of cases, users may not be able to formulate information requirements because they have no existing model (either normative or experiential) on which to base requirements. They may find it difficult to deal in abstract requirements or to visualize new systems. Users may need to anchor on concrete systems from which they can make adjustments.

Another approach to information requirements determination is, therefore, to capture an initial set of requirements and implement an information system to provide those requirements. The system is designed for ease of change. As users employ the system, they request additional requirements. After initial requirements establish an anchor, additional requirments are discovered through use of the system. The general approach has been described as prototyping or heuristic development;[17] it is described in more detail in Chapter 18.

SELECTING A STRATEGY FOR DETERMINING INFORMATION REQUIREMENTS

Four strategies have been described for determining information requirements, with each strategy having a number of methods that may be employed. This section will present an approach to the selection of an appropriate primary strategy. The selection procedure is contingent on characteristics of the environment in which the determination of requirements is conducted.

The underlying basis for selecting a strategy is uncertainty with respect to the requirements determination processes. The uncertainty is based on four factors: characteristics of the utilizing system, the information system or application, the users, and the analysts.

The approach to selecting an information requirements determination strategy consists of five steps (Figure 15-4). The steps represent a series of evaluations to establish a basis for selection. The evaluations are not precise, but do provide guidelines for judgment. The steps are listed in Table 15-2 and explained in more detail below.

---

[15]Ross and Schoman, "Structured Analysis for Requirements Definition."

[16]M. Lundeberg, G. Goldkuhl, and A. Nilsson, *Information Systems Development: A Systematic Approach*, Prentice-Hall, Englewood Cliffs, NJ, 1981.

[17]T. R. Berrisford and J. C. Wetherbe, "Heuristic Development: A Redesign of Systems Design," *MIS Quarterly*, 3:1, March 1979, pp. 11–19.

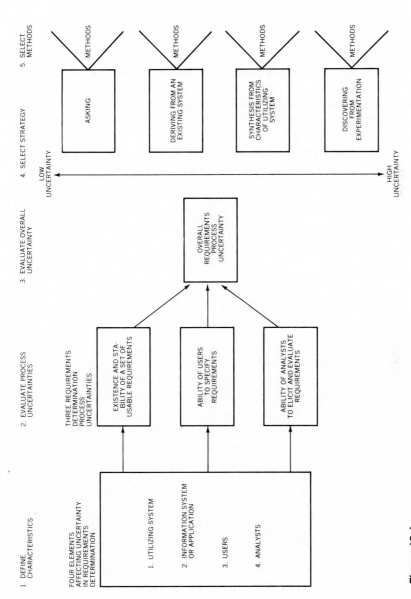

Figure 15-4
Selection of a strategy for the determination of information requirements.

TABLE 15-2: STEPS IN SELECTING A STRATEGY AND METHODS FOR DETERMINING INFORMATION REQUIREMENTS

1 Identify those characteristics of the four elements in the development process that affect uncertainty in the determination of information requirements:

- Utilizing system
- Information system or application
- Users
- Analysts

2 Evaluate the effect of the characteristics of the four elements in the development process on three process uncertainties:

- Existence and availability of a set of usable requirements
- Ability of users to specify requirements
- Ability of analysts to elicit and evaluate requirements

3 Evaluate the combined effect of the process uncertainties on overall requirements uncertainty.

4 Select a primary strategy for requirements determination based on the overall requirements uncertainty.

Uncertainty	Strategy
Low	Asking directly
↑	Deriving from an existing system
↓	Synthesis from characteristics of utilizing system
High	Discovering from experimentation

5 Select one or more methods from the set of methods to implement the primary strategy.

Identifying the Characteristics of Elements in the Development Process that Affect Uncertainty

Four elements in the development process affect the level of uncertainty of a strategy for determining information requirements: the utilizing system, the information system or application system, the users, and the analysts. As summarized below, for each of the elements there are characteristics that reduce expected uncertainty as to requirements determination; there are opposing characteristics that increase expected uncertainty.

Elements in development process	Characteristics that reduce uncertainty	Characteristics th . increase uncertainty
Utilizing system	Stable, well-defined system not in process of change Programmed activities or decisions	Unstable, poorly understood system in process of change Nonprogrammed activities or decisions
Information system or application system	Traditional, simple set of requirements Clerical support system	Complex or unusual set of requirements Management support system

Users	One or few users High user system experience	Many users Low user system experience
Analysts	Trained and experienced with similar information system	Little prior training or experience with similar information system

Evaluating the Effect of the Characteristics on Process Uncertainty

The characteristics of the four elements in the development process affect the uncertainty of determining information requirements by affecting three process uncertainties:

1 Uncertainty with respect to existence and stability of a usable set of requirements.
2 Uncertainty with respect to users' ability to specify requirements.
3 Uncertainty with respect to analyst's ability to elicit requirements and evaluate their correctness and completeness.

The first uncertainty can arise from a number of characteristics of the utilizing system. Some examples are

- Lack of a well-understood model of the utilizing system. This lack may be reflected in confused objectives, unclear organization, and poorly defined operating procedures.
- Lack of stability in structure and operation of the utilizing system.
- Lack of stability in use of information system. Nonprogrammed activity has a low level of predefined structure, and, therefore, changes in user personnel may create unstable use patterns.
- The existence of a large number of users. The large number can affect the existence and stability of requirements if all users participate in specification of requirements and there is no mechanism to arbitrate differences or achieve consensus.

The second process uncertainty about the ability of users to specify requirements is a result not only of human limitations in developing specifications but also of characteristics of the information system or application. Examples are

- Lack of user conceptual model of the utilizing system.
- Lack of structure for activity or decision being supported.
- Changes in the utilizing system.
- Changes in the use of information.
- A complex system.
- A large number of users which will affect level of participation and users' feelings of responsibility in specifying requirements.
- Types of users doing the specifications. Clerical users may be able to specify procedure requirements but not overall content; managers may be better able to specify content than procedures.
- Lack of user experience in the utilizing system and lack of experience in type of application being proposed.

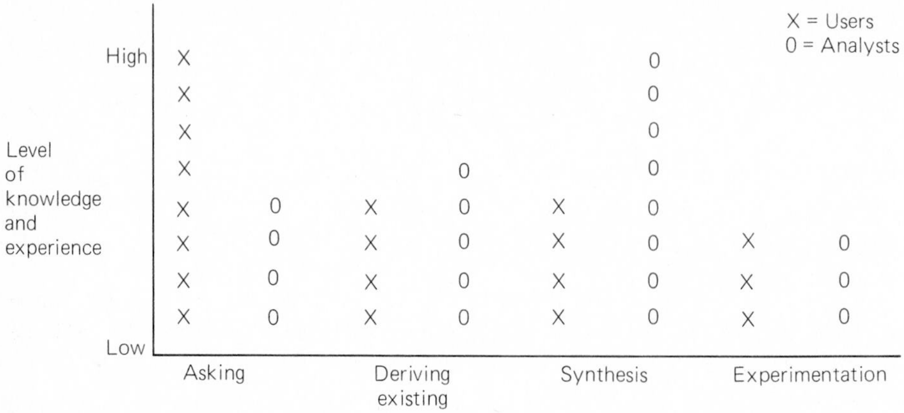

Figure 15-5
Relative estimated level of knowledge and experience by users and analysts to employ the four requirements determination strategies.

The third uncertainty with regard to the ability of the analyst is related to the personal characteristics of the analysts, their general level of training, and prior experience with the same or similar applications. The characteristics of the application that affect users described above also affect the performance of the analyst.

The level of knowledge and experience needed by users and analysts tends to differ for different strategies in the determination of requirements. As illustrated in Figure 15-5, an asking strategy requires a higher level of user knowledge and experience than an experimental strategy.

Evaluating the Combined Effect of the Process Uncertainties on Overall Requirements Uncertainty

The expected overall requirements uncertainty might be estimated directly from the characteristics of the object system, the information system, the users, and the analysts. However, it is useful to make this evaluation in two steps:

1 Evaluate the effect of the characteristics of the four elements on the three process uncertainties.

2 Evaluate the three process uncertainties to arrive at an estimated overall level of requirements process uncertainty.

The expected overall level cannot be estimated with certainty, but the insight gained in the three-step evaluation allows a reasonable basis for selection of a strategy.

Selecting a Primary Strategy for Determining Requirements and One or More Methods

The selection of a primary strategy is based on the level of uncertainty in requirements determination. When a strategy has been selected, one or more methods are selected for use. The selection of a primary strategy and associated method(s) does not preclude the use of a secondary strategy and other supplementary methods, but it does assist the analyst in understanding how to deal with the expected level of uncertainty regarding requirements.

Many installations have adopted a single development methodology to be used for all applications. This has training, supervision, and quality assurance benefits for the organization. It may, however, mean that some applications are developed with a methodology that is not optimal. In such cases, the strategy selection approach outlined above may aid in encouraging analysts to use alternative features of the standard methodology or to modify, adjust, or supplement it.

In order to clarify the concept of uncertainty and its effect on determining information requirements, the use of the selection approach will now be illustrated for both the organizational information requirements and application requirements.

THE CONTINGENCY APPROACH APPLIED TO DETERMINING ORGANIZATIONAL INFORMATION REQUIREMENTS

The set of characteristics that apply to the four elements in determining organizational-level requirements are described in Table 15-3.

TABLE 15-3: EVALUATING UNCERTAINTY FOR ORGANIZATIONAL-LEVEL REQUIREMENTS

Elements in process	Characteristics affecting requirements determination uncertainty
Utilizing system	Stability of technology and operational systems Stability in management and control Maturity in use of information systems
Information system	Extent to which higher-level management applications are included in scope of systems Complexity and level of integration of information
Users	Level of experience in utilizing system Experience in planning information systems
Analysts	Experience in planning information systems

One item of special interest is organizational maturity in the use of a computer-based information system. This item reflects the fact that organizations exhibit a learning process as discussed in Chapter 14. It is not feasible to implement a complex information system until the organization has reached a "mature" stage of information processing.

Three examples illustrate the use of the contingency approach for selection of a strategy for determining information requirements for the organizational level.

    1 Company A is a small company with a stable technology that has not used computers before. It expects to apply computer processing first to accounting and inventory control. It has an analyst with two years experience. In the list below and in those of the succeeding examples, the second column indicates whether an item increases or reduces uncertainty.

Characteristics of company	*Effect on uncertainty*
Stable technology	Reduces

Characteristics of company	*Effect on uncertainty*
Stable management control	Reduces
Low maturity in computer use	Increases
Clerical level applications	Reduces
Complexity and integration low	Reduces
Experience of analysts	—
Experience of users low	Increases

Based on these characteristics, process uncertainties are classified in the following ways:

- Low uncertainty as to existence and stability of requirements
- Moderate uncertainty as to the ability of users to specify requirements
- Moderate to low uncertainty as to the ability of analysts to elicit and evaluate requirements

The overall evaluation is moderate to low uncertainty. A requirements strategy might be to derive an initial set of organizational requirements from the existing manual systems.

2 Company B has used computers for traditional accounting but would now like to have management-support applications, decision-support applications, query capabilities, and planning applications. The requirements uncertainty analysis is:

Characteristics of company	*Effect on uncertainty*
Stable technology and operational systems	Reduces
Management control changing	Increases
Fairly mature in use of computers	Reduces
Management-level applications	Increases
Complexity and integration high	Increases
Experience of users low	Increases
Experience of analysts moderate	Increases

An evaluation of these characteristics suggests a moderate to high uncertainty in existence and stability of requirements, a fairly high uncertainty as to the ability of users to specify requirements, and a moderate uncertainty as to the ability of analysts to elicit and evaluate requirements. Overall, there is a moderately high degree of uncertainty in determining requirements, which suggests a strategy of synthesizing organizational information needs from the characteristics of the utilizing system.

3 Company C has a very unstable environment and very poorly developed planning and control information. Management wishes to improve its information system to provide better information for planning and control.

Characteristics of company	*Effect on uncertainty*
Unstable operational processes	Increases
Management control changing	Increases
Low maturity in use of computers	Increases
Complexity and integration high	Increases
Experience of analysts low	Increases
Experience of users low	Increases

An evaluation of the characteristics suggests a high degree of uncertainty for existence and stability of requirements, the ability of users to specify, and the ability of analysts to elicit and evaluate. With this high level of overall uncertainty, the appropriate strategy for determining organizational requirements might be to use experimentation with an evolving planning and control system.

THE CONTINGENCY APPROACH APPLIED TO DETERMINING APPLICATION INFORMATION REQUIREMENTS

The characteristics that may be considered in evaluating the uncertainty of requirements processes for an application are summarized in Table 15-4.

TABLE 15-4: EVALUATING UNCERTAINTY FOR APPLICATION-LEVEL REQUIREMENTS

Elements in process	Characteristics affecting uncertainty in determining requirements
Utilizing system	Existence of a model of the system Stability of system Nonprogrammed versus programmed activity Stability in information use
Application	High-level versus low-level application Complexity Number of users
Users	Experience with utilizing system Experience with application
Analysts	Experience with utilizing system Experience with application

The following examples illustrate the use of the contingency theory to select a strategy for determining requirements for an application. In each example, the second column of the list indicates whether an item increases or reduces uncertainty.

1 A balance forward billing and accounts receivable application system for a retail store.

Utilizing system has stable, programmed activity	Reduces
Application has stable requirements with fairly small number of users in accounting department	Reduces
User familiarity with system is high	Reduces
Analyst familiarity and experience is reasonably high	Reduces

There is very little uncertainty with respect to the requirements themselves, little uncertainty with respect to the ability of users to provide requirements, and little uncertainty as to the ability of analysts to elicit requirements and evaluate their correctness and completeness. Given this overall low degree of uncertainty, the analyst may use a primary strategy of asking users to define requirements (using open or closed questions). An alternative primary strategy is to derive requirements from an existing billing and accounts receivable system (existing system in this organization or in another organization).

2 An integrated online order entry transaction system and management order tracking application to replace a traditional batch system having little management reporting.

Utilizing system is stable, mainly programmed activity	Reduces
Application has stable requirements for clerical users and moderately stable requirements for management users. Medium number of users.	Reduces

Well defined model of requirements for order entry procedures	Reduces
Less well-defined model of tracking requirements	Increases
Complex system	Increases
User personnel are familiar with order entry requirements	Reduces
Experience of analysts is at least moderate for online systems	Reduces

The overall uncertainty level is moderate, based on the evaluation of the three processes:

- Little uncertainty with respect to the order entry functions to be performed and requirements related to these functions. Some uncertainty as to management functions to be supported.
- Little uncertainty as to the ability of users to define transaction entry requirements and medium uncertainty as to ability to define management reporting. Because of online systems, there may also be new social system considerations and human behavior considerations that users cannot define clearly and completely.
- Moderate uncertainty as to the ability of analysts to elicit requirements and evaluate their correctness and completeness.

Given this overall moderate degree of uncertainty, the analyst may choose to synthesize from the characteristics of the utilizing system as the primary strategy for requirements determination. Examples of methods appropriate to this situation are:

- Input-process-output analysis
- Sociotechnical analysis for social and behavioral requirements
- Decision analysis or critical factors analysis for management reporting

3 A management report application for problem identification and problem finding with respect to sales. It includes content of some existing informal, private information systems but does not replace an existing information system application.

Supports mixture of programmed and nonprogrammed activities	Increases
Requirements not stable because they are dependent on experience and decision style of users	Increases
No well-defined model of utilizing system and its requirements	Increases
Users somewhat unsure of requirements	Increases
Analysts inexperienced in specific application because it is unique	Increases

Based on these characteristics, there is uncertainty with respect to processes for determining requirements:

- High uncertainty as to necessary and desirable requirements
- High uncertainty as to the ability of users to specify requirements
- High uncertainty as to the ability of analysts to elicit requirements and assess correctness and completeness

The high level of uncertainty suggests a discovery methodology in which requirements are identified iteratively as the application system evolves.

SUMMARY

The chapter describes factors relevant to the selection of a strategy for determining information requirements. The chapter defines three levels of requirements: organizational information requirements, application-level requirements, and database requirements. The constraints on humans as specifiers of information requirements are explored. Four broad strategies for determining information requirements encompass groups of methods. These strategies are (1) asking directly, (2) deriving from an existing information system, (3) synthesizing from characteristics of the utilizing system, and (4) discovering from experimentation with an evolving information system.

The selection of a strategy is based on uncertainties with respect to processes for determining information requirements. The uncertainty focuses on (1) uncertainty with respect to the existence and stability of a set of requirements, (2) uncertainty with respect to the ability of users to specify requirements, and (3) uncertainty with respect to the ability of analysts to elicit requirements and evaluate their correctness and completeness. These three uncertainties as to the best process for determining information requirements are associated with certain characteristics of the utilizing systems, the information system or application, users, and analysts.

The selection of a strategy for determining requirements for both the organizational level and the application level is thus based on an evaluation of the characteristics that determine the three areas of uncertainty. The selection of a primary strategy for determining requirements that satisfies the level of uncertainty points to a set of methods for use. An analyst may choose to use other strategies and methods to supplement the primary determination strategy.

MINICASES

1 THE VERY NEW COMPANY

The company had just been established by a group of engineers. The product was a line of software for microcomputers. None of the founders had any accounting or finance experience. An experienced bookkeeper was hired and a CPA was engaged to provide advice when needed. Rather than begin with a large-scale information system, management and the bookkeeper decided to automate only the essential bookkeeping functions. The requirements for the information system are to be formulated and the information system plan developed. The basic idea is to use software packages and tailor them only as much as absolutely necessary.

Question

Analyze this company in terms of the contingency theory for obtaining organizational information system requirements.

2 THE MODERATELY NEW COMPANY

Two years have gone by and the company is over the initial stages of growth. Everything has grown, and the president realizes that the company must enter a new phase of management that is less casual. As part of this, the president wants a budgeting and responsibility reporting system installed. The company now has a controller and a small data processing staff with two analysts (one of whom is very experienced). Most of the executives concerned have had some experience with management budgeting and control in the company they were with before they started the new company, but they have all operated for two years with private information and control systems.

Question

Analyze, in terms of the contingency theory, how the company might perform the process for determining information requirements for the budgeting and control application.

3 THE DECISION SUPPORT APPLICATION

The marketing manager of a software company is concerned about special software deals. Sales representatives are very innovative in coming up with "deals." At first, the tendency was to accept them because they always represented marginal income. Lately, however, there has been significant concern that deals may spoil the regular market and interfere with existing contracts. For example, the government pricing schedule requires that it be the lowest price the company sells for. The marketing manager would like a decision support system to aid representatives in the analysis and to aid him in reviewing the deals.

Question

Analyze, in terms of contingency theory, how the requirements for the decision support application might be determined.

EXERCISES

1 What is the relationship between the three levels of information requirements determination?
2 Why can't an analyst just ask users for requirements and always expect to get a correct and complete answer?
3 Under what conditions can an analyst ask users for requirements and expect to get a correct and complete answer?
4 How can an analyst derive requirements from an existing system? What existing systems can be used for this purpose?
5 An analyst argues that it is never a good idea to simply ask or take requirements from an existing system. She says that the only correct way to obtain requirements is by analysis of the object system (the utilizing system). Make a pro and con list of arguments for her position.
6 The methods presented in the chapter for deriving requirements from characteristics of the utilizing system represent a variety of methods that are not all competitors in the sense that one is used to the exclusion of all others. More than one may be used in combination. Select three pairs of methods that appear to be complementary and explain why.
7 An organization has adopted the "Only Way Analysis Methodology." All analysts are to use the methodology for all application development. It contains a method for determining requirements based on input-process-output analysis. Significant documentation is generated using the method which also results in user signoffs for information requirements. Examine the following incidents. Explain why they may have happened and what might be done to avoid cases like these in the future.
   a The accounting department needed a fairly straightforward accounting report. They became very frustrated with the delays caused by the requirements determination method. They said, "We know what we want; just do it!"
   b The finance area is working hard to make sense of the foreign exchange problem. The rules seem to keep changing, and the situation is very volatile. They have asked for an information system application to support their work. When asked to sign off on the information requirements, they said they weren't sure whether they were right. Information systems then closed the project saying they couldn't design a system that wasn't specified.
8 The accounting department was in trouble with accounts payable. Vendors weren't being paid on time, and the analysis of accounts payable was very inadequate. The department requested some assistance. The decision was made to prototype an application, both to get it working and

also to clarify requirements. The system is now in and working. Accounting doesn't want to spend any more time to have the system redesigned and recoded with more traditional development procedures. Evaluate their position.

9 Why is uncertainty the basis for an information requirements strategy? Why not something else—size, complexity, etc.?

10 The contingency theory provides some guidance, but the measurements are imprecise, and it is difficult to sum up the effect of low and high measurements. Given these difficulties, does it help at all to have such a theory? Discuss.

SELECTED REFERENCES

Bowman, B., G. B. Davis, and J. C. Wetherbe: "Modeling for MIS," *Datamation*, July 1981, pp. 155–164.

Business Systems Planning—Information Systems Planning Guide, Application Manual, GE20-0527-3, Third Edition, IBM Corporation, July 1981.

Carlson, Walter M.: "Business Information Analysis and Integration Technique (BIAIT)—The New Horizon," *Data Base*, Spring 1979, pp. 3–9.

Couger, J. Daniel, Mel A. Colter, and Robert W. Knapp: *Advanced System Development/Feasibility Techniques*, Wiley, New York, 1982.

Gordon, L. A., and Danny Miller: "A Contingency Framework for the Design of Accounting Information Systems," *Accounting Organizations and Society*, 1:1, June 1976, pp. 59–69.

Gorry, G. A., and M. S. Scott Morton: "A Framework for Management Information Systems," *Sloan Management Review*, 12, Fall 1971, pp. 55–70.

Hedberg, B., and E. Mumford: "The Design of Computer Systems: Man's Vision of Man as an Integral Part of the Systems Design Process," in E. Mumford and H. Sackman (eds.), *Human Choice and Computers*, North-Holland, Amsterdam, 1975, pp. 31–59.

Jenkins, A. M., and R. D. Johnson: "What the Information Analyst Should Know about Body Language," *MIS Quarterly*, 1:3, September 1977, pp. 33–47.

Kerner, David V.: "Business Information Characterization Study," *Data Base*, Spring 1979, pp. 10–17.

King, W. R.: "Strategic Planning for Management Information Systems," *MIS Quarterly*, 2:1, March 1978, pp. 27–37.

King, W. R., and D. I. Cleland: "The Design of Management Information Systems: An Information Analysis Approach," *Management Science*, 22:3, November 1974, pp. 286–297.

London, K.: *The People Side of Systems*, McGraw-Hill, New York, 1976.

Lundeberg, Mats, Goran Goldkuhl, and Anders Nilsson: "A Systematic Approach to Information Systems Development—I. Introduction," *Information Systems*, 4, 1979, pp. 1–12.

Lundeberg, Mats, Goran Goldkuhl, and Anders Nilsson: *Information Systems Development—A Systematic Approach*, Prentice-Hall, Englewood Cliffs, NJ, 1980.

Lynch, Hugh J.: "ADS: A Technique in Systems Documentation," *Data Base*, 1:1, Spring 1969, pp. 6–18.

Markus, M. Lynne: *Systems in Organizations: Bugs and Features*, Pitman, Boston, 1984.

Miller, J. C.: "Conceptual Models and Determining Information Requirements," *Proceedings of the Spring Joint Computer Conference*, 25, 1964, pp. 609–620.

Mumford, E., and M. Weir: *Computer Systems in Work Design: The ETHICS Method*, Halsted (Wiley), New York, 1979.

Munro, M. C., and G. B. Davis: "Determining Management Information Needs: A Comparison of Methods," *MIS Quarterly*, 1:2, June 1977, pp. 55–67.

Rockart, J. F.: "Critical Success Factors," *Harvard Business Review*, March–April 1979, pp. 81–91.

Shneiderman, B.: *Software Psychology: Human Factors in Computer and Information Systems*, Winthrop, Cambridge, MA, 1980.

Vitalari, N. P., and G. W. Dickson: "Problem Solving for Effective Systems Analysis," *Communications of the ACM*, 26:11, November 1983, pp. 948–956.

Yadav, Surya B.: "Determining an Organization's Information Requirements: A State of the Art Survey," *Data Base*, 14:3, Spring 1983, pp. 3–20.

Young, J. W., and H. Kent, "Abstract Formulation of Data Processing Problems," *Journal of Industrial Engineering*, November–December 1958, pp. 471–479.

DATABASE REQUIREMENTS

One approach to definition of data requirements in an organization is to specify data only in relation to particular information system applications. There are several difficulties with that approach:

1 Having data ''owned'' by individual applications may lead to difficulties in data access for other uses, duplicate data, and inconsistencies between data in different files.

2 New applications may be more costly to develop because of the need to build new files, redesign files, or develop interfaces with existing data.

3 Frequently, data needed for analyses and for responding to queries will not be available because no existing application has provided it.

4 Some data may be available for applications, but it may be very difficult and costly to access it for ad hoc query or analysis.

The solution (introduced in earlier chapters) is to establish databases and use a database management system to manage data as a general use resource. However, even with a database, there may be data items that are not available because their use was not anticipated. Much of the data in the database may be derived from the requirements of data processing applications, but many data items that should be in a database are not part of the normal transaction processing or reporting applications.

The subject of this chapter is how to determine the information requirements for organizational databases. The chapter provides conceptual background on databases and reviews the data concepts and terminology introduced in Chapter 4. Alternatives for determining current and anticipated database data requirements are reviewed, and two methods for data modeling are explained.

DATABASES AND DATABASE MANAGEMENT SYSTEMS

The database is central to a management information system. Although the term ''database'' is often used to refer to any data available for information processing or retrieval operations, the term implies a particular structuring of the data, both conceptually and in physical storage. This section will provide definitions and background concepts related to databases and database management systems.

The Database Approach

A *database* is a mechanized, formally defined, centrally controlled collection of data in an organization.[1] The data records are physically organized and stored so as to promote shareability, availability, evolvability, and integrity. The database approach is made operational by a *database management system*, or DBMS, a software system which performs the functions of defining, creating, revising, and controlling the database. It provides facilities for retrieving data, generating reports, revising data definitions, updating data, and building applications. Many different end users and a variety of application programs can access the database, and it is desirable to have an organizational function to exercise control over the database. This function is known as *database administration*; the person performing the function is a *database administrator*.

The database management system controls the interaction between the database and

---

[1]Gordon C. Everest, *Database Management: Objectives, System Functions, and Administration*, McGraw-Hill, New York, 1985.

application programs prepared by programmers and between the database and nonprogramming or ad hoc users. Accessing or updating items in the database is performed only through the database management system. The overall model of the database management system is shown in Figure 16-1.

There are three classes of users who interact with database management systems. There are languages and instruction procedures appropriate for each of them:

1 *The nonprogramming user.* User who is not writing a program to use the database. Usually an analyst or end user with special training. Programs ad hoc queries and reports using a database query language.

2 *The programming user.* An applications programmer who does the analysis and programming of applications. Uses special database interface instructions to program application access to the database through the database management system. The instructions call the database management system to request data, perform updates, etc. The programming user can also use the database query language for special assignments.

3 *The database administrator (DBA).* The DBA uses special instructions and facilities of the database management system (a *data definition language* or DDL) to define, create, redefine, and restructure the database and to implement integrity controls.

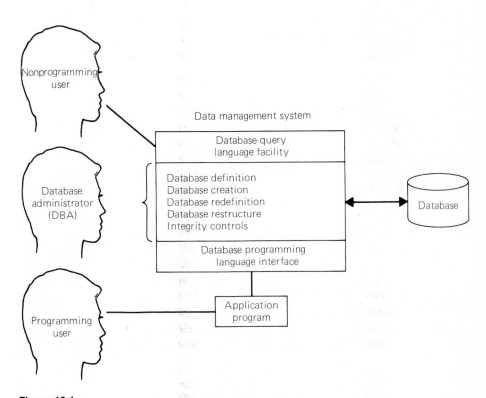

Figure 16-1
Conceptual model of a database management system. (Adapted from Gordon C. Everest, *Database Management: Objectives, System Functions, and Administration*, McGraw-Hill, New York, 1984.)

Installing a database requires procedures to determine data requirements to be stored in the database and use of software to build the initial database, maintain and reorganize the database, provide data to applications programs, and execute ad hoc queries and report requests. The database administration function performs or oversees these activities. The focus of this chapter is on the first activity of determining data to be stored. The database administration function will be described further in Chapter 20.

Objectives of Database and Database Management Systems

The objectives of the database approach are listed below;[2] they provide a guide to the database requirements process and data modeling.

Database objective	Description
Availability	Data should be available for use by applications (both current and future) and by queries.
Shareability	Data items prepared by one application are available to all applications or queries. No data items are "owned" by an application.
Evolvability	The database can evolve as application usage and query needs evolve.
Data independence	The users of the database establish their view of the data and its structure without regard to the actual physical storage of the data.
Data integrity	The database establishes a uniform high level of accuracy and consistency. Validation rules are applied by the database management system.

Data independence is achieved by separating data from the programs that use it, providing facilities for different user views of the data, and the separation of logical design from physical design. The raw material for the physical design is the logical database design that describes the data as perceived by the users of the database. The shareability objective results in a minimization of unplanned redundancy. Redundancy occurs when the same data item is stored multiple times. With a database system, it need only be stored once. This reduces inconsistencies and also aids in achieving the objective of data integrity. The data integrity objective is also achieved by having data in the database controlled through the database administration function and data creation, access, and updating controlled by the database management software.

An explanation of the physical design of the database is beyond the scope of this chapter. However, there are many trade-offs to be made in deciding on how to physically structure the data, provide access paths, etc. These trade-offs are between storage utilization, speed of access, ease of maintenance, and availability of data for a variety of uses. The physical trade-offs may mean that some user requirements are met with fast access times while others are allowed to take significant time to process. The database is not a huge file drawer in which everything is available with equal accessibility. Access paths must be established. By analogy, automobile and truck traffic uses a network of

[2]Everest, *Database Management*.

highways, secondary roads, and streets that are predefined. If there is no direct route to a location, a relatively inefficient route may be found using secondary roads and streets. In some cases, no route can be found. In the same way, the physical database design must provide highways for fast data access for the most common needs. Other needs must use less efficient, less direct access paths.

The Data Dictionary

A data dictionary, as the name implies, is a repository of information about data. In some database systems, the stored definitions of data (called schemas) provide all necessary data dictionary information; in others, the data dictionary is supplementary. Although it might be possible in a very small limited database to prepare a manual dictionary, the term refers to a dictionary maintained by special data dictionary software. It contains such information as the following about data:

1 The name of the data item.
2 A description of the data item. The description can be a language description (such as "a unique 9-digit identification code") or a data processing description (such as PIC X(12) for type and number of characters in a field). The descriptions may also specify allowable values (numeric, range of values, etc.), edit and validation criteria, security, calculations to determine value, classification, aliases, owners, and number of occurrences.
3 Source of data—various sources of input.
4 Impact analysis—users of the data including screens, reports, programs, and organizational positions that access and use the data item.
5 Key words used for categorizing and searching for data item descriptions.

The information in the data dictionary is about both types of data and uses of data. It relates both to the documentation of design requirements and to design decisions. As shown in Figure 16-2, entities and attributes document design requirements about types

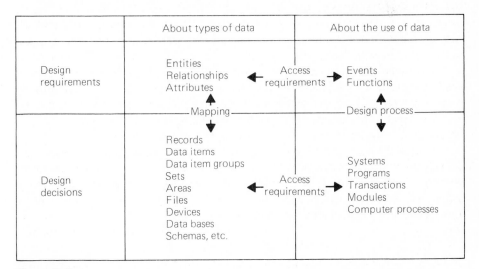

Figure 16-2
The information in a data dictionary, (Source: "The British Computer Society Data Dictionary Systems Working Party Report," *Data Base*, 9:2, Fall 1977, p. 5. ©1978, Association for Computing Machinery, Inc. By permission.)

of data; data items and records document physical design decisions. Events and functions document the end use of data; programs and modules document the physical information processing use of data.

A DATA ITEM NAME MAY NOT MEAN WHAT IT SAYS

The COBOL programming language made a step forward in handling of data in programs by separating the data (DATA DIVISION) from the processing procedures (PROCEDURE DIVISION). The DATA DIVISION documents a name for each data item and a description of its format (numeric, alphabetic, decimal point, etc.). The data names can be 30 characters in length, so very descriptive names are possible. For example, a data item name may be NET-PAY-AFTER-ALL-DEDUCTIONS.

When establishing a data dictionary, a bank found that the COBOL naming feature did not always work the way it should. For example, a data item was named AVERAGE-ACCOUNT-BALANCE, but the data item values were the ending balance for the account. The programmer had chosen a descriptive name, but the definition of the content was changed and the name was not altered.

There are three general types of facilities in a data dictionary:

1 Report facility. There is detailed reporting on data items and their uses. Cross-reference reports show relationships, and summary reporting provides various summary data.

2 Control facility. This detects violations of standards for user authority, documentation, etc.

3 Excerpt facility. Specific tasks are performed such as preparation of test data, copying of code from existing programs and inserting in programs under development, and copying documentation into source code.

The data dictionary provides lists of data items sequenced alphabetically by classification, keyword, etc. The dictionary provides a consistent official description of data as well as consistent data names for programming and retrieval. For example, the data dictionary can provide a response to specific queries such as all data items describing "product."

The advantages of a data dictionary are not only consistency of data descriptions and naming, but also ease of updating where one data description serves many purposes. For example, if a change is to be made to a product code, some data dictionaries identify every program, input screen, and report in which the data item appears.

Data dictionaries may be used by the database administrator to enforce standards for names and descriptions; those who create data must follow these standards. Creating a data dictionary requires significant effort to remove past inconsistencies and ambiguities. The same data items in different applications will have different names, so synonyms must be specified. Also, the same name may have been used in different applications to refer to different data items.

A DIFFICULT CONVERSION TO A DATA DICTIONARY

A medium-large company is considering a data dictionary for documenting existing data and supporting development. The company uses 3,000 programs that access 2,400 files.

However, there has been no consistency of naming, so a file may be referred to by as many as five different names. With an average of three records per file and an average of 10 fields per record, there are a maximum of 12,000 file names, 36,000 record definitions (under the file names), and 360,000 items. There are significantly fewer in actual fact because of the high number of aliases, but there are still a large number. Extracted from Christopher J. Coulson, "People Just Aren't Using Data Dictionaries!" *Computerworld*, August 16, 1982, In Depth, p. 16.

DATA MODEL CONCEPTS AND TERMINOLOGY

Database design can be divided into three phases:

Phase	Description
Requirements determination	Determination of the data requirements (views) of individual users and applications.
Conceptual (logical) design	Integration of the individual user and application views into an overall conceptual view that resolves view conflicts. There are two parts to this phase: an unconstrained or natural conceptual design and a conceptual design constrained for a particular DBMS.
Physical design	Translating the conceptual design into physical storage structures.

The data modeling procedures described in the chapter refer to requirements determination and development of an overall, natural conceptual model.

Review of Definitions

As explained in Chapter 4, a *data model* is a model describing the data in an organization. It provides a framework for abstracting the essential qualities or characteristics of data. *Data modeling* is the process of abstraction and documentation using a data model.

Data modeling creates hierarchies of abstraction along two dimensions: aggregation and generalization (Figure 16-3). Aggregation identifies data items as parts of a higher-level, more aggregate descriptor. For example, project number is associated with (part of) a project which is part of an assignment. Generalization creates categories into which a data item may be classified. For example, employees may be categorized as to age, type of job, type of pay plan, etc. Examples of generalization of employees by type of job are secretaries, truck drivers, and salespersons.

A data model may be a conceptual model designed to provide user-understandable specifications of data or a physical data model designed to aid in physical database design. The two types of models have also been termed infological (for the human understanding and requirements level) and datalogical (for physical design and implementation).[3] Models can contain some elements of both. For example, the hierarchical, network, and relational models described in Chapter 4 contain not only conceptual requirements aspects but also physical aspects of data related to implementation.

---

[3]Bo Lundgren, *Theory of Data Bases*, Mason/Charter, New York, 1975.

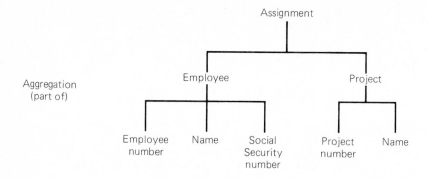

Figure 16-3
Concepts of aggregation and generalization.

Some definitions of terms used in describing logical data structures were defined in Chapter 4. They are summarized below:

Term	Definition
Entity	Any type of "thing" about which information is maintained. A more formal definition is "a category, arbitrarily defined (but agreed to) so that membership within the category can be established (at least at a point in time)."[4]
Attribute	A characteristic of an entity.
Instance	A specific instance of an entity or relationship. Consists of a set of values for attributes of an entity or relationship.
Relationship	Association between entities.
Identifiers	Set of attributes which uniquely identify an instance of an entity or relationship.

[4]Salvatore T. March, "Techniques for Structuring Database Records," *ACM Computing Surveys*, 15:1, March 1983, p. 46.

An explanation of the relationship among these terms may clarify their meaning. An entity is a category or grouping of things; instances of an entity are members of that category (e.g., EMPLOYEE is an entity and a person who works for the company is an instance of that entity). The description of an entity-instance is a set of values for selected attributes (data items) of the entity-instance (e.g., ''John Doe'' is the value of the attribute EMPLOYEE-NAME for an instance of the entity EMPLOYEE).

Relationships

There are three types of relationships among entities. These are recorded during conceptual data modeling and also affect physical database design (Figure 16-4).

Relationship	Explanation
1:1	In a one-to-one relationship, an instance of an entity has a given relationship with only one instance of a second entity. For example, the entity PROFESSOR had the relationship HOLDS for the entity ENDOWED-CHAIR and the ENDOWED-CHAIR entity has the relationship IS HELD BY with the entity PROFESSOR. Since only one professor holds an endowed chair and the endowed chair is held by only one professor, the relationship is 1:1.
1:M	In a one-to-many relationship, an entity has relationships with many instances of another entity. For example, the entity UNIVERSITY has many STUDENTs. but each STUDENT entity instance IS ATTENDING only one UNIVERSITY. Note that if a student can attend many universities, the data model should define a many-to-many relationship.
M:N	In a many-to-many relationship, an entity has relationships with many instances of another entity; and that entity has relationships with multiple entity instances of the first. For example, the entity instances for STUDENT may be REGISTERED IN many different CLASSES, the relationship is many-to-many since each CLASS also has many students.

Constraints

Constraints define conditions that must be met for the data to be complete and correct. Three major types of constraints are on values, dependencies, and referential integrity.

Constraint	Description
Values	The allowable, valid values for attributes may be stated as a list, a range, types of characters, etc. For example, values may be 1, 2, or 3 only, range from 0 to 60, or be numeric only.

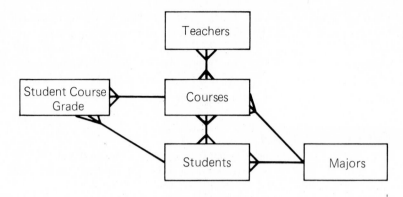

One-many relationship (there is one accounting
major with many students)

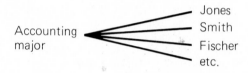

Many-many relationship (there are many courses associated with many students)

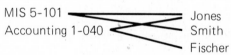

Note that Student Course Grade is
an attribute of this relationship.

Figure 16-4
Entities in a university and relationships among them.

Constraint	Description
Dependencies	The allowable values for attributes may depend on some other value. For example, the allowable values for an employee skill classification are determined by the allowable skills that are part of the employee's department. An employee's eligibility for overtime pay (value for overtime wages) is dependent on his or her employee status code.
Referential integrity	Entities and relationships often have reference conditions that must be met. For example, there may be existence dependencies, in which for one entity to exist, a second entity must also exist. An illustration of this is a sales order; for an order to exist, there must be a customer.

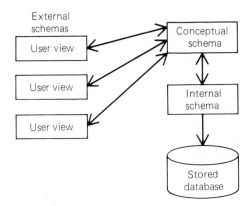

Figure 16-5
A general model of a database system.

Schemas and Mappings

Three schemas[5] were introduced in Chapter 4. These define categories of data and their properties. The different schemas reflect different views of the database (Figure 16-5):

- *External schema* or *user schema* is the user's view of a part of the database
- *Conceptual schema* is the overall logical view of the database
- *Internal schema* or *data storage definition* is the way the data is physically organized in storage

Each user of the database (an application program or a person formulating a query) is concerned with only a small portion of the database. Each user is interested in only a part of the entities in the database, only part of the attributes of those entities, and certain

---

[5]T. C. Tsichritzis and A. Klug (eds.), "The ANSI/SPARC DBMS Framework Report of the Study Group on Database Management Systems," *Information Systems*, 3, 1978, pp. 173–191.

relationships among the entities. The external schema is the user's schema or *user's view* of the data being used.

The conceptual schema (or conceptual model) is the logical view of the entire database. Ideally, the conceptual schema represents as closely as possible the real entities and their relationships. It contains integrity rules and authorization rules, but it does not contain information about how the data items are stored.

The internal schema (or physical data model) describes how the database is organized for physical storage and access. The internal schema includes information on ordering of records, block sizes, storage indexes, use of pointers, and access strategies being used.

A *mapping* is a translation from one schema to another. In order for a user to access data, the user view of the data as reflected in the external schema must be translated into the overall conceptual schema. This is accomplished through *external/conceptual mapping* (Figure 16-6). In the same way, the *conceptual/internal mapping* translates logical descriptions of data in the conceptual schema to physical locations and access paths in the internal schema.

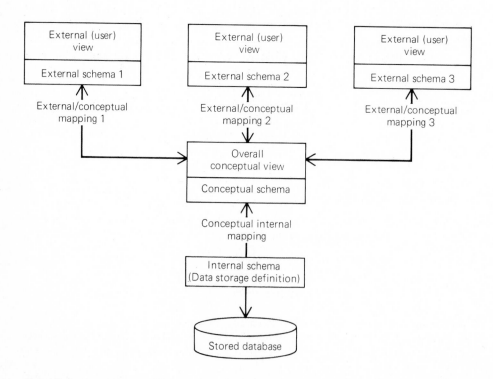

Figure 16-6
Mapping between schemas.

External schemas that describe overlapping portions of the database in different ways are resolved through the external/conceptual mapping. For example, one application may describe the data item "MAJOR" as having 11 characters while another external schema describes it has having 12 characters. These differences can be handled through the external/conceptual mapping. It first translates each view into the conceptual schema for that field (which may, for instance, be 10 characters). When the data item is retrieved, its format can be translated to conform to the definition given by the external schema before it is displayed to the user.

NORMALIZATION IN DATABASE DESIGN

One of the issues in database design is achieving a well-defined model of data to avoid update anomalies. This is aided by *normal forms* and normalization rules. All of the database models described in Chapter 4 can make use of the concepts of normalization. The normal forms are easily understood in terms of relational database design. The relational database model describes the database as tables or relations. Each relation consists of rows (called *tuples*) representing entities and columns representing attributes. Normalization is used to determine how to cluster data items.

There are five normal forms,[6] although fourth and fifth forms are rarely used in practice. They are summarized below and then explained in more detail with an indication of the importance of each. As defined in Chapter 4, a *key field* in a record is a unique identifier that differentiates the record from any others. The key field may consist of subfields. For example, the key field for a part could consist of two subfields for part number and warehouse number. The other fields in the record are nonkey fields.

Form	Explanation
First normal form	By definition, all fields in a record in first normal form are atomic or single valued. There are no repeating groups of items.
Second normal form	"Second and third normal forms deal with the relationship between nonkey and key fields. Under second and third normal forms, *a nonkey field must provide a fact about the key, the whole key, and nothing but the key.*"[7]

---

[6]This section is based on William Kent, "A Simple Guide to Five Normal Forms in Relational Database Theory," *Communications of the ACM*, 26:2, February 1983, pp. 120–136. The examples are also from the article.

[7]William Kent, "A Simple Guide to Five Normal Forms in Relational Database Theory," p. 120.

Form	Explanation
	In second normal form, no nonkey field is a fact about (depends on) a subset of a key.
Third normal form	No nonkey field is a fact about (depends on) another nonkey field.
Fourth normal form	The key of a record type (that already satisfies third normal form) does not contain two or more independent multivalued facts about an entity.
Fifth normal form	A record in fifth normal form is the same as fourth normal form except in special cases where there is a symmetric constraint.

The discussion here will focus on second, third, and fourth normal forms. Second and third normal forms deal with single-valued facts, i.e., one-to-one or one-to-many relationships. Fourth normal form is associated with multivalued facts or many-to-many relationships.

A record in first normal form can only violate second normal form if the key consists of multiple fields (composite key). Design problems occur when there is a composite key and a nonkey data item is a fact about a subfield of the key. For example, if the composite key for a record is PART and WAREHOUSE, a nonkey data item for WAREHOUSE-ADDRESS is a fact only about WAREHOUSE. The record is normalized as follows:

```
                           ┌─── Depends on ───┐
┌──────────────────────────┴──┬──────────────┬┴──────────────────────┐
│  PART     WAREHOUSE         │  QUANTITY    │  WAREHOUSE-ADDRESS     │
└─────────────────────────────┴──────────────┴────────────────────────┘
.....KEY . . . . . . . . . . . . . . .
```

The record is replaced by two records in second normal form:

```
┌─────────┬──────────────┬──────────────┐
│  PART   │  WAREHOUSE   │  QUANTITY    │
└─────────┴──────────────┴──────────────┘
.....KEY..
```

```
┌──────────────┬──────────────────────┐
│  WAREHOUSE   │  WAREHOUSE/ADDRESS   │
└──────────────┴──────────────────────┘
.....KEY . . . . . . . .
```

The third normal form eliminates cases in which a nonkey field is a fact about another nonkey field. For example, if the key field is EMPLOYEE (say, an employee number) and there are nonkey fields for DEPARTMENT and LOCATION of department, the LOCATION is a fact about DEPARTMENT. To place in third normal form, the record definition is replaced by two record types:

```
                Depends on ┐
                     ┌─────┴──────┐
┌──────────────┬─────┴────────┬───┴──────────┐
│  EMPLOYEE    │  DEPARTMENT  │  LOCATION    │
└──────────────┴──────────────┴──────────────┘
....KEY . . . . . . .
```

The record is replaced by two records in third normal form:

EMPLOYEE	DEPARTMENT

....KEY.......

DEPARTMENT	LOCATION

....KEY.........

To look back at the examples for second and third normal forms, the basic problems caused by violation of the forms are the same:

- The item in violation is repeated in every record; therefore, if it changes, every record containing the item must be updated. For example, if the address of the warehouse or the location of a department is changed, every record must be updated. There is significant opportunity for the updating to miss a record and for the records to become inconsistent.
- If there are no records associated with the field violating the normal form, there may be no record in which to store the data. For example, if there are no parts stored in the warehouse, there is no record to keep the warehouse address. Likewise, if a department has no employees, there may be no record in which to store the department location.

Fourth normal form eliminates cases in which the composite key of a record type contains two or more data items that are independent, multivalued facts about an entity. The fields are independent if there are no combinations that are logically related. For example, in the following example, SKILL and LANGUAGE are multivalued (many different skills and many different languages), but there is no logical dependency between a language and a skill. To put into fourth normal form, the data must be represented by two records.

EMPLOYEE	SKILL	LANGUAGE

....KEY..............................

is replaced by:

EMPLOYEE	SKILL

....KEY...............

EMPLOYEE	LANGUAGE

....KEY....................

Normalization is a powerful approach to defining the grouping of data items into records. The process of normalization of records or relations provides both conceptual insight and practical procedures for database design, especially when the database model is relational. Ideally, the database should be in fourth or fifth normal form, but for many situations second or third normal form is acceptable.

APPROACHES TO DETERMINATION OF DATA
REQUIREMENTS FOR DATABASES

The development of requirements for a database consists of an overall planning strategy and processes to define an overall architecture, existing requirements, and anticipated requirements. Based on these three processes, there are three alternative requirements development strategies:

- Development strategy based on overall architecture
- Evolutionary development strategy based on existing files
- Anticipatory development design strategy

Regardless of the strategy chosen for database requirements determination, it should be preceded by an overall planning strategy which defines the basic architecture of the database. The degree of variation between the existing defined database (or files) and the planned overall architecture determines the best strategy for specific requirements development.

The overall architecture for a database is based on two types of requirements:

1 Transaction processing requirements. These are generally defined by existing data processing applications.

2 Management requirements. These include requirements derived from transaction processing as well as new requirements to support management needs not based on transactions or routine reports.

The second type of requirements is the most difficult to obtain. Eliciting these requirements may use a technique such as the one described in Chapter 14 or similar techniques for requirements elicitation and architecture design.

The result of such planning is an architecture defining databases, classes of data, attributes, and users or uses for the data.

Development Strategy Based on Overall Architecture

The requirements development strategy may be based primarily on an overall architecture for the databases. As individual applications are defined based on the overall architecture, the database requirements of those applications are explicitly defined. All data items do not need to be defined initially, but no data items are added unless there is an identified need either from a new application or from unmet queries.

The data flow diagramming method for application design illustrates an approach to systematic additions to a database based on an overall architecture and a specific application. Data flow diagramming defines application processing and data required to accomplish them. A logical data model is developed that includes all data items identified as being required for the application. The data items are grouped and analyzed using normalization to ensure a nonredundant model of data. They can be integrated with existing data items using the data dictionary. If data items do not exist, they are added to the database. The data items for the application are analyzed as to frequency of access and volume of occurrences, and physical database specifications are prepared.

Evolutionary Development Strategy Based on Existing Files

Some organizations have chosen to not do an overall architecture based on requirements eliciting procedures but to follow an evolutionary strategy. The reasoning is that it is difficult and expensive to develop an overall architecture and that it is better to let the databases evolve through usage. The evolution may occur both from application development and unmet query needs.

1 In the evolution from application development, the existing data files are used as the initial database. As more applications are defined, existing data items are assigned more uses and new data items are added. This approach has special appeal for a database that is expected to show little change in content or pattern of use.

2 In the unmet query evolution, a small initial database is prepared. As it is used, requests for new data items and new data relationships are made. Some items are found to have little or no use. There are additions, deletions, and reorganization at frequent intervals. The approach is especially useful for small, local databases.

Anticipatory Development Strategy

Rather than only responding to requirements defined by applications or unmet queries, an alternative strategy is to define database requirements in a general way that includes both existing needs and anticipated needs. The approach will be referred to as *conceptual data modeling* to distinguish it from physical data modeling. Other terms are frequently used, such as *semantic data modeling* or *data structure modeling*.

The data requirements in the conceptual data modeling strategy are developed from a description of the entities and relationships among entities in the organization or other object system requiring databases. Two alternative approaches to conceptual data modeling described below illustrate current thinking. There are other alternatives or variations on these approaches, but these will provide a basis for understanding the conceptual and practical issues in defining a complete set of database requirements including anticipated requirements. The two methods that will be explained illustrate graphic methods and use of a sentence-predicate calculus. The graphic approach is the entity-relationship (E-R) model usually associated with Chen; the sentence-predicate calculus approach is Nijssen's information analysis. Neither will be explained in enough depth for operational use; rather, the objective is to illustrate concepts and ideas of conceptual data modeling and how they are being implemented.

CONCEPTUAL DATA MODELING

The common characteristic of conceptual data modeling methods is the definition of database requirements based on the the development of a conceptual model of the organization (referred to as the ''enterprise'') and its operations. The general flow of work from conceptual data modeling to database design is shown in Figure 16-7.

Advocates of conceptual data modeling argue that the most stable parts of a data processing system are data and the data relations. Processing applications and processing functions are more changeable. The fundamental approach to requirements definition should therefore be based on the data. The data structure is theoretically more general

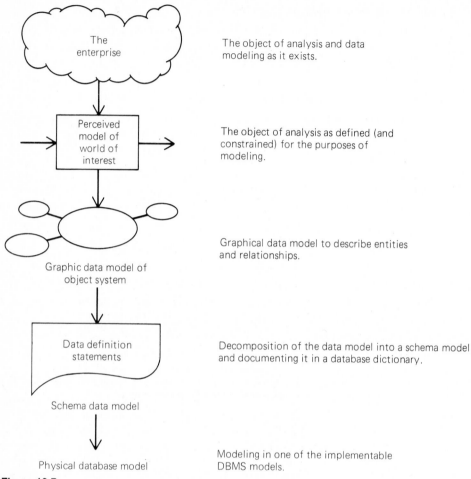

The object of analysis and data modeling as it exists.

The object of analysis as defined (and constrained) for the purposes of modeling.

Graphical data model to describe entities and relationships.

Decomposition of the data model into a schema model and documenting it in a database dictionary.

Modeling in one of the implementable DBMS models.

Figure 16-7
Flow of work from conceptual data modeling to database design.

than processes because data entities and relationships are based on the way the enterprise operates and the way the participants view data. If the enterprise does not change its operations or users do not change the way they view data entities and relationships, any data or relationship a user may request currently or in the future will have been included in the database.

Chen Entity-Relationship Data Model

The idea of an entity-relationship (E-R) data model was first proposed by Senko[8] and others. A publication by Chen[9] prompted significant added interest. The E-R model

---

[8]M. E. Senko, E. B. Altman, M. M. Astrahan, and P. L. Fehder, "Data Structures and Accessing in Data-Base Systems," *IBM Systems Journal*, 12:1, 1973, pp. 30–93.

[9]Peter P. Chen, "The Entity-Relationship Model: Toward a Unified View of Data," *ACM Transactions on Database Systems*, 1:1, March 1976, pp. 9–36.

contemplates an enterprise schema which is the data view of the entire enterprise.

The E-R data model uses a few basic concepts in producing an entity relationship diagram (ERD).

Element in E-R model	Description and diagram
Entity set	An entity set representing a type of thing about which information is maintained. Represented by a rectangular labeled box. [Professor]
Relationship set	A relationship set defines a type of relationship between entity sets. Represented by a diamond labelled box. Professor —1— ◇Advisor— N— Student In the above diagram, a PROFESSOR, in an ADVISOR relationship, may relate to many (N) STUDENTS; a STUDENT, in the ADVISOR relationship, has only one advisor PROFESSOR.
Attribute	An attribute associates a set of values (a value set) with an entity set or relationship set and provides an interpretation of the set of values in this context. Represented by a labeled elipse. (Name)

Figure 16-8 uses E-R data model notation to diagram a PROFESSOR who has a NAME (FIRST NAME and LAST NAME) and a SOCIAL SECURITY NUMBER. In other words, the entity PROFESSOR has FIRST NAME as an attribute. There is a set of first names that are the value set for FIRST NAME. There are additional rules and

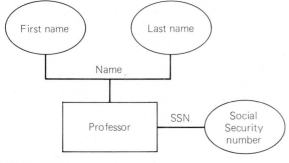

Figure 16-8
Value set in E-R diagram.

procedures for creating an E-R diagram and interpreting it. A complete exposition of this modeling approach is beyond the scope of the chapter.

A DIALOGUE

Questioner: "I saw a brochure coming around for a database system called...
and I found it strange—in this brochure, they actually
suggested you use an entity relationship model to design your
database."

Expert: "I don't see anything strange about being advised to use the
entity-relationship model as a design tool and having a
relational database as the end result."

Excerpted from "The Database Debate," *Computerworld*, September 13, 1982,
In Depth, p. 12.

An E-R diagram is read by using the names of the entity set plus words that describe the relationships among them. Arcs without labels are read with words such as: of, has, belongs to, and is in. For example, the diagram below could be read as "A university has (enrolls) students" and a "student is at (is enrolled at) a university." The university has attributes of university name and university # with university number being an identifier. A student has attributes of student name, student ID #, and social security # with student ID # being part of a unique identifier, the other part being the university name. This simple data model also illustrates the limitations that are incorporated in any data model. The model shows a student with only one university. If a student is attending two or more universities, the data model cannot show it.

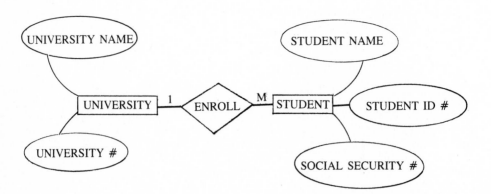

The analyst working with a user (or a user working alone who has received training in data modeling) can use a diagramming technique such as the ERD to develop a user data view of the enterprise and to document that view. For example:

1 The user starts by identifying entity sets (entity types) that are significant for his or her view of the enterprise. Each entity set is given a name and enclosed in a rectangle on a chalkboard or paper.

2 Relationship sets (relationship types) are identified. Each is given a name and graphed with a diamond. The entity sets that participate in a relationship set are indicated by connecting with an arc. The relationship is specified as 1, M, or N.

3 The attributes that establish values for the entity are elicited and diagrammed with arcs that connect attributes to sets.

4 The process continues until all entity sets, relationship sets, attributes, and value sets have been elicited and diagrammed. The diagram is a tool which allows the analyst and user to discuss the data model and resolve ambiguities.

The drawing of a diagram is only one part of the process of designing a database. However, it can be a useful and significant step in preparing the requirements from which to design the physical database.

Nijssen's Information Analysis[10]

A number of database researchers have suggested other methods for conceptual data modeling. The one chosen for illustration is information analysis by G. M. Nijssen.[11] Other researchers such as William Kent of IBM have proposed similar ideas. Kent describes his approach as "fact-based analysis."[12]

The fundamental data model in the Nijssen approach consists of *deep structure elementary sentences*. These sentences exhibit "deep structure" in the sense that they can be transformed into a variety of other representations (called surface structures). The sentences can be viewed as an extension of a predicate calculus formula. Each sentence takes the form:

$$S = P (NOLOT, LOT, LOI....)$$

where S = sentence instance
       P = sentence predicate
       NOLOT = nonlexical object type
       LOT = lexical object type
       LOI = lexical object instance

---

[10]This section, including Figures 16-9 and 16-10, is based on a working paper by Peter Seddon of the University of Melbourne, Australia, "Database Schema Using Information Analysis and RM/T," 1984.

[11]G. M. Nijssen, "Current Issues in Conceptual Schema Concepts," in *Architecture and Models in Data Base Management Systems*, North Holland, New York, 1977, pp. 31–65. Also, G. M. A. Verheijen and J. Van Bekkum, "NIAM: An Information Analysis Method," in T. W. Olle, H. G. Sol, and A. A. Verrijn-Stuart (eds.), *Information Systems Design Methodologies: A Comparative Review*, North-Holland, Amsterdam, 1982, Appendix E.

[12]W. Kent, "Fact-Based Data Analysis and Design," in *Proceedings of the Third International Conference on the Entity-Relationship Approach*, Anaheim, CA, October 1983.

There is a clear distinction in this approach between entities (nonlexical), that is, kinds, classes, categories or types of things (NOLOTs), and the naming conventions or kinds of names (lexical) for things (LOTs). Each instance of a naming convention is a LOI.

Each sentence may be presented as an equation; it may also be transformed to natural language, a table, or a graph. The following example is a natural language sentence (arranged to show the deep structure):

The EMPLOYEE	(a kind of thing, a NOLOT)
with EMPLOYEE NUMBER	(a naming convention, a LOT)
37891	(instance of a name, a LOI)
WORKS FOR	(logical predicate, an IDEA)
the DEPARTMENT	(a kind of thing, a NOLOT)
with DEPARTMENT NUMBER	(a naming convention, a LOT)
468	(instance of a name, a LOI)

The *role* of every object type in every relationship is defined in the information analysis. In the above sentence, the relationship of EMPLOYEE and DEPARTMENT is explicitly defined as the role "works for."

The example presented in a natural language sentence above is shown below as a table (extended tabular format) with an added set of instances:

EMPLOYEE	DEPARTMENT	(NOLOTs)
EMPLOYEE NUMBER	DEPARTMENT NUMBER	(LOTs)
WORKS FOR	EMPLOYS	(NOLOT ROLEs)
37891	468	Sentence 1
28932	470	Sentence 2

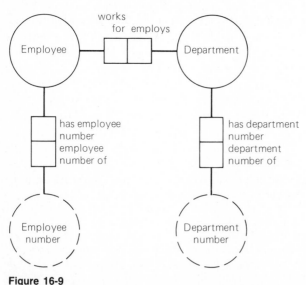

Figure 16-9
Information analysis conceptual schema in graphic form. (From Peter Seddon, "Database Schema Design Using Information Analysis and RM/T.")

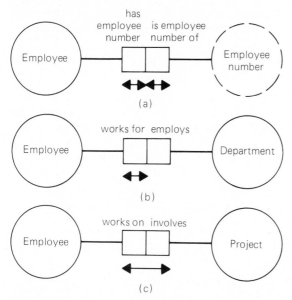

Figure 16-10
Representing cardinality constraints of 1:1, 1:m, and n:m in information analysis graphics. (From Peter Seddon, "Database Schema Design using Information Analysis and RM/T.")

Figure 16-9 shows the conceptual schema for the same information in graphic form. Since the LOI information is missing, the graph is a general template for all sentences of the same type, in the same way as the table headings above. A NOLOT is graphed as a solid line circle or elipse; a LOT is diagrammed as a broken line circle or elipse. The rectangles linking the object type symbols specify role information. Uniqueness is defined for roles by a bar with arrowheads underneath the box. For example, a 1:1 relationship is unique for both roles (thinking in terms of a table with rows, either role defines a unique row in the table), so each has a bar underneath. For a 1:m relationship, the unique role is the "one" role, and a bar underneath it shows this role on the graph. In Figure 16-10, employee works for only one department, but the department employs many employees. In the case of n:m relationships, a unique row is specified by a combination of both roles, so an underline is placed under both role boxes.

There are additional conventions and rules for both E-R modeling and information analysis, but they are beyond the scope of the chapter. The brief introduction to the two modeling approaches should illustrate the differences between them. In the case of the Chen E-R model, entities, relationships, and attributes are associated and graphed; in the Nijssen information analysis, sentences are formulated and illustrated using natural language, tables, or graphs.

Limitations of Conceptual Data Models

The conceptual data model approach to database requirements has some limitations in arriving at a complete and correct database. Two major limitations are:[13]

---

[13]Based on W. Kent, "Data Model Theory Meets a Practical Application," *Conference on Very Large Databases*, 1981, Institute of Electrical and Electronics Engineers, pp. 13–22.

1 There are many ways to view an enterprise and many ways to model it. These do not yield exactly the same result. Different analysts and users look at the same thing differently, and they will model it differently.

2 General knowledge is the basis for many data elements. These are not specifically derived from analysis of the enterprise.

For these reasons, a top-down conceptual enterprise approach may be combined with other analyses such as analysis of data requirements for specific applications. The combination of high-level factoring plus low-level application data analysis may provide a more complete data model.

A SCHEDULE FOR DATA MODELING

A large manufacturing company established a project team of eleven users and eleven data processing personnel to develop a data model for a database for part of its plant. The chronology and volume of activity are instructive.

End of period	Activity completed
January	2800 attributes identified.
March	Normalization.
May	Complete data model with 3700 data attributes and 530 data entities representing 40 subject databases and 40 application systems.

Based on Clive Finkelstein, "Information Engineering," *Computerworld*, In Depth, 12, 1981, pp. 11–12.

SUMMARY

Database is a central concept in the design of organizational information systems. The objectives of a database are availability, shareability, and evolvability of data plus data independence and data integrity. The database concept is made operational by a database management system, or DBMS. A supplementary data dictionary is also frequently used.

A data model is a model about the data in an enterprise. It can provide user-understandable specifications of data and physical data specifications. There are three views or schemas in building and using databases: the external schema is the user's view of the data, the conceptual schema is the overall logical view of the database, and the internal schema or data storage definition is the way the data items are actually stored. Conceptual design of databases is the development and integration of individual user and application views into an overall conceptual view. Physical design is the translation of the conceptual design into physical storage structures.

Normalization is the process of forming records with key fields and nonkey fields that meet criteria for five normal forms. The normal forms are useful in analyzing data, removing unwanted redundancies, and forming logical records prior to physical database design.

Ideally, a database should contain all data items that will be needed by any user of the system, stored in such a way that they can be retrieved. This ideal can rarely be achieved completely; the purpose of information requirements determination for databases is to establish the requirements for data to be stored in a database and the access connections that should be established for retrieval.

A database architecture can be developed by a high-level requirements determination and architecture definition process. Three alternative strategies may be used subsequent to the planning strategy (or in place of it): development based on overall architecture, evolution from existing data files, or anticipatory development based on conceptual data modeling. Each method has its advantages and disadvantages. The conceptual data modeling approach is described in the chapter because it provides an approach to obtaining requirements that is independent of the functions in data processing applications.

Several researchers have contributed to the concepts of conceptual data modeling: the work of Chen and Nijssen are presented in the chapter as examples of graphics-oriented and sentence-predicate calculus-based methods. The elements of the Chen entity-relationship or E-R model are entity set, relationship set, and attributes. With the concept of an enterprise schema, a graphical E-R data model is used to describe entity set relationships, attributes, and value sets. In Nijssen's information analysis, data is defined by sentences having deep structure. The sentences may be presented as natural language statements, tables, or graphs.

MINICASES

1 AN E-R MODEL

"The Imported Products Division of the Widget Corp. has 10,000 customers who place orders against 5,000 products. An average of five orders is outstanding at any time for each customer, with 20 percent of these orders having back orders to be filled. Each order is made up of an average of five product items, but this can range from one to ten product items per order. An average of two invoices are used to cover two shipments (on average) per order."

From Clive Finkelstein, "Information Engineering," *Computerworld*, In Depth, 12, 1981, pp. 11–12.

Question

Prepare an entity-relationship diagram for this enterprise.

2 UNRAVELING THE JARGON

The consultant's reply was: "In my investigation of your applications portfolios, I've applied...to the logical data structures and have discovered a very high frequency—approximately 93.286%—of data embedded in application program logic which is largely responsible for the integrity and synchronization problem currently being encountered. As a solution, I would recommend the design of a master database each of which would employ relational technology to reduce the database to third normal form. This would eliminate the possibility of semantic disintegrity upon querying the database."

From Paul R. Hessinger, "Database Viewed from a People Perspective," *Computerworld*, Special Report, October 27, 1980, pp. 20–21.

Question

Explain (using concepts from the chapter) what the consultant said.

EXERCISES

1 Discuss data redundancy with respect to:
  a Updating of records
  b Error detection
2 Explain the difference between:
  a Logical database and physical database
  b Entity and data item
  c Relation and record
3 Explain the value of data independence.
4 Why not just ask everyone what they want in the database and put it in?
5 Explain the characteristics of a data dictionary.
6 Why do some installations not use a data dictionary?
7 Define:
  a Data model
  b Entity
  c Attribute
  d Relationship
  e Schema
  f Aggregation
  g Generalization
8 Explain the three schemas. What is their value?
9 Explain three strategies for identifying data for the database.
10 What is the relationship of the Chen enterprise schema and conceptual schema?
11 Explain the basic elements of the E-R model.
12 Explain the basic elements of the information analysis model.
13 Convert the data in the invoice in Figure 16-11 to third normal form. Show each stage.
14 Write statements and prepare information analysis tables and graphs for data in Figure 16-11.

		XYZ COMPANY			
		St. Paul, Minnesota			
Order Number			Customer Number		
Date			Billing Address		
Delivery Date					
Discount			Ship to Address	Same	
Product Number	Description		Quantity Ordered	Unit Price	Extension
				Total	

Figure 16-11
Invoice.

15 Convert the data in the diagram from question 14 into third normal form.

16 Formulate descriptions for five of the entities in Figure 16-11. For each, specify reasonable descriptions that might appear in a data dictionary:

- Input or calculation to obtain instances of the entity
- Where entity used
- Description (number of characters, etc.)
- Integrity rules (values, dependencies, and referential integrity)

SELECTED REFERENCES

ANSI/SPARC Study Group Data Base Management Systems: "Framework Report on Data Base Management Systems," AFIP Press, Montvale, NJ, 1978.

Association for Computing Machinery: "The British Computer Society Data Dictionary Systems Working Party Report," *Data Base*, 9:2, Fall 1977, and *SIGMOD Record*, 9:4, December 1977.

Borkin, S. A.: *Data Models: A Semantic Approach for Database Systems*, M.I.T. Press, Cambridge, MA, 1980.

Chen, Peter P.: "The Entity-Relationship Model: Toward a Unified View of Data," *ACM Transactions on Database Systems*, 1:1, March 1976, pp. 9–36.

Chen, Peter P. (ed.): *Entity-Relationship Approach to Systems Analysis and Design*, North-Holland, Amsterdam, 1980.

Codd, E. F.: "A Relational Model of Data for Large Shared Banks," *Communications of the ACM*, 13:6, June 1972, pp. 377–387.

Codd, E. F.: "Relational Database: A Practical Formulation for Productivity," *Communications of the ACM*, 25:2, February 1982, pp. 109–117.

CODASYL Systems Committee: *Feature Analysis of Generalized Data Base Management Systems*, Technical Report, published by several organizations such as the Association for Computing Machinery, New York, May 1971.

Curtice, R. M., and P. E. Jones: "Fundamentals of Data Element Definition," *ACM SIGMOD International Conference on Management of Data*, Ann Arbor, MI, April 29–May 1, 1981, pp. 49–55.

Date, C. J.: *An Introduction to Database Systems*, Third Edition, Addison-Wesley, Reading, MA, 1981.

Davis, C. G., S. Jajodia, A. Ng, and R. T. Yeh (eds.): *Proceedings of the Third International Conference on the Entity-Relationship Approach*, Elsevier, New York, 1983.

Everest, Gordon C.: *Database Management: Objectives, System Functions, and Administration*, McGraw-Hill, New York, 1985.

Flavin, Matt: *Fundamental Concepts of Information Modeling*, Yourdon, New York, 1981.

Kent, W.: "A Simple Guide to Five Normal Forms in Relational Database Theory," *Communications of the ACM*, 26:2, February 1983, pp. 120–125.

Kent, W.: *Data and Reality*, North-Holland, Amsterdam, 1978.

Kent, W.: "Data Model Theory Meets a Practical Application," *Conference on Very Large Databases*, Institute of Electrical and Electronics Engineers, 1981.

Lundgren, Bo: *Theory of Data Bases*, Mason/Charter, New York, 1975.

March, S., D. Ridjanovic, and M. Prietula: "On the Effects of Normalization on the Quality of Relational Database Designs, or Being Normal Is Not Enough," *Proceedings Trends and Applications 1984: Making Databases Work*, IEEE Computer Society Press, 1984, pp. 257–261.

McCarthy, William E.: "An Entity-Relationship View of Accounting Models," *The Accounting Review*, 54:4, October 1979, pp. 667–685.

Nijssen, G. M. (ed.): "Current Issues in Conceptual Schema Concepts," in *Architecture and Models in Data Base Management Systems*, North Holland, New York, 1977, pp. 31–65.

Nijssen, G. M. (ed.): *Modeling in Data Base Management Systems*, North-Holland, Amsterdam, 1976.

Smith, J. M., and D. C. P. Smith: "Database Abstractions and Aggregations," *Communications of the ACM*, 20:6, June 1977, pp. 405–413.

Smith, J. M., and D. C. P. Smith: "Principles of Database Conceptual Design," *NYU Symposium on Database Design*, New York University, New York, May 18–19, 1978, pp. 35–49.

Tsichritzis, D. C., and F. H. Lochovsky: *Data Models*, Prentice-Hall, Englewood Cliffs, NJ, 1982.

Wong, Harry K. T., and John Mylopoulos: "Two Views of Data Semantics: A Survey of Data Models in Artificial Intelligence and Database Management," *INFOR*, 15:3, October 1979, pp. 344–383.

USER INTERFACE REQUIREMENTS

Computer-based information systems increasingly involve online interaction between the human user and the machine; a critical element of the design of these systems is the user interface. The interface consists of screens, keyboards, devices, languages, and other means by which the human user and the computer system exchange inputs and outputs. Because of the importance of a well-designed user interface in the effective use of a system, a separate chapter is devoted to the topic.

User interface design has received significant attention in recent years. Many "principles" of good user interface design have been developed, much of it focusing on "user friendly" systems and ease of use. Research in this area is frequently characterized as *human factors engineering* or *ergonomics*. Some research related to humans as information processors (reviewed in Chapter 8) has been the basis for certain interface design principles; research dealing more specifically with user interface design is reviewed in this chapter.

This chapter provides an overview of important features of user interfaces and develops a contingency approach to the selection of design features. There are many options in user interface design, and the choice of appropriate options depends on factors such as the experience and knowledge of the user and the type of task to be performed. Several guiding principles hold throughout: the system should be flexible, it should be consistent, and it should be perceived as being under the user's control. These principles are discussed in more detail below.

CLASSIFICATION OF USERS

This section discusses several different ways of characterizing users. They are not exclusive classifications, in that a user may be characterized in several different ways at the same time.

Shift to human effectiveness from machine efficiency
Human should control interface - Not machine

Developers versus Nondevelopers

An obvious but important distinction in user interface design exists between the developer of the system and the target end user. System developers are those who develop information processing applications and tools for use by other workers, whereas end users are workers who input, manipulate, or retrieve information using the applications and tools. The distinction is particularly important when developers are professional systems analysts who must deal with large, complex systems (for example, a large transaction processing system). This causes an emphasis on technical considerations and system control; it often inhibits emphasis on the user interface. In other words, it is often difficult for a system developer both to see the overall technical system and to take a user's view.

To the user, the system is represented primarily by the interface. A complex interface reflects a complex system to the user; a simple interface suggests a simple system to the user. One of the problems illustrated by this distinction is difficulty in communication between system developers and users. Methods for improving the communication process so that systems developers can see the user's view and interpret it appropriately for user interface design are discussed in Chapter 18.

For many types of systems the distinction between developers and nondevelopers is blurred by the introduction of users in the development process. In end-user development, discussed in Chapter 13, the user and developer can be the same person. Frequently, the developer may be a full-time analyst who is an expert in the user function.

Novices versus Experts

An important distinction directly affecting interface design is the experience level of the user. This experience has two components: the frequency of use of the particular system and the user's general knowledge of computer system concepts. The first component may be referred to as syntactic knowledge and the latter as semantic knowledge.[1]

Ideally, a system should be flexible enough to accommodate both a novice and an expert user. A novice who is unfamiliar with both the system's specific syntax and generalizable (semantic) knowledge about use of computers should be able to get explanations or assistance through the system. On the other hand, an expert who has internalized the system's syntactic structure or has considerable semantic knowledge should be permitted rapid interaction and not be held up by explanations or details that are only required by the novice. (See Chapter 8 for discussion of semantic and syntactic knowledge.)

A key design feature of user interfaces is *consistency* in relating to users' general or semantic knowledge. A user faced with a request for a response in a dialog with a computer and an unclear set of choices may borrow from the experience of other computer systems with similar interfaces to make "an educated guess." Developers can establish reasonable consistency of interfaces through the development of organizational guidelines and standards for user interface design.[2] For example, all applications needing to save a program or file should use the same command (such as SAVE).

WHAT IS THE COMMAND TO RELEASE A FILE?

This is a report of a conversation with a user of a timesharing system. "I had SAVEd a file, but was now through with it. I had been instructed to release all files no longer needed, because they resulted in storage charges. I couldn't find the release command in my manual, so I searched my memory. I tried UNSAVE, REMOVE, RELEASE, and DESTROY. Nothing worked, so I just left it. Later, I found the command was PURGE."

Occasional versus Frequent Users

Another way of categorizing of users, related to novices and experts, is occasional versus frequent users. In general, a frequent user will become more expert, particularly in

---

[1]B. Shneiderman, *Software Psychology: Human Factors in Computer and Information Systems*, Winthrop, Cambridge, MA, 1980.

[2]For an example of user interface guidelines developed internally for IBM, see F. H. Otte, "Consistent User Interface," in Y. Vassilou (ed.), *Human Factors in Interactive Compuer Systems,* Ablex Publishing, Norwood, NJ, 1984.

syntactic knowledge, than an occasional one. However, there are other aspects of frequency of use besides the need for training. An occasional user will probably use the system for ad hoc, nonrepetitive processing. A system receiving frequent use is more likely to be used for routine, repetitive activities.

Frequency of use determines directly the amount of training required of the user: the more the expected use of the system, the greater the justification for investment in training time. The amount of training in turn determines the user's skill level after the training period.

After initial training, there is a significant decay in knowledge of system use. Occasional users therefore need to be able to refresh their knowledge of system functions and commands. Commands that use words common to the user and formats that are fairly natural aid in this recall and refreshing of memory. The occasional user has a significant need for online assistance, manuals that have comprehensive indexes, and examples of command use. Frequent users are more willing to learn and use ''unnatural'' commands and command structures.

Primary versus Secondary Users

A final distinction is the type of user or reason for utilizing the system. In general, a *primary user* is one who benefits from the system's output, while a *secondary user* is responsible for input into the system and sometimes for output but does not use the output directly in his or her job. In end-user systems and in the support systems described in Chapters 12 and 13, the two roles are frequently combined; the person who utilizes the system output also develops it. In some situations, the end user may employ an intermediary. For example, many managers prefer to have the system actually operated by an assistant.

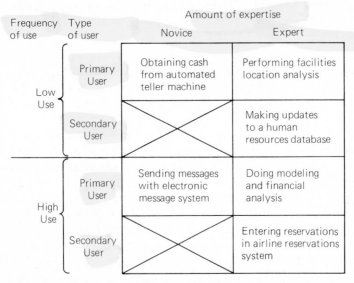

Figure 17-1
Classes of users and examples of system uses.

As a contrast to end-user systems that combine primary and secondary user roles, other applications separate the functions. *Data entry* is the term normally used for jobs doing input (and often validation) of large volumes of data. However, data entry of transactions often takes place at the point of origination of the transactions, and those who input data also use the system for inquiry purposes. For instance, a retail sales clerk enters all information about a sale into the computer via a "point-of-sale" terminal as part of the process of creating a sales receipt. The same system is utilized for validation of the customer's credit on a charge account.

Secondary users such as data entry personnel typically perform data input as a major part of their jobs. Therefore, secondary users would be classified as experts rather than novices and as frequent users. As mentioned previously, none of these classes of users is exclusive. Figure 17-1 shows some typical tasks for some combinations of user classes.

DIVISION OF FUNCTIONS BETWEEN USER AND SYSTEM

An important decision which dictates many user interface requirements is the division of functions between the user and the computer system. This issue is related to topics discussed in earlier chapters. For instance, in Chapter 9 there was a discussion of the relationship between the computer as a relatively closed, deterministic system and the human as an open, probabilistic system. It was recommended that a human-machine system should be designed to take maximum advantage of the characteristics of each. In Chapter 11, the need for variety and challenge in human job design was explained.

The division of functions between person and machine, regardless of application, has shifted over the last decade from emphasis on machine efficiency to enhancement of human effectiveness. The primary reason for this shift has been the declining cost of hardware relative to the cost of human labor. This shift is also reflected in the replacement of many batch processing applications by online, interactive systems. The cost of the hardware and software for the user interface may be a major component of the total cost of application development and operations. However, these costs are small relative to the typical improvement in the performance of the human system.

The distinction between the negative and positive effects of a computer system on individual quality of work life is related to the division of function between human and machine. A system which gives the user very little discretion in terms of selection of tasks or pace of work may have apparent cost advantages, especially if the skills required of the human operator are minimized. However, these cost advantages may be lost due to added costs of increased turnover of personnel and reduced job commitment. Therefore, whenever possible, a system should be designed so that the user controls the interaction rather than the system. In the long run, a system that is designed well from the user's point of view will result in increased overall performance. The implications of the division of function between person and machine are discussed in more detail in a later section of this chapter. The sociotechnical approach to requirements (discussed in Chapter 15) and to job design (Chapter 18) is one method to achieve application designs that take advantage of the strengths of both humans and machines to achieve improved quality of work life.

CONSIDERATIONS IN DESIGN OF A USER INTERFACE

In this section, the general components of user interface design are discussed. The next section presents some alternative approaches to interactive user dialog. Underlying the discussion is the premise that selection of an appropriate interface is contingent on the type of user and the type of task to be performed.

The design of user interfaces is the major factor in ease of learning and ease of use. One research study that compared nine text editors showed significant variation in performance of both experts (in terms of error-free time and time spent correcting errors) and novices (in terms of time to learn a core editing task).[3]

Screen Design

A good screen design is clear, uncluttered, and free of irrelevant information. Two useful guidelines for deciding what information should be put on a single screen are the following:[4]

> **1** Provide only information that is essential to making a decision or performing an action.
>
> **2** Provide all data related to one task on a single screen. The user should not have to remember data from one screen to the next.

The placement of text and data on a screen affect the user's task of responding. The following are some guidelines for placement based on human information processing limitations plus culture-based habits for processing.

- Place items together that logically belong together (name and address).
- Place items in customary processing order (in the United States: city followed by state followed by postal code).
- Position most important items (preferably) at left side and arrange in importance from top to bottom.
- Leave sufficient space so that items do not get confused.
- Position items across close enough that the eye does not change rows in moving across. Use guide strips of lines, dots, or dashes if necessary.

Some examples of good and poor placement of information on a screen are shown in Figure 17-2. The availability of graphics and of color extend the options available in terms of enhancing clarity of screen design.

Design of data entry tasks for secondary users requires special consideration. The most important issue is whether data items will be keyed from a specially designed source document. If such a document is used, the primary visual focus of the user will be toward the document, and the screen should be designed to reflect the form of the document. Forms-based screens for use with documents are discussed in a later section of the chapter. If data entry does not follow a document, the user's primary focus is

---

[3]T. L. Roberts and T. P. Moran, "The Evaluation of Text Editors: Methodology and Empirical Results," *Communications of the ACM*, 26:4, April 1983, pp. 265–283.

[4]W. O. Galitz, *Human Factors in Office Automation,* Life Office Management Association, Atlanta, GA, 1980, p. 108.

Poor Formatting	Better Formatting	Comments
AMOUNT DUE: $104.00	AMOUNT DUE: $104.00	Don't break a label unless necessary
NAME: KAREN JONES ADDRESS: 310 BLEECKER ST CITY: NEW YORK	NAME: KAREN JONES ADDRESS: 310 BLEECKER ST CITY: NEW YORK	Use alignment to visually separate labels and responses
IN STOCK: 10 ON BACK ORDER: 20	IN STOCK: 10 ON BACK ORDER: 20	Line up numeric output to support visual comparison
(412) 285-6078	TEL: (412) 285-6078	Use label to avoid misinterpretation
082184	08/21/84	Separate subitems with symbols

Figure 17-2
Examples of good and poor formatting of text and data on a screen.

toward the screen, and prompts from the system elicit the necessary information. The latter would be the case in any type of telephone request or system where the input values are being captured at the source of the transaction. Examples are point-of-sale retail transactions or banking through an automated teller machine.[5]

In working with a screen, a user must often look aside at other data or instructions while retaining (and returning to) the original screen. This can be accomplished by *split screens* or *windows*. In the split screen, a portion of the screen, say at the bottom, is used for instructions and reference data. Windows are small areas, overlaid on the screen, in which data or instructions are displayed. Another window may be overlaid on the first, etc. For example, a user may be composing a paper and wish to refer to another text. Using a window, a second text may be read while retaining the original on the screen (obscured in part by the window). When the user is finished, the window may be removed. Or, while reading the window with the second text, the user may desire access to the set of instructions for copying a text. This may be called up in a second window (smaller than the first) which is overlaid on the first window.

Feedback and Assistance

The human need for feedback was discussed in Chapter 8. Two types of feedback should be part of a user machine dialog:

1 The system should acknowledge every user request in some way
2 Additional assistance (such as system status) should be available upon request

---

[5]Galitz, *Human Factors in Office Automation*, p. 148.

In the first case, the most common form of acknowledgment is the result from the request. However, if the request requires a long time to process, acknowledgment of receipt of the request may be appropriate (see discussion of response times below). For instance, if a user submits a complex query to a large database and the processing time is expected to be fairly long (say 30 seconds), the system may respond, ''Your query is being processed; there will be a short delay,'' or ''...there will be about a 30 second delay.'' The user's psychological need for feedback is satisfied by the knowledge that the system has received the query and is not sitting idle.

Further reassurance meeting the psychological need for feedback is provided by system status requests. For instance, a user has sent a request for a report, and the request has been sent to a ''print queue.'' By typing a simple command such as ''information output,'' the user may see a list of all reports in the print queue and the status in the queue of the report in question.

```
I D A  (V.TOPS20.091580)

> ?
YOU CAN HAVE HELP ON ANY OR ALL OF THE FOLLOWING :

 1. GENERAL COMMENTS ABOUT IDA
 2. DATA DEFINITION
 3. DATA EDITING
 4. DATA DISPLAY (PRINT)
 5. DATA DISPLAY (PLOT)
 6. TRANSFORMATIONS
 7. SUMMARY STATISTICS
 8. ONE SAMPLE STATISTICS
 9. TABULAR ANALYSIS
10. REGRESSION ANALYSIS
11. TIME-SERIES ANALYSIS
12. PROBABILITY COMMANDS
13. MISCELLANEOUS COMMANDS

FOR HOW MANY OF THE ABOVE 13 CATEGORIES DO YOU NEED HELP ? 1
* CATEGORY NUMBER(S) :  1

WANT ALL OUTPUT FOR "GENERAL COMMENTS" ? NO

1.  GENERAL COMMENTS:
WANT INFO ON SIZE OF DATA MATRIX ? YES

A.  MAXIMUM SIZE OF DATA MATRIX IS NORMALLY  500 BY 19.
    COLUMNS OF THE DATA MATRIX ARE REFERRED TO AS VARIABLES
    AND ROWS AS OBSERVATIONS.  UNIVARIATE DATA SHOULD BE
    STORED IN A SINGLE COLUMN.  IF YOU HAVE MORE THAN  500
    ROWS IN YOUR MATRIX, YOU MAY REDIMENSION THE SIZE BY
    EXECUTING THE COMMAND "RDIM".

WANT INFO ON PROMPTS ? NO

WANT INFO ON ERROR RECOVERY ? NO

WANT INFO ON ACTIVATING DATA ? NO

WANT INFO ON UPDATING DATA ? NO

END OF GENERAL COMMENTS

> QUIT
STOP
```

Figure 17-3
Example of user-machine dialog with system prompts.

```
@help rdmail
Type in a date and time in TOPS-20 format as follows:

              MMM DD,YYYY HH:MM
or
              MMM DD,YYYY
or
              HH:MM

       The second case will assume time 00:01, and the last case
       will assume today's date.  (For example, a valid date and
       time is MAR 16,1976 15:30)

or     Type an empty line and get all messages since the last
       reading of the message file.

/HELP Print this text
/ALL Types all messages in the file
/PERUSE For perusing messages only
/STOP Will cause RDMAIL to pause after each message typed
/MESSAGE-OF-THE-DAY Will use the message of the day file for message type out
/LIST Will output messages to the line printer
```

Figure 17-4
Example of program documentation accessed online by means of "HELP" command.

Another type of feedback provided in user-system dialogs is system prompting. Prompting guides a user step by step through a task. It also may give the range of options available. Prompting is very helpful for novice users, but it may be frustrating to experienced users who have internalized the sequence of steps. Ideally, an experienced user should be able to "turn off" such prompting. Figure 17-3 shows a sample dialog with prompting.

Online assistance is frequently available in the form of optional prompts for help. The help may consist of detailed online documentation or a reference to external documentation. A common method of receiving online assistance is the "HELP" function. For instance, a user wishes to run an electronic mail program called "RDMAIL." Rather than searching the computer center or terminal user library for the system documentation, she types "HELP RDMAIL" on her terminal. The system responds with a brief introduction of the RDMAIL program and the basic commands for using it. An example description of a response to a HELP request is shown in Figure 17-4.

The word HELP may be a poor term, since it connotes distress or emergency. EXPLAIN, INSTRUCT, ASSIST, or a question mark may be used instead. There are several types of help that may be available.[6] These are summarized below:

Type of help	Description
Command assistance	Provides an explanation of how to formulate a specific command. For example, asking for HELP PRINT on one system obtains a brief

[6]Raymond C. Houghton, Jr., "Online Help Systems: A Conspectus," *Communications of the ACM*, 27:2, February 1984, pp. 126–133.

Type of help	Description
General help	explanation of the PRINT command and a list of parameters that can be specified with the command. Provides a list of commands. When a user identifies the command needed, a command assistance HELP may be used. Research indicates that specific command names are remembered more easily than general names. Another method of online assistance is a request for options. In a system where prompts do not appear automatically, a user may type a request for options (such as a question mark) to see a list of alternative responses to a system request. Figure 17-5 shows the use of requests for system options during a user-system dialog.
Error assistance	Error codes or error notes are frequently insufficient for understanding the error. The HELP facilities may include further explanation of error codes. For example, a user might enter HELP ERROR FORTRAN 31 for an explanation of error 31 in a FORTRAN program execution.
Prompting	When an error is detected, some systems will attempt to prompt the user with information to make a correct entry. For example, if a command is used incorrectly, the response will be an explanation of how to use the command.
Online tutor	A new user (or an infrequent user) may not know how to perform basic operations, so general help and command help are insufficient. The online tutor help provides a lesson on how to use the system.
Online documentation	The manual is online in addition to or instead of a document manual. The online documentation serves much the same purpose as a command help, but may be in more depth. There is some evidence that written documentation is more effective than online documentation.

Error Control

A basic objective of user interface design is to minimize the errors of the human in the information dialog. A fundamental meaning inherent in "ease of use" and "user friendly systems" is adequate error control.

Regardless of the language structure used, a well-designed user interface should have appropriate error detection mechanisms. The *law of requisite variety* (Chapter 10) applies to interface design. There should be a system response not only to every correct input but also to every incorrect input.

A well-designed user interface should have four distinct dimensions of error control:[7]

---

[7]Galitz, *Human Factors in Office Automation*, pp. 101–102.

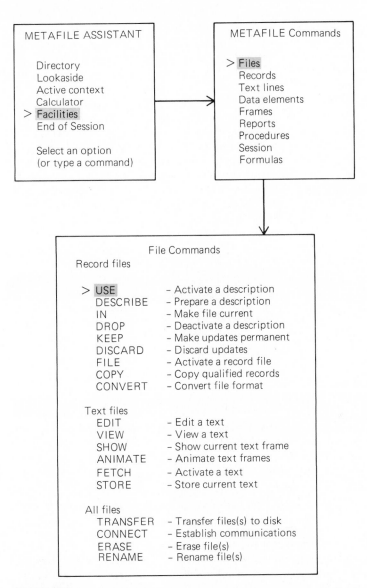

Figure 17-5
Example of use of requests for system options in a user-system dialog. First selection of an option gives detailed set and selection of one of these gives a more detailed set of options. (Example from *Metafile*, courtesy of Sensor-Based Systems, Chatfield, MN.)

1 *Error prevention*. As much as possible, the system should provide specific instructions (e.g., prompts, help facilities) so that the user knows exactly what to do and avoids making errors.

2 *Error detection*. When an error is made, the system should identify it clearly and explicitly. However, "polite" error messages are favored. Common messages such as "FATAL ERROR, RUN ABORTED" and "INVALID COMMAND" are neither polite nor helpful.[8] Notification that an error has been detected should occur immediately. The user should be able to easily identify the error. Finally, no error should cause the system to terminate abnormally; following the law of requisite variety and designing an appropriate control response for every possible input (no matter how incorrect) prevents abnormal program termination from occurring.

3 *Error correction.* Correction should be straightforward and should require rekeying only the portion of the data in error. There is debate over whether systems should attempt correction themselves. For instance, if a system has a total of 50 commands and a user types in a misspelled command, the system can be programmed to estimate through pattern matching which command was meant. In systems where error correction is programmed, the correction is usually posed as a question and the user verifies the correction before it is made.

4 *Error recovery.* Once a command has been accepted, it may still be in error and cause an incorrect action. An important feature of a well-designed system is the ability to "undo" something which has been done. For instance, a user sends an incorrect update to a database. "Undoing" the update is difficult because the old data item was replaced by the new, incorrect data item. However, transactions and before-and-after images of the record being updated are logged by the system, and a procedure should exist to reconstruct the prior state of the database using this data. Having an easy and natural "undo" command can relieve a significant element of stress for novice users who are afraid of doing something wrong that will "wipe out" the system. It is also an important feature of a system used by an expert user who may do things very quickly and need to backtrack as part of the thought process; examples of systems needing this feature are decision support systems and other knowledge work support systems.

Response Time

Response time in an interactive system is the time that elapses between the user keying in a command and the system beginning to display a response. Response times are affected by the system's capacity, the number of other users (if it is a timesharing system), and the complexity of the user's request.

Usually a system design will specify a minimum or average expected response time for a given type of transaction. The response time goal should not necessarily be as fast as possible. It is often more important to have consistent response times for a given level of user expertise for the task to be performed. Some useful guidelines are the following:[9]

1 Frequent, simple commands should take less than a second.

2 For a given command type, response time should be as consistent as possible, even if it takes slightly longer. A maximum response time deviation of no more than 20 percent from the mean has been suggested.

3 Short response times to relatively complex requests may actually increase error rates or inhibit learning.

4 If a response will take a long time (say greater than 10 seconds) a message should be issued within 1 or 2 seconds to give the user feedback. A novice user, in particular, may become frustrated or anxious if the system appears to be idle and waiting for an action.

---

[8]B. Shneiderman, "Direct Manipulation: A Step Beyond Programming Languages," *Computer*, August 1983, pp. 57–69.

[9]Shneiderman, "Direct Manipulation."

Another feature of system performance that interacts with response time is display rate. This is the rate at which characters (or graphics) are displayed on the screen. In a terminal connected to a remote computer, display rate is a direct function of the communication speed or baud rate (see Chapter 3). Display rate is most critical for word processing functions, when an entire screen of text may be redisplayed every time an edit command is issued. With such functions, a display rate of 300 baud (30 characters per second) is extremely slow and can seriously impair performance. At the other extreme, 9,600-baud communication speed (or use of a personal computer or intelligent workstation where no data communication is required) permits the entire screen to be redisplayed very quickly and does not impair typing performance. When a person is composing text at a terminal rather than performing bulk typing, slower display rates are generally acceptable. Consistency is also important with display rates in that erratic display rates can be disturbing to users and increase errors.

Workstation Design

Much ergonomics research related to computer system use has been concerned with physical aspects such as furniture design, office layout, noise, and lighting. In terms of workstations, guidelines have been developed for size, color, and positioning of visual display terminal (VDT) screens, measurements of furniture, and keyboard layout.

There have been some concerns that the use of VDTs might adversely affect the health of workers. In a study of 248 office workplace VDT users (and 85 nonuser counterparts) sponsored by the National Institute for Occupational Safety and Health, the results did not support the major concerns. However, certain aspects of working conditions were judged less favorably by VDT users. The chair and workstation configuration affected workers' complaints about musculoskeletal disturbances. Workers who use monofocal reading glasses were most affected. Fixed keyboards were also a factor in discomfort. Visual stress was found to be correlated with the illumination levels at both the keyboard and the workplace site.[10]

One example of the evolution of ergonomically designed workstations is the detached keyboard. Many terminals and personal computers in the late 1970s had keyboards fixed to the front of the display screen. Most terminals are now designed with detachable, lightweight, adjustable keyboards.

Some major points to consider in choosing appropriate screens and keyboards for particular applications or for general use are highlighted here. References at the end of the chapter provide more detailed guidelines on ergonomic considerations in workstation design.

Considerations in a visual display terminal are the following:[11]

    1 The screen should usually be fixed at an angle of 10 to 15 degrees from the vertical, away from the user. Preferably, the tilt should be adjustable, horizontally as well as vertically.

---

[10]S. L. Sauter, M. S. Gottlieb, K. C. Jones, V. N. Dodson, and K. M. Rohrer, "Job and Health Implications of VDT Use: Initial Results of the Wisconsin-NIOSH Study," *Communications of the ACM*, 26:4, April 1983, pp. 284–294.

[11]C. Raftering and J. Keener, "Providing Terminal Comfort," *Mini-Micro Systems*, August 1981; and Galitz, "*Human Factors in Office Automation*," p. 134.

2 Characters should not flicker or move on the screen.

3 Glare and reflections on the display surface should be minimized.

4 Resolution must provide a sharp image.

5 Character-to-background brightness contrast should be greater than 50 percent. Preferably, the brightness should be adjustable. Screens may offer alternatives of dark on light or light on dark.

Keyboard considerations focus on the physical feel and placement of the keyboard as a whole as well as the placement of individual keys. Keyboard design preferences are often highly individualistic; for this reason an ideal keyboard has as many adjustable features as possible. The following are some examples of ergonomic considerations in the physical design of the keyboard:[12]

1 *Key force*: A range of 15 to 125 grams pressure.

2 *Key spacing*: 18 to 20 millimeters between keys.

3 *Key displacement and activation*: This results in the "feel" of a key when it is pressed. Suggested displacement is 3 to 5 millimeters, with a key activation point requiring an increasing force until contact is made at 65 to 75 percent of downward travel, then a decrease in force so that the point of contact can be felt.

4 *Key shape*: Concave shape, with a matte finish to prevent reflection.

5 *Keyboard slope*: 10 to 15 degrees, preferably adjustable.

Another aspect of keyboard design is a separate numeric keypad. This feature is particularly important if data entry is heavily numeric.

The importance of a well-designed workstation is partially influenced by the amount of time spent on the system. For secondary users, who may spend several hours keying data without breaks, physical features such as lighting and furniture design are especially important.

THE GERMAN ERGONOMIC STANDARDS

The West German ergonomic standards are the most detailed in the world. The regulations are becoming a *defacto standard* in the United States as well. The Deutsch Industries Norm spells out 30 different requirements. The following are a few examples:

- VDT screens that display dark characters on a light background
- Clear and unambiguous characters that do not touch
- No red or blue characters
- No flicker; minimum screen glare
- A nonglossy finish on keyboards and housings
- Detachable keyboards and adjustable screens
- A keyboard height at the middle row of keys of no more than 30 millimeters and a slope of less than 25 degrees

Excerpted from Jeffrey Tarter, "Ergonomics: A Primer," *Business Computer Systems*, June 1983, pp. 55–72.

The layout of the keyboard should fit the convenience of the operator and the task. The keyboard should have all essential keys, and they should be grouped for

---

[12]Galitz, *"Human Factors in Office Automation,"* p. 135.

convenience. Most keyboards have a standard QWERTY keyboard layout because it is the one most skilled typists have learned. Another keyboard layout called the Dvorak, which is based on frequency of character usage, reduces the distance a typical typist's fingers travel by as much as a factor of ten. To date, the Dvorak keyboard has not received widespread acceptance because of the amount of retraining as well as keyboard replacement that would be required. However, its features have now been standardized. Also, microcomputers and word processors can be easily designed to allow the user to specify QWERTY or Dvorak. These developments suggest possible significant future use for the Dvorak layout.

THE ORIGINS OF THE QWERTY KEYBOARD

"In the late 1860s, engineers at Sholes & Co., the country's leading typewriter manufacturer, discovered they had a design problem. The keys on their newfangled lever-action machines were jamming up whenever skilled typists put on a burst of speed. Sholes & Co.'s pre-ergonomic solution: change the keyboard to slow down typing speed. Thus, revised typewriters went on the market with a keyboard layout that deliberately separated common letter combinations and placed frequently used letters (like O, I, A, and S) where they could be reached only by the weakest fingers on the typist's hand. This layout, called the QWERTY keyboard because of the sequence of letters on its top row, eventually became the modern standard."

Jeffrey Tarter, "Ergonomics: A Primer," *Business Computer Systems*, June 1983, p. 64.

A common feature of most terminal and personal computer keyboards is a set of function keys. Often these are placed separately from the frequently used keys, either to one side or along the top. Function keys are marked, often in a different color. They are used to replace keyed commands for frequently used functions. Function keys are usually assigned by the program in operation, although some systems allow the user to assign function keys to tailor the system. For instance, a frequent user of a text editing program may assign certain cursor-positioning functions (end of line, next line, next word, etc.) to function keys.

In summary, workstation design should be carefully considered in light of the type of task to be performed. The overall design should emphasize flexibility or easy adjustment to suit individual preferences. The keyboard design, in particular, should emphasize speed, accuracy, comfort, and flexibility.

INTERACTIVE USER DIALOG

The dialog between user and machine can follow many different structures: command languages, menus, forms, graphics, and natural language. The characteristics of each of these language structures are described in this section. In general, considerations in choosing an appropriate language structure are the expertise of the user, the user's knowledge about the particular problem domains for which the system is used, the physical constraints of the computer and the terminal, and consistency with other dialogs in use.

Command Languages

The most common method of user interface dialog is the command language. Most basic computer operating systems utilize a command language to access other applications and perform basic system functions.

A command language generally has a prespecified format for each command. Typically, a command to perform an operation is followed by one or more *arguments* that specify the details for it. For instance, there may be a command to rename a file. The user specifies the command RENAME followed by the user-defined current file name and the new file name. Two methods are commonly used:

1 *Keyword.* The user specifies keywords for the arguments:

RENAME OLD = TEXTFIL2 NEW = TEXTFIL3

2 *Position.* The meaning of the arguments is determined by their position:

RENAME TEXTFIL2 TEXTFIL3

The advantage of the keyword format is that the user does not have to remember the order of the arguments, whereas in the position format the order is significant and must be memorized. However, the keyword format requires considerably more typing, and the user must remember not only the appropriate arguments but also their associated keywords. The position method tends to be preferred by expert users who know the command formats. Two methods for making position format commands easier for novice users are system prompts and system defaults.

With system prompts, the user types the command, such as RENAME, and then presses a key (such as RETURN or ESC) designated for a prompt. The system then prompts with a keyword indicating the expected argument. For example:

RENAME ?   *FROMFILE* TEXFIL2 ? *TOFILE* TEXFIL3

In the example above, *FROMFILE* and *TOFILE* are system prompts given as a result of the user typing a question mark.

Use of system defaults can increase the efficiency of command language. Typically, the command default represents the broadest range for the command and specific arguments are required to narrow the range. For example, a user may wish to list a directory of file names under his account. If the user only specifies "DIR," the system defaults to printing a directory of all files in the account. If he is interested in only those files with the suffix "DOC" or only those created after a certain date, range arguments would follow the command "DIR."

An issue in command language interface design is whether to require the user to enter the full command words or to allow abbreviation. Command abbreviations reduce input time and annoyance associated with system use. In research reported by Benbasat and Wand,[13] truncation was supported as the preferred method for abbreviation. It was found easy to use and implement, it generated few errors, and it led to more abbreviations when commands increased in length or usage.

---

[13]Izak Benbasat and Yair Wand, "Command Abbreviation Behavior in Human-Computer Interaction," *Communications of the ACM*, 27:4, May 1984, pp. 376–382.

A simple SQL query to select and list the name and address of alumni who have a PhD. degree.

```
SELECT   NAME, ADDRESS
FROM     ALUMNI
WHERE    DEGREE = 'Ph.D' ;
```

An SQL query to select and list the names of alumni who are not donors.

```
SELECT   NAME
FROM     ALUMNI
WHERE    ID NOT IN
         ( SELECT ID
           FROM    DONORS );
```

AN SQL query to list the sum of donations from alumni from Chicago.

```
SELECT   ALUMNI.NAME, SUM(DONORS.AMOUNT)
FROM     ALUMNI, DONORS
WHERE    ALUMNI.CITY = 'CHICAGO' AND
         ALUMNI.ID   = DONORS.ID
GROUP BY DONORS.ID ;
```

Figure 17-6
Examples of database query language (SQL) to access information from a database. Example
database contains data on alumni of a university.

Command language formats are commonly used in database query languages. Commands have a syntax using natural language words but are restricted to a very specific set of keywords and often a specific ordering. An example of a dialog using a database query language (SQL) based on command language processing is shown in Figure 17-6.

Menus

With the menu format, the user is shown a list of options, usually numbered, and is expected to choose the appropriate option by positioning a cursor or by keying the associated number. A series of menus allows the user to step through a series of hierarchical levels of increasing specificity. Refer back to figure 17-5 which shows a series of menus by which a specific transaction is completed.

The advantage of a well-designed menu is that it provides a familiar format and a clear set of choices which are well understood by the user. Menus therefore require less training to use than command languages. One important feature of a menu structure is the capability of backtracking to a higher (more general level) or of returning to the highest level and starting over. Another useful feature is to refer to similar commands by similar numbers.

One of the major drawbacks to menu selection is its inefficiency for the expert user who wants to go directly to a specific command. An ideal menu interface should have shortcuts. Examples of shortcuts are a menu of menu names so that a user may immediately specify a lower level menu and a feature to permit direct writing of a complex command that bypasses the menu displays.

Forms

In a forms-based interface design, the user "fills in the blanks" on a screen. This type of interface dialog is particularly appropriate for data entry of transactions. As explained earlier, the design of a screen for transaction processing should differ depending on whether the user is working from a transaction document. If a document is used, the screen format should reflect the document layout; if no document is used, the dialog format simulates a form. In both cases, data entry often reflects a "fill in the blanks" philosophy, with automatic positioning of the cursor to the next field for entry and captions indicating what information goes in each space. Often color or foreground (bright) and background (dim) character printing differentiates system prompts from user-supplied information on the screen. Two examples of forms-based screens for transaction processing are shown in Figure 17-7. (See selected references at the end of the chapter for guidelines for caption format, alignment between caption and data entered, spacing, etc.)

The design and programming of screen dialog can be time consuming and difficult if performed using procedural languages such as COBOL. There are software packages that simplify design and programming. Some application development tools have screen generators which facilitate screen design; an example is shown in Figure 17-8.

Icons, Graphs, and Color

The availability of graphics was discussed in Chapter 5. Graphical symbols commonly called *icons* may be used in system dialog instead of menus or command languages. A workstation display may show a menu of icons: a desk, an in box, an out box, a file cabinet, a wastebasket. The user moves the cursor to the icon representing the desired function and presses a key to select that icon; either the function is executed or a new set of icons is displayed. Icons and graphics functions may also be used as the basis for creation of complex graphical images that may be displayed on the screen or incorporated in a document. Figure 17-9 shows examples of drawings created through these functions as well as a free-form "paint" function which allows the user to "draw" on the screen using a physical manipulation device (explained later in this chapter). Note icons at left of screen.

Graphics interfaces have had limited use in database query systems via a method known as *spatial data management*.[14] A combination of graphical images, color, and a joystick manipulation device (explained in the next section) permit the user to traverse through a hierarchical menu by "zooming" in to greater levels of detail. An example of progressive "zooming" is shown in Figure 17-10.

---

[14]C. F. Herot, "Graphical User Interfaces," in Vassilou, *Human Factors in Interactive Computer Systems*.

```
FILE: EMPLOYEE                          RECORD UPDATE

  EMPNO ................: 45584
  EMPNAME .............: PETERSON, N. M.
  UNIT ....................: 2000
  JOBCODE ...............: 0110
  LEVEL .................: HEAD
  TITLE ..................: DIVISION MANAGER
  SEX ......................: M
  BIRTHDATE ............: 280607
  PSKILL .................: 0110
  SSKILL1 ................: 6130
  SSKILL2 ................: 6625
  SSKILLS ................: 6040
  ACTSALARY ...........: 56000

  ARROWS move cursor to change values; RETURN to accept.
```

a Screen design not based on a paper form.

```
                              INDIVIDUAL
INDIVIDUAL NUMBER  :_____:               HOUSEHOLD NUMBER :____:

NAME— LAST  :_____:       FIRST NAME (S)  :_____:
      TITLE  :___:       SUFFIX  : ___:   ALTERNATE LAST NAME  :_____:

PERSONAL— SEX :_:           BIRTHDATE  :___/___/___: ROLE IN HOUSEHOLD* :_:

MARITAL— STATUS* :_:   LAST TRANSITION DATE  :___/___/___:

MEMBERSHIP— STATUS* :_: METHOD* :_:    DATE :_____:
        FORMER CHURCH (DEN LOC CHNAME)* :_____:

RELIGIOUS DATES—  #1  :___/___/___:     #2 :___/___/___:   CHURCH SCHOOL LEVEL :_:

EDUCATION—  ACTIVITY/DIFFERENTIAL* :_:  CURRENT/LAST SCHOOL  :_____:
              LEVEL ATTAINED* :_:  CURRENT/LAST MAJOR :_____:

OCCUPATION— EMPLOYER  :_____:        WORK PHONE :___-___-___x___:
        GENERIC TITLE * :_____:
                                          XREF TO SPECIAL NEEDS  :__:
OFFICE—  DATE OF LAST CHANGE  :___/___/___:   LAST REVIEW BY INDIVIDUAL  :_____:
```

b Screen design based on a corresponding paper form.

Figure 17-7
Examples of forms-based interface designs.

The ability to combine graphics with color provides potential for enhancing communication. Color can be used to highlight a particular aspect of a cluttered display, highlight a change, or separate information categories. Color is especially valuable in tasks involving identification, searching, and counting.

There can be some problems with using color. Since it is very noticeable, it can distract a person by highlighting unimportant items or associating different items that are really unrelated. Color should generally be used carefully, consistently, and sparingly, since irrelevant colors can interfere with the ability to perform tasks. (See Ives in selected references for a summary of graphical user interfaces.)

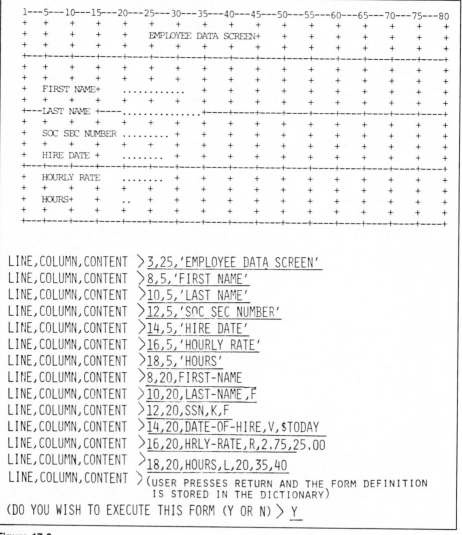

Figure 17-8
Example of use of a screen generator to create screens for transaction processing. (Courtesy of Henco Software, Inc., 100 Fifth Avenue, Waltham, MA. 02154.)

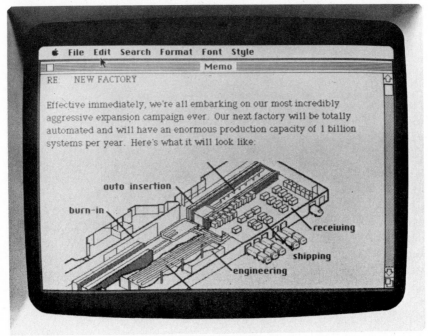

Figure 17-9
Using functions specified by icons and menus to create drawings. Top shows drawing and shading; bottom shows insertion of drawing in a memorandum. (Courtesy of Apple Computer, Inc.)

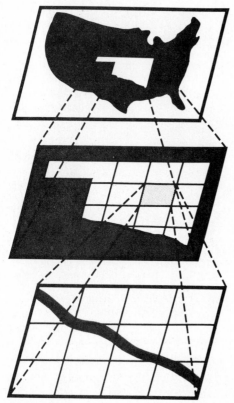

Figure 17-10
Illustration of progressive "zooming" through a spatial data management system. (Figure 2.2 from Christopher Herot, Richard Carling, Mark Friedell, David Kramlich, and Ronni Rosenberg, "Overview of the Spatial Data Management System," Computer Corporation of America, Technical Report CCA-81-08, November 1981.)

Natural Language

The development of natural language interfaces is generally considered part of the domain of artificial intelligence. The goal is for a novice user to communicate with the computer through a natural language such as English. The ultimate objective is for computers to be able to understand natural language in the spoken voice, which would make many of the interface designs already discussed in this chapter unnecessary. In practical terms, natural language interfaces are extremely difficult to implement, although considerable research and development is in progress. An example of a commercial product is *Intellect* from Artificial Intelligence Corporation.

The primary barrier to development of useful natural language systems is the imprecision of language itself. The objective is to be flexible in stating a query rather than to be forced into the positional or keyword limitations of a command language. However, many ways of phrasing a query (in English for instance) are ambiguous if considered word for word but very understandable to another human. For instance, "Doctor Livingstone, I presume" is understandable in spoken English (in part because of verbal clues such as emphasis and pauses), but in logical analysis, it is incomplete. The words "I presume" require an object to be complete. The analysis that the sentence means "I presume you are Doctor Livingstone" is not impossible, but is very difficult.

Natural language systems now being developed are "restricted natural language" systems. That is, they are based on a limited domain of inquiry and contain a data dictionary of words and meanings referencing that limited domain. Even within that domain and a given grammar, many phrases which the user would consider "natural" will not be understood. Thus, the language cannot be completely "natural" even within that domain, and the user may become easily frustrated.

Even with the difficulty of a limited domain of specialized knowledge, applications can be developed that "understand" a set of queries greater in scope than command language statements. The statements below are a dialog using a prototype natural language system. The information desired is exactly the same as that accessed by the command-based query language shown in Figure 17-6.

- What are the names and addresses of the alumni who graduated with a PhD?
- Who are the alumni who are not donors?
- List the sum of donations for each alumnus from Chicago.

It should be clear from the example that a restricted natural language is ideal for a novice user with no technical knowledge and no previous training. However, an important drawback of such systems is that they are not efficient for repeated queries or for expert users, since natural language is very verbose and the query requires a great deal more keying than any of the other interfaces discussed in this section.

Several other drawbacks to the practical implementation of natural language systems should be noted:[15]

- The creation of a dictionary and grammar for a particular application is very labor-intensive and the finished product is tied to the particular database and database management system in use. This work must be redone every time the system is installed on a new database.
- One of the advantages of a database is that it can be changed easily. This requires new words to be understood by the natural language interface that were not in its original vocabulary. The interface needs to evolve over time through additions to and changes in its grammar and data dictionary, a problem which is presently difficult.
- A computer system is deterministic and relatively closed, even with a natural language interface. Therefore, it can give a literal answer which may actually be misleading. For instance, an answer to the question, "Which managers make over $15,000 per year" may yield a list of 1,000 names when the more appropriate answer would be "all." Or a response of "none" to the query "How many stores showed a profit on sales of speedboats in region Y?" would be misleading if region Y does not carry speedboats at all.

---

[15]S. J. Kaplan and D. Ferris, "Natural Language in the DP World," *Datamation*, August 1982.

The problems discussed above are technically solvable in the long run. However, it seems likely that applications of natural language systems will continue to be domain-specific.

ALTERNATE INTERACTION MECHANISMS

The preceding section focused on screen formats for carrying out an interactive dialog with the computer. For the most part, interactive dialog is based on the use of alphanumeric displays and the keyboard. In this section, some alternative interactive mechanisms are considered that do not necessarily emphasize keying skills. The major alternatives are direct manipulation and speech.

Direct Manipulation Systems

With the types of support systems described in Chapter 13, the typical user is an expert who uses the system intensively for long periods of time to do many different tasks. Many of the systems developed for this type of support have a common set of interaction principles. Termed *direct manipulation systems*, they are characterized by the following:[16]

- Visibility of the object of interest
- Rapid reversible actions
- Replacement of a command language by direct manipulation of the object of interest

Many of the examples already described in this chapter and in Chapter 13 reflect direct manipulation. The approach does not necessarily require new technological devices; however, it reflects a philosophy that interaction between the user and the system is performed by a direct interaction of the user with visual presentations or physical manipulation devices.

The system encourages the user to explore its more powerful aspects. Some examples illustrate the philosophy of direct manipulation systems:

1 *Visual display editors*. These editors reflect the notion that "what you see is what you get." Text can be manipulated and viewed on the screen, and the results of an action are displayed immediately. The cursor is moved to the point in the text to be changed; it is manipulated physically by function keys or physical objects, such as a mouse or joystick, that have an intuitive relationship to the movement of the cursor. Commands are easily reversible through the ability to insert or delete characters, words, or lines directly at the point of error.

2 *Electronic spreadsheets*. The electronic spreadsheet simulates visibly traditional accounting spreadsheets. Manipulation of one part of the spreadsheet results in visible changes in the rest, so that the user can readily see results.

3 *Spatial data management*. The notion of using a graphical interface to a database was discussed in the previous section. Actions are easily reversible in that one can zoom back to a higher level of generality and then zoom down to another level of detail on some other object of interest.

4 *Video games*. Video games use color graphics and even sound to create a rich interface. They are also direct manipulation systems in that commands are directed through physical rotation of knobs or joysticks and results are shown directly on the screen.

---

[16]Shneiderman, ''Direct Manipulation.''

Figure 17-11
A mouse physical manipulation device plus a keyboard. (Courtesy of Apple Computer, Inc.)

Several of the preceding examples incorporated not only keyboard manipulation, but physical devices whose analogous movement is reflected immediately on the screen. Such devices have been commonly used in video games but are also available for personal computers and personal workstations.

Device	Explanation
Joystick	A handle that can be angled verically and horizontally to move the cursor on the screen.
Mouse	The device is a small box with a ball that moves as the box is moved on a hard surface. Shown in Figure 17-11, the mouse allows the cursor to be moved rapidly to position it at a point or to draw on the screen. For example, the mouse is used to position the cursor over an icon or menu item and a button on the top of the mouse activates a command to select it.
Pointing device	The most common pointing device is the light pen. It can be used to point to and select a menu item; in some cases, they can also be used to draw on the screen. Disadvantages are the awkwardness of use and obstruction of part of the screen when pointing.
Touch-sensitive screen	Touch sensitive screens can be activated by a grid within the screen surface that responds to touch or to a grid of light beams just over the surface of the screen that is broken when a finger or other object comes close to the screen surface.

DAYTON'S BRIDAL REGISTRY USES TOUCH SENSITIVE SCREEN

A bride or groom about to be married can register gift preference items at Dayton's department store in the Twin Cities of Minneapolis and St. Paul. The list of gifts are not restricted to a few items such as china or crystal. The gift preferences are listed under both bride and groom.

A user of the computer-based gift registry inputs via a touch sensitive screen. The user touches a designated spot on the screen to indicate bride or groom. The next touch is to indicate the first letter of the last name of the bride or groom. The system displays the persons who have a last name beginning with that letter. The user touches a spot opposite the person being selected. An attached printer provides a list of the gift preference items; when a buyer reports a purchase made, a notation is placed in the list beside the item.

Speech Recognition and Synthesis

The advantages of voice recognition for data entry are significant: it is fast and accurate, requires minimal training, and frees the user's hands for other operations. Voice recognition systems for limited vocabularies (100 to 400 words) are relatively inexpensive and are very useful for such applications as inventory control inspections. Usually, such systems are speaker-dependent in that the recognition is based on a recording of the speaker's voice patterns.

General voice recognition is a much more difficult problem because the normal spoken voice is continuous and often ambiguous. The notion of a "listening typewriter" which can compose a correct written manuscript from speech input is still far from reality, although significant efforts to accomplish it are being made in research laboratories.

Speech synthesis, or the ability of a computer to translate words into speech output, is utilized in telephone information systems. The use of speech output is currently limited to short messages such as telephone numbers, attention-getting devices, and aids to the blind.

SUMMARY

This chapter has explained information system requirements for the user interface. As systems are more commonly used directly by those who benefit from their outputs and who may know very little about their internal aspects, a well-designed interface is critical to the success of a system. Three basic principles that should be incorporated into all interface designs are consistency, flexibility, and user control.

Characteristics of the interface vary according to the degree of expertise of the user and the nature of the task to be performed. The amount of time the user will spend on the system and whether or not he or she benefits from system outputs (primary user) or is responsible primarily for system inputs (secondary user) are also considerations.

The components of the user interface that need to be considered in determining requirements are the language structure, the layout of the screen, the amount of feedback and assistance required, the degree of error control, response time, and ergonomics in workstation design. In terms of interactive dialog design, the most commonly used structures are command languages, menus, and forms images; icons, graphics, color and natural language are also used.

Physical system interface concepts not using the keyboard are direct manipulation and speech. Direct manipulation systems incorporate a manipulation of a visual representation (what you see is what you get) or a manipulation of a physical device. Physical manipulation of objects such as a joystick or mouse are translated into cursor control. Other direct physical manipulation technologies are light pens and touch-sensitive screens. Speech recognition systems are in limited use for specific applications.

MINICASES
1 A SYSTEM LOG-IN
Consider the following interaction with a commonly used operating system. The user made the connection through telephone lines. On the screen appeared:

TERMINAL =

The user typed in the name of the terminal on which he was working, and the system responded:

?

The user began again from the point of dialing in. This time when he received the message

TERMINAL =

he skipped it by hitting the carriage return. Then the system responded with:

@

He tried typing a few things but only received the response

?

Finally he gave up.

Question

Without being concerned about what the user is trying to accomplish, describe what is wrong with the user interface and make suggestions for improving it.

2 AN ENGINEER'S VIEW OF A USER INTERFACE
"I remember the first time I used the computer. Our data processing department gave me an account number. Two days later, a terminal was moved into my office and half of my desk disappeared. To help me get acquainted with my new assistant, I was handed something called a user's manual. It was two inches thick, filled with pages of diagrams, boxes, examples. It had long black lines in the left-hand margin. I tried to read it that afternoon, but got bogged down after the first two pages.

"The next day, manual in hand, I started to explore the system. After I turned the terminal on, the following message appeared:

VERSION 3.3 3/10/81

ENTER LOGON/PASSWORD:

A "LOGON"? What was that? No one had ever mentioned a LOGON. I could not even find it in the unabridged dictionary. After spending 15 minutes searching through the manual, I realized a LOGON was my account number. Why couldn't the data processing department and the computer agree on what they call an account number? Why don't they say what they mean?

"As I began to type, everything seemed to be going fine, until I pressed the "/" key; then the computer stopped printing. I hit the return key, but nothing happened. The computer simply told me

ACCESS DENIED

"I attempted to revive the computer a few times with no success. When I called the woman from the computer center, I was told that the computer would not print my password, but it read it anyway. How could the computer read something if it was not printed? The answer: the printing is not important; it's the pressing of the keys that sends information to the machine. In fact, the computer looks at each key as it is pressed. Suddenly, I knew why the computer did not print my password. When I pressed the key marked "/", the computer turned off the printing for the rest of the line. From then on, I avoided using that key; I wanted to know what I typed.

"A few minutes after I typed the next line I was treated to the following information:

**** THE SYSTEM WILL BE DOWN FOR PM FROM
     1000 TO 1130.

**** USER SHOULD REFER TO LIB.$SYS.NEW.PROC
     FOR UPDATED PROCEDURES.

**** THERE HAVE BEEN REPORTS ABOUT
     PROBLEMS WITH XLIBSTA. IF YOU HAVE
     EXPERIENCED ANY PROBLEMS CONTACT BOB
     AT EXTENSION 8425.

**** DUE TO THE HEAVY LOAD ON THE SYSTEM,
     GAMES WILL NOT BE ALLOWED FROM 10:00 TO
     17:30.

At least I understood the last part of the message; where were the games?

"During the next two weeks I worked on a number of different jobs, each requiring a different program. Each program looked different; each worked differently; one could not communicate with another. What bothered me most was that I had to think in different terms for each program. Not only were the same items called by different names in different programs, but operations I could do on the same item in one program were impossible in another. As an engineer I had learned well-defined methods for designing cars. Why couldn't computer people do the same thing?"

Michael L. Schneider and John C. Thomas, "The Humanization of Computer Interfaces," *Communications of the ACM*, April 1983, p. 253.

Question

Apply the principles learned in this chapter to justify the engineer's complaints.

EXERCISES

1 Describe the characteristics of the following types of users and identify the most important principles of user interface design for each.
   a A novice occasional user
   b An expert occasional user
   c A frequent primary user
   d A frequent secondary user
2 How has the balance between human and machine in the performance of a task changed over the last decade?
3 How should a screen design differ for secondary users depending on whether they are working from a document?
4 Why is feedback important? How is it incorporated into a user interface?
5 Identify how each of the following types of online assistance could be a nuisance to the user.
   a Requests
   b System status requests

c Prompting
d A "HELP" function

6 What are the four dimensions of error control that should be incorporated into a user interface and what methods are used to incorporate them?

7 What is the relationship between response time and display rate?

8 Describe a task environment where a slow response time (i.e., greater than 30 seconds) would be advantageous and one where a very fast response time (i.e., one second or less) would be necessary.

9 What is the advantage of a Dvorak keyboard over a standard QWERTY keyboard? Why has it not been adopted more readily? With current technology, what could be done to remove these barriers to adoption? How long would this take?

10 How are ergonomic problems in workstation design related to job design?

11 What are the trade-offs between the keyword and position methods of specifying arguments in a command language?

12 When are forms-based systems appropriate? What factors should be considered in their design?

13 How does use of color in displays affect individual perceptions and processing of information?

14 What is a restricted natural language system? What are its advantages over other dialog methods? What are its disadvantages?

15 What are the characteristics of a direct manipulation system? Give an example of a direct manipulation application other than one of those cited in the text.

16 Analyze the user interface of a text editor with which you are familiar, considering:
a Consistency
b Flexibility
c Degree of user control

17 Information systems personnel typically are users of online systems to write programs, execute test runs, and perform other related tasks such as documentation. Describe the ideal interfaces for a programmer.

18 The text emphasized clear, direct responses from the computer. Some applications for novice users use a style that simulates a friendly human. For example, the user inserts a name and all messages use it.

- I CAN'T UNDERSTAND THIS INSTRUCTION
- GORDON, YOU FORGOT THAT THE LAST COMMAND NEEDS A SOURCE FILE
- SORRY, GORDON, YOUR FILE IS TOO LARGE FOR THE SPACE YOU HAVE BEEN ALLOCATED

What are arguments for and against this type of computer response?

19 Degradation in response time reduces job satisfaction. What is the effect of slow response versus variability in response time?

20 A major microcomputer vendor is advertising the benefits of a touch-sensitive screen, so that users can avoid keyboarding.
a List advantages and disadvantages.
b Identify two "good" applications for touch-sensitive screens and explain why.

SELECTED REFERENCES

Workstation Design

Bailey, Robert W.: *Human Performance Engineering: A Guide for System Designers*, Prentice-Hall, Englewood Cliffs, NJ, 1982.

Barber, Raymond E., and Henry C. Lucas, Jr.: "System Response Time, Operator Productivity, and Job Satisfaction," *Communications of the ACM*, 26:11, November 1983, pp. 972–986.

Dreyfus, H., and Associates: *Measures of Man: Human Factors in Design*, Second Edition, Whitney Library of Design, New York, 1967.

Galitz, W. O.: *Human Factors in Office Automation*, Life Office Management Association, Atlanta, GA, 1980.

Koffler, Richard P.: "The Ergonomic Art," *Datamation*, June 1983, pp. 235–238.

Sauter, S. L., M. S. Gottlieb, K. C. Jones, V. N. Dodson, and K. M. Rohrer: "Job and Health Implications of VDT Use: Initial Results of the Wisconsin-NIOSH Study," *Communications of the ACM*, 29:4, April 1983.

Tarter, Jeffrey: "Ergonomics: A Primer," *Business Computer Systems*, June 1983, pp. 55–72.

Williams, G.: "The Lisa Computer System," *Byte*, February 1983, pp. 33–50.

Interface

Benbasat, Izak, and Yair Wand: "Command Abbreviation Behavior in Human-Computer Interaction," *Communications of the ACM*, 27:4, May 1984, pp.376–382. Brown, P. J.: "Error Messages: The Neglected Area of the Man/Machine Interface?" *Communications of the ACM*, 26:4, April 1983, pp. 246–249.

Card, S., T. Moran, and A. Newell: *Applied Information Processing Psychology: The Human Computer Interface*, Earlbaum, Hillsdale, NJ, 1983.

Card, S., T. Moran, and A. Newell: "Computer Text-Editing: An Information-Processing Analysis of a Routine Cognitive Skill," *Cognitive Psychology*, 12, 1980, pp. 32–74.

Card, S., T. Moran, and A. Newell: "The Keystroke-Level Model for User Performance Time with Interactive Systems," *Communications of the ACM*, 23:7, July 1980, pp. 396–410.

Card, S., T. Moran, and A. Newell: *The Psychology of Human-Computer Interaction*, Earlbaum, Hillsdale, NJ, 1983.

Carey, T.: "User Differences in Interface Design," *Computer*, 15:11, November 1982, pp. 14–20.

Christ, Richard E.: "Review and Analysis of Color Coding Research for Visual Displays," *Human Factors*, 17:6, December 1975, pp. 542–570.

Computing Surveys, 13:1, May 1981. Entire issue.

Ehrenreich, S. L.: "Query Languages: Design Recommendations Derived from the Human Factors Literature," *Human Factors*, 23:6, December 1981, pp. 709–725.

Embly, D., and G. Nagy: "Behavioral Aspects of Text Editors," *Computing Surveys*, 13:1, March 1981, pp. 34–70.

Gould, J., J. Conti, and T. Hovanyecz: "Composing Letters with a Simulated Listening Typewriter," *Communications of the ACM*, 26:4, April 1983, pp. 295–308.

Houghton, Raymond C., Jr.: "Online Help Systems: A Conspectus," *Communications of the ACM*, 27:2, February 1984, pp. 126–133.

IBM Systems Journal, 22:2, 1981. Entire issue.

Ives, Blake: "Graphical User Interfaces for Business Information Systems," *MIS Quarterly*, Special Issue, December 1982, pp. 15–48.

Jacob, R. J. K.: "Using Formal Specifications in the Design of a Human-Computer Interface," *Communciations of the ACM*, 26:4, April 1983, pp. 259–264.

Norman, Donald A.: "Design Rules Based on Analyses of Human Error," *Communications of the ACM*, 26:4, April 1983, pp. 254–258.

Psychology Today, 17:12, December 1983. Entire issue is on "user friendly" machines.

Roberts, Teresa L., and Thomas P. Moran: "The Evaluation of Text Editors: Methodology and Empirical Results," *Communications of the ACM*, 26:4, April 1983, pp. 265–283.

Schneider, Michael L., and C. Thomas (eds.): "The Humanization of Computer Interfaces," *Communications of the ACM*, 26:4, April 1983.

Shneiderman, B.: "Direct Manipulation: A Step Beyond Programming Languages," *Computer*, August 1983, pp. 57–69.

Shneiderman, Ben: *Software Psychology: Human Factors in Computer and Information Systems*, Winthrop, Cambridge, MA, 1980.

Vassiliou, Yannis (ed.): *Human Factors in Interactive Computer Systems*, Ablex Publishing, Norwood, NJ, 1984.

Williges, R. C., and B. H. Williges: "Modeling the Human Operator in Computer-Based Data
  Entry," *Human Factors*, 24:3, 1982, pp. 285–299.
Woodson, Wesley E.: *Human Factors Design Handbook*, McGraw-Hill, New York, 1981.

DEVELOPMENT, IMPLEMENTATION, AND MANAGEMENT OF INFORMATION SYSTEM RESOURCES

Information is a resource that should be managed. Information management includes development and implementation of information applications, quality assurance, and the organization and management of the information resources function. This section contains a chapter on each of these three elements. The final chapter provides an overview of significant technology and information system developments and their effect on organizations and society.

The development and implementation of information applications is an organizational change process. Organizational procedures and processes change as a result of or in connection with new information systems. Jobs and tasks are altered. The development and implementation of applications therefore should be managed in order to achieve desired results without undesirable organizational and behavioral consequences. The basic approach to application development management is the system development life cycle, but other strategies are in use. The development approach to a specific application should be the one that is most effective, considering the characteristics of the application and the application development environment.

Organizations usually follow quality assurance procedures for manufacturing operations, but frequently do not apply the same principles to information systems. Control and quality assurance procedures can be applied within the organization to assure information system quality. Analysis of value of information systems and post-audit evaluation of applications are methods for applying cost and benefit criteria to information system applications. There are also methods to evaluate existing and proposed hardware and software.

The organization and management of the information resources function applies well-known organization and management principles, but there are also some unique features. Centralization versus decentralization has been a frequent, recurring issue, so it will be explored in detail.

The section contains four chapters:

Chapter	Title	Notes on content
18	Developing and Implementing Application Systems	Describes the life cycle and prototyping approaches for managing application development. Explains the organizational change process.
19	Quality Assurance and Evaluation of Information Systems	Describes quality assurance duties and processes. Explains evaluation ofinformation system value.
20	Organization and Management of the Information Resources Function	Describes information resources management, organization of information processing, management of information systems personnel, and management of end-user computing
21	Future Developments and Their Organizational and Social Implications	Brief descriptions of current technological trends and potential changes in organizational and societal use of information systems.

CHAPTER 18

DEVELOPING AND IMPLEMENTING APPLICATION SYSTEMS

In Section Five, techniques for specifying information system requirements were described. The purpose of this chapter is to describe the *process* of system design and implementation. It focuses on action-oriented techniques for carrying out the process of design and managing it. The underlying theme of the chapter is that different strategies are available for the design and implementation of information systems, and the selection of the appropriate strategy depends on the situation. In the first section, a contingency approach to choosing the appropriate development strategy is described. In the following sections two major system development strategies (prototyping and life cycle) are discussed. Project management and implementation processes are surveyed.

A CONTINGENCY APPROACH TO CHOOSING AN APPLICATION DEVELOPMENT STRATEGY

As discussed in Chapter 15, information requirements determination may employ a variety of techniques, the appropriate technique being dependent on the situation. Development should encompass a process to accommodate requirements changes and provide assurance that the application as developed is an accurate and complete reflection of user requirements. A fundamental purpose for application development methods is therefore *requirements development assurance*. However, application development approaches or strategies differ in their power to achieve requirements assurance. A contingency approach to choosing the appropriate strategy is described below. Once a strategy is selected, methods appropriate to it can be selected. Subsequent sections of this chapter describe the prototyping and life cycle development methods and relate them to the contingency approach to requirements development assurance.

Contingencies Contributing to Requirements Development Uncertainty

This contingency theory for a development strategy is closely related to the contingency theory for an information requirements determination strategy described in Chapter 15. The underlying basis for the selection of a requirements determination strategy was uncertainty as to the ability of users and developers to know and elicit requirements. In the selection of an appropriate development strategy to assure correct and complete application development, there is uncertainty of requirements prior to and during development. During application development, four contingencies affect the degree of uncertainty with respect to achievement of an application to deliver "real" information requirements. These are summarized and described below.

Contingency		Contribution to uncertainty (plus or minus)
Type	Degree	
Project size	Small	−
	Large	+
Degree of structuredness	Structured	−
	Unstructured	+
User task comprehension	Complete	−
	Incomplete	+
Developer-task proficiency	High	−
	Low	+

1 *Project size.* The project size contingency has two characteristics: duration and total cost. These characteristics are usually, but not necessarily, collinear; that is, a high-cost project usually requires an extended time period. Large project size increases the difficulty of assuring that requirements are met because of the number of persons involved in establishing and modifying requirements, the volume and complexity of communications, and changes over time in both user and developer personnel.

2 *Degree of structuredness.* One dimension of the Gorry and Scott Morton[1] framework for information systems is the relative structuredness of the decisions to be supported by an information system. Uncertainty about the structure of the decision process or other process to be supported is thus an important factor in uncertainty about initial requirements and about alteration of those requirements during development.

3 *User task comprehension.* Distinct from degree of structuredness is the comprehension that the user or users have of the task to be performed by the information system. User task comprehension affects requirements determination and development uncertainty in much the same way as the degree of structuredness. If users have a low degree of understanding, or do not agree on the task for which a system is intended, the level of uncertainty for accuracy and completeness both in initial requirements and requirements modification is high.

4 *Developer-task proficiency.* Developer-task proficiency is a measure of the specific training and experience brought to the project by the development staff: project management, liaison staff, systems analysts, systems designers, programmers, and so on. It is not a measure of ability or potential but rather of directly applicable experience. This contingency indicates the degree of certainty with which the developer will be able to understand requirements accurately and completely and develop an application to achieve them.

[1]G. A. Gorry and M. S. Scott Morton, "A Framework for Management Information Systems," *Sloan Management Review*, 13:1, Fall 1971, pp. 55–69.

Selection of Development Strategy for Requirements Development Assurance

A common organizational response to requirements development uncertainty is to add control by adopting a single requirements development assurance method. Rather than forcing all projects to use a single requirements development assurance strategy, an alternative approach, which recognizes the differences in project-related factors, is as follows:

1 Measure contingencies and determine the level of development uncertainty.
2 Select a development assurance strategy suitable for the observed level of uncertainty.

Four basic development assurance strategies, and the contingencies under which they are appropriate, are described below:

1 *Acceptance assurance strategy.* This strategy is to accept user statements of requirements as complete, correct, and firm and to develop as defined. There are no procedures to gain assurance that initial requirements are correct or complete or that requirements do not change during development. Examples of appropriate use of the ''accept'' strategy are file conversions, reports from existing files or databases, and some simple, single-user decision models. The contingencies these examples have in common are small size, high degree of structure, users who understand what the systems are to do, and developers who are experienced in this kind of task. When appropriate, the acceptance assurance strategy will lead to greater responsiveness to users who have well defined needs, elimination of frustrating assurance procedures for such users, and an increase in development efficiency.

2 *Linear assurance process.* If application requirements can be determined through a straightforward process with little or no subsequent modification, a suitable assurance strategy is to proceed from requirements specification to final development. As each step is completed, there are assurance procedures to verify conformance with requirements. There are ''sign offs'' to this effect. This is a linear assurance process and is used in most formal life cycle methodologies. The linear assurance process is an effective strategy under a combination of contingencies that lead to a very low level of requirements changes after the initial sign-off on specifications. Application requirements for systems that are highly structured and for which user task comprehension and developer task proficiency are high may be effectively developed by this process. If the system is also small and involves only one or a few users, the linear assurance strategy may be effectively equivalent to an acceptance assurance strategy. On the other hand, requirements achievement for even a relatively small system might not be assured by this process if the decisions to be supported are relatively unstructured, the user does not comprehend the task, or the developers have not previously produced such a system.

3 *Iterative assurance process.* Where requirements uncertainty during development is moderately high, the linear assurance strategy may not assure that application development meets real information requirements. For such applications, the linear assurance process of traditional life cycle methodologies can be modified to include iteration. Whenever requirements are found to be wrong or inadequate during development, the specifications are revised by a return to the requirements determination process with users. The sequence of activities in the life cycle can therefore be repeated as often as necessary in order to obtain the requirements and develop a system to achieve them. This approach assumes that a correct and complete specification of requirements can be obtained if sufficient iterations are used. Examples where the iterative assurance process is applicable are large multiple-user systems and application areas that are new to the user or developer organization.

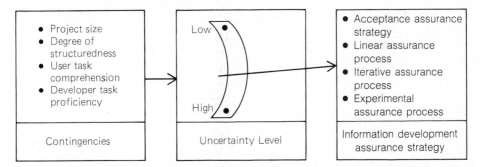

Figure 18-1
A contingency model for choosing an information requirements development assurance strategy. (Reprinted by permission of the publisher from "Determining Information Requirements: A Contingency Method for Selection of a Requirements Assurance Strategy," by J. David Naumann, G. B. Davis, and J. D. McKeen, *Journal of Systems and Software*, Vol. 1, page 227. ©1980 by Elsevier Science Publishing Co., Inc.)

4 *Experimental assurance process.* A high level of requirements and achievement uncertainty during development may indicate the need for an experimental assurance process in which requirements development assurance is obtained through actual user experience with the system being developed. This experience is achieved by prototyping or simulation of the application. The prototype design method reduces uncertainty by producing successive approximations. Users and developers can readily identify the shortcomings of a prototype even when they were unable to specify application requirements in advance. Examples of applications with high uncertainty include decision support systems for upper management, interactive forecasting models, and unstructured systems to be implemented for multiple users. Conscious selection of the experimental assurance strategy may be the only effective approach to assurance that requirements are met when the level of uncertainty is very high.

A contingency model for selection of a development assurance strategy selection is depicted in Figure 18-1. Application of the contingency model requires measurement of the level of each contingency, estimation of the overall level of uncertainty determined by the contingencies, and selection of an appropriate strategy.

Note that, putting aside the acceptance assurance strategy, there are two general approaches to proactive application development requirements assurance: application development life cycle (applied in a linear fashion or with iterations) and an experimental, prototyping approach. Prototyping is described below; the traditional system development life cycle method is described in subsequent sections of this chapter.

PROTOTYPING APPROACH TO APPLICATION SYSTEM DEVELOPMENT

As explained above, the strategy of experimental assurance in development of information system applications may be achieved by an evolutionary design method commonly called *prototyping*.[2] Prototyping is used when requirements are difficult to

---

[2]The material in this section is adapted from A. Milton Jenkins, "Prototyping: A Methodology for the Design and Development of Application Systems," Working Paper, School of Business, Indiana University, Bloomington, 1983.

specify in advance or when requirements may change significantly during development. The prototyping methodology is based on the simple proposition that people can express what they like or do not like about an existing application system more easily than they can express what they think they would like in an imagined, future system. A prototyping methodology is initiated by a user who conceives of a problem or an opportunity to be solved by an information system. The user seeks assistance from a professional system designer who is competent in the prototyping methodology.

A Model of the Prototyping Process

Prototyping an application system is basically a four-step process, as described below and depicted in Figure 18-2. There are two significant roles: the user and the system designer.

Step 1: Identify the user's basic information requirements. In this stage, the user articulates his or her basic needs in terms of output from the system. The designer's responsibility is to establish realistic user expectations and to estimate the cost of developing an operational prototype. The data elements required are defined and their availability determined. The basic models to be computerized are kept as simple as possible.

Step 2: Develop the initial prototype system. The objective of this step is to build a functional interactive application system that meets the user's basic stated information requirements. The system designer has the responsibility for building the system using very high level development languages or other application development tools. Emphasis is placed on speed of building rather than efficiency of operation. The initial prototype responds only to the user's basic requirements; it is understood to be incomplete. The early prototype is delivered to the user.

Step 3: Use of the prototype system to refine the user's requirements. This step allows the user to gain hands-on experience with the system in order to understand his or her information needs and what the system does and does not do to meet those needs. It is expected that the user will find problems with the first version. The user rather than the designer decides when changes are necessary and thus controls the overall development time.

Step 4: Revise and enhance the prototype system. The designer makes requested changes using the same principles as stated in step 2. Only the changes the user requests are made. Speed in modifying the system and returning it to the user is emphasized.

As illustrated in Figure 18-2, steps 3 and 4 are iterative. The number of iterations may vary considerably. There may be one of two reasons that iterative modification is ceased. First, the user determines that the prototype is not useful and the working prototype is discarded. Second, the user is satisfied with the system and it becomes an "operational prototype." It may be modified at a later stage, but at this point it is considered usable and may be distributed to other users. Alternatively, it may "seed" the idea of a new major application and be used to provide initial specifications for the application development effort.

The prototyping methodology, as outlined above, has several significant advantages in development of applications having high uncertainty as to requirements:

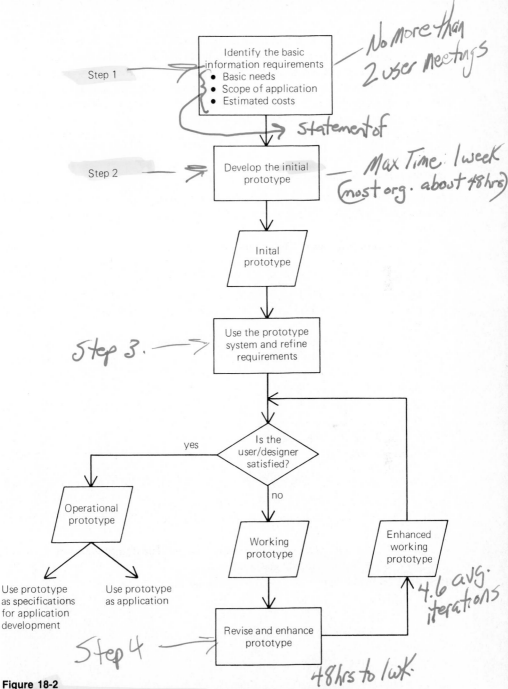

Figure 18-2
Application system prototype development model. (Adapted from A. Milton Jenkins, "Prototyping: A Methodology for the Design and Development of Application Systems," Working Paper, School of Business, Indiana University, 1983.)

- Ability to "try out" ideas without incurring large costs
- Lower overall development costs when requirements change frequently
- The ability to get a functioning system into the hands of the user quickly
- Effective division of labor between the user professional and the MIS professional
- Reduced application development time to achieve a functioning system
- Effective utilization of scarce (human) resources

A major difficulty with prototyping is management of the development process because of frequent changes.[3] Also, there may be a tendency to accept a prototype as the final product when it should only be the basis for a fully-specified design. For example, a prototype may not handle all exceptions or be complete as to controls. It "works," but it is not complete.

Variations on the Prototyping Model

The model described above assumes only two participants: a user who is a functional expert and a system designer who is expert at the development of prototypes. The prototyping methodology may be modified to accommodate a greater number of participants.

Multiple users may be involved in prototype development when the application is useful across a broad area with many different users, or when it is so complex as to require input from several specialists. Both situations require added time for communications and negotiation among users. They do not significantly affect the designer's time required to build the prototype. If an application requires complex technical or analytical skills, it may be necessary to have more than one designer, and this may add time to the prototype-building process.

As users become more familiar with very high level development languages and gain experience with the use of prototypes, it will become more common for the user to also function as the system designer (discussed in Chapter 13). In such cases, it is important that the user have access to computing resources. One approach is a service organization such as an information center (discussed further in Chapter 20). Having users as developers introduces special development risks, which are described in Chapter 13.

LIFE CYCLE APPROACH TO APPLICATION SYSTEM DEVELOPMENT

Although there are a growing number of applications (such as decision support systems) that should be developed using an experimental process strategy such as prototyping, a significant amount of new development work continues to involve major operational applications of broad scope. The application systems are large and highly structured. User task comprehension and developer task proficiency are usually high. These factors suggest a linear or iterative assurance strategy. The most common method for this large class of problems is a *system development life cycle model* in which each stage of

SDLC

---

[3]Maryam Alavi, "An Assessment of the Prototyping Approach to Information Systems Development," *Communications of the ACM*, 27:6, June 1984, pp. 556–563.

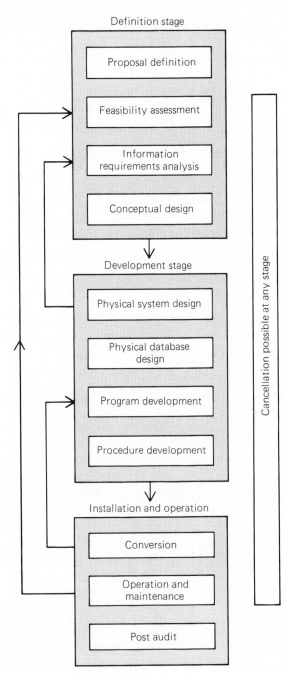

Figure 18-3
The application system development life cycle.

development is well defined and has straightforward requirements for deliverables, feedback, and sign-off. The system development life cycle is described in detail since it continues to be an appropriate methodology for a significant part of new development work.

The basic idea of the system development life cycle is that there is a well-defined process by which an application is conceived, developed, and implemented. The life cycle gives structure to a creative process. In order to manage and control the development effort, it is necessary to know what should have been done, what has been done, and what has yet to be accomplished. The phases in the system development life cycle provide a basis for management and control because they define segments of the flow of work which can be identified for managerial purposes and specify the documents or other deliverables to be produced in each phase.

The phases in the life cycle for information system development are described differently by different writers, but the differences are primarily in amount of detail and manner of categorization. There is general agreement on the flow of development steps and the necessity for control procedures at each stage.

The information system development cycle for an application consists of three major stages:

Definition

Development

Installation and operation

The first stage is the process which defines the information requirements for a feasible cost-effective system. The requirements are then translated into a physical system of forms, procedures, programs, etc., by system design, computer programming, and procedure development. The resulting system is tested and put into operation. No system is perfect, so there is always a need for maintenance changes. To complete the cycle, there should be a post audit of the system to evaluate how well it performs and how well it meets cost and performance specifications. The three stages of definition, development, and installation and operation can therefore be divided into smaller steps or phases as follows:

Stages in life cycle	Phases in life cycle	Comments
Definition	Proposal definition	Preparation of request for a proposed application
	Feasibility assessment	Evaluation of feasibility and cost-benefit of proposed application
	Information requirements analysis	Determination of information needed
	Conceptual design	User-oriented design of application

	Physical system design	Detailed design of flows and processes in application processing system and preparation of program specifications
Development	Physical database design	Design of internal schema for data in database or design of files
	Program development	Coding and testing of computer programs
	Procedure development	Design of procedures and preparation of user instructions
Installation and operation	Conversion	Final system test and conversion
	Operation and maintenance	Day-to-day operation, modification, and maintenance
	Post audit	Evaluation of development process, application system, and results of use

At completion of each phase, formal approval sign-offs are required from the users as well as from the manager of project development. Each phase also results in formal documentation. The information system development cycle can follow an iterative assurance strategy (Figure 18-3). For example, the review after the physical design phase may result in cancellation or continuation, but it may also result in going back to prepare a new conceptual design.

The following percentages provide a rough idea of the allocation of effort in the information system development life cycle from inception until the system is operating properly (i.e., excluding operation and maintenance). These percentages will, of course, vary with each project. The ranges shown are indicative of the variations to be expected.

Stages in life cycle	Phases in life cycle	Rough percentage of effort	Range in percentage of effort
Definition	Proposal Feasibility assessment	5	3–10
	Information requirements analysis	15	10–20
	Conceptual design	5	3–7
Development	Physical system design	15	10–25
	Physical database design	5	3–7
	Program development	25	20–40
	Procedure development	10	5–15
Installation and operation	Conversion	15	10–20
	Operation and maintenance	(not applicable)	
	Post audit	5	2–6

It is instructive to note that upon completion of coding of programs and beginning of program testing (about half way through the program development phase), the application is probably only about 60 percent complete. For complex systems involving much testing, completion of coding may mark about the halfway point. Many errors in estimation of project completion dates can be attributed to failure to allocate adequate time to program testing and conversion.

THE LIFE CYCLE DEFINITION STAGE

Ideally, a major system development project is conceived as a component of the information systems planning process, as described in Chapter 14, but a proposal may come from other sources such as users and data processing personnel. After a project is proposed, the next step in the definition stage is feasibility assessment, which is discussed briefly here. Once a proposed alternative is approved, the next phase is information requirements analysis, which was explained in Chapter 15. Following requirements analysis, a conceptual design phase produces a high-level design emphasizing the application as seen by its users.

Upon completion of the definition stage most of the key decisions that affect the user have been made. The definition stage is therefore critical in making sure the application will meet user needs. Although perhaps only 25 percent of total effort has been expended, the important decisions that shape the remainder of the effort are in place. The definition stage must therefore not be neglected if applications are to satisfy the users. In a study by McKeen,[4] it was found that projects which spend more time in the definition (analysis) phase were more successful regardless of the outcome measure used. Both user satisfaction and ability to develop the application within budget were enhanced.

Proposal Definition

The proposal definition phase is not necessary if the application was defined as part of information system planning. Otherwise, a simple procedure may be used for proposal of an application. Proposals may be for entirely new applications or for enhancements to existing applications. The proposal should not be complex but in a short one- or two-page document should provide sufficient justification to support a decision to proceed with a feasibility analysis. Examples of items that may be included are the following:

- Identification of those proposing the project and others who have an interest in the application
- The organizational need for or benefit from the application (the business reason)
- Organizational support (budget, sponsor, management support, etc.)
- Schedule considerations (date needed, availability of user personnel, etc.)

Following user management approval, the proposal is reviewed by the management authority responsible for allocating information system development resources (user management, a steering committee, or the information systems executive).

Feasibility Assessment

When a new application is proposed, it normally goes through a feasibility study before it is approved for development. If the application is part of the predefined MIS master plan, it still should go through the feasibility assessment phase in order to evaluate alternative approaches to its development, even though the general idea has been approved with the

---

[4]James D. McKeen, "Successful Development Strategies for Business Application Systems," *MIS Quarterly*, 7:3, September 1983, pp. 47–65.

rest of the plan. If a proposal is submitted outside of the plan, the feasibility study includes whether it is consistent with the existing plan and whether it should override the priorities of other applications already planned.

Five types of feasibility are addressed in the study. They result in recognition of both the benefits and risks inherent in the development and implementation of the proposed application system:

1 *Technical feasibility.* Can the proposed application be implemented with existing technology? Analysis of project risk relative to technical feasibility includes not only whether the technology is available on the market but also its "state of the art" both in absolute terms and relative to the company's current technical sophistication.

2 *Economic feasibility.* Will the system provide benefits greater than the costs? The feasibility study presents intangible as well as tangible benefits in a formal way. A relatively detailed analysis of the costs of both development and operations of the various alternatives is also presented.

3 *Motivational feasibility.* The probability that the organization is sufficiently motivated to support the development and implementation of the application with necessary user participation, resources, training time, etc. This motivation is usually demonstrated by an owner or champion for the application who has sufficient organizational power to provide the resources and motivate others to assist and cooperate.

4 *Schedule feasibility.* The probability that the organization can complete the development process in the time allowed for development. Adding development resources does not always reduce the development time; in fact, adding staff who cannot be used effectively may impede development because of time spent in communication.

5 *Operational feasibility.* Will it work when installed? This analysis may involve a subjective assessment of the political and managerial environment in which the system will be implemented. In general, the greater the requirements for change in the user environment in which the system will be installed, the greater the risk of implementation failure.

The feasibility study may be staffed in different ways. Some alternatives are:

1 Evaluation group with representatives from users, information systems, and other groups affected by the system. The head of the study group may be a user or from information systems.

2 Evaluation person or group from information systems.

3 Evaluation person or group from users.

Each of the alternatives has advantages and disadvantages, and the selection of the staff for evaluation may depend on the type of project and the organizational culture with respect to responsibility. For example, an evaluation group with many representatives has advantages when the application will have significant impact on several groups or on the fundamental operations of the organization. The evaluation by information systems may be appropriate for highly centralized organizations in which the evaluation is primarily technical. The feasibility evaluation by users is consistent with user responsibility for information system resources. It establishes user commitment to the new system, and requires that user management be "sold" by the user evaluators.

The feasibility report covers items such as the following:
- General description of the application
- Expected development schedule
- Schedule of resources and budget required for development

- Schedule of expected cost and benefits from operations (economic feasibility)
- Summary of evaluation with respect to technical, motivational, schedule, and operational feasibility

If the feasibility study includes several alternatives, the report should present the budget, expected benefits, schedule of resources required, etc., for each (including the alternative of "do nothing"). The choice of alternative is based on the relative feasibility of each of the alternatives. For instance, the following alternatives were considered for an accounts receivable system for one division of a large multidivisional company (after rejecting "do nothing"):

1 Dedicated minicomputer system with modification of a purchased software package
2 A minicomputer system for data entry with processing on the central computer using a generalized transaction processing package
3 Online data entry to the central computer using an accounts receivable system developed by another division and modified as required

The feasibility report is reviewed by the management of information systems and by the requesting department. If not part of the master plan (and of significant impact), it may also be reviewed by the information systems steering committee. Once the feasibility study has been accepted and an alternative is approved, information requirements analysis can begin.

Information Requirements Analysis

The process of information requirements analysis was described in Chapter 15. A contingency approach to selecting one or more methods for determining information requirements was outlined. In order to effectively obtain a complete and correct set of requirements, it is necessary to use a method or methods that take into account the extent to which requirements are already known versus their needing to be searched out or discovered.

The result of the information requirements analysis or requirements determination phase of the application development life cycle is a report detailing the requirements for the application. The requirements consist of items such as the following:

- Reports (including the data items on the reports)
- Queries (both regular and ad hoc)
- Conceptual schema for database (from data modeling or other analysis)
- Functional requirements (including operational characteristics)
- User interface requirements

Conceptual Design

In the proposal definition, some user needs were specified; in the feasibility assessment phase, additional requirements were identified and some fairly general design alternatives were evaluated. The information requirements analysis phase elicited and documented a more detailed set of requirements. The conceptual design phase establishes a more complete user-oriented design for the application.

It is useful to divide application design into a conceptual design phase and a physical design phase. These two phases can also be characterized as external design and internal design or general design and detailed design. The conceptual design emphasizes the application as seen by those who will operate or use the outputs of the system; the physical design translates those requirements into specifications for implementing the system. The conceptual design establishes the inputs and outputs, functions to be performed by the application, and application audits and controls. In general terms, conceptual design treats the actual processing functions as "black boxes"; physical design specifies the actual processing given in conceptual design. Conceptual versus physical designs in application development are loosely analogous to conceptual versus physical modeling in database development.

Typical contents of a conceptual design report are the following:

- User-oriented application description. Documents the flow of the application activities through the organizational units providing inputs and using outputs. Distinguishes manual operations from automated operations performed by the application system.
- Inputs for the application with general description of each (visual display screens, source documents, forms, queries, etc.).
- Outputs produced by the application with general description of each (visual display screens, query responses, printed outputs, reports, etc.).
- Functions to be performed by the application system.
- General flow of processing with relationships of major programs, files, inputs, and outputs.
- Outlines of operating manuals, user manuals, and training materials needed for the application.
- Audit and control processes and procedures for ensuring appropriate quality in the use and operation of the application.

THE LIFE CYCLE DEVELOPMENT STAGE

The development stage of the system development life cycle consists of four classes of activity which may occur somewhat concurrently: physical system design, physical database design, program development, and procedure development.

Physical System Design

The physical system design phase, also called internal or detailed design, consists of activities to prepare the detailed technical design of the application system. The physical system design is based on the information requirements and the conceptual design. In turn, it provides the basis for physical database design, program development, and procedure development. Testing is sometimes defined as a separate phase, but testing is really part of each phase. Some life cycles include physical database design in the physical system design phase; however, since the trend is toward more independence between programs and data and specialized skills are often required for physical database design, it is considered a separate design phase in this explanation. The results of the physical system design phase are specifications and designs for the following:

- System design showing flow of work, programs, and user functions
- Control design showing controls to be implemented at various points in the flow of processing
- Hardware specifications for the applications if new hardware is required
- Data communications requirements and specifications
- The overall structure of programs required by the application with procedural specifications on functions to be performed by each
- Security and backup provisions
- An application test or quality assurance plan for the remainder of the development

The physical system design work is performed by systems analysts and other technical personnel (such as controls specialists, quality assurance personnel, data communications specialists, etc.). Users may participate in this phase, but much of the work requires data processing expertise instead of user function expertise.

The work of the physical system design phase is to take the fairly high level, user-oriented requirements of the conceptual design phase and produce a specific technical design. This process is generally one of defining the "black boxes" that will produce the required outputs based on the inputs defined in conceptual design. There are a number of different methods an analyst may employ. By supporting the systematic process of expanding the level of detail and documenting the results, the methods aid in reducing the complexity and cost of developing application systems and in improving the reliability and modifiability of the designs.

Generally, physical system design techniques achieve simplicity by subdividing the application system into small, relatively self-contained modules. System modules can be programs or procedures which are subsections of programs. System complexity is reduced because each module can be developed, coded, and tested relatively independently of the others. Reliability and modifiability are enhanced because a change (whether a change in specifications, an enhancement, or a repair) can be made to a system module with minimal, well-understood effects on the rest of the system. The techniques are thus based on well-understood principles of systems theory as described in Chapter 9.

As illustrations, some of the available techniques are summarized below:

Technique	Description
Top-down design (Stepwise Refinement)[5]	A processing unit (system, program, module) is defined by a general statement of its purpose, then broken down into smaller and smaller refinements. The design is depicted as a hierarchy chart with general control modules at the top and detailed modules at the bottom (see Figure 18-4). The resulting program is also hierarchically structured.

[5]N. Wirth, "On the Composition of Well-Structured Programs," *Computing Surveys*, 6:4, December 1974, pp. 247–259.

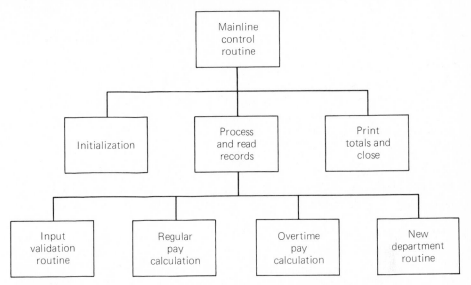

Figure 18-4
A hierarchy chart illustrating top-down design of a payroll validation report program.

Structured design[6]	Each module of a program is defined by the specific function it performs. Emphasis is on decoupling or minimizing the integration between modules; each module is highly cohesive, meaning all the statements within it are functionally related. Structure charts, similar to hierarchy charts, show module definition. The transformation of data is represented by data flow diagrams (see Figure 18-5).
SADT[7]	Structured Analysis and Design Technique is a proprietary system utilizing a graphical modeling language to describe, in a top-down fashion, the functions of the system and the data utilized.
HIPO[8]	Hierarchy-Input-Process-Output is a documentation technique which can also be used to communicate system specifications to project participants throughout the design process. The three types of charts, each depicting a finer level of detail, are in Figure 18-6 on pp. 582-583.

[6]E. Yourdon and L. L. Constantine, *Structured Design*, Prentice-Hall, Englewood Cliffs, NJ, 1979.

[7]SADT is a proprietary methodology of Softech, but a public version was delivered to the Air Force: AF Wright Aeronautical Laboratories, Integrated Computer-Aided Manufacturing project (ICAM): Function Modeling Manual, Dynamics Modeling Manual, and Information Modeling Manual, Wright-Patterson AFB, Ohio, June 1981.

[8]*HIPO—A Design Aid and Documentation Technique*, International Business Machines, GC20-1851, White Plains, New York, 1974.

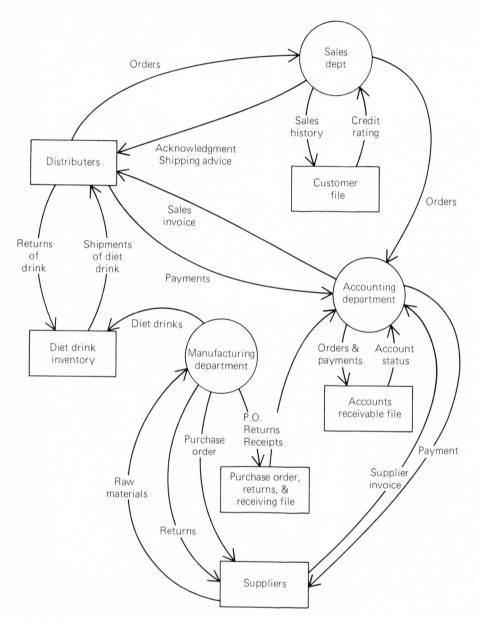

Figure 18-5
Example of a data flow diagram.

Technique	Description
Warnier-Orr[9]	The methodology was originally developed in France by Warnier; it has been adapted and expanded by Orr. The methodology assists in defining the hierarchical structure of systems. It can be used in defining the logical structure of the processing system, data structures, and control structures and flow of control in programs. Nested braces are used in documenting the hierarchical structures.

The objectives of these examples of techniques for detailed design are similar, but each has unique features for defining and communicating system specifications. They can be used in communicating the design specifications to users, although they are not necessarily easy to understand for a person untrained in the technique. Another advantage of these physical design approaches is that they support the use of *structured programming*, to be described later in this chapter. One problem with all of the techniques is that they require a large investment in training analysts and converting to the new procedures. Each requires a rather complete commitment and changeover; it is not easy to "borrow" elements from each and combine them.

Since the early 1960s there has been ongoing experimental work in techniques for automating the system design process. The intent of these efforts has been to provide a means for specifying the information requirements of a system and automatically generating program code and database specifications. The problem is to develop a requirements language which is rich enough to provide the necessary information yet easy to understand. Another problem is developing adequate tools to generate code and organize data structures automatically.

The most comprehensive research project to date has been ISDOS (Information System Design and Optimization System) at the University of Michigan. The ISDOS approach begins with a problem definer who defines the information needed, specifies timing and volume requirements, and provides algorithms and logic to produce output. The requirements are written in a Problem Statement Language (PSL). The software system (Problem Statement Analyzer or PSA) analyzes the problem statements and in a limited sense performs system design, compiles programs, organizes files, and directs execution of the resulting application system. In other words, information requirements determination and conceptual design must be performed prior to writing the problem statements. The ISDOS system thus performs tasks associated with physical system design, physical database design, program development, some procedure development, conversion, and operation phases of the system development life cycle. The system is in limited experimental use.

---

[9]Jean-Dominique Warnier, *Logical Construction of Systems*, Van Nostrand Reinhold, New York, 1981; and Kenneth D. Orr, *Structured Requirements Definition*, Ken Orr and Associates, Topeka, Kansas, 1981.

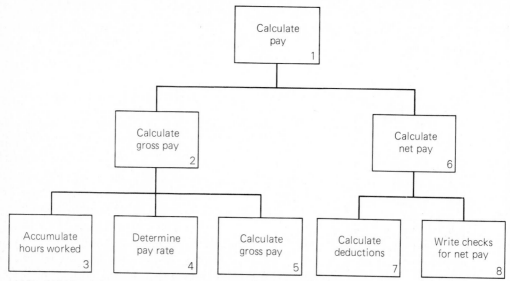

a Visual Table of Contents (VTOC) for HIPO documentation technique. Each block refers to a diagram. (Courtesy of International Business Machines Corporation.)

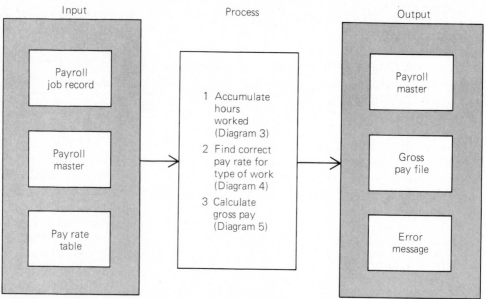

b Overview diagram for block 2 of table of contents (Figure 18-6a). (Courtesy of International Business Machines Corporation.)

Figure 18-6
HIPO documentation

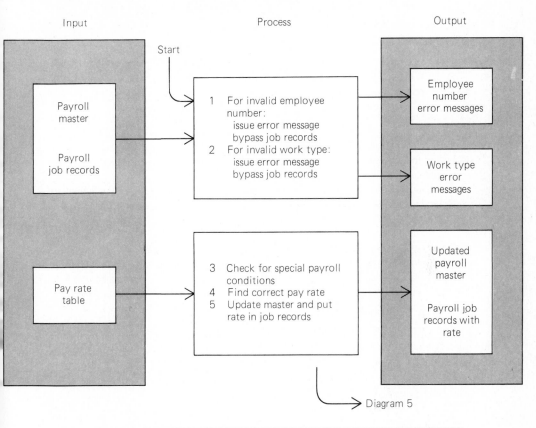

| | Input | Process | Output |

	Extended description	Routine	Label
1	The program checks for valid employee number. If invalid, job records for that number are by passed and an error message is printed.	IODNA	DETR
2	A check is made for correct type of work. If invalid, bypass job records and print error message.		
3	Special conditions, such as overtime, shift pay, vacation pay, or holiday pay, are checked to help determine correct rate.		
4	The master record, job records, and pay rate table are all referenced to determine correct pay rate.		
5	When all conditions are checked, payroll job records are rewritten with proper rate and the payroll master is updated.		

c Detail diagram for block 4 of table of contents (Figure 18-6a) and extended description. (Courtesy of International Business Machines Corporation.)

Physical Database Design

The approach to physical database design for an application depends on the existing database and the approach followed for database requirements determination, as described in Chapter 16. There are three major approaches to meeting the data requirements for an application.

1 *Create a new physical file or database.* This is appropriate if no database is used or a database is dedicated to the application; in either case the application "owns" the data and objectives of a database (shareability, data independence) are violated. New data may be required and the files or database must be designed and created from data collected specifically for the application.

2 *Using and modifying an existing database.* This method is appropriate if an evolutionary strategy for database development is followed. It may require special functions to be evoked by the database administrator for restructuring the existing database as well as adding necessary data.

3 *Access an existing database by means of a user schema.* This approach is possible if a complete conceptual model of the enterprise, anticipating new application needs, was used as the basis for physical database design. New data may need to be added to the database, but the connection between the logical description of the data needed by the application and the physical database is easily made through the database management software.

The third alternative assumes that a complete data model of the enterprise will anticipate further application requirements. The second alternative is more likely even if a data modeling approach to database definition was followed. Fortunately, one of the advantages of database management systems is that the database can be restructured to accommodate evolutionary application requirements.

Program Development

A primary output of the physical design process is a set of specifications that define programming tasks. The goal of the program development phase is to code and test programs required for the application. Testing of each module is performed on test data representing a fairly complete set of variations in input data in the user environment.

Problems encountered during the programming phase are typically a result of lack of complete specifications provided during conceptual or physical design. This often results in extensive reprogramming efforts when specifications are changed. The techniques for formalizing the conceptual and physical design process are aimed at alleviating this problem. Another problem in this phase is inadequate program testing prior to system test and conversion. A number of program development techniques reduce program complexity and aid in achieving program correctness. Important examples are modularity, structured programming, application generators, and tailoring of application packages.

The concept of *modularity* has already been discussed. The practice of subdividing a program into small, relatively well defined modules is generally accepted. Modularity aids in reducing program complexity and in enhancing reliability and modifiability. In most programming languages, modules can be programmed as subprograms with well-defined procedures for passing data values between them. Each module can be coded and tested by itself before being integrated and tested with other modules.

In *structured programming*, a small set of basic coding structures is used for all program code, which generally results in programs that are straightforward in flow of logic. Structured programming is related to modularity in that use of the coding structures ensures well-defined modules. Structured programming is often termed "GOTO-less" programming because GOTO statements are discouraged or prohibited. The reason is that use of GOTOs can introduce unnecessary complexity. However, structured programming is not simply prohibition of GOTOs; correct use of coding structures results in code which does not require GOTOs. The three primary coding structures in structured programming are illustrated in Figure 18-7.

Testing represents a critical factor in application development. It can take up from 15 to 50 percent of the total development effort depending on the size and complexity of the application. Formal approaches to system testing involve a discipline which begins early in the program development phase. There are three distinct phases of program testing:

> **1** *Module testing*. Each individual program module is tested using dummy routines (or *stubs*) for calls to other modules.
>
> **2** *Integration testing*. Groups of program modules are tested together to determine if they interface properly. This may be done incrementally as they are developed until the entire program system is tested.
>
> **3** *System testing*. This involves testing of the complete set of application programs.

There is debate over what constitutes a correct or adequately tested program. Some errors will be revealed only after the system is in production; however, a system that is put into production with too many errors can be disastrous in terms of corrective activity required and organizational acceptance of the application. Criteria for program correctness vary widely and tend to be related to the method of generating test data.

It is useful to distinguish between reliability and correctness for programs.[10] A *correct* program meets specifications; a *reliable* program operates in an acceptable manner under both intended and unintended input data and operating conditions. In other words, a reliable program will perform satisfactorily (even to the extent of rejecting further processing) under a wide range of correct and incorrect inputs; a correct program need only perform satisfactorily as long as the inputs are as specified. Reliability of programs is therefore a broader and more useful concept; reliable programs meet the law of requisite variety as described in Chapter 10.

An alternative approach to application development with high potential payoff in productivity is to purchase generalized software packages and modify them to meet the unique needs of the organization. Many applications, such as payroll, have similarities across organizations and across industries, suggesting the possibility of using generalized software instead of writing unique application software. There are two alternative approaches to the use of generalized application software packages:

> **1** *Have organization adapt to the package*. The application software procedures are fixed and the operating procedures of the organization are modified to conform to the software. This alternative may be desirable for an organization with applications where there are no significant

---

[10]M. A. Zelkowitz, "Perspectives on Software Engineering," *Computing Surveys*, 10:2, June 1978.

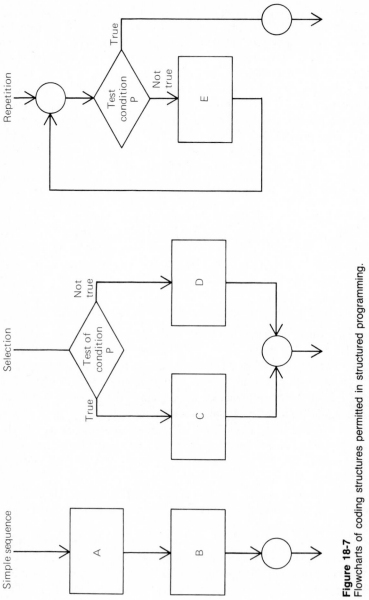

Figure 18-7
Flowcharts of coding structures permitted in structured programming.

unique organizational requirements or internal training is less expensive than modifying the software. Another situation is when cost limits or the urgency for the system to be implemented offsets the benefits of unique requirements that can be obtained only through delay and extra cost associated with unique application development. Small businesses, for example, can frequently afford the cost of conforming to a package but not the cost of unique development.

2 *Adapt package to organizational needs.* Recent trends, accepted by software vendors and purchasers, have been to provide general packages that can be easily modified because of modular design to fit unique organization requirements. The increasing cost of software development (primarily the cost of personnel) relative to packages makes it cost-justifiable to purchase a package and spend the same amount as the acquisition cost (or sometimes more) to modify it. Some vendors "tailor" packages themselves; others provide the source code for their clients to modify. The tailoring alternative is suited for situations in which the essential features are found in a package, but the purchasing organization desires unique features.

When the choice is made to purchase a software package rather than to develop in-house, it is still important to have complete, accurate system design specifications. The specifications provide the guidelines for evaluating different software packages and choosing the one that most closely meets the specifications. They also dictate how the chosen package should be modified, providing a basis for estimating the cost of modifications and assuring that it is done adequately.

THE NOT-INVENTED-HERE SYNDROME

The application development group was charged with developing a new online student registration system for a large university. The idea was to develop a system that would handle the unique requirements of an urban university and be state of the art.

Significant time was spent in eliciting and documenting requirements. Development turned out to be very expensive; large cost overruns and delays were experienced. The resulting system did not appear to have major advantages over systems of other universities.

Near the end of the requirements phase, at a presentation on the requirements process, the team was asked if they had looked at the existing operational systems available immediately that they could purchase or lease at a fraction of the cost of development. They said "No" and indicated they were not interested in them.

Procedure Development

Procedure development (manuals, instruction sheets, input forms, HELP screens, etc.) can take place concurrently with program development. Procedures should be written for all personnel who have contact with the system. This includes the following:

1 *Primary users.* This includes instructions for how to interpret a report, how to select different options for a report, etc. If the user can execute the system directly, as in online queries, it includes detailed instructions for accessing the system and formulating different types of queries.

2 *Secondary users.* This includes detailed instructions on how to enter each kind of input. It is more oriented to "how to" and less to "what" for different inputs (when compared with the instructions to primary users).

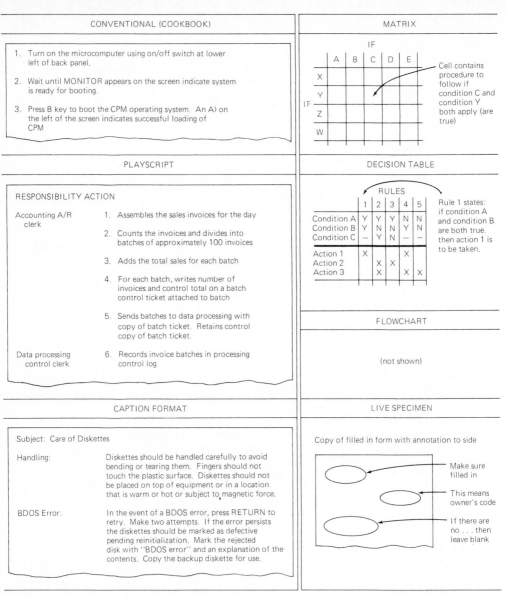

Figure 18-8
Alternative methods for documenting procedures.

3 *Computer operating personnel.* There are generally maintenance procedures to be performed by computer operators and/or control personnel. Procedures include instructions for quality assurance, backing up system files, maintaining program documentation, etc.

4 *Training procedures.* In some cases, a separate training manual or set of training screens is developed for the implementation stage and subsequent training.

One of two groups may be responsible for writing procedures: analysts or users. The advantages of analyst-written procedures are technical accuracy, project control over completion, and conformance to the overall documentation; disadvantages are the tendency of analysts to write in technical jargon or technical abbreviations and to assume users have knowledge of the technical environment. The advantages of user-written procedures are an appropriate level of technical description and instructions that are understandable; disadvantages are the difficulty of assuring clear, complete instruction. A mixed strategy is one in which analysts and users work together to produce a technically correct, understandable manual.

An effective procedures manual, one that communicates well and can be referenced easily, must be well designed. Several alternative layouts are shown in Figure 18-8. Conditions under which each are most appropriate are the following:[11]

Format	Conditions for use
Conventional (cookbook)	Sequenced set of instructions for one job title or unit. Possible use for policy statements.
Playscript	Sequenced set of instructions involving several job titles or units.
Caption	Unsequenced procedures or policies.
Matrix	Two conditions determine a procedure or an action (IF and IF).
Decision table	Several conditions and one or more procedures or actions.
Live specimen	Supplement for all of above.
Flowchart	Supplement to playscript, matrix, or decision table.

It is important that procedures be kept current to coincide with changes to the information system. A document numbering system that ties procedures to particular programs, modules, or data files is useful for this purpose.

THE LIFE CYCLE INSTALLATION AND OPERATION STAGE

The third stage of the information system development life cycle begins with conversion to the new application system. The rest of the system development life cycle refers to the life of the system in use. After the system is in production, changes and enhancements are made during the operation and maintenance phase of the system. Periodically, a post audit of the system is conducted; based on this activity, the system may be modified, enhanced, or replaced.

Conversion

Conversion to the new application system begins after all programs and procedures have been prepared and individually tested. Three major activities prepare for actual conversion: acceptance testing, file building, and user training.

Acceptance testing is testing of the completed application and comparing it to specifications. It verifies to the user that the system meets performance criteria and operational requirements. The testing includes user inputs, operating and control procedures, and outputs. Differences between what users expected and what the system delivers are identified and resolved. The acceptance test was developed as part of the planning for the system.

File building refers to the collection and conversion to machine-readable form of all new data required by the application. File building can be a long and tedious process, and careful planning is important. Ad hoc file conversion programs may be employed if the

---

[11]C. I. Haga, "Procedures Manuals," *Ideas for Management*, Systems and Procedures Association, Cleveland, OH, 1958, pp. 127-154.

required data is already in computer-readable form. If not, the data must be gathered, coded, and entered into the database. Sufficient time and human resources should be provided to "clean up" the data, that is, remove inaccuracies and inconsistencies and make the data complete.

User training may be relatively straightforward or a critical effort, depending on the degree to which the new application system affects existing jobs. If techniques such as job design, discussed in Chapter 11, are used, training will involve substantial reorientation of the users to their jobs. Proper user training is an important factor in overcoming user resistance to new systems. In a later section of this chapter, training as a subset of the implementation or change process will be discussed.

Conversion from the old system to the new takes place after acceptance testing, file building, and user training are complete. Conversion can be accomplished in several ways. The most careful method is to run the old and new systems in parallel; the new system is run under actual conditions and the results are compared with the old system for reliability and accuracy. After the new system has shown consistent results for a reasonable period of time it becomes operational and the old system is dropped. The drawback to this method is that it is expensive; both machines and employees work double time. Machine time can be costly if new hardware is replacing old and both must be maintained. More important, employees are required to perform essentially two full-time jobs, one of them being new and unfamiliar. Moreover, if the system has not been sufficiently tested and errors are detected during conversion, costly delays and employee frustration can cause serious problems.

If parallel processing of the old and new systems is not feasible, the new system should be tested under simulated conditions of full volume before cutting over from the old. Complete cutover is often referred to as "burning the bridges" because it is usually impossible to return operations to the old system once cutover takes place. Problems with the new system are corrected by "brute force" since no alternative is available. This is frequently a risky strategy, especially for systems such as payroll where very little delay can be tolerated. If possible, conversion should take place gradually, one portion of the system at a time.

CONVERSION TURNS TO DISASTER

A shoe manufacturer and importer, a division of a large company, wanted a computer. The company hired a consultant to recommend computer hardware, prepare programs, and convert company records. The invoicing and inventory systems were to be the first applications, followed by accounts receivable and accounts payable.

The first computerized invoices resulted in customer complaints. The inventory reports could not be compared with the parent company reports. The consultant was terminated, and he filed a lawsuit for fees due.

Some errors in development were highlighted in pretrial discovery:

1 The company had no experience with computers but still decided to implement all major applications at one time.

2 The manual system of inventory control had been developed by employees without formal training, resulting in somewhat unique features. The consultant never fully understood the existing system.

3 Live data items were used in the testing. This produced huge test outputs which could not be checked adequately.

4 The parent company system and the company's new system were not compatible, so the parent company inventory files were not copied. Instead, temporary input clerks were brought in to prepare data, but no programs were available to validate this input. The input data quality was poor.

5 No audit trails were included to identify corrections. No one knew what had changed or who made the changes.

6 No company personnel were assigned to the project. Lower-level employees were afraid to contradict the consultant; higher-level employees refused to participate at all.

Excerpted from Marcia Ann Bowles, "The Wise Manager's Basic Guide to Conversion," *Computerworld*, June 13, 1983, In Depth, pp. 20–21.

Operation and Maintenance

When the system appears to be operating without difficulty it is turned over to the information processing production function. This often requires not only approval by the user stating that the system meets predefined acceptance criteria, but also approval of the system operations and maintenance groups stating that it meets standards for documentation and maintainability.

Any subsequent changes in the application are handled as maintenance. Maintenance of an application can be classified as repairs or enhancements. Repairs are required when incomplete or incorrect coding renders the application defective. Enhancements are additions or improvements. Repairs dominate the maintenance activity for the first few months of operation. Later, most of the maintenance is enhancement. Sometimes maintenance is performed by the system developers, but often it is the responsibility of a separate maintenance group.

Post Audit

A desirable part of the system development life cycle is a review of the application after it has been in operation for a period, such as a year. An audit team with representatives from users, development, maintenance, operations, and perhaps internal audit review the operation, use, cost, and benefits of the application. Recommendations from a post audit include specific recommendations for dropping, repairing, or enhancing an application and suggestions for improving the development process on subsequent applications. The post audit is described in chapter 19.

PROJECT MANAGEMENT

When an information system project is approved, its consequences are not certain;[12] there are risks associated with it. The anticipated benefits may not be achieved, costs may be higher than planned, time for implementation may be greater than estimated, or

---

[12]This section is based on Chapter 7 of F. Warren McFarlan and James L. McKenney, *Corporate Information Systems Management: The Issues Facing Senior Executives*, Irwin, Homewood, IL, 1983.

performance of the hardware and software may be lower than anticipated. There are three factors, recognizable prior to implementation, that affect the inherent risk in a project: project size, the degree of structure of tasks to be automated, and the level of technology of the project relative to the organization. Note that the first two are similar to the factors contributing to uncertainty of information requirements. The level of company-relative technology introduces risk in system implementation but is relatively independent of requirements definition. Using combinations of high and low (or large and small) for these three factors, there are eight possible risk estimates for projects.

Relative level of technology used	Structure	Size	Risk
Low	High	Large	Low
		Small	Very low
	Low	Large	Low
		Small	Very low
High	High	Large	Medium
		Small	Medium–low
	Low	Large	Very high
		Small	High

In other words, a large project using high technology (relative to the organization's experience) for an application having low structure for the tasks to be automated has a very high risk. A small project using a low relative technology and high structure for tasks has a very low risk.

The contingency approach to project management is to organize and manage a project according to the level of risk in the project. Four types of tools and techniques are applied to obtain appropriate project management.

    1 External integration tools and techniques to link the project with users. Examples are user project managers, users on project team, and user steering committee.

    2 Internal integration tools and techniques to keep the project team working as a unit. Examples are project review meetings, minutes, and team participation in decisions.

    3 Formal planning tools and techniques to structure and sequence tasks. Examples are critical path scheduling, milestones, and project approval processes.

    4 Formal control tools and techniques to evaluate progress. An example is a series of formal status reports with variance analysis.

In general, the lower the structure of the tasks to be automated, the greater the need for high levels of external integration with user involvement. High level of technology relative to the organization generally is aided by high internal project integration and fairly low formal planning and control. High formal planning and control tend to be most useful for large projects with low technology.

Project characteristic	Project management technique to handle risk
Low structure of tasks	High external integration
High structure of tasks	Low external integration

High technology relative to organization	High internal integration
Low technology relative to organization	Low internal integration
Large project with low technology and high structure	High use of formal planning and control
Large project with high technology or low structure	Low to medium use of formal planning and control
Small project with high technology or low structure	Low use of formal planning and control
Small project with low technology or high structure	Medium to high use of formal planning and control

Management may choose a portfolio of projects to balance the overall development risk. Typically, a high-risk project will also have the greatest expected benefits if implemented successfully. For instance, a balanced portfolio might include one or two high-risk, high-benefit (potential) applications as well as several low-risk applications with more modest expected benefits. A mixture of projects with different risks and different project organization and management will allow an organization to achieve acceptable results while taking some risks to implement large projects, unstructured projects, and using relatively high technology.

IMPLEMENTATION OF INFORMATION SYSTEMS AS AN ORGANIZATIONAL CHANGE PROCESS

In one organization a well-designed system fails; a similar but poorly designed system in another organization succeeds. The reason can usually be traced to human rather than technical problems. *Implementation* of information systems is a process of organizational change; in this sense, implementation refers to the ongoing process of preparing the organization for the new system and introducing it in such a way as to assure its successful use. Recent research has focused on those human and organizational factors that affect the successful (or unsuccessful) implementation of a new information system.[13]

Theories of Organizational Change

In Chapter 11, Lewin's three-stage process of organizational change was reviewed. This

---

[13]H. C. Lucas, Jr., *Implementation: The Key to Successful Information Systems*, Columbia University Press, New York, 1981; contains a complete review of the research on implementation.

theory has formed the basis for most implementation research and is reviewed briefy below:

Stage	Description
Unfreezing	Increasing the receptivity of the organization to a possible change.
Moving	Choosing a course of action and following it.
Refreezing	Reinforcing the "equilibrium" of the organization at a new level after the change has occurred.

Another model of organizational change that elaborates on the Lewin stages has been proposed by Kolb and Frohman.[14] According to this model, an organizational "consultant" establishes a relationship with the "client" through a series of seven stages. The term "consultant" is used to refer to a person outside of the unit where the change is to occur. This key person is often termed a "change agent" and may be thought of as a catalyst for the change process. The success with which the consultant and client deal with important issues at each stage of the process determines the success of the overall change effort. The Kolb-Frohman model, with its relationship to the Lewin stages, (and also elaborated by Schein) is shown in Figure 18-9.

The Change Agent

Models of organizational change are useful because they identify issues that must be faced in new information system design and implementation. Projects differ in their organizational impact. If a project is well defined at the outset and involves minimal organizational change, a purely technical solution may be adequate. However, most large application systems involve considerable organizational change and require many redefinitions and reformulations before they are complete. These conditions increase the likelihood that the system will not be implemented successfully without explicit change procedures.

If the systems analyst is viewed as a "change agent" rather than a technician under organizational change conditions, the dangers of system failure can be reduced. An active change agent can assure better communication with the user and minimize the possibility of misunderstandings. He or she stays involved through all stages of the process to assure that "refreezing" takes place, rather than leaving as soon as the technical system is installed correctly. Moreover, in the role of change agent, the analyst can recognize when his or her change skills and the project requirements do not match and take the necessary action to involve others with the required skills in the implementation effort.[15]

---

[14]D. A. Kolb and A. L. Frohman, "An Organization Development Approach to Consulting," *Sloan Management Review*, 12, 1970, pp. 51–65.

[15]M. A. Ginzberg, "A Study of the Implementation Process," *TIMS Studies in the Management Sciences*, 13, 1979, pp. 85–102.

Kolb/Frohman stage	Activities	Underlying Lewin/Schein stage
Scouting	Client and consultant assess each other's needs and abilities; entry point is chosen	Unfreezing
Entry	Initial statement of problem, goals, and objectives; develop mutual commitment and trust; establish "felt need" for change	Unfreezing
Diagnosis	Data gathering to define client's felt problem and goals; assessment of available resources (client's and consultant's)	Unfreezing
Planning	Defining specific operational objectives; examination of alternative routes to those objectives and their impact on the organization; developing action plan	Moving
Action	Putting "best" alternative solution into practice; modifying action plan if unanticipated consequences occur	Moving
Evaluation	Assessing how well objectives were met; deciding to evolve or terminate	Moving and Refreezing
Termination	Confirming new behavior patterns; completing transfer of system "ownership" and responsibility to the client	Refreezing

Figure 18-9
A comparison of the Kolb/Frohman and Lewin/Schein models of organizational change. (M. Ginzberg, "A Study of the Implementation Process," *TIMS Studies in the Management Sciences*, 13, 1979, p. 88.)

Mechanisms for Successful Implementation

A recent study of implementation success and failure across multiple information systems[16] revealed that the probability of successful implemention of an MIS can probably be increased if special attention is paid to the following three key issues:

1 Gaining management and user commitment to the project
2 Gaining user commitment to any changes necessitated by the new system
3 Assuring that the project is well defined and plans are clearly specified.

Generally, user participation in the system design process is advocated in order both to increase commitment and to assure accuracy of requirements specifications. Involvement of primary users is usually advocated, particularly when system use is voluntary. The more active the users in information requirements determination and in approval of user interface design, the more likely they are to accept the system and utilize it appropriately. Research has shown that user involvement in development can subsequently increase their satisfaction with the system, but a relationship between user

---

[16]M. A. Ginzberg, "Key Recurrent Issues in the MIS Implementation Process," *MIS Quarterly*, 5:2, June 1981, pp. 47–60.

involvement and propensity to use a (voluntary-use) system has not been clearly demonstrated.[17]

A significant problem with organizational change is resistance to the change by those affected. User resistance to new information systems can be a serious problem. If use is voluntary (for instance, use of a decision support system by primary users), resistance will be manifested by avoidance of the system. If use is not voluntary (for instance, data entry by secondary users), user resistance can cause significant problems in the way of disruptions, increased error rates, deliberate sabotage, or increased turnover. There are different approaches to overcoming user resistance, depending on the situation as well as the implicit theories of management and system designers. Three implicit theories to explain resistance are the following:[18]

1 *People-oriented theory*: resistance occurs because of factors internal to the users as individuals or as a group.

2 *System-oriented theory*: resistance occurs because of factors inherent in the design of the system to be implemented.

3 *Interaction theory*: people or groups resist systems because of an interaction between characteristics related to both people and systems.

Strategies for implementation that are implied by different views of the problem of resistance are:

Theory	Implementation strategy
People-oriented	Educate users (training) Coerce users (edicts, policies) Persuade users User participation (to obtain commitment)
System-oriented	Educate users (better technology) Improve human factors Modify packages to conform to organizational procedures User participation (to obtain better design)
Interaction	Fix organizational problem before introducing system Restructure incentives for users Restructure relationships between users and designers User participation (not always appropriate)

The significant point of the interaction theory is that for a system with a large number of users who are impacted differently by the system, the first two approaches are too simplistic to overcome all resistance. Although user participation is often advocated for either obtaining greater commitment or improving system quality or both, there are

---

[17]B. Ives and M. H. Olson, "User Involvement in Information System Development: A Review of Research," *Management Science*, 30:5, May 1984, pp. 586–603.

[18]M. L. Markus, "Power, Politics, and MIS Implementation," *Communications of the ACM*, 26:6, June 1983, pp. 430–444.

situations where it is not appropriate. For instance, if a new design is mandated even though it is unpopular, an appearance of user involvement without substantive user influence in the design can increase user resentment and resistance. According to the interaction theory, the best prescriptions for an implementation strategy as well as system design will follow from a thorough diagnosis of the organizational setting in which the system will be used. One approach to system design and implementation which directly reflects the interaction theory discussed above is *sociotechnical design*.

Sociotechnical Approach to System Design and Implementation

The sociotechnical approach was introduced in Chapter 11 and also discussed in Chapter 15. In this section, specific techniques for implementing information systems using a sociotechnical approach are described.

The goal of sociotechnical system design is to produce systems which are both technically efficient and have social characteristics which lead to high job satisfaction. It is most suitable for transaction processing systems where a large number of operating personnel will be affected; their direct participation in design is emphasized. The steps, as defined by Mumford,[19] are the following:

> *Step 1: Diagnosis.* Questionnaires are utilized to diagnose human needs in the job setting. The results of the questionnaires show what employees like and do not like about their jobs and what they would like to have in an ideal job.
>
> *Step 2: Sociotechnical system design.* Human objectives for the system are set as a result of step 1. Based on these and the technical objectives of the system (generally specified in advance), broad design objectives for the system are specified.
>
> *Step 3: Define alternative solutions.* Technical and social solutions are set out separately. Each is evaluated based on the criteria established in step 2, and a short list of feasible social and technical solutions is developed.
>
> *Step 4: Define possible sociotechnical solutions.* Proposed technical solutions are compared with proposed social solutions, and those that can be combined into one solution are proposed as "sociotechnical" solutions.
>
> *Step 5: Rank sociotechnical solutions.* A cost-benefit analysis of each proposed sociotechnical solution is undertaken. The "best" solution is then evaluated against the social and technical objectives formulated in step 2.
>
> *Step 6: Prepare a detailed work design.* Specific task structures are considered to determine the appropriate mix of tasks and organization of work groups for the new system. Job design principles, discussed in Chapter 11, are employed for this purpose.
>
> *Step 7: Accept the best sociotechnical solution.* When the solution/system is implemented, the affected employees should see that the objectives of the system have been met. Follow-up diagnosis of job satisfaction and productivity measures are two mechanisms to measure improvements brought about as a result of the new system.

With the sociotechnical approach, direct participation by many users in design which affects their jobs directly should both increase commitment to the system and ensure its technical quality. Productivity goals should be met without sacrificing social needs and values.

---

[19]Enid Mumford and Mary Weir, *Computer Systems in Work Design: The ETHICS Method*, Chapter 3, Halsted (Wiley), New York, 1979.

SUMMARY

The process of system design and implementation was described in this chapter. The appropriate development strategy depends on several factors which contribute to the degree of uncertainty with respect to application development: project size, project structure, user task comprehension, and developer-task proficiency. Four basic strategies for assuring that an application will meet real user requirements are: acceptance of user requirements and development as defined, linear assurance process, iterative assurance process, and experimental assurance process.

An experimental assurance strategy is generally accomplished by *prototyping*. The prototyping methodology is an iterative process carried out by a user and designer. Very high level development languages are used to build a system quickly and iterate modifications based on the user's actual experience with the prototype.

The most common methodology applied to large, highly structured application systems is the *system development life cycle*. This represents a linear assurance strategy but can be modified to an iterative assurance strategy. The life cycle consists of three major stages: definition, development, and installation and operation. The phases in the life cycle provide a basis for system management and control by breaking the process down into small, well-defined segments.

In the definition stage, a proposal definition initiates a project. A feasibility assessment is made to analyze alternative approaches. Once a solution is selected, information requirements are determined (discussed in Chapter 15). A general user-oriented conceptual design is prepared in the conceptual design phase.

The development stage includes four types of activities: physical system design, physical database design, program development, and procedure development. Physical system design involves translating information requirements and conceptual design into technical specifications and general flow of processing.

Physical database design includes procedures to define or redefine the database or files needed by an application. Program development includes the coding and testing of individual programs. Procedure development includes preparation of procedures for users of output, data input preparation, operations, and training. Program testing represents a critical factor in the development stage.

The final stage of the system development life cycle includes conversion to the new system, ongoing operation and maintenance, and post audit. Conversion activities are acceptance testing, file building, and user training.

Project management techniques for a project can be determined by a set of contingencies that establish project risk. Four classes of techniques for project management can be combined in different forms to achieve a desired level of project management, depending on the type and level of risk inherent in the project. The techniques are: planning, control, internal project integration, and external project integration.

The implementation of an information system can be viewed as an organizational change process. The system designer may be viewed as a change agent to the user community. One common suggestion for improving the probability of successful implementation is user participation, which may increase user commitment to the system and/or improve system quality. An alternative approach, based on a theory of interaction between users and systems, suggests that understanding the structure of the relationship between users and designers is critical to successful implementation; user participation is not justified in all cases. One interaction approach to design is sociotechnical design, which uses participation to create a system that both is technically efficient and leads to high job satisfaction.

MINICASES

1 LEGISLATING A DEVELOPMENT ASSURANCE METHOD

The legislature of a midwestern state was concerned about control of application development, so that state government systems would be properly developed. They legislated that all applications would follow a well-known application development control method (usually applied in a linear fashion).

The result was not as intended. For some projects, it worked well—primarily when requirements were understood by the users. The requirements caused difficulty with applications for which requirements were uncertain or not known.

Various methods were used to circumvent the legislative requirement.

Question

Explain this in terms of the contingency theory in the chapter.

2 THE TEMPORARY PROTOTYPE THAT BECAME PERMANENT

The company embraced the idea of prototyping as a method of developing applications, but management wanted to use the prototypes only to identify requirements; working systems were then to be developed with proper controls and with consideration to efficiency. This followed the concept of heuristic development. (See T. Berrisford and James C. Wetherbe, "Heuristic Development: A Redesign of Systems Design," *MIS Quarterly*, 3:1, March 1979, pp. 11–19.)

The policy didn't work out for many applications. The users didn't want to proceed with a project to move from the prototype to a regular working version.

Question

Why didn't users follow the heuristic development policy? What are the costs and benefits of full development and the users' alternative of using only the prototype?

3 THE OWNERLESS APPLICATION

The information systems area of a major corporation was working on a large-scale accounting application affecting several functions in the organization. A consultant, in reviewing the projects, recommended that the project be dropped because there was no "owner."

Question

Discuss this in terms of both project risk and implementation theory.

EXERCISES

1 Explain the contingencies leading to uncertainty of the system development process and how they increase or decrease uncertainty.

2 When is an iterative assurance strategy appropriate, as opposed to an experimental assurance strategy?

3 What are the benefits of a prototyping approach to system development? When is it appropriate? What are the costs?

4 Identify and describe the outputs of the phases of the system development life cycle.

5 Describe the elements of project risk that can be identified by a feasibility study.

6 What are the advantages and disadvantages of having users develop their own feasibility studies?

7 What is the significance of modularity in a technique for physical system design?

8 Describe ISDOS. What technical problems are encountered with such an approach to system design?

9 What are the advantages of selecting a software package over designing a complete system in-house? What are its drawbacks?

10 What factors should be considered in the design of a procedure manual?

11 Describe the difference between program correctness and program reliability. Under what circumstances would a user prefer to emphasize a correct program over a reliable program?

12 Why is the time required for conversion from the old to the new system usually underestimated?

13 Describe the four types of tools and techniques for project management and project contingencies contributing to the appropriate use of each type.

14 Describe the Lewin theory of organizational change. How is this theory relevant to a system designer?

15 Why is user participation in system development commonly advocated? Why is it difficult?

16 Define the steps in the sociotechnical approach to system design. Does it conflict with the system development life cycle approach to system design? Why or why not?

17 Compare the contingencies affecting project risk with the contingencies affecting choice of a system development strategy.

18 Contrast the conceptual design phase with the physical design phase.

19 "Improve human factors and users will accept the system." What is the theory underlying the statement, and why might it be inadequate?

20 For a given application development project, define a policy for selecting:
   a a development approach
   b a project management approach

SELECTED REFERENCES

Alavi, M., and J. Henderson: "Evolutionary Strategy for Implementing a Decision Support System," *Management Science*, 17:11, November 1981, pp. 1309–1325.

Alter, S., and M. Ginzberg: "Managing Uncertainty in MIS Implementation," *Sloan Management Review*, 1978, pp. 23–31.

Beath, Cynthia: "Models for Managing MIS Projects: A Transaction Cost Approach," *Proceedings of the Fourth International Conference on Information Systems*, Society for Information Management, Chicago, 1983, pp. 133–147.

Berrisford, T., and J. Wetherbe: "Heuristic Development: A Redesign of Systems Design," *MIS Quarterly*, 3:1, March 1979, pp. 11–19.

Colter, M. A.: "A Comparative Examination of Systems Analysis Techniques," *MIS Quarterly*, March 1984, 8:1, pp. 51–66.

Couger, J. D., and R. W. Knapp: *Advanced Systems Development/Feasibility Techniques*, Wiley, New York, 1982.

Curley, Kathleen F., and Lee L. Gremillion: "The Role of the Champion in DSS Implementation," *Information and Management*, 6, 1983, pp. 203–209.

DeMarco, Tom: *Structured Analysis and System Specification*, Yourdon, New York, 1978.

DeSanctis, Gerardine, and James F. Courtney: "Toward Friendly User MIS Implementation," *Communications of the ACM*, 26:10, October 1983, pp. 732–738.

Dijkstra, E. K.: *A Discipline of Programming*, Prentice-Hall, Englewood Cliffs, NJ, 1976.

Gane, C., and T. Sarson: "Structured Methodologies: What Have We Learned," *Computerworld/Extra*, 14:38, September 17, 1981, pp. 52–57.

Gane, C., and T. Sarson: *Structured Systems Analysis: Tools and Techniques*, Prentice-Hall, Englewood Cliffs, NJ, 1979.

Ginzberg, Michael J.: "Early Diagnosis of MIS Implementation Failure," *Management Science*, 27:4, 1981, pp. 459–478.

Ginzberg, Michael J.: "Key Recurrent Issues in MIS Implementation Process," *MIS Quarterly*, 5:2, June 1981, pp. 47–60.

Ginzberg, Michael J.: "Steps toward More Effective Implementation of MS and MIS," *Interfaces*, May 1978.

Ives, B., and M. H. Olson: "User Involvement in Information System Development: A Review of Research," *Management Science*, 30:5, May 1984, pp. 586–603.

Jenkins, A. Milton: "Prototyping: A Methodology for the Design and Development of Application Systems," Working Paper, School of Business, Indiana University, Bloomington, 1983.

King, W. R., and J. I. Rodriguez: "Participative Design of Strategic Decision Support Systems: An Empirical Assessment," *Management Science*, 27:6, June 1981, pp. 717–726.

Lucas, Henry C., Jr.: *Implementation: The Key to Successful Information Systems*, Columbia University Press, New York, 1981.

Keen, Peter G. W.: "Information Systems and Organizational Change," *Communications of the ACM*, 24:1, January 1981, pp. 24–33.

Kolb, D. A., and A. L. Frohman: "An Organization Development Approach to Consulting," *Sloan Management Review*, 12, 1970, pp. 51–65.

Markus, M. L.: "Power, Politics, and MIS Implementation," *Communications of the ACM*, 26:6, June 1983, pp. 430–444.

McKeen, James D.: "Successful Development Strategies for Business Application Systems," *MIS Quarterly*, 7:3, September 1983, pp. 47–65.

Mumford, Enid, and Mary Weir: *Computer Systems in Work Design: The Ethics Method*, Halsted (Wiley), New York, 1979.

Myers, G. J.: *Composite/Structured Design*, Van Nostrand Reinhold, New York, 1978.

Myers, G.: "The Need for Software Engineering," *Computer*, February 1978.

Naumann, Justus D., and A. Milton Jenkins: "Prototyping: The New Paradigm for Systems Development," *MIS Quarterly*, 6:3, September 1982, pp. 29–44.

Orr, Kenneth D.: *Structured Requirements Definition*, Ken Orr and Associates, Topeka, Kanas, 1981; see also Kenneth D. Orr, *Structured Systems Development*, Yourdon Press, New York, 1977.

Parnas, D. C.: "On the Criteria to be Used in Decomposing Systems into Modules," *Communications of the ACM*, 15:12, December 1972, pp. 1053–1058.

Peters, L. J., and L. L. Tripp: "Comparing Software Design Methods," *Datamation*, 23:11, November 1977, pp. 89–94.

Wetherbe, J. C., and G. W. Dickson: *MIS Management*, McGraw-Hill, New York, 1984.

Wirth, N.: "On the Composition of Well-Structured Programs," *Computing Surveys*, 6:4, December 1974, pp. 247–259.

Yourdon, E., and L. Constantine: *Structured Design: Fundamentals of a Discipline of Computer Program and Systems Design*, Prentice-Hall, Englewood Cliffs, NJ, 1979.

Zelkowitz, M. A.: "Perspectives on Software Engineering," *Computing Surveys*, 10:2, June 1978, pp. 197–216.

Zmud, Robert W., and James F. Cox: "The Implementation Process: A Change Approach," *MIS Quarterly*, 3:2, June 1979, pp. 35–43.

Glenn Vaughn – 4:00

CHAPTER 19

QUALITY ASSURANCE AND EVALUATION OF INFORMATION SYSTEMS

Since information is a critical organizational resource, low-quality information has an adverse effect on organizational performance. Therefore, quality control or quality assurance of information products is critical. Quality control for information processing includes duties and functions in the organizational structure, activities and design features in applications, and policies and procedures for user-developed systems. These define a comprehensive organizational response to the problem of information system control and quality assurance.

Information systems compete for organizational resources against alternative uses for these resources. Therefore, the value of information systems must be assessed to compare with estimates of cost. This tends to be difficult, since many factors of information system value are qualitative. As discussed in Chapter 18, evaluations of system benefits are included in the feasibility analysis phase of new system development. It is also necessary to evaluate the efficiency and effectiveness of existing applications and hardware. Proposed additions are evaluated by comparison to alternative, competing hardware and software.

This chapter thus has a theme of quality assurance, control, evaluation, and audit to establish and maintain value and quality of information resources.

THE CONCEPT OF QUALITY IN INFORMATION SYSTEMS

Quality is defined as excellence or fitness. It is not an absolute concept; it is defined within a context. An application has quality relative to its primary and secondary users, operations personnel, control personnel, maintenance personnel, and so forth. Perfect quality is very costly and virtually impossible. Quality should be within acceptable limits as defined by the organization. The quality limits reflect the consequences of lack of quality and the cost of achieving it. For example, lack of quality in the development process may result in applications that are not used or that have a very high level of maintenance repairs and enhancements, but a development process that seeks to make sure the application is perfect will never be completed.

Quality in information systems has a number of characteristics. The importance of each depends on the application and its context. The following are some of the characteristics included in the concept of quality in information systems:

Information system quality characteristic	Implementation of quality concepts
Complete data	All data items are captured and stored for use. Data items are properly identified with time periods.
Accurate data	The correct data values are recorded.
Precise data	Measurement of variables meets user needs for precision
Understandable output	The output of the system is understandable to the users.
Timely output	The output of the application is available in time for actions and decisions.
Relevant output	The outputs are relevant to the actions and decisions to be taken.
Meaningful output	The format, labeling, data provided, and context in which data is presented makes the output meaningful for actions and decision making.
User friendly operation	The system provides user interfaces that are understandable and designed to conform to human capabilities.
Error resistant operations	Suitable error prevention and detection procedures are in place. There are procedures for reporting and correcting errors. Various audit procedures are applied.
Authorized use	Only authorized personnel have access to facilities, applications, and data
Protected system and operations	The system and its operations are protected from various environmental and operational risks. There are provisions for recovery in the event of failure or destruction of part or all of the system.

The quality defined above is achieved by a comprehensive approach consisting of organizational functions with responsibility for quality and various procedures and activities to incorporate quality in information systems and to assure that quality is achieved.

ORGANIZATIONAL FUNCTIONS FOR CONTROL AND QUALITY ASSURANCE

The basic organizational mechanisms for control and quality assurance in information systems follow the patterns established for other activities such as production. There are management duties relative to quality and control, and there are also special functions within the information systems organization. The users of information system resources also have responsibilities for quality assurance.

Top Management Information System Control and Quality Assurance Duties

The role of top management in information system quality control is to establish the overall organization structure, select the information system executive, approve the information system plan and budget, and evaluate performance. Some examples of top management duties are:

- Establish domain of responsibility and authority of information systems function
- Select information systems executive
- Approve (often through negotiation) the information system charter, the information system long-range plan, and the yearly budget
- Approve major hardware and software systems
- Approve major applications
- Review results against plan and evaluate information system performance
- Review and approve information system procedures for quality assurance and control

The top management responsibilities listed above may be exercised by individual top management personnel, or a committee structure may be used to do much of the work prior to final decision making by top management. In the committee approach, an information system steering committee composed of top management of the organizational functions performs evaluations and makes recommendations for action.

Information Systems Management Control and Quality Assurance Duties

The information systems executive has the responsibility for organizing and supervising the various control and quality assurance activities in information systems. Examples of duties are:

- Establish and supervise quality assurance procedures for applications developed in-house or obtained as packages
- Establish and supervise various information system control functions
- Establish and monitor procedures to measure and report evidence of quality: errors, downtime, reruns, application repair maintenance, etc.

Information System Control and Quality Assurance Functions

There are certain control and quality assurance functions that need to be performed in information system operations. In large installations, performance of these functions may require a special staff; in small installations, they may be part-time duties for an individual performing other activities. The major functions are:

1 *Librarian.* This function maintains custody of programs, files, and documentation. These resources are issued based on an authorized schedule of use or special authorization. The custodial activities include record keeping.

2 *Processing control.* This includes logging in and checking input, checking progress of jobs, reconciling control information for applications, checking output and distributing it to authorized recipients, maintaining error logs, and following up on error correction.

3 *Access control.* This function is responsible for control of physical access to the installation and control of access through terminals. Duties include followup on violations of system access rules.

4 *Database administration.* This includes control over access to and use of the database, enforcement of data integrity rules, and establishment and enforcement of standards.

5 *Backup and recovery.* This function is responsible for preparing backup copies of programs, files and databases, etc.

6 *Application development quality assurance.* This function includes review of controls planned for an application and review of adequacy of testing during development.

User Control and Quality Assurance Duties

Users have quality assurance duties as participants in application and database development and maintenance. There are also special control and quality assurance considerations when users develop their own systems, to be discussed later in the chapter.

User quality assurance duties require knowledge of context of data, user participation in both input and output, and the organizational control principle of separation of functions. Knowledge of context means that users are able to identify invalid data because it does not fit or is not reasonable. This ability represents situation-dependent data validation because the validation criteria may not be formulated until the user is faced with the specific invalid instance. For example, the user may recognize a personnel record showing that a person was born in 1961 and graduated from a university in 1975 as probably being in error. A validation test for this relationship could have been designed, but it is likely to have been overlooked (of course, there is also the small probability that it is correct). The user should be responsible for reporting such probable invalid data; procedures should exist to facilitate reporting of such instances and provide feedback that they have been corrected.

When a user prepares input for a batch system and also receives the output, this is one basis for quality control duties. For instance, the user may develop a control total of input data provided to data processing and check control totals on output against the input control total. The user may check output with other data such as checking the total on a listing of accounts receivable with the accounting ledger total for accounts receivable.

The organizational control principle of separating functions (or division of duties) is that a person should not be responsible for incompatible functions in terms of ability to make errors or commit fraud. The same person should not have custody of assets and do all accounting for the assets. The initiation of transactions should be separated from the data processing of the transactions to produce financial records. The separation of functions increases the probability that an error by one person will be detected by another. Also, separation of function reduces the likelihood of fraud because it would require collusion. In the case of information processing, the division of functions is manifest in:

- Requirements that a transaction in error be returned to the initiating area rather than being corrected by data processing.
- Policy that data processing may not initiate transactions or master file changes.
- User controls and user control duties in applications.

THE CONTROLS THAT FAILED

A savings bank had an online transaction system for tellers to enter deposits, withdrawals, etc. Since errors may occur, one terminal at a branch is designated as a supervisory terminal for the head teller to use to make adjustments and corrections. The supervisory terminal is then subjected to special controls:

- The supervisory transactions are listed and the manager of the branch is given responsibility to review the list.
- The supervisory terminal listings for all branches are reviewed by a special control function to detect unusual activity.

The tellers and the customers have implied control duties. If customers find errors (because of carelessness or fraud), they are expected to complain to a teller and the resulting investigation should detect unauthorized or fraudulent activity. Vacation time is enforced, so the duties of a person are performed by another person for at least some time during a year.

The head teller at a branch stole over a half million dollars by using the supervisory terminal to make fraudulent transfers among accounts. The fraud was not detected by any of the controls; his name was found in a police raid on a bookie, and investigation of his betting activity of about $20,000 a week uncovered the fraud.

The controls failed because they were organizationally in place, but the duties were not performed as expected.

- The manager of the branch was nearing retirement. He did not understand the online system and failed to review the copy of the supervisory terminal log of transactions.
- The person at the control unit with responsibility to review the supervisory log was told to check for unusual activity. She said "that branch always had a lot of transactions, and there was no unusual activity."
- The customers did complain, but the tellers always turned over the complaints to the head teller (as he instructed them). Even when he was on vacation, the customers were asked to wait for corrections until he returned, and they did.

QUALITY ASSURANCE FOR APPLICATIONS

A large proportion of the procedures related to an information system application relate to quality assurance. These include handling of exceptions, detection of errors, error correction, and various exception, error, and control reports. In a typical application, from 25 to 50 percent of activities and program code are for quality assurance. The same factors apply to databases. Quality assurance is therefore a significant issue in application design, operation, and maintenance.

Conditions for Quality Assurance

There are three conditions that underlie quality control in applications: organizational commitment to quality, information processing discipline with respect to operations, and redundancy to achieve error control in the application design. Specific quality assurance procedures rely upon these three conditions.

The organizational commitment to quality in the results of information processing is not merely a statement of support; quality assurance requires extra effort and extra expense both in development and in operation. However, there are significant differences in quality requirements among applications. There are different quality requirements by different organizations and different functions within the same organization. This means the commitment to quality may differ among organizations and applications, but the commitment should be appropriate to the conditions.

Information processing discipline is an element in overall organizational discipline. The term "discipline" is used in the sense of diligently following established procedures. It implies an acceptance of the need for careful attention to quality. Information processing discipline is institutionalized in the use of forms, screen design, and procedures for input, output, and error handling. It is transmitted to new employees by training, supervision, and example. For example, an older employee tells about the time she stayed until midnight locating an error caused by a sloppy transaction document. This transmits a message about the seriousness of errors and the diligence expected of employees in locating and fixing them. As a new employee gains experience, acceptance of data processing quality assurance procedures is strengthened. The success of many quality assurance procedures depends on the existence of such information processing discipline in the organization.

Redundancy was explained in Chapter 7 in connection with information concepts. Redundancy in information processing consists of an extra element, process, or procedure that would not be required if there were complete assurance that the data and procedures were without error. Some examples of redundancy in computer data processing are:

- Parity bit to detect errors in electronic circuitry or data communication lines
- Longitudinal parity bit (check characters) on magnetic tape blocks to detect and correct errors
- Check digit added to identification codes
- Control totals on batches of data
- Run-to-run control totals
- Echo of input at VDT entry
- Verification of input data by rekeying and comparing

Redundant data or redundant processing procedures provide the basis for very effective quality assurance procedures. However, there are three costs associated with the redundant elements: the cost of obtaining the redundant data or doing the redundant processing, the cost of error detection and error correction for the redundant elements, and the cost of the assurance procedures themselves. For example, a control total comparison used to detect loss or nonprocessing of data in a batch of data items requires the control total to be computed, the control total to be recomputed if there is a difference between the control total and the processing total (because the error can either be in the control total or in the processing total), and either manual or programmed comparison of the two totals.

Quality Assurance in Application Development

The application development life cycle was described in Chapter 18. The development cycle is designed to support quality assurance in terms of developing a system that meets requirements. Some quality assurance processes are:

- Information requirements determination processes to ensure complete and correct requirements.
- Sign-offs at each phase of development to assure adequate review and agreement on the system to that point.
- Program development procedures for quality control. These include structured design, structured programming, independent review of program logic, and program testing.
- Conventional installation testing.
- Post audit evaluation, to be discussed later in the chapter.

Development quality assurance procedures can be operated in a cooperative mode, an adversary mode, or a combination. In the cooperative mode, quality assurance is considered a responsibility of the entire development group. Finding errors is viewed as an aid to assist members of the group to achieve a better result. An example of the cooperative approach is a structured walkthrough for programmers. A member of the project team "walks through" program logic and procedures with the rest of the group; the objective is to improve the program, not to evaluate the programmer or analyst.

In the adversary mode, a separate quality assurance or testing function is established. The persons doing the quality assurance and testing receive organizational rewards for finding weaknesses and errors and identifying the source of the errors. The staff of the quality assurance function monitors application development projects and evaluates them in terms of processes being applied to achieve quality (such as technical reviews, testing, walkthroughs, and approvals) and in terms of the quality of the result. The separate function provides an independent evaluation of both project management relative to quality assurance and the application that is produced. The quality assurance staff first does a review when the project plan has been formulated. The review consists of an independent evaluation of project risk and project plans in the light of the risk. Project reviews are conducted on a periodic basis during the development to assess progress. Special reviews may be made to deal with problems that arise.

The advantages of the separate quality assurance function are independence of the function, demonstration of organizational time and resource commitment, and specialization in quality assurance. The disadvantages are primarily that quality assurance is then divorced from application development and resistance to separate quality assurance personnel may reduce their effectiveness.

Application Design for Quality

Applications designed with high regard for quality assurance in operation tend to have low error rates. Some examples of features that aid in assuring quality and low error rates are the following:

- Design of input documents and screens to elicit input in natural sequence with labels, boxes, and menus that clearly identify what is to be input.
- Expanded echo of input data to provide opportunity for visual verification. For example, code 3175 is input; the echo of the input is: ''Code 3175: engine mounting.''
- Presentation of sufficient information on output for recipient to verify processing. ''70 dozen widgets at $0.72 per dozen = $50.40.''
- Control totals on output to allow checking against other control totals.
- Audit trail references to allow tracing of end result back to constituent parts or tracing a part up to the result.

As discussed in Chapter 7, the cost of data increases with the quality requirements. A tendency to request higher quality of data than is required can be costly. Accounting data on cash, customer billing, etc., needs to be very exact; data on sales by product by area can be less exact and yet be completely satisfactory. Additional accuracy and completeness are achieved at the cost of redundant data and controls at a variety of points in the processing cycle.

Maintenance of Application Quality

According to system theory (Chapter 9), a system will run down and become disorganized unless matter and energy (negative entropy) are applied to overcome the natural tendency to entropy. For information system applications, the negative entropy is application maintenance; this refers to either repairs of errors or enhancements. If repairs are not made, users lose confidence in the system and fail to use it or to provide inputs. If enhancements are not made, users may switch to alternative sources of information.

The process of maintenance follows a cycle of identification, analysis, performing change, and testing. The identification of errors and proposed enhancements is crucial to the maintenance of system quality. Procedures need to be established for feedback from users on need for changes and from maintenance personnel to users. If the application is ''owned'' by one function, this function can assign responsibility for working with maintenance personnel. If there are many users, there may need to be a user group responsible for resolving conflicts.

Maintenance of Data Quality

The principle of entropy also applies to stored data. The maintenance of data quality requires continuous inputs of resources. In assessing the establishment of databases, an important factor to be considered is the probability that the integrity of the data (accuracy, completeness, etc.) can be maintained.[1] The assessment should also consider

---

[1] Jim Highsmith, ''Synchronizing Data with Reality'' *Datamation*, November 1981, pp. 187–193.

the risk from a degradation of data quality. The ability of an organization to maintain data quality depends on both organizational factors and data factors.

1 *Length of error-effect cycle.* If errors have an immediate effect, organizational resources will be applied more readily than if the effect of error is longer term. Errors in the billing file are therefore more likely to receive attention than errors in the employee information file (e.g., address).

2 *Regularity of measurements.* Data collection that is scheduled at frequent, regular intervals is more likely to be regularized through institutional procedures. Occasional, ad hoc data collection is likely to be forgotten or done poorly. A regular, weekly report of competitor intelligence from sales staff as part of expense reports is more likely to have high integrity than an occasional intelligence report.

3 *User-provider link.* It is more difficult to maintain high quality data when the function providing the data has no organizational link with its users. If the data is received from an external source, the organization cannot impose its own quality control standards.

4 *Provider data discipline.* The extent of data discipline (following practices that achieve complete, accurate data) in a function is a result of the background, training, and culture of the function. For example, the accounting function tends to have greater data discipline than marketing.

5 *Ease of verification.* Some data items can be easily checked by comparison with other stored data or by comparison with physical evidence. The credits to accounts receivable are easily verified by the debits to cash (plus other adjustments).

Given these factors affecting data quality and the difficulty of maintaining data quality over time, organizational procedures can be applied to increase the probability of maintaining suitable quality. There can be regular comparisons with physical evidence, such as inventory counts. The objects of data collection (employees, customers, clients, etc.) may be requested to review their records for correctness and completeness. Records may be reviewed on a cycle basis (a portion of each period) by persons who can recognize errors. For example, the purchasing department may review two percent of the vendor files each week. Training and supervision may be utilized to instill an appropriate level of data discipline.

CUSTODIANS FOR NONACCOUNTING DATA

In seeking to provide more data in support of strategic management one organization found that much of the data needed by the top executives was already being collected and stored by the organization. The procedures for collection and storage were often casual and undisciplined. There were frequent lapses in data collection and file maintenance. Most of the data in question was collected and stored outside of accounting.

The first step in a solution was to identify the data for which there was executive need and to appoint a custodian for the data from the same function (or perhaps the same person) who had been collecting and storing it. Responsibility of custodians includes collection, storage, maintanance, and providing part or all when requested. In the future, part of the data assigned to custodians may be added to the organization database. In the meantime, it is available.

QUALITY ASSURANCE WITH USER-DEVELOPED SYSTEMS

As explained in Chapter 13, user-developed applications are an approach to overcoming problems of backlog of new applications, systems that do not meet user needs, and implementation failure. Users are provided with application development tools and given training and assistance; they take over the responsibility for requirements determination, development, implementation, and maintenance. There are unique quality assurance problems associated with user-developed systems, primarily because of the elimination of the analyst role in the design of controls for the application.

The quality assurance procedures for user-developed systems were explained in Chapter 13. To summarize the explanation in that chapter, there are two approaches: development tools and policy. Development tools can be used which automatically include control procedures or prompt users to include them. Some also provide appropriate documentation as a by-product of user development.

The policy approach is to establish policy for adequacy of testing and documentation. For example, a policy may establish different testing and documentation guidelines depending on the importance of the problem, the duration of the system, and the task interdependencies involved. Four levels of testing might be:

- No testing or non-developer review
- Minimal testing and peer review
- Medium testing and external review
- High level of testing and formal external review

The quality assurance procedures summarized above reflect a balance between letting users have complete responsibility for developing their own systems without organizational controls and having a formal quality assurance process that must be applied to all user-developed systems. The same level of formal process for all cases would stifle creativity and experimentation, but the lack of any organizational controls subjects the organization to an unacceptable level of risk.

POST AUDIT EVALUATION OF INFORMATION SYSTEM APPLICATIONS

As discussed in Chapter 18, the last phase of the system development life cycle is a post audit. This is a review by a task group (composed, for example, of one or more users, representatives from the internal audit staff, and analysts from information systems). The audit group reviews the objectives and cost-benefit representations made on behalf of the project and compares them with actual performance and actual costs. It also reviews the operational characteristics of the system to determine if they are satisfactory. Documentation is reviewed for backup and maintainability considerations. Control and security provisions are examined. The results of the post audit are intended to assist in improved cost justification and management of future projects, improvements in the application under review, or cancellation of the application if it is no longer justified.

Applications may be evaluated in terms of measures of system value. They may also be compared with the reports of technical, operational, and economic feasibility by which they were originally justified.

Evaluation of System Value

One of the most severe problems with the post audit evaluation is the difficulty of determining system value. The ideal measure, as of any investment of organizational resources, is a determination of the impact of the system on organizational effectiveness. Since few changes can be isolated so that their effects on overall organizational functioning can be measured, substitute indicators must be used. The most logical place to look for such measures of system value is the immediate environment where the system is being used. Methods can be determined for measuring the *effectiveness* of the user as a result of having received the output or service from the system. Some methods of indirectly measuring system value are:

Significant task relevance	Results of system use are directly observable. For instance, an office support system results in improved turnaround of documents. For a decision support system, task relevance is *improved decision quality*, which is often difficult to observe but sometimes possible to approximate through users' subjective estimates.
Willingness to pay	Users may be asked to specify how much they are willing to pay for a specific report or system capability (such as ad hoc query). This type of estimate will be very imprecise unless it is linked to an actual transfer price (see Chapter 20).
System usage	System logs may permit measures of system use, or users may be asked to estimate their use of the system. This is only appropriate for systems whose usage is voluntary.
User information satisfaction[2]	Users are asked to rate their satisfaction with such aspects of the system as response time, turnaround time, vendor support, accuracy, timeliness, format of outputs, and confidence in the system.

Measures developed according to any of the above methods are probably most effective if given both before and after a new system or system enhancement is introduced. This provides a comparative indicator of improvements. System value assessments should not be made shortly after a system is implemented; an excess of program errors, difficulties in learning and adjusting to new procedures, and general resistance to change may bias significantly both user satisfaction and system usage. With many voluntary-use systems, initial use may be very high and will gradually taper off to a steady level once the novelty of the system has worn off. Another caution is that some applications cause subtle changes in the structure and behavior of organizations in ways that were not anticipated, and these changes may be difficult to uncover through the simple measures described above.

---

[2]B. Ives, M. Olson, and J. Baroudi, "The Measurement of User Information Satisfaction," *Communications of the ACM*, 26:10, October 1983, pp. 785–793.

CHANGING THE TECHNOLOGY CHANGES DUTIES AND ROLES

An information system faculty member who did significant amounts of writing plus some administrative duties acquired two microcomputers. One (with letter-quality printer, hard disk, and floppy disk) was provided to his secretary. The other one (with only floppy disks and a matrix printer) was placed in his study at home where he did much of his writing. Communication was established for transfer between the two machines. After a year and a half of experience, some roles and duties had changed.

- The faculty member now composes at the keyboard where previously all keying was done by the secretary.
- Faculty member frequently keys in all text and data for a document and secretary puts in final form, including page breaks, checking for misspelled or mistyped words using software, and printing on letter-quality printer. Previously, he read for errors and format.
- Faculty member sometimes dictates to secretary who keys text. To do further work, he either takes diskette or receives text over communications line. He makes corrections directly at his microcomputer and sends corrected text back to secretary. Previously, he always marked changes in pen which secretary keyed.
- Secretary writes programs, using microcomputer application development system to do complex reports.
- Secretary builds files on the microcomputer for administrative lists, mailings, etc.
- Secretary has learned to send files to a large computer for special printing and to prepare graphical output. Previously, faculty member was responsible for all computer technology.

Technical Evaluation

The questions asked during a technical evaluation are similar to those used to determine whether the application was technically feasible. Some examples are:

- Is the data transmission rate fast enough to handle the data?
- Is there sufficient secondary storage to keep the necessary data?
- Does the CPU respond to all requests within the specified time period?

When applications are installed, subsequent evaluation may disclose that they operate ineffectively because the technical capabilities of the hardware or software cannot support them properly. An online realtime operation may be very slow because the computer involved has insufficient capacity to handle the workload. A communications network may adequately handle the workload but be more costly than had been anticipated. Another common problem is that transaction volumes were underestimated, so that secondary storage for online processing has inadequate capacity.

Operational Evaluation

Operational considerations relate to whether the input data is properly provided and the output is usable and used appropriately. Evaluation of applications should examine how well they operate with special reference to input, error rates, timeliness of output, and utilization. Some research on utilization of output suggests the need for periodic evaluation of applications. In a study by Gee,[3] 64 line managers at the middle

---

[3]Kenneth P. Gee, ''Specifying and Satisfying the Control Information Requirements of Middle Management,'' unpublished paper, University of Manchester, England.

management level of manufacturing companies were interviewed and asked to evaluate control information items they received as being used substantially or as being irrelevant or background information. Of 579 items, 46 percent (267) were considered to be irrelevant or useful only for background. In a further investigation, 49 middle managers were asked to classify items of control information as vital (admitting no delay), important (used for reference and delay or inaccuracy generally not significant), or background (items rarely used). The results from 383 items were as follows:

Vital	32%
Important	36%
Background	32%

There is a tendency not to terminate a report once it is started. Even though it may not be used, there often is a feeling that it might have utility in the future. This is consistent with the concept of the value of unused information described in Chapter 8. Various methods can be used to identify unused reports:

- Termination of the report to see if anyone asks for it when it does not arrive
- Periodic review of all reports by a task force
- Transfer pricing for reports to provide incentives for managers to eliminate those that are unnecessary

Economic Evaluation

The original proposal for an application included an economic evaluation. In the post audit economic evaluation, the actual costs are compared with actual benefits. The costs can be estimated with reasonable accuracy at post audit, but many benefits may still be difficult to measure. After making these estimates, an economic evaluation may be computed. For example, a revised return on investment may be calculated.

The economic evaluation may be useful beyond the specific application examined. For management purposes, the evaluation may aid future decision making to identify the costs of applications for which an economic return was not expected or could not be estimated. For example, the reasons for the application may have been:

- Mandated by law or changes in external systems (such as changes in zip codes)
- Required in order to meet competition
- To establish or maintain a competitive advantage or innovation
- Improvements in organizational performance that are expected but are difficult to measure

If economic evaluation shows that the return-on-investment objective will not be achieved or other benefits are less (compared with cost) than anticipated, the economic analysis required to decide whether or not to drop the application uses only future costs and benefits. In other words, the costs of development already incurred are no longer relevant; they are sunk costs and cannot be altered by the decision. Frequently, therefore, an application that has less benefit than anticipated may still have sufficient future benefit to pay for operating costs and future maintenance costs.

EVALUATION OF EXISTING HARDWARE AND SOFTWARE

The purpose of evaluation of existing hardware and software is to determine if all resources are needed, if some resources should be replaced with improved hardware or software, if a rearrangement of resources will improve effectiveness, or if additional resources will increase the effectiveness of the system. Some examples of actions resulting from performance evaluation of the existing hardware-software system are:

- Addition of a new data channel or dropping a data channel not being used
- Replacement of a low-speed data channel with a high-speed channel
- Addition to main memory capacity
- Change in disk storage units
- Change in disk storage organization
- Change in database management software
- Change in communication network
- Replacement of order entry application package

The methods and tools for evaluation of the hardware-software system are hardware and software monitors, system logs and observations, and simulation.

Evaluation by Use of Performance Monitors

Hardware monitors are sensing devices attached to selected signal lines in the computer hardware to measure the presence or absence of electrical impulses. For example, a sensor might be attached to measure the time that the CPU is in wait state. Another sensor might measure channel activity. The monitoring device does not affect the operation of the computer hardware. It requires no primary storage and no CPU cycle times. The data from the sensor probes is routed to counters. Periodically the data in the counters, together with the time determined by an internal clock, is written onto magnetic tape or other output medium in computer-readable format. It is periodically summarized by use of a computer program and reported in an analytical format.

Monitors can collect data on both CPU and peripheral device activity such as disk storage. The major shortcoming of hardware monitors is that they cannot identify the program which is being measured unless the location of the program in memory is known. Most computers of reasonable size use relocatable programs and have more than one program in memory at a time; this reduces the effectiveness of hardware monitors for measuring specific program efficiency. The operating system normally resides in a fixed partition in memory, so its activity can be measured.

Software monitors are computer programs. They reside in main memory and require execution time; they interrupt the program being executed to record data about the execution. They therefore slow down the execution of the programs they are monitoring. One approach to reduce the amount of interruption is to sample the activities being executed rather than to measure them continuously. Software monitors can identify particular programs or program modules within the operating system environment. Peripheral device activity is not measured directly but can be estimated from the CPU commands.

Hardware and software monitors can be used to detect idle resources, bottlenecks, and load imbalance. Inefficient use of resources owing to excessive wait time can be measured. This wait time may be caused by insufficient channel capacity, excessive seek time by disk storage devices, inefficient overlapping of input-output and processing, etc. The monitors assist in identifying the causes of inefficiency.

Some remedies to be applied following performance monitoring and analysis of the results include:

- Changes in equipment
- Recoding of program segments
- Redesign of disk storage files
- Restructuring of access to disk storage records

The results from "tuning" of hardware-software systems have been significant. A 25 percent reduction in execution time for the few jobs which normally take most of the processing capability is not unusual.

Evaluation by Use of System Logs and Observation

The system log may provide data useful for evaluation. This is especially true of small installations which maintain simple logs of jobs, job times, etc. An analysis of the system log may indicate problems with reruns, variations in job running times or excessive machine failure. The log may also be used to develop a distribution of jobs by time required. Such a list generally reveals the impact of, for example, a few large jobs or a stream of small jobs.

Observation of computer operations is useful in detecting inefficient scheduling of resource use and inefficient applications. Some signs of inefficient scheduling or poor operating procedures are:

- Processing delays for operator to locate files, mount tapes or disks, load forms, or perform similar functions
- Excessive requirements for operator response at console
- Delays caused by lack of training in proper restart procedures when processing is interrupted

---

EVALUATING DISK STORAGE UTILIZATION

A large data center of a major manufacturing firm was experiencing problems with inadequate disk storage space. An analyst was assigned to determine whether increases in volumes were more than anticipated and to project future disk storage needs. The analyst began by analyzing the file directories of the disk storage packs in use. He quickly discovered that, because of inadequate and careless procedures for assigning file space, only 35 percent of the available space was in actual use.

Simulation

Simulation is used primarily to choose a new system but can also be used to study the effects of proposed changes or additions to existing installations. In this approach, the analyst defines mathematical models of representative computer runs and descriptions of the existing or proposed computer configuration and operating system. These are input to a software package which produces a series of reports representing how the workload will be processed. Simulation is useful, once a problem has been identified, in analyzing various alternative solutions. Its drawbacks are that it is expensive to set up and run.

EVALUATION OF PROPOSED HARDWARE AND SOFTWARE

A frequent decision in information systems is the acquisition of new or replacement hardware or software. These are often major purchases with significant organizational implications. The process of evaluation for a new or major replacement hardware-software system will vary depending on the level of experience by the organization using computers, the urgency of replacement, and other factors. A general approach consists of steps such as the following:

Requirements study
Preparation of specifications
Obtaining vendor proposals
Evaluation of proposals

The basis for this approach is that the organization should undertake sufficient analysis to specify its requirements and request proposals from vendors based on the specific requirements. The vendor proposals are systematically evaluated relative to the requirements, and a decision is made. This approach is in contrast to a common method of asking a single vendor to propose hardware and software without any organizational study and specification.

The Study Group

If the hardware or software acquisition is major, a high-level study group or committee should be formed. Some smaller acquisitions may benefit from an advisory group of users. The high-level study group will be described as the model for both groups. A high-level committee should usually consist of middle-management personnel who represent the principal functions of the business, plus an executive from the systems function.

The study group should be provided with technical staff support. For an organization that already has a computer installation and is studying the value of a new or expanded system, this support can come from the data processing systems staff. For an organization without prior experience, the use of outside consultants for support is frequently advisable.

Requirements Study

The purpose of the requirements study is to investigate the present hardware or software system, evaluate the need for a new or replacement system, outline the characteristics of a tentative system, evaluate the cost and effectiveness of the tentative system, and evaluate the impact of the tentative system on the organization.

The requirements study may make use of the master plan (if it exists), procedures

NEW COMPUTER COST ANALYSIS

Estimated initial cost of new computer system

Cost of site preparation	$xx	
Analysis and programming of basic applications	xx	
Cost of training, file conversion, parallel operations, etc.	xx	
Total one-time costs		$xx

Estimated annual operating costs

Computer and related equipment lease or amortization and maintenance	$xx	
Software lease	xx	
Analysts and programmers	xx	
Operating personnel	xx	
Space charges, supplies, power, etc.	xx	
Total operating costs		$xx
Annual savings (displaced costs plus value of operation efficiencies less annual operating costs)		$xx
Rate of return (rate at which present value of savings equals present value of one-time costs)		xx%

Other intangible benefits (list)

Figure 19-1
Preliminary cost/benefit analysis.

described in Chapters 14 and 15, and study of the existing system. Data on the cost of operating the current system is collected in order to make a cost/benefit analysis for a new system.

From the information obtained in the requirements study, the group formulates the characteristics of one or more tentative hardware and software systems, then makes rough estimates of cost and ability of each alternative to meet performance objectives. From these tentative systems, one of which should usually be a modified version of the system in use, a tentative system having the specified characteristics is selected as the preferred solution and is then analyzed further in terms of personnel impact, cost-benefit, and suitability to the firm's needs. The system solution is by necessity very general, since it is not tied to a particular hardware or software vendor.

The cost-benefit study summarizes the benefits to be expected from the system, the expected cost, and expected savings, if any. Figure 19-1 shows a summarized analysis for a computer for a first-time user. This should be supported by an analysis showing more detail. The figures are rough because specific equipment has not yet been selected. Equipment life has tended to be fairly short because of technological obsolesence. A reasonable life estimate for medium- to large-scale equipment is five years; for microcomputers, the life before obsolescence is considered about three years.

The results of the hardware-software requirements study together with the recommendations of the study group are summarized and presented for top-management approval. If the project is approved, the next step is to prepare a manual of specifications for use in procurement.

Preparation of Specifications and Obtaining Proposals

The manual of specifications defines specifically what is to be accomplished by the proposed hardware-software system. It is a fairly detailed document based on data collected in the requirements study. The document serves both as a summary of the proposed system for internal purposes and as a statement for use in inviting proposals from vendors of hardware and software.

On the basis of a preliminary screening, four or five vendors may be invited to submit proposals. Each vendor is provided with a copy of the manual of specifications and the rules for submitting proposals. There may be follow-up interviews with vendors to clarify any misunderstandings or uncertainties in the specifications. The vendor's representative is usually provided with an opportunity to make a presentation to the study group, in order to summarize the proposal and answer questions. An example outline of a vendor proposal for a computer system is shown in Figure 19-2. The proposed vendor contract for a system is usually based on their standard contract form, but companies have found there is room for negotiation.

```
1 Proposed equipment configuration
  a Equipment units
  b Equipment operating characteristics and specifications
  c Options or alternative configurations
  d Ability of the system to expand (modularity)
  e Special requirements as to site and other installation costs
2 Cost of proposed configuration
  a Rental, lease, and purchase price by unit
  b Extra-shift rental (if applicable)
  c Maintenance contract
  d Software lease
3 Software availability for specified software and special
  software packages
4 Systems support
  a Systems analysis included; cost for added services
  b Programming services included; cost for added services
  c Customer maintenance engineer availability
  d Education support and schedule of rates
  e Backup availability
5 Terms
  a Acceptance of specified delivery date or proposed alternative
    delivery date
  b Payment terms
  c Lease-purchase and other options
  d Amount of test time to be provided
6 System performances for specified applications
  a Changes in design if different from that specified in requirements
  b Timings (how long each application takes)
  c Changes in timings using optional equipment
7 Other information
```

Figure 19-2
Outline of a vendor proposal for a new computer system.

		Proposals		
Criteria for evaluation	Possible points	A	B	C
1 System performance (42%)				
a Hardware performance	60	60	41	42
b Software performance	60	39	43	31
c Communications performance	30	21	25	15
d Expansion capabilities	25	20	23	15
2 Vendor capabilities (25%)				
a Vendor performance	40	25.	32	21
b Maintenance and backup	20	14	18	13
c Installation support	20	12	18	12
d Staff preference	25	15	20	5
3 Cost (33%)				
a Purchase or lease price	50	35	23	40
b Maintenance	20	17	5	18
c Ongoing educational cost	25	21	9	17
d Backup and recovery	20	15	10	14
e One-time system and education cost	20	18	11	14
	415	312	278	257

Figure 19-3
Summary sheet for point-ranking method of computer evaluation.

Evaluation of Proposals

Evaluation may be simple if only one vendor can satisfy the specifications, but in general several vendors will respond with proposals worthy of consideration. Since there are a number of considerations, both quantitative and subjective, one evaluation method is to rank each supplier by a point system. For each criterion for evaluation, a number of points is assigned as a potential total, and then each vendor is rated by being awarded part or all of the potential points. A summary of such an analysis for a computer acquisition is given in Figure 19-3. Supporting analysis should be supplied for each of the summary criteria. For example, software evaluation might include such subcriteria as:

Operating system evaluation
Very high level language evaluation
Procedural language evaluation
Database management system evaluation
Software package availability evaluation
Other software evaluation

The major questions that need to be addressed are whether the proposed hardware or software will perform the job in the time allowed, its relative cost, and its flexibility to expand as more applications are needed. Most computer systems can provide for growth by the addition of equipment options. For example, a stripped-down minimum-memory computer may have its power increased by addition of faster input-output units, more storage, or special software packages. A compatible ''family'' of computers allows the organization to move from one computer in the family to a larger size without reprogramming. The evaluation should include not only the existing software but also the probability of promised software being available on schedule.

In evaluations of hardware and software it is usually desirable to run test programs. The vendor will usually provide time for testing.

When equipment is being evaluated, the alternative of a mixed system should be considered. Several firms offer ''plug compatible'' peripherals (for instance, a disk unit) which have higher performance at a lower cost than the computer vendor's units. The main disadvantage of these independent peripherals is in the added management problems of dealing with more than one vendor and coping with responsibility for equipment-caused failures.

For a new computer system or major software package, the study group should conduct an independent analysis of system performance. The real criterion for measuring system performance is throughput; if actual jobs cannot be run and timed, then substitute measures must be used. There are several substitute comparison methods, but the most common is standard benchmark analysis in which standard problems of a type normally performed are coded and time to perform the standard task is estimated or measured by running it. For example, a standard problem might be to read 10,000 records sequentially from disk storage and print them. Standard benchmark problems usually reflect typical jobs but are not a sample of the complete processing system as it will operate.

AUDITING OF INFORMATION SYSTEMS

Organizations use auditors as independent evaluators. There are basically two types of auditors: independent (external) auditors and internal auditors. Auditors who specialize in auditing activities related to information systems are generally termed EDP auditors. The roles of independent and internal auditors are different, although they perform many activities that are similar. Auditors can have a significant effect on quality and control of computer processing.

Independent Auditors

A major role of independent auditors is to attest to the fairness of financial statements. This professional judgment is based on evidence obtained and evaluated by the auditor during an examination.

If computers are used in activities that affect the financial statements, independent auditors must include a study of internal control in EDP systems as part of the overall study and evaluation of internal control. This process includes the following procedures:

1 Preliminary phase of the review in which an initial assessment is made of the role of computer data processing in the preparation of financial records. A preliminary evaluation is made of the existence of general controls over data processing and controls in applications relevant to the audit. The assessment from the preliminary phase is the basis for planning the completion of the review. The result may be to tentatively rely on the internal control in data processing and proceed to complete the review or not to rely and to collect alternative evidence.

2 Complete the review of internal control in computer data processing by more detailed study of controls. By interviews, checklists, study of documentation, and observation, the auditor determines the set of controls the company says are operating. If these controls provide a reasonable basis for internal control, the auditor proceeds to test whether the controls are functioning.

3 Compliance tests of the controls. Controls may be established but not operating or operating improperly, incorrectly, or irregularly. The purpose of the compliance tests is to obtain evidence on how well the controls are operating. The tests include examination of evidence of compliance such as signatures when they are required, control total comparisons, library control records, etc.

4 Evaluation of the reliance that can be placed on internal EDP control and decision on the substantive tests that need to be performed to provide evidence other than internal control.

Substantive tests by the independent auditor can be performed by manual procedures; they can also make use of both independent, auditor-supplied software and company software. For example, an auditor may make use of a generalized audit software system to test files by counting records, summing dollar amounts, selecting records for followup, analyzing characteristics of data in the file, etc. An auditor may also make use of system software to select records, print files, etc., and database management software to retrieve data from databases.

The procedures followed by an independent auditor will generally provide sufficient evidence for making a judgment about the financial statements of the organization; it is not sufficient to detect all instances of fraud or other misconduct. Presumably, major frauds that have a significant effect on the financial statements will be discovered, but relatively minor ones will not. If fraud is suspected, a special fraud audit may be conducted. Independent auditors can also be engaged to perform management advisory services with respect to data processing. Examples are evaluation of information services, evaluation of security procedures, and performance evaluation.

Internal Auditors

Internal auditors are employees of the company. They usually have a reporting relationship within the company that provides independence from those they are auditing. Internal auditors perform control assignments, do more detailed auditing than that performed by external auditors, and do evaluations. Internal auditors may perform frequent testing of data processing using software where appropriate. They may participate in post audit evaluations of applications and periodic tests of security and backup procedures. They are available for assignment by management to investigate problems such as excessive error rates in billing. Internal EDP auditors combine auditing skills with knowledge of computers and information processing.

SUMMARY

Quality for information systems is defined as excellence or fitness of the system in serving the purposes for which it was developed. There are a number of characteristics that establish overall quality. Quality is achieved by organizational functions that establish quality and perform quality assurance activities. Quality assurance for applications includes quality assurance activities in development and design of quality assurance features into applications. There are specific activities to maintain the quality of applications and to maintain the quality of stored data. There are special quality assurance procedures with user-developed systems.

Post audit evaluations of information systems should include assessments of system value as well as technical, operational, and economic evaluations. Four methods of assessing system value are observation of the system's relevance to specific task improvements, determination of users' willingness to pay for system capabilities or outputs, logs of voluntary system usage, and measures of user information satisfaction. Technical evaluations focus on the system performance criteria established in the feasibility study. Operational considerations relate to whether the input data is properly provided and the output is usable and used. Economic evaluation provides a current assessment of cost-benefit.

Existing hardware and software should be evaluated for efficiency and to determine if additional resources are required. Methods of hardware evaluation are hardware and software monitors, use of system logs and observations, and simulation.

Proposed hardware and software should be evaluated through a systematic requirements study, preparation of specifications, and evaluation of vendor proposals responding to those specifications.

Auditors can have a significant role in quality assurance and control of computer processing. Independent auditors perform a study of internal control in EDP systems as part of an evaluation of internal control in an organization. They may also perform management advisory services relative to information systems. Internal auditors may perform a variety of control assignments and evaluations.

MINICASES

1 FOR ACCURACY OF STUDENT DATA, ASK THE STUDENT

A university is faced with the problem of maintaining the accuracy and completeness of data in student transcripts. The providers of the data are removed from the users. In fact, many uses may occur after the student has graduated. The cycle from the time an error is made to the error's having an effect can therefore be very long. There is no natural, easy verification of the transcript data. All these factors contribute to quality problems. Offsetting these are good data discipline in the transcript office and well established, regular procedures.

One university sends each student a copy of his or her transcript with a request that the student identify any errors and return the transcript for correction.

Questions

a Is this procedure a good example of quality assurance over data? Why or why not?
b What other quality assurance procedures might be necessary or feasible?

2 MISSING CONTROLS LEAD TO MISSING CHECKS

Builders' Appliance Distributors (BAD) is a supplier of kitchen appliances to building contractors. A contractor or home owner chooses from a variety of models on display then places the order in person at the order desk or by telephone. The order desk clerk fills out an order form, marks it "ship," and submits one copy to the warehouse and one to the computer for processing and invoicing. Contractors are usually billed monthly, but sometimes they pay by check when they come to pick up their appliances.

An order desk clerk figured out a simple embezzlement scheme. When a contractor paid by check, he marked "ship" on the warehouse copy of the order and "cancel" on the copy sent to the computer. He then pocketed the check and later deposited it in a special bank account.

Eventually, one order paid by check at the order counter was mistakenly entered into the computer, and the contractor was billed. He protested, and brought in his cancelled check to prove he had paid for the merchandise. On the back of the check was the order clerk's signature. By this time, he had successfully embezzled nearly $100,000.

Questions

a Analyze the order clerk's responsibilities. What principles were violated?

b When the embezzlement was discovered, BAD had just passed an independent audit. Why did the auditors not discover the fraud?

c What checks could be built into a computer system to prevent or detect such a scheme?

3 THE CONVERSION CUTOVER INTEREST BONUS

The Ohio State Federal Savings and Loan Association credited more than 2,000 customers with over $100,000 in extra interest. The bank discovered the error and reclaimed the interest within a few days.

The error resulted when the Association took over another savings and loan that had a different computer system. A year was allowed for the conversion to the Ohio State Federal computer system. Sunday, October 22 was the date chosen for the cutover. However, the old computer system projected interest to the end of the week rather than cutting off on Sunday, and the Ohio State Federal computer system started crediting interest on Monday of the week. In other words, there was a double credit of interest. Based on James Connolly , "Interest Bonus Proves Bogus for Bank's Customers," *Computerworld*, January 9, 1984, p. 27.

Questions

a What organizational units in Ohio State Federal Savings and Loan should have been involved in quality assurance for the cutover?

b Outline some procedures the controller could have followed to detect the error.

c How could Internal Audit have been used in quality assurance for the conversion?

EXERCISES

1 What should top management do to assure information system control and quality?

2 What reports might an information system executive use to monitor quality of information systems?

3 Describe the control and quality assurance components of the following positions:
   a Librarian
   b Processing control
   c Access control
   d Database administrator
   e Backup and recovery
   f Application development quality assurance

4 A small business with four people in the accounting office plus one secretary is purchasing a microcomputer for a variety of information system applications. The office manager has read about control functions and recognizes he does not have the necessary staff. Describe the control functions for this operation and make assignments to the five people.

5 A new employee comes into inventory control. A computer system is in place. Define user control duties for the inventory control area.

6 What comparative advantage does a user have for error control?

7 In the story of the controls that failed (page 608), what could management have done to ensure the controls were working as expected?

8 Given the concept of a data processing discipline, why do accountants have it more than sales personnel? What can be done to achieve data processing discipline among sales personnel?

9 In a study of budget officers, one researcher found they received a psychological "reward" by finding and reporting mistakes made by others. The result was an adversary relationship with other functions. What possibilities are there for adversary relationships in data processing?

10 Sometimes poorly designed systems succeed because users want them to succeed and well-designed systems fail for the opposite reason. Does this mean that application design for quality is a waste of effort, that the only thing that matters is user attitude?

11 How does systems theory explain the need for system maintenance?

12 Use the factors affecting data quality to explain:
a Data quality of financial data for the annual report
b Data quality of customer complaint report prepared from complaint forms filed by sales personnel

13 Why should eliminating the role of the systems analyst affect the quality of user-developed application systems?

14 Two different user-developed applications were prepared by a user. How should he test and review the two applications?
a A spreadsheet projection (using VisiCalc) of costs by month for a five-month renovation of the executive offices. Results are used for cash requirements forecasting.
b A spreadsheet projection of sales and profit by product line using assumptions provided by product line managers. The results are to be used to terminate or sell off some product lines.

15 The engineering department of a firm has a $4,000 microcomputer for each of 20 engineers and a $30,000 engineering graphics unit. The graphics unit replaced one draftsman, but the microcomputers have ill-defined benefits. Describe some reasoning and some measurement processes to use in convincing management that the $60,000 for the microcomputers was well spent.

16 How can user information satisfaction be an indication of improved organizational effectiveness?

17 How can a post audit be helpful rather than an exercise in "finding the guilty"?

18 Why shouldn't an installation just install performance monitors and see what comes out?

19 Examples in the text for evaluation of proposed hardware and software refer to computer hardware. Describe contents of the documents for an evaluation of a new personnel-payroll software application package.

20 Why should a company prepare specifications for hardware-software acquisition? Why not let the vendors identify problems and propose solutions?

SELECTED REFERENCES

Anderson, L. G., and R. F. Settle: *Benefit-Cost Analysis: A Practical Guide*, Lexington Books, Lexington, MA, 1977.

Chandler, John S.: "A Multiple Criteria Approach for Evaluating Information Systems," *MIS Quarterly*, 6:1, March 1982, pp. 61–74.

Davis, G. B., D. L. Adams, and C. A. Schaller: *Auditing & EDP*, Second Edition, American Institute of Certified Public Accountants, New York, 1983.

Hamilton, S., and N. L. Chervany: "Evaluating Information Systems Effectiveness—Part I: Comparing Evaluation Approaches," *MIS Quarterly*, 5:3, September 1981, pp. 55–69.

"Information Resources Management," Special Section, *Business Week*, March 29, 1982.

Institute of Internal Auditors: *Standards for the Professional Practice of Internal Auditing*, Altamonte Springs, FL, 1978.

Ives, B., M. H. Olson, and J. J. Baroudi: "The Measurement of User Information Satisfaction," *Communications of the ACM*, 26:10, October 1983, pp. 785–793.

Matlin, G. L.: "How to Survive a Management Assessment," *MIS Quarterly*, 1:1, March 1977, pp. 11–18.

Matlin, G. L.: "What Is the Value of Investment in Information Systems?" *MIS Quarterly*, 3:3, September 1979, pp. 5–34.

Merten, A., and D. Severance: "Data Processing: A State-of-the-Art Survey of Attitudes and Concerns of DP Managers," *MIS Quarterly*, 5:2, June 1981, pp. 11–32.

Nolan, R. L.: "Managing the Crises in Data Processing," *Harvard Business Review*, 57:2, March–April 1979, pp. 115–126.

Timmreck, E. M.: "Computer Selection Methodology," *Computing Surveys*, 5:4, December 1973.

CHAPTER 20

ORGANIZATION AND MANAGEMENT OF THE INFORMATION RESOURCES FUNCTION

ORGANIZATION AND MANAGEMENT OF END-USER COMPUTING
  Microcomputer Acquisition and Use
  End-User Software Support
  Information Centers
SUMMARY
MINICASES
EXERCISES
SELECTED REFERENCES

The organization and management of the information systems are based on fundamental principles of organization and management. However, there are some unique characteristics in the information systems environment. The chapter focuses on several major issues and organization and management alternatives. A major issue is centralization versus decentralization. The issue is manifest in organizational design, in allocating information systems resources, and in maintaining service levels. The chapter will survey these issues and also explain the unique problems of information systems personnel. An important underlying concept is that the organization and management of an information system should fit the organizational structure of which it is a part. Information system culture should fit organizational culture; information system level of centralization should fit the organization level of centralization, and information system management philosophy should be consistent with the organizational management philosophy.

THE CHANGE FROM INFORMATION SYSTEMS MANAGEMENT
TO INFORMATION RESOURCES MANAGEMENT

The management of information systems in many organizations is experiencing a transition from computers and data-based information processing to information as a strategic resource and to an expanded role for information technology. This has resulted in an expanded responsibility for the information systems executive. This expanded role is often termed *information resources management* (IRM). The term usually includes the related activities of data processing, data communications, and office automation.

Reasons for the Shift in Emphasis to
Information Resources Management

There are two reasons for the shift in emphasis from information processing to information resources management. One is the stage of development of the information systems function; the other is based on technological developments.

The Nolan stage theory, presented in Chapter 14, described stages of information system use in organizations. In the six-stage version of the theory, the idea is presented that after the first three stages of initiation, contagion, and control, there is a transition from management of computers to management of organizational data resources.[1] The stages that follow the transition are integration, data administration, and maturity. In the maturity stage, the application portfolio mirrors organizational processes, there is joint information systems-user accountability for information resources, and there is a match between information system structure and organizational structure.

EXXON HAS ORGANIZATION FOR COMPREHENSIVE INFORMATION RESOURCES SUPPORT

Exxon Corporation has a Communications and Computer Sciences Department that includes a large number of information resources functions. The organizational breakdown is shown in Figure 20-1. Under the application development and coordination function, there are functional coordinators, office systems, decision support, and client support centers. As part of the data center, there is an emerging data resource management function to link traditional applications and end-user computing.

There are 16 information centers (called CSC—Client Support Centers). These provide direct user training and consulting. A breakdown of CSC activity is shown in Figure 20-2.

Source: Richard T. Johnson, "The Infocenter Experience," *Datamation*, January 1984, pp. 137–142.

The technology explanation for the shift to information resources management is that technologies which in the past could be managed separately are now highly interdependent and should be the responsibility of a single organizational authority. For instance,

---

[1]R. L. Nolan, "Managing the Crises in Data Processing," *Harvard Business Review*, March–April 1975, pp. 115–126.

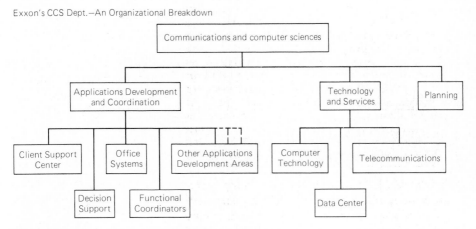

Exxon's CCS Dept.—An Organizational Breakdown

Figure 20-1
Organization of Exxon's Communications and Computer Science Department. (Source: Richard T. Johnson, "The Infocenter Experience," *Datamation*, January 1984, p. 137.)

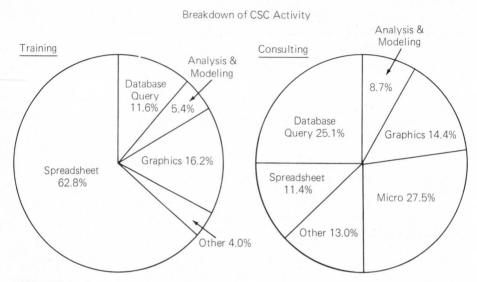

Figure 20-2
Breakdown of Exxon's Client Support Center activities. (Source: Richard T. Johnson, "The Infocenter Experience," *Datamation*, Janaury 1984, p. 140.)

the technologies for voice and data telecommunications were separate. Now an organizationally efficient telecommunications system must consider both forms as highly interdependent. Office automation, when first introduced, typically referred only to the replacement of typewriters by word processors; now office automation is highly interrelated with both data processing and telecommunications. Therefore, there is an organizational theory basis for assigning all three functions to a single organizational function, namely, information systems or information resources.

The Information Resources Function

Figure 20-3 shows the component activities that make up the overall information resources function. The three general components are the following:[2]

    1 *Data Processing.* In a traditional information systems environment, information resources are synonymous with data processing. In organizations where information systems have a broader charter, data processing continues to play a significant role. Development of major applications, ongoing operations of "production" systems, operation of the corporate database, and cost control over major system expenditures (i.e., mainframe computers) are part of data processing.

    2 *Telecommunications.* Traditionally, data communications have been the responsibility of data processing operations, while voice communications were assigned elsewhere. The

---

[2]F. W. McFarlan and J. L. McKenney, "The Information Archipelago: Maps and Bridges," *Harvard Business Review*, September–October 1982, pp. 109–119.

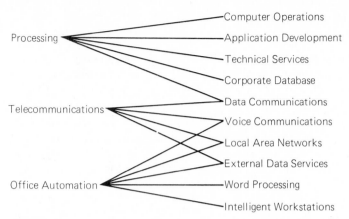

Figure 20-3
Functional components of information resources management.

advances in communication technology (discussed in Chapter 3) support corporate-wide telecommunications capabilities that integrate voice and data communications. Data communications are also an integral component of both data processing and office automation applications.

3 *Office automation*. This component typically began as the word processing function under the responsibility of office administrators who were separate from data processing. Intelligent workstations (discussed in Chapter 13) integrate word processing with data processing and frequently involve access to the corporate database. Local area networks and wide area communications are key components for integrating office automation functions and providing access to data processing facilities.

PROBLEMS OF THE AUTOMATED OFFICE

In a 1983 office automation survey, responses from 352 managers, 362 employees, and 16 office automation experts rated problems with automation in the office. The six top-rated problems were:

1 Maintaining a human perspective in an automated office setting
2 Designing meaningful and satisfying jobs
3 Ensuring that automated office systems are user oriented
4 Changing management's orientation to long-term strategic planning
5 Helping employees maintain job satisfaction
6 Ensuring that computer files of key personnel are available to others in the company

Source: Harold T. Smith, "High Tech Future," *Exchange*, Winter 1984, p. 4.

The Information Resources Executive

The management of information as a corporate resource requires a high-level organizational executive. This executive has been called the "management information systems director," the "information resources executive," or the "chief information officer." The position of this executive responsibility in the organization varies, but there is evidence that it is moving away from reporting to a functional authority (e.g., production) or control authority (e.g., accounting) to becoming an autonomous organizational unit, either one or two levels below the chief executive officer.[3]

The responsibility of the organizational unit headed by the chief information officer in the "mature" information resources environment may be characterized as the following:

1 Operational responsibility for central data processing and data communications systems

2 Coordination of organization-wide information systems planning, use, and evaluation

3 Maintaining infrastructure for technical services and assistance to all organizational units

4 Acquisition and dissemination of knowledge and expertise regarding new technology, including the research and development function of testing high-risk, leading-edge applications

5 Establishment and enforcement of standards and guidelines for all major information system applications and databases acquired throughout the organization

6 Aiding of adequate placement of information systems expertise and responsibilities in areas of decentralized information application control

ORGANIZATION OF THE INFORMATION RESOURCES FUNCTION

There are a number of alternatives in centralization versus decentralization of the information systems function because centralization or decentralization can be applied independently to the functions within information systems: system operations, application system development, and overall planning and control. Alternative organization designs for these three functions within information systems will be described with emphasis on advantages and disadvantages of each. It is important to keep in mind in the discussion of alternatives that a major consideration in the selection of an alternative is fitting the information system organization to the overall organization. In many cases, this consideration will dominate technical and operational factors being explained in this section. Also, centralization versus decentralization should not be considered absolute alternatives but extreme points along a continuum from highly centralized resources to highly decentralized.

---

[3]P. Ein-Dor and E. Segev, "Information Systems: Emergence of a New Organizational Function," *Information and Management*, 5, 1982, pp. 279–286.

Pressures for Centralized versus Decentralized Control of Information Resources

All other factors being equal, organizational units requiring information resources tend to prefer to have those resources directly under their control, thus encouraging decentralization. There are, however, other pressures favoring a centralized authority.

Pressures for decentralized control:

1 Availability of low-cost technology. Personal computers, intelligent workstations, and terminals plus software for end-user computing permit many applications to be user-developed that previously required centralized development and permit many tasks to be user-operated and user-controlled that previously required centralized operation.

2 Backlog of development work. The shortage of qualified information systems professionals combined with increasing user demand for new major applications has created a three- to five-year backlog of new development in many organizations. Users' perceptions that centralized information systems management is unresponsive to their needs makes acquisition of user-area hardware and user-function development of applications more attractive.

3 User control over operations. Having direct control over their own information systems operations is very attractive to users, particularly if information systems play a measurable role in their performance. Users may be willing to pay increased costs in return for control. Increased experience of users with computing, primarily through personal computing, increases their confidence in being able to develop, implement, and maintain their own systems more quickly and easily than through the centralized information systems function.

4 Organizational behavior. As explained in Chapter 8, there are psychological and organizational behavior reasons for the accumulation of information (even if not needed). Some of the same reasons may explain pressures for local control of information resources. These include:

- Psychological value of unused information. Knowing it is there if needed or "just in case" seems to have a positive value.
- Information is often gathered and communicated to persuade (and even to misrepresent). This function is most easily performed by information systems under local control.
- Information use is a symbol of commitment to rational choice. Local control of information resources thus represents local competence.

Pressures for centralized control:

1 Staff professionalism. A large development and operations support staff provides challenging work, creates an environment of shared expertise and learning, and provides alternative career paths. It also makes standards for information system development and operation easier to enforce.

2 Corporate database control. The philosophy behind development of a corporate database is centralized control over data accessibility, integrity, and security. User-designed systems with their own databases are incompatible with the global database approach.

3 Technical competence and research. A central unit can specialize and thus develop sufficient expertise to evaluate technologies. It can also function as a research unit for high-

risk, leading-edge pilot projects that an individual user would not be able to undertake. In a highly complex technical environment, systems professionals with highly specialized skills are required. Such specialists could not be supported economically in a decentralized organizational unit.

4 Comparative cost advantage. When extra communications costs required with decentralization are included, the net comparative cost advantage of centralized facilities may be relatively small. Each system must be evaluated to determine whether or not there is a cost advantage; it cannot be assumed. The cost advantage from centralization of personnel with technical expertise persists.

Alternative Organizational Forms for Information Systems

The basic organizational forms described in Chapter 11 (functional, product, and matrix) apply to the organization of information resources. Each of these forms may be implemented in a centralized environment; modified forms may be appropriate in a decentralized environment, depending on the size of each organizational unit.

The most common organizational structure for information systems is a functional organization. Personnel are grouped by the function they perform such as application system development and operations. Figure 20-4 shows a typical functional organization. There are three managers reporting to the manager of information systems: a system development manager, an operations manager, and a technical services manager. Within systems development, a functional organization will have managers for separate development functions such as systems analysis and applications programming. Under technical services, there may be functions, with managers, for program maintenance, communications network services, and systems programming. Under operations (not shown), a possible functional breakdown is data preparation and data entry, data center operations, and data control.

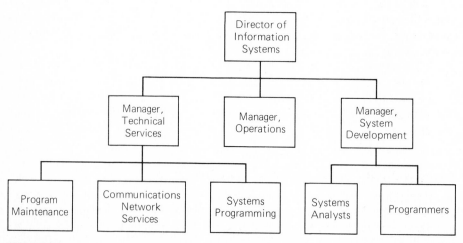

Figure 20-4
Functional information system organization

The advantage of a functional organization is specialization of personnel. In information systems, specialization is important for training and maintaining technical competence. As the organization grows, there can be fairly narrow specialization to meet specific technical requirements. The disadvantage is the narrow view promoted by specialization.

Alternatively, the information systems function may be organized by product; this would typically be appropriate in an organization which is also product-oriented. For instance, a major consumer products firm has a food products division, a clothing division, and a cosmetics division. Each division operates autonomously under an umbrella corporate management structure; each division also has its own data center and system development staff.

The advantage of product organization is that information systems tend to be more responsive to user needs because they report to user management. The disadvantages tend to be the difficulty of user management supervising a function that employs a technology they do not understand well and the difficulty of providing career development opportunities for information systems personnel. Specialization is reduced by the smaller information systems units, and variety in work assignments is limited. Also, there may be significant problems of coordination if the organization has an organization-wide database, major applications that cross organizational boundaries, or organization-wide systems such as a data communications network.

The matrix organization is an organizational structure approach to the problem of coordination when the information system function is dispersed among different organizational units. Each information systems function reports to the management of the organizational unit it supports; it has a "dotted line" relationship to a central information systems director who provides technical direction, coordination, standardization, etc. The matrix organization can be applied to all parts of the information systems function or only to some. For example, Figure 20-5 illustrates a matrix organization in which each major business function has its own application development staff; a manager of application development for a function reports directly to the manager of that function and reports on a dotted line basis to the corporate information systems. In this example, only application system development is decentralized; the functions of system operations and technical services are centralized.

The issue of centralization or decentralization is not "either or." There can be various combinations of centralization or decentralization. Using system operations and system development as the two major parts, both or either may be centralized or decentralized. Within system operations or system development, there are centralization-decentralization alternatives.

Centralization-Decentralization of System Operations

There are three elements of system operation that may be centralized or decentralized: computer hardware location, computer processing control, and location of data.

There are a number of factors that may affect the location of computer hardware (other than organizational fit mentioned earlier):

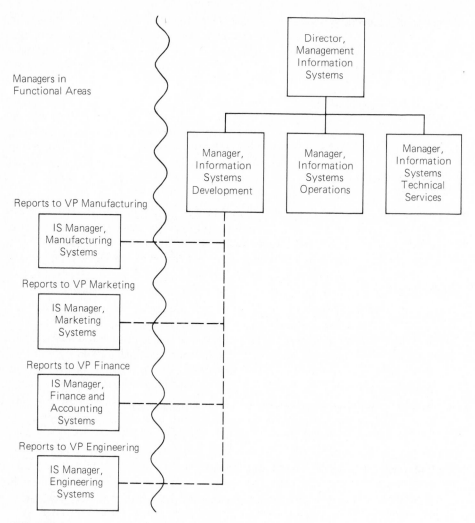

Figure 20-5
Matrix structure for information system development.

Factor affecting location	Comments
Economies of scale for computer equipment	As mentioned earlier in the chapter, historically, economies of scale strongly favored large, centralized computers. This is no longer true. In fact, considering communications costs as well as overhead required for operating a large complex computer, there may be diseconomies of scale for hardware; large, central computers may be justified by the need for speed and power but not by lower cost per unit of processing.

Integration of processing	If there is significant integration of processing performed for different locations or functions (i.e., applications are highly interdependent), a central computer facility reduces the problems of incompatible hardware interfaces.
Data communications costs	Data communications costs reflect the type of processing, the configuration of equipment, and the distances between locations. Dispersing equipment may increase or decrease communication costs depending on all of these factors.
Technological expertise to support computer operations	There must be a certain level of technological expertise to support the use of computer equipment, and the level of expertise tends to be higher with larger, more complex hardware configurations. The large installation requires on-site expertise; smaller installations must be assured of access to expertise when needed.
Hardware installation risk	A company with a single, large hardware installation can maintain adequate security, but the entire data processing capacity of the organization is at risk in the event of disasters such as fire, tornado, explosion, riot, etc. It is more difficult and costly to arrange backup for a single large installation than for smaller ones. With multiple small installations, work can be shifted temporarily to where there is unused capacity if one installation is out of service

SPREADING THE COMPUTER INSTALLATION RISK

A large international company with a centralized computer facility studied the risk associated with its large, centralized computer center. As a result of the study, a second computer center was located about 10 miles away. The distance allows efficient data communications between the two but also spreads the risk from flood, tornado, fire, etc. Both centers have compatible equipment, and there is continuous communication. Either center has sufficient capacity to do all time-sensitive processing.

There are a number of alternatives for hardware location and control. The list below is arranged in approximate order from highly decentralized to highly centralized.

- Distributed computer hardware with no central control over configurations and no communications
- Distributed computer hardware with central control over equipment configurations
- Distributed computer hardware with communications network for communicating between hardware at different locations
- Distributed computer hardware for local processing and a central computer for larger jobs

- Distributed computer hardware with communications network controlled by a central computer that allocates jobs to local computers
- Centralized computer hardware with remote job entry stations for input/output
- Centralized computer hardware with remote terminal access to specify jobs to be run
- Centralized computer hardware with remote terminal access only for input and output

---

A POLICY ON THE USE OF MICROCOMPUTERS

In a 1983 survey of 100 companies, sponsored by the National Association of Accountants, 52 percent have established policies covering the use of microcomputers. However, only 19 percent provide guidance on data security and only 22 percent provide users with a manual setting management policy.
Source: *The CPA Letter*, 63:22, December 26, 1983, p. 3.

The distributed hardware configurations tend to provide local processing control, but central computer hardware can also allow local processing control. A central computer with remote job entry equipment essentially allows the remote site to send a job when it is ready (although the schedule for the central computer may constrain this). The remote site may also receive its outputs (i.e., reports) directly through its own printer. Online processing of database query on a centralized computer may be user-controlled through their own terminals.

Another aspect of system operations that can be centralized or decentralized is storage of and access to data. As with hardware, there are a number of alternatives for achieving central or local storage and control. They are arranged below in approximate order from decentralized to centralized.

- Each distributed computer has its own files, and there is no interchange or central control.
- Each distributed computer has its own files, but there are organization-wide standards on naming, integrity checks, etc.
- Each distributed computer has files, but the data can be accessed by other computers.
- There is a centrally controlled network of distributed files and databases. A file or database is assigned to a local computer, and data records are transferred to other computers as needed.
- There is a central database with subfiles downloaded to local computers for local use; file changes and transaction data are sent to the central computer for updating of the database.
- A central computer has all files and databases.

The ultimate decentralization is for each user to have a microcomputer and files. However, individual users have need for data developed by transaction processing. This data may be downloaded from the computer used for transaction processing. The management and control of end-user computing is discussed in a later section of the chapter.

Centralization-Decentralization of System Development

Centralization-decentralization of application system development is achieved through the organizational location of systems analysts and programmers or other control mechanisms. Locating systems analysis personnel within the user organization has the advantage of making the analysts more responsive to the needs of the using group. In general, they can design applications and interact with operating personnel much better than systems analysts coming in from outside groups. Managers tend to be more responsive to information processing if they have someone on their staff with whom they can work. Some offsetting disadvantages are the fact that systems analysis personnel who operate in decentralized units tend not to have the amount of cross-fertilization of ideas, the training, or the opportunity for specialization that occurs in a centralized group. Development of technical expertise and a career path in information systems is difficult. Standards are also more difficult to enforce than when a centralized group is used.

If systems analysts remain in a centralized group, project organization may be used to gain some of the advantages of decentralization. Each application to be developed is organized as a project with a project leader and systems analysts assigned to it. The advantages are reduction in communication difficulties between project phases and the focusing of responsibility for system success on a single group. In addition, the project team helps users identify which analysts are responsible for ''their'' projects. Having a user as a member of the project team is commonly suggested as a way to increase user input and user responsibility for the final product.

Companies with a large development staff can organize their analysts into permanent project teams responsible for all projects in a particular user division. This arrangement has advantages and disadvantages similar to those of the decentralization alternative; the responsibility for hiring and reassigning staff remains with information systems management, so training and provision of career paths may be facilitated.

Another common mechanism for maintaining a centralized development group while improving responsiveness to user needs is the role of a *user liaison*. A person in this position typically reports to a centralized function but may have ''dotted line'' responsibility to the user group for which he or she is responsible. The reverse is also possible. The user liaison's most important task is translation and communication of user requests into data processing specifications and of data processing ''jargon'' into terms understandable to the user. The user liaison typically does not do any actual system design or programming but may be actively involved in the definition stage of a project (feasibility study and information requirements definition).

ALLOCATING SCARCE INFORMATION SYSTEM RESOURCES

A significant management task is the allocation of scarce resources. In the case of information systems, there are more demands for information resources than can be provided. There must be some mechanism for allocating them. This will often be a part of the information system planning process, but allocation often takes place outside of formal planning. The two major alternatives are a central authority method and a decentralized authority method.

Central Authority for Resource Allocation

The central authority approach to resource allocation is to assign the allocation to a central person or body. The central person can, for example, be the chief information systems executive. This executive has a broad information resources view and may be able to make allocations that improve overall organizational information resources; however, there are many political factors in such allocations and coalitions of managers within the organization may not be recognized by the information system executive.

The use of a central body that reflects the political environment of the organization is illustrated by a steering committee. It is made up of representatives from major users and therefore can take into account overall needs of the organization and yet operate within the political constraints. The steering committee may have difficulty in assessing the technical importance of applications and in balancing the portfolio with projects having a range of risks as well as benefits.

The central authority approach is consistent with a service center[4] concept for information systems. Users are not permitted to turn to outside services. The chargeback mechanism, if it exists, is geared to full or partial cost recovery but does not reflect market demand for the services requested. (Chargeback systems are discussed in the next section.) Final approvals of system development priorities are centrally controlled by the steering committee or information systems management. One significant advantage of this approach is that it facilitates integration and an overall balance of development of information system applications; it also facilitates close adherence to an overall MIS master plan. Some central control is necessary for implementing an organization-wide database.

Decentralized Authority for Resource Allocation

Rather than a central authority trying to decide among competing projects, an alternative is to provide users with the basis for making such decisions. This requires a chargeback system that makes users responsible for their own information system costs. Under a chargeback system, users are charged full or partial cost for system operations and new application development. The algorithms for establishing costs for services are complex and vary widely depending on the objectives of the chargeback system. Among these objectives are:[5]

1 Meet the basic accounting objective of cost recovery
2 Ensure equitable computer resource allocation among users
3 Satisfy contractual or legal requirements
4 Regulate the demand for scarce computer resources
5 Assist management in planning
6 Decentralize control of information resources to users

---

[4]A. R. Wheelock, "Service Center or Profit Center?" *Datamation*, May 1982.

[5]M. H. Olson and B. Ives, "Chargeback Systems and User Involvement in Information Systems: An Empirical Investigation," *MIS Quarterly*, 6:2, June 1982, pp. 47–60.

There are a variety of methods for handling information systems costs. They can be classified into five alternatives:[6]

1 *Overhead* (no chargeback). All costs are absorbed by the information systems function.

2 *Allocation of expense.* Time reporting or CPU records are used to arrive at a rough percentage of use for each department. Usually 100 percent of all costs are allocated.

3 *Standard resource rates.* Users are charged by type of service used according to a fixed rate schedule established in advance.

4 *Standard rate per unit processed.* Users are charged a prespecified rate for particular units of input or output, i.e., transactions processed, online inquiries, reports requested.

5 *Fixed price.* Users pay a fixed fee for usage of a block of time on a dedicated system or for new system development where the final product is relatively well defined.

It can be seen that not all the methods of chargeback result in decentralization of planning and control to users. A chargeback system whose objective is simply to provide a cost recovery function will probably use allocation of expenses or, at most, standard resource rates.

In order to serve decentralized planning and control, a chargeback system should have the following characteristics:[7]

- Understandability: Users should be able to associate costs with specific activities.
- Controllability: Charges should be under the control of the user/manager.
- Accountability: Costs and utilization of information system costs should be a factor in user employee performance evaluation.
- Cost/benefit incidence: The user receiving the bill for services should also receive (directly or indirectly) the benefits of those services.

In order to have these characteristics, a chargeback method for system operations should be based on a standard rate per unit processed, such as transactions, inquiries, or reports; fixed price is generally appropriate for development. A user should be able to cancel production of a report, for instance, and see it reflected in the bill for services. Such a system is very complex because actual costs may vary widely depending on transaction volumes and other demands on the system. Furthermore, if the information systems function is organized as a profit center, rates charged must reflect market rates since users have the option of utilizing external resources. A good example is the use of fixed prices for new system development. The internal development group must submit a "bid" which is realistic in terms of actual cost but is also attractive relative to external resources (both in cost and in time to completion).

Thus different goals of chargeback systems may be in conflict and cannot be met by the same method. A method which adequately allocates all data processing expenses will most likely not meet the criterion of being an adequate tool for user planning and control. On the other hand, a system which establishes standard rates and/or fixed prices relative to market rates may not allocate all costs.

---

[6]R. P. Popadic, "Design of Chargeout Control Systems for Computer Services," in R. L. Nolan and F. W. McFarlan (eds.), *Information Systems Handbook*, Dow Jones-Irwin, New York, 1975, pp. 154–175.

[7]R. L. Nolan, "Effects of Chargeout on User/Manager Attitudes," *Communications of the ACM*, 20:3, March 1977, pp. 177–184.

Many chargeback systems are implemented based on allocation of expense using standard resource rates in order to give users feedback on their expenses. There is some evidence that such an approach may be dysfunctional.[8] Users frequently do not understand the charges, which are often based on such items as CPU utilization and disk storage costs. Even if they do understand the charges, they do not know how to affect those charges through system usage. Information systems are usually seen as expensive but necessary. Chargeback systems that are implemented for purposes other than to affect user requests for information services probably do not result in more effective decentralized planning and control of those services.

The decentralized, chargeback approach is consistent with a profit center concept for information systems in which the center operates in parallel with an outside competitive market. Prices for services are competitive with alternative services external to the organization, and users are free to "shop around" for a better price. Furthermore, information systems may sell its excess capacity (machine or human resources) to users outside of the organization. In keeping with the profit center strategy, all decisions regarding system development priorities are decentralized to users, and they have responsibility for cost-justifying their decision to local management.

One disadvantage of the profit center approach is the difficulty of accommodating it to a corporate database or corporate telecommunications requirements. In fact, the development of nonintegrated divisional databases should be expected. Furthermore, it is difficult to reconcile user-controlled decisions to an information system master plan. Finally, users must be considerably sophisticated about information systems in order to determine their own information system needs and evaluate competitive alternatives for meeting them.

MANAGEMENT OF INFORMATION SYSTEMS PERSONNEL

Given the past growth rate in data processing and information systems jobs, one of the most difficult responsibilities of information systems managers has been to attract and retain competent employees. While some of the work of systems professionals may be shifting to users, recruiting and retention of technically trained employees is still a major management task. This section of the chapter describes major job categories in information systems, the motivation of information systems personnel, job design considerations, and career path planning.

Information Systems Job Positions

The following illustrates the types of positions found in a functional information systems organization in which jobs are designed around technical specialization:

Position	Description
Information analyst	Works with users to define information requirements. Requires ability to work with people and understanding of organization, management, and decision-making functions. Requires more organizational knowledge and analytical skills than technical skills.

[8]Olson and Ives, "Chargeback Systems and User Involvement in Information Systems."

System designer	Designs computer-based processing system (files, program specifications, etc.) to provide the information specified by the information analyst. Requires higher technical capability than information analyst. Knowledge of programming is helpful.
Systems analyst	Combines duties of information analyst and system designer.
Application programmer	Designs, codes, and tests programs based on specifications from system designer. Requires ability to design, code, debug, and document computer programs.
Maintenance programmer	Works on the maintenance (repairs and enhancements) of existing applications programs.
Program librarian	Maintains library of programs and documentation. Schedules changes to production applications after completion of testing and maintains records of changes.
Systems programmer	Maintains specialized software such as operating systems and data management systems. Writes specialized system-level routines. Requires technical proficiency in hardware and software, usually specialized by the particular type of hardware in use.
Data communications specialist	Designs systems for data communications support. Requires expertise in data communications hardware and software and distributed processing.
Database administrator	Administers and controls the corporate database.
User liaison	Coordinates communication flows between users and systems analysts, primarily for long-range planning and the definition stage of application development.
Office automation coordinator	Provides assistance in development of office applications. Requires expert knowledge of all hardware and software related to office automation.
Information center analyst	Provides guidance and training to users in solving user-defined problems, particularly using personal computers and very high level languages.
Operator	Operates the mainframe computer equipment.
Data control clerk	Establishes control over jobs and input data to be processed. Checks controls on processing and distributes output to authorized recipients.
Data entry clerk	Enters data into machine-readable form for processing, using data entry devices or online terminals.
Security coordinator	Establishes system security procedures, monitors security, and investigates security violations.

One reason for the diversity of positions is the range of skills, training, and aptitude required. For example, successful analysts tend to have different aptitude and require different training than programmers. They also need a broader organizational perspective. Analysts need to deal with people as well as systems; programmers deal with programming languages, compilers, and documentation systems. This does not mean a person cannot be both a good analyst and a good programmer, but it does suggest that different recruiting criteria and different training are necessary.

Not all of these positions will be found in every installation. Certain duties will be combined or not performed in small installations. In some cases, organizations have combined positions for performance purposes. The most common example is combining the duties of analyst and programmer into a programmer-analyst position. The rationale is that this provides continuity for system development and reduces communication difficulties inherent in two positions.

Motivation of Information Systems Personnel

Some research has shown that the problem of motivating information systems personnel may be significant. Turnover among information systems professionals is dysfunctionally high.[9] Organizational commitment tends to be low and to be replaced by commitment to one's profession. Research by Couger and Zawacki[10] concluded that information systems personnel have higher growth needs and lower social needs than average. In other words, they like the impersonal world of the computer system but need a challenging environment in which they can learn and develop.

Another problem is the wide variation in the difficulty, challenge, and intrinsic interest between one system development project and another. For instance, system maintenance is generally considered routine and noninteresting and usually does not require learning advanced state-of-the-art technology. Thus, it is widely believed (although the evidence is inconclusive) that information systems personnel prefer to work on the development of new applications and dislike doing maintenance of existing applications. If this view is correct, there is a significant personnel problem in information systems because 50 percent or more of all personnel time is devoted to maintenance. In many organizations, maintenance is an entry-level programming job; programmers must advance to assignments in new system development. However, some managers are concerned that they may lose programmers with the most potential because the work is not sufficiently challenging.

Couger and Colter[11] have identified four factors related to the work of systems analysts and programmers that will affect the motivation of information systems personnel in the coming years:

---

[9]J. J. Baroudi, *Job Satisfaction, Commitment, and Turnover Among Information Systems Development Personnel: An Empirical Investigation*, unpublished doctoral dissertation, New York University, New York, 1984.

[10]J. D. Couger and R. A. Zawacki, *Motivating and Managing Computer Personnel*, Wiley, New York, 1980.

[11]J. D. Couger and Mel A. Colter, *Motivation of the Maintenance Programmer*, CYSCS, Colorado Springs, Colo., 1983.

1 The nature of the work is changing to maintenance instead of new development.

2 There is an increase in the availability of package software which requires tailoring (similar to maintenance) rather than new development.

3 The information center concept supports user-developed systems and deprives the information system development staff of interesting application development.

4 The availability of very high-level languages and application development facilities reduces the skill level for application development and makes the work less challenging.

Given the relatively high growth need of people in information systems, the low perceived challenge of maintenance, and high turnover, keeping personnel motivated appears to be a major problem. However, Couger and Colter found that some companies were able to keep motivational levels high by matching richness of motivation and challenge in a job with individual needs for motivation. In other words, programmers with low growth needs might continue to work on maintenance while those with greater needs for challenging work would be assigned more difficult, technically complex new development work.

Considering individual motivation as a major factor in assignment of personnel to projects is difficult for three reasons:

1 Methods of determining individual motivational needs are very subjective and often inaccurate; an employee who shows little motivation or interest in maintenance work might become highly motivated if given a more challenging assignment or increased responsibility but might never be given that chance.

2 Many information systems professionals are motivated by projects which are technically sophisticated, with state-of-the-art equipment and applications. Organizations whose business is information processing (such as banks and insurance companies) may have difficulty retaining their most motivated and productive personnel to work on large, rather mundane applications supporting organizational operations.

3 Personnel resources are generally so scarce that many other constraints affect assignment of projects; if 50 percent of the work to be done is maintenance, it is unlikely that all of the personnel assigned to maintenance would prefer it over other assignments.

A research study by Bartol[12] showed that turnover of information systems personnel was related to professional reward criteria, job satisfaction, and organizational commitment. The research suggests that to achieve lower turnover, management needs to focus attention on reward systems and the job satisfaction of information system professionals. The opportunity to participate in professional organizations was also shown to enhance the commitment of information systems professionals to the organization.

A point often made in relation to the information system executive is that it is a high-stress job. Based on a self-report measure of stress and health behavior, Ivancevich, et al., reported that stress levels of information system executives were not excessive.[13] Other research shows that information systems managers have lower social support from others within their organizations than other managers at the same level; where social

[12]Kathryn M. Bartol, "Turnover among DP Personnel: A Causal Analysis," *Communications of the ACM*, 26:10, October 1983, pp. 807–811.

[13]John Ivancevich, H. Albert Napier, and James Wetherbe, "Occupational Stress, Attitudes, and Health Problems in the Information Systems Professional," *Communications of the ACM*, 26:10, October 1983, pp. 800–806.

support does not exist, the strain of the job is significantly higher than for those with social support.[14]

Career Path Planning

There is a tendency to a hierarchical career ladder in organizations. An employee starts in a functional area job, rises to a management position in the function, and finally becomes a general manager. There are several difficulties with this model. Not everyone can become a manager, and many very productive employees may not have strong managerial skills but may be pressured to become managers because that is the only career path to greater responsibility and income. Two alternatives to this hierarchical career path within information systems are the dual ladder and the career stage model.[15] Another alternative is to use information systems as a step into a functional area career path.

In a dual ladder approach to career paths, a technical path is created that is parallel to a managerial path. A hierarchical set of positions defines a technical career with increasing technical responsibility, but no management. In the case of information systems, the dual ladder concept might have a technical path where an employee starts with programming and works to systems programming and senior technical specialist; a systems analyst path might lead to a management level.

The career stage model was developed by Dalton and others from a study of engineers.[16] They found that engineers varied significantly in their value to the organization, and this value did not necessarily increase with years on the job. On the basis of characteristics of different engineers classified according to their productivity and value to the organization, a four-stage career path was proposed in which an individual increases in value to the organization as progression is made through the stages.

Stages	Comments
Apprentice	Works under supervision.
Colleague	Works independently and establishes competence in doing a job. Develops contacts in function.
Mentor	Assists apprentices and colleagues to develop. Makes a range of contacts within the organization.
Sponsor	Demonstrates ability to organize resources and cause projects to be established. Network of contacts outside the organization that aid in getting information and sponsoring activities.

---

[14]M. Weiss, "Effects of Work Stress and Social Support on Information Systems Managers," *MIS Quarterly*, 7:1, March 1983, pp. 29–44.

[15]P. H. Chesebrough and G. B. Davis, "Planning a Career Path in Information Systems," *Journal of Systems Management*, January 1983, pp. 6–13.

[16]G. W. Dalton, P. H. Thompson, and R. L. Price, "The Four Stages of Professional Careers: A New Look at Performance by Professionals," *Organizational Dynamics*, Summer 1977.

The power of the career stage model for information systems is that it explains how an individual may become more valuable to the organization without becoming a manager. It identifies the stages that an individual must go through to demonstrate higher value. The individual planning a career should demonstrate competence at the job assigned in order to move into the colleague stage. A willingness and ability to be a mentor is demonstrated in programming and analysis by those who share their expertise with those who are newer. There are individuals who are sought out for their mentoring; others refuse to do it and never move into this stage. The person who develops the range of contacts that allows a project to be formulated, information made available, and talents assembled is a sponsor. For example, a company is planning to do a study of word processing. A sponsor-type person will be able to make contacts with persons in other companies who have done similar studies, with vendors, and with key personnel in the organization who must approve of the study. The study will gain credibility because it is being proposed by a person who has a reputation as one who can assemble the resources and get things done.

An alternative to a career path that remains within the information systems function is to use information systems as one step in a multifunction career path. For example, an analyst may be assigned to a user area for a project or as a user liaison. After demonstrating competence and becoming familiar with the function, the analyst may choose to accept a position in the line organization of the function and continue in that career path. This line of career paths is easier to establish in organizations where system development is decentralized or organized by permanent project teams.

Job Design

The influence of job design on job satisfaction has been noted in terms of the design of information systems applications. The same concept applies to information systems personnel. Data entry positions can be enriched by changes in job design to provide some variety and place appropriate responsibility with the data entry operators.

The job of a programmer may be enriched by a programmer workbench—a set of tools for writing code, documentation, and testing. Online programming provides a more motivating environment because of reduction in test time and improved feedback on program errors, etc. The job of an analyst may be enhanced by various tools for automating some of the more mundane tasks.

Programmer-analyst jobs that interact with user areas and accept responsibility for results may be an improved job design because the programmer-analyst has a better understanding of the reasons for the system and a greater commitment to its success. Recent research showed that analysts who were fulfilled a liaison role between users and a central systems group had higher commitment to the organization than analysts with little interaction with user areas.[17]

---

[17]Baroudi, *Job Satisfaction, Commitment, and Turnover among Information Systems Development Personnel: An Empirical Investigation.*

ORGANIZATION AND MANAGEMENT OF
END-USER COMPUTING

The trend to end-user computing discussed in Chapter 13 also represents a significant shift to decentralization of information systems resources. The motivations for decentralization have been noted earlier in the chapter. The organization of end-user computing can be highly decentralized or somewhat centralized. Responsibilities can be allocated to fit the organizational philosophy. The following are examples of allocations of responsibility and authority (ranging from highly decentralized to somewhat centralized):

- Decentralized end-user computing with no central coordination or control.
- Decentralized end-user computing with centralized responsibility for overall planning, major resource allocation, and enforcement of standards. Selection and training of technical specialists may also be centralized.
- The operation of an information center that provides analysts who go to users to work with them
- The operation of a centralized information center to which users come as needed for training and assistance.
- The operation of a centralized information center for end users in conjunction with a centralized computer and centralized databases. Access to the facilities of the information center and the databases of the central computer is subject to centralized standards and procedures.

Three organizational issues that are important in the context of end-user computing are organizational policy and procedures for acquisition and use of microcomputers, end-user software support, and the organization of the information center.

Microcomputer Acquisition and Use

Prior to the availability of low-cost microcomputers, the centralized information systems function could maintain control over computer acquisitions, since they were major expenditures requiring formal approval processes at fairly high levels in the organization. Microcomputers are relatively low in cost and can be acquired by departments or individuals as part of their budget without the need for higher-level review. In the context of organizational innovation and experimentation, these users represent innovators, and they perform a technology transfer function in the organization. However, they also cause several problems:

- The microcomputers may be incompatible. At first, this may not be a problem, but as use expands, there is a need to transfer software and data.
- The microcomputers may need to access data in the main computer, but this requires special software and introduces new data control problems. A variety of microcomputers makes this more difficult.
- A variety of software packages and microcomputers makes training difficult and inefficient.
- A variety of vendors for hardware and software systems increases maintenance difficulties.

Because of these difficulties, many organizations have established a policy on microcomputers. A limited set of hardware, software, and vendor options are established. These options are supported by the training, consulting, and maintenance staffs of the computer center or information center.

COMPANY AVOIDS MICRO CHAOS

"The acquisition of personal computers within a corporation can often result in chaos when users discover that their machines cannot communicate with the corporate mainframe or with other micros. But a strategic plan can prevent this high-tech Tower of Babel—at least it did at Union Oil of California, according to the senior computer services planning adviser there.

"Among the regulations suggested by the plan was standardization of operating systems and communications protocols for specific applications. On the division level, vendor-specific machines were recommended to departments."

Source: Jim Bartimo, "Union Oil Tells How It Avoided Micro Chaos," *Computerworld*, June 6, 1983, p. 11.

End-User Software Support

A problem similar to microcomputer acquisition is central support for software (other than standard packages defined by the acquisition policy). Users may develop their own software, they may acquire software packages, or they may contract with the information systems development staff for software. There is little opportunity to follow the strict procedures of a system development life cycle. Continuing maintenance for such software is a particular problem. The persons who developed or acquired the software may move to other positions or other organizations and leave the software without knowledgeable user support. Vendors may provide upgrades or changes that require expertise to install. These factors suggest the need for organizational policy and procedures to define the role of users and the role of the information systems function with respect to end-user software. One approach is to define classes of software support that will be provided:

Class of support	Explanation
Complete support	Software developed and documented by information systems staff. Software acquired from outside vendors but reviewed and approved by information systems function as having adequate documentation and other features for maintainability. User-developed systems that meet standards for documentation and have been reviewed and approved by information systems function.
Negotiated support	Software acquired from outside vendors or developed by users that is documented but has not been reviewed and approved for complete maintenance. Support must be requested and negotiated.
Support will not be provided	Software without documentation. This may also include software written in languages that are not supported by the installation.

The advantage of a policy such as the one above is that users can experiment with undocumented packages or write undocumented programs, but they know these will not be supported. If they want complete support, they must go to the trouble of review and approval. If they buy a package that does not appear to need support, they may choose to wait to negotiate support in the event it is needed.

Information Centers

Information centers were described in Chapter 13. They provide users with ready access to facilities and consultation in order to perform their own analyses, develop systems, access data, etc.

Information center staff need to be technically knowledgeable about the latest development tools for end-user computing on mainframes and personal computers. Many information centers support only one or the other, but many support both. As very high level languages become more portable and communications between microcomputers and mainframes is facilitated, the distinction between the two types of end-user services will become blurred. Information center staff also need to be good communicators and trainers; in many organizations a position in the information center is considered desirable because staff utilize the most current technology. The position may lead to a career path either within information systems (i.e., technical) or within a user area (i.e., as an information specialist).

There are differences of opinion as to the future of the information center within organizations. One view is that it is a transient phenomenon and will not be needed as information systems are decentralized more completely and users become more knowledgeable. The other view is that the functions of the information center, facilitating technology transfer and providing technical expertise, are long-term. It is reasoned that most users will never develop sufficient expertise to use information systems facilities without assistance from an expert. Occasional users will continue to need help to refresh their understanding and to aid them in using new or unusual features.

SUMMARY

The chapter summarizes major issues and alternatives in the management of information resources in an organization. There is a transition taking place that is defining a broader scope to information systems management. Some have termed this broader scope "information resources management." There are two major reasons for this shift: a stage theory of information processing which places organizations in a resource management stage and a search for organizational supervision for emerging office automation and telecommunications technologies. The information resource function contains traditional data processing, telecommunications, and office automation. The information resources executive has a broad role that extends beyond the traditional data processing executive.

There are a number of pressures based both on information technology and on organizational behavior for a decentralized information systems function; there are also pressures for a centralized function. There are three basic organizational forms used in information systems: functional, product, and matrix. In all cases, an important consideration is making the information systems organization conform to the organization and culture of the organization it serves.

The information systems functions that can be centralized or decentralized are operations and application development. Elements of system operation subject to centralization or decentralization are hardware location, processing conrol, and location of data. Systems development personnel may be centralized and organized functionally or decentralized to report directly to users. A hybrid approach is centralized development with analysts permanently assigned to certain user functions. Planning and control of centralized information resources may be centralized through a service center approach or decentralized through a profit center approach.

Allocating scarce information resources is a major management problem. One alternative is the use of a central authority such as the information system manager or a steering committee. A second alternative is the use of decentralized authority mechanisms such as chargeback for services. A chargeback system which decentralize control to users must be understandable to and controllable by the user. The best methods for accomplishing this are standard rate per unit processed for system operations and fixed price for system development.

Management of information systems personnel may be changing because of fundamental changes in job content. A major problem is motivation of information systems personnel. Career path planning is important both for employees who wish to plan their careers and for managers who provide opportunities. Various career path alternatives are hierarchical path, dual career, and career stage. Information systems personnel can also consider information systems as a path to a functional area position.

End-user computing and personal computers support a trend to decentralization of information system operations and development. Information centers are one approach to training and facilities support for end-user computing.

MINICASES
1 THE MIS MANAGER HAD A PROBLEM

All data processing operations were under centralized control at Company XYZ. Although they had moved to a distributed processing structure in the last five years, user divisions were not permitted to purchase their own computing equipment. In two or three isolated cases, users had requested their own dedicated minicomputers to run departmental applications. After a careful study of the alternatives, the data processing department had installed a minicomputer in the user department, but all programming and installation had been done by the central programming staff, and the user department did not even have its own programmer.

The policy of centralized control had evolved in line with an organizational policy of centralized controls as well as a strong concern on the part of top management about rising data processing costs. Last year, the data processing budget had increased 30 percent. When the MIS manager presented the budget to the board, their response was, "What are we getting for our money?" She was hard pressed to give them an adequate response. They approved the budget but only with a stern warning about showing improved performance and/or cost reduction the following year.

Now a new problem lay on the data processing manager's desk informing her of the fact that in the last six months over *one hundred* small business and personal computers had shown up in user departments without her knowledge. She had become dimly aware of a problem when several users withdrew new system requests they had considered urgent and not given her an explanation. Apparently they had gotten tired of the long backlog for system requests and, realizing the price of hardware had gone down dramatically, found room in their own budgets for equipment. The MIS manager was horrified. Not only were they purchasing incompatible equipment, they didn't know the first thing about designing or programming systems! With the board of directors' warning echoing in her ears, she tried to find a solution to regaining control over data processing.

Question

What should she do?

2 SOMETHING IS CRAZY HERE

The principle was clear. Each business unit was a profit center and therefore should be charged with its share of the cost of information processing being performed on a large central computer. The approximate cost was estimated in advance, but each business unit received its final cost when all actual costs of data processing were calculated. Total costs were divided by usage to give the actual cost share for each unit.

The company bought a new, larger computer that was to reduce the cost of processing. The business units refused to authorize applications to be placed on the new equipment. The reason was the cost allocation method. The first users of the new computer would be charged for all actual costs and this would be much larger than a share of the fully utilized older equipment. For example, if the actual cost on the older equipment was $120 an hour and an application took 10 minutes of time, but all time was used, the cost share would be $2 per minute times 10 minutes, for an allocated cost of $20; if the new equipment cost $240 an hour and the application took only 2 minutes of time, but only 20 percent of the time was being used, the cost share would be 240/12 minutes times 2, for an allocated cost of $40.

The president said, "Let me get this straight! The new computer costs less to run an application, but the business unit gets charged more. Something is crazy here."

Questions

a What are the advantages of actual cost allocation? What are the disadvantages?
b Suggest a chargeback method that will allow the business units to act in their own interests and also ensure that these decisions are good ones from a total organizational standpoint.

3 EFFICIENT BUT DANGEROUS TASK ALLOCATION

The financial institution made large loans to farmers. The data processing requirements were fairly modest, so the data processing installation was fairly small. The manager of data processing performed all programming, all system software maintenance, all training of operators and data entry personnel, and all management activities. The remaining employees were operators and data entry personnel. The manager prepared and maintained all documentation and had all interaction with users regarding reports and corrections.

Questions

a What efficiencies are present in the current task division?
b What internal control dangers are present in the current arrangement?
c How should tasks be restructured to provide adequate internal control without significantly increased costs?

EXERCISES

1 Explain the technological reasons for the information resource concept. If the information systems area does not expand its scope to include voice and data communications and office automation, what other organizational function can take that responsibility?

2 Write an analysis of the way the Exxon organization differs from a traditional information systems organization. See pages 631-632.

3 Describe the skill requirements for the information resources executive. Discuss the relative need for technical and managerial skills.

6 The areas of data processing, telecommunications, and office automation, traditionally separate, now require integrated coordination and control. Explain.

7 Grosch's law states that computer power varies according to the square of the price. In other words, for double the price, performance is increased four fold; for triple the price, performance increases by nine times, etc. Discuss the cost pressures for centralization given this law. If the law no longer holds across the range of computers from microcomputers to supercomputers, how does this affect the decision to centralize? Why might an organization still centralize its computer facilities, using a very large computer rather than many small ones?

6 What are the advantages and disadvantages of the following organizational structures for information systems?
   a Functional
   b Project
   c Matrix

7 Describe an information systems function with the following:
   a Centralized operations and decentralized development
   b Decentralized operations and centralized development
   c Decentralized operations and development

8 How has the introduction of personal computers occurred in large organizations? How could personal computers be introduced under central control? Under decentralized control?

9 What are the advantages of a functional versus a project organization for system development?

10 Explain the reasons for functional specialization versus more of a generalist position. Use the alternatives of separate programmer and analyst positions versus a programmer-analyst.

11 Information system application development can be compared with designing and building a machine or a building or even a work of art. When there are few rules for how to build, the developer of systems is an innovator; when the rules are established, the developer is an engineer. Assuming the above concept holds, how does this affect the type of people who will be challenged by information systems? If tailoring of packages and maintenance of existing applications are the dominant activities, how does this affect the motivation of analysts and programmers?

12 Why is provision of a career path in information systems a significant problem?

13 If a person likes analysis and programming and does not want to become a manager, how would the career stage model aid in career development in order for the person to become more valuable to the organization? Explain what the person should do to move from one stage to another.

14 It is not clear whether very high level languages and development facilities enrich the job content for programmers. Develop arguments for and against the proposition that these tools enrich the job.

15 The procedures for allocating scarce information resources should reflect the organization and management philosophy of the organization. Explain the allocation mechanism that best fits the following organizations:
   a A highly centralized organization in which budget allocations are made by the owner-manager
   b A highly decentralized organization in which each business unit is a profit center
   c A moderately centralized organization in which committees are used to resolve many issues

16 As a user, what would you expect in a chargeback system whose purpose was to help you control costs of system operations for your division.

17 How do information centers improve service levels for users of information system services?

18 As a user, would you welcome or resist the distribution of information system functions to user areas? Why?

19 For the following situations, explain how you would organize the information system operations, development, and allocation of information system resources.

a The Alpha Company has 20 retail stores in a midwestern state. The stores are essentially identical in layout and items stocked. A manager is responsible for the operations of each store, but decisions on the items to be stocked, prices, etc., are handled from the central office. Each store has cash registers that do pricing based on a stock number input by the checkout clerk. The cash registers can also input purchase data into a computer. Employees are paid by a central office; the local store prepares input forms. The company is organized into three geographical divisions each headed by a district manager. The organization chart shows a sales VP, a controller, a human resources VP, and a purchasing VP. The information systems manager reports to the controller.

b The Beta Company has 20 stores in a midwestern state. The stores are tailored by the manager to suit local conditions. The manager decides pricing and what to stock. There is a standard catalogue, but the manager can buy from outsiders as well. The stores are organized into three groups, each headed by a vice president. Each group has its own marketing manager, controller, human resources manager, and purchasing agent. The central office has a small staff plus a marketing VP, a controller, a human resources VP, and a purchasing VP. They have overall technical direction for these functions in the groups, but each manager reports to the group VP.

20 The Gamma Company manufactures and sells toys. The president believes in user responsibility for and control of information systems. He abolished the central information systems function and assigned all personnel to functional units of manufacturing, marketing, purchasing, and finance, which each have their own information systems organization and equipment. The hardware consists of small computers in each case. Any executive may have a microcomputer. Evaluate the benefits and costs or risks of this action.

SELECTED REFERENCES

Baroudi, J. J.: *Job Satisfaction, Commitment, and Turnover among Information Systems Development Personnel: An Empirical Investigation*, unpublished doctoral dissertation, New York University, New York, 1984.

Bartol, Kathryn M.: "Turnover among DP Personnel: A Causal Analysis," *Communications of the ACM*, 26:10, October 1983, pp. 807–811.

Bernard, D., J. C. Emery, R. L. Nolan, and R. N. Scott: *Charging for Computer Services: Principles and Guidelines*, Petrocelli, New York, 1977.

Buchanan, J. R., and R. G. Linowes: "Making Distributed Processing Work," *Harvard Business Review*, September–October 1980, pp. 143–161.

Chesebrough, Pamela H., and Gordon B. Davis: "Planning a Career Path in Information Systems," *Journal of Systems Management*, January 1983, pp. 6–13.

Couger, J. D., and Mel A. Colter: *Motivation of the Maintenance Programmer*, CYSCS, Colorado Springs, Colo., 1983.

Couger, J. D., and R. A. Zawacki: *Motivating and Managing Computer Personnel*, Wiley, New York, 1980.

Dalton, Gene W., Paul H. Thompson, and Raymond L. Price: "The Four Stages of Professional Careers: A New Look at Performance by Professionals," *Organizational Dynamics*, Summer 1977.

Ein-Dor, P., and E. Segev: "Information Systems: Emergence of a New Organizational Function," *Information and Management*, 5, 1982, pp. 279–286.

Kahn, Beverly K.: "Some Realities of Data Administration," *Communications of the ACM*, 26:10, October 1983, pp. 794–799.

McFarlan, F. W., and J. L. McKenney: "The Information Archipelago: Maps and Bridges," *Harvard Business Review*, September–October 1982, pp. 109–119.

Nolan, R. L.: "Effects of Chargeout on User/Manager Attitudes," *Communications of the ACM*, 20:3, March 1977, pp. 177–184.

Nolan, R. L.: "Managing the Crises in Data Processing," *Harvard Business Review*, March–April 1975, pp. 115–126.

Olson, Margrethe H., and Gordon B. Davis: "Getting in Sync," *Datamation*, February 1981, pp. 125–132.

Olson, Margrethe H., and Blake Ives: "Chargeback Systems and User Involvement in Information Systems: An Empirical Investigation," *MIS Quarterly*, 6:2, June 1982, pp. 47–60.

Popadic, R. P.: "Design of Chargeout Control Systems for Computer Services," in R. L. Nolan and F. W. McFarlan (eds.), *Information Systems Handbook*, Dow Jones-Irwin, New York, 1975, pp. 154–175.

Weiss, Madeline: "Effects of Work Stress and Social Support on Information Systems Managers," *MIS Quarterly*, 7:1, March 1983, pp. 29–44.

Wetherbe, James C., and Gary W. Dickson: *MIS Management*, McGraw-Hill, New York, 1984.

Wheelock, A. R.: "Service Center or Profit Center?" *Datamation*, May 1982.

CHAPTER 21

FUTURE DEVELOPMENTS AND THEIR ORGANIZATIONAL AND SOCIAL IMPLICATIONS

There is continuing discussion about the "information revolution" and "new information society." Dramatic organizational and societal changes may (or may not) occur over the next several decades as a result of developments in information technology. In this chapter a modest view of the next decade is given, highlighting a few basic, significant issues. The selected references provide more in-depth discussions of future issues.

THE FIFTH GENERATION COMPUTER

The concept of a fifth generation computer is evolving from research and development in the United States and Western Europe plus a concentrated, large-scale government-sponsored research and development effort in Japan. The Japanese fifth generation project is the most publicized and best defined. It will be used as the basis for the discussion of the fifth generation.

Definition of the Fifth Generation

According to the Japanese plan, the fifth generation computer systems will have the following functions:[1]

- Increased intelligence and ease of use. The system will support human judgment and decision making.
- Input or output via voice, graphics, images, and documents
- Processing using natural language
- Specialized knowledge bases
- Learning, association, and inference capabilities

The fifth generation is a radical departure from past computer systems. The computers will mirror human recognition systems, so that there can be input and output in many forms. The processing will be knowledge-based with high level problem solving and "learning" capabilities.

The hardware configuration envisioned for the fifth generation consists of three machines:

- Problem solving and inference machine. Roughly comparable to the CPU, the machine will have speeds 1,000 to 10,000 times faster than current computers.
- Knowledge base machine. The storage component with 100 to 1,000 billion bytes of storage.
- Intelligent interface machine for input and output.

Expert systems, discussed in Chapter 12, can be considered part of the conceptual basis for the fifth generation. Expert systems currently are limited in technology and methodology for representing knowledge, efficiently processing many inference rules, and communicating with users in natural forms. The goal of the fifth generation is to overcome many of the limitations.

---

[1]The discussion in this section is based on E. Feigenbaum and P. McCorduck, *The Fifth Generation*, Addison-Wesley, Reading, MA, 1983; E. Feigenbaum and P. McCorduck, "Land of the Rising Fifth Generation Computers," *High Technology*, June 1983; and "Japan's Fifth Generation," *Computerworld*, In Depth, June 18, 1982.

Knowledge-Based Representation and Inference

Expert systems developed to date utilize several different methods for storing expertise, or "knowledge representation." The method utilized must allow for easy modifications and efficient search of very large amounts of data (called "objects") and inferences (sometimes called "rules," "production rules," or "inference rules"). The goal of the Japanese fifth generation is a knowledge representation capacity of thousands of inference rules and one hundred million objects.

Inference processes are the methods to construct and process inference rules in a knowledge-based system. The goal of the fifth generation is an efficient approach to inference processing coupled with a new machine architecture, in this decade, that will execute one million logical inferences per second (LIPS). The long-run target is a machine architecture capable of performing one hundred million to one billion LIPS. Current computer architecture, by contrast, processes in the range of 10^4 to 10^5 LIPS.

Human-Machine Interaction

Current developments in user interfaces were discussed in Chapter 17. The goals of the Japanese Fifth Generation computer project include a much broader machine capability for interaction than is possible today. One goal is true "natural-language" understanding, which includes not only access to a large knowledge base but understanding of continuous speech rather than isolated words. In other words, a user should be able to speak as naturally to the computer as to another human being and expect it to understand and respond intelligently. Further goals in terms of human-machine interaction include the ability to understand graphs and other pictorial images.

Technological Support

In current computer architecture, referred to as "von Neumann" after the mathematician, data and instructions are passed back and forth through a single link to the central memory. This architecture forces instruction to be processed one at a time, even when conceivably they could be done in parallel; this has been referred to as the "von Neumann bottleneck."[2] Using very-large-scale-integrated (VLSI) circuitry with thousands of processors on a single chip, the challenge is to design an architecture that will take advantage of the ability to process many instructions, and data, in parallel. The significant problem is handling data dependencies: programs need to be structured so that required data is there when needed, even if accesses to that data are widely scattered throughout a large program or previous operations.[3]

Development of computer architectures that take advantage of the power of parallel processing is a very difficult task. Several alternative approaches are briefly described below:[4]

---

[2] The term was first used by John Bachus in his 1977 Turing Award Lecture.

[3] J. H. Douglas, "New Computer Architectures Tackle Bottleneck," *High Technology*, June 1983.

[4] Douglas, "New Computer Architectures."

Dataflow	Separate copies of data are attached to every instruction needing them. Instructions execute automatically when all data is available.
Reduction	The computer reduces program instructions to their most fundamental parts before execution. Each part is assigned to a different processor and executed relatively independently.
Pipelining	A variation on the von Neumann architecture where processors are spread out like an assembly line and each processor executes one step of an instruction. Sequential processing is speeded up because synchronization of each step is not required.

A more detailed discussion of these architectures is beyond the scope of this text, more explanation is found in selected references cited at the end of the chapter.

Prospects for the Japanese Initiative

The Japanese strategic initiative is a ten-year plan aimed at domination of the "knowledge industry," the successor to the computer industry which the United States has dominated. The budget for the ten year period is estimated to be as high as one billion dollars. The Japanese expect these machines to have a significant impact on society: powerful reasoning and knowledge will be easily available at low cost to users, in factories, offices, stores, and homes. The most significant resource for dominating this industry is human (rather than natural resources such as energy supplies).

JAPANESE MOTIVATION FOR THE FIFTH GENERATION

Japan has had a period of significant productivity. It has 2.7 percent of the world's population, but produces about 10 percent of the world's production. However, there are serious impediments to continued prosperity. Land area, energy, and natural resources are scarce. The population is aging. There are demands on Japan to play a greater role in international problems. At the same time, Japan has a highly educated population committed to work.

Information technology is seen as the way to improve the productivity of the work force. Japan can make a contribution to international problems by information technology. Computer technology will aid efficiency in energy use and development of new energy sources. The industrial system can shift to a knowledge-intensive information industry that uses little energy. The problems inherent in an aging population can be ameliorated by use of information technology to provide services and support for the aged.

Based on Shohei Kurita, "What to Expect for the Fifth Generation Computer," *Computerworld*, In Depth, June 14, 1982.

Reaching the goals entails several significant technological breakthroughs whose potential difficulties cannot be predicted easily in advance. Since Japanese management is traditionally conservative and risk-aversive, changing its orientation to tackle this plan may be a formidable task. The significant work required is primarily in software in which the Japanese have never excelled; rather than hardware; they may also lack the necessary supply of qualified computer scientists.

However, the Japanese strategy has been very carefully planned and is recognized as a key economic strategy. The project is a cooperative effort of eight major high-technology companies and the government. The planning horizon of ten years, long for technology developments, is significant.

In the United States, two major cooperative research and development efforts are now under way: the Department of Defense's "supercomputer" project and a consortium of microelectronics firms called the "Microelectronics and Computer Technology Corporation" (MCC). However, no efforts of the size of the Japanese initiative are currently being considered in the United States.

MERGING OF COMPUTER AND COMMUNICATIONS TECHNOLOGIES

Technological, economic, and government policy developments are already affecting the traditional separation of the computer and communications industries. This text has emphasized developments in information processing technology; communications has been viewed primarily as the vehicle for transmitting information processing capabilities. In this section, some future developments in telecommunications technology are highlighted. Changes in regulatory policy in the United States and their potential effects on the computer and telecommunications industries are briefly discussed. The potential for an integrated services digital network (ISDN) capability is presented.

Developments in Telecommunications

The telecommunications industry includes not only data communications, but voice, broadcast (radio and television), and cable as well. Three related technological developments are rapidly changing the nature of telecommunications: substantial increases in capacity (bandwidth) of telecommunications channels, substantial decreases in costs for those capabilities, and the increasing use of digitized signals.

Satellite transmission, in particular, permits relatively low-cost transmission of voice, data, and images; the cost of transmission is relatively independent of distance. Furthermore, other developments in land-based network technology, such as fiber optics, have substantially increased capacity over traditional forms at significantly lower costs.

Until this decade, the primary communication network was the telephone network, using analog transmission; public packet-switched networks were commonly used for data communications. Now telephone network transmission itself is becoming digitized, primarily with fiber-optic technology and the use of digital switches in analog networks. This evolution permits more flexibility with regard to telecommunications services, particularly data transmission.[5] In the near future, image, voice, and data transmission will commonly take place over the same telecommunications network.

Increased demand for information processing services, through personal computers

---

[5]L. D. O'Neill, "Converging Communications Services," *Computerworld on Communications*, 17:20A, May 18, 1983, pp. 77–84.

and office automation, has created an increased need for telecommunications services within organizations. PABX systems have replaced some intracompany demand for public telephone services. Public-access data banks and public information services are growing rapidly.

Figure 21-1 shows the important developments that have contributed to an integration of computer and communications technologies. One term that has been used to refer to this merger is "telematics."[6]

---

[6]S. Nora and A. Minc, *The Computerization of Society*, MIT Press, Cambridge, MA, 1980.

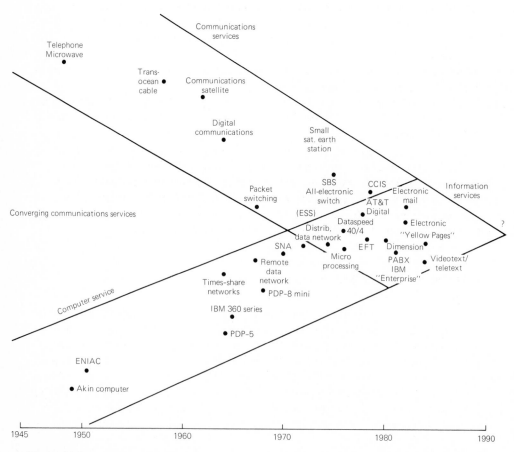

Figure 21-1
Integration of computer and telecommunications technology. (From L. D. O'Neill, "Converging Communication Services," *Computerworld on Communications*, 17:20A, May 18, 1983, pp. 77-84.)

The Role of Government Regulation

The recent history of government regulation and the telecommunications industry in the United States is complex. Until 1968, AT&T had a virtual monopoly on all telecommunications services and related equipment. Then, in a series of changes, competition was permitted in data communications and long-distance transmission. Independent microwave networks, packet-switching and satellite transmission services were allowed to compete with specific segments of the market.

In 1984, the major telephone utility in the United States, American Telephone and Telegraph (AT&T), was broken into several large regional, regulated telephone companies that offer local telephone service and long distance within their regions plus a company (AT&T) that competes with other vendors for long distance services, telecommunications equipment, and services. The net effect of the change in the United States is to increase the cost of local telephone services (that had been subsidized by long distance rates) and to reduce the cost of long distance service. There are many more options in equipment, and the costs of equipment are lower. At the same time that new competitors have entered the market for long distance communications, the new AT&T has entered the computer market. The distinction between communications companies and computer companies has now been removed. IBM is a vendor for communication equipment and a supplier of satellite communications services (through its share of Sattelite Business Systems).

The deregulation of the telephone system is not typical of other industrialized countries. Although there are some changes in competition in Great Britain, the general trend throughout the world is for a government controlled communications utility that is effectively merged with the postal service. The dominant trend is for this utility to expand its control of new technology. France, in particular, has taken a strong policy initiative to utilize the telecommunications agency in government to improve development of the economy. One result of this initiative is the development of Teletel, a videotex system. Dissemination of the service into homes was accomplished via the availability of a low-cost terminal to replace telephone directories.[7]

Integrated Services Digital Networks

A clear trend is the merging of the telecommunications and information services industries. The potential exists for an integrated services digital network (ISDN) utility. With such a service, multiple networks and services, public and private, are interconnected with a full range of terminal devices. Network access is invisible to the user, and information input, storage, and processing functions are located either where user needs require or where access is most efficient. Voice, data, and image transmission are integrated. Some information processing services are carried by the network itself. In the ideal ISDN environment, a single communications utility fulfills all telecommunications requirements and provides access to all necessary information processing services.

---

[7]S. Nora, "Experimental Approaches Toward Telecommunications in France," in D. Marschall and J. Gregory (eds.), *Office Automation: Jekyll or Hyde?* Working Women Education Fund, Cleveland, OH, 1983.

Current difficulties with implementation are lack of standards, incompatibility of interfaces, and the number of providers competing for a share of the communications services market.

IMPACT OF INFORMATION TECHNOLOGY ON ORGANIZATIONS AND SOCIETY

In this section some broader issues regarding the impact of information technology over the next decade are highlighted. The view is short-term; no sweeping societal restructuring is predicted.

Impact on Individual Jobs

The impact of information technology on clerical and professional jobs was discussed in Chapter 13. The general trends are highlighted here. There is some concern that new information technology, particularly office automation, reduces the skill levels of many clerical jobs and increases the opportunity for electronic "surveillance."[8] On the other hand, it is possible that the traditional office as a satellite of another function with no room for promotion may give way to an administrative hierarchy with opportunities for individuals to improve their skills as "information specialists" and move into supervisory or management positions.

Several recent surveys[9] of secretarial workers have shown that the majority feel that the addition of word processing has improved their overall skills and their chances for advancement. However, there is little indication that new career opportunities have actually developed as a result.

As information technology moves into the realm of professional work, it is possible that the distinction between it and clerical work will be less noticeable. It is hard to generalize about changes in professional work, but it is clear that some tasks that are repetitive in nature but required some technical expertise will now be automated. One example is the creation of engineering drawings by computer-aided designs (CAD). The remaining tasks require a high level of professional skill, but fewer of these jobs are required and there are few apprentice positions to provide training and a natural career path.

Some tasks considered today to require professional expertise will have their overall skill levels reduced. An example is programming: the use of very high-level languages means that less training is required to master the language and become a programmer. The skills required to do programming itself are reduced, but programming in very high level languages may open a career growth opportunity for clerical employees.

Studies of managers, including middle management, have shown that their jobs are

---

[8]J. Gregory and K. Nussbaum, "Race Against Time: Automation of the Office," *Office: Technology and People*, 1:2&3, September 1982.

[9]Minolta Corporation and Professional Secretaries International Research and Educational Foundation, *The Evolving Role of the Secretary in the Information Age*, 1983; Kelly Services, *The Kelly Report on People in the Electronic Office*, Troy, MI, 1983; 9 to 5 National Association of Working Women, *National Survey on Women and Stress*, Cleveland, OH, 1984.

characterized by short, fragmented tasks which are frequently interrupted (see Chapter 8). Furthermore, they spend the majority of their time in verbal communication. Although there has been much speculation about improving managerial productivity through office automation, the nature of the job seems to resist it. However, information tools that enhance the communication capabilities of managers, particularly electronic mail and voice store-and-forward message systems, are becoming accepted for managerial use.

Impact on Organizational Structure

In 1958, a now-classic article predicted the impact of information technology on middle management.[10] The article predicted a recentralization of authority within top management, while middle management jobs would become more structured and the boundaries between middle and top management would become more rigid.

Recently, a set of predictions have focused on the impact of office automation. Generally, the notion is that since communications between the bottom and the top of the organization will be streamlined, there will be less need for middle management to filter and pass on information. It is possible that information technology will reduce the need for middle management jobs in many organizations; some anecdotal examples of the shrinking of middle management ranks now exist.[11] However, numerous organizational examples show that information systems can support, or even influence, either a centralized or decentralized organization, depending on the organizational philosophy under which they are implemented.

Location and Schedule of Work

As more white collar jobs require access to computers and communications technology, other physical materials become less important. Electronic and voice mail extend the capability of the telephone to contact another person without being physically present; many contacts can be completed and information received without needing to be connected at the same time. Thus, theoretically, information technology removes the physical constraints of being "in the office from 9 to 5." This location and time independence of office jobs permits a greater number of options for physical location of organizational facilities. The term "telecommuting" has been used to reflect this phenomenon. Three possibilities are in various stages of discussion and experimentation: satellite work centers, neighborhood work centers, and work at home. There are some forces supporting these options, but factors of organizational need for social interaction are in opposition.

One option when considering office location may be near where employees live, thus reducing commute times. The term *satellite work center* refers to a location, typically an

---

[10]Leavitt and Whisler, "Management in the 1980s," *Harvard Business Review*, November–December 1958, pp. 41–48.

[11]See, for instance, R. Dasey, "Training: The Magic Cure for All Ills?" in D. Marschall and J. Gregory (eds.), *Office Automation: Jekyll or Hyde?* Working Women Education Fund, Cleveland, OH, 1983.

office, in or near a residential area. Employees may go to the satellite work center, which is equipped with terminals, printers, facsimile machines, and teleconferencing facilities, rather than commuting to the central office.

Another option is a *neighborhood work center*. This is a facility providing the equipment of a satellite work center, but it is shared by employees of many organizations. The concept is similar to that of a shopping center: a variety of facilities (including day care) are available on an "as-needed" basis.

There has been some discussion of the potential for computer and communications technology to support *work at home*. Although a number of companies have experimented with a few employees, primarily programmers and word processors, the total number working at home as a substitute for attending an office is not significant. Many employees prefer the social interaction the office provides to the isolation of being at home. Moreover, many managers feel uncomfortable supervising employees they can not see. The potential exists for exploitation, particularly of clerical workers, in the same way that industrial homework has been exploitative: employees are willing to accept significantly lower wages, especially on a piece rate, since they are not required to pay commuting or day care expenses.

On the other hand, many employees are increasingly motivated to demand more flexible work options from their employers, (including work at home), flexible work hours, and extended leaves of absence. Their reasons for needing increased flexibility are clear: increasing numbers of dual-career families and single-parent families, the increasing number of mothers of small children who are entering the work force, and the lack of adequate day care facilities in the United States. However, work at home is a generally inadequate solution to combining work and child care.

Shifts in Employment

The impact of automation on employment has been debated since computers were first introduced in organizations in the 1950s. In the short term, it is predicted that the trends that began in the 1950s will continue: a shrinkage of jobs requiring minimal skills and growth in occupations requiring some technical skills. Potential shifts in white collar employment within organizations has already been discussed.

A shift away from jobs in manufacturing to the service sector has been well documented. Figure 21-2 shows that the most rapidly growing sector of employment in the United States has been the "information sector." Over 50 percent of all jobs are related to the production or dissemination of information, and the information component of all jobs is increasing.

Electronic Services in the Home

The developments in telecommunications described earlier in this chapter may have significant effect on the information services available in the home. Personal computers are available in a significant percent of homes. The number of services available to home users is growing: videotex, home banking, home shopping, electronic mail, educational services, and video games. Several trials of videotext services are being conducted, primarily by newspaper publishers and television broadcast organizations.

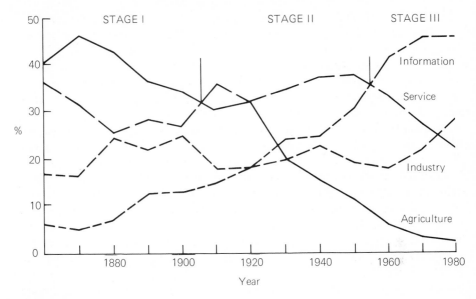

Figure 21-2
Growth of the information sector in United States employment. (Courtesy of Mark Porat.)

SURVEY OF COMPUTERS IN THE HOME

In 1984, according to a poll of 811 people, 15 percent have a home computer and 20 percent plan to buy one or upgrade present equipment. "Home computers are most popular among young, highly educated people." Having a computer at the office (45 percent have one at work) influences the decision to have one at home.

The top four services people want their home computers to provide are basic education, access to encyclopedia-type data, management of finances, and preparation of income taxes.

Based on a story in *USA Today* by John Hillkirt and Mark Lewyn, "1 in 5 of Us Wants to Buy a Computer," Thursday, May 10, 1984, pp. 1 and 81.

Impact on Lifestyles

In the long run, the impact of information technology on general quality of life is difficult to predict. Futurists predict potentially dramatic changes in lifestyles; the reader is referred to the selected references for detailed discussions of these changes.

For instance, those who advocate "telecommuting" see a return to the community, instead of the workplace, as the critical social unit beyond family. Individuals can choose to live in a particular community independent of their work, since the work can be performed anywhere. It is also possible to see an increase in contract work. Companies purchase specialized skills on an as-needed basis (perhaps through an electronic ''bulletin board'' of skills); individuals provide the skills, frequently from remote locations, and remain autonomous from the organization.

A potential concern of many is a growing gap between the ''information rich''and the ''information poor.'' Those who have access to electronic services in the home, for instance, may have social benefits not available to those who cannot afford such services. Another issue creating a potential information gap is that of education. Personal computer use in schools, even elementary schools, is growing rapidly, but accessibility of that educational resource is not evenly distributed. It is possible that differential education in information technology will create an even greater gap between the employable and those with inadequate technical skills.

There are many more issues that could be addressed here. The essential point is that information technology continually increases the number of options for improving productivity, the quality of work life, and the quality of life. It also has the potential for detrimental personal and social effects.

The Threat to Privacy

Privacy in the information age has a new meaning: it is the right of the individual to control the use of information about his or her activities, habits, health, finances, and so forth. The danger to privacy arises from the incremental gathering of data by many organizations and the loss of individual control over the ultimate use of the data. In the United States, for example, there is legislation governing the rights of individuals with respect to credit information companies and the rights of citizens to information on the activities of public agencies, but significant gathering of information on individuals by private organizations is not regulated. The use of computers to match different files of information on individuals (where the information was obtained for other purposes) raises serious societal issues. There is a need to promote governmental efficiency and compliance with laws; there is also a need to protect individual privacy. Organizations need to collect information in order to make decisions; they also need to obtain corroborating information to verify the completeness and accuracy of the data collected. Yet, data collected for one purpose, such as obtaining a mortgage, should not necessarily be available, without permission, for a potential employer. These issues have yet to be resolved.

COMPUTER MATCHING MARCHES ON

Computer matching is the use of files from various sources to identify people with certain characteristics important to the organization doing the matching. It is used by governmental agencies to identify individuals who are not obeying certain laws or regulations. It is estimated that in 1984 there were 85 United States federal agencies doing computer matching and twice as many stage agencies. Some examples are:

- The Internal Revenue Service is matching commercially available lists such as property assessment lists, vehicle registration lists, etc. against the list of taxpayers to identify those not filing tax returns.
- The Selective Service System is matching Social Security files against files of those registering for the draft to identify those failing to register.

- The Massachusetts Department of Welfare has matched its welfare rolls with lists of holders of bank accounts to identify welfare recipients who have sizeable bank balances and therefore may not be eligible for assistance.
- The Internal Revenue Service matches income tax refund lists with lists of those delinquent on child support payments. Those who are delinquent will have the delinquency offset against the income tax refund.
- The federal government matched its payroll records against the file of those delinquent on federally guaranteed student loans. Those who are delinquent must pay or have the loan payments deducted from their wages.

Based on John Gallent, "Computer Matching: An Ethical Exchange," *Computerworld*, December 26, 1983/January 2, 1984, pp. 88–95.

SUMMARY

There is a diversity of opinion regarding the potential impacts of computer and communications technology on individuals, organizations, and society. The fifth generation computer may provide access to vast amounts of knowledge in a usable form for many people. Developments in telecommunications and changes in regulatory policy in the United States are creating a merging of the telecommunications and information processing industries and making many forms of information readily available at significantly lower costs. A significant development is an integrated services digital network, a utility that accommodates a broad spectrum of communications and information needs.

Information systems services and technology are likely to continue to impact jobs and organizations. Clerical and professional work may be reduced in skill level or become more enriched, while the character of managerial work will change less. The impact of technology on organizational structure probably depends most on the organizational philosophy under which it is implemented. The potential exists for many jobs to be performed remotely from a central site, at a satellite or neighborhood work center, or at home. On a societal level, there will be continuing shifts in employment toward the "information sector." The availability of electronic services in some homes and the emphasis, in some economic sectors, on computer education may help to create a society of "information rich" and "information poor." There is a continuing concern about the information processing threat to privacy.

MINICASES

1 UPCOMING AND OUTGOING TECHNOLOGY

Jim Bartimo, Senior Editor/Communications for *Computerworld*, identifies technologies that are upcoming (hot) and those that are fading. Some of his conclusions are:

Chip technology

Upcoming:	Wafer technology to place all circuits on a single 2 1/2 inch wafer instead of wiring individual chips to boards
	Biochip technology to produce microchips from large protein molecules
Fading:	Josephson junction circuits based on supercooling

Displays
  Upcoming: Liquid crystal or plasma flat-panel displays that take
                     very little space behind the display

Storage
  Upcoming: Optical disk storage. One disk storage system can store
                     the entire *Encyclopedia Britanica*.
                     Vertical recording technology to increase density of
                     storage on magnetic media (up to 100 times more)
                     Nonvolatile memory that allows stored data to remain and uses a
                     very small power source
  Fading: Magnetic bubble memory because of high cost and lack of
                     support

Software
  Upcoming: Windowing and integrated software packages
  Fading: Dumb terminals to timesharing

Communications
  Upcoming: Nonblocking private branch exchange (PBX) that switches
                     both data and voice. Nonblocking means each port can
                     access every other.
  Fading: Video teleconferencing

Source: Jim Bartimo, "What's Hot! What's Not!" *Computerworld*, January 2, 1984, pp. 15–18.

Questions

a Describe the impact of each of the upcoming developments on the computer systems available for information processing.

b Describe how the future availability of these developments may affect the long range MIS plan.

2 PREPARING TO BE AN MIS MANAGER

In a 1983 Delphi study of important information system (IS) management issues, conducted jointly by the Management Information Systems Research Center (MISRC) at the University of Minnesota and the Society for Information Management, 54 leading practitioners responded. The top ten issues for management of information systems were:

- Improved IS planning
- Facilitation and management of end-user computing
- Integration of data processing, office automation, and telecommunications
- Improved software development and quality
- Measuring and improving IS effectiveness/productivity
- Facilitation of organizational learning and usage of information systems technologies
- Aligning the IS organization with that of the enterprise
- Specification, recruitment, and development of IS human resources
- Effective use of the organization's data resources
- Development and implementation of decision support systems

Source: G. W. Dickson, R. Leitheiser, M, Nechis, and J. Wetherbe, "Key Information Systems Issues for the 1980s," *MIS Quarterly*, 8:3, September 1984.

Questions

a What academic courses or other preparation would prepare a student to deal with these important IS management issues?

b How do these issues impact organization and staffing of the IS function?

3 THE ROLE OF INFORMATION AND INFORMATION SYSTEMS IN MEGATRENDS

In the bestselling book, *Megatrends* (Warner, New York, 1982), John Naisbitt identified 10 major trends or directions affecting our lives:

- The change from an industrial society to an information society
- The parallel response of high technology and human response (high tech/high touch)
- The change from a national economy to a global economy
- Restructuring from short term to long term considerations and rewards
- The change across society from centralization to decentralization (from top down to bottom up direction)
- The shift in emphasis from institutional help to self reliance and self help
- The shift from representative democracy to participatory democracy
- The move from hierarchical organizational and power structures to networking
- The North to South shift of population and economic activity (to West, Southwest, and Florida)
- Multiple options instead of "either/or"

Questions

a Identify how computers and information systems are influencing each of the megatrends.
b Describe how each of the megatrends influences the direction of information systems in organizations.

SELECTED REFERENCES

Benjamin, Robert I.: "Information Technology in the 1990s: A Long Range Planning Scenario," *MIS Quarterly*, 6:2, June 1982, pp. 11–32.

Feigenbaum, E., and P. McCorduck: *The Fifth Generation*, Addison-Wesley, Reading, MA, 1983.

Forester, Tom (ed.): *The Microelectronics Revolution: The Complete Guide to the New Technology and Its Impact on Society*, MIT Press, Cambridge, MA, 1981.

Hiltz, S. R., and M. Turoff: *The Network Nation*, Addison-Wesley, Reading, MA, 1978.

Johansen, R.: *Teleconferencing and Beyond: Communications in the Office of the Future*, McGraw-Hill, New York, 1984.

Marschall, D., and J. Gregory (eds.): *Office Automation: Jekyll or Hyde?* Working Women Education Fund, Cleveland, OH, 1983.

Masuda, Yoneji: *The Information Society as Post-Industrial Society*, Institute for the Information Society, Tokyo, Japan, 1980.

Moreau, Rene: *The Computer Comes of Age: The People, the Hardware, and the Software*, MIT Press, Cambridge, MA, 1984.

Naisbitt, John: *Megatrends*, Warner, New York, 1982.

Nora, Simon, and Alain Minc: *The Computerization of Society*, MIT Press, Cambridge, MA, 1980.

Uhlig, R. P., D.J. Farber, and J.H. Bair: *The Office of the Future*, North Holland, New York, 1979.

NAME INDEX

SUBJECT INDEX

About The Book

This is an extensive revision of one of
the most authoritative and widely read
books in the field. It discusses the
design of organizational information systems and the concepts underlying their
fundamental structure. The book is
designed to help readers develop a
strong conceptual grasp of management
information systems. It includes practical
information on such topics as determining information requirements, implementing systems, and managing information resources.

An excellent selection of problems reinforces concepts discussed in the book
and describes practical concerns to
which material can be applied. The addition of short case problems makes the
concepts more concrete and shows how
they are applied to information systems.
Overall, the new second edition features
a greater emphasis on user participation, user concerns, and decision and
knowledge work support systems. More
examples and case illustrations demonstrate the applicability of the concepts
discussed to information systems.